FREEDOM OF INFORMATION

THE MACMILLAN COMPANY
NEW YORK • BOSTON • CHICAGO
DALLAS • ATLANTA • SAN FRANCISCO

MACMILLAN AND CO., LIMITED
LONDON • BOMBAY • CALCUTTA
MADRAS • MELBOURNE

THE MACMILLAN COMPANY
OF CANADA, LIMITED
TORONTO

HERBERT BRUCKER

FREEDOM
OF INFORMATION

THE MACMILLAN COMPANY

New York · 1949

Material used in this book is quoted from publications that are protected by the following copyrights:
Copyright 1945 and 1946 by The American Association of Schools and Departments of Journalism and the American Association of Teachers of Journalism; Copyright 1941 by the American Newspaper Guild; Copyright 1938 by Maxwell Anderson; Copyright 1927 by Willard Grosvenor Bleyer; Copyright 1928 by The Bobbs-Merrill Company; Copyright Feb. 1944 by Broadcasting Publications Inc.; Copyright 1941 by Delbert Clark; Copyright 1931 by Columbia University Press; Copyright Feb. 1942 by The American Jewish Committee; Copyright 1942 by Kent Cooper; Copyright 1937 by F. S. Crofts & Co., Inc.; Copyright 1934 by Walter Duranty; Copyright 1932 and 1942 by Editor & Publisher Company; Copyright 1930 by Alfred A. Knopf, Inc.; Copyright 1942 by Matthew Gordon; Copyright 1940 by Oliver Gramling; Copyright 1942 by The Greystone Press, Inc.; Copyright 1920 by Harper & Brothers; Copyright 1946 by The Hartford Courant; Copyright 1915 and 1937 by Henry Holt and Company; Copyright 1943 by The International Longshoremen's and Warehousemen's Union; Copyright 1936 by Will Irwin; Copyright 1943 by Louisiana State University Press; Copyright 1944 for The (Louisville) Times; Copyright 1922, 1937 and 1941 by The Macmillan Company; Copyright 1931 by Walter Millis; Copyright 1933 by The Muncie Evening Press; Copyright 1941, 1942, 1944 and 1946 by New York Herald Tribune Inc.; Copyright 1914, 1921, 1922, 1923, 1924, 1925, 1926, 1927, 1928, 1929, 1930, 1931, 1932, 1933, 1940, 1941, 1942, 1943, 1944, 1945 and 1946 by New York Times Company; Copyright Nov. 1921 by North American Review; Copyright 1932 by W. W. Norton & Company, Inc.; Copyright March 1942 by The Omaha World-Herald; Copyright 1923 by Oxford University Press American Branch; Copyright 1940 by The Newspaper PM Inc.; Copyright 1929 by Frank Presbrey; Copyright 1941 by Everett Rich; Copyright 1942 by Robert St. John; Copyright 1942 by The St. Louis Post-Dispatch; Copyright 1939 by Stackpole Sons; Copyright 1940 by Edmund L. Taylor; Copyright 1939 by Time, Inc.; Copyright Sept. 1943 by United Feature Syndicate; Copyright Apr. 9, 1942, by United Press Associations; Copyright 1941 by The Vanguard Press, Inc.; Copyright 1931 by Yale University Press.
For permission to quote from various books, publications, periodicals, papers and documents, acknowledgments and thanks are made to the following:
The American Historical Company, Inc.; The American Society of Newspaper Editors; D. Appleton-Century Company, Inc.; The Associated Press; The Bobbs-Merrill Company; R. R. Bowker Co.; Broadcasting; Charles B. Brophy; Mrs. R. C. E. Brown; Sevellon Brown; Chapman & Hall Ltd.; Mitchell V. Charnley; Chatto & Windus; Columbia Broadcasting System, Inc.; Columbia University Press; Commentary; Doubleday & Company, Inc.; Editor & Publisher; The Economist; The Emporia Gazette; Fortune; The Guild Reporter; Harcourt, Brace and Company, Inc.; Harper & Brothers; Harvard University Press; Henry Holt and Company, Inc.; Houghton Mifflin Company; Palmer Hoyt; Journalism Quarterly; Alfred A. Knopf, Inc.; J. B. Lippincott Company; Liveright Publishing Corporation; Longmans, Green & Co., Inc.; Louisiana State University Press; The Louisville Times; The Macmillan Company; The Manchester Guardian; Dwight Marvin; The Muncie [Indiana] Press; The New Statesman & Nation; New York Herald Tribune; The New York Times; New York World-Telegram; W. W. Norton & Company, Inc.; Oxford University Press, New York; Drew Pearson; Westbrook Pegler; James S. Pope; Presses Universitaires De France; Rinehart & Company, Incorporated; Elmo Roper; The St. Louis Post-Despatch; Charles Scribner's Sons; William Sloane Associates, Inc.; The Telegraph Press; New York Star; Union Amicale des Maitres-Imprimeurs de France; United Feature Syndicate; United Press Associations; The Vanguard Press, Inc.; The Viking Press, Inc.; Morris Watson; Whittlesey House; The [Omaha] World-Herald; and Yale University Press.

To S. C. B.

CONTENTS

CONTENTS

WE LIVE IN TWO WORLDS

THIS fifth largest planet of the solar system, our earth, is so big that no one man can know it. To be sure, it is one world in the sense that Wendell Willkie meant—one world, in which what any single nation does has its impact on all others—whether we like it or not. Yet in another and equally real sense each of us lives in two worlds. One is the actual world of six continents and two billion human beings. The other consists of the pictures of that world we carry about in our heads.

The difference between these two worlds is the subject of this chapter. And the ways of getting information about the physical world into our mental world is the subject of this book.

Throughout the early fall of 1914 life on Direction Island went on in peaceful tropic routine. And why not? Once the shock of the news that Europe was at war had worn off, there was nothing to ruffle the life of this tiny atoll, one of the Keeling, or Cocos, Islands, five hundred miles southwest of Java. Except for the fact that Direction Island was a relay station on a cable from Europe to Australia, it was an insignificant spot in the hot emptiness of the Indian Ocean.

Suddenly, at six in the morning on Monday November 9, a

four-funneled cruiser cut at full speed through the blue sea and anchored at the entrance to the lagoon. The employees of the Eastern Telegraph Company on the island became suspicious, for the cruiser flew no flag, and her fourth funnel was obviously a canvas dummy. As they watched, an armored launch and two boats were put over the side. In them came three officers and forty men, armed with rifles, revolvers, and four Maxim guns. They were Germans; the raiding cruiser was the *Emden*. The invaders from the boats rushed up to the cable station, turned out the operators, smashed the instruments, and set an armed guard over the buildings; they then blew up the stores of electrical supplies. The crew of the launch, meanwhile, was grappling offshore for the cable, to cut it.

After about three hours of destruction, the *Emden* blew its siren. This was apparently a signal for the landing party to return, for the men at once rushed for the boats. The cable was still not cut. But even before the landing parties could gain the *Emden's* side she steamed away, leaving them there.

Looking eastward, the cable company employees soon saw why. The heavier Australian cruiser *Sydney* was coming near. While both ships were still in plain sight the *Emden* opened fire. One hit put the Australian's range finder out of action. But even so the *Sydney's* heavier guns found their mark; and by the time the *Emden* steamed over the horizon two funnels and a mast had been shot away, and she was on fire. Before long she was run aground on North Keeling Island, a flaming wreck.*

The *Emden* had been trying to cut communication between the British homeland and Australia. Its raid was merely of nuisance value, for the damage was local and was soon repaired. The *Emden* and similar German marauders were trying, without much success, to emulate an example of cable-cutting set by the British and French in the first days of the war. Because the British Navy controlled the Atlantic Ocean, the Allies could cut such cables as they desired, and keep them cut. In 1914 Kaiser Wilhelm's Germany was linked by six direct cables to

---

* Though there are plenty of footnotes in succeeding pages, they are henceforth banished to the back of this book. The reader may safely skip them all, confident that he is missing no interesting sidelights or added information. Footnotes contain nothing but citations of sources, like this one for the origin of the account of the *Emden's* adventures: *Telegraph and Telephone Age,* Dec. 1, 1914, p. 642.

Britain (which the coming of war immediately made useless) and by five other cables to the rest of the outside world. Two of these longer cables connected Germany with North America, but within three days of Britain's entry into the war the *New York Times* reported:

Since 1:30 o'clock yesterday morning, the German Empire has been isolated so far as communication with America is concerned. At that hour the cables leading from the United States to Emden, Germany, were cut, and since then no messages have been received here from that country, unless they have come through German wireless stations in this country.[1]

Thus all five of Germany's links to the outside world had been severed. The Allies' brusque action caused confusion and indignation in this country. Even Secretary of State Bryan lost contact with Ambassador James W. Gerard in Berlin. After some days a circuitous route was established from Washington through New York, London, Copenhagen, and Stockholm to Berlin; and this route was used by President Wilson for his notes of protest to Germany.[2] It is to be noted that this led through the British capital.

The world has not yet recovered from the imprint left by that relatively simple act of war. Because wireless was then in its infancy as a transocean service, cutting the cables was all that was necessary to hold Germany incommunicado. Except in nearby neutral countries, like Switzerland or the Netherlands, Germany could present neither the facts about what it was doing nor its arguments in its own behalf, except to the extent that the Allies were willing to pass them, censored to their satisfaction. Inevitably the picture of Germany in the minds of the outside world during that four-year-long war was a picture painted by the Allies.

It was different in World War II. Once more the British cut the cables; but this time, they were the ones left helpless. Long before 1939 the Nazis, fully aware of what had happened a generation before, had begun to build the world's most ambitious broadcasting system. Thirty miles outside Berlin, between the villages of Königs Wusterhausen and Zossen, Dr. Goebbels erected a battery of short-wave transmitters that broadcast daily entertainment and news and argument in fourteen languages.[3]

Technology, which in the earlier war by its vulnerability had silenced Germany, now made it possible for the Third Reich to speak to the entire world at will.

The contrast in German experience between the first and second World Wars offers an object lesson, even though German militarism dulled its edge. Except for the atrocity stories of 1914–1918, Kaiser Wilhelm's Germany actually resembled the picture the Allies painted. It was a powerful military nation dedicated to the theory that might makes right. In World War II, when the Nazis had ready access to the world's ear, they themselves openly boasted of atrocities more vicious than any manufactured about the Kaiser's Germany. Had Germany had a better case in World War I, Allied control of the cables might have kept it from reaching the rest of the world. Had Germany had a better case in World War II, the development of short-wave broadcasting would have enabled it to spread that case around the world. But the political failure of Germany in 1914 and 1939 in no wise alters the fact that both the Allies and Germany struggled to control the mind of mankind.

This struggle was predicated on two fundamental truths: first, that a fact that cannot reach a man's mind from the out-side world simply does not exist, as far as he is concerned; and second, that what a man has in his head as a fact is a fact, as far as he is concerned, whether or not it exists in the world outside. On these two truths, all that follows in this book is based.

If we reflect upon these things, we discover that each of us moves in an orbit that is woefully small in relation to the world as a whole. We circle about between home, the job, and near-by familiar points. Few of us come into daily contact with more than a handful of the teeming hosts of our fellow men. Unless we are exceptional travelers, we know at first hand only a pin point of the earth. That is why we must get most of our information about the world we really live in by artificial means. Those artificial means are what we call journalism—newspapers, radio, books, magazines, and a complex array of new facilities for learning what is going on out of eyesight and out of earshot. Journalism, then, is the instrument we use to stock our heads with information about the world that we can never know for ourselves.

Dr. Goebbels's information system for Germany, like the Soviet system of today, was based on the fundamental principle that what a man thinks is true, for him *is* true. The object was and is to make an entire nation live in a desired mental world, which to it seems to be the real world. And since the entire nation has essentially the same view of the facts, it tends to react in the same way toward them.

Those who see the solution of today's problems in a totalitarian state consider journalism to be a servant of government, instead of an independent means of bringing information about the outside world to the individual. Rather than trust to the babel of conflicting reports, the doubts and dissensions that follow from an unregimented reporting system, totalitarians want to present to their people a unified view of the world. And the fact that a press free from government control is open to manipulation by economic, political, or social interests confirms them in their preference for a mental world made to order by a benevolent state.

As citizens of a democracy we feel ourselves infinitely superior to the citizens of totalitarian states. Curiously, it never occurs to us that our own mental world may not be an exact copy of the real one. Democratic society, of course, is predicated on the search for truth. We struggle mightily to see things as they are. That is why most of us take for granted that we at least see the world steadily and see it whole. Yet under the infinite complexities of the modern economic, industrial, and social organization of the world we ourselves are only relatively better off than the citizens of totalitarian states. Our mental world, while bearing more than a coincidental resemblance to reality, is nevertheless only a fuzzy approximation of it. Like the victims of Nazi and Soviet rule, we think we know the real world we live in. But we don't.

If this seems extreme, consider one characteristic bit of evidence. Three months after the well remembered OPA launched its program of wartime ceiling prices—months marked by a national barrage of publicity about price control—a representative cross section of citizens in a midwestern city of more than 400,000 was questioned about it. The three daily newspapers and four radio stations of this city had hammered home the facts about OPA for ninety days. But, reports Elmo Roper, conductor of the *Fortune* poll:

. . . 21.8 per cent of all adults—one out of every five people—did not even know . . . that there was any such thing as government regulation of prices! Among women, who have more to do with day-to-day purchases, the number was even greater—one out of every four were unaware of government price regulation.[4]

It is not willful stubbornness, nor a preference for ignorance, that makes us take our inadequate mental world for the real thing. We do so for the fundamental reason that our conception of the world is the only one we know or can ever hope to know. In this we are all somewhat in the position of a Dr. William Beebe, when he descended into the depths of the sea in a bathysphere. Except for occasional sights revealed by our attempts to illuminate the surrounding gloom, we see nothing. The difference between Dr. Beebe and us is that he can have himself hauled up into the light. We, on the other hand, are condemned to spend our lives in the world that exists only in our heads. We are at the mercy of the news we get, of the facts—true or false, adequate or not—that come to us from the outside world.

Sir Norman Angell once defined the citizen of a democracy as manager of civilization in his spare time.[5] Even if Sir Norman puts it a little unkindly, we do put something like that task upon our own shoulders in believing in democracy. It follows that, impossible though it may be for us ever to know enough of our world, we are condemned by our own faith in democracy to try. We must somehow get into our heads a reasonably accurate facsimile, at least, of the real world. The survival of democracy is predicated on our doing so.

How adequate, then, is the method by which democracy seeks to inform itself, seeks to make the minds of its citizens comprehend the real world? Ours is a complex information system. At bottom it rests, for better or for worse, upon the daily newspaper and the radio. Therefore, we can best make a beginning at evaluating the modern world if we stop to think what it would be like without either of them. Newspaperless and radioless communities in this industrial and highly integrated world are hard to find. In 1945, when newspaper strikes in New York and Seattle left the public hungry for facts and dissatisfied for want of the accustomed voluminous and permanent printed

record,[6] radio tided them over in sketchy fashion—Mayor La
Guardia of New York even reading the "funnies" into the
microphone. I have one example of a modern American city
without either newspaper or radio. It goes back to 1932, when
Butte, Montana, also because of a strike, was without a newspaper for two weeks. The radio did not cover local news.
According to a contemporary summary:

> One rumor spread through the town that a terrible murder had
> been committed in the suburbs.
> Another report carried the dismal tidings that the bonus men
> had blown up the White House.
> A third terrifying rumor, widely spread through the city, was
> to the effect that President Hoover had been assassinated.[7]

Another example of the newspaperless community is the regiment or division, or other large military unit. The elusive
ubiquity of rumors in such military groups is familiar to all
who have served in them. And rumors are prevalent in military organizations precisely because the normal democratic machinery of information, with the written newspaper record as
its backbone, does not exist.

In the United States our supply of daily news is so large and
so reliable that few of us have occasion to think what life
might be like without it. We absorb news so regularly, so much
as a matter of course, that we are no more conscious of the
process than we are of the mechanics by which our eyes let
us see. One who has lived in an academic environment is
privileged, however, to see, as from the outside, the unconscious
absorption of news by an elite group of thinking citizens.
Scholars in all fields damn the press over the day's luncheon
table as superficial and inaccurate, if not willfully untruthful.
Yet the next moment they will discourse on what Russia has
just done or on what the President ought to do—totally oblivious
that it is only from the daily newspaper that they themselves
know of Russia's action, or are aware of the President's dilemma.

Seen in this light, democracy's information system takes on
new stature. The daily newspaper, though merely skimmed and
thrown aside, is more than a scrap of paper; the news program,
half listened to while we play bridge, is more than an anonymous voice. They link the two worlds we live in. In fact, we

all, even the most learned, are little better off than Will Rogers. The difference is that he admitted that all he knew was what he read in the papers.

THE FOURTH BRANCH OF GOVERNMENT

ON WEDNESDAY May 30, 1787, the Federal Convention that was to draw up the Constitution of the United States finally got down to business in the State House at Philadelphia. Enough belated delegates had arrived to make a quorum, and the preliminaries were out of the way. The Convention, acting as a Committee of the Whole, was ready to revise the Articles of Confederation.

Edmund Randolph, Governor of Virginia, arose to address his fellow delegates. This thirty-four-year-old Virginian had previously presented fifteen resolutions, laying down a tentative plan for the new government. He now proposed a substitute for the first of these resolutions, moving that the Convention at its very outset commit itself to the following proposition: "That a National Government ought to be established consisting of a supreme Legislative, Executive, and Judiciary." [1]

As every American schoolboy since has learned, the division of the United States government into these three basic parts survived the debates of the Convention, the risks of ratification by the states, and the strains of a century and a half of national growth. Orators dwell upon this constitutional trinity, scholars of each new generation analyze it afresh, and every alien seeking naturalization must learn it. As one man, the American nation seems to regard it as fixed for all time that the checks and balances among legislative, executive, and judiciary are all there is to our government.

But are they? How can one legislate, or execute, or judge, if one does not know what is going on? How indeed can the people choose their representatives in government without a bedrock of information on which to base their votes? In sum, upon what meat doth this our democracy feed? It feeds upon facts brought into the minds of its citizens by the press, the radio, and the supplementary media of information. This information system of our democracy constitutes a little recognized but indispensable fourth branch of the United States government.

Perhaps it is not wholly accurate to refer to our information system as part of the government. The function of this system is less that of an integral member of government than that of an outside agent, a catalyst. To put it another way, the information system serves democratic government as the bee serves a flower, by pollinating it. Adequate information provides the only environment in which democratic government can live. Without information, Congress, President, and courts cannot function.

Perception of this fundamental principle, that without information government cannot govern, is hardly a twentieth century discovery. The Greeks—as usual, in matters of human wisdom—saw the need of it. At least Aristotle, in discussing the ideal state, noted that there must be a limit to its size, set by the fact that everyone must know what is going on. As he explained it:

> What should be the limit will be easily ascertained by experience. For both governors and governed have duties to perform; the special functions of a governor are to command and to judge. But if the citizens of a state are to judge and to distribute offices according to merit, then they must know each other's characters; where they do not possess this knowledge, both the election to offices and the decision of lawsuits will go wrong. When the population is very large they are manifestly settled at haphazard, which clearly ought not to be. . . . Clearly, then, the best limit of the population of a state is the largest number which suffices for the purposes of life, and can be taken in at a single view.[2]

Aristotle speculated on these matters long before newspapers were developed. He could see no way to ensure information adequate to government other than to hold down the number of citizens to the limits of personal acquaintance. This formula was later made familiar to us by the New England town meeting.

Our national government, however, was another matter. It was formed some twenty centuries after Aristotle, when mankind had arrived at the age of the Rights of Man. And by this time, the late eighteenth century, newspapers were part of the accepted furniture of civilization. Though far different from ours in size and in manner, the newspapers were the same in purpose. Frank Luther Mott, outstanding historian of American journalism, points out that "as we look back, down the long vista of three and a half centuries or more of printed news, we find that the papers have been devoted mainly to the satisfaction of the fundamental need of human beings in any society to know what is happening in the world about them." [8]

In other words, when in the seventeenth and eighteenth centuries the world grew more populous and complex, at the same time that technological developments made possible printed journalism, the newspaper began to assume its modern task of stretching the mental world of the individual beyond that limit of personal observation and acquaintance envisioned by Aristotle as a permanent maximum. It began to report to the citizen what went on in the next valley, in the farther parts of his own land, and even overseas. This being so, it is not surprising to find that, by the time our Constitutional Convention met in the late eighteenth century, a man of insight should insist that the newspaper was indispensable to government. Thomas Jefferson was such a man. In a statement that has endeared him to generations of newspapermen, Jefferson held newspapers to be even more necessary than government itself. When the Federal Convention met in Philadelphia he was not there as a delegate. Instead, he was in Paris as our Minister to France. Distance did not, however, keep him from thinking of the constitutional issues under debate at home. Thus, on January 16, 1787, some months before the Convention met, he wrote to his friend Edward Carrington, the Revolutionary general, jurist, and statesman:

The way to prevent these irregular interpositions of the people [into the actions of Congress] is to give them full information of their affairs thro' the channel of the public papers, & to contrive that those papers should penetrate the whole mass of the people. The basis of our governments being the opinion of the people, the first object should be to keep that right: *and were it left to me to decide whether we should have a government without newspapers or newspapers without a government, I should not hesitate to prefer the latter.* But I should mean that every man should receive those papers & be capable of reading them.[4]

Unlike Jefferson, the Constitutional Convention gave little thought to the imperative necessity for providing accurate information in order to put flesh on the constitutional skeleton. That brilliant assembly of thinkers and statesmen appears instead to have assumed without question that Nature had endowed officials and people alike with all information necessary to intelligent action. As Gunning Bedford of Delaware told his fellow delegates, in words reminiscent of Aristotle, "The representatives of the people were the best judges of what was for their interest." [5] And after all, the Convention delegates themselves did know enough to write the Constitution with an insight into fundamentals seldom equaled in the history of government. As for the future of the country under the Constitution, they could guide themselves only by the America they themselves knew. Therefore they took for granted that every citizen and every officer of the tripartite government now to arise would know all he needed to know to make the structure work.

In the rural, leisured life of those days this assumption was natural. The population of the entire thirteen states at the time was only 3,100,000,[6] or only half again as much as the 2,000,000 who inhabit the city of Philadelphia today. This made it possible for the population of that time, and for its representatives in government, to attain in their mental worlds a workable approximation of the relatively simple physical world they lived in.

Through the years since then the physical world, as we are learning by bitter experience, has grown more and more complex. It is therefore a matter of some surprise that, as the world gradually became more intricate, so few should be aware of the need to examine anew the fundamental requirement of information that already had been apparent to Thomas Jefferson. To be sure, Oliver Wendell Holmes, Sr., once pointed out that in time of war "news is as necessary as bread." [7] But, by and large, the assumption that information would be on hand without anyone's doing anything about it—as though by virtue of some spontaneous combustion within the breast of the citizen —has persisted from the eighteenth century to this. The public tends to regard newspaper work as being valuable but not invaluable, at least in principle. It gives lip service to the press. But, if actions speak louder than words, those of our body politic are not exactly stentorian about the indispensability of newspapers to government.

It was with some comfort, therefore, that early in 1942 American newspapermen read that a new Canadian Selective Service plan would consider newspapers and press associations as essential services, even in wartime. "Nothing will be done to deprive them of the necessary qualified persons to insure their efficient publication," said Elliott M. Little, director of Canada's National Selective Service. [8]

This was balm to Americans in the craft. Alone of skilled groups and professions, they had been classed by their own draft system as superfluous in wartime. Later modifications remedied this, but still did not hold a newspaperman to be as essential to his country as the man who sprayed paint on a tank. So, too, a wartime questionnaire designed to compile a national roster of professional and scientific workers, and those in skilled occupations, left newspapermen out entirely. [9] Unlike a hundred and fifty varieties of mechanics, from airplane fabric worker to woodworking machine operator; unlike professional men (thirty-six categories of them, from accountant and bacteriologist), nine kinds of engineers, historians, lawyers, social workers, and so on through veterinarian, there was no place for reporter or editor to mark his X. As a nation, we are still not aware, apparently, that the fourth branch of government exists, and that the other three cannot function without it.

Meanwhile, embarrassingly loud creaks continue to issue from the machinery of democracy. Certainly since 1918, if not before, we have had occasion to wonder whether a framework of government designed in an era of wooden wheels could survive in a world of stainless steel and vacuum tubes. But except for the challenge of that modern version of the ancient tyrant, the totalitarian leader who rises with a microphone in one hand and a blitzkrieg in the other, little has been offered by way of change.

This may be startling when one thinks of it, but it is true. Few in the democratic camp have examined closely the question whether democracy's sources of information are adequate to the needs of today. One of the handful to do so was Walter Lippmann. And he, writing as long ago as 1922, concluded that it was the inadequacy of our information system that gave rise to democracy's twentieth century ailments:

The press . . . is like the beam of a searchlight that moves restlessly about, bringing one episode and then another out of darkness into vision. Men cannot do the work of the world by this light alone. They cannot govern society by episodes, incidents, and eruptions. It is only when they work by a steady light of their own, that the press, when it is turned upon them, reveals a situation intelligible enough for a popular decision. The trouble lies deeper than the press . . .

. . . the troubles of the press, like the troubles of representative government, be it territorial or functional, like the troubles of industry, be it capitalist, cooperative, or communist, go back to a common source: to the failure of self-governing people to transcend their casual experience and their prejudice, by inventing, creating, and organizing a machinery of knowledge. It is because they are compelled to act without a reliable picture of the world, that governments . . . make such small headway against the more obvious failings of democracy.[10]

The cure Lippmann proposed reminds one of the elderly sociologist's greeting to the young one: "Good morning. And how are you since you left off thinking and began to count?" For what Lippmann suggested was that some one begin to count the facts. Information should be obtained *for* the press rather than *by* the press. There should be an independent audit of the facts, he argued, by bureaus of governmental research, by specialized lobbies of corporations and trade unions and public groups, by legislative reference libraries, and by committees for this and associations for that. Democracy ought to be put wise to its own needs—in short, by means of all the paraphernalia of modern research.

The decades since Lippmann made his thoughtful suggestion have seen an explosive growth of research. But in today's lexicon the term "research" covers a multitude of sins. The research departments of interested groups have a way of merging themselves with departments of public information. The amount of specialized information put out for the press by press bureaus, information directors, counselors on public relations, publicity men, and plain press agents would, if laid end to end in our news columns, crowd out everything else many times over. But still we do not seem to be much the wiser.

In recent years, especially after total war loaded new burdens on our democracy and therefore also upon our errant press, there has been further effort to organize intelligence. One suggestion carried the principle to its apogee. This was to construct a machine that might have been a nightmare dreamed by the editors of *Fortune* after a visit to New York's prewar World's Fair. The idea called for an illuminated globe that should tell all in terms of many-hued pictorial data and geopolitical charts. It was to answer all questions from "Where is the Navy?" to "What is today's weighted index of German morale?" at the press of a button.

Somehow this incandescent dome of many-colored glass turned juke box never materialized. Nor, on the more serious side, did research make democracy any less befuddled. The physical world has continued to defy man's efforts to reduce it in size and complexity enough to get it into his mental world. All the schemes for educating democracy up to the point of consistently intelligent decisions have left us pretty much where we were. Awkward though this system may be in democracy's hours of trial, the alternative is a Führer or Generalissimo whose inner voices enable him to see all and know all. And somehow, when democracy faces an issue that has become acute, information on which to base a decision usually turns up. Then that restless beam of the press's searchlight shines upon it. And until now, at least, this system has kept democracy's head above the rising flood waters of ever new complexities and intricacies.

In other words our democracy, for better for worse, for richer for poorer, seems destined to stick by its ancient principles of representative government and delegated powers. The necessary corollary is that it will retain essentially the information system it now has, and like it. Whether this information system—

this unofficial fourth branch of government consisting of press, radio, and all the rest—is adequate to the task of enabling democracy to get along, is the central question of our time.

There remains for consideration another question, that of how this machinery of information is to be controlled—if at all. Controlling the information system, as against recognizing it as a part of government, came before the Philadelphia Convention in that hot summer of 1787; for, though the delegates to the Federal Convention assumed that a certain amount of information was every American's birthright, they debated briefly the press's right to freedom from government control. At least one proposal for a bill of rights in the Constitution itself began with the phrase, "The liberty of the press shall be inviolably preserved." [11] And the Convention in the end failed to write a free-press clause into the Constitution itself not because the delegates opposed a free press. Far from it. The Convention held such a clause unnecessary: "For why declare that things shall not be done, which there is no power to do?" as Hamilton wrote later in the *Federalist*.[12]

As it turned out, the omission from the new Constitution of a bill of rights similar to those already written in eight state constitutions formed the chief ground for reluctance to accept it. Therefore, as part of the contract under which the states adopted the Constitution, a bill of rights—known to us as Amendments I through X— was ratified less than three years after the Constitution itself. The very first of these amendments began, and begins today, with these words:

Congress shall make no law respecting an establishment of religion, or prohibiting the free exercise thereof; or abridging the freedom of speech or of the press . . .

Commenting on this fact Harold L. Ickes, former Secretary of the Interior and the most zestful gadfly of the press in our time, has written: "Except the press, no other private institution is specifically mentioned in the Bill of Rights. This places the press and its problems in a special suspense file." [13]

CHAPTER III

PLUS ÇA CHANGE

MELVIN J. STRONG, meat packer's agent of Fort Worth, had done pretty well in 1956 in spite of the times. Not many in the trade had been able to turn in a sales record like his in the face of the new regulations of the National Beef Authority. Not many homes in town were as sumptuously furnished. Hence Strong was able, one evening after dinner, to seat himself before the television screen of his new Superfidelity Communications set. This was a cabinet no bigger than his old radio, that had in it everything from a phonograph that played wire records to a facsimile attachment that ground out three copies of the family's morning *Star-Telegram* right there in the home, while everyone slept.

As the television tubes of the set grew warm and the images of a news program appeared on the screen, Mr. Strong's temperature rose. For there, all but filling the screen, was a face he had come to dislike intensely—that of Adalbert Hasenschmaltz. Adalbert was a supposedly reconditioned survivor of the Nazi educational nightmare, who had passed his United Nations examinations, including the social aptitude test, brilliantly enough. He was also doing a good job, Strong conceded, as Meat Administrator in Buenos Aires. But what was good for Argentina wasn't

17

necessarily good for the Texas cattle industry. Besides, Strong just didn't like Hasenschmaltz's looks.

The scene before Strong's eyes shifted to another camera angle, disclosing the administrator seated in his handsome office in the superb new United Nations Building. By now Strong knew that building well. Even though he had never flown to B.A., he knew the look of things down there, as in other capitals around the world, ever since the weekly World Economic Roundup television programs had been on.

On the screen, an Administrative Assistant in Charge of Information presented to Herr Hasenschmaltz a typewritten sheet, and the two fell to discussing it. Fascinated, Strong forgot he was at home in Fort Worth, and not on the twenty-third floor of that gigantic magnesium-coated edifice on the Avenida del Mayo. Though his Spanish was not of the best even after considerable television practice, Strong tried to catch the drift of the conversation that accompanied the scene before him. As he began to understand the burden of Hasenschmaltz's argument, and saw what it meant in the way of further trouble for American packers, his anger rose even higher. Before witnessing this scene with his own eyes, he had, in spite of all that had happened, discounted the alarmist stories about the Argentine as so much newspaper talk. But the vision now unfolded before him—revealing the fixed purpose of those damned administrators to insist on their world-trade outlook no matter what happened in the United States—changed all that.

Strong snapped off his set, strode to his desk, and sat down to compose a sizzling telegram to his congressman.

It need hardly be said that several aspects of the imaginary scene just described are still remote. Among other things, intercontinental television, while achieved in experiments, is still a dream. And, even if it were possible technically, no such temperature-raising sight would appear on the American television screen. Government officials do not invite television engineers, any more than newspaper correspondents, broadcasters, or photographers, to be present when they are formulating policies in the privacy of their offices.

Nevertheless there is a resemblance between Mr. Strong's television program and journalism as we know it. For a program like the one imagined is merely the ultimate perfection of journalism toward which we have, in past centuries and in this one, been advancing. It is the ultimate in the sense that, if it came to pass, the citizen could peer at will into any distant corner of the earth, and into nearer imponderables as well; he could see what was going on anywhere, to inform, to guide, or merely to amuse himself. The individual would know the physical world as well as he now knows his mental copy of it, and this would make the two, for practical purposes, the same.

This is the goal toward which journalism has ever struggled, and presumably ever will struggle without quite reaching it. The history of journalism is the history of man's striving for ways and means of learning what is going on in his world.

To us, of course, journalism seems to be merely the business of reporting the distant scene by means of printed newspapers, magazines, and radio. Writers on public affairs from Jefferson to date have as one man noted that printed publications constitute the only sources from which the individual could get the information about his world that is the prerequisite of democracy. Recently we have begun to say that "the newspapers and radio" have done this, or ought to do that. This recognition that the rotary press is not the only mechanical contrivance that can serve as a medium for distributing news is a reminder that journalism is bigger than ink on newsprint. It is, indeed, merely an accident of technological history that, from the invention of printing until this century, journalism was synonymous with printed matter. Today's sociologists tell us that what we are pleased to call human progress comes not so much from the inspiration of an inventor's genius as from the sociological climate of his time. No one can invent anything until civilization is ready for it. Applying this view to the mechanics of journalism, one notes that throughout history a new method of communication has turned up whenever the times have changed enough to warrant it, and whenever evolving technics have made it possible. Specifically, if Gutenberg had not developed movable type and the printing press at the time he did, someone else would have.

This cultural framework determined that Western civilization should be ready for printing, but not for radio, in the fifteenth century. Printing grew slowly at first, but began to come into its own in the seventeenth century. This made it inevitable that journalism, ripe for development at that time, should fasten itself to printing. The two grew up together. And, because through three centuries of growth there was no other technical process that could carry its burden, journalism was nourished solely on a diet of print.

This circumstance has obscured the fact that journalism existed before the printed newspaper. For the journalistic function has existed, and has been carried on by one means or another, since man came down from the trees. I suppose we shall no more be able to rid ourselves of associating printed newspapers with journalism than we have been able, four centuries after Copernicus and three after Galileo, to rid ourselves of the notion that the sun rises while the earth stands still. Nevertheless, if a radio news program and a radio commentator's interpretation of the news are not journalism, what are they?

Today, moreover, radio is not the newspaper's only fellow worker in the field. Other mechanical gadgets, in part at least, perform essentially the same service. And older and more familiar ways of finding out what is going on ought to be identified as a part of journalism. Here, for example, is a list of the channels of information that exist today:

1. Background sources
       Education and environment
       Conversation
       Lectures, forums, sermons
       Books
       Magazines
2. Newspapers
3. Public opinion polls and communications research
4. Radio
5. Facsimile
6. News photographs and picture magazines
7. Motion pictures
8. Television

All but the first two are new with this century. Two of them, facsimile and television, are so new that they have not yet begun to carry their share of the burden. Also some of the newcomers, like radio and the movies, are instruments of entertainment rather than of journalism. Nevertheless, to some extent at least, each of these instruments of information discharges the journalistic function. Hence it seems only proper to identify them as members of the journalistic family, to the extent to which they have become so in fact.

The *Time*-financed Commission on Freedom of the Press recognized the desirability of doing this. "The Commission decided," says the foreword to its report, "to include within its scope the major agencies of mass communication: the radio, newspapers, motion pictures, magazines, and books. Wherever the word 'press' is used in the publications of the Commission, it refers to all these media." [1] But even though contemporary facts make such a definition self-evident, it was greeted rather churlishly by defenders of the journalistic *status quo.* Thus Frank Gannett, the chain publisher, characterized the whole report as "erroneous, inconsistent, ineffective and dangerous," and denounced this obvious definition of contemporary journalism as a misuse of the word "press." [2]

Perhaps the Commission was careless in choosing the word "press" rather than the more inclusive "journalism" or "media of mass communication," or something similar. Yet the Commission stated its definition clearly, and the reasons for it are patent. Surely the existence of today's varied array of carriers of information makes it high time to redefine journalism as the *function,* rather than as any particular *instrument* through which that function is discharged. Journalism, then, is the enterprise of collecting and distributing current information, and of explaining and interpreting that information. In practice, too, the heavy weight of information and interpretation must be seasoned with enough entertainment to induce the customers to come and get it. Since Homer began to spin his tales, and probably before that, too, the ability to entertain has been at a premium in journalism. Therefore we ought to widen the definition and say that journalism is the collection and distribution of current information, interpretation, and entertainment.

If it is right to take journalism as the function rather than its means of execution, and so to include in it everything from newspapers to television, then we have a right to expect that henceforth journalism's work will be done better than ever before. The new technics of radio, photography, and television extend the range of our eyes and ears. Their reporting of the distant scene makes it seem more direct and more real than does writing. It ought to follow that our mental and physical worlds will match a little better in the future than in the past.

This point has an interesting corollary. Since today's journalism is tomorrow's history, history in the years to come will be based on more than newspaper accounts, diaries, letters, state documents, and other written records. It will be based also on photographs, on newsreels, on the films that will be used to fix in time television's direct coverage of news, and on recordings of radio broadcasts. From World War I we have only photographs and crude movies, in addition to the written record. But World War II is well documented on all kinds of film and recordings. The early triumphs of the Nazi Army, the disaster of Pearl Harbor, the voices of Hitler, Churchill, Roosevelt, and the rest, the sights and sounds of the London blitz, of Stalingrad and the war in the Pacific—indeed, all the big and little sights and sounds of the war have been fixed on these newer incunabula. The smells of the war are the only part of it that has not been preserved.

All this should make the study of history more exciting for future generations than it has been for us. It is difficult for the schoolboy of today to see the Civil War, for example, as something alive. It is a lot of words in a book, plus perhaps some line cuts and a stiff Brady photograph or two. At most, it is the emotional understanding that comes out of the pages of a *Gone with the Wind*. Only the scholar who specializes in an era really gets under its skin deeply enough to feel its life and to know its characters as living people. Only by such efforts can Gettysburg again become something tense—as real as that sinking feeling we had when France collapsed in 1940— instead of something musty, with the odor of old books and papers.

By contrast, the schoolboy of the future, if the schools are on their toes, will not know Hitler as desiccated in written records, but with his own ears will hear him ranting as he harangued the mob at a Nazi pageant, and with his own eyes will see him as he looked when he danced in the garden on hearing of France's surrender. So, too, tomorrow's schoolboy can live over again the dark hours of the Battle of Britain by hearing for himself Winston Churchill's voice as he promised nothing but "blood, toil, tears, and sweat," or as he paid tribute to the few in the RAF to whom so many owed so much. And if our future schoolboy is shown the American Army's indoctrination films, like "Prelude to War" and "The Nazis Strike," he ought to begin not only to see the war as the fiercely living thing it was, but to feel for himself at least something of what we who lived through it felt. If so, perhaps future generations can learn more from history and its repeating pattern than we have learned.

To us, of course, the graphic intensity of the reporting done through the new instruments of journalism is important not alone as source material for future historians. Through it we can see the distant scene more directly, and perhaps understand it better, than if we merely read about it. This makes it supremely important that we realize fully that, whatever else they may be, radio, moving pictures, and all the rest are authentic parts of journalism. As such they ought to be guaranteed the benefits of a free press under the First Amendment to the Constitution. In return, the whole battery of democracy's new instruments of information must learn to breathe the traditions of the Fourth Estate by struggling to report and interpret facts independently of the social and economic groups that make up our body politic. Only if they are free from control by government, and only if they realize fully their own obligations as objective reporters, can they function as the integral parts of journalism they are.

CHAPTER IV

MR. MACAULAY'S FOURTH ESTATE

THE fact that, of all the private enterprises in our economy, only newspapers receive protection from the Constitution forces them to lead a double life. On the one hand they are profit-making businesses, just as self-seeking as any other business. On the other they are an integral part of democracy. Inevitably the fact that they thus stand with one foot in the cash register and the other in government gives them a Jekyll-Hyde personality. And just as inevitably the public, seeing in the newspapers now the Dr. Jekyll and now the Mr. Hyde, is confused as to what their position in our society is and what it should be. Nor is this confusion lessened by the nonsense contributed from both sides of the discussion.

Perhaps we can begin to penetrate the confusion by following the details of an interesting encounter between a critic of Mr. Hyde and a friend of Dr. Jekyll. The critic is Harold L. Ickes, whose joy in his avocation as banderillero to newspapers has already been mentioned. The friend is a reporter, Winifred Mallon of the *New York Times*. The occasion of their encounter was a press conference held a few days after the Roosevelt-Willkie election of 1940, when the bitterness of that campaign was still fresh in everyone's mind. Although the exchange

took place some years ago it is still pertinent because any discussion of the press today is likely to raise the same cloud of dust.

Secretary Ickes opened his conference with the remark that
although the people had elected the same man President three
times, that man had had the active support of only 40 per cent
of the press in 1932; 36 per cent in 1936; and less than 23 per
cent in 1940. (Four years later, he said the figure had sunk to
a mere 17.7 per cent.) The Secretary thereupon observed to
the assembled reporters: "I am convinced that our democracy
needs, more than ever before, a truly free press that represents
no class or economic group and one that will rewin the confidence of our citizens because it is worthy of rewinning that
confidence." He then commended the situation as he had posed
it to the publishers, "for calm self-examination and comment." [1]

The result, he said later, was the "vicious snarl" with which
many newspapers habitually reply to criticism. But at the press
conference Ickes, no mean vicious snarler himself, was subjected
by Winifred Mallon to a searching request for light as to how
a "more truly free press" might be achieved. The dialogue is
so interesting that it is reproduced here in full, as published
in the *New York Times* next day.[2] The spark that started it
was Ickes' insistence that publishers were, despite their dis-
claimer, responsible for the opinions expressed by their columnists. Then the fun began:

Mr. Ickes was asked if he thought the press would be freer if it
could not print such a column as the one under discussion, to which
he replied:

"I don't think it goes to the question of the freedom of the press
at all."

"But that," said the reporter, "is what—"

Mr. Ickes interrupted and the following discussion ensued:

Mr. Ickes: "You are implying that a newspaper, in order to be
free, has to print sewage, aren't you?"

Reporter: "There is such a difference of opinion as to what is
sewage."

Mr. Ickes: "Well, I agree with that, but there isn't that difference
between olfactory nerves."

Reporter: "Well, if the paper isn't going to be the judge, who
would be, to make it free?"

Mr. Ickes: "You are the judge."

Reporter: "What?"

Mr. Ickes: "Well, we are getting down to another question. What do you mean by the paper's judgment? The man who happens to own it, or the editorial staff?"

Reporter: "Both. It wouldn't last long if it wasn't both."

Mr. Ickes: "Well, how many people, how many members of the editorial staff, are consulted as to policy? I can go further than that—editorial and reportorial staff. What is a newspaper?"

Reporter: "What interests me is just what you mean, sir (reading): 'Although we are fortunate in having free communication over the air, I am convinced that our democracy needs more than ever a truly free press.' That is what I mean. You pointed out something you think is wrong, and maybe it is, but what is there about it that isn't free?"

Mr. Ickes: "Well, maybe if any comment is made on this statement—perhaps the editors will raise that question. When it is raised, why, perhaps I will have something to say about it. I don't think a press is free that represents one economic group or one social group or the two combined."

Reporter: "And again we come down to who is going to decide it."

Mr. Ickes: "I am sorry if you don't like what I say there, but I have said it anyhow."

Reporter: "No, Mr. Secretary, please. We all want freedom of the press. If you don't think it is free now, how would you go about making it more free than it is now?"

Mr. Ickes: "What is a newspaper supposed to represent? Its readers—have they any rights? The editorial staff? They have all the rights there are. A newspaper used to say it represented its readers—it represented public opinion."

Reporter: "When it stops having readers it will cease to be a newspaper."

Mr. Ickes: "Oh, no. My point is that they are not representing any constituency at all."

Reporter: "Well, if it represents a constituency, that begs the whole question. It would be representing one class and not readers generally."

Mr. Ickes: "Well, that is all right, if that is what you think a newspaper ought to be."

Reporter: "I truly want to know what you have in mind."

Mr. Ickes: "I think a newspaper ought to represent as honestly as it can, at any rate to some degree, and not unreasonably, the views of its readers because that is a newspaper's constituency, just as the voters in a Congressional district are the constituency of the Congressman."

Reporter: "Mr. Secretary, the constituency of a newspaper can take the power of any newspaper away by refusing to read it and buy it, and the newspaper then is forced to quit."

Mr. Ickes: "In other words, you say that misrepresentation is defensible so long as people continue to buy the newspapers? Well, I don't."

Reporter: "I am just pointing out that you made that parallel between a newspaper and a Representative in the House and the constituents of that Representative in the House."

Mr. Ickes: "Well, of course they don't have to buy. I can admit all that, but does that absolve the newspaper of all responsibility for trying to represent fairly, especially if they have such mast headlines as 'All the news that is fit to print' and then enhance one side of the campaign and suppress another?"

It is unfortunate that at this point a question on a different subject broke off the colloquy. For it seems to me that here a critic and a defender of our present American press were close to the source of our confusion. It is apparent that they were really talking about two different things. Ickes used the words "free press," but he was not talking about a free press. Rather he was talking about the fact that the contemporary American newspaper is, whatever else it may be, a big business. At the same time the reporter, using the same words, was talking about a free press in the historic sense. Ickes, clearly annoyed that the politics of most of our newspapers were different from his own, concluded that they were not truly free. In the sense that they had pocketbook nerves and so were not free from a predilection toward political and economic conservatism, he was right, and there is the source of much of our trouble with the press today. But that has nothing to do with the theory of a free press as embodied in the Constitution. In fact, what really bothered Ickes was that, in the precise meaning of the words "free press," our newspapers *were* free—free to oppose the administration in power, free to fight a political battle from the opposite side of the party fence from which the redoubtable Secretary had swung his campaign haymakers at the opposition.

Here, I think, is the reason for much of the muddled thinking and talking about our newspapers. Apologists for our contemporary journalism fall back on an eighteenth century term, the "free press." They use it in its original and accurate sense,

of a press uncontrolled by authority, though they often overlook the possibly embarrassing question as to whether the eighteenth century concept is adequate to today's society. Conversely,
critics of our press use the same eighteenth century term to
mean something wholly different—namely, a journalism cast
loose, in some way they never define—from the oversized
modern version of its classic economic foundation.

In an effort to clear the ground for an examination into the
resulting conflict of opinion, I am devoting the rest of this
chapter to an analysis of the theory of a free press as it evolved
in Anglo-Saxon history. The reader whose sympathies range
him alongside Ickes is warned that he will find here nothing
about the contemporary economics of journalism. He will, however, find a great deal about the governmental framework within
which newspapers operate today, and within which they must
operate tomorrow in any society that deserves the name "democracy." The economics of journalism are reserved for Chapters 6 and 7. Even so, I trust that the critic of today's newspaper
in particular will thread his way through the argument that
follows, because innumerable discussions have shown me that
critics who are most troubled about the faults of the press
today are precisely the ones who are most likely to fail in understanding the historic doctrine of the free press, and therefore
in appreciating its priceless value even in today's world.

There follows, then, not an analysis of the American press
today, but an examination of the *theory* of a free press. And
we can best begin to grasp that theory if we forget for the time
being the words "free press," and instead look into another
term sometimes applied to the newspapers; namely, the "Fourth
Estate."

In all the nations of Christendom, society has usually been
divided into three estates, using "estate" in the sense of an
order or class of society that participates in government. In
former days a large part of the population, being serfs or
belonging to similar lower orders, did not qualify as an estate
because its members were uninvited to the seats of government.
In Great Britain, whence we inherited the term, the composition
of the three estates varied as it did elsewhere. But after some
fluctuations it came to be accepted that the realm was made

up of these three: the Lords Spiritual, or the Church; the Lords Temporal, or the aristocracy; the Commons, the representatives of the rising commercial civilization of the towns.

It is hardly surprising that this acceptance of three estates led from time to time to half-humorous suggestions as to what other estates there might be; so the Spanish Civil War of the late thirties gave us the term "Fifth Column," and we soon invented sixth and seventh columns. Thus Henry Fielding in 1752 wrote of "that very large and powerful body which forms the Fourth Estate in this community . . . The Mob." Others called the Army—surely at times a powerful arm of the government— the Fourth Estate. And William Hazlitt, the essayist, in 1821 referred to the reformer William Cobbett as "a kind of Fourth Estate in the politics of this country."[3]

Some time in the early nineteenth century this unofficial designation of Fourth Estate became attached to the press. Certainly by Tuesday May 19, 1840, when Thomas Carlyle made his fifth lecture on "Heroes and Hero-Worship" on a public platform in London, he used it seriously in this sense. Speaking of the hero as a man of letters, Mr. Carlyle pointed out the change printing had wrought in government:

Witenagemote, old Parliament, was a great thing. The affairs of the nation were there deliberated and decided; what we were to *do* as a nation. But does not, though the name Parliament subsists, the parliamentary debate go on now, everywhere and at all times, in a far more comprehensive way, *out* of Parliament altogether? Burke said there were Three Estates in Parliament; but, in the Reporters' Gallery yonder, there sat a *Fourth Estate* more important far than they all. It is not a figure of speech, or a witty saying; it is a literal fact,—very momentous to us in these times. Literature is our Parliament too. Printing, which comes necessarily out of Writing, I say often, is equivalent to Democracy: invent Writing, Democracy is inevitable.[4]

Edmund Burke never said what is ascribed to him by Carlyle. At least, the Oxford Dictionary reports,[5] "We have failed to discover confirmation of Carlyle's statement attributing to Burke the use of the phrase in the application now current." It seems most likely that this serious rather than jocular use of

"Fourth Estate" had first found its way into print a dozen years before Carlyle's lecture, in the essay Thomas Babington Macaulay wrote on Hallam's *Constitutional History of England;* for there Macaulay wrote:

> The gallery in which the reporters sit has become a fourth estate of the realm. The publication of the debates, a practice which seemed to the most liberal statesmen of the old school full of danger to the great safeguards of public liberty, is now regarded by many persons as a safeguard tantamount, and more than tantamount, to all the rest together." [6]

The fact that in his very next sentence Macaulay referred to a speech by Burke makes it seem likely that Carlyle found the source of his misquotation here. But however fascinating the exact origins of this usage may be, it is pertinent that more than a century ago these two distinguished writers soberly applied the term "Fourth Estate" to the press. Since then the press, and especially the newspaper press, has appropriated it. Sincere editors use the term when pouring out their hearts about their profession; and publishers who don't like a Wages and Hours Act find in it a convenient shield against the future.

The conception of the newspapers as the Fourth Estate in a society provides an understanding of the place of the information system in democracy. More than that, it gives the key to democracy in our time. And this is the reason for the fact noted by Secretary Ickes, that newspapers are the only private business institution mentioned in the Bill of Rights.

At this point it becomes necessary for critics of present-day American newspapers to remember that we are discussing not the Hearst newspapers or the *Chicago Tribune,* but the philosophical framework within which democracy's information system operates—or perhaps we had better say, should operate. Proceeding then upon this plane, we begin to sense something profound in the conception of journalism as an entity apart from all other groups that make up society, as a reporter of all kinds of events, but a reporter free from partisan interest in any one segment of society as against any other segment.

Essentially, of course, such a separate and disinterested Fourth Estate is what was described in a preceding chapter as the fourth branch of government. Yet it is something more too. It is something more because all other estates of the social order, and all other branches of government stand together on one side of a line while the Fourth Estate remains on the other. For example, though Congress and President may be jealous of their powers and their dignity in relation to each other, each has more in common with the other than with the Fourth Estate. In a dispute between President and Congress, the Fourth Estate —not necessarily your newspaper—prints on its front page what the President said, and what the senators or representatives said, without arguing for one or the other. It will tell the reader what the CIO demands, and what the industrialist thinks of that demand, without coloring its accounts with interpretation of the kind made familiar by editorial pages and columnists. It will report defeats and victories in war, the news of science, education, the Church, sports, and all the other interests of all the groups that make up the body politic—but it will not identify itself with any one of them.

The usefulness of the Fourth Estate, therefore, lies in its independence from all other groups into which man has organized himself. And if the Fourth Estate is to bridge the gap between our physical and mental worlds, then this independence must be its backbone; for, if the information we get comes to us charged with the partisan emotions of any particular fraction of society, it is poisoned. Our information machinery will then no longer bring us, with (reasonably) honest intent and a (fairly) pure heart, news of those further horizons we cannot see, but which yet form the larger part of the environment with which we must deal in our work and in our government.

Even though we are concerned here with an ideal Fourth Estate rather than with its practical expression, we can find something of that ideal embodied in the journalism of the past, at least. What instrument was most powerful in helping man break the shackles of the Church from his mind? The printing press. What was the particular issue of many of the individual battles in the seventeenth and eighteenth century wars for liberty? The printing press, used to bring facts and opinions from the physical world into the mental world. For no ancient order of priests, no modern totalitarian tyrant wired for sound, can suppress thoughts in a man's head. Thoughts can be suppressed only at the point of utterance. And until thirty years ago the only effective way to get an idea beyond range of your own voice was to print it.

We tend to think that our predecessors in Anglo-Saxon lands fought for some glorious abstraction called Liberty. They didn't. They fought for smaller but more specific objectives. And often that specific objective involved the right to use the printing press in the service of the Fourth Estate. The heroes of liberty fought for the right to publish a particular book without the imprimatur of an Inquisition. Or they fought to reseat in Parliament a certain man named John Wilkes, convicted of seditious libel for criticizing a speech from the throne in his *North Briton*. Liberty and the printing press are inseparable. One has no meaning, the other little use, without its partner.

Let not some irritated patron of contemporary journalism begin to fidget and say: "This is all very well as an ideal, and perhaps even as a workaday practice in bygone days, but what has it to do with today's American newspaper?" It must be admitted that all but the best of our journalism today is still a long way from the ideal of the Fourth Estate. Not only is it closely associated with our present-day Lords Temporal, our economically and politically conservative groups, but everyday journalism seems hardly to improve in either morals or skill on our ministers, doctors, lawyers, entrepreneurs, or indeed anyone else.

In spite of all this, some pride in the Fourth Estate, some feeling for its import, pervades our newsrooms. The feeling is no more visible than electricity, but it is just as real. Perhaps only working newspapermen, and by no means all of them, share it. Cynical and disillusioned though they may be—enough so to make them keep such pride to themselves—this sense of being part of the Fourth Estate must be reckoned with in the practical councils of men. The working newspaperman— the reporter or copy reader, that is, rather than the columnist or publisher—is entitled to a certain pride in his calling. I can testify from experience that, other things being equal, his employment is less commercial than that in other institutions of private profit. Your reporter may look with envy on the higher rewards that come to those who forsake journalism for publicity or advertising, but at least he knows he has not sold his soul to a tooth paste.

This holds true even under the abuses to which the Fourth Estate is subject as an instrument handled by erring human beings who are an integral part of our enterprise-for-profit system. Even the veteran desk man who wrote the headline and shaped the lead of the story in last night's paper that made you bilious—even he feels it. He probably doesn't like that particular story any better than you did, but he did it that way because it touched a subject toward which the paper's management had a policy. Nine-tenths of the time he does his impartial best. You benefit by it, but do you give him credit for it? Not unless you are different from other newspaper readers, who take the 90 per cent of accurate and objective reporting as a natural part of the scenery, but utter loud cries at the 10 per cent that is either seemingly or really bad.

Presumably this spirit of the independent Fourth Estate was felt, in spite of what he had to do, by even the legendary rewrite man on the Communist *Daily Worker,* the one who was tossed an item about a collision between two automobiles, with the injunction: "Here, class-angle that!" For there is inherent in the trade of writing news some inner compulsion toward the truth. It makes even the man whose business it is to make the facts fit the party line—no matter whether that line is Communist or Big Business—squirm, because he feels that inner compulsion.

This force that tends to make the newspapers, with all their faults and failures, present us with a reasonably accurate report, comes to us out of our political and social inheritance.

Most of us are agreed that, though man has struggled toward the truth through all the ages, he has never found it. What he has found, after countless generations of labor, is a way of approaching the truth. Surely so far as concerns the facts on which government decisions are based, at least a method has been evolved during the last three centuries. By this method we can use the truth, even though it may never be captured and measured.

The method was put into words in 1644 by John Milton in his unspoken and at the time unsuccessful address to Parliament, *Areopagitica.* The idea somehow sprang out of the soil of England in the seventeenth century. Others had aired it before Milton,[7] but it was he who dressed it in eloquent phrases and thereby bequeathed to us the formula that we still use today.

Briefly, what Milton said was that while truth might assume more shapes than one,[8] we could yet find it and make it serve our needs. For practical purposes, finding the truth was simple. All you had to do was to let all versions of the truth fight it out among themselves. No matter how highly colored an opinion a man might have as to what was truth, let him utter it without hindrance:

And through all the windes of doctrin were let loose to play upon the earth, so Truth be in the field, we do injuriously by licencing and prohibiting to misdoubt her strength. Let her and Falsehood grapple; who ever knew Truth put to the wors, in a free and open encounter.[9]

Milton here phrased his plea as though there were one pure truth and a variety of erroneous versions. They were like knights on the jousting field, all dressed in armor with visors down. You could tell which was Truth at the end of the tournament, for Truth was the one that unhorsed all the others.

What Milton was pleading for was no universal formula. He sought a specific object: unlicensed printing. He wanted no Court of the Star Chamber, no Company of Stationers, to say beforehand what was truth and what error, and to license for printing only that which they certified as the truth. Yet here is the germ of a profound principle—a principle that has been validated by three hundred years of experience. Anglo-Saxon society, at least, has gotten where it is by permitting substantially all facts, and all opinions as to what were facts, to compete openly in the market place for public acceptance. By and large, Truth, somewhat battered but still recognizable, has eventually emerged triumphant.

When Milton published his argument—without a license, incidentally—printed newspapers, recognizable as such, had existed in England for scarcely more than two decades. Milton's concern was for pamphlets like his own and for books, rather than for newspapers as we know them. His argument has been appropriated ever since, however, as a plea for free newspapers. Here, then, is the origin of the now debatable term, "free press." And while technically it still covers all products of the printing press, for practical purposes it has come to mean simply newspapers uncontrolled by government. On a still broader plane we use it to mean the absence of control by any authority, sacred or profane, within the whole framework of society.

Now, in practice, freedom of the press has been no more absolute than any other freedom. Specific encroachments have been made upon it from time to time, as upon all liberties. For the American newspaper press one of the major historical encroachments was the trial of John Peter Zenger in New York, in August, 1735. Zenger was an immigrant printer from Germany. He used his *New York Weekly Journal* as a mouthpiece of opposition to the authoritarian regime of Governor William Cosby, representative of the British Crown. Cosby had him put into jail and tried on a charge of libel. Under the English law of the time, which was the law of the colonies too, Zenger could not plead the truth of his newspaper articles as a defense against the charge of libel. As the prosecuting attorney argued, "It is not less a libel because it is true."

To the surprise of Chief Justice James De Lancey, handpicked as Cosby's man in the colony's court system, there appeared in defense of Zenger an old man of nearly eighty, known to be one of the great lawyers of the colonies. He was Andrew Hamilton of Philadelphia—not to be confused with Alexander Hamilton, who was not born until twenty-two years later.

Justice De Lancey, basing his decision on Star Chamber precedents, refused to let Hamilton prove that the facts as Zenger had printed them were true. Thereupon the defense attorney, in an address to the jury that became a classic, neatly made the verdict turn upon the truth none the less. "And were you to find a Verdict against my Client," argued the elderly Hamilton, "you must take upon you to say, the Papers referred to in the Information, and which we acknowledge we printed and published, are *false, scandalous, and seditious*." [10] They knew that what Zenger had written was substantially true, and agreed with such bias as it had. So their verdict was, Not Guilty. Thereby this jury of American colonists established for themselves and for us the right to which Andrew Hamilton had appealed in his peroration: the right "both of exposing and opposing arbitrary Power . . . by speaking and writing Truth." [11]

During the two centuries since Zenger's trial, the independent Fourth Estate in this country has suffered many other trials,

many other limitations, on its freedom. Yet thus far it has survived in its essential character of an unmuzzled check on government. The reason was put into a few words by another eighteenth century Englishman, Thomas Erskine. Defending Thomas
Paine in a British court some half a century after the Zenger
trial, again on a libel charge, Erskine said:

> In this manner power has reasoned in every age; government,
> *in its own estimation,* has been at all times a system of perfection;
> but a free press has examined and detected its errors, and the people
> have from time to time reformed them. This freedom has alone
> made our Government what it is; this freedom alone can preserve
> it.[12]

All governments from that day to this—all the Goebbelses of
Nazism, all the thinkers of the Communist revolution, all the
recent upheavals in our own America—have yet to disprove the
validity of the theory of a free press as Erskine stated it. Therefore we must accept it as fact that no man, however farreaching
the information that is his by virtue of his office at the center
of government, however deep his understanding of the temper
of his time, is wise enough to judge himself and his acts before
the people. He must always be subject to criticism by the press,
however sincerely he may believe that he is right and the press
wrong, however convinced he may be that in the people's own
interest a hostile newspaper's opinion ought to be made to conform to the sympathetic opinions of his own supporters. That
is what John Stuart Mill must have had in mind when he wrote
that "we can never be sure that the opinion we are endeavoring
to stifle is a false opinion." [13] And that is why we cannot approach the faults of contemporary journalism without first
accepting the major premise that, no matter what else is done,
we cannot have democracy without a Fourth Estate, sheltered
behind the principle of a free press in the precise meaning of
that term as hammered out in Anglo-Saxon history.

THE FOURTH ESTATE IN ACTION

THAT eighteenth century crusader for reason and justice, François Marie Arouet de Voltaire, is popularly believed to have written his fellow philosopher, Claude Adrien Helvetius, this ringing declaration: "I disapprove of what you say, but I will defend to the death your right to say it." A noble thought, surely. Unfortunately, Voltaire never uttered it. The phrase was invented and ascribed to Voltaire in 1906 by the English writer, E. Beatrice Hall, of *The Friends of Voltaire*.[1] Even so, those eighteen words aptly phrase the principle behind the ideal of a press that is free in the historic sense.

Unfortunately, no human society has yet reached that level. Voltaire himself violated the rule ascribed to him on at least one occasion. In a letter dated February 13, 1759, he protested hotly because a certain bookseller had published a pamphlet that Voltaire called "contre les môeurs, contre la religion, contre la paix des particuliers, contre le bon ordre." [2] Here the great man was unmistakably disapproving what another said, but he was hardly defending to the death the other's right to say it.

Voltaire's annoyance when he encountered liberty of opinion in the flesh is characteristic of us all. That the attitude can be enacted into law even here in the land of the free is shown by the Sedition Law of 1798, and the Alien Law coupled with it. During World War I we reenacted the idea in the 1918 amendment to the Espionage Act of 1917; and the alien restrictions were again made stiffer as World War II came on, though this time their administration was far more enlightened. All this is simply a reflection of the fact that throughout our national history we have never hesitated to restrict freedom of expression when something else has seemed to matter more. The public will to do this has expressed itself in all kinds of ways, from lynching a former Revolutionary general when he sought to help an editor distribute an unpopular newspaper during the War of 1812 to the criminal syndicalism laws enacted by many states. Nor is the halter on freedom merely a temporary aberration during crises; the long history of our libel laws shows that, while we may want a press that is free, we don't want what we consider abuse of freedom, at any time.

Nor is this surprising. Who would "defend to the death" the right of a Colonel Robert R. McCormick, publisher of the *Chicago Tribune,* to call his own country's government an enemy while we were deep in the greatest war of our history? TRIBUNE CHECKS FILES ON FORMER AIDS TURNED FOES, said a *Tribune* headline on May 24, 1942.[3] This sounded as though some *Tribune* correspondents abroad might have turned traitor and gone to work for the Axis. A reading of the story itself, though, shows that nothing of the kind had happened. Instead, four journalists once on its staff were now "foes" of the *Tribune* and therefore, apparently, enemies of their country, presumably because the *Tribune* was champion of the American Way of Life. Their seditious activity—to follow the paper's line of reasoning—consisted of a campaign made under "the respectable cloak of the Russian war effort" against that way of life. The fascinated reader discovered that one of them was carrying out his nefarious designs from the shelter of "a fat government 'information' job." This reprehensible character, it turned out, was none other than Edmond L. Taylor, distinguished author of that exposé of the Nazi war of nerves, *The Strategy of Terror.* The others were William L. Shirer, Jay Allen, and George Seldes.

This kind of thing surely crosses over the invisible line that delimits responsible use of the press's right to freedom. Yet the

Tribune, even though the item referred to was just one sample of many, was not suppressed. By contrast, Father Coughlin's *Social Justice* was suppressed, and from the contrast we can perhaps see more clearly how we ourselves consent to practical limits on the freedom of the Fourth Estate. *Social Justice* was a weekly journal of opinion, the personal mouthpiece [4] of the well known demagogue Father Charles Edward Coughlin, pastor of the Shrine of the Little Flower in Detroit. Even though *Social Justice* was obviously fascist-minded, it was suffered to live, under the supposed Voltaire philosophy, until war came. Then, on May 4, 1942, it was suppressed. Government evidence indicated that *Social Justice* "had by direct statement and implication sought to blame the United States and President Roosevelt for the war, and had called on the people in the name of 'reason' to bring it to an end, and had in other ways repeated the propaganda line of the Axis." Accordingly Postmaster General Frank C. Walker, using the means by which the federal government has long controlled questionable advertising, denied *Social Justice* further access to the mails under our postal laws.[5]

Where then was Milton's thesis that Truth could not be put to the worse in a free and open encounter? The answer is, I think, that we did not care to wait for Father Coughlin's falsehoods to be overtaken by what seemed to us the truth, because to do so would have gotten in the way of our will to fight. With the national life itself in danger we would rather suppress *Social Justice* than live up to the letter of our free-press principle. And so long as suppression is on the unmistakable ground of disloyalty in war, who will quarrel with it?

This is vastly different from doing the same thing in time of peace, or for any reason less momentous than overt opposition to a life-and-death war. So, in practice as distinct from theory, one does arrive at this modification of the free-press principle: that in time of war it may be abrogated on the ground of sedition (agitation in the direction of treason stopping short of an overt act) or of treason (an overt attempt to overthrow the government). Even so, suppression is dangerous, even in time of war, because only later generations can tell "whether the opinion we are trying to stifle is a false opinion."

It is of course true that in peacetime too we make compromises with freedom. As Harold J. Laski put it: "The meaning of liberty will vary with every age. Each generation will have certain things it prizes as supremely good and will demand that these, above all, should be free." [6] The things a generation does not want free it will suppress either directly—by mob action if need be—or more usually through sanctioning the legal actions of its courts, legislatures, and executives.

The long history of our willingness to negate in detail the broad theory of the free press, however, brings one up short. Looking at past suppressions with the perspective of hindsight, one comes to the conviction that the more nearly inviolable free speech and free press are, the better for the common good. The risk of persecution, in denying them, is too great. The censor is all too likely to squelch a minority that speaks for a future majority. Therefore the burden of proof should lie always on him who would suppress, rather than the other way around. A publication must be presumed innocent until proved guilty.

This view was well expressed a few years ago in the dissenting opinions of the Supreme Court's five-to-four decision upholding the right of communities to tax the sale of religious literature by the rather bumptious sect known as Jehovah's Witnesses. As Associate Justice Murphy wrote at the time, "If this court is to err in evaluating claims that freedom of speech, freedom of the press, and freedom of religion have been invaded, far better that it err in being overprotective of those precious rights." Or, as the American Bar Association's Committee on the Bill of Rights put it in connection with the same case:

The philosophy of free institutions is now being subjected to the most severe test it has ever undergone. Advocates of totalitarian government point to the speed and efficiency with which such systems are administered, and assert that democracy can offer nothing to outweigh these advantages. The answer is to be found in the value of certain basic individual rights and the assurance afforded by free institutions that these shall not be required to yield to majority pressure, no matter how overwhelming.[7]

When a man sees in a newspaper some fact or opinion that offends him, he is likely to follow the real Voltaire into scandalized irritation. He will ask: "Why this freedom of the press? Why should this newspaper writer have constitutional protec-

tion for doing what he damn pleases, when neither I nor anyone else have anything like it in my business?"

Freedom of the press thus appears to be a license granted to
the writer or publisher, and not what it really is—a right that
belongs to and protects the people; for, as Professor Zechariah
Chafee, Jr., said of freedom of speech, it is really valuable not
to the minority that wants to talk, but to the majority that does
not want to listen.[8] In practice, the benefits of the Fourth Estate
do not come to us directly and visibly, as do the newspaper items
that offend us, but indirectly. This happens because somehow,
out of the free-for-all of fact and opinion, there usually emerges
when needed the corrective fact or argument that holds government in line when it strays from the path of virtue. It is this
almost automatic corrective quality that has proved, through
the centuries, to be man's safest insurance that his rulers will
not err too greatly.

If this seems an exaggeration, consider a few examples now
far enough in the past to be viewed with reasonable objectivity.
On December 17, 1941, President Roosevelt issued Executive
Order No. 8982, transforming the Economic Defense Board into
the Board of Economic Warfare. On April 13, 1942, he defined
the functions of the BEW in Executive Order No. 9128, which
he promulgated without showing it to any of the victims of its
changes within the government.[9] No one objected openly when
the text was read in the government departments and agencies
affected. Certainly the public, busy with its own worries, accepted Order No. 8982 either in complete ignorance or at most
as one of those myriad new things needed to get on with the
war. Not so the Fourth Estate. The *New York Times'* chief
Washington correspondent and political writer, Arthur Krock,
wrote in his column:

> After detailed inspection and checking with government officials,
> the deeper effect of this extraordinary document is revealed as sup-
> planting the State Department in the formulation of fundamental
> foreign policy.[10]

The rest of the column went on to explain why and how. In
subsequent days the wheels of the free-press machinery continued to grind, with Krock returning to the charge on April
30, and with others taking up the cause. In due course, the

President, who apparently had been unaware of this effect of the order he had signed, issued a statement on May 21, 1942, saying:

In the making of decisions the board and its officers will continue to recognize the primary responsibility and position, under the President, of the Secretary of State in the formulation and conduct of our foreign policy and our relations with foreign nations.[11]

The Fourth Estate had once again served as monitor of the government.

At this point, the reader who is less interested in a free press than in the hostility of many newspapers to liberalism is likely again to become impatient. I can only remind him once more that his turn is coming in the next chapter, and point out here that the concept of a Fourth Estate, like all the rest of the apparatus of democracy, is predicated less on the assumption that man will follow some altruistic ideal than on recognizing and making use of the push-and-pull among self-interested groups. Therefore, although at that time, at least, Krock had earned from many a Roosevelt supporter the title of New Deal baiter, he was nevertheless putting into practice the theory of the free press. Let us say that he merely took an unholy joy in shying rocks at the White House. Even so, his published criticism was a perfect example of the Fourth Estate in action, for it was his act and not his motive that mattered. Roosevelt's own remedial action as regards the BEW and the State Department was an admission that an error had been committed by government. That error was made public by a representative of the Fourth Estate; and, at least in part because this brought the affair out into the open where all could see it, a change was made in the public interest.

Time and again, in matters high and low, this process takes place. Half a year before Pearl Harbor, Secretary Ickes was able to keep valuable war supplies from going to a Japan that already seemed a probable enemy. As defense oil coordinator, he halted a shipment of 252,000 gallons of lubricating oil to Japan on the *Azuma Maru,* which was awaiting its cargo at a Philadelphia dock. Why? Because a private firm had brought the proposed shipment to his attention. And how did the private firm know about it? A newspaper story had revealed it.[12]

Again, it was not until more than two months after the outbreak of war that American aircraft manufacturers were given priority ratings on a par with those enjoyed by producers of tanks and ships. Donald M. Nelson, chairman of the War Production Board, finally ordered the change. Why? You've guessed it: "His action followed the publication of a magazine story charging that the priority system was obsolete and that its application to airplanes was hampering production." [13]

This is a process that goes on unobtrusively day in and day out, in peace as in war. For example, some time after the war the United Nations Military Staff Committee, long deadlocked between the conflicting desires of the Russians and the rest of the world, finally agreed on a report as to the composition of the U.N. world police force, but still kept the report secret. All its work had been done under wraps. But after a competent reporter unearthed the report and published the gist of it, the Staff Committee finally adopted a policy of letting the public in on what it was doing in the public's name.[14]

It is not always the free press alone that initiates these corrections of government. Often an interested official, or a disgruntled Congressman, or an honest lawyer, or a pressure group, or some other fragment of an estate strikes the initial spark, with motives ranging from black to white. But without the facilities of our information system for spreading facts throughout the community, it would be extremely difficult, probably impossible, to enforce the correction. This may be seen in the famous fight over the Supreme Court bill in 1937. Formal opposition came from self-interested political opponents on the Senate Judiciary Committee, but it was publication of their objections that made the fight a national issue. The question was thus debated on a continental scale. Publicity reenforced existing political pressures, and Congress, in the end, defeated the bill.

It is not alone the Executive who errs and is called to account by an aroused Fourth Estate. Any other authority—governmental, religious, or lay—may fall foul of the watchful eye of the press. Congress is a favorite victim of the Fourth Estate's delight in keeping others on the strait and narrow path. Again to choose examples from the early impact of war on the nation, consider both the congressional pension scheme and the flurry over unlimited gasoline for congressmen in the first confusion over rationing. Now, congressional pensions are not evil in themselves. In fact, they seem highly desirable. But a weary and irritated Congress voted them to itself and to members of the executive departments at the turn of the year 1941 to 1942. This was the time when Bataan followed Pearl Harbor, when Malaya, Singapore, Java, and the Philippines were falling, one after another. Everywhere the United Nations were retreating. Gradually the awful need for "blood, toil, tears, and sweat" came home to the American public. It was this moment of national sacrifice that Congress chose to vote itself pensions. The House passed the bill without debate or roll call, the Senate by 42 to 24. The President protested, but signed it on January 27, 1942. Then the newspaper campaign that had begun with the House's original vote reached a crescendo. It was too much for Congress. By February 19 the Senate reversed itself, 75 to 5. The House followed along, 289 to 7. By March 9 the President signed the repeal.

In the same way, when gasoline rationing began along the East Coast with the system of A, B, and X cards, Congress held itself entitled to X cards. These carried the right to unlimited gasoline, and were intended, like the later C cards, for doctors and those who had to get about no matter what. The people were expected to be content with an A card, then worth three gallons a week, or, if more essential to life or defense work, with the various B cards. But when the press published what senators and congressmen said about being entitled to X cards, the legislators responded with a flood of irritated oratory. Characteristic was Senator La Follette's assertion that this was part of "a deliberate campaign to undermine faith in Congress, which might even destroy our representative form of government"; and Senator Bankhead's annoyed suggestion that the Attorney General investigate critical newspapers, which he said had been guilty of seditious conduct.[15] As Raymond Clapper wrote, our representatives were "handing out personal abuse to rationing officials and . . . denouncing the press for reporting the fact that they are chiseling unlimited gasoline cards."[16] The issue finally died down when a new and more workable method of rationing was set up. But once again we had seen the Fourth Estate in action.

By observing the press as it has functioned day in and day out, through the years, the decades, and even the centuries, we can deduce a corollary of the principle of the Fourth Estate. It is this: There must reside in the newspapers—and now too in the other media of information—a suspicious curiosity and perpetual skepticism about all things.

The press can never, as we have seen, be wholly free; but, to make sure that neither authority nor the public itself carries restriction too far, it must maintain the balance of forces by constant pressure in the opposite direction. This investigatory proclivity may be likened to a coiled spring, ever ready to snap into action at the least excuse. Whenever a news event happens, as it does a thousand times a day, this force must work as swiftly and as blindly as a reflex action of the nerves.

Such an attitude on the part of newspapers is probably difficult for laymen to understand. They see it work harm at times, and are troubled. Also they see individual newspapers abuse it by prying into private matters that turn out to be none of their business. The public remembers the exceptions and abuses, which are easier to comprehend than the steady, unspectacular force in the press that keeps democracy from atrophying.

Let us look for a moment at what happens when the press is politely unquestioning. At the time of the collapse of France in the early summer of 1940, a correspondent of the *Manchester Guardian,* who had lived through the debacle, put much of the blame for it on absence of a free and critical press:

> The result of it [the rigorous French censorship] was eight months of perfect complacency followed by a fearful shock, which was all the more demoralizing as the public—and even the troops—had been completely unprepared for it. The censorship was one of the chief causes of France's collapse; let us not forget it.[17]

In the same way, Thomas Mann, distinguished author and refugee from Germany, warned America to guard the vigilance of its press. An interviewer quoted him as saying:

> It is when fear enters the lives of a nation's citizens that the danger of totalitarianism is upon it. . . . Dictatorship is essentially based on terror. The press can be in fear long before any actual control is exercised over it, so that its freedom may be surrendered in effect even before it is lost in actuality.[18]

Here, then, we can see what happens when the Fourth Estate stops prying into things after scandalized cries from the great and the respectable that, in so prying, it is wrecking the nation and destroying all things good in the sight of God and man.

The service rendered by a vigilant Fourth Estate stands out when it is placed against a background so vast as the disintegration of a nation; but it is harder to appreciate on the smaller scale of daily life. One reason may be that the district-attorney habit of the press often works blindly. It leaps into action when the signal comes. One cannot always tell at the time whether it will work for good or ill. Only later—perhaps years later, when the historians have thoroughly worked over ground long neglected by the living—can we find out whether in this particular event the Fourth Estate's innate suspicion of man and his actions was justified.

Regrettably, newspapers sometimes so far forget their obligation that, instead of prying into dark corners, they cover them up by deliberately suppressing news. But the fact remains that newspapermen have acquired a tendency to ask, in even the most ordinary circumstances, Why? They have learned from their fellow men, whom it is their business to observe at first hand, that it is necessary to look under the rug for dust, to peep behind the brilliant façade for what may or may not lie behind —even though official guardians try to keep them out. The upright and the respectable may assure the world that all is well, yet it is the business of a somewhat misanthropic press to see for itself. Experience on experience has shown that the man who stacks the neatest and the biggest woodpile is often likely to hide something in it.

Unfortunately, such a power to investigate, such a tendency to pry, is open to abuse. It has led the press into moral cellars in which it seemed desirable to hound a President Cleveland with publicity on his wedding trip, to steal from a private house or office the photograph of someone whom tragedy has suddenly brought into the news. It has twice caused Mrs. Charles A. Lindbergh the anguish of living mentally through a second kidnaping of a child, only to learn that the supposed kidnapers were news photographers under orders to get a picture.[19]

Presumably it was a reaction against such treatment of respected personages that led the London journalist Albany Fonblanque to write a century ago: "The mobbing in the streets does not seem to us a whit more annoying and unmannerly than this mobbing in the Press. In both there is the same low, vulgar, prying spirit." [20]

The Vassar historian Lucy Maynard Salmon has pointed out that matters of taste and selection enter here, since what is a legitimate power of inquiry into matters of government seems less legitimate if applied to ordinary people merely for the human interest there may be in their lives. "It is impossible to touch pitch without being defiled," she writes. "The representatives of the press that lower their standards to minister to vulgar taste are themselves thereby debased." [21]

Objection sustained. The press does at times poke its nose into dirt that were better left covered, or into affairs which, even though God allows them to happen on this good green earth, were better not exposed before a gawking public. The result has been a trend in recent years to erect legal barriers around the individual's right to privacy—another limitation on the press's freedom that the public seems ready to sanction.

And yet—who is to set the standard? Who is to decide where the line shall be drawn between what the press should not publicize and what, in the long-run public interest, it should lay open? For example, shortly after Pearl Harbor, troubled friends asked me how the press could justify what they called the smear campaign of the *New York Post* against the wartime chairman of the Senate Naval Affairs Committee. If you have forgotten the details, better let them stay forgotten. Suffice it to say that the *Post* had been radically prowar before Pearl Harbor, and the senator had been one of our confirmed isolationists. The charges by the *Post* focused on this point. But they hinged more largely on a point of personal conduct by the senator that was outrageously libelous to print.[22] Why not, asked my friends, concentrate on the question of the senator's insight or his patriotism? Why not let his personal life alone, at least?

To answer that the personal life of a public figure is *ipso facto* also public—whether we like it or not—did not quiet their doubts. It is hard for laymen to understand the meaning of the statement that Caesar's wife must be above suspicion. And in this particular episode there was the further fact that the circumstances linked both the public and the private aspects of the charges inextricably. It was impossible to make charges in the patriotic interest without dragging in the personal matters too.

So there you are again. How does one distinguish between vulgarity and public service? Who is to decide? A board of censors? But human experience with censors has not been happy. The accused? But the history of jurisprudence has shown that the guilty rarely decide against themselves. Or is the point which we have reached on balance the best—that the press itself should be free to decide, free to make up its own mind, even at the risk of making mistakes?

In passing, one may offer a suggestion to those who themselves become the victims of the newspapers' habit of prying. The best defense is to come clean. If somebody wants your picture, let them take it, even though it seems obvious to you that it is none of their damned business. If a reporter asks a question, answer it frankly. With nothing to conceal, few who respond with honesty and fairness rather than with hostility and a desire to tell the press where to get off suffer greatly from its nosiness. It is with shutting the door that trouble begins, for that makes it look as though there were something to hide; and then the hounds are on the trail with a vengeance.

It is best to be broad-minded about this. Human institutions are rarely perfect, and newspapers are no exception. The nearest we can get to perfection is a balance of forces that works reasonably well. So if you are troubled by the impersonal and almost amoral pressure of the Fourth Estate to find out what is going on, come hell or high blood pressure, the best thing is to grin and bear it. To do so is, in the long run, in your own interest. The Fourth Estate, the free press, the prying press—they are all one and the same thing—is like rain that soaks you to the skin. The soaking may annoy you, but without rain you could not live. Without a press free to pry, democracy cannot live.

THE FOURTH ESTATE IN THE
TWENTIETH CENTURY

IN THE eighteenth century, when America was a nation of farmers, the doctrine of the free press fitted neatly into the scheme of things. Any good American, having gotten himself a wife and a place to live, was likely to start a newspaper. Perhaps, indeed, the eighteenth century pamphleteer considered his right to self-expression even more important than a wife or a home.

At the very least, the Revolutionary American could, if he did not himself own a newspaper, contribute to existing ones. Lawyer, parson, teacher, doctor, merchant, farmer—all who had something to say could say it. Sports, comics, columns, women's pages, and feature pages did not clutter the papers, so that contributions were welcome. Though circulations were small, less than 1,500 for the most part, the practice of reprinting from contemporaries made it relatively easy for the literate citizen to make himself heard before a state-wide and even a nation-wide audience. In this way Alexander Hamilton, James Madison, and John Jay put the *Federalist* papers before the whole America of their day by contributing most of them to a New York semiweekly, the *Independent Journal; or, the General Advertiser.*

Throughout the nineteenth century the doctrine of the free

press continued substantially to suit the country. As recently as 1895, one of our great editors, William Allen White, bought the *Emporia Gazette* as a poor young man of twenty-seven. As he used to put it, in those days anybody with a shirttail full of type and $200 could start a paper. He himself arrived in Emporia with $1.25 of his own in his pocket, having borrowed all of the $3,000 with which he bought the *Gazette*.[1] And as he said later:

> . . . when I bought the *Gazette* . . . I could do everything in that little one-room office . . . that I asked anyone else to do. I could set type, put the paper to press, feed the press, kick the jobber, set the meager advertising that was used in those days, keep the books, solicit the advertising, take charge of the circulation, deliver the paper, solicit subscribers, and run the bank account, such as it was.[2]

Already by that time, however, the far different journalistic economics of today had cast their shadows before them in the big cities, where starting a newspaper had ceased to be a task for a man with ambition, and had become one for a man with a fortune. The new pattern was dramatized early in this century by the late Frank Munsey, a self-made magazine publisher who bought his way into the newspaper field, and during a busy career took over, merged, or killed seventeen newspapers in five cities. Among the New York papers that passed through his hands were the *Press*, the *Sun*, the *Evening Sun*, the *Globe and Commercial Advertiser*, the *Evening Telegram*, and the *Herald*. Of these six only one, the *Sun*, survives today, and two others live on as names in the merged properties of the *Herald Tribune* and the *World-Telegram*.

So, too, when some years later (early depression years) the *Washington Post* went into a decline and threatened to disappear, it was revived not by a bright young editor-publisher, but by the wealthy Eugene Meyer, who rescued it with a non-journalistic fortune. Again, when soon after its founding in 1940 it became necessary to save the adless *PM* from extinction, it was not editorial ingenuity, but support from the Marshall Field fortune that did the trick. And the dominant *Chicago Tribune* was given brief competition in the morning field only because Field, thanks again to his non-journalistic fortune, was able to do it.

The reactions of America's liberals as they watched our newspapers becoming fewer and richer were summed up in that brief obituary William Allen White wrote:

Frank Munsey, the great publisher, is dead.
Frank Munsey contributed to the journalism of his day the talent of a meat packer, the morals of a money changer, and the manners of an undertaker. He and his kind have about succeeded in transforming a once-noble profession into an 8 per cent security.
May he rest in trust.[3]

As the control of journalism became increasingly the prerogative of the rich, a profound change took place—something came between the newspapers and their readers. Today the people still read the papers avidly, to be sure. But they no longer feel so much at one with them—a fact dramatized in Mr. Roosevelt's procession of election campaigns, in which a majority of the voters were regularly on his side and a majority of publishers as regularly on the other. For the most part, the publishers insisted that in this ideological split it was the people and not the papers that were wrong. Occasionally, however, a doubting voice was raised even within their ranks. One arch-Republican publisher, James E. Stiles of the *Nassau Review-Star* on Long Island, had this to say in a moment of self-examination:

Why should the press be afraid of the President or the New Deal, if it had the leadership and influence it should have? We have the largest constituency of any force in the country. The President when he ran for a third term received more than 20,000,000 votes, but the press sells more than 40,000,000 copies of the daily papers every day in the week and we take for granted that each copy is read by an average of four persons.
If the press, as a source of information and guidance, held the respect and confidence of its readers, it would be a more powerful force than the President, the Congress, or that entire aggregation that we term the New Deal. It would not be a case of the press fearing the New Deal. The New Deal would appreciate and respect the power of the press. The fact that we are the ones who have been doing the worrying shows that we are not sure of our position and certainly not sure of our audience. . . .

The press has missed a wonderful opportunity in not embracing and clarifying the President's program, exerting its prestige as a positive influence, to steer it unfalteringly along the lines I have described. . . . Here is the cause of the ages brought up to date, the deathless, unending struggle of the common man for recognition of the dignity of the individual. And the press of America has thrown it out of the window.[4]

Whether the press has thrown the cause of the common man out of the window, or whether the common man has gone chasing after other gods than those of Anglo-Saxon liberalism—or both—is beside the point here. What matters is that the honored theory of the free press has come to seem remote from reality. It is an anachronism as it wanders through the twentieth century dressed in its eighteenth century clothes. The change has made it inevitable that the liberals among us, those very persons whose prototypes in previous generations fought for the freedom of the press, now battle against the press instead.

Clearly, something about the Fourth Estate is out of whack.

In liberal and academic circles the legend persists that advertising is the villain who betrayed the once virgin Fourth Estate. The theory is beautiful in its simplicity. In the old days, it holds, the press was a modest affair, with little or no advertising. Therefore its prime interest was to serve the people. But today the press draws the bulk of its huge income from advertising. Therefore it listens to its advertisers rather than to its readers. Q.E.D.

Support for this view comes, moreover, from high places. For example, when the New York *Star* was founded in New York in 1940 as *PM,* with the war cry "We Sell No Advertising"—since abandoned—President Roosevelt took enough interest to remark:

As you know, I have been critical at times of a part of the daily press. Too often the news of this part of the press has been colored because of front office prejudice or "business" reasons.

Your proposal to sustain your enterprise simply by merchandising information, with the public as your only customer, appeals to me as a new and promising formula for freedom of the press.[5]

Support for the thesis that advertising is the root of the trouble can also be found within the journalistic ranks. Early in the depression years, for example, the magazine *The Purchasing Agent,* changing its name to *Purchasing* as a symbol of the reform it was about to undertake, made this ringing declaration:

In common with all business journal publishers, we have heretofore depended on advertising for our major income. For the most part advertisers are fair in their attitude toward publications they support, and that is particularly true of the class of advertisers with whom we have dealt. Nevertheless, we assert that no journal can be truly independent, critical and untrammeled so long as its existence depends primarily on the favor and good will of advertisers. In every publishing office there arise constant problems of whether or not to print facts, comment or opinion which may adversely affect the interests of advertisers. . . . Our purpose in abolishing advertising from the pages of *Purchasing* is to be free from the most remote or subconscious form of influence over editorial policies.[6]

It is also possible to find examples of advertising pressure. Most persons who have had experience in the business, notably on newspapers or magazines whose economic foundations are shaky, have encountered it occasionally. Not many cases, to be sure, are particularly significant in themselves. They are of the kind, probably more common a generation ago, in which newspapers would ignore accidents that happened in department stores, or would discreetly pass over encounters with the law by substantial advertising clients or their sons. Sometimes, however, the suppressions really matter. You can find examples in Upton Sinclair [7] and George Seldes.[8] Or consider this personal letter from an editor, which I present with several blanks, changes, and fictitious names out of respect for the laws of libel:

I did not sleep right and my mind was in a constant state of turmoil over such damn things as Black's advertising and whether or not Green's advertising was not being menaced by things I was saying. The break came over . . . [an] editorial. . . . It was only a ten-line swat, but said what I had in mind. The Black management demanded my head. My publisher put up a fight and then all Black's advertising was withdrawn. My publisher called a meeting and said he proposed to cut expenses, that is, take out of the staff any loss he might suffer because of the Black withdrawal. I said, "Here's my head." He replied, "Unthinkable," but he didn't say it quickly enough and I knew that he meant "thinkable." So, I insisted and he did it, and by this time has no doubt delivered the old coco on a silver platter to Smith and Jones and all the rest of the hard-boiled gang, and they are having the laugh of the season. . . .

The simple fact is that we have permitted Green, Brown, White and Black . . . to get away with murder, and our own advertising has been the real reason. I cannot stomach it.

In other words, there is such a thing as advertising pressure. Yet, the more one studies the subject, the more one becomes convinced that advertising pressure on editorial integrity is a symptom rather than a cause of the present economic orientation of the press. Regrettably, the whole matter is not so simple that, if only advertising were banished from journalism, the press would automatically assume the independence characteristic of the true Fourth Estate.

We can best see why by glancing backward over the history of newspaper advertising. And the starting point is that advertising, far from being a twentieth century phenomenon, has been an integral part of journalism since the beginning. In printed journalism it all began shortly before the end of the sixteenth century when Seigneur Michel Eyquem de Montaigne, philosopher and essayist, suggested that there ought to be some means by which sellers could tell buyers what they had to offer. If someone had pearls to sell and another wanted to buy them, if someone sought a servant and a servant sought a job, and so on, the lot of them ought to have some place in which they could meet.[9]

About this time such a meeting place for buyers and sellers appeared in the rudimentary printed newspaper. A German newsbook of 1591 contained a poem recommending a book.[10] It is not known who first discovered that newspaper notices to prospective buyers would be paid for by prospective sellers, but the newspapers' motive in printing them—namely, to help defray the cost of editorial matter—is clear; for, since the very beginning, printed journalism has been characterized by an economic fact that those who criticize advertising and its influence on newspapers choose to ignore. Yet this fact—that *readers have never been willing to pay the cost of the news they read, so that at no time and in no country in the world has circulation revenue alone paid for making and distributing a nation's newspapers*—is basic to an understanding of journalism. The deficit has had to be made up somehow, for as the *Journal des Débats* of Paris confessed in 1799, "*Il faut bien vivre.*" [11] Thus journalism is peculiar in that, unlike the other goods and services of our economy, which pay their own way, it has to a varying extent earned its living through sale of a by-product. And a study of what has happened in many countries in the last three centuries will show that a healthy volume of predominantly honest advertising, such as we have in this country now, is a cleaner by-product than the political subsidy familiar in the United States more than a century ago and in French journalism up to the Second World War, or the outright government subsidy of totalitarian states.

Tracing further the facts of Anglo-Saxon journalism's economic history, let us note that during the first half of the seventeenth century, about the time of John Milton's plea for unlicensed printing in *Areopagitica*, there grew up the practice of inserting in the embryo newspapers notices essentially like our classified advertisements. Consider this early specimen from the Dutch *Courante uyt Italian en de Duytschland* of July 23, 1633:

> With the last ships from the East Indies have been brought an elephant, a tiger, and an Indian stag, which are to be seen at the Old Glass house, for the benefit of the poor, where many thousands of people visit them.[12]

Even patent medicine advertising is not a corrupting influence peculiar to the press of the machine age, to judge by notices like this one, which appeared in Britain's *Mercurius Politicus* in December, 1660:

> Most Excellent and Approved *Dentrifices* to scour and the Teeth, making them white as Ivory, preserves from the Toothach; so that, being constantly used, the parties using it are never troubled with the Toothach; it fastens the Teeth, sweetens the Breath, and preserves the mouth and gums from Cankers and Imposthumes. Made by *Robert Turner,* Gentleman; and the right are onely to be

had at *Thomas Rookes,* Stationer, at the Holy Lamb at the East end of St. Paul's Church, near the School, in sealed papers, at 12d. the paper.[13]

By the beginning of the eighteenth century a different kind of advertising began to appear. It was not merely a notice that something was for sale, or that a new play was on, or that a slave had been lost, but a public argument on the merits of a product. Joseph Addison noted the trend in *Tatler* No. 224, of September 12–14, 1710:

A Second Use which this Sort of Writings have been turned to of late Years, has been the Management of Controversy, insomuch that above half the Advertisements one meets with now-a-Days are purely Polemical. The Inventors of *Strops for Razors* have written against one another this Way for several Years, and that with great Bitterness; as the whole Argument *pro* and *con* in the Case of the Morning-Gowns is still carried on in the same manner.[14]

In America, newspaper advertising ran much the same course, though, as with other journalistic matters, developments came some years later. Benjamin Franklin advertised in his newspapers, along with many other things, a Super Fine Crown Soap made by his brothers:

It cleanses fine Linens, Muslins, Laces, Chinces, Cambricks, etc., with Ease and Expedition, which often suffer more from the long and hard rubbing of the Washer, through the ill qualities of the soap than the wearing.[15]

Paul Revere, too, advertised one of his many talents in this fashion in the *Boston Gazette* for September 5, 1768:

Whereas many Persons are so unfortunate as to lose their Fore-teeth by Accident, and otherways, to their great Detriment, not only in Looks, but speaking both in Public and Private:—This is to inform all such, that they may have them re-placed with false Ones, that looks as well as the Natural, and answers the End of Speaking to all Intents, by PAUL REVERE, Goldsmith, near the Head of Dr. Clarke's Wharf, Boston.
All Persons who have had false Teeth fixt by Mr. John Baker, Surgeon-Dentist, and they have got loose (as they will in Time) may have them fastened by the above, who learnt the Method of fixing them from Mr. Baker.[16]

It is significant, too, that it was an excess of *advertising* rather than of news that brought about the appearance of the first daily in America. This was the *Pennsylvania Packet and Daily Advertiser,* which went from triweekly to daily publication on September 21, 1784. Pages 1 and 4 of the first four-page issue consisted of solid advertising. Page 3 was about evenly divided between news and advertising, and page 2 alone, was devoted to editorial matter exclusively.[17] Equally significant, the word "Advertiser" appears in the name of many early dailies, which were devoted largely to the interests of the mercantile class. Thus, the second daily in this country was the *South Carolina Gazette and General Advertiser.* New York's first was the *New York Daily Advertiser;* and Boston's, the *Polar Star and Daily Advertiser.*

In Chapter 18 we shall have occasion to see that Samuel Adams, Thomas Paine, and others demonstrated by their propagandist activities during the Revolution that newspapers could serve a cause. Since a cause might be that of a party as well as of patriotism, there followed a profound revolution in American journalism. Newspapers became political organs rather than primitive chroniclers of fact, and in so doing they tapped a new source of revenue—subsidies by political parties. This made the journalism of the half-century after the Revolution—which today may appear to the nostalgic citizen to have been the glorious heyday of the free press—actually the low point in our journalistic history. Whatever venality may today be traceable to the corrupting influence of advertisers is as nothing compared to the bias which in the late eighteenth and early nineteenth century came out of the party coffers. Vituperation and vilification, plus a blind disregard for any facts that did not suit party purposes, were the order of the day. Let any critic of today's press pick his pet hate among our newspapers and compare it with any paper of the party-subsidized days. Today's sinner will seem a paragon of honesty and accuracy by comparison. This is a fact established beyond question in the history of American journalism, though for some reason it goes unnoticed among today's critics of our newspapers.

Behind the growth of the party press, chronologically, another fact makes it difficult to sustain the theory that advertising corrupts the press to an important degree. For it was precisely the development of modern advertising that freed the press from the political purse, and so enabled it to become an independent news-gatherer. Here, as in news-gathering itself, James Gordon Bennett, who founded the *New York Herald* in 1835, was a pioneer. He and the other publishers of the penny press—that is, the large-circulation one- or two-cent papers addressed to the masses, as against the previous small-circulation four- or six-cent papers serving the mercantile and political classes—revolutionized advertising. Instead of charging $32 a year for unlimited advertising space, which merchants were apparently not bright enough to take full advantage of, Bennett charged by the square, a column-wide unit of space which in the *Herald* was sixteen agate lines deep. Rates were jacked up to meet the unprecedentedly large circulation—Bennett claimed 5,000 after six weeks—to 50 cents a day or $30 a year per square. Bennett was also Scot enough to insist on a doctrine new to advertising, payment right away instead of at the leisured pleasure of the advertiser.[18]

The result was a surprisingly rapid change from the party-kept press toward the modern newspaper that enjoys extensive news-gathering facilities because of its prosperous advertising schedule. We are so used to the modern and vastly improved version of the new type of newspaper introduced in the second quarter of the last century that we do not realize how profoundly the vulgar penny press changed journalism for the better. Yet it is the almost universal experience of newspaper workers today that papers with the heaviest advertising, far from being the most corrupt, are the ones most willing to tell advertisers to keep their noses out of editorial matters. Only those newspapers and magazines near the financial precipice can afford to give in to advertising pressure.

British experience, incidentally, duplicates our own; it was only after a heavy tax on newspapers and newspaper advertisements had been removed in 1855 that British papers came out from under the party wing and began to report events with a semblance of objectivity.

The situation has a logical basis. Advertising is now placed through advertising agencies—that is, through professionals, to whose advantage it is to get the most for their client's money. Agencies are interested in selling something in a particular region, or to a particular class or mass of customers. Hence they place their advertising in the media most likely to reach the group of readers they are after. In terms of newspapers, this means that the paper that best pleases its group of readers, who in turn show their satisfaction by buying it in large numbers, is the best buy for the advertiser. And a newspaper that trims its editorial sails to accommodate advertisers, even to a fraction of the extent to which the party press trimmed its sails toward its political masters, is so much less likely to please an extensive group of readers. Only the newspaper that is financially free— that stands on its own feet—has the fundamental prerequisite for reporting the news accurately and interpreting it honestly.

In trying to drive home this point, the publisher of the *New York Times,* Arthur Hays Sulzberger, spoke as follows:

Our income from circulation last year (and all my figures are for 1944) was some $7,000,000, or slightly less than one-third of our total. The balance of our revenue, aside from investments, is derived from advertising. This advertising revenue, in turn, can be broken down roughly as follows: 24 per cent comes from classified advertising; 46 per cent from national, and 30 per cent from retail. Now, the classified income came from approximately one million and a quarter individual advertisers or, it would be better to say, that number of individual advertisements—since if you are looking for a maid in these days it may be necessary to repeat the same advertisement forever.

Our national business represents many thousands of separate advertisers who have no association but are scattered about the country. Only in the retail group, which accounts for less than one-third of our business, could you pick out, say, twenty-five merchants who might hope by economic pressure to influence the freedom of our editorial expression. Well, I admit they might try it, but I can tell you very definitely that they have never done so; and I would point out further that since these are advertisers who deal directly with a mass of consumers, every business instinct must suggest to them the avoidance of interference in matters on which their customers differ.

I have gone into this at length, for I should like to knock down once and for all the fallacious notion that advertisers are a venal influence upon editorial policies and point out, conversely, that it isn't the advertising but the lack of advertising of which you should be fearful. When advertising revenue is nonexistent or insufficient, as was conspicuously the case in France before the war, then watch out! [19]

But, if advertising revenue tends to give independence, what of circulation revenue? We have already noted that throughout history, in all countries, readers have refused to pay in full the cost of gathering, editing, printing, and distributing the news they read. But they do contribute something. How much? And what is the influence of this presumably pure source of revenue on editorial policy?

The figures below indicate how small a part of newspaper revenue is derived today from subscribers. These percentages, based on the experience of ten California dailies, show the proportion of income derived from circulation in prewar years; [20] the rest of their revenue came from advertising:

1933	29.3%	1938	28.4%
1934	26.4	1939	29.7
1935	27.4	1940	28.3
1936	24.9	1941	29.4
1937	25.7	1942	33.6

While these ten papers are in no sense a scientific cross section, we may take them as typical of contemporary American newspapers. It has for decades been safe to assume that newspapers get from a quarter to a third of their income from circulation, the rest from advertising. During the war years there was a tendency for circulation revenue to rise even higher, a condition that has continued during the post-war period.

The influence of the two sources of newspaper income, advertising and circulation, on editorial policy has received an interesting analysis by Sevellon Brown, editor and publisher of the Providence *Journal* and *Bulletin*. His conclusions, presented in numerous speeches and writings, have not, so far as I can find, had the attention they deserve from those who are concerned with journalism.

Brown has assessed the relative influence of reader and advertiser on editorial policy, in the light of the principle that he who pays the piper calls the tune. He argues that the newspaper editor serves the reader under the creed of the late Melville Stone, "The newspaper is owned by the man who pays two cents for it"—though nowadays the price is likely to be three, four, or five cents rather than two. The business manager or publisher, on the other hand, watches the economic health of the

paper, and so keeps an eye on advertising revenue and matters
of interest to advertisers generally. It follows, says Brown, that
journalism is a profession within a business. As a business, it
lives on the sale of a by-product—advertising; but advertising
has value only because of the professional labor of the editorial
staff, carried on independently and perhaps in the face of advertising interests. He goes on:

> This is so complicated a performance that probably many news-
> papermen do not thoroughly understand it, so that it is not infre-
> quently the case that the editor knows his professional task and
> does it, and the publisher knows his job and does that, but neither
> of them quite understands the other fellow's performance. Yet the
> relationship is intimate and the independence is absolute. This is
> so true that there is a force almost intuitively felt in newspaper
> organizations compelling a balance between business interest and
> professional performance.
> It is this force—this balance, this dualistic motive—which gives
> the American newspaper its peculiar character. It is this which
> makes of the newspaper a reformer, but a responsible and cautious
> reformer.[21]

From the push and pull of this dualism, argues Sevellon
Brown, follows an interesting fact—that, as the current of
public affairs swings from right to left and back again, the newspaper tends to swing, as a counterbalance, to the opposite side.
The newspaper is always off center, first to the right and then
to the left of the national political trend.

We today are so painfully familiar with the depression and
the war that followed, which together covered more than a
decade and a half, that we tend to forget the fabulous twenties.
But in those years, as Brown points out, the newspapers tended
to be left of center. For all their fat revenue, their institutional-
ization, their peddling of syndicated entertainment, the leaders
among newspapers, at least, were predominantly on the side of
the man who owned the paper because he paid two cents for it.
With Calvin Coolidge in the White House, a policy of doing
nothing about fundamental domestic and foreign problems was
the national will. This tended to free the newspapers to move
politically to the left of government. Their advertising revenue
was secure and plentiful, and they could afford to remember

their heritage of the Fourth Estate and to be liberal in comparison to the rest of the national community. So, too, forty years ago a good part of American journalism, believing its economic life to be secure and not threatened by a high public debt, resulting high taxes, and a hostile administration, enjoyed going along with the first Roosevelt. It brought forth the muckraker, and it cartooned the trusts as predatory, potbellied monstrosities wearing clothes covered with dollar signs. Yes, even Hearst himself, the latter-day symbol of reaction, did that.

But after those days and after the twenties came the depression. For a little while—during the days of fright which the newspapers as well as the rest of us had in 1932 and early 1933—the press was on the side of the people, whooping it up for Franklin Roosevelt. The conservative *New York Sun,* as I recall it, devoted one day's entire front page to the dull and legal text of one of the early New Deal financial measures—so much did the President appear as the savior of our economy.

Once the implications of the New Deal became clear, however, the counterbalance of advertising revenue—to follow Sevellon Brown's thesis—swung around and carried a good part of the American press over to right of center. For the editors as well as the publishers became convinced that the New Deal was, for all the good it was doing, tearing down the America we knew. They tended for the most part to a social outlook that was the opposite of the view they had held during the days of Theodore Roosevelt and Taft, and during the smug era of Coolidge and Hoover.

Brown's diagnosis of the relative influence of advertising and circulation income offers a healthy corrective to the somewhat naïve assumptions of our liberals, who tend to date the beginning of political wisdom from March 4, 1933, because it helps to put the effect of advertising on editorial policy into perspective. But it does not, I submit, go to the heart of the trouble. For, granted that in time of social stability our newspapers have tended to be left of center, and that in time of upheaval they have tended to be right of center, advertising is not the factor that makes them swing to liberalism in order to counterbalance a Harding or a Coolidge, and to conservatism in reaction against a Franklin Roosevelt. Other far more fundamental facts, I think, explain why the twentieth century Fourth Estate is not the

consistently independent element of society—free to report and
to comment on the doings or misdoings of any other estate for
the benefit of all—that it should be. Let us look at those facts.

The real devil is nothing more sinister or obscure than the
effect on newspapers of the profound change that has taken
place in the whole of America during the last half-century.
For newspaper properties, just like railroads, automobile companies, corner groceries, and nearly everything else, have been
and still are metamorphosing themselves into ever bigger and
ever fewer units. Journalism was practically a one-man job in
the eighteenth century, and a highly individualistic and essentially small enterprise in the nineteenth. In the twentieth century it is just another big business.

The first thing to note in seeking the facts about this transformation is the growth, in spite of radio and the depression, of
the over-all circulation of American newspapers. Here are the
figures as to total daily circulation of all English-language papers
in recent decades: [22]

Year	Circulation	Year	Circulation
1921	28,423,740	1934	36,709,010
1922	29,680,328	1935	38,155,540
1923	31,453,683	1936	40,292,266
1924	32,999,437	1937	41,418,730
1925	33,739,369	1938	39,571,839
1926	36,001,803	1939	39,670,682
1927	37,966,766	1940	41,131,611
1928	37,972,592	1941	42,080,391
1929	39,425,615	1942	43,374,850
1930	39,589,172	1943	44,392,829
1931	38,761,187	1944	45,954,838
1932	36,407,679	1945	48,384,188
1933	35,175,238	1946	50,927,505
		1947	51,673,276

Thus, despite a serious eight-year slump after 1930, total circulation continues to grow. At first glance this seems to indicate
more outlets for free expression. A check soon indicates, however, that it means only that those newspapers that survive are
growing still larger and more powerful, because since World
War I the number of dailies in this country went down steadily,
at least until 1944. With the post-war inflation there came
a slight rise to a total of 1,769 by October 1, 1947.[23]   This

was twenty-five more than at the 1944 low point. But it was not yet up to 1942's then-diminishing total of 1,787. Moreover, although figures are not available, it is almost certain that this hopeful but modest increase did not keep pace with the growth of population. Nor has there appeared anywhere an indication that in the long pull there will be a reversal of the twentieth century trend toward a decline in the number of daily newspapers.

American newspapers began to be a social force during the two decades from 1770 to 1790, the decades of the Revolution and the Constitution. We can see why, by watching their numbers grow through our earlier years, as in the following graphic portrayal:

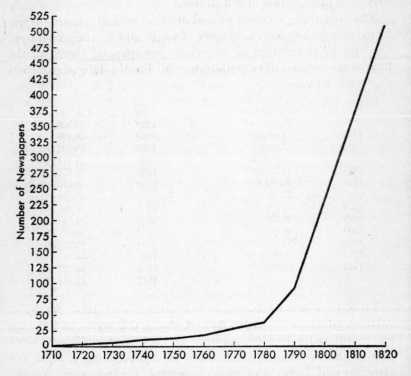

The explosive increase in the number of newspapers after the Revolution shows unmistakably that the basis of the free-press theory, as it had by that time taken shape, was sound.

It was sound because a rapidly growing number of newspapers provided outlets by which the people could with reasonable ease and directness air their views on government and other public matters. In fact, if one compares the number of post-Revolutionary newspapers with the population one finds that newspapers grew faster than the nation. For example:

Year	Population (millions)	Newspapers [24]	Papers per Million Population
1790	3.9	92	23.6
1800	5.3	235	44.3
1810	7.2	371	51.5
1820	9.6	512	53.5

The significant figures appear in the final column of this table, for they show that the *proportion of papers to population* rose continuously through the early years of the United States.

An identical pattern appears throughout the nineteenth century. Here, however, it is desirable to take a slightly different basis of calculation—daily newspapers only. The table above includes both weeklies and newspapers of more frequent appearance. The number of weeklies, of course, also continued to grow through the nineteenth century, and there are now some ten thousand. At some indefinable point in the nineteenth century, however, the daily newspaper surpassed the weekly as the dominant voice in public affairs. Therefore we can more conveniently trace the center of gravity of the free press by concentrating on the dailies alone. Here is the record:

Year	Population (millions)	Daily Newspapers [25]	Dailies per Million Population
1820	9.6	42	4.4
1830	12.9	65	5.0
1840	17.0	138	8.0
1850	23.0	254	11.0
1860	31.0	387	12.5
1870	39.0	574	14.7
1880	50.0	971	19.4
1890	63.0	1,610 [26]	25.5
1900	76.0	2,226 [26]	29.3
1910	92.0	2,600 [26]	28.2
1920	106.0	2,441 [26]	23.0
1930	123.0	2,086 [26]	16.9
1947	143.5	1,769 [27]	12.3

Examination of this table immediately reveals a difference from the earlier one. For while the number of dailies continued its steady growth through the decade ending in 1910, it thereafter began a decline, which so far appears to be relentless. Yet our population continued its lusty growth. And a comparison of the two shows that the *proportion of papers to population,* that significant index of the validity of the historic free-press theory, as revealed in the number of dailies per million inhabitants, began its decline at the turn of the century. Here is the final column in the table above, shown graphically:

This means that throughout what is virtually the first half of the twentieth century there was a reversal of the historic trend. The proportion of journalistic outlets to population shrank steadily and swiftly, and it is still shrinking.

We can glimpse something of what this decline means in practical terms by noting a few significant facts brought to light by the Office of Radio Research at Columbia University for the Newspaper Radio Committee in 1941. Take this contrast in the number of newspapers per town at the beginning and end of the depression decade: [28]

The totals show that the number of towns and cities enjoying daily newspaper service grew; but it tended to be the service of a single newspaper. The number of communities that had the luxury of two or more dailies shrank from 294 to 167 during the decade, while the number of those in which the free press was limited to a single daily grew from 1,096 to 1,268.

	1930		1940	
	No.	%	No.	%
Communities with two or more daily English-language papers	294	21	167	11.6
Communities with only one daily English-language paper	1,096	79	1,268	88.4
Totals	1,390	100	1,435	100.

Another study, by Raymond B. Nixon, director of the Division of Journalism at Emory University,[29] fills in later details in this picture of a shrinking supply of outlets for free expression. Professor Nixon points out that while we have more than 1,700 English-language dailies, if we allow for combinations and chains, the present maximum number of separate newspaper ownerships does not exceed 1,300. He gives this revealing information of the way concentrated ownership makes a bottleneck through which all the views expressed in our press have to pass:

Total number of cities with daily newspapers	1,394
One-daily cities	1,103
Other one-owner cities	161
Cities whose newspapers are partially merged	13
Total number of cities without competing newspapers	1,277
Total number of cities with competing newspapers	117

Professor Nixon's tabulation shows that ten states (Arizona, Delaware, Minnesota, Montana, New Hampshire, North Dakota, South Carolina, South Dakota, Virginia, and Wyoming) have no competing newspapers. Since his study was published John and Anna Roosevelt Boettiger turned a Phoenix shopping news they bought into a daily (since sold),[30] thus giving Arizona a solitary example of newspaper competition. Nevertheless the over-all condition indicated by the last two lines in the tabulation above, showing 117 American cities with daily newspaper competition while more than ten times as many, or 1,277, have none, tells the story of the Fourth Estate in the twentieth century.

One wonders, indeed, what is happening to the premise on which the doctrine of the free press was founded. Standard-broadcast radio in the United States is limited to some 2,000 stations because there is physically room for only that many in the spectrum. It may be that during this first half of the twentieth century a comparable economic spectrum has come into existence, and that there is room in the United States for only a fixed or perhaps even a shrinking number of daily newspapers.

This goes to the roots of democracy, and some of today's editors are scratching their heads over it. As Dwight Marvin, editor of the *Troy Record* newspapers, put it a few years ago:

I can remember . . . when the little city of Troy had seven regular newspapers, five of them dailies and two Sundays. . . . Today the *Record* newspapers (one morning and one evening paper under single ownership) are the only dailies left and there is a small Sunday paper. . . .

What then becomes of the freedom of the press? It represents in this city my right—or, if he wishes to exercise it, the publisher's— to say my say. If I wish to be decent enough I can let people write me letters on the other side; but I don't have to do this. Nobody can speak his mind in Troy except on the platform or on my say-so. Why? Because I don't want him to? Not at all! That is just what we are facing today in the trend toward concentration. If a man wants to say anything of which the newspaper doesn't approve he must hire a printer, print his broadside, distribute it at his own expense, and be considered queer.

As a matter of fact, because we believe in the freedom of the press, we open our columns willingly to the other side. But this makes freedom of the press less a constitutional right than a privilege we graciously grant to the other fellow.[31]

There are some thoughts here to which we must return at the end of this volume. For the present, let us state that freedom of the press seems to mean only the right of fewer than 1,800 newspaper publishers and their editors to impose their own picture of the physical world upon the minds of 145,000,000 Americans.

That is why I insist that it is not advertising, but the fact that we live in an era of fewer but richer newspapers that makes us question the contemporary validity of the free-press theory. For if modern journalism tends to speak the language of corporate business instead of that of the little fellow, it does so not because it is corrupt and venal but because it is itself a big business, a powerful institution with its interest vested in conservative economics. Its publishers and editors live in the same residential districts as the men who run the rest of big business. Publishers and editors, like their colleagues in the upper strata of our economy, look upon government from the higher income-tax brackets. In other words, journalism now tends *of its own accord* to think the same way and feel the same way as business. Humbert Wolfe neatly hit off the similar situation in Britain:

> You cannot hope to bribe or twist,
> Thank God, the British journalist;
> But seeing what the man will do
> Unbribed, there's no occasion to.[32]

The result is that John Milton's winds of doctrine, on which the theory of the free press is founded, no longer blow at will through the press. More than that, the concentration of daily journalism into fewer and bigger units has removed the free press from the people; for, though the humble citizen can still get a letter printed in his newspaper, it is exceedingly difficult for him to make himself heard by a national audience. Nor, failing that, can he feel sure as did his forefathers that the editor, being a neighbor in circumstances similar to his own, will speak his thoughts.

I am indebted to Paul F. Lazarsfeld, Director of the Bureau of Applied Social Research at Columbia University, for a simple way of visualizing what journalism's economic transformation has done to the theory of the free press. When that theory was young one could represent the facts graphically by connecting two points with a line, thus:

Individual o————o **Government**

The line between the two, representing relations between citizen and government, also represented freedom of the press, because for practical purposes the press and the individual were identical. In fact, the newspaper was hardly more than an artic-ulate individual with access to a printing press. Hence freedom of the press was directly and intimately a civil liberty of the individual.

Today's mighty engines of journalism, however, have changed the situation into a triangle like this:

The press, though it still fights its inevitable battle with government, and thus serves the citizen better than he realizes, has nevertheless grown to be an institution in its own right, and so is just as remote from the individual as is government. Instead of identifying himself with it, therefore, the citizen regards it as a big, powerful, and remote entity, with motives and interests that may well be entirely different from his own. The contemporary newspaper, he feels, represents him no more directly than United States Steel or any other large corporation. Thus freedom of the press has become an issue not between the individual and government, but between the press and government. As for the individual, he has just as much interest in freedom *from* the press as he has in freedom *of* the press.

This is, I submit, the key to the contemporary citizen's distrust of the press, and the reason for the contemporary liberal's frustrated desire somehow to make it behave. And when a depression comes along, bringing with it a New Deal that says for the common man what he wants said, while the erstwhile tribune of the people and palladium of their liberties speaks against what he sees as his own interest—when that happens, the citizen is inclined to go along with the government rather than with the press. He believes in the free press still, but no longer with fire in his eye.

CHAPTER VII

MONOPOLY

ALTHOUGH the concentration of newspapers into fewer and bigger units has altered the foundation on which the free press was built, that is not the only change forced upon democracy's information system by the twentieth century. For journalism now includes other means of mass communication such as radio, moving pictures, and television. And these newer instruments of journalism have approached closer than the newspapers to monopoly. For example:

We are concerned that the number of daily newspapers has shrunk to less than 1,800; but there were only 1,962 radio stations in the United States on January 1, 1948.

FM radio, by its technical provision of room on the air for more broadcasters, has raised the number of stations considerably. So may the still experimental system of pulse-time modulation, which makes it possible to broadcast more than one program on a given radio channel. Even so, it is doubtful whether economic factors will allow more than a handful of radio networks.

Television now offers the possibility of still more information outlets to the public. But because of astronomical production expenses it too is likely to be limited to a handful of networks.

Most national and foreign news comes to both newspapers and radio from three large press associations.

In another form, concentration is appearing even among the magazines. At least, fear of it led the *New Yorker,* early in 1944, to refuse to renew its agreement permitting the *Reader's Digest* to reprint *New Yorker* material. In a note to contributors the *New Yorker* explained that the *Digest* was no longer a reprint magazine. Not only did it now frankly originate a large portion of its material, but it also originated much more that it first farmed out to other publications, and then presented in its own pages as reprint material. Said the *New Yorker:*

> The effect of this (apart from spreading a lot of money around) is that the *Digest* is beginning to generate a considerable fraction of the contents of American magazines. This gives us the creeps, as does any centralization of Genius. The fact seems to be that some publications are already as good as subsidized by the *Digest.*
> . . . We object to the *Digest's* indirect creative function, which is a threat to the free flow of ideas and to the independent spirit.[1]

The *New Republic* followed suit in part. It announced that it would "no longer use material which originates in the *Digest* office and is intended for eventual reprint there." It would, however, permit its own original material to be reprinted in the *Digest,* though it thought the *Digest's* editorial policy now too conservative for that to happen often.[2]

Finally, on top of this extensive concentration within the individual media of mass communication, there has arisen a tendency toward cross-monopoly between the media. Thus a single owner controls not only the magazines *Time, Life, Fortune,* and *Architectural Forum,* but also the moving picture "March of Time," and for a time owned an interest in station WQXR and the ABC radio network.[3] Again, by January 30, 1941 (the last date for which the Federal Communications Commission has figures), 249 radio stations were more or less closely affiliated with newspapers. If, as is likely, the ratio has not changed greatly since, about one-quarter of our radio stations are now connected with newspapers.

Thus there is not only a movement toward concentration

within each of the mass-communications industries that make up today's Fourth Estate, but also the beginnings of joint control among them. Where does this march toward monopoly leave the theory of a free press?

Fear of monopoly rests on the premise that concentrated control of the means of public information corrupts what would otherwise be pure information brought to the mental world of the citizen. If that premise is sound, then there is grave risk that the trend toward concentration will fix a false view of the physical world in our mental world.

We are not yet sure, however, that the premise is sound. Whether it is or not depends, after all, on facts. Regrettably, we do not have the facts. We simply do not know what difference diversified ownership as against concentrated ownership makes in what people read, hear over the air, and see on the screen. There has been no thorough comparison of chain with independent newspapers in their handling of the same controversial issues. We have no idea whether listeners to network stations are, or are not, more accurately informed than listeners to independent stations. Nor has anyone measured what effect it has on a community for a single man or a single corporation to control the only newspaper and the only radio station in it. Therefore, though many persons loudly voice their opinions on both sides of the monopoly argument, they actually don't know what they are talking about.

The facts remain obscure because they are exceedingly difficult to get. The science of content analysis—that is, of finding out what is being said in our media of information—is only beginning to take form. I had occasion to learn, while serving in the Office of War Information, that we are not even sure of what methods to use in trying to measure the cascade of news and opinion that pours from our newspaper presses, radio transmitters, and newsreel cameras every day. And only when we know how to measure can we begin the exceedingly complex, painstaking, and expensive process of comprehending what the various parts of democracy's information system tell us.

Therefore an answer to the question whether or not monopoly of the media of information makes us live in false mental worlds cannot be given, no matter how earnestly pleaders for one side or the other assure us that such concentration as exists is a scandal, or perfection, or something in between. Nevertheless, we can and should look into what is being said and done about it.

As for the newspapers, one factor remains to be added to the analysis in the preceding chapter, of the basic trend toward fewer and bigger units; namely, the newspaper chains. For though newspaper mergers and consolidations go back as far as 1735,[4] that is, almost to the beginning, chains are relatively new. The first newspaper chain in the modern sense was formed for political purposes by J. W. Forney, who founded the *Philadelphia Press* in 1857 and the *Washington Daily Morning Chronicle* in 1861, and for nine years thereafter owned them both. The first of the modern chains was built by E. W. Scripps, from humble beginnings with the *Detroit Evening News,* founded in 1873. After the turn of the century the chain idea really took hold, and by 1910 there were 13 known chains controlling 62 newspapers. This gave an average of not quite 5 papers per chain. By 1930 there were as many as 55 chains controlling 311 papers.[5] Since then there has been a reduction in the number of chains paralleling the reduction in the number of newspapers, for the chains recently listed in the *Editor & Publisher* Year Book add up to 46, controlling some 231 daily papers.[6] This gives an average of almost 5 papers per chain, scarcely more than the 1910 figure. Probably more important is the fact that, both in number of papers and in total circulation, a few chains have attained a size that is significant if monopoly control does alter content. Thus by 1943 there was the Hearst chain of 17 papers, most of them fairly large ones; the Scripps-Howard chain of 19, some of them smaller, and the Frank E. Gannett chain of 19, most of them smaller. These are the facts as to chains, in so far as we know them. But it must be said again that we have no evidence, one way or another, as to whether the readers of any of these chains would be more, or less, accurately informed if each of the papers concerned were independently owned.

Another aspect of monopoly in the newspaper business, which is perhaps more important than the chains, is the government's antitrust suit against the Associated Press, oldest and largest of the wire services that supply newspapers and radio stations with state, national, and foreign news. This suit was decided in favor of the government—at least, the most hotly debated point at issue—by a special three-judge Federal district court in New York. A horrified AP appealed to the Supreme Court, which in June, 1945, upheld the lower court, and therefore the government, by a five-to-three decision. Once more the AP tried to stave off the inevitable by asking for a rehearing; but on October 9, 1945, the Supreme Court denied its request, thus exhausting the last of the legal recourses available.

Many AP members are convinced that the suit was brought primarily because of President Roosevelt's hostility to the newspaper publishers, and in particular to favor Marshall Field's *Chicago Sun,* which has since died, as against Robert R. McCormick's vitriolically opposed *Chicago Tribune.* As Joseph M. Patterson, publisher of the *New York Daily News* and cousin of Colonel McCormick, put it: "This suit . . . is patently a revenge suit, the object being to wreak revenge on the AP for having refused to grant Marshall Field III the [Associated Press] franchise which the Administration wanted him to have." [7] In support of their belief these AP members point out that it had existed in substantially its present form for more than forty years before the suit was brought. If it was a monopoly now, why wasn't it before? Why bring suit only after the *Chicago Sun's* application for an AP franchise was voted down?

In view of the bad temper that existed between President Roosevelt and much of the press, it is not difficult to accept this interpretation of the origin of the AP suit. At the same time it takes an extreme myopia to see behind it nothing more than a presidential pique. For at bottom this was only one more challenge by the majority of our people, as represented by the Administration they elected four times, against a concentration of private power that had grown so strong as to raise the question whether its usefulness to the public outweighed its disadvantages. If the AP suit had not grown out of the *Chicago Sun's* application, it would have grown out of something else. It was the times, rather than the AP, that had changed.

In any case, on August 28, 1942, the Department of Justice filed a complaint in the Southern District of New York against the Associated Press, thirty-five member publishers and papers individually. The nub of the matter as far as both the AP and the government were concerned lay in a provision of the AP bylaws that gave members a protest right against admission to AP membership of rivals in their field—that is, in the same city and in the same morning, evening, or Sunday publication period. This right had been liberalized slightly several times since the present Associated Press was founded, and notably when the government's suit began to threaten; but, even so, no rival had ever been elected to membership over a member's protest.

What gave the charge of monopoly its sting was the fact that within the elect circle of AP there is an exclusive exchange of news. The member papers pour into the common pool news originating in their areas, but withhold it from other newspapers and press associations. Thus an AP member newspaper that also subscribes to the United Press has to give the news it develops in its territory to the AP, but may not give it to the UP. Since the AP membership is large and well distributed, and consists in good part of strong newspapers, this cozy arrangement has a tendency to give the AP news report greater completeness and authenticity than that of any rival press association.

At the same time it is true that the very exclusiveness of the AP was largely responsible for the rise of the other major wire services, the United Press and the International News Service. Here was a point of which the AP and its members made much when the suit was brought. How could the AP be a monopoly if its very existence had fostered competition?

It was with a shock that the members heard on October 6, 1943, that a two-man majority of the court, consisting of Judge Learned Hand and his cousin, Augustus N. Hand, had decided in a summary judgment that the protest right unlawfully restricted the admission of members. While upholding the right to impose some conditions as to membership, the court stipulated:

. . . members in the same "field" as the applicant shall not have power to impose, or dispense with, any conditions upon his admission, and that the by laws shall affirmatively declare that the effect of admission upon the ability of an applicant to compete with members in the same "field" shall not be taken into consideration in passing upon his application.[8]

The AP membership found what comfort it could in the minority opinion of Judge Thomas W. Swan, who held the AP's membership bylaws had no tendency to create a monopoly in news-gathering, and had not stifled competition. "Not a single instance has been adduced," he wrote, "where a newspaper failed because it lacked AP membership or was not started because the intending publisher could not obtain one." [9]

It was not long before the AP appealed to the Supreme Court, as did the *Chicago Tribune,* independently.[10] Incidentally, Colonel McCormick's capacity to view such matters objectively may be gauged from the comment he made the day the government first filed its complaint against the AP. "Marshall Field," he said, "is not a legitimate newspaperman and *The Sun* is not a legitimate newspaper. It is part of an alien and radical conspiracy against our republican form of government." [11]

The Justice Department likewise appealed to the Supreme Court, apparently feeling that the special district court's verdict was not tough enough.[12] The American Newspaper Publishers Association also intervened.[13] But the Supreme Court, unimpressed, endorsed the lower court's decision as it had been given.

The AP now had no alternative but to give in. Accordingly, a special meeting amended the bylaws to conform to the court's decision, and Marshall Field got his membership for the *Chicago Sun*.[14] The redoubtable Colonel McCormick, however, refused to accept the inevitable. He called a meeting of like-minded newspaper publishers, and urged that they seek relief in Congress from the Supreme Court's decision. Accordingly, the meeting approved, by 114 to 30, a resolution calling on Congress to amend the Federal antitrust laws so that they "shall not be construed to prohibit any press service company from exercising its own discretion in the selection of its customers." [15] Such a proposal, embodied in the Mason bill, was actually introduced in the 80th Congress.[16] Even so, it is doubtful whether Congress will grant so conspicuous a favor. The AP is doing business just as successfully after its defeat in court as before.

In the course of American news-gathering since the AP's original predecessor was founded in New York a century ago, there has been much to offset the AP membership's hostility to newcomers. One commentator said, before the Supreme Court decision: "In the folklore of AP banquet speakers and their con-

gressional echoes, the organization's membership-limiting provisions have been no more than a device for excluding the unworthy and ensuring that admission shall be restricted to the
finest flower of American journalism. Actually, they are a device for protecting individual newspapers against competition
in their own localities." [17] As we have seen, the Supreme Court
accepted this estimate as sound. Yet it is also pertinent that one
of the weapons used by the AP in its fight to conquer earlier
rivals was the pioneering for those standards of accuracy, integrity, and impartiality in the news that we now take for
granted. And that fact must be weighed in the balance with the
Supreme Court's ruling that a press association that was
patently not a monopoly was, nevertheless, too monopolistic.

To a considerable extent the four national networks, the
American Broadcasting Company, the Columbia Broadcasting
System, the National Broadcasting Company, and the Mutual
Broadcasting System, have made American radio what it is.
Because of the dominant position of these networks, radio presents an even clearer picture of concentration than newspapers.
Hence it is not surprising that here, too, the Justice Department
moved in with an antitrust suit. On December 31, 1941, it
charged NBC and CBS with having "been engaged . . . in a
wrongful and unlawful combination and conspiracy . . . to
attempt to monopolize the . . . interstate commerce in radio
broadcasting" in violation of the Sherman Act.[18] These suits
were dismissed in the fall of 1943, without harm to the networks.[19] But even before this another, and as it turned out a
more serious, attack had been made on them by the New Deal's
task force in the communications sector—the Federal Communications Commission. There had been a long series of preliminary moves that had had their original impetus in Congress; [20] but now the FCC took the ball and on May 2, 1941,
issued a five-to-two majority report designed to lessen the networks' dominant position in broadcasting.

The FCC's majority had two objectives: first, to make NBC
get rid of either its Red or its Blue network, both of which it
had built up from the beginning; and second, to loosen in
several specific ways the bonds with which the networks bound
their affiliated stations into broadcasting chains. It has been the

custom for networks to own outright only a handful of their stations. The others were joined to them by contracts. And these contracts, the FCC majority ordered, must henceforth leave the individual stations far freer than before. For one thing, contracts should run for one year rather than five, as most of them did. Then, too, networks should no longer refuse to send a program to another station in an area served by an affiliate, even though the affiliate rejected it. Nor should the stations be bound, in the future, to take the programs of only a single network; they should be able to choose between networks.

These and the related regulations, said James Lawrence Fly, then chairman of the FCC, might be called a Magna Charta for American broadcasting stations. They would open the way to new networks, and in general would foster and strengthen network broadcasting by stimulating free competition. The FCC minority of two, on the other hand, feared that the majority's proposals, instead of resulting in free competition, would create anarchy, or a business chaos in which the service to the public would suffer.[21]

Both CBS and NBC, which as parent of the Red and Blue networks felt particularly hit, at once protested loudly and sought an injunction restraining Chairman Fly from swinging his ax upon their necks. Mutual, a later and less tightly organized arrival on the network scene, for the most part sided with the FCC. The attitude of NBC and CBS was reflected by the Association of National Advertisers, which protested to the Supreme Court that the proposed regulations would inevitably result in "the destruction of network organizations." [22] The Supreme Court was not impressed, for on May 10, 1943, it upheld the FCC in a five-to-two decision.

Justice Murphy, in a dissent for the two-man minority consisting of himself and Justice Roberts, held that the Commission was supposed merely to allot the limited supply of broadcasting frequencies to individual stations. It had no business extending its authority over the business activities of the networks. But the Court's majority ruled that the FCC had acted within the limits of power granted to it by Congress, and told the networks that if they did not like what the FCC was doing they should apply to Congress, not the Court, for relief.

In short, those social and political forces that were resisting the concentration of the means of communication won hands down. The networks were forced to liberalize their relations with the individual stations that made up their chains. Far from being destroyed as they had protested in the beginning, they proceeded in the very next year, 1944, to make more money than they ever had before. And, to this writing, they have continued to do the same.

The FCC victory included splitting the ownership of NBC's Red and Blue networks. For although the commission had said it would not force NBC to sell one of its two networks until after the war, a purchaser for the Blue appeared late in 1943 in the form of a new company formed for the purpose. And the Blue, long known as a money-loser in contrast to the lucrative Red when both were controlled by the same ownership, took a new lease on life under its separate ownership as the American Broadcasting Company, and began to prosper.

Thus in the radio industry a balance has been struck, for the present at least, between the seemingly inevitable pressure toward concentration and government resistance to that pressure. Meanwhile, there have been preliminary maneuvers for a similar battle between industry and government over television. Television is now at last peeping around that corner behind which it has hid ever since the 1920's. But the FCC, noting the interest of both the radio and the motion-picture industry in this new means of communication, and scenting another attempt at excessive concentration of control, has long cast a displeased eye upon television's economic background. When on July 1, 1941, by setting certain standards of transmission and reception under which television might operate commercially, the Commission finally gave it a green light technically, it put up a red light economically. It forbade any one person or group to own or operate more than three television stations. Presumably this will not prevent the formation of networks, which might be arranged by means of contracts with individual stations like those that are the basis of radio networks. It is to be hoped, indeed, that such networks will be allowed to grow, since for technical reasons television consumes program funds with a voraciousness that makes radio and even Hollywood seem modest. Television simply will not be able to produce good programs unless their fantastic cost can be spread over a large number of stations. Here, then, is a powerful force that will tend to concentrate control of this industry, too, in relatively few hands.

There remains one other medium of mass communication in which the universal pressure toward centralization and concentration has been at work: the moving-picture industry. Moving pictures date from the late nineteenth century in technical development. Therefore the industry was able to begin with a democratic, not to say raffish, gold rush among a multitude of individuals, and so for a time duplicated those many outlets for expression on which the theory of a free press is predicated. Yet here again the dominant survivors of today are few and powerful. Of more than a hundred American producers, only eight are important: Paramount Pictures, Loew's (MGM), Radio-Keith-Orpheum, Warner Brothers, Twentieth Century Fox, Columbia Pictures, Universal, and United Artists. Of these, the first five are the really powerful ones. They produce pictures, distribute them, and own their own theaters. The remaining companies produce and distribute but do not exhibit, and hence constitute a little three among the big fellows.

If we may believe a monograph prepared for the Temporary National Economic Committee, an antimonopoly offshoot of the New Deal element in Congress, mere mention of which has a catnip-like effect on almost any industry, the major film companies use their control of strategic strong points in the industry not so much to form a visible monopoly as to achieve the substance of one by killing effective competition:

Competition in the motion picture industry is far different than when the industry was composed of a great many small units. At the present time there is competition between the large producer-distributor-exhibitor units, but it is limited. . . .

In lieu of competition between the leaders of the industry, there is in many respects a very definite cooperation. This is illustrated by the Hays organization, the avowed purpose of which is self-government of the industry. Through the many divisions and services of this organization, the major producer-distributor-exhibitors engage in many common activities, and present a united front against any influence which would tend to change the status quo. . . .

The state of competition in the industry is epitomized in the utterance of Spyros Skouras, executive of one of the affiliated exhibition companies and himself owner of a large theater chain. After urging an increase of admission prices to a minimum of 50 cents in all principal key cities, he added: "For we are no longer fighting each other, nor is there any longer such a thing as competition, but a question of establishing solidarity or perishing.[23]

There can be little doubt that the going is tough for the independents. The freedom of the dominant companies was, to be sure, circumscribed somewhat by a huge antitrust suit begun by the Department of Justice on July 20, 1938, against the 8 big producers, 25 of their affiliates, and 132 officers and directors.[24] This suit ended not victoriously, like the FCC's challenge to the radio networks, but inconclusively, in a consent decree agreed to by the government and the five large companies but not the little three. After the war, prosecution was once more resumed,[25] and there followed various restrictions. There has also been discernible a growth of small independent producing units. But the fact is that they are small, and therefore weak. Their independence is more apparent than real. The pictures they make are still subject to the existing distribution system. All in all, the top-dog position of the large companies has not changed greatly.

Since bigness is inherent in our technology, this is hardly to be wondered at. One can conclude only that in moving pictures, in radio, and in television, control of the instruments that bring information and entertainment to America's millions is destined to rest in few hands. Clearly this offers opportunity for the small controlling group of predominantly conservative men to color the picture of the world presented by the communications industries. Yet here we must remember the fact with which we began; namely, that there is as yet little evidence that concentrated control has, in fact, resulted in such coloring. Until we have further evidence from scientific analysis of the content of the picture of the world presented by our communications industries, then, we ought to suspend judgment.

At the same time we must live with our newspapers, radio, moving pictures, and the rest as they are. Even though concentrated ownership may not alter the views presented, this amounts to practicing democracy without that diversification of ownership that constitutes the historic backbone of democracy. Somehow it must be done. And we can best see what is involved by inspecting the monopolistic tendency to reach over from one communications industry to the next that was mentioned at the beginning of this chapter. It is a tendency most spectacularly demonstrated in the existing degree of affiliation between newspapers and radio.

There are, naturally enough, two opposing views of joint control of newspapers and radio. Those who fear the march toward monopoly accept the premise that if a relatively small group holds in its hands a substantial share of the instruments through which the public gets its news, then it will color that news in its own interest. Like medieval robber barons perched in strongholds on the hilltops, the barons of publishing and radio dominate the news traffic that passes by. Therefore—according to this view—they will inevitably make us all their mental slaves by giving us only the picture of the world they want us to have.

The opposing point of view is that the experience and discipline inherited from three centuries of journalism, that is, the Fourth Estate's fumbling but fundamentally valiant battle in search of the truth, plus its established position and economic stability, combine to make newspapers peculiarly fitted to operate the sister service of radio. After all, this argument runs, journalism is journalism. What difference does it make whether its agent happens to be a rotary press or a broadcasting transmitter?

By nature the New Deal accepted the first of these opposing views. But since newspapers were protected by the First Amendment from government molestation, it could not get at them. Radio was different. Because room on the air is limited, radio cannot be open to all, even in theory. Hence radio had to be made subject to government regulation, and exists today under the administrative supervision of the Federal Communications Commission. And since in prewar days the Commission had a five-to-two New Deal majority, it made a handy tool not only to get at the suspicious liaison between newspapers and radio, but in so doing also to peep into the forbidden preserves of the newspapers themselves. And while the FCC acted with an out-

wardly punctilious respect for its nonpartisan obligations, many
newspaper and radio people convinced themselves that the
Commission, and notably James Lawrence Fly, its chairman
at that time, were essentially hatchet men sent out by the New
Deal to get them. The line-up was, in short, much like that in
the contemporary battle between the Department of Justice
and the Associated Press.

The question of joint newspaper-radio affiliation had long
been agitated, but Chairman Fly took as the immediate occasion for his inquiry the fact that by June 30, 1941, forty-three,
or nearly half, of ninety-nine applications for FM radio licenses
before the Commission came from newspaper interests.[26] "These
newspaper applications," he said, "raise the common question
of the extent to which and the circumstances in which grants to
newspapers will serve the public interest." So it was that on
March 20, 1941, the FCC directed itself, through its Order No.
79, to look into the matter. Before long there began a series of
hearings that stretched from July, 1941, to February, 1942.
Some 3,500 typed pages of testimony were put into record by
both sides.

The burden of the testimony offered by witnesses called by
the FCC make it clear that the Commission was conducting not
so much an investigation as a prosecution. It sought to get into
the record reasons that might justify rulings that would divorce
newspapers from radio. But the FCC's case rested not on evidence that joint ownership did in fact result in twisted news,
but on showing the extent of affiliation between newspapers
and radio, and in then arguing on the assumed premise that
such overlapping was *ipso facto* evil. Typical of the host of Commission witnesses was Morris L. Ernst, New York lawyer and
associate counsel for the Civil Liberties Union, who began his
argument by expounding what was essentially the theory of a
free press as detailed in Chapter IV. As he put it, "We are
gambling in this country and our society on the thought that
if there is a market place in thought, truth will win out."[27]
But, he said, newspaper-radio affiliation automatically cut
down the number of items offered in the market place of
thought:

I don't think you can maintain our philosophy of the market place
of thought, that the truth will win out there, unless you have as

decent and as complete a market place as society permits; and the best way to prove it is that nobody would favor having all of the radio stations owned by the newspapers. . . . So the only dispute is at what point should we be frightened, at what point should we stop—300 out of 800, or should we wait until 700, 600? There can be honest differences of opinion as to just where is the frightening point. I am telling you my prejudices. I am frightened when I see one. I am frightened if I think of the motion picture companies owning television. I am frightened as to any interlocking of the controls because I want the greatest possible variety of prejudices in that market place, whether I agree with them or not, and then they are going to correctly criticize each other.

Ernst described the newspapers, radio, and other means of communication as pipe lines to human minds. We could not maintain the Bill of Rights, he contended, if the number of persons who controlled those pipe lines got to be fewer and fewer.[28]

Another of the many witnesses who expressed preference for separate ownership, though he declined to take sides on the question of a flat rule forbidding newspaper ownership of radio stations, was Professor Zechariah Chafee, Jr., of Harvard. A Commission witness, Professor Chafee nevertheless made an observation that must be scored on the newspapers' side. The FCC, he said, was not in charge of the national welfare as a whole, but in charge of radio only. Not only that, but the Commission was fighting its battle on the border line between two industries, one of which—the newspaper industry—was outside its field. "The use of a political power established for one purpose in order to produce a result of a different sort," said Professor Chafee, "is always risky."[29]

When the time came for witnesses on the publishers' side to speak, they made more of this point. In particular, Arthur Garfield Hays, national director of the Civil Liberties Union, forcefully expressed this thesis, thus opposing his fellow apostle of civil liberties, Morris Ernst. It surprised many to find a veteran battler for the underdog, like Hays, turning up on the side of the Bourbons of the press; but he did so because of his convictions on the fundamental political issue involved. His argument makes required reading for anyone who wonders how the historic principles of democracy apply to the society of today. For example:

What I am afraid of is an extension by law, or by any Commission, which would lead to a violation of rights, because of a desire to bring about more equal opportunities. I feel that, under a democratic system, . . . so long as we have equal rights under the law, most of us can take care of ourselves. . . .

If everybody is given equal rights, it is up to those who want radio stations to run them properly and convince the Commission that they are the people who are best qualified to have them.

Just as soon as you favor one group over the other, under the law, whether it is to protect somebody or help somebody, it seems to me you are denying the underlying principles of democracy.

Of course, everybody who starts out with the idea of denying these principles does it with good motives. The purpose, unquestionably, is to bring about a desired end. But the theory of democracy is that, if you let people alone, they will get farther by their own efforts, so long as you treat them alike, and that no government can safely lay down methods that will bring about as beneficial results as giving people equal rights under the law.[30]

So the arguments went. Innumerable facts, statistical and otherwise, subtle theories as to the functions of administrative agencies as distinct from legislative bodies, journalistic history, radio history, all were put into the record. Many distinguished persons testified. At length, on February 6, 1942, Chairman Fly recessed the hearing *sine die*.

The fundamental fact that emerged from the hearing was that there was no concrete evidence of bias stemming from newspaper control of radio. FCC investigators had been sent out on a nation-wide hunt to get the goods on newspaper-owned radio. They searched the stations of the country through and through with fervor and diligence, but still they could find no example of monopoly-colored news caused by joint newspaper-radio control. They did bring into the hearings, to be sure, a suspicious situation in Charleston, South Carolina. Here radio station WCSC had complained about its local competitor, WTMA, which was owned by the two newspapers in town. And the newspapers had, for a time, published the program listings of their own station but not those of the rival—an old habit of the years when the press fought radio that still persists in some areas, hardly reinforcing the newspapers' protestations of purity and objectivity. Even so, the most strenuous efforts of the FCC produced nothing in the way of evidence of bias in the general dissemination of news and opinion. One witness for the complaining station (State Senator Cotesworth P. Means) probably put his finger on the truth of the whole matter when under cross-examination he said that the monopoly dangers complained of were feared for the future rather than evident in what had happened to date.[31]

A comparison of what actually goes out over the air from newspaper as against non-newspaper stations can be found in a study made by the Office of Radio Research, affiliated with Columbia University, at the request of the publishers' Newspaper-Radio Committee. This study compares news and educational programs as broadcast by newspaper and non-newspaper stations, and also the political allegiance of newspapers with radio affiliations and without any. It is based on the output of fifty newspaper-owned stations, fifty non-newspaper stations, and fifty newspapers without radio connection, all matched as closely as possible. The assumption was that any differences that appeared might be due to the newspaper-radio connection or lack of it.[32]

This study revealed that in towns with only one paper and only one station, where each was independent of the other, the papers tended to discriminate against the stations by not printing a log of all their programs—the vicious and shortsighted policy on the part of publishers noted in Charleston. But so far as the quality and quantity of news and social service programs was concerned, and also the time of day at which they were broadcast, there were only negligible differences. All in all, this study, one of the tiny bits of factual light on this much agitated question, proved little. It did hint, however, at what anyone familiar with journalism and radio would suspect in the first place: that individual newspapers and individual radio stations are pretty much what circumstances and their owners make them, and that affiliation between the two makes little difference one way or another.

As time went on word began to get around that the Commission found itself without much of a case for that enforced separation of newspapers and radio which, in spite of Chairman Fly's disclaimers at the time the hearings had begun, the newspapers insisted had been the purpose of the whole rumpus.

Besides, by 1943 elements in Congress opposed to the New Deal were talking of clipping the financial wings of the Commission, and observers began to wonder whether he would find it expedient to make a move as controversial as divorcing press and radio. Then, one day late in 1943, FCC Commissioner Tunis Augustus Macdonough Craven, a retired Navy communications officer, appeared before the Senate Interstate Commerce Committee. He predicted that his colleagues would soon issue an order forbidding joint ownership of newspapers and radio stations.[33]

The full story of what happened next has not yet been told. There is some evidence that a five-to-two or six-to-one majority of the Commission was on the point of coming out with a stiff anti-newspaper regulation. Apparently, however, Craven appeared at the Commission's private sessions with a hard-hitting minority report which he was prepared to release simultaneously, and which therefore threatened to add fuel to the flames that hostile congressmen had already built under the FCC.

Meanwhile, the temperature of the opposition in Congress was rising, and in addition the uncertainties of the campaign year of 1944 were at hand. Chairman Fly finally went to the White House to consult the President, to whose inspiration the whole attempt to divorce newspapers and radio is commonly credited.[34] Thereafter the whole three-year crusade was suddenly abandoned. On January 13, 1944, the Commission closed the record and dismissed the proceedings. Chairman Fly and the other six Commissioners joined unanimously in saying:

The Commission has concluded, in the light of the record in this proceeding and of the grave legal and policy questions involved, not to adopt any general rule with respect to newspaper ownership of radio stations.[35]

So far as the FCC investigation is concerned, then, the battle was won by the publishers. It was won, if you will, by the forces of monopoly. Or, should your predilections run that way, it was won by the forces of equal rights under law, on behalf of a group that, if it abused its obligations in operating radio stations, could be penalized just like anyone else.

In Chapter XIX we shall have to return to the issue of what

to do about monopoly in democracy's information system. For while the FCC's most zealous efforts failed to get the goods on the newspapers so far as performance is concerned, the fact remains that joint newspaper-radio ownership does exist, and will probably grow through newspaper acquisition of FM licenses if in no other way. So, too, technical and economic pressures promise to concentrate radio, moving pictures, television, and the newspapers themselves still further. Already they are held in fewer hands than were dreamed of when the free-press theory was born.

ENTER THE PLANNERS

BECAUSE the relentless trend toward concentration of power examined in the two previous chapters is changing not only the newspaper, radio, and other communications industries but our entire economy, we cannot make an intelligent decision as to the place of the Fourth Estate in twentieth century society without first orienting ourselves among the stresses and strains of contemporary democracy as a whole. Democracy's information system is, to be sure, its brain, and without a democratic information system we cannot have democracy. But unless we understand the disease that attacks the whole, we cannot diagnose the difficulty that afflicts our information system.

While the issue is infinitely complex, it takes no great insight to see that the great issue of the twentieth century is to determine the extent to which government shall dominate the concentrations of private wealth and power. For this generation's political reformers seek to fight the concentration of power in private hands with a bigger and better concentration of power —namely, government. Thus the liberal of today is the antithesis of the original liberal, whose aim was to free man as far as possible from government.

Whatever we may think of this tendency we can agree, I think, that the reason for it was neatly summed up by a student of journalism during the late depression years. Asked whether liberty or security seemed more valuable to him, he replied unhesitatingly in favor of security. "It doesn't make so much difference what comes out of the mouth by way of free speech," he explained, "as long as something goes into it by way of food." Here is summed up the contemporary generation's distrust of the attempt to operate today's economy under the classic rules of liberty. For however admirable liberty and democracy are—and in our time many have rediscovered the deep fires of meaning that burn within them from Hitler, Mussolini, the Japanese, and totalitarian Russia—somehow they seem remote if food and shelter are not forthcoming under them.

This dominant political issue of our century is so surcharged with emotion, so overlaid with the different meanings each of us reads into words, like Communist and Fascist, liberal and conservative, radical and reactionary, that it is exceedingly difficult to penetrate to the core of the issue and to weigh the benefits of the new service state while yet being sensitive to its sinister possibilities. Yet only if we make the effort, only if the man who voted for Hoover, Landon, Willkie, and Dewey can find at least a temporary meeting ground with the man who voted for Roosevelt, Roosevelt, Roosevelt and Roosevelt, can we achieve a solid premise on which to hang our decision as to where the Fourth Estate belongs in the twentieth century economic democracy. It is an issue that cut across 1948's four-cornered presidential race of Dewey, Truman, Wallace, and Thurmond of the Dixiecrats. And though we have difficulty seeing it through the overhanging war clouds, it is inherent in at least some of our differences with Soviet Russia.

We can, I think, find this neutral meeting ground if we abandon for the moment our contemporary political labels and seek the basic reasons why there should be a tendency toward centralization in countries as diverse as Britain and Russia, the United States and Holland. And we shall find, I think, that at bottom this universal pressure toward centralization arises from two principal causes: first, a rapid and vast increase in the world's population; and second, the changing technics of our civilization.

Though we hear much more of this latter, we must not overlook the first. In the early years of this century the German economist Werner Sombart stressed the phenomenal growth in numbers, at least in Europe. More recently the Spanish philosopher and essayist, José Ortega y Gasset, pointed to Sombart's figures as the source of what he deplored as "the revolt of the masses." The increase in population is, says Mr. Ortega y Gasset, a "very simple" but overwhelmingly important fact:

. . . from the time European history begins in the sixth century up to the year 1800—that is, through the course of twelve centuries —Europe does not succeed in reaching a total population greater than 180 million inhabitants. Now, from 1800 to 1914—little more than a century—the population of Europe mounts from 180 to 460 millions! [1]

So, too, the United States mushroomed from hardly more than five million in 1800 to 145 million in 1948. Even as late as 1920 we numbered only 105 million, a fact that helps explain why it is only recently that we have felt the social and political repercussions of our tremendous growth. For it is inevitable that jamming so many human beings into the space formerly occupied by so few was bound to cause some annoying elbow-rubbing.

To this must be added the other factor mentioned, the changing technics by which we live. We have been told over and over again, especially since World War I, that countless new inventions, plus the pressures of mass industrialization, have made the physical world infinitely complex and tightly interrelated. In fact, it does seem obvious that the change from the buggy and its horse, locally raised and locally fed, to an automobile mass-produced from raw materials from all over the world, typifies a universal economic change that necessitates a political change to match it. Not only that, but there is another product of today's technics that the mass of people all over the world seem to sense, even if they understand neither the reasons for it nor the political consequences that flow from it. This new and startling factor was once succinctly summed up by Donald M. Nelson, a recruit from Big Business to the wartime New Deal, in these words:

For the first time in the history of the human race there can be enough of everything to go round. Poverty is not inevitable any more. The sum total of the world's greatest possible output of goods, divided by the sum total of the world's inhabitants, no longer means a little less than enough for everybody. It means more than enough.[2]

Slowly the tremendous significance of this fact is becoming understood. Repeated public opinion polls, indeed, show that the general public is far ahead of industrial and business management in appreciating its significance. There are, of course, many industrial leaders who see that we cannot do the work of today with the shibboleths of the past; but they are clearly a minority. Such a one is Dr. Charles F. Kettering, inventor of the automobile self-starter and former vice president of the General Motors Corporation. In an address before the American Association for the Advancement of Science he put his finger on a specific aspect of the situation. "We have the scientific knowledge," he said, "to provide an adequate diet for every one of the 2,000,000,000 inhabitants of the globe if the information were properly applied." The reason three-fourths of the world's people lack so elementary a thing as enough proper food, said Dr. Kettering, is the familiar lag of social and political thinking behind science:

The false barriers erected by man himself are responsible. The antiquated social systems, ignorance, stupidity, and fear prevent a large percentage of the peoples of the world from enjoying even the most fundamental of the benefits of science.[3]

The results are curious, not only among starving and disease-ridden peoples in remote corners of the earth, but right here in the most advanced and most powerful nation in all history. From 1940 to 1945 we showed that, despite the war's extraordinary demands upon us, we could maintain our supremacy over man's historic enemies—famine, disaster, and pestilence. Some eleven million of our most productive citizens were a dead loss to our productive system because of their service in the Army or Navy, and nearly half our remaining workers were turning out not consumption goods but engines of destruction. Nevertheless we fed, housed, clothed, and kept healthy not only the entire United States but a good part of the rest of the world as well. Our military and naval engineers built fully grown seaports on the hostile beaches of Normandy, carved airports out of mountains or jungles, built highways and rebuilt cities, with never a delay. No one said, "You can't do that," or "It's unconstitutional." Instead, the whole nation seemed to adopt for its own the motto of the Navy Seabees: "Can do."

With such an amazing spectacle a part of our history, this nation is not going to be quite what it was before. Despite the confusions of post-war adjustment, we have a new concept of what we can do. Peace does not have the urgency of war, nor does it summon up so much energy so swiftly. We may be baffled for the moment over inflation or housing. But in the long run if we need houses or economic brakes, if we want to clear slums or build new TVAs, we shall be disposed to have them. We are not going to let another great depression come without acting at once, no matter what party happens to be in office. If a skeleton working force in wartime can carry much of the weight of the world on its shoulders, an entire nation is not going to stand by while farms are idle, factory chimneys are cold and lifeless, and millions of our people lack food, health, and a place to live. We are going to do something about it.

This determination took root long before the war. All that this century's two world wars have done, indeed, is to reenforce the conviction that it is silly to tolerate poverty when we have shown we can have plenty. The people of this and other countries have long felt this in their bones. And this feeling is, I submit, the primary source of the epochal surge that has forced governments everywhere to manifest, in varying degree and in varying manner as determined by national traditions, the same underlying tendency toward a service state.

It was inevitable that there should be trouble when this new force collided with our political traditions, for historically the American has been pretty much what Maxwell Anderson pictured him to be in *Knickerbocker Holiday:*

> He hates and eternally despises
> The policeman on his beat, the judge at his assizes,
> The sheriff with his warrants and the bureaucratic crew
> For the sole and simple reason that they tell him what to do.

And again:

> He hates both the guts and the faces
> Of the people who can order him and put him through his paces,
> The assessor with his taxes or the colonel at review
> Or any fool official who can tell him what to do,
> And he won't go to heaven and he won't go to hell,
> And he will not buy and he will not sell
> According to the precepts of a governmental plan—
> And that's an American!

To be sure, "planning," the catchword of the new order, is an attractive word. Is it not foolish to try to get anything done without planning it in advance? Under contemporary conditions classic liberalism may give freedom of action to our industrialists; but it has also given us alternate periods of boom and bust. Laissez faire produced too much cotton at prices that were too high, too few cheap shoes and shirts, seven million new radio sets in a year when only two million had the money to buy them, and so on all up and down the line. Is it not smarter, then, to plan things in advance in orderly fashion? What could be more sensible than matching production to fit consumption? Would it not be still better, indeed, to plan increased consumption? After all, we have long since been forced to give up the unplanned method of the gold standard, yet we have survived under a currency at least partly managed. Why not a completely managed economy, designed in advance to desirable specifications?

The difficulty is that planning and bureaucracy are Siamese twins—as depression and war have amply demonstrated. Government cannot set foot over the line between historic liberalism and planning without calling in a host of administrators, directors, and managers, plus their innumerable underlings, to execute its plan. Thus, when laissez faire is hurried out at the door, bureacracy flies in at the window. The governmental plan to which Maxwell Anderson's historic American objects brings with it the bureaucratic crew he likes no better. Moreover, most of us are convinced that political liberty and economic liberty are mutually exclusive. Perhaps it will turn out that they need not be. But most of us want to be shown.

To be sure, the milder prophets of collectivism assure us that the two are not incompatible, that our liberties are divisible into two classes. Thus, as John Chamberlain once put it in an analysis of President Roosevelt's nine young men on the Supreme Court, "The 'left' in modern parlance means giving a green light to big government in economic matters while at the same time it signifies putting up a contrary stop sign when government tries to say *verboten* in matters of the civil liberty." [4]

It may be that Supreme Court justices, concerned with the finer points of law, can make this nice distinction. In the rough-and-tumble of political action, however, it has thus far not worked out. Big government, given the green light in economic matters, tends to ride blindly over the individual's right to go his own way. In this country such big government as we have had still allows the citizen to shout bloody murder at what it is doing; but it tells him where to get off, just the same.

Thus we have begun to see that the political struggle of the second half of the twentieth century will not be the epic battle between Communism and Fascism that was anticipated before the Second World War, but a battle to integrate democracy and collectivism. We are faced with the problem of preserving the values of freedom from the drift toward centralization. No one yet knows whether political liberty can survive when government is given vast economic power over the individual. No one yet knows whether we can deliver the economic benefits promised to the mass of men by Soviet Russia without substituting for our basic concept that the state is made for man the Russian premise that man is made for the state. We have yet to make certain, in other words, whether "the ultimate sanction of planned economy is the hangman." [5] The example of Soviet Russia seems to indicate that planning is impossible without the hangman to force the citizenry to accept the plan. But we must not forget that Soviet Russia is Russian as well as Soviet, and that the hangman and the political police were indigenous to Russia long before Lenin and Stalin. It may be that in America the ultimate sanction of a planned society would be nothing more sinister than the familiar figure of the corner cop.

There are in motion in the world today profound changes

of which we in this country—living in what is virtually a pre-war island in a postwar world—are only dimly aware. The destruction of Europe obliterated more than its cities. National gold and dollar reserves, individual savings, and political tradition disappeared in the dust. Because there was hardly any accumulation of private capital left in those countries, they could not avoid adopting programs of nationalization that remain anathema to us. Over the entire Continent it is the same. Even Britain's Tories have accepted some of the Labor Party's nationalization program. But it is important to realize that, for all the abruptness of Europe's postwar lurch to the left, the war was little more than a catalyzing agent. It merely gave Europe a push in a direction in which all of us are moving anyway.

If this is correct, it is futile to argue whether centralization is desirable. We are going to have some of it whether we like it or not. Our technology drives us irresistibly toward production on a huge scale, and the resulting centralization of economic power in private hands inevitably calls up a corresponding centralization of governmental power. This means that the battle of the remaining half of the twentieth century is not going to be between the right and the left as we still conceive of them —that is, between those who would force us into centralization and those who would prevent it. Because we are going to centralize to some extent anyway, the real fight is as to how, not whether, we are going to do it.

At bottom, it comes down to a struggle between those who believe in civil liberties and those who do not. Russia is the archetype of those who do not. Britain and the United States are the protagonists of those who do. No matter what happens, we are going to keep free elections, independent courts, and the basic rights of the individual. The individual may have to fill out ever more paper forms, and he will surely never go back to the good old days when taxes were only a minor irritant; but his vote, and above all his mind, will remain free. The free American is not going to endorse excessive government; he will hold back. It is instinctive with him, and properly so, to resist the trend to centralization, to ask questions, to insist that it be house-broken in the ways of democracy. But the American citizen is not going to let his country repeat the history of the dinosaurs, whose wits were not adequate to coping with a changing environment.

All this poses a question. If there is going to be more centralization, if the planners and the managers and the bureaucrats are to be with us—is there not a risk that they will want to centralize and plan and manage our news too?

MANAGED NEWS

NOWHERE are the planners and managers who seem destined to be an integral part of our society more out of place than in the Fourth Estate. For the earmark of the Fourth Estate is, as we have seen, its independence from the rest of society, notably government.

Those of us who during the war served in the Office of War Information and other war agencies became familiar with the reasons for news-managing—because war is by nature totalitarian. The OWI under Elmer Davis, its wartime head, was oriented toward as full and as free publication of the facts as military necessity permitted. A vindictively partisan press tried to make out otherwise, but such was Davis's purpose.

Even so, those in the OWI whose job it was to channel news (that had its source in the war or in government) to press and radio felt constantly that we were in a war for national survival. The supreme necessity then seemed to be not so much to publish the facts regardless of their import, but to judge them constantly in reference to the supreme necessity of winning the war. Would this fact, if published, help or hinder the prosecution of the war? That was the question. Was the news of the early Pacific fighting so frighteningly gloomy that it would dishearten the people if published *in toto*? Could the people take it? Should not the facts be toned down before publication? Or was the public not too complacent? Perhaps stressing the black side of the picture could shock it into realizing how serious a business the war was. Always there was this compulsion to further the ultimate aim of winning the war, rather than to publish the facts —good, bad, or indifferent—come what might.

Similar influences were at play in wartime Britain. The inevitable consequences inspired the British wit who uses the pseudonym Sagittarius to compose a barbed parody of Rudyard Kipling's "L'Envoi," of which this is a sample:

When the last newspaper is printed and the ink is faded and dried,
And the oldest critic is muzzled and the youngest croaker has died,
We shall pass to a tranquil era of government by decree,
When every voice shall be silenced but the voice of the B.B.C.
We shall hearken to Government spokesmen, we shall listen to
    Government news;
And no one will doubt or question, and none shall express their
    views. . . .[1]

Even though war exaggerates it, government news is not exclusively a wartime phenomenon. One can pick any convenient day as the one on which the first government news-manager clambered over the fence that marked the hitherto inviolate boundaries of the Fourth Estate. Perhaps as good as any is the cold, rainy, winter day in 1902 described by the Washington correspondent Delbert Clark, the day on which President Theodore Roosevelt took pity on the newspapermen hanging around the White House gate in the hope of picking up news from visitors to the inner sanctum, and directed that a room be set aside for them in the Executive Offices.[2] Or it may have been the day in April, 1917, when President Wilson issued an executive order setting up the Committee on Public Information, that First World War combination of the Second World War's Office of Censorship and the Office of War Information.

Whatever the exact day on which government first began to take an official hand in controlling the news it created, it was the success of private business in managing news that gave government the idea. For business found in the hiring of publicity men the answer to its discovery that it had grown too vast, too complex, for the general-assignment reporter to grasp the significance of the news about itself in the few hours or minutes before deadline. Besides, the news about business that resulted from catch-as-catch-can reporting was not always fortunate. Why not take steps to see that the press appreciated business's point of view? Why not, indeed? And when business hired former reporters as publicity men, private news management was born.

If business was so big it had to be explained and interpreted, government was bigger. So, with the best intentions in the world, the government hired publicity men also. President Hoover began it on a large scale; [3] but his efforts were modest in comparison with those of the New Deal when, meeting the depression's demand for planners and managers all along the government front, it set the stage for big-time news management. Clark thus sums up the inevitable result:

When President Roosevelt assigned his secretary, Stephen T. Early, to organize press services in the various departments and important non-Cabinet agencies, the avowed purpose was to provide full and accurate publicity for all the government's activities, without propaganda in the invidious sense, and without suppression. "Do your job just as if you were working for a newspaper," Early told the press agents.

Obviously no such high-minded ideal could last for long. . . . To each administrative official truth is what he believes; and what he does not believe, does not approve of, or would prefer to forget, is not generally considered fit material for the press.[4]

It is not easy to find out how many of the publicity tribe there are in our peacetime government today. At the height of the war there were in Britain, according to one observer, "more people to 'help' journalists than there are members of the National Union of Journalists." [5] So far, at least, we have not reached that point. Some time ago the Bureau of the Budget, in a report to the House Committee on Appropriations for the fiscal year ending June 30, 1941, put the total publicity cost for that year at $27,769,940. One hundred and fifty-three agencies of the Executive Department had services of information, education, and contact with the public.[6]

Not all the results were beneficial. Senator Millard F. Tydings of Maryland, chairman of a special committee on economy and efficiency in government, complained of the government's "daily deluge" of news releases. "A careful reading of these releases," he said, "clearly shows that here is one of the most wasteful activities of the federal bureaucracy." For example:

The Office of Emergency Management put out an article entitled "How to Spend the Week-End Without a Car." This opus was divided into five parts. Part 1 pointed out that a citizen could work in his garden, where he could "dig for fun, for health, for good living, for economy, and for patriotism." Part 2 advised the organization of discussion groups in each community. Part 3 advised hiking, bicycle riding, and the use of street cars in place of automobile riding. Part 4 dealt with the playing of games, and Part 5 advised former auto drivers to take up a hobby such as "stamps, coins, and autographs."

Consider that valuable office space, many government employees, much office machinery and much money is in this critical hour of the world's history being devoted to such foolish propositions as the one mentioned.[7]

The Senator's remarks, it must be noted, were presented to a somewhat unimpressed public through a publicity release of the very type to which he was objecting.

Mere government publicity, even if wasteful, is not necessarily hostile to the democratic process. Some among us become incensed on learning of the mere existence of a government information specialist—or "bungling bureaucrat," as he is known to the opposition—who is fattening himself on the public pay roll. But if he contents himself with gathering and issuing statistics and other information in his field he may be helping rather than hindering the process of getting news of the government into the citizen's head. It is only when he goes beyond this, striving to put over a point of view, to smooth the way for some government project, to suppress some item because he does not deem the public ready for it, that he engages in news-managing proper. For here he does come into conflict with the fundamental principle of a press free to report the facts independently. But again, we can best see what is involved by studying government news in war.

Although antedating the outbreak of war by more than two years, the Office of Government Reports, as a separate information agency, was the first sign of what was to come. Headed by the former newspaper editor Lowell Mellett, it was set up under the ever expanding Executive Office on July 1, 1939, to replace a less formidable National Emergency Council that dated from November of 1933—the New Deal's first year. The *United States Government Manual* of March, 1941, listed OGR's functions as preparing reports on the programs of government departments and agencies, studying progress toward the objectives of these programs, recommending ways to overcome obstacles— thus opening the door to news-managing proper—and related activities. Shortly before OGR was merged into the still more ambitious Office of War Information, it achieved a $530,000 building of its own, familiar to Washington and its visitors as "Mellett's Madhouse." Moreover, OGR's alphabetical designation easily led suspicious newspapers to refer to it as OGRE, and at least one responsible Washington correspondent saw in it a school for government censors.[8]

Next in order was Colonel William J. Donovan's Office of the Coordinator of Information, founded July 11, 1941. The Colonel's job was listed officially: "to collect and analyze all information and data which may bear upon national security."[9] The COI was, thanks to its military responsibilities, a hush-hush agency, principally concerned with gathering intelligence data abroad and exporting American propaganda in return.

More noise surrounded the brief but active life of the third of these mushrooming agencies, the Office of Facts and Figures, born by executive order October 25, 1941, and known to newspaper and other critics as the "Office of Fads and Fancies," or by variations on that theme. The *New York Herald Tribune* celebrated its coming with a famous editorial headed "Here's Where We Get OFF," which said:

Here, obviously, is the answer to the prayers of a bewildered people. The Office of Facts and Figures, or OFF, will coordinate the Office of the Coordinator of Information (or OCI), report on the Office of Government Reports, . . . press-agent the innumerable Press Agents of the Individual Departments (often called the PAIDS) and will under no circumstances do anything whatever that anybody else is doing already. . . .

OFF is just going to superimpose its own "well organized facts" upon the splendid confusion, interpret the interpreters, re-digest those who now digest the digesters, explain what those who explain what the explainers of the explanations mean, and coordinate the coordinators of those appointed to coordinate the coordinations of the coordinated. Before this example of the sublime administrative genius which now rules in Washington, the mind can only reel with admiration. . . . When the Office of Utter Confusion and Hysteria (to be referred to as OUCH) has finally been created, then the capstone will have been set upon the pyramid and we can all die happy, strangled in the very best red tape.[10]

OFF had its origin in the brain of a newspaperman, Robert E. Kintner, who sensed the need for some single agency to make available to members of the government, if not the public, accurate information on the progress of what was then known as the defense effort. But in characteristic fashion OFF was set up in addition to, rather than in place of, the OGR, COI, and the publicity bureaus of the various departments and agencies of the government. Its head was Archibald MacLeish, Librarian of Congress, poet, and ex-writer for *Fortune* magazine.

When OFF was set up we were still formally at peace. But six weeks later Japanese carrier planes came out of the Hawaiian sky, and our sentiments changed. The need for some order among the conflicting statements that came out of a confused Washington was painfully obvious. But President Roosevelt paid no attention until, more than half a year later, he gave in to the almost universal sentiment as voiced in a news broadcast by Elmer Davis: "Almost anybody would be better than half a dozen heads." [11] Davis was persuaded to accept the job for which he had thus unwittingly recommended himself, and became director of a still bigger and better agency, the Office of War Information.

Thus at long last was born a single strong government information bureau. Instead of being built on top of the ramshackle structure of the existing overlapping agencies, OWI swallowed whole the Office of Facts and Figures and the Office of Government Reports. Colonel Donovan fought long and stubbornly against merging his office with the others in the OWI, with the result that only the half· of his COI that produced propaganda for foreign consumption disappeared into it. He kept the half devoted to incoming intelligence in a freshly constituted, and later justly famous, Office of Strategic Services.[12]

The appointment of Elmer Davis as Director of War Information seemed ideal. He had made an honorable record as a newspaperman and radio commentator; and he was an independent, rather than one of the New Deal zealots so often preferred. Moreover, in OWI's regulation No. 1, he laid down the principle that the public should have as much information as strictly military considerations made possible.

This is a people's war and to win it the people should know as much about it as they can [he said]. This office will do its best to tell the truth and nothing but the truth, both at home and abroad. Military information that would aid the enemy must be withheld; but within that limitation we shall try to give the people a clear, complete, and accurate picture.[13]

It is to be noted that Davis promised "the truth and nothing but the truth," but omitted "the whole truth." Thus his prescription stretched the Fourth Estate principle of free access to the news as far as war would let him. Fresh from the newspaper and radio ranks, he saw the need of giving the public continuing access to the events of the world that as citizens of a democracy they had to know. This attitude was in sharp contrast to the usual news-manager's reaction, which is that he has a tough job to do and so, by God, he's going to do it without any nonsense from reporters, photographers, radio commentators, and other self-appointed representatives of The People.

But alas, even though Davis thus publicly and forthrightly abjured the temptation of all planners and managers to tell the people only what he decides is good for them, it was not long before the old guard, both in and out of the newspapers, was denouncing him as though he had been a commissar straight from Moscow. Those of us who fought the Battle of the Social Security Building in Washington, and the Battle of Fifty-seventh Street in New York with the OWI, had opportunity to appreciate the considerable malice and the gross ignorance that lay behind most newspaper and political criticism of OWI. It left me, at least, with the feeling that Davis, hung between New Dealers on one side and die-hards on the other, bore one of the war's heavier crosses. How well he bore it, how well he performed the delicate task that was his, is for the historians to decide. For our purposes it is enough to note that the OWI was a mechanism well designed to manage news, even though it did not do so to an extent greater than that necessitated by the war.

We have noted that war, with its irresistible demand for totalitarian ways, gave us a preview of what peacetime managed news could be. In the gloomy earlier days of the war there was a tendency to conceal our reverses and failures. Later, as the war news got better, there was concern on high lest the home front grow too complacent—a concern that led to official efforts to shock us into realization of the war's continuing seriousness. This tendency to play down or play up the truth for a purpose was for the most part a normal manifestation of wartime censorship, for, as we shall see later in examining the subject, censorship always starts with the obvious necessity of military secrecy and then imperceptibly drifts into manipulating public opinion, whether to conceal mistakes and failures from the home public or to gain some other objective—all under the plea that straightforward publication of the facts would give aid and comfort to the enemy.

Nowhere have the values involved in this dilemma been better stated than by Palmer Hoyt (now publisher of the *Denver Post*) when in 1943 he was director of the domestic branch of OWI. What he had to say is required reading today, because even though the war is long since over the problem remains. We have yet to resolve the clash between the big state, which a democracy sees in exaggerated form in war, and our fundamental freedom. Here is what Hoyt said:

Last fall, speaking before the Southern Newspaper Publishers Association, I suggested that our greatest single need is a play-by-play account of the war. We approached that goal in Tunisia, came closer at Salerno—but not until Tarawa did we receive the first real play-by-play account of a major battle. . . .

This was followed a little later by almost a spectacular coverage by the Army in connection with the occupation of New Britain. Again the American public was vicariously at the scene. Again the people of these United States lived with their sons, their brothers, their husbands and fathers, the horror of battle and the glories of victory.

This was real reporting. And this kind of war coverage, incidentally, will do more to bring home the seriousness of this global struggle than all the lectures of all the high government officials combined. . . .

What does all this add up to? Simply this, that the best way to give the people of this country an understanding of the war is not to preach to them but to spare no effort in giving them full and fast reportings of events as they occur. People understand events and learn from them. One event in a war such as ours when properly and adequately reported is worth ten thousand sermons.

Let us interrupt long enough to say again that what is true of government news in war is every bit as true now in peace. Hoyt continued in words that ought to be written on the heart of every public official:

Too many people who have no understanding of the nature and character of news and information, or of its importance, also have a complete misconception of what an organization like the Office of War Information ought properly to do. Many of them have the notion that it is the job of an office of war information to spoon-feed the public with whatever ideas or attitudes are considered desirable at the moment. They regard the Office of War Information as a sort of thermostat on national morale, warming up the national ardor for the war whenever it cools, and cooling it off when it gets too high.

The first trouble with that notion is that no one can have sufficient wisdom to know with exactitude and certainty what attitudes people ought to have at a given moment.

The second trouble with it is that even if you knew what effect you wanted to create, you couldn't do it successfully without the type of pervasive control that characterizes a dictatorship.[14]

In short, what the people of a democracy must know, whether in war or in peace, is not what official opinion holds good for them to know, but what has happened. If something has happened, or has been said in important places, or has been decided on, the people have an inalienable right to know it. We should be shocked if a government sought to pollute the air we breathe, or to poison the food we eat. Yet managing the news, even with the best intentions in the world, poisons the information the public gets.

The errors and inadequacies of the press blind us, I think,

to what is happening. For three centuries we have developed a Fourth Estate skilled in ferreting out the news; and despite its excesses and abuses that Fourth Estate has served us well by revealing to us the essential facts of the world we live in. But with the advent of the Big State there has been raised up a host of highly skilled suppressors and distorters of the news. The motives with which they do it do not matter. The fact that they do it matters supremely.

It will not do to say that in today's world this is characteristic of Russia and its satellites alone, that with the end of the war the United States returned safely to its accustomed ways, and that therefore government-managed news is nothing to worry about. We forget that peace, too, has its threats. They may seem just as unreal as the threats of war—until war comes. It is living in a fool's paradise to assume that we have permanently escaped another great depression, or an unprecedented international economic collapse, or some other catastrophe that can bear upon us personally like the depression of 1929–1933 or the war itself. In such a crisis, all the old alarms will return, and with them demands upon the government to do something. Then in turn the temptation will visit government itself to make the news not an honest report but some sort of combined censor and morale-builder for the people.

That is why it is essential to convince the American people that managed news does not meet the need, noted in earlier chapters, for bringing the historic principle of the free press into line with the economics of the twentieth century. The remedy for the concentration of control over our newspapers, radio, and the rest, in the hands of a relatively few men must lie elsewhere.

CHAPTER X

MOVING THE NEWS

At 5:47 on April 9, 1942, a commuter, homeward bound from Manhattan, settled into a seat on his nightly train just before it pulled out of the station. He unfolded the 7th Sports Final Edition of the *World-Telegram* he had bought at the news stand. Across the top of the page, in two-inch letters, were the words JAPS OVERWHELM BATAAN. And down the right-hand side of the page, in boldface type, two columns wide, ran this story:

By the United Press.

WASHINGTON, April 9.—Massive Japanese fighting forces, heavily outnumbering the 36,800 American and Filipino troops, finally overwhelmed the gallant defenders of Bataan Peninsula today and Secretary of War Stimson said it appeared doubtful any substantial number could be evacuated to continue the fight from the fortresses of Manila Bay.

Mr. Stimson, disclosing for the first time the number and plight of the Bataan defenders who fought on despite exhaustion, short rations, disease and lack of relief, was unable to say how many of the 36,853 Yanks and Filipinos would be in each of the categories of casualties—killed, captured, or wounded.

He said that every effort was being made to get as many of them as possible to Corregidor and other American fortresses that still hold out in Manila Bay.

The story went on with two more crisp paragraphs of information. Then it quoted the Secretary of War directly:

"Our troops, outnumbered, worn down by attack, exhausted by insufficient rations and disease prevailing in that area, had their lines broken and enveloped by the enemy," Mr. Stimson said.

"Our defenses on Bataan have been overthrown. Corregidor is still fighting.

"A long and gallant defense has been worn down and overthrown.

"There is nothing but praise for the men who have so ably conducted an epic chapter in the history of the Philippines."

As President Roosevelt and General Douglas MacArthur before him, Mr. Stimson pledged that the United States would win back the Philippines from the Japanese and restore independence to the Filipino people who had acquitted themselves so gallantly in the hopeless fight.

The story, grim with the details of that milestone in the dark days of the war, ran on down the page and over to page 2 for another column and a half.

The fall of Bataan is now a yellowing page in the history of World War II. I cite it here to illustrate, by examining that page in detail, how the machinery of the Fourth Estate moves the news from the scene of action to the mind of the citizen. Any one of a thousand later stories might do as well. But it happens that I have at hand a completely documented file on the origin, development, and transmission of this particular item of news by the three large press associations, all the New York newspapers, and the four large radio networks. This is a rare treasure, whose existence I owe to the skill and persistence and powers of observation of my collaborator on this chapter. It is rare, because journalism, like the flower in your buttonhole, blossoms for a day and then is gone. The dusty cellar of a single press association, newspaper, or radio network may contain the files of its own coverage of a story; but I believe they never before have been assembled all in one place.

Let us therefore use this unique exhibit to observe a process that goes on twenty-four hours a day for three hundred and sixty-five days a year—a process so incidental to the import of the news that we are hardly aware of it. Without this process of news transmission, bearing day in and day out a stream of facts from the physical world into our mental world, modern society could not exist.

Whence, then, came this story about Bataan? And how did it get into the hands of our commuter?

Actually it came by Army radio from Lieutenant General Jonathan M. Wainwright in the rocky tunnels of Corregidor to the War Department. But for our purposes it came from stuffy, fluorescent-lighted Room 2045 in the Munitions Building on Constitution Avenue in Washington. There, in pre-Pentagon days, Secretary Stimson received the press. At 10:45 that morning—fifteen minutes late because he had just been conferring with the President—he entered the room. He was accompanied by Major General A. D. Surles, in charge of Army public relations, and Colonel Stanley Grogan. Fifty-odd reporters—slightly more than usual—and fifty Army officers were waiting. They were hushed and grim.

The Secretary wasted no time. "The communiqué issued this morning shortly after four o'clock," he said, "contained the latest information we have." He was referring to a special communiqué, long since sent out over the press association wires, that read:

A message from General Wainwright at Fort Mills just received at the War Department states that the Japanese attack on Bataan Peninsula succeeded in enveloping the east flank of our lines, in the position held by the Second Corps. An attack by the First Corps, ordered to relieve the situation, failed due to complete physical exhaustion of the troops.

Full details are not available but this situation indicates the probability that the defenses on Bataan have been overcome.

Secretary Stimson went on: "Our troops were outnumbered and worn down by successive attacks by fresh troops. They were exhausted by insufficient rations and the tropic diseases prevailing in that region and had their lines broken and enveloped by the enemy. Our defense on Bataan has been overthrown. A long and gallant defense has been worn down and overthrown."

He repeated the phrase several times, as though talking to himself. Then:

"We have nothing but praise and admiration for the commanders and their men. They have made this an epic chapter in the history of their country. I believe this to be a temporary loss. This country, in fulfillment of its pledge to the Philippines, will ultimately drive out the invaders. We shall not stop until that is done."

The Secretary's voice broke as he said this. Then he went on:

"During the long defense we have heard from General MacArthur and General Wainwright a great deal about the soldiers on Bataan, and the generals have had nothing but praise for the Filipinos who have been fighting side by side with our soldiers in that battle. The Philippines now have been united with us in battle as well as linked by the cooperation between the United States and the Philippines during the last forty years."

A reporter interrupted to ask whether he might quote the Secretary as saying that the Japanese would be driven from the islands.

"We shall not stop until that is done," replied the Secretary.

For thirty-five minutes the colloquy went on. At one point Secretary Stimson began talking off the record. This is the first degree of information under the folkways of Washington press conferences. An official gives out information so that the reporters may orient themselves among the facts, but they must not use it in their stories. In response to requests from the reporters Stimson relented enough to say that the facts in question might be used but not attributed to him—the second degree of information. Further importuning led him in the end to consent to the third category, direct quotation.

As he talked, he not only rounded out the background of the early morning special communiqué, but gave information that had hitherto been closely guarded. There were, as of the day before, he said, 36,853 effectives on Bataan, including Filipinos and American sailors and marines. There were also 6,000 Filipino workmen, and some 18,000 to 20,000 refugees—almost all Filipinos—who had gone to Bataan with MacArthur. The 36,853 figure did not, however, include troops on Corregidor and the other fortresses in the bay.

These posts, Secretary Stimson said twice during the session, were all holding out and still fighting. The President had left to General Wainwright the decision as to what to do next, and had told him that any decision he reached now would be in the interest of the country and that of the splendid troops he commanded.

The Secretary also divulged that strenuous efforts had been made under Patrick Hurley, himself a former Secretary of War, to break the blockade of Corregidor and Bataan. Hurley was successful in finding ships and supplies, and got several shiploads to the Philippines. "But for every ship that arrived, we lost nearly two ships," Stimson said. However:

"I am glad to say that the defenders were never short of ammunition because of Hurley's work. Up until the very last word from them, they had plenty of small arms and artillery ammunition. But they had been on short rations since MacArthur put them in effect on January 11. This fact and the long strain were a very potent factor in wearing down our troops, making them unable to rebound to the counterattack as at first."

So it went, now off the record, now on. How many were American soldiers, how many Filipinos? Air power? A month before the end MacArthur had had only four pursuit planes left. The Americans had fought the battle without air support.

At length the story was told, the conference ended. The Army officers began distributing War Department news releases dealing with R.O.T.C. units, mechanizing cavalry, and other subjects that had no relation to the big story. Some of the reporters took these releases, but many didn't wait. They were already racing to the press room.

This press room was just down the corridor from the conference room. From thirty to forty men were there, the press association men and reporters for Washington's afternoon papers already at the telephones. Others stood gazing at the notes they had scribbled on pieces of folded gray copy paper as Mr. Stimson spoke. A few were comparing notes. Several were clustered around an officer near the door. Still others were waiting for the phones to be free.

INS—that is to say, the International News Service, the Hearst press association—was the first to get word of what Mr. Stimson said on the wires to its subscribing newspapers and radio stations. It was first largely because the editors in the Washington bureau deemed the story worth a flash. Accordingly, a rewrite man in the INS office at once typed a few words on a slip of paper and handed them to a teletype operator, while the INS man in the Munitions Building was still phoning in details.

The teletype operator tapped the bell key on his machine four times. In newspaper offices and radio stations throughout the country bells on the receiving teletypes went *bing, bing, bing, bing* in warning that something big was coming. Then the Washington operator unhurriedly, but without waste motion, typed out the message. By 11:22, two or three minutes after Mr. Stimson had finished talking, it was on the wires:

> FLASH
> WASHINGTON—36,800 TRAPPED ON BATAAN—STIMSON
> 1122 AEG   INS TX

Simultaneously in newspaper and radio offices, from New York to Los Angeles, the teletypes clacked out those six words on endless rolls of yellow paper.

Meanwhile, the news had been telephoned just as fast to the Washington headquarters of the Associated Press and the United Press Associations. In both, the responsible editors decided that, in view of the early morning communiqué foreshadowing what Mr. Stimson said, the news was worth not a flash but only a bulletin. Both services had their bulletins on the wires right behind the briefer INS flash.

Now a flash is not any bit of gossip nervously rattled out, as you might think from Walter Winchell's radio program. It is a rare news item of top importance. The essence of such news is phrased in ten words or less that are put on the circuit forthwith, interrupting whatever other news may be in transmission. A bulletin is a similar item of just less than top importance. It is told in about twenty-five words, and likewise has precedence on the wires. While individual press associations use variations or subdivisions of this terminology, the distinction between flash and bulletin is enough for our purposes. We must also note that, naturally enough, all three press associations supplement both flash and bulletin on the teletype with detailed information. This is sent out in units of one, two, or more paragraphs, interspersed if necessary between similar takes from other stories, as soon as they are written and approved.

But let us return to the INS bureau in Washington. There the flash had been followed within two minutes by a bulletin giving a few details. Despite the speed at which it was written, this bulletin could be set in type by the subscribing newspapers as the first paragraph of the story. Forewarned by the flash and preparing to use the Stimson news under big headlines on page one, the newspapers were awaiting it:

> TXA55 BUN SUB FLASH AND SECOND LEAD
>
> BY JOSEPH A BORS
> INTERNATIONAL NEWS SERVICE STAFF CORRESPONDENT
> WASHINGTON, APRIL 9— (INS)—BATAAN FELL BEFORE THE
> FURIOUS ONSLAUGHT OF NUMERICALLY SUPERIOR JAPANESE
> FORCES TODAY ENTRAPPING 36,800 AMERICAN AND FILIPINO
> TROOPS WHO HAD VALIANTLY WITHSTOOD THE ENEMY FOR
> 90 DAYS.
>
> (MORE)   1124 AEG

One minute later (the numerals at the end of the items indicate the time at which transmission was completed) this addition had been received by the subscribers:

> TXA56 ADD 2ND LEAD BORS
>
> ANNOUNCEMENT OF THE FALL OF BATAAN WAS MADE BY
> THE WAR DEPARTMENT IN A SPECIAL COMMUNIQUE AT
> 5:15 A.M. EWT AND A FEW HOURS LATER SECRETARY OF WAR
> STIMSON REVEALED THE NUMBER OF AMERICAN-FILIPINO
> TROOPS WHO WENT DOWN WITH THE PENINSULA.
>
> (MORE)   1125 AEG

There followed in rapid succession two more takes giving further details, all written so that with a little editing to make them conform to the individual paper's typographical style and to spell out symbols like EWT into Eastern War Time, or to add "Secretary" or "Mr." before Stimson, they could be rushed into type:

> TXA57 BUN ADD 2ND LEAD BORS
>
> "I BELIEVE IT WILL BE A TEMPORARY LOSS," STIMSON SAID.
> "WE WILL ULTIMATELY DRIVE OUT THESE INVADERS. WE
> SHALL NOT STOP UNTIL THIS IS DONE."
>
> (MORE)   1126 AEG

TXA58 ADD 2ND LEAD BORS

AT THE SAME TIME THE SECRETARY SAID THAT CORREGI-
DOR AND OTHER ISLAND FORTS ARE FIGHTING ON AND
THAT PRESIDENT ROOSEVELT HAS LEFT TO LIEUT. GEN.
JONATHAN M. WAINWRIGHT THE DECISION FOR FUTURE
ACTION IN THE PHILIPPINES.

(MORE)

This was followed by numerous additional takes, some of
which carried corrections to be made in the earlier ones. And
as the newspaper clients received the later parts of the story
the headlines and the edited earlier parts were already being
put into type. At the same time radio stations were rewording
the teletype news for spoken presentation on the air. It was
11:49—twenty-seven minutes after the flash, half an hour after
Secretary Stimson had finished speaking—when subscribers on
the West Coast, like those elsewhere in the country, had received
the complete story.

Once the Stimson news was out of the way, other items could
again be tapped out on the teletype for those clients that sub-
scribe to only a single-wire service. They can, of course, receive
but one take from one story at a time. The larger papers sub-
scribe to a multiple-wire service, so that sports, finance, and
regional items, as well as general news, can all pile into the office
at the same time. Some of the metropolitan papers and the big
networks take the full reports of two or more press associations.

But back to the INS office once more. In the course of the
early afternoon it sent out items that included the releases
handed out at the Stimson conference, together with fresh subsidiary stories on Bataan, like the statement from the Philippine Commissioner in Washington. There were also advance
stories for use in the papers of April 10, the next day.

By four o'clock INS's afternoon-paper service closed, and the
morning wire opened. First item on the schedule was the Stim-
son-Bataan story again, this time a more polished and far longer
piece on which Eric Friedheim of the Washington staff had
worked while Bors was batting out his hurried story for the
afternoon editors. By this time, too, there were more subsidiary items, carrying comment by President Roosevelt and
General Wainwright's wife, and giving the reactions of other
United Nations capitals.

Meanwhile, much the same news was being speeded out from the Washington bureaus of the Associated Press and the United Press with the same unhurried swiftness. The AP had sent out two leads on Bataan based on the War Department's early morning communiqué. The first, carried on the day report at 5:15, told of "the probability that the defenses on Bataan have been overcome." The second lead, a few minutes afterward, gave such other details as were in the communiqué. Then, when late in the morning the Stimson story was telephoned in, this item went out to New York, Kansas City, and other AP junction points for immediate relay over the regional circuits:

A175 WX

BULLETIN

THIRD LEAD PHILIPPINES

WASHINGTON, APRIL 9— (AP)—SECRETARY OF WAR STIMSON REPORTED TODAY THAT LIEUTENANT GENERAL JONATHAN WAINWRIGHT'S FORCE ON THE PHILIPPINES BATAAN PENINSULA NUMBERED 36,853 EFFECTIVE TROOPS WHEN THEIR RESISTANCE APPARENTLY COLLAPSED.

SU1124AEW

There followed other items giving full details. By 12:24, or just an hour after the Stimson bulletin, a fifth and final lead on the Bataan story for the afternoon papers was on the wire. This fifth lead stayed unchanged through the afternoon, except for an insertion to the effect that Bataan was probably the severest loss in a foreign war in the history of American arms, and that officials believed the man-power loss might be the heaviest sustained by an American force in any single engagement with a foreign foe.

Before the morning-paper service opened at four P.M. other developments were rushed to the wire. Around the world AP men were already hunting out related material. Thus, by three o'clock the AP was able to put on a dispatch from Clark Lee, then its correspondent in Melbourne, who used as a news peg the fact that General MacArthur had been informed of the fall of Bataan. For the most part, however, Lee's dispatch was an eyewitness account of conditions on Bataan that Lee was able to file because he had himself been there, having only recently been smuggled through the Japanese blockade as had General

MacArthur himself, Philippines High Commissioner Francis B. Sayre, President Quezon, and a handful of others.

Here again it is necessary to digress for a moment and go into a detail of press association procedure. Lee had sent his story from Australia to San Francisco, at the urgent rate of 59 cents a word, in cablese. This is a skeletonized English used by foreign correspondents to help cut cable tolls. In it the two words "this morning" become a single and therefore cheaper word, "smorning." A downpour comes out of "rainiest" skies. The Foreign Minister doesn't look something up, he "uplooks" it. Bobby Jones used to win by "oneputting" on "sixteenhole." And should a prewar duke be motoring back from the shooting in Scotland, he would be "Rollsroycing Londonwards." I have before me a wartime clipping from the *New York Times,* giving an eyewitness description of an American attack in the Pacific, that says at one point, "Now the Japanese are incoming." A hurried copy reader must have let that slip by without changing it to "are coming in." For in the newspaper offices, or at receiving points for press association cables like New York or San Francisco, cablese is translated into normal English for relay on the domestic wires. And that was what was done with Clark Lee's dispatch from Melbourne in April, 1942.

The AP held the Bataan collapse so important, morever, that it gave the morning papers EOS beginning at 2:22 P.M. That abbreviation stands for "extraordinary occasion service," which had been put into effect with the *Titanic* sinking in 1912 [1] to permit morning papers to publish news at once even though by agreement it was still during afternoon-paper hours, or vice versa. Because radio now so largely discharges the function once served by newspaper extras, EOS has in practice become largely an advance service that enables newspapers to organize thorough coverage of outstanding events. With its morning-paper service on the news from Bataan the AP showed what it could do for sheer volume of news. Instead of following that, however, let us briefly examine the UP report that became the basis of the account in the *New York World-Telegram* with which this chapter began. Ever since the previous war, which matured it as one of our great news services, the UP has been restive at the AP's longstanding assumption that the AP report alone ranks with the tablets brought down from Sinai. The UP staff does not resent that assumption the less because on occasion the AP's gold standard of news has been marred by those lapses into error— such as its false D-Day flash in 1944 and its authentic but premature news of the surrender at Rheims a year later—to which all press associations, being manned by human beings, are liable despite the most rigid safeguards.

Anyway, on with the story. Actually the big press associations are with occasional exceptions all within a few minutes of one another in sending big news, day in and day out. Thus on the day of Bataan the UP happened to be the slowest of the three, but even so got off its bulletin only one minute after the AP. Here is what it said:

UP187

BULLETIN

WASHINGTON, APRIL 9.— (UP)—SECRETARY OF WAR HENRY L. STIMSON SAID TODAY THAT A FORCE OF 36,800 AMERICANS AND FILIPINOS WENT DOWN FIGHTING AGAINST OVER- WHELMINGLY SUPERIOR JAPANESE FORCES ON BATAAN.

MORE   JL1125A

And one minute later:

UP188

ADD STIMSON WASHN X X X BATAAN

HE PROMISED THAT THE FIGHT WILL NOT BE ENDED UNTIL THE INVADERS EVENTUALLY ARE DRIVEN OUT.

MORE   JL1126A

Here we can already recognize some of the elements that survived in the copy of the *World-Telegram* bought by our commuter more than six hours later. Toward the end of the bulletin is the word "overwhelmingly," which, changed back into the word Mr. Stimson had himself used, figured in the paper's banner headline, JAPS OVERWHELM BATAAN. Again, the round number 36,800 appears in this bulletin just as it does in the first sentence of the newspaper's story, which does not give Mr. Stimson's exact figure until later. Finally, in the add (for addition) to the UP's bulletin appears the Secretary's promise that we would not stop until the Japanese were driven out, which also survives in the *World-Telegram's* story.

The UP, like the other two press associations, followed its first statement with additional bulletin matter, and then with smoother and more connected stories. The first four paragraphs of the first of these detailed stories were filed by 11:52. It is interesting to note that these paragraphs, hurriedly written though they were, appeared almost verbatim in the finished *World-Telegram* account. From here on, indeed, the UP's cascading paragraphs are almost word for word what was printed in the *World-Telegram* to tell our home-going commuter what had happened that day in the Philippines. In fact, the whole account in the newspaper, when checked against Secretary Stimson's words at the press conference, graphically demonstrates the accuracy with which the story of Bataan was moved from its origin in the Munitions Building, via telephone to the United Press's Washington office, by teletype to the newspaper in New York, then quickly across the copy desk and so on to printing, delivery by truck to news stand, and finally to our homeward-bound commuter. Such accuracy is by no means reserved for the occasional big story. It is routine for the press associations, a fact often forgotten by the critics of the press, who pounce on the newspapers' lapses from fairness and accuracy in the news but ignore its day-in and day-out performance.

The work of the newspaper copy desk, too, is little appreciated by those who read its products every day. Again, only the errors seem to stand out where we can see them. What happens is that incoming news, like the AP and UP bulletins on Bataan this particular day, are torn off the teletypes by a copy boy and given to the telegraph editor. On a story as big as this the telegraph editor confers with the managing editor, the news editor, or whoever has the making of page 1 in his hands. They decide quickly that Bataan not only is the leading story for the remaining editions that day, but deserves an eight-column headline in the largest type.

The telegraph editor then passes the press association bulletins to the "man in the slot" as the head of the copy desk is known, because of his post in a niche on the inside of the desk, on whose rim sit the copy readers. He scans the copy swiftly, but notes accurately its essence. He then glances about at his copy readers, whom the British designate more accurately as "subeditors," to see who among those competent to handle a big wire story is free. Because only minutes are left, it does not take him long to note down a symbol indicating the style of headline to be written, and to slide the copy across the desk to the man he has selected.

Henceforth that man handles every new paragraph, every correction, and every subsidiary item of the story in question. He takes the early material, quickly sizes it up, and makes notes on the chief facts. On them he will base his headline, unless, because the time is short or because it is the most important headline in the paper, the head of the desk or the telegraph editor has already taken it in hand. That headline must be written in a matter of minutes determined by the nearness of press time. Not only that, but it must present the heart of the news at once to the uninformed reader who skims it, and at the same time fit neatly into a limited space that a mere count of letters is usually too crude to measure.

As for the story, the copy reader assembles the press association "takes" in proper order, underlines two or three times each letter that is to be set in capitals, marks the paragraphs, inserts a "Mr." here or a first name there, makes the figures and other details conform to the paper's typographical style, corrects spellings, dates, and other facts out of his head if possible and out of a reference source if not, watches for libel with his subconscious self, and otherwise assumes responsibility for the story's readiness to appear in public. If the next edition is only minutes away the takes are sent individually to the composing room as they are edited. If there is time, they are kept together in the form in which they are to appear as edited.

Newspapers that receive more than one press association report, plus perhaps a dispatch from their own correspondent, select the story that seems best to convey the news, and lead off with it. If other matter is occasionally inserted, it is carefully set off by brackets, indentation, or some other typographical device, and clearly credited to the new source. A more common device is to follow the leading story with one or more stories from other sources, trimmed to present only additional material, and again clearly identified as to source.

In the Bataan story the decision was made on the *World-Telegram's* desk to use the UP version, which that paper often does when other things are equal. The copy reader took the bulletin matter on the Stimson conference, plus a "Third Lead Philippines" that came in later from Mack Johnson (the UP's War Department correspondent), and assembled them. He then rewrote the first two paragraphs, and simply edited the rest. Over them went the headline we saw in the beginning, JAPS OVERWHELM BATAAN.

It is to be noted, however, that even though the first two paragraphs were rewritten, all the facts are to be found in the United Press file. This is because the press associations are adamant in insisting that no client paper tamper with the facts as it reports them. Smoothing out the phraseology, leaving out details at the end to save space, or even changing the order of facts is permissible. But a change in fact, or the introduction of other facts gathered by another press association or by the paper itself, brings a sharp protest backed by the press association's power to cut off service. This insistence that the news be used substantially as it comes over the wires not only protects the press association itself, but puts its guaranty on the integrity of its account of the news.

The files of the press associations and of the New York papers on the news of Bataan's fall are so voluminous that merely reprinting them textually would fill a good part of this book. Because the excerpts given above are fair samples, I think we have seen enough to indicate the mechanics of the complex, swift business of news transmission and news editing whose fruits we enjoy daily, but of whose workings we are usually unaware. At the very least, I trust we have seen enough to give the lay reader a glimpse of the accuracy, dispatch, and faithfulness to detail of the press association reports on which we depend for much of the daily bread in our information.

To illustrate the work of the press associations I have postulated a New York commuter who did not learn that Bataan had fallen until he opened his evening newspaper on the way home. Actually, of course, much of America had heard the news hours earlier by radio. The War Department's early-morning communiqué, which hinted broadly at what Secretary Stimson explicitly confirmed a few hours later, had been on the day's early news programs and in the first editions of the afternoon papers. And soon after the teletype operators of the big press associations spelled out their first bulletins for the newspapers, special circuits from AP's subsidiary, Press Association, from the radio department of the UP, and from smaller units like Transradio Press had carried the news to the microphones of the country.

In radio studios the problem was not to assemble a detailed and orderly account of what Secretary Stimson had said, but to rephrase the news briefly in words suitable for spoken presentation over the air at the earliest appropriate moment. The smaller stations usually rely on the press associations' radio circuits, which send out news already written in radio form. Or, if affiliated with a newspaper, they can rewrite the paper's press association reports. But big networks, like the National Broadcasting Company and the Columbia Broadcasting System, get the works—the newspaper wires from AP, UP, and INS, from which the networks like to rewrite their own copy, and a radio wire or two. And the news programs of the big networks, NBC, CBS, ABC, and Mutual, are available to most of the United States at the same moment and in the same form as in New York itself. Therefore we can better see how radio handles the news, I think, by concentrating on what happened on the day of Bataan in one of the big network newsrooms than by scattering our observation among the networks and the independent stations, big and little, around the country. So, as the announcers might say, we take you now to CBS in New York.

The wartime newsroom on the seventeenth floor of CBS's Madison Avenue building is compact. Along two walls stand rows of teletypes, bringing in the press associations' reports. Three AP machines are ranged along the wall next to the news studio. Above them is a glass window through which you can see into the studio. And in the studio is a table from which emerge three movable arms holding microphones. At the far end is a couch, used by the early-morning announcers who have nothing to do between the five-minute shows they read every hour on the hour. Over the couch is another plate-glass window, through which can be seen a small studio with a single microphone. This one is seldom used, being needed only if two news broadcasts—one for WABC (the later WCBS) locally and the other for the network, one sponsored and one not—are on the air at the same time. The main newsroom has two other plate-glass windows—one opening into the control room, the other looking into the office of Paul W. White, then CBS Director of News Broadcasts.

Normally the news announcer sits with his back to White's office. He must be able to watch both the production man in the control room and a large clock, for should he run over his time the production man might have to cut him off in the middle of a sentence. Even the news of the world is less sacred than clock to radio, whose devotees will trim anything except the "Star-Spangled Banner" to suit the second hand.

At a quarter past eleven on the morning of April 9, 1942, that is to say shortly before Secretary Stimson ended his press conference in Washington, the main CBS studio was empty. The next news broadcast, a part of the Kate Smith hour, did not go on until noon, and anyway it originated in Washington, not in the New York studio. At typewriters in the New York newsroom were two writers and a copy boy, preparing the news for the afternoon shows.

At 11:22 the bells on the INS machine jangled out sixteen strokes in groups of four. One of the writers, Jesse Zousmer, rose from his typewriter and strode across to the machine. He ripped off the flash, walked quickly across to the office of the director. Mr. White was ill that day, but Robert Wood, then second in command, was at White's desk.

"Flash," said Zousmer, handing Wood the six-word item from INS. Wood glanced at it, looked at the electric clock. It was 11:24, and already the bell on an AP machine was ringing. Peggy Miller, the other writer, walked over to see what was up.

"What's on now?" asked Wood.

"Soap opera," Zousmer replied.

Wood's decision was not to interrupt the program, a practice reserved for events pretty well in the Pearl Harbor and V Day class. Mr. Stimson's news would have to wait the remaining few minutes until 11:30.

"We'll handle it at station break," Wood said. "Write me about fifteen seconds."

Zousmer went to his desk, to which Miss Miller brought the AP bulletin. As he began to type, Wood picked up a phone to call production:

"We've a flash coming up for a station break. Who've you got?"

"Marble," said production.

"O.K., we'll send it right up. Fifteen seconds."

"O.K."

The announcement was to be made upstairs by the announcer on the job in the studio where the program was on. By the time Wood had gone to Zousmer's desk the item was ready. Wood approved it, wrote "Bulletin" at the top, because CBS does not use the term "flash" on the air, and sent it upstairs by compressed-air tube. It was now 11:28.

In the upstairs studio Harry Marble, the announcer, took the item from its container, read it to himself, then read it aloud. He went into a little studio off the control room. It was 11:29:45. From the control room the production man waved, then cocked his right hand with forefinger in the air and thumb pointing over his shoulder. As the second hand reached 11:30 he flipped a switch with his left hand, brought down his poised forefinger to point at Marble. The announcer read:

"Bulletin.

"Washington—Secretary of War Stimson announces that most of the 36,000 American and Filipino troops on Bataan Peninsula have been killed or captured by the Japanese.

"But Stimson adds that the defenders went down fighting and the defense of Corregidor goes on."

The fifteen seconds were up.

By this time the news for the Kate Smith program in Washington had been trimmed to leave room for Secretary Stimson's information, even though it had been almost all written before the bells on the network's teletypes in Washington began ringing. At the appropriate time the revised script was ready, with this paragraph included in the program's budget of news:

"The worst [news] of all comes in this late dispatch from Washington. Secretary of War Stimson has just told a press conference that 36,800 Americans and Filipinos went down fighting. Most of them, probably killed or captured. Mr. Stimson promised that the fight will not be ended until the invaders are eventually driven out."

CBS's next news show was on at three o'clock. Ten minutes before that time Miss Miller had turned her script for it over to

Mark Hawley, the announcer, so that he might read it to see how it would sound. It led off with some six hundred words based on the Secretary of War's statements, and on the press associations' follow-up news, all now translated out of newspaper style into conversational sentences, with smooth transitions between news items. Radio's news is not scattered about typographically, so that the eye may select first one, then another. It must form a smooth-running, continuous pattern that can be taken in from beginning to end.

At 4:45 another CBS news program told the now familiar story to a new audience, adding such further reactions from around the world as had come in. This was followed at six by Frazier Hunt's commentary, written by Hunt himself but based once more on press association raw material. And this in turn was followed by the high point in CBS's news coverage, the evening news roundup at 6:45.

On the night Bataan fell, the roundup was to call in Washington, London, and Sydney. This had been arranged by cable a week in advance, subject to modification by transatlantic telephone. On the job in the New York newsroom was John Daly, a tall, brown-haired news announcer who prides himself on never having read a commercial over the air. The words that covered the transitions in the program were written for Daly by Henry Wefing, former newspaperman, who also wrote stand-by copy for the points abroad should sunspots or anything else prevent the overseas voices from coming in clearly enough to be understood. If so, Daly would apologize to the radio audience and say, "But here are the latest reports from London," and read the stand-by copy. Such emergency copy is hardly ever needed for Washington, which comes in by land wire instead of short wave, though a press association dispatch may be kept on hand against the unexpected.

By 6:35, ten minutes ahead of time, everything was ready. Daly was in the newsroom's main studio, rehearsing his opening and transitions, checking his stand-by copy for Philippine and other unpronounceables. Behind him in White's office the night editor, at that time Matthew Gordon, was at the desk. A bell rang and Gordon picked up one of the three telephones at the edge of the desk.

"Hello. Washington? Oh, hello, Al." It was correspondent Albert Warner. Gordon continued:

"Anything cooking? You're first, Al. You come up at 6:45:30 —right from here to you. Yes. You handle George's introduction down there." (George Fielding Eliot was also to speak from Washington.)

As Gordon glanced over a sheet on which the points to be called in were listed together with the time down to the second, a loud-speaker near the ceiling began to talk: "Reading from the *Daily Express:* 'The recent developments on the Continent indicate that Hitler . . .' " It was Bob Trout, correspondent in London, testing. At RCA the engineers listened, to check the quality of reception. The New York engineers were telling the London engineers, and Trout, how he was coming in. The phone rang again, and Gordon answered:

"Yes, Gordon. Oh, how's the signal in San Francisco?" That is where the short-wave broadcast from Sydney is picked up, to be brought to New York by wire. "That's good. . . . Yes, at 6:51:30. If it's bad, cut 'er quick. . . . No, we'll fill in here unless you've something hot to report from the coast. . . . No? O.K., we'll fill."

By now it was 6:41. Gordon beckoned through two glass windows to the production man with Daly in the studio. The man came in.

"It's Washington, London, and Sydney," Gordon told him. "San Francisco says the signal is good from Sydney. That's second—Washington, Sydney, London. And Bob sounds good from London. O.K.?"

"O.K."

Gordon leaned over and reached for the silver cue-channel mike on the telephone ledge at the edge of the desk. Through it he could talk to Trout in London. "CBS, New York," he said.

"Oh, hello, Matt," said Trout from his bombproof BBC studio in London. "Everything neat and tidy?"

"Sure. What's for tonight, Bob?"

"Oh, bit about the Indian Ocean, bit about Bataan. You know."

"O.K., you're coming through fine tonight, Bob."

"Swell. Oh, say, I'm up at 6:56:30?"

"Yes. John'll give it to you on name cue anyway."

Trout's voice had been coming in not by telephone receiver, but through the loud-speaker at the ceiling. Now Gordon switched Trout off, and with another switch brought in WABC on the same loud-speaker. He heard WABC, upstairs, in the process of station identification. The second hand on the clock was covering the last few seconds to 6:45:00. Gordon picked up a phone and asked for San Francisco again.

In the control room an engineer, his hand cocked in the air with upraised forefinger, was looking through the glass at Daly in the studio. As the second hand pointed straight up he brought his finger down to point at Daly, again flipping a switch with his other hand. Over each of the studio's three doors signs, reading "On the Air," glowed red. The commercial announcer sitting at a microphone at Daly's left began: "The World Today. Brought to you by the United Fruit Company. And now, John Daly and the CBS news."

Daly glanced at the yellow copy paper in his hand, and read:

"The story of the fall of Bataan, where for three months a relatively small number of gallant American and Filipino troops held out against numerically overwhelming Japanese forces, dominates tonight's news. So, first, a detailed report on the Philippine situation from Albert L. Warner, and then an analysis of its military significance by Major George Fielding Eliot. . . . Now to Washington, and Mr. Warner."

The engineer threw a switch, and after a two-second pause Warner's steady voice came in. He began by saying that there were no further details from Corregidor, and then he gave the news as it stood in Washington at the moment. He, in turn, brought in Major Eliot, who ended with ". . . and the fiercer determination that those that fell in the defense shall not have died in vain."

In the New York studio Daly read the transition to Australia. Promptly on time, through a faint buzz of atmospheric disturbance came the voice of John Raleigh from halfway around the world in Sydney. He began with unofficial reports that "a major naval action has taken place in the Bay of Bengal between a Japanese fleet and Allied defensive units." Then Bataan, with what fresh light there was on it in Australia.

Then came a similar transition to London, with Daly in New York picking up between the two. In London, Trout too led off with the naval battle, saying London was waiting for more details on the loss of the cruisers *Dorsetshire* and *Cornwall*. As he spoke, Gordon hung up his phones and pushed away the cue-channel microphone, to go into the studio with Daly. Trout's voice came clearly through another loud-speaker there. He was telling about London's reaction to the day's news from Bataan, ending ". . . that's from tomorrow's London *Times*. I return you to Columbia in New York."

Daly signed the program off with the copy prepared. The red warning signs went out, the mike was dead.

"Oh, well," said Daly to Gordon, "another holler, another dollar."

Meanwhile, a gray-haired, tanned man in his shirt sleeves had been jotting down notes at the news printers, and keeping an ear cocked for significant statements from Columbia's overseas reporters. It was Elmer Davis, as yet unaware that in a little more than two months he would be in Washington at the head of a new agency to be called the Office of War Information. Davis wrote his scripts himself, in a little office next to Paul White's. At 8:55 on the night of Bataan he was ready with sixty-eight typewritten lines of copy, and on the air: "There is no later news from Bataan than Secretary Stimson's statement this morning . . ."

CBS put two more news programs on the air before midnight, and another as the new day began. But still the story was, "There is no late news from the Philippines . . ."

The story that had come from Secretary Stimson's press conference thirteen hours before had done its duty. Long since, it had been put into ordered, final form by the morning papers.

While newspapers and radio were getting the news of Bataan to the country, the press association teletypes were bringing the facts into the editorial offices of the news magazines. There researchers and writers and editors put the wire copy together with newspaper clippings, reference material, and dispatches from their own correspondents. They sweated over it; compressing and arranging the actual happening, its antecedents, and its meaning, into a far more ordered perspective than the most care-

ful morning paper can give. In the offices of the general magazines other editors read the newspaper stories about Bataan.
This was a routine part of their task of keeping up with the
news so that they might arrange articles and pictures for their
own pages. In the universities, the professors were reading the
same items, either for their own information or for use in their
classes. Lecturers, too, were making clippings for talks on current events. And you may be sure that the printed versions of
the AP, UP, and INS stories mentioned earlier in this chapter
will be scanned once more when the time comes to write formal
histories of the war in the Pacific. Against that time the bound
or microfilm copies of the newspapers carrying them arrived
in due course in the libraries.

The news of Bataan was, in short, moving into the background phase, from its origin with Secretary Stimson and its
transmission as spot news over the press association, newspaper,
and radio teletypes.

The newsreels, while also as much a background as spot-news
medium, found little they could do with the news of Bataan's
fall. Picturewise, the Stimson conference was only another of
the kind that Washington has at a dime a dozen. Nor would the
Army films, showing the actual fighting, be coming in to be
censored, edited, and used. For the fall of Corregidor still lay
ahead, and whatever films the Signal Corps made in the Philippines and took to Corregidor became temporary booty for the
Jap. Here was one unit in the machinery of information that
could not use the press association reports except to keep up
with the news.

However, had facsimile and television been functioning in
the news machinery—as they are now finally beginning to—
they would have built their programs on those bulletins and
detailed stories sent over press association teletypes; for facsimile is simply another way of reproducing printed and other
graphic matter, and television, unless it can train its elec-
tronic cameras on the action itself, must build its images on the
skeleton of the written words that come in by teletype.

It all comes down to this: the whole machinery of information
that constitutes contemporary journalism depends on the press
associations for its contact with a great part of the physical
world. Radio, moving pictures, still photography, and television

can, in proper circumstances, report directly from the scene of action. But the proper circumstances attend only a minority of the news developments about which the citizens of democracy must know. Hence the press association, and the related newspaper and radio reports that give color, details, and background, are the old reliables.

Make no mistake about it: the press associations do the bulk of the work. Only a handful among even the larger American newspapers maintain their own staffs of foreign correspondents. These are papers like the *Times* and *Herald Tribune* in New York, the *Tribune, Daily News,* and *Sun-Times* in Chicago, and the *Christian Science Monitor* in Boston. Other metropolitan papers, like the *Baltimore Sun* and the *New York Sun,* maintain a few foreign correspondents of their own. The big radio networks, as we saw in examining CBS's coverage of Bataan, have their own men abroad, and so does an occasional large station, like WLW in Cincinnati.[2] Sometimes, too, these correspondents for individual newspapers or networks do double duty, as when the *New York Times* sells its own foreign service to the *Boston Herald* and other papers. Again, individual correspondents will be on the staff of a newspaper bureau in a news center like Cairo, and will at the same time broadcast from there for a network when there is occasion. These special correspondents have latitude to supply the detailed and thoughtful coverage that tends to interest the speakers and writers at home who follow the news professionally. But it is the press association men who supply the bulk of the news to the bulk of American readers and listeners.

What these press association reporters do rarely resembles the romantic notion of the foreign correspondent. Press association men are on an assembly line. They have deadlines to meet twenty-four hours a day because somewhere there is always a paper going to press or a news program going on the air. Hence, press association correspondents have little time for the moving prose or the cogent analysis of which the correspondents for individual newspapers can often deliver themselves. Their job is to get the facts in solid form, suited to clients of all political, economic, and even national colors—and then to get those facts moving. Familiarity with alternative means of communication is more useful to them than ability to turn a phrase. For only if the facts as pried loose at the source are constantly sped on their way can the teletypes of America go *bing, bing, bing, bing,* when the big news comes.

For the burden it has to carry, the press association structure is amazingly small. True, these agencies could not operate without drawing on the reporting facilities of the newspapers they serve. In that sense every newspaper and its staff is helping to do the press association's work. It is also true that each press association—like the newspapers and networks with their own foreign staffs—has a host of "string," or part-time, correspondents, paid only when they have news to deliver, scattered around the world; but, day in and day out, the work is done by the regulars, and of these, on editorial, mechanical, and business staffs together, the AP and UP have perhaps 2,000 each, INS far fewer, and the smaller news agencies a comparative handful. A total of 6,000 men and women exclusively in the business of collecting and transmitting American press association news is probably a liberal estimate.

How much would the publicists and the lecturers, the college presidents and the bishops, the writers of editorials, articles, and books—how much would any of them know about those world affairs concerning which they deliver their opinions, without the press associations and their co-workers of newspaper and radio? How much would even government officials, relying on direct but strictly limited sources of information, be able to understand of what was happening in the world? Without the press associations and their fellows America would live in darkness.

CHAPTER XI

AMERICAN MINISTERS

OF POPULAR ENLIGHTENMENT

FORTUNATELY the United States has never yet had a Minister of Propaganda and Popular Enlightenment after the manner of Nazi Germany's Dr. Goebbels. Of course, George Creel of the Committee on Public Information in World War I and Elmer Davis of the Office of War Information in World War II were called Administration propagandists by politicians, editors, and businessmen whose spleens were more active than their brains. But despite the totalitarian pressures of war, and the present universal trend toward centralized government, we have not yet remotely approached official management of the news that makes the world as we see it in our heads.

The shoe is, indeed, on the other foot. Not only is there that preponderant identification of our press, radio, and other media of information with the political and economic old guard as noted in Chapter VI, but such rigging of the news as we have comes more from business interests and pressure groups than from government; for the United States is the world's most fertile breeding ground of press agents, publicity men, vice presidents in charge of information, and counselors on public relations, who have no other purpose than to alter our mental worlds in the interests of their clients. These unofficial ministers of popular enlightenment have so prospered, multiplied, and become a part of the scheme of things that if you want to start an organization to manufacture widgets, sell peanuts, abolish labor unions, wipe out capitalism, or merely to band together a loyal lodge of undertakers, the first thing is to get yourself a publicity man. No publicity, no organization; for, in a world of mass populations dependent on mass communications, any enterprise whose influence goes beyond walking distance of the home office is lost unless it becomes known, understood, and to some extent approved by its public.

Government, of course, has long since joined the procession, and employs publicity men by the thousand. Their output may be sampled from a table in Washington's National Press Club, where mimeographed releases from government agencies and bureaus arrive fresh every day if not every hour, to provide a governmental publicity *smörgåsbord*. The White House itself has not escaped the habit. The Red Cross, the National Tuberculosis Association, the American Society for the Control of Cancer, and innumerable other causes, all go in for publicity— that is to say, for propaganda on behalf of themselves and their objectives. Even the American Library Association makes awards for "distinguished publicity" to libraries.[1] So unbelievably huge is the resulting barrage of releases that newspaper editors on the receiving end have been frenetic on the subject for a generation. This blast from Edward W. Sowers, co-publisher and editor of the *Excelsior Springs Daily Standard* in Missouri, is typical:

> If all the editors of all the newspapers and periodicals in the United States would do what I am doing . . . we would in twelve months eliminate the . . . paper shortage, lift the post office department out of the red, save $13,688,340.64 in wasted postage, save an additional $27,376,681.28 in paper and labor gone-for-naught.[2]

Mr. Sowers' remedy was simple: to put all publicity material into the wastebasket instead of into the paper.

Perhaps, however, it is not so simple as that. Publicity and propaganda differ only in degree, and not in kind; and for all the waste involved, propaganda is to a greater or lesser extent effective. The waste of paper in publicity is merely the by-product of the amazing potency of propaganda in favorable circumstances. Samuel Adams, Thomas Paine, and a handful of others committed an undecided majority of the American colonists—almost in spite of themselves—to independence. Again, it was not alone the corruption and confusion of Czarism and war that turned Russia Bolshevist; it was the propagandists Lenin and Trotsky. In the same way the German people did not become Nazis all by themselves; a frustrated nobody with a devilish vision and fanatic purpose led them to it. Or, to descend to a less majestic scale, it was the publicity genius William H. Anderson of the Anti-Saloon League who, within a few months after his arrival in New York in 1914, changed the entire political line-up of the state.[3] In sum, propaganda and its little brother publicity, alike in that they can channel the wavering minds of men into a predetermined course, have been an exceedingly powerful force throughout modern times.

One can indeed trace propaganda back as far as one likes. The Apostle Paul himself is in many ways a prototype of the propagandist, as is many another leader of man's historic causes. Harold Lasswell, an authority on the subject, has discovered traces of the propaganda technic in *The Book of War* by Sun Tzu in the fifth century B.C., and in the Indian classic, Kautilya's *Arthasastra,* of the fourth century B.C.[4] Perhaps a more convenient beginning, however, is June 22, 1622, when Pope Gregory XV established in Rome the Sacra Congregatio de Propaganda Fide, or Sacred Congregation for the Propagation of the Faith. Gregory was succeeded the following year by Urban VIII, who founded the College of Propaganda to train priests for missionary work in the expanding world of explorers, conquerors, and colonists of the seventeenth century.[5] This is a convenient beginning not only because it gave us our word "propaganda," but also because it reveals what propaganda really is; for, though in World War I the word acquired the connotation of putting over something false, the original propaganda was the missionary work of the Roman Catholic Church. Etymologically, then, propaganda is simply the propagation of a creed and, by derivation, the propagation of any idea or purpose. As Elmer Davis told the House Appropriations Committee in 1942 when asking funds for the Office of War Information: "Propaganda is an instrument; it may employ truth instead of falsehood in its operation . . . and it may be directed to worthy instead of unworthy purposes." [6] Therefore it is immaterial whether we ourselves think a particular concept that is being propagandized is good or bad. Human weakness calls it propaganda if someone does it to us, and education if we do it to others; but, good or bad, true or false, old or new, big or little, it is all propaganda.

The war of 1914–1918 gave propaganda something far more important than an undeserved connotation of evil, and that was its present place in the scheme of things. Before the war only the Imperial German Government had an official press bureau, one stemming from Prince Otto von Bismarck himself; [7] but during that war other major governments acquired them, and far improved on the original. As spectacularly successful as any was America's Creel Committee, the Committee on Public Information. Basing its activity primarily on a propaganda of truth, the committee mobilized America and, with the help of the gospel of Woodrow Wilson, influenced the thinking of the world. Speeches, articles, releases, photographs, posters, moving pictures, news services, the four-minute speakers of the Liberty Loan drives—all the now familiar technics—were united for the first time on a grand scale. It was not only the success of government propaganda in that war, however, that gave publicity its modern stature. Its taproot goes deep into American history. It goes back at least as far as Phineas Taylor Barnum, the nineteenth century's genius of the large crowd, grand master of exploiting the curious, and father of press agentry. As Barnum himself said of one of his magnificent triumphs—the tempest of acclamation that greeted Jenny Lind at her first American concert at Castle Garden:

She was effectually brought before the public before they had seen or heard her. She appeared in the presence of a jury already excited to enthusiasm in her behalf. [8]

There was a reason:

I had put innumerable means and appliances into operation for the furtherance of my object, and little did the public see of the hand that indirectly pulled at their heart-strings, preparatory to a relaxation of their purse-strings. . . . [9]

One of Barnum's "innumerable means and appliances" was something new. This was a use of newspapers to get publicity for commercial enterprises, not only by paid advertising but also by secretly stimulating letters, news reports, reviews, and editorials about the Barnum shows. We can see the method clearly in one of his earlier ventures, his exploitation of what he called the Fejee Mermaid. This supposed mermaid was a black, dried-up monstrosity about three feet long, with a bestial, monkey-like head, arms, and trunk joined to a fish's body. Its origin was dubious, but close inspection revealed no obvious joint between the two dissimilar halves, or other patent evidence of fakery.

Soon after the exhibit came into Barnum's hands a newsletter from Alabama appeared in the *New York Herald*. After giving several items of local news, the letter mentioned casually that a Dr. Griffin, of the Lyceum of Natural History in London, had arrived with a most remarkable curiosity, a real mermaid, found and preserved by Chinese in the Fiji Islands. In subsequent days many letters, from Charleston and Washington, came to other New York papers; and in due course Dr. Griffin himself arrived in Philadelphia, where he graciously allowed his hotel keeper to see the curiosity and show it to a few friends. Naturally, by the time he stopped off in New York on his way to London, reporters flocked to see him and his exhibit. And at last, when these and many similar devious doings had run their course in the New York press, Barnum announced he had persuaded the genial Dr. Griffin to allow him to exhibit the curiosity in Barnum's own American Museum, without extra charge.

The letters, written by Barnum himself, had been forwarded to friends in the South for mailing. Dr. Griffin was a Barnum assistant. By a dodge, Barnum had even planted engravings showing the mermaid—not as it actually was but as mermaids appear in song and story—in three New York papers. All this increased the profits of Barnum's Museum from around $1,200, in the four weeks before the mermaid's arrival, to more than $3,300 in the four weeks after.[10]

Barnum sensed, too, a fundamental principle, one that still escapes many who cultivate publicity: there is only one kind of publicity. For in the deeper sense there is neither good publicity nor bad publicity. Unfavorable publicity helps just as much as favorable publicity to build strength for a cause.

Hence Barnum did not mind occasional denunciations of his ways. Later masters of the art have appreciated this point of view. Joseph Pulitzer is reputed to have been pleased if, riding down to work on the New York Elevated, he overheard an incensed fellow citizen say, "Did you see that damn article in the *World* this morning?" because it was a sign that the *World* was read and was a vital part of the life of the city. So, too, Huey Long and Father Coughlin throve on the abuse heaped upon them by politicians and editorial writers, and boasted of it to the mob. Finally Dr. Goebbels, much as he cultivated strictly favorable publicity, also relished denunciations of the Nazis' treatment of the Jews. Else why were there virtually no restrictions on sending reports of Jewish persecution out of Germany? Goebbels well knew that such articles were a sure way of keeping "the Jewish question" alive, of getting Gentiles to fight among themselves about the Jews, and were thus a means to anti-Semitism.[11]

But that is getting ahead of the story. Barnum's use of press agentry throughout a life that stretched from 1810 to 1891 was not lost upon other enterprising Americans. Accordingly, strange things began to happen, notably in the late nineteenth and early twentieth centuries, and particularly in New York, metropolis of the show business and of so much else. One morning, for example, an elephant stumbled out of the waters on Staten Island's shore and lay down in great weariness just as a policeman patrolling the beach came along. In due course this strange arrival was entered on the local police blotter, where the news-hounds found it. The wonder was proclaimed to the world, and soon it was discovered that the elephant had disappeared during a storm from Luna Park, a place of amusement about to be opened on Coney Island. For days the event ran through the columns of an interested New York press, which among other things sent reporters to interview scientists as to whether an elephant could or could not swim from Coney Island to Staten Island. The episode had, of course, been engineered by a press agent, who transported the elephant to Staten Island at night by boat, after it had been trained to stay in water and to come out and lie down on signal. All this, in the interest of attracting attention to Luna Park.[12]

Innumerable examples of this sort of thing, each one more

ingenious than the last, in order to hoodwink an increasingly suspicious press, appeared in the papers. Thus in the space of a few months in 1920, Sari, a mysterious Turkish girl, wept and bellowed in the Hotel Majestic until a Broadway theater was ready to show a moving picture called the *Virgin of Stamboul.* A lion put on a scene at the Hotel Belleclaire for another movie. Finally the suicide of a heartbroken Japanese maiden named O. Yuki was reported. After policemen had dragged the lake in Central Park for her body for two days, however, District Attorney Edward Swann became suspicious enough to question a press agent, Harry Reichenbach. Reichenbach denied that the non-existent suicide, again staged in the interests of a moving picture, was his handiwork. He admitted authorship of similar dodges, however, and remarked disarmingly, "I went abroad for the Creel Bureau, doing exactly this same type of work." [13]

It is of course not accurate to call the work of the Creel Committee "exactly the same type" as press agentry. The committee conducted propaganda on the level of statecraft. Press agentry is the use of tricks to get free news space in newspapers for commercial enterprises. There was by this time a third stratum of the business, usually designated "publicity." It had arisen in a small way before World War I to meet a need different from that of plugging forthcoming plays, pictures, and their stars; for the presidents of railroads and other large corporations had discovered that unpopularity with the public did not pay. Hence a few pioneers like Alexander J. Cassatt of the Pennsylvania Railroad sought to induce trained newspapermen to leave the Fourth Estate at salaries that were princely by comparison, for the service of a corporation. At one end of the scale their trade bordered on press agentry and concealment, at the other on frankness and a sincere regard for the public interest. An example of the most poisonous kind of their work was published in the *Springfield Republican,* April 18, 1905. It was a letter from the Boston Gas Company, enclosing copy for an advertisement decrying an enterprise called the Public Franchise League. The letter said:

Enclosed you will find copy for a reading matter ad. to be used in your paper Tuesday, April 18th. It is understood that this will be set as news matter in news type, with a news head at the top of the column and without advertising marks of any sort. First page position is desired unless your rules debar that position, in which case give it the best position possible. Please send your bill at the lowest net cash rates to the undersigned at the above address.[14]

Such bald attempts to disguise paid advertising as news were rare even in those days. Today, thanks to the purgative effects of experience, corporations are rarely tempted to do that kind of thing, and if they are newspapers have found it to their interest not to permit it. Instead the corporations, and for that matter labor unions and Zionist groups and committees for this and that as well, now openly buy space in the papers and fill it, not with the accustomed snappy display advertising, but with what they call "public relations advertising"—solid columns of words in which they unburden their hearts to the public. There remains, nevertheless, a continuous effort of stupendous proportions to place in the news columns all sorts of items that, whether or not they qualify as news, do serve a special interest. The following letter from the National One-Cent Postage Association, before World War I, illustrates the older less-than-frank type of publicity that to some extent still survives:

In conjunction with the prosecution of our campaign for one-cent letter postage, we find we secure invaluable assistance from the newspapers by their publishing articles in regard to one-cent letter postage.

We also find that if we send these articles direct they are often disregarded, while if we secure some of our friends to send the articles to them, the newspapers use them very promptly.

Because of this fact, we are asking the assistance of friends of the movement to secure publicity for our work. I am taking the liberty of enclosing herewith an article which I have had prepared, and in which I have had your name inserted, and would appreciate it very much if you would place this in the hands of one of your local newspapers.[15]

There followed two more paragraphs saying how this might be done most effectively.

It must be made clear, however, that the great bulk of today's publicity is far less devious. It consists in good part of the wholly legitimate function of making a cause or a company articulate among the multifarious intricacies of the contemporary world. Our society is now so full of a number of things that the ordinary newspaper staff needs help to cope with everything from tax policy, union security, juvenile delinquency, educational theory, and suicides, to Persian oil, grade labeling, the United Nations, and nuclear physics. Usually there is a publicity man who is delighted to help. The newspaper's reliance on private publicity departments is just what the corporations, government departments, and other practitioners of the private propaganda that is publicity want. The corporation president who reads over the letters he dictates to his own secretary before signing them does not trust his company's appearance before the public to the mercy of a fifteen-minute conversation with half a dozen reporters he has never seen before. He prefers to prepare in advance a considered statement that he discusses with his associates—and notably with his assistant in charge of public relations—before issuing it to the public. Only by doing so can he feel certain that his company's activities will be presented to the public in what seems to him a just light.

The newspapers recognize this, and ever since World War I their columns have been full of what corporation presidents call "considered statements," and what bilious editors call "handouts." The result is that contemporary American journalism is divided over the issue. It gladly uses publicity statements because it knows that often they are sources of accurate news, yet it distrusts them because they are self-interested statements rather than the product of independent reporting. The distrust makes our newspaper copy desks death on one thing in particular—free advertising. A handout that is an honest public statement of a private interest's point of view is one thing. A handout that seeks to make customers out of the readers is another. This skeptical watchfulness, born of long and painful experience with spacegrabbers, is an assurance of integrity in the news columns. It does, however, leave us with some curious survivals. Thus we still read daily accounts of accidents in which "a large black sedan" sideswiped "a small coupé," or something equally vague; for no self-respecting newspaper would identify the sedan as a Packard and the coupé as a Ford. To an automobile-crazy America this might seem like omitting a vital part of the news. No matter; to editors it is a stern suppression of free advertising. Just how the statement that, say, a Buick has been smashed with the resultant death or maiming of its occupants will sell more Buicks is not clear. No matter what the commercial product involved, young reporters all have to learn that to soil the news columns with a trade name is desecration.

Well and good. Yet the same newspapers that fly into a frenzy over some innocuous trade name regularly print racing results on their front pages and jam their sports departments with news of baseball, professional football, prize fights, and other sporting industries. This, although these distinctly non-amateur sports are just as commercial as Mobilgas or Buicks or department stores or another young lady from Hollywood on the make. So we must put the news of commercial sports down as an example of journalism's schizophrenia over free publicity.

Long ago, fortunately, many editors and publishers after earnest pondering of their dilemma reached an eminently sensible conclusion on how to handle most day-to-day issues. They saw that a given item of news may have two aspects. It may, that is, serve a purely selfish or commercial purpose, and so constitute free advertising; yet at the same time it may be of interest to a large number of newspaper readers, and so qualify as news. One cannot carry this test too far, because department-store advertising, for one thing, obviously has great news value to women readers, and publishers could hardly stay in business if they printed it as news rather than as their bread and butter. Yet the test is an excellent rule-of-thumb for news desks. If a story has news value, print it as news, regardless of its capacity to sell goods. If on the other hand it has a predominantly commercial value, don't admit it to the paper except as advertising, so identified, and duly bought and paid for. In sum, as long as our newspapers and other media of information devote their editorial space to matters of honest interest to their readers, it does not matter much whether a commercial or political purpose is also served in the process.

The war of 1914–1918 marked the introduction of what in the war of 1939–1945 was called "psychological warfare." We call it that now, because the new name has more agreeable overtones than "propaganda," which has not yet recovered from its World War I stigma; but, whatever we call it, the thing itself is an attack on the mind of the enemy that can be just as forceful and just as well organized as the attack on his armed forces, his economic life, and his political stability. World War I's example of propaganda on this scale, of publicity on behalf of a mighty nation conducted from the shadow of the White House itself, raised up a new vision of the potential dignity and power of the business of shaping men's minds toward a desired end. Accordingly, after that war the publicity efforts that constituted the propaganda of private organizations took on new ways. And just as the publicity man had sought to dissociate himself from press agentry by a more dignified name, so the practitioner of the new technic adopted titles like "counselor on public relations" and "vice president in charge of public information" to symbolize their advance over mere publicity.

We can glimpse the breadth of the vision which that earlier war laid before the tribe of minor propagandists by looking at the work of the Creel Committee. Take, for example, the use put to President Wilson's decision to make the speech in which he laid down the Fourteen Points. Edgar Sisson, a member of the committee, had this to say about the Wilsonian ability to appeal to the mass of men:

The fact is, historical, spiritual, or what you will, that once or twice in a century there comes along a man able to express his own great thoughts with such grace, clarity, and simplicity that they are heard and cherished by the folk of all the world—of every plane of life and of every race. In his utterances Woodrow Wilson had, supremely, this quality of universality. I often have wondered if Americans knew this, as assuredly, the rest of the world does. I know it, because whatever he said could be turned into other languages, any other language, without losing any of its content, whether of charm, of force, or of idea.

With that background, Sisson went enthusiastically to work when the text of the Fourteen Points was cabled to him in postrevolutionary Russia, a Russia that was obviously still far from the iron curtain. As he told the home office five days after the speech was delivered:

President's speech placarded on walls of Petrograd this morning. One hundred thousand copies will have this display within three days. Three hundred thousand handbills will be distributed here within five days. Proportionate display Moscow by end of week. Y.M.C.A. agreed distribute million Russian and million German copies along the line. Other channels into Germany being opened. *Izvestia*, official government newspaper nearly million circulation throughout Russia, printed speech in full Saturday morning with comment welcoming it as sincere and hopeful. Other newspaper comment still cynical but shifting rapidly as speech makes its own mighty appeal. German version in hands printer now.

The whole of Russia was blanketed with posters, handbills, and pamphlets containing the speech. But there remained the greater problem:

The military utility was against Germany, our first heavy and organized attack upon her morale. That late winter and spring we circled her in the neutral countries with mediums for feeding to her through the newspapers of those countries (certain of steady penetration into Germany) the utterances of the President and also the news of the inevitability of defeat from the oncoming crushing power of the United States. Persistently through the summer we visualized that power with facts, an army of two million coming, a million there, and a million and a half there, the others hastening on. Germany had campaigned with falsehood. We met it with the truth. Germany made the error of continuing to say we were liars and bluffers, so that when the truth was evident, it broke the confidence of the German people in their leadership, and immediately their morale.[16]

Sisson summed up the effect of this and similar work by the Creel Committee by quoting Dr. William T. Ellis, a traveler and writer, on his return to this country from a trip six years after the 1918 Armistice. Dr. Ellis said:

It may sound like an exaggeration to say so, but I think it is true that no other mortal man has ever attained so nearly absolutely universal fame as President Wilson. . . . Shakespeare's name and Caesar's and Alexander's are unknown to two-thirds of the human race. Even contemporary military figures, like Foch and the Kaiser, had only a relatively limited circle of fame.

But because of his magic appeal to the deepest sensibilities of all human life, which were given the wings of the morning by the unprecedented propaganda of the Allies, the Wilson principles quickly spread to the uttermost parts of the earth. There the innate vitality of the ideals caused them to take root and grow. As no other wholly human man has ever done before Woodrow Wilson voiced the basic instincts and desires of the race.

So it has come to pass that far-faring travelers nowadays can tell of ignorant Bedouins of the desert judging Government by the Wilson standards.[17]

The careful reader will note two hints in this testimony as to why our propaganda in World War I established the modern technic. First, the thorough manner in which, for the first time in history, propaganda material from a nation at war was "given the wings of the morning" and spread to the uttermost deserts and mountains of the earth; and second, the striking concept that the propaganda thus broadcast was effective *not so much because of the efforts to spread it as because of the inherent appeal of the doctrine itself.*

The World War I example of what propaganda could do, from the impact of Wilsonian ideals upon the Bedouin mind to the dispatch and thoroughness with which Liberty Loan drives siphoned money out of America's pockets, was not lost upon those interested in the business of manipulating public opinion. As one of them, Edward L. Bernays, said later: "It was only natural, after the war ended, that intelligent persons should ask themselves whether it was not possible to apply a similar technique to the problems of peace." [18]

It was. And the great discovery that the more capable ones like Bernays made was this: that effective policy makes effective propaganda. Instead of seeking to gain favor with the public by making an existing cause seem attractive, the new propaganda technic first made the cause itself attractive to the public. If, in other words, the particular object of your propaganda is so set up, or so altered, as to become inherently sound from the public's point of view, favorable publicity will pour in of its own accord with relatively little further effort on your part. While this may seem self-evident, it is in truth a revolutionary discovery. In fact, even now, nearly three decades later, it is yet to be grasped by most of the bigwigs in business, politics, labor, education, and indeed all other important fields of human endeavor.

Our leaders' conception of the public as something to be put upon accounts for much of the distrust in which the bulk of our citizens still hold a great part of what is done by the ownership and management of our industry, commerce, and finance. To some extent the same is true, of course, of efforts to publicize existing policies of government, labor, farm organizations, and the whole assortment of pressure groups. For despite efforts to persuade the bulk of our people of the desirability of a particular pressure group's point of view, the people sense that much in modern publicity is synthetic. They distrust the tricks of the bosses and their propagandists, whether it is a matter of getting leaders of fashion to wear wool dresses in the interest of the woolen industry, or of wrapping a vicious antilabor policy in the cloak of liberty. The public does not like to see slick professional writers preparing speeches for big shots in business or government. And it resents ghost-thinking even more than ghost-writing.

Yet time and again we see our leaders put up a false front before the public instead of changing their habits and methods in the interest of the public. This mental myopia on the part of our betters sometimes has its amusing aspects. For example, the American Newspaper Publishers Association, long troubled by the comparative unpopularity of the American newspaper as an institution, seems to think that the people's attitude toward the newspaper, and not the newspaper's attitude toward the people, ought to be changed. "We have devoted our columns to publicity for everyone else," the ANPA apparently mused to itself. "Why don't we put on a public-relations campaign in our own behalf?" Accordingly, during the prewar depression years there began a campaign that still continues, to make the newspaper, just as it is, more palatable to the public. Students were encouraged to enter essay contests, in which they dwelt on the blessings of a free press—which few doubt anyway, and which are not the point at issue. Statistical studies of newspaper readership were made, which incidentally proved to be interesting and valuable. Advertising was prepared that asked, "Where do people get most of their information?" and then answered (surprise!), "People get most of their information from the newspapers." [19] It seems never to have occurred to the publishers that perhaps the way to endear themselves to the mass of men was to get it through their heads that twentieth century

Americans no longer identify the newspaper's attitude toward public issues with their own interests, and that a vast majority hold it to be, as often as not, actually hostile to their interests. Yet after two decades of depression, war, and reconversion most of our publishers have not yet admitted in their inmost consciousness the dread thought that the era of Horace Greeley is dead, and will never come back. They are not aware that what is needed to restore the newspaper in the day of large circulations to the popularity it held in the day of the proliferous party organs, each with its small circle of devoted readers, is an editorial policy that convinces the ordinary citizen who cannot afford membership in the best clubs in town that the newspaper is on his side as much as on the side of the wealthy. The whole spectacle is a subject for a Disney film, in which a porcupine scurries about with all its quills bristling, wondering why the rest of the wood folk do not show it more affection.

Happily, this attitude, widespread though it is among our leaders in all sorts of endeavor, is not universal. The new principle of getting favorable publicity by acts and policies that arouse public respect and approbation has begun to make changes far more fundamental than the original substitution of a publicity man for a public-be-damned policy. Where it was understood, it has actually changed the policies of causes and corporations. Henry Ford's classic decision to pay a minimum wage of five dollars a day for the first time in history was an early spectacular example. The wartime practices of Jack & Heintz, a circus involving everything from free medical care and permanents to paying fabulous wages, is another example—of which there have been, regrettably, all too few. One might visualize the old publicity technic as painting over the outside of a company or a cause with a coat of whitewash, in the expectation that people would think it was pure within no matter what dirt might be concealed. The new technic actually cleans up the inside, and then invites the public in to see. Or one might put it this way: The old type of publicity man represents the organization before the public; the new type of public-relations strategist represents the public within the organization.

Where the new concept has been put into effect the results were naturally so favorable that the older method could not hope to approach them. Thus there was a reason why the practitioners of the new method often appeared as vice presidents and other high officials in charge of public relations. For unless the new type of propagandist operates on the highest level of strategy and can talk with the topmost executives on equal terms, the benefits of the method remain elusive. It will not work unless the expert on public relations is brought into action before policy decisions are made, and is given a large voice in making them. He must be on the job before trouble arises and not merely be called in afterward to clean up a mess.

This means that in its highest form propaganda, whether commercial or political, *consists in acting in the interests of the public*. For when decisions of policy are made in the public interest—whether that involves a Wilsonian dream for a new world, a public utility's decision voluntarily to apply for lower rates to consumers, or a labor union's determination to open its books and its politics to public view without the pressure of a Taft-Hartley law—then, even though at bottom the propaganda purpose is selfish, the net effect is desirable.

CHAPTER XII

IT'S ONLY A NEWSPAPER STORY

DURING World War II a Marine sergeant, struck by the contrast between American war news and the reality of battle, observed gloomily, "The war that is being written in the newspapers must be a different one from the one we see." [1] That sergeant was undergoing an experience common to many a civilian who witnesses an event and then reads about it in the papers. And even those of us who lack personal experience of the disparity that sometimes exists between an event and the news of it, nevertheless also take that disparity for granted.

How can this be, in view of the fact that newspapers are forever boasting that they tell only the truth? And did not the American Society of Newspaper Editors, as long ago as 1923, adopt a set of highly moral Canons of Journalism? No. IV of these reads as follows:

Sincerity, Truthfulness, Accuracy.—Good faith with the reader is the foundation of all journalism worthy of the name.

1. By every consideration of good faith a newspaper is constrained to be truthful. It is not to be excused for lack of thoroughness or accuracy within its control or failure to obtain command of these essential qualities.

149

2. Headlines should be fully warranted by the contents of the articles which they surmount.[2]

Non-newspaper people tend to sniff at these canons, and perhaps to remark that they are honored more often in the breach than in the observance. In fact, whenever a question of newspaper accuracy comes up we one and all tend to shrug our shoulders, smile to show how wise we are in the ways of the world, and say, "It's only a newspaper story." This attitude is by no means peculiar to our times. It goes back pretty much to the beginnings of printed journalism. The redoubtable Samuel Johnson remarked in 1758 that "contempt of shame and indifference to truth are absolutely necessary" in a news writer.[3] Today we hear much the same thing from our public men. We can even find them quoted in our newspapers—these particular reports being, no doubt, an exception to the universal rule of newspaper mendaciousness. The public's attitude toward the press, moreover, is not without justification. The careful reader will note seemingly deliberate lapses from honesty in even our greatest journals, as when on page 17 of the late city edition of the *New York Times* of November 21, 1938, there appeared an advertisement of George Seldes' *Lords of the Press.* In fine print toward the bottom of the ad there was a partial table of contents, one fragment of which read, " 'Treason' in the Press." Yet in the book itself this item reads " 'Treason' on the *Times.*" [4] The copy for the advertisement must have mentioned the *Times,* and someone on the *Times* must have changed it deliberately.

Even when it is not a question of calculated misrepresentation in the interests of a particular political or economic point of view, there is universal feeling on the part of newspaper readers that our papers have an inherent, and apparently incurable talent for error. Certainly it seems so whenever the public-opinion pollers sample the national attitude toward the press. Most ambitious of these inquiries was a 1939 *Fortune* Survey substantially confirmed by subsequent studies. The answers make discouraging reading for those who would like to defend the newspapers. For when the public was asked, "If you heard conflicting versions of the same story from these sources, which would you be most likely to believe?" The newspapers came out on the short end. Here are the answers, tabulated in percentages:

A radio press bulletin	22.7%	⎫ 40.3%
A radio commentator	17.6	⎬
An authority you heard speak	13.0	⎭
An editorial in a newspaper	12.4	⎫
A news item in a newspaper	11.1	⎬ 26.9%
A columnist in a newspaper	3.4	⎭
Depends on paper, writer, speaker	11.6	
Don't know	8.2	

Radio, in other words, was appraised as far more believable than the press. And when a direct question as to the accuracy of newspapers was asked, the answer, while not utterly damning, were hardly cheering either:

In your experience do newspaper headlines usually give you—

An accurate idea of what really happened	59.1%
Or a misleading idea of what really happened	29.4
Qualified or don't know	11.5

Do you feel that the news story itself—

Is almost always accurate as to its facts	23.3	⎫
Is usually accurate as to its facts	45.1	⎬ 68.4%
Is not accurate in many instances	24.7	⎭
Qualified or don't know	6.9	

While this indicates a substantial belief in the accuracy of newspapers, it would be difficult, as *Fortune* commented, for a newspaper promotion manager to sound boastful with slogans like: "Nearly three out of five newspaper readers find that our headlines tell what happened." [5]

A Gallup poll after the 1940 election [6] asked a question bearing on the newspapers' impartiality rather than their accuracy. This question read, "Do you think the paper (or papers) you read regularly gave both Roosevelt and Willkie an even break in its headlines and news accounts of the Presidential campaign?" Once again the newspapers got no overwhelming endorsement from their customers:

Papers considered giving even break to Roosevelt and Willkie	54%
Papers not considered giving even break	36
Don't know	10

All in all, the American public does not seem to be impressed with either the accuracy or the impartiality of its press. Perhaps we should reverse a former cigarette company slogan, and say of the newspapers, "Such unpopularity must be deserved."

Sometimes newspaper inaccuracies hurt, and they hurt particularly if it is not carelessness but political prejudice that accounts for the error. When I was with the Office of War Information, the *New York World-Telegram* ran a cartoon by Will B. Johnstone holding the OWI up to ridicule. The caption read: "NEWS ITEM: Senator Burton K. Wheeler suggests that the OWI should be eliminated as a blessing to the American people." There were six panels in the cartoon, of which the first was typical. It showed a room full of cigar-smoking bureaucrats, all with their feet on their desks, wasting their time reading newspapers. In the foreground a particularly pompous one held a paper with a large headline, "Abolish OWI." He was saying: "The idea! Trying to clean out us New Deal press agents with a 4th term coming up!" Alongside was a sign "We pay the highest prices for news men—you don't have to be good to work for OWI—Reds preferred."

As one of the OWI staff I read this with resentment. In the first place, I knew from personal experience that the charge that the OWI was trying to put over fourth-term propaganda was, to put it politely, inaccurate. The fact that I myself had happened to be strenuously opposed to the third and fourth terms did not make me feel more kindly about it. And, having long been put down by my friends at Columbia University and elsewhere as hopelessly conservative, I got hot under the collar at the snide suggestion that the OWI preferred Reds.

Having shown in the two paragraphs above the existence of newspaper ways that lead to many charges of distortion and lying, let me say that we can get a valid estimate of the extent of newspaper inaccuracy only by ruling out all emotionally charged material of this kind. Cartoons, editorials, columns, political articles, feature stories—these are deliberately and openly devoted to opinion rather than information. They are a colorful frosting on the solid cake of news. Because they are all in the realm of opinion, we cannot test them objectively to tell whether they are true or not. Only later generations can point to one opinion as having been substantially in accord with the facts and another as false. Furthermore, the sins that stem from political, social, and economic bias have already been pointed out in Chapter VI, "The Fourth Estate in the Twentieth Century." We must, therefore, look elsewhere for a basis of fact on which to judge newspaper accuracy.

But where can we find it? Repeated experience indicates that the most furious denunciations of newspaper inaccuracies, even when made by the great of the earth, are not always well founded. Diligent search reveals that while opinions as to newspaper inaccuracy are a dime a dozen, facts are scarcer than the critics say they are in newspapers. The *Time*-University of Chicago Commission on Freedom of the Press set down as a first requirement that the press should not lie,[7] thereby implying that it does. Elsewhere in its report, in fact, it says so in so many words,[8] and many will no doubt agree with its assertion that newspaper columnists and radio commentators in particular sin by spreading lies.[9] Yet this is in the field of opinion we have ruled out, and anyway here again there is no bill of particulars.

There was, of course, the classic "A Test of the News," [10] in which Walter Lippmann and Charles Merz measured the validity of the *New York Times*' news of the Russian Revolution from 1917 to 1920, with results so unfavorable that the *Times* changed its news-gathering methods and even, many years later, made Merz its editor. That test, however, not only is old but is in the realm of politics that we have ruled out in an effort to isolate the pure journalistic germ. In fact, as far as I have been able to discover, the only systematic, objective study of newspaper accuracy was made by Professor Mitchell V. Charnley of the University of Minnesota in 1936.[11] It was a pioneering effort partly intended to devise a method. Regrettably, that method has not yet been applied on a wider scale. The Charnley test consisted in sending clippings of news stories—short items, long ones, reports of speeches, and reports of interviews—to the sources of the news contained in them. The assumption was that these authorities were 100 per cent right in their judgment as to what constituted accuracy in the stories that concerned them. Since they might be considered as interested parties in the cause they were judging, this assumption must have weighted the scales against the press.

In any event, a thousand news items from three Minneapolis dailies were sent out, each pasted to a pretested questionnaire by means of which the respondents' comment as to accuracy could be classified. Of the 591 clippings that came back, 54 per cent were certified as completely accurate. This meant that they were not only free from typographical errors but also pure as to every name, title, age, address, place, time, and date mentioned in them; that quotations were approved as completely accurate; that spelling and even grammar were right; and on top of that the stories as a whole were deemed correct as to meaning. This last was described to the respondents as follows:

If the story errs in implication—in the impression it gives the reader, in emphasizing any point unduly or in failing to give any points due emphasis, in omitting information or details necessary to give the reader a fair understanding of its subject—please describe such errors below.

Anyone who has been a reporter, and knows from experience how widely the judgment of news values varies—for example, between a minister whose sermon is written up and the reporter who writes the item—will not be surprised that Charnley found the errors in meaning to lead all the rest. Indeed, he himself warns us against accepting this verdict at its face value.

Since, therefore, the test was made on so strict a basis, with every opportunity given to potential critics to detect the minutest flaw, a score of 54 per cent of the stories completely error-proof might be considered highly creditable for so wayward a creature as the daily newspaper. Nevertheless, because the newspaper is our basic means of knowing what is happening round about us—that is, our chief link with the world we live in—this half-and-half performance leaves much to be desired. Some of the breakdowns, in particular, are not encouraging. For example, Charnley found by setting the total number of errors against the total number of stories returned that we could expect about three errors in every four stories. Again, errors in names and titles seem to be entirely too high. But read the worst for yourself in one of Mr. Charnley's tables, which gives an over-all view of the results:

FREQUENCY OF DIFFERENT TYPES OF ERROR

	SHORT STRAIGHT NEWS STORIES	LONG STRAIGHT NEWS STORIES	SPEECH STORIES	INTER- VIEW STORIES	TOTAL
Stories accurate	245	47	17	10	319
Stories inaccurate	205	35	20	12	272
Total stories	450	82	37	22	591
Errors in meaning	76	18	21	6	121
Errors in names	80	6	6	1	93
Errors in titles	62	16	5	0	83
Mechanical errors	21	7	1	0	29
Errors in figures	18	3	0	0	21
Errors in times	18	1	0	1	20
Errors in places	14	3	0	0	17
Errors in quotations	7	2	4	4	17
Errors in addresses	12	1	0	0	13
Errors in dates	12	0	1	0	13
Errors in spelling	9	2	0	2	13
Errors in grammar	8	1	0	0	9
Errors in ages	3	0	0	3	6
Total errors	340	60	38	17	455
Previous errors repeated	48	11	5	2	66

A base of fewer than 600 news stories from three papers all in one city in a short period of time is not large enough to support an indictment of the entire American press. Yet I doubt if many newspapermen would be disposed to argue that Charnley's findings are unrepresentative of our journalism as a whole, good, bad, and indifferent. Besides, there is enough in the test itself to hint that the common attitude toward newspaper accuracy has at least a ponderable basis in fact. And finally there are confessions from within the ranks, like this one from James S. Pope, managing editor of the *Courier-Journal* in Louisville:

I do not think you can successfully deny that most of the newspapers in this country have grossly neglected the fundamental principle of accuracy. If I were going to generalize on this question, I am afraid I believe that a miserable job of reporting is being done.[13]

Now that we have an airtight case against that culprit, the newspaper, let us see what there may be in the way of extenuating circumstances. For while extenuating circumstances cannot lessen the crime, they may lead us to look upon the guilty with understanding and perhaps even compassion. In similar circumstances the courts usually look into the environment of the delinquent. If we do that we find a ready source of error in the complexities amid which journalism must be practiced. With a daily Niagara of words to be rushed through the process of writing, transmitting, editing, headlining, typesetting, and make-up mistakes are inevitable. Perfection is impossible in the face of the task to be done in the time available.

Speaking once of how charitable we ought to be in weighing the daily newspaper's many sins, Dr. Douglas S. Freeman, editor of the *Richmond News Leader,* pointed to the size of its task. There were probably, he said, 5,000 statements of fact in the ordinary newspaper. I asked my collaborator on this chapter to make an independent audit of Dr. Freeman's estimate by counting the number of facts in a sample newspaper. He took a copy of the *Omaha Morning World-Herald* (circulation 100,-000)—a Saturday issue and therefore a thin one, running to eighteen standard-size pages. Then came the question as to what constitutes a fact. In order to make the task manageable, he decided to count each unit of information as a fact, rather than to split the news into its basic atoms. Splitting it that fine would have been justified, of course, because each fragment might be wrong and might therefore count as a separate error, as it did in Professor Charnley's survey mentioned above. My collaborator's count of facts was, then, exceptionally conservative. Here, for example, is a sample fact from one front-page story. It was counted as one though its opportunities for error were multiple:

NEW YORK, March 27 (AP)—William S. Farish, president of Standard Oil Company (New Jersey), declared in a prepared statement

tonight synthetic butyl rubber samples developed by the company
and the German firm of I.G. Farben Industrie were submittted to
the United States government and private American concerns in
1939, but ruled to be "of doubtful quality." [14]

That is, to be sure, about as comprehensive an example as
any of what was counted as a single fact. Others were considerably shorter. Anyway, with such a rough unit as his guide, my
collaborator went through the paper from beginning to end—
except for the advertisements—and found there were 3,078
straight-news facts in it. The market pages, where stock and
grain and similar prices were listed, naturally produced a
further multitude of smaller facts. These came to 2,389, making
a total of 5,467 statements of fact in this single edition of a newspaper. Dr. Freeman's estimate is, therefore, more than corroborated. Even if we omit the market tables—every item in which
offers an opportunity for error—we still find that the ordinary
medium-sized newspaper is likely to have some 3,000 statements of fact in every edition.

What this means in the way of opportunities for error can be
grasped if we break down the sample unit of fact quoted above
into its component parts. Instead of counting that item as a
single fact, then, it might have been scored as at least eleven, as
follows:

1. William S. Farish
2. president of Standard Oil Company (New Jersey)
3. declared in a prepared statement
4. tonight
5. synthetic butyl rubber samples
6. developed by the company
7. and the German firm of I.G. Farben Industrie
8. were submitted to the United States government
9. and private American concerns
10. in 1939
11. but ruled to be "of doubtful quality"

All this, let us say it again, does not lessen by one bit the
misstatements, the distortions, the confusions, that daily appear
in our press. But taken together with the fact that the ordinary
newspaper is put out in about eight hours, and some of its im-

portant news in a matter of minutes, it does begin to show why newspapers make mistakes.

Scholars in particular forget the journalistic handicap of time when shaking their heads over newspaper inaccuracies. They contrast the newspapers' sloppiness with their own discipline in the search for truth. They know what it is to take a relatively simple subject and track down its sources and penetrate its intricacies; to ponder, to adjust and readjust, and then check and double-check for error. It is natural that so severe a standard of correctness should be kept in mind when trained minds contemplate the carelessness of the press—natural, but not fair. A news item is not the product of two years of hard work in the scholar's study. It is the product of a few hours, or even minutes, of sweat.

It is this time factor as well as carelessness that accounts for the prevalence of typographical errors. The results, obviously, are sometimes embarrassing as well as annoying. For the difficulties of attaining typographical perfection will make the *Guild Reporter,* organ of the labor union known as the American Newspaper Guild, quote a Guild executive as saying, "We have got to realize that we are dealing with the toughest, greediest, most reactionary set of employees in the United States," when it is obvious, seeing who was speaking, that he meant employers, not employees.[15] Again, a newspaper as careful as the *New York Herald Tribune,* when reporting a statement of Leon Henderson as head of OPA, will make him say: ". . . don't blame your Government. Blame it on the Germans and the Jews." [16] Obviously again, it was a forgetful linotyper or some other erring human who made Henderson appear to say "Jews," when he had actually said "Japs."

Related errors are those examples of mistaken identity, sometimes embarrassing in the extreme, that pop unexpectedly out of typewriters, or get into print because someone going through a file of pictures forgets that eternal skepticism is the price of accuracy. Thus, when Charles H. Taylor of the *Boston Globe* died, one New York paper illustrated his obituary with a picture of his father, General Charles H. Taylor, long since dead. Not to be outdone, another New York paper used a wholly irrelevant cut of the very much alive Walter M. Dear, publisher of the neighboring *Jersey Journal.*[17]

Far more important than mechanical and near-mechanical obstacles to accuracy, however, is the nature of journalism itself. The newspaper has to take in its stride anything under the sun. It cannot confine itself to the routine chitchat of home-town happenings, but must also report on the latest events in abstruse fields like science, economics, government, diplomacy, scholarship, art, and a thousand other specialties. Inevitably its attempts to do so get it into trouble. In the first place, it has to try to reduce all news, no matter what its intricacy, to a common denominator so low that the young lady from the deep South who didn't graduate from high school has a chance of getting its drift. This is the penalty of democracy, but the resulting oversimplification and error irritates the specialist. Moreover, every reader, whether specialist or not, considers himself an authority on practically everything in the paper.

In this, journalism differs sharply from other human enterprises requiring professional skill. If, for example, we suffer from a wheezy bronchial tube and consult a doctor he will mumble a few Latin words at us by way of identifying the ailment. We accept the evidence of his learning and meekly go to bed if he tells us to. So, too, a lawyer can make learned reference to the significance for our cause of the precedent established in Higginbottom *v.* Heathertop. We are helpless before him, and accept his superior authority without question. By contrast, a newspaper, even though it boasts a staff as disciplined, informed, and competent in its field as are the doctor or the lawyer in theirs, cannot fall back on professional abracadabra. Instead of hiding its mistakes as the lawyers do, if they can, or burying them as the doctors do, it flaunts them before the world in several different editions a day. Inevitably, then, the mistakes of the professions or of business, with which we unthinkingly compare journalistic mistakes, remain comparatively obscure. By contrast everyone knows about the newspapers' mistakes. It is nothing short of amazing how the sins of the reporter will find him out. Newspapermen may sometimes regret that the public does not read their offerings more eagerly, but let them make one mistake and, even though the mistake is so recondite that only one living expert knows enough to spot it and he is at the moment traveling in Zamboanga, you may be sure that some relentless attention-caller, knowing his interest in the subject, will send him a clipping. Thereupon the paper gets one more letter regretting the lamentable inability of the press ever to get anything straight.

Errors seem more prevalent in newspaper work than in other callings because of the publication before a universal audience. This means that each tyro reporter, whatever the subject he writers about, offers it for the inspection of the world's greatest expert in that field. It holds true even if he writes a paragraph about a local fire, because some layman, seeing that fire, became in his own eyes an authority on it—even though his excited version, told to the neighbors in scorn of the newspaper that got it all wrong, is wholly subjective. At least it is not the distillation, as is the newspaper's story, of what the police and the firemen and a host of contradictory witnesses said about it.

One extenuating circumstance is the fact that accurate information is sometimes hard to come by. Laymen find it difficult to comprehend this. An acquaintance will tell them of some event, apparently out of his personal experience, in graphic detail. Coming thus directly from a person known to be honest, the story is fixed in the recipient's mind as true. Yet systematic investigation might show it to be wholly fiction.

We can see what tracking down this kind of thing involves from newspaper experience. John Lewellen, a feature writer for the *Muncie Evening Press* in Indiana, got a tip from his city editor about what sounded like a heartrending human-interest feature. It went like this:

A Muncie man (name unknown) was driving into Muncie two or three days ago. A short way from the town he picked up two adults, a man and a woman. The woman had a baby at her breast. The couple was destitute and the motorist, feeling sorry for them, offered to get them something to eat when he reached Muncie. "Don't mind the baby," the woman said. "It's dead."

Well, the baby had been dead for two days. The couple was trying to get to Indianapolis to give the dead infant a decent burial. They had relatives there. The motorist was so touched he took the man and his wife and the body of their baby on to Indianapolis.[18]

Lewellen was told that the manager of a typewriter office knew the motorist personally. He started there, but found himself shunted from person to person—fifteen in all. Each one in turn was convinced that the man from whom he had heard the story had been the one who actually knew the motorist. This, by the way, is characteristic of the word-of-mouth stories that we accept with such faith from friends while we scorn what the papers print. But with much difficulty Lewellen checked his story through families, a church, a school, a business office, a barber shop, a garage, until he finally traced it to a cigar store. The manager had heard it from a cigar salesman traveling through. The manager was not fully convinced of the truth of the tale, as had been the others who passed it on toward the other end of the line, but his version did specify that the body of the baby had been turned over to the Marion County coroner at Indianapolis. At last Lewellen thought he had an authentic clue. But when he telephoned the coroner he once more drew a blank. The man had never heard of such a dead baby.

Exhausted, Lewellen let it go at that. Instead of writing up the story he wrote an account of his efforts, beginning:

The next time anyone cracks the inaccuracy of newspapers, I'm liable to crack him, unless I'm not feeling well.

More than likely the guy who moans over the inaccuracy of the newspapers, the same day has repeated half a dozen stories he couldn't verify with the aid of the Technocrats' research department.[19]

A similar tale making the rounds during the war years was finally pinned down by the *Redlands Daily Facts,* a small California paper. This time the story concerned a Los Angeles woman who, driving through Pomona with a friend, gave a soldier a lift to town. Since the soldier had no particular plans for spending his evening away from camp, the woman took him home to supper. On leaving, the soldier said her simple friendliness had given him the most pleasant experience he had had since joining the Army. And a few days later the woman was surprised to receive a complete set of table silver, which came to her house with the visiting card of Marshall Field IV, son of the department-store heir and publisher. He had been the soldier.

Frank E. Moore, editor of the *Daily Facts,* decided to investigate. Here is the result:

In the first place, the woman who had brought the story to the paper had heard it from her husband, who had heard it from his father, who had heard it from his packing-house manager. The latter claimed to have heard it from Mrs. Corwin (the friend driving with the heroine of the tale when the soldier was picked up) or perhaps from somebody else. Mrs. Corwin laughed merrily at the editor's telephone inquiry, and said that it hadn't happened to her friend. She said she had heard it while six Highland women were driving to the Red Cross blood bank in Fontana, but she couldn't remember which one had told it. Possibly it was Mrs. Kyle Alexander, who, she thought, was a friend of the lady Samaritan. A call to Mrs. Alexander, however, showed only that she herself had heard it at a meeting in Los Angeles but couldn't recall who had told it. And there the trail seemed to end.

Next day, however, a friend called up Editor Moore, who had printed the tale with qualifications indicating his skepticism. The friend chided him for his doubts, assuring him that his own wife had seen the chest of silver, and that the story was true. A call to this supposed first actual witness brought no answer. But next day another caller arrived with the information that the woman to whom it had happened lived not in Los Angeles, but in Laguna, and that she had befriended the soldier not once, but several times. Furthermore, the silver had come not from the Marshall Field who was a World War II soldier but from his father. The baffled editor decided that this bit of information offered a way to find out for sure, and so wrote to Field himself. This was the reply:

Dear Mr. Moore:

Thank you for checking up on the story about my son. The story is not true. I think it actually springs from a story about myself in the last war, in which I sent a bunch of flowers to my hostess the next day. It did not include any silver.

Yours very truly,
Marshall Field [20]

Man is a perverse creature. He repeats as gospel the most baseless rumor, yet complains that what is in his paper is only a newspaper story.

Not only does everyone object to the weather, but in objecting to it everyone blames the newspaper for a fault that is clearly not its own. For who has not celebrated some miserable day with an exchange of greetings along these lines?

"Good morning. My, isn't it raining!"

"Yes. And the paper said it was going to be nice today."

"Oh, well, you never can believe what you read in the papers anyway."

A moment's reflection, time for which is somehow never taken, shows that the newspaper has but one source of weather predictions, the nearest United States Weather Bureau. If, therefore, your paper prophesies that today will be sunny and warmer with gentle winds, and if on the strength of that you leave your umbrella at home only to be soaked in a downpour later, then your righteous indignation ought to be directed at the Weather Bureau, or perhaps at the imperfect state of meteorological science, but certainly not at your newspaper. It was merely reporting truthfully and accurately exactly what the Weather Bureau had said.

The weather news is, moreover, a simple illustration of a common but mistaken reason for the belief that newspapers are inaccurate. We think of the paper not as the reporter that it is, but as the originator of what we read in it. Yet, whatever newspapers report, they get from some source; and, while they get their facts wrong all too often, nevertheless it is frequently the source and not the newspaper that is in error. Suppose that a wartime news story had read: "Two Japanese cruisers, a destroyer, and three large merchant vessels have been sunk off New Guinea by an American task force at a cost of one escort vessel, the Navy Department announced tonight." Then suppose, as happened in the first two years of the war, that it turned out that our own losses had actually been heavier than those of the Japanese. Most readers, not making the distinction between the newspaper and the source, would say once more that the war news was just a newspaper story. Yet the newspaper story in this particular example was 100 per cent correct. The newspaper did not say the Japanese losses were heavy, and ours light. It merely reported that the Navy Department gave out those figures—which was precisely what happened.

There is a corollary to this tradition of heaping the sins of others upon the head of journalism, and that is the habit public men have of calling the newspapers liars when they themselves are lying. It is a habit peculiarly common to men in governmental office, including the highest. Successive British Prime Ministers and successive American Presidents have indulged in it.

Sometimes, painful though it is, there is no alternative; for, if a reporter publishes a truth that is politically inexpedient or perhaps even nationally disastrous when it leaks out, the official concerned feels he simply has to deny it. The trouble is that we all are inclined to see a national disaster in a published report which actually is nothing but a personal embarrassment to us. Perhaps it is not even that, but only a case of the cat being let out of the bag before we are ready to startle the world with the news ourselves. In any case, it is an occupational propensity of men in public office to hold close to their chests information that it would do no harm to publish, or in which the harm caused by denial may be greater than that caused by forthright publication. Nor are men in government the only sinners, for the same is done by businessmen, labor leaders, university presidents, and, indeed, by men prominent in all callings. The temptation seems to seize all who emerge from obscurity far enough to get themselves into the news.

This is not to say that persons who deny the truth of published reports are always wrong, and that the newspapers always right. Far from it. I have before me a 1940 clipping from the responsible *New York Times,* with the headline, "Miss Perkins Quits Cabinet; Views Her Job as Finished." The story goes on to say with equal finality: "Miss Frances Perkins, Secretary of Labor since 1933 and only woman member of President Roosevelt's Cabinet, has resigned and the President has accepted her resignation, it was learned authoritatively last night." [21] Where there was that much smoke there was doubtless some fire. The *Times* must have been convinced by the source of its information, obviously close to Miss Perkins, that her resignation had occurred. Yet it was only after President Roosevelt's death—more than four years later—that Miss Perkins resigned.

The public assumes this kind of error to be the norm, when actually it is not. Certainly, I have had no difficulty in gathering examples of official denials of published statements known to be true by those who denied them. Take this characteristic one from Louisville. The *Courier-Journal* published a local story to the effect that residents of a community known as Beechmont were annoyed by the unpleasant sights and smells in their streets growing out of a lack of garbage collection.[22] Prime source of the paper's story was O. E. Hoffman, secretary of the Beechmont Civic Club. No sooner was the item published, however, than Mayor Wyatt branded the story as false. "I was at their meeting last night myself," remarked His Honor, "and the garbage collection situation was not discussed. There were no fireworks at all." The account of his remarks, as published in the afternoon *Louisville Times,* went on:

Several club members, headed by O. E. Hoffman, Secretary, called at his office this morning and expressed amazement at the story, saying they did not recognize the quotations attributed to them, Wyatt added.[23]

Next day there was another long story in the *Courier-Journal.* The officials concerned seemed to be much more polite about calling the paper a liar. The reason, says the managing editor, was this:

You will notice that although we invited the Mayor to specify any falsity in our original story, nobody ever found anything false in it. Those who tried to hedge quickly closed up when they discovered that our reporter had taken down everything they said in shorthand. This is a secret weapon we are going to use more and more.[24]

Another example, on a more important subject but no whit different in principle, is given by Westbrook Pegler. Here it is as he cited it:

On June 21, 1917, American newspapers carried a United Press dispatch from Queenstown, Ireland, reporting that an American destroyer had fought a submarine and, "according to the belief expressed by the crew," had rammed and sunk it. The story had passed censorship by a lieutenant commander on the staff of Vice-Admiral William S. Sims in the presence of the post censor, a British lieutenant commander. Two days later, that is, on June 23, the Associated Press carried a Queenstown dispatch reporting that

Admiral Sims, questioned about the UP story, had called it "absolutely false." The UP reporter, thus publicly humiliated by an accusation of faking, was sent back to London.

That reporter's name was Westbrook Pegler. Twenty-three years later he came upon official Navy records that showed that on June 20, 1917, or three days before Admiral Sims had publicly called the story absolutely false, the Admiral had reported to the Navy as follows: "It is reasonably certain now that the *O'Brien* [the destroyer in question] destroyed the submarine mentioned." Pegler also turned up a report dated June 19 from the *O'Brien's* skipper that unmistakably confirmed the truth of his story.[25]

Why would an American admiral, obviously an honest and an upright man, do such a thing? Possibly because Pegler's 1917 story mentioned depth bombs—at that time secret weapons. Perhaps, even though the censors had passed it, the Admiral judged it a matter for secrecy. Certainly, some such private judgment as to what is the public interest often prompts public men to deny what they know to be true, and leads them to hold honest men up to contempt as fakers when they know them to be right.

Possibly the tendency to discredit the press as a source of information does more harm than good. For if the assumption of this book is sound—namely, that the press and the related media of information constitute a fourth branch of government, unofficial but essential to its functioning—then the official habit of hiding behind "It's only a newspaper story" undermines a part of democracy itself. Perhaps, therefore, democracy would be healthier if the men whose positions get them into the news would come clean more often. It can be done. A month before the invasion of Sicily, for example, Winston Churchill said in public that "brilliant prospects lie before us." Apparently, the phrase called up one of those waves of overoptimism for which the people of wartime Britain and America were so often taken to task by their officials. But instead of denying that he had uttered the words in question, or taking refuge behind a complaint about "the mystifying misinterpretations of my remarks in the press" or other familiar circumlocutions, Churchill stood before the House of Commons and said:

I am sorry that a few days ago, in the press of travel and affairs, I let slip the expression "brilliant prospects lie before us." I would prefer to substitute the words "brighter and solid prospects lie before us." That, I think, would be more appropriate and becoming in such anxious days.[26]

Unhappily, such public confessions of error are rare.

By now the reader is, I trust, thoroughly confused. Beginning with an indictment of newspaper accuracy that piled evidence on evidence to show the Fourth Estate could do little better than reach halfway toward perfection, this chapter has gone on to show how difficult newspaper accuracy is, and even to argue that newspapers are often right when the most honorable call them liars. Yet that confusion, that duality, represents the situation as it is. Newspapers are by no means so accurate as they ought to be, but they are far more accurate than most persons give them credit for being.

Perhaps we can sum it all up with a tale told by Vilhjalmur Stefansson.[27] Exhaustive research by Stefansson turned up an amazing series of facts that started in the *New York Evening Mail* of December 28, 1917, with an article by Henry Louis Mencken on the history of the bathtub in America that read as though it were based on the utmost knowledge of bathtubs. It told how in the 1830's Adam Thompson of Cincinnati, seeing a bathtub on a trip to England, had been so impressed that he had a seven-by-four-foot beauty made of mahogany and lined with lead for his home in 1842. There followed a long history, with minutiae about ordinances in Philadelphia and Boston, forbidding bathing as dangerous to health, medical disapproval of bathing, a tax of $30 a year on bathtubs, and so on, in full detail.

For all its learned appearance, Mencken's tale was a hoax. And yet, as the years rolled on, the supposed facts continued to reappear in the most respectable of places. A former Health Commissioner of New York used some in a broadcast over WEAF (now WNBC). One of its spurious dates crept into Hans Zinsser's *Rats, Lice and History*. Feature articles, technical articles, scholarly articles, all showed traces of Mencken's spoofing. The *New York Herald Tribune,* in 1946, quoted some of its more colorful, but wholly false, dates and facts in an editorial.[28] All this still goes on, despite the fact that Mencken long since became alarmed at the way his spoofing was accepted as history. In 1926, nine years after his original sin, he wrote a retraction of the tale, pointing to inconsistencies and absurdities in it as proof, hoping in this way to make the truth more prominent in the record than the original fiction. And, sure enough, at the time, the denial received far more space than the *Evening Mail* feature had had in 1917. It was published in thirty newspapers. One of them, the *Boston Herald,* put the story of Mencken's retraction, with its clear exposure of the falsity of all the original misinformation, on a prominent page under a four-column headline. "Three weeks later," comments Mr. Stefansson, "the same paper reprinted, as a piece of news, the substance of the story as it had originally appeared in 1917."

CHAPTER XIII

CENSORSHIP: SOLDIER VS. FOURTH ESTATE

IN THE twenty-four centuries since the republic of Rome gave them their name, censors have sought to regulate an amazing range of human conduct. Even today, in this land of freedom, there is considerable state, church, and unofficial censorship of moral, social, and political matters. This chapter, however, is not concerned with such manifestations of sumptuary censorship; it seeks only to evaluate what happens when, under the compulsion of war, we censor information that is of value to the enemy. Though World War II has long since become history, there is more than historical value in such an evaluation. It is a necessary introduction to a study of the continuing psychological warfare of peace, otherwise known as the cold war.

Military censorship, as a whole, is too vast a subject for examination here. Let Byron Price, director of the wartime Office of Censorship, explain:

The way our budget is set up, 86½ per cent is for the censorship of international mail, 11½ per cent is for the censorship of cablegrams, radio telegraph, radio telephone and land wires; 1½ per cent is for administration, and one-half of 1 per cent is for . . . censorship of all domestic media of news dissemination.[1]

169

The censorship of press, radio, and other instruments of the Fourth Estate that took only one-half of 1 per cent of Director Price's budget is our subject.

There is an irreconcilable conflict between the soldier and the newspaperman; for, while it is the business of the newspaperman to dig continually for the news, it is the business of the soldier, in wartime at least, to keep dark what he is doing. The soldier's disinclination to publish anything is justified by the necessity for victory. He knows from experience that the most innocent bit of information, when the enemy puts it with similar bits, can betray him. Accordingly the soldier dislikes a reporter who snoops around for information with what seems to him to be a careless regard for the nation's security. Besides, the soldier's training leaves him largely innocent of the values of the Fourth Estate, so that he is likely to think of it—as did Brigadier General Johnson Hagood during World War I—as made up of persons whose heads "are full of mush about the God-given rights of a free press." [2] Therefore, he asks to be let alone in accomplishing the task for which he has been trained.

There is, however, an equal justification for the newspaper's desire to publish. War does not suddenly confer upon the political, military, and naval leadership of the state a monopoly of wisdom it did not have in peace. Censorship not only conceals military information from the enemy, but also hides from the people any mistakes, incompetencies, corruption, or political manipulation there may be in high places.

One can see this by looking back. In the early years of World War I the Northcliffe papers bitterly attacked the British government. Their campaign was publicizing truths that were hidden behind the wall of censorship and complacency. In order to reveal the desperate shortage of high-explosive shells and the need for conscription, the papers attacked even Lord Kitchener, the Secretary of State for War. "Shush!" replied the Asquith government, the rival newspapers, and the Better People generally. "Shush! We are doing the best that can be done; but you are betraying the country." There was a burst of anger against such a journalistic upsetting of the patriotic applecart; but in the end the new post of Minister of Munitions was given to Lloyd George, production of shells and machine guns was increased, and conscription was adopted.[3] It is possible that, had the Northcliffe press been muzzled, the British—and we— would have lost the war.

Inevitably, the struggle between secrecy and publication lasts as long as the war. Its effects are far from happy. For much is published that were far better kept quiet; and much is suppressed that were better published. You may remember, for example, when the French liner *Normandie* burned and turned over at its pier, just before it was to go into the service of our navy. Shortly before, a reporter for *PM* had gotten on the ship without authorization, there to find much carelessness and laxity, with the accompanying risk of sabotage and fire. When *PM* submitted the reporter's story to the Navy for publication, however, permission to use it was forbidden and the reporter was warned to watch his step. Had the paper thumbed its nose at the censor and published the story, there might have been enough of a public outcry to force a tightening of supervision. In other words, disregard of the censor might have saved this ship at the time of our greatest need.

War censorship, then, constitutes a dilemma, in which we are damned if we do and damned if we don't. Faced with such a choice, most of us decide to be damned if we do. We favor the soldier, as against the Fourth Estate, and cheerfully allow the news to be suppressed; for, as Mr. Price himself put it, our basic consideration is "that none of us shall provide the enemy, by design or inadvertence, with information which will help him kill Americans." [4]

Yet it remains true that, other things begin equal, censorship is a confession of weakness. We can see this in our own moves toward a less stringent suppression of strictly military news, as we turned from the defeats of the 1941–1942 toward victory. In the spring of 1942, when the gargantuan bomber plant at Willow Run was completed, Charles E. Sorensen, Ford vice president, saw no reason for censoring its secrets. "Bring the Germans and Japs in to see it— Hell, they'd blow their brains out," he said.[5] By 1943, even with victory two years away, Donald M. Nelson of the War Production Board said that our production situation had become so favorable that publishing figures about it, instead of giving aid and comfort to the enemy, would do just the opposite.[6] The same principle could be seen in a strictly military setting when, shortly before the capitulation of Japan, our B-29's dropped leaflets over eleven Japanese cities, warning the residents that they were to be bombed.[7] This advance warning of the atomic bomb was a spectacular reversal of army policy in the early days of the war. We can set it down that the better a war—or anything else—is going, the less censorship there is.

While censorship works in a variety of ways, it is divisible into three basic patterns: preventive censorship, punitive censorship, and censorship at the source.

The first, preventive censorship, is what most of us think of when the subject is discussed. It is typified by a stock figure, who with blue pencil cuts the heart out of a piece of writing before it is cabled, printed, or otherwise disseminated among the people. Preventive censorship was, incidentally, the first to be hit upon when the invention of printing made the spread of ideas to the mass of people possible, and so gave the authorities of church and state occasion for suppressing writings that seemed subversive. The Borgia Pope Alexander VI's original Bull of 1501 against unlicensed printing was a form of preventive censorship. And the *modus operandi* of this kind of censorship was well stated in one of the early secular censorships, a ruling of the Scottish Estates in 1551. Under it, all printing was prohibited "unto the tyme the samin be sene, vewit and examit be sum wyse and discreit persounis depute thairto." [8]

In comparison with preventive censorship, punitive censorship seems liberal. Instead of forbidding publication of an unapproved text it leaves the decision to the individual who wants to print. He is, however, held responsible. Our peacetime libel laws are an example; under them an author or publisher is free to say anything he likes, but is accountable if later he is adjudged to have violated the law. Again, our censorship in both world wars belonged to the family of punitive censorships. No censor was physically present in editorial offices and broadcasting studios to say what might or might not be published. Newspapers and newscasters were merely "requested" by the Office of Censorship not to reveal certain kinds of information. Behind that request, however, were the Espionage Act of 1917, as amended, and the first War Powers Act of 1941. Thus even though no penalties were invoked, our so-called "voluntary censorship" was actually a punitive censorship.

When liberally administered as was our wartime censorship, punitive censorship is less formidable than preventive censorship. But the severity of any censorship depends more on the spirit and purpose with which it is enforced than on the particular brand used. Nazi Germany prided itself on using punitive rather than preventive censorship upon American and other foreign correspondents. Indeed, the Goebbels ministry boasted that Germany had no censorship, for were not the correspondents free to cable anything they chose? They were; but they had to send only the kind of copy considered fair by Dr. Goebbels, and punitive action, in the shape of expulsion—frequently resorted to—was always there.

The Nazi version of punitive censorship was reinforced, moreover, by a management so extreme that no news, except the Nazi product, was available. This was a manifestation of the third kind of censorship, censorship at the source. It is not usually catalogued as censorship, because it applies to news and not to the propagation of heretical ideas that has kept busy so many of the censors of history. The churches, for example, have had little need for censorship at the source. Their problem has been to prevent the spread of ideas deemed false or dangerous, and because such ideas hardly originate in church headquarters, there is little occasion for bottling them there.

It is different with political and military news. Here headquarters produce the hottest kind of information. Hence military authorities formulating strategic plans must, and political news managers do, sit on the news at the source as the easiest means of preventing its circulation. Furthermore, censorship at the source, while obviously practiced from antiquity, has become increasingly important with the growth of mass communications. Because, in modern warfare, the home front is just as important to victory as the fighting front, the definition of military information has been so widened that it is often impossible to say whether a given item of information is military or political. Sometimes it is both. Therefore, those in authority hide facts on the plea of patriotism and military information, while the opposition complains that the facts are concealed for political purposes. During the last war the tangled situation caused much irritation in this country and in Britain. The storms that beat about the Roosevelt administration in the war years are still not forgotten. Apparently it was the same in Britain. At any rate, the anonymous Sagittarius was moved, after two years of war characterized by suppression of the facts, to contribute six biting stanzas on the subject to the *New Statesman and Nation,* of which this is a sample:

> What are the facts? Are they sunny or sinister?
> Ignorant queries are here out of place;
> All we can read is the face of a Minister
> Pallid from looking the facts in the face.[9]

When we turn to the uses to which censorship has been put in American wars, we soon see that, however irritating suppression of the facts may be, there is all too often justification for it. There are interesting precedents and examples from 1776, 1812, and 1846, but the Civil War provides the object lesson for those who grow restive at censorship. On the Southern side, the newspapers were, for the most part, well behaved. Because they were less ambitious and less efficient news-gatherers than the Northern papers, they rarely revealed important information to the enemy, and never meddled unduly in the prosecution of the war.[10] In fact, the Northern generals and the Lincoln administration were envious of the comparative discipline of the Southern press. But one factor that made that discipline possible, an official press association, was not imitated by the North.

On the contrary, the Federal authorities indulged in arbitrary suppressions, falsifications, and stupidities. These were more than matched, however, with irresponsibility and indeed disaffection by the press. Throughout the war, the Army complained that the newspapers betrayed its attempts to take advantage of secrecy and surprise. No wonder that William Tecumseh Sherman, when told at Vicksburg that a shell had killed three correspondents, is said to have remarked: "Good! Now we'll have news from hell before breakfast."

More amazing even than the newspapers' disregard of the elementary necessities of censorship was the unsympathetic attitude of many a Northern editor. One of the worst of the Copperheads was the *Chicago Times,* bought in 1861 by Wilbur F. Storey, who announced it as his purpose "To Raise Hell and Sell Newspapers!" [11] He succeeded in doing both, and was so traitorous in the process that in 1863 General Ambrose E. Burnside suppressed the paper by military force—an action promptly reversed by President Lincoln. One can sympathize with the General, even though his method has become a landmark in the record of how not to handle a recalcitrant press.

More than thirty years after the Civil War, when for a few ebullient months we fought Spain, we made an even poorer showing. One historian of that compound of tragedy and *opéra bouffe,* Walter Millis, sums it up this way:

> The war correspondents, flocking into every camp, every naval station and every possible or impossible theater of action, loaded down the wires with detailed accounts of every move made or contemplated. Any feeble opposition put up by the browbeaten authorities on the score of secrecy was imperiously brushed aside. After all, if it was not the newspapers' war, whose war was it? [12]

When less than two decades later we found ourselves in World War I we were a different nation. The United States, and indeed the world of 1917, had already assumed a family resemblance to the world of today, and one reflection of that fact was our newspapers' essentially responsible treatment of war and war news. Both the cynically irresponsible Civil War journalism and the comic-opera journalism that had fanned the flames of the war with Spain were left behind. Months before we plunged into that war, the Army, Navy, and other branches of the government had become concerned because there was no provision for censorship in event of war. As early as 1916 a joint Army-Navy board had recommended a law under which censorship of military information might be established during a national emergency by presidential proclamation. And on June 9 of that year the War Department actually began to censor military information by bottling it up at the source, in a Bureau of Information. Chief of that bureau was a young officer, a certain major named Douglas MacArthur.[13] And when the Congress that was to declare a state of war met on April 2, 1917, there began a long debate over censorship by law.

Happily, no press-censorship law was passed, largely because, before the debate ended, the press had already been taken care of by a voluntary censorship. This was something new and peculiarly American in the history of censorship, and despite the forebodings of the soldiers and the high-pressure patriots, it worked. In fact, it worked so well that it became the model for security regulations in World War II. This 1917 variation on the ancient theme of censorship grew out of requests for voluntary cooperation by the press, made by the Army and the Navy before the war came, when they found themselves without legal means for compelling suppression. There followed a considerable debate over what form of censorship might be desirable, and within a week after the congressional declaration that a state of war existed the Secretaries of State, War, and Navy recommended, in a letter to the President, the formation of a committee that would both censor military information and publish legitimate war information. "It is our opinion," they wrote, "that the two functions—censorship and publicity—can be joined in honesty and with profit, and we recommend the creation of a Committee on Public Information." [14] On the following day the President set up such a committee by executive order. It consisted of a Wilsonian journalist, George Creel, as chairman, plus the three secretaries that had made the recommendation. Because the committee was charged not only with administering a voluntary censorship on information of value to the enemy, but also with conducting an informational campaign about the war here and abroad, it combined the functions that in World War II were lodged separately in the Office of Censorship and the Office of War Information. As for censorship, however, Creel protested later in his apologia that there had been no such thing:

The fantastic legend that associated gags and muzzles with [the Creel Committee's] work may be likened only to those trees which are evolved out of the air by Hindu magicians and which rise, grow and flourish in gay disregard of such usual necessities as roots, sap, and sustenance. *In no degree was the Committee an agency of censorship, a machinery of concealment or repression. Its emphasis throughout was on the open and the positive. At no point did it seek or exercise authorities under those war laws that limited the freedom of speech and press.* [15]

The italics are Creel's, and his statement is emphatic. Yet, what he meant by denying the existence of censorship was only that there was no preventive censorship. He himself confesses two pages later that there was an unmistakable censorship:

A voluntary censorship agreement safeguarded military information of obvious value to the enemy, but in all else the rights of the press were recognized and furthered.

This censorship was embodied in a statement specifying "what the government asks of the press," sent by the Creel Committee to editors and publishers. It was a list of eighteen types of information (beginning with "advance information of the routes and schedules of troop movements") that the papers were asked not to mention.[16] The whole proceeded, as Creel said, properly and inevitably from the necessities of war.

His brand of censorship, then, took care of the standard news about military plans and happenings. Unfortunately, that was not all there was to censorship in World War I. In the Espionage Act of June 15, 1917, the Trading with the Enemy Act of October 6 that year, and the amendment to the Espionage Act known as the Sedition Act of May 16, 1918, there was far stronger medicine. Though Creel denies that the Committee on Public Information had occasion to use them, these statutes stood behind the voluntary censorship and so provided the accustomed punitive sanction for it. More important, they were the occasion for the unhappy list of oppressions of pacifist, leftist, labor, and liberal groups by the Post Office Department and the Department of Justice that darkened World War I and the years immediately after it. These un-American laws, some of which are still in force today, demonstrated that whenever censorship is applied for military and patriotic reasons it brings censorship for social and political reasons in its train.

Censorship in World War II also began before war itself. The first step was taken December 31, 1940, when Secretary of the Navy Frank Knox broadcast what he called a confidential letter to 5,000 newspaper, radio, and picture editors, asking "avoidance of publicity" on practically all Navy news except recruiting, unless officially announced.[17] The following March 24 the

Secretary enlarged his original request to include news, photographs, or broadcasts of British ships that came to our ports for repair under the newly passed Lend-Lease Act.

A few days later, April 6, H.M.S. *Malaya* steamed into New York harbor. Commuters, strollers on Staten Island or the Battery, and the German Consulate had an excellent view of the battleship and of the collision mats covering the hole made by a torpedo. That night, British sailors, with the telltale "Malaya" on their hatbands, talked in New York's restaurants and bars of having been torpedoed March 20 while on North Atlantic convoy duty. It is possible that the British deliberately flaunted the *Malaya's* arrival in order to dramatize their life-and-death struggle, from which so many Americans still felt themselves remote. In any case, the morning after her arrival, the isolationist *New York Daily News* splashed an air photo of the damaged ship on its front page, and the interventionist *New York Herald Tribune* ran a story illustrated with a stock picture of the *Malaya*. The other New York papers heeded Secretary Knox's request to keep mum, despite the fact that no fourth-rate spy could have missed the facts. Thereupon Secretary Knox praised the silent papers, and said of the *News* and *Herald Tribune,* without mentioning them by name, "This sort of reporting is of inestimable value to the Germans." [18] The *Daily News* retorted editorially that, because papers could differ in their judgment as to the need for suppressing such a public event, there should be an official censorship that would say Yes or No. President Roosevelt joined in to remark that such excuses were the lamest he had ever read; and only after weeks of bickering was the incident filed away as experience.

Before long, other requests were made of the press. But it was not until the attack on Pearl Harbor that the debate over censorship was settled as an incident to settling the long and acrimonious debate over whether we should, or would, get into the war. The shock of the Japanese attack led the White House at once to clamp down a censorship at the source, reminiscent of the old skipper who wanted nothing but silence, and damn little of that. In fact, the President announced a censorship at the source in so many words; for at a press conference on December 9 he reserved to himself and the heads of the War and Navy departments the right of decision over what news might be released. He also laid down two general rules for the press: first, the news it published must be true; and second, it must not give aid and comfort to the enemy.[19] And the coming of open warfare automatically put into effect the wartime provisions of the laws surviving from World War I, and led to passage of the first War Powers Act, signed by the President, December 18, 1941. The net effect was to give us laws that, while wide open to abuse, were more liberal than those of the previous war, because the Sedition Act was not revived. In addition, the administration of these laws did far less violence to civil liberties in World War II than in 1918. They were, however, on the books, and provided a club with which to hold in line anyone who might jump over the traces of voluntary control.

Censorship of press and radio was put into effect December 19, 1941, sixteen days after Pearl Harbor. On that day, the President, acting under the first War Powers Act, established an Office of Censorship and appointed a director. The man picked was Byron Price, able executive news editor of the Associated Press. It was an excellent choice, for both press and radio knew him as one of themselves, and had full confidence in him. They were, furthermore, reassured by the tone of the President's announcement, which began:

All Americans abhor censorship, just as they abhor war. But the experience of this and of all other nations has demonstrated that some degree of censorship is essential in wartime, and we are at war. The important thing is that such forms of censorship as are necessary shall be administered effectively and in harmony with the best interests of our free institutions.[20]

Within a month—that is, on January 15, 1942—Price issued codes of wartime practices for press and radio. They constituted a censorship as gentle as the necessities of war allowed, being offered, like Creel's, not as commands but as practices "which the government feels are desirable for effective prosecution of the war." Price based the practices on two points: first, that the outcome of the war was of vital concern to every American; and second, that information that helped the enemy weakened the security of our armed forces and even of our homes and liberties. After asking editors to accept these points, he added:

The result of such a process will hardly represent "business as usual" on the news desks of the country. On the contrary, it will mean some sacrifice of the journalistic enterprise of ordinary times. But it will not mean a news or editorial black-out. It is the hope and expectation of the Office of Censorship that the columns of American publications will remain the freest in the world, and will tell the story of our national successes and shortcomings accurately and in much detail.[21]

As the war went on, and particularly after it took a turn for the better, Price issued successive revisions and clarifications of his code that were progressively more liberal. For example, the revision of February 1, 1943, promoted to the inside cover of the texts, under the heading "Special Note," a point that had been put obscurely at the end of the original newspaper code. It made curious reading in the light of continued editorial restiveness at censorship, for it pointed out that, should any authority anywhere in the country request a suppression that seemed unreasonable, "you are at liberty to appeal at once to the Office of Censorship." Here was the boss censor asserting his authority against self-appointed helpers—of whom there were many among the local satraps of Army, Navy, and civilian government about the country, as well as in the seats of the mighty in Washington. Price went further. In a note to editors sent over the press association wires, December 10, 1943, on the eve of another revision, he cautioned editors against accepting orders as to what they might or might not publish. Here was news of the man-bites-dog type, for the censor was worried lest the editors censor too much:

> I solicit your continued cooperation to see . . . that a dangerous psychology of overcensorship is not created throughout the land by the activities of a miscellany of volunteer firemen. . . .
> Many of you have been led by overzealousness to withhold information having no security value, on the advice of persons having no authority.[22]

On occasion, Price had to vary his tone by issuing warnings to the press, such as gossiping on the eve of the invasion of Western Europe.[23] But one begins to see why, under Price and his staff, censorship has worked as well as it can ever work. He understood his new job; but he also understood from lifelong experience the intangibles that go to make up the Fourth Estate. Being a newspaperman, he could reconcile, so far as they can be reconciled, the opposing needs of soldier and press. In this way he avoided the mistakes many censors make.

It is, in fact, far easier to make good censors out of newspapermen than it is out of soldiers or militarized laymen. The reason is, I think, that all of us are censors at heart anyway. Put into uniform or otherwise, given authority to say what may or may not be printed, and backed by the majesty of the fact that the nation is in danger, we take pleasure in saying No to the reporters, editors, and publishers we have long wanted to tell off anyway. Besides, most of us accept as authoritative our own judgment on matters of writing, news, public opinion, and censorship. We all read and write. We all hear and read the news every day. There seems to be nothing esoteric about it, as there is about other professions. Hence it never occurs to us that matters of writing news, public opinion, and censorship may constitute a discipline as complex as that of law or medicine, which a lifetime of experience and study is not enough to encompass. The result is that men in authority see no inconsistency in appointing as censor a man without training in this discipline, or without realization of how and why it forms the backbone of democracy. They would never dream of putting a reporter on the bench, in charge of a power plant, or in command of an aircraft carrier; but they see no harm in taking a lawyer, an engineer, or an admiral and making him a censor, with absolute power over some segment of the news that goes to make the world in which the nation lives. Hence the annoyance of editors, and the frustration of correspondents at the fronts and in the warring capitals, who during the war tried to give the American people an account of how their fate was being decided.

It was, I submit, because Byron Price understood thoroughly the fundamentals of the Fourth Estate that he was able to make the part of the censorship under his jurisdiction—that is, everything but the political, military, and naval censorship at the source, in Washington and in the field—work as well as it did. The confidence of press and radio had its counterpart in the unnatural self-restraint with which the media of information

kept secrets that they would normally shout from the house-
tops. Thus when in the summer of 1942 there came to Washington the Soviet Foreign Commissar, Viacheslav M. Molotov,
hundreds of newspapermen and broadcasters knew about it.
The visit was an early incident in the temporary *rapprochement*
that took place during the war between Soviet Russia and the
United States. Molotov's arrival was big political news, affecting the future of the American citizen to such an extent that
normally it would be unthinkable that the press could be
restrained from popping out with it. It was, moreover, difficult
to see how it could be classed as military information whose
publication would endanger our armed forces. Nevertheless, the
papers and radio said not a word, except the *Philadelphia
News*,[24] which printed it in the guise of gossip. In Washington,
too, press photographers, waiting at the White House to picture
the Duke and Duchess of Windsor, watched Molotov stroll by,
and not a single shutter clicked.[25] Here was a conspicuous example of what went on every day during the war: the suppression
by newspapers and radio of information that every professional
instinct called for publishing at once, and prominently. Everything, from events like this to the total suppression for four
years of the slightest hint of the atomic bomb, showed how well
our censorship worked during the war.

The fact that Byron Price and his Office of Censorship got
what was, for a censorship, a lyrically good press presents an
interesting study in contrasts; for his World War I predecessor,
George Creel, had received only brickbats from those he censored. So, too, his World War II colleague, Elmer Davis of the
Office of War Information, was treated by many editorial writers,
columnists, and radio commentators almost like an enemy
agent rather than director of his country's wartime information
service. When Davis got on the job six months after Pearl
Harbor, there was, to be sure, a chorus of approval from a press
that had been justifiably irritated at the patchwork confusion
of OWI's predecessors. But within six months editorial and
political rotten eggs were being thrown at the OWI, and
before long even its respected director began to be on the receiving end of a barrage from a largely hostile press whose fury
increased as the war continued.

This was strange, since Price and Davis both had been respected members of their profession, free from identification with the New Deal and therefore not unduly suspect by the political opposition, before taking their war assignments. The reason for the contrast may be found, I think, in their functions. Price was a censor, and nothing but a censor. Creel had likewise been a censor, but he had been a propagandist as well. And Davis was nothing but a propagandist. From this we can deduce that it is wartime propaganda rather than wartime censorship, that sets ill with Americans, and particularly with their conservative press. Reasonable censorship is tolerated for protecting military secrets, but the need for conducting psychological warfare against the enemy, and still more for officially channeling government news at home, is less widely accepted. And since war adjourns politics to only a minor extent, it was easy for a political opposition that was as undiscriminating as it was virulent to see in Davis, as in Creel, a propagandist for the reigning administration rather than for the country as a whole. Creel's functions as a propagandist lost him what credit he might have had as a censor. As for Davis, he took the job for patriotic reasons and for the duration only. Those of us who, by working in the OWI, had direct and personal experience with what it did —an advantage the complaining editors, commentators, and politicians did not have—knew that, though the OWI was staffed by persons of all political predilections, the charge that it was engaged in propagandizing the New Deal was bunk. It had many faults, notably the creaking inefficiency common to bureaucracies, but on the side of political prejudice it erred only infinitesimally in comparison with its critics. Nevertheless, the fact remains: Price, the censor, got off well; Creel and Davis, the propagandists, did not. One can only conclude that, despite the evils it brings in its train again and again in history, a competent wartime censorship will receive substantial public support.

What, then, is all the shouting about? Why not simply resolve the perpetual struggle between the soldier and the Fourth Estate in favor of the soldier for the duration? The answer is that, while the soldier must and will be top dog in wartime, a democracy simply cannot afford to have him rule unchecked. It must constantly be reminded of the dangers that are inseparable from censorship, the better to find its way through not only the perils of war but the ensuing battles of peace.

Some of censorship's inherent evils have already been pointed out, but there are others. For one thing, it has a perverse habit of giving rise to rumors. President Roosevelt brought this into the open immediately after Pearl Harbor, when he read newspaper and radio this lesson:

You have a most grave responsibility to the nation now and for the duration of this war.

If you feel that your government is not disclosing enough of the truth, you have every right to say so. But—in the absence of all the facts, as revealed by official sources—you have no right to deal out unconfirmed reports in such a way as to make people believe it is the gospel truth.[26]

Despite the popular conviction to the contrary, newspapers and radio do not make a practice of dealing out rumors as truth. Regrettably, some columnists, commentators, and editorial writers do at times pass them on, but news columns and news programs do not. Besides, rumors circulate unaided. Let that pass, because President Roosevelt in his comment after Pearl Harbor was laying down a highly desirable, not to say ideal, course of action. Unfortunately, the fact that it was desirable did not make it attainable, for there is an inevitable train of action and reaction between censorship and rumor. One might formulate it this way: Rumors exist in direct proportion to the degree of censorship. Just as air pressure used to be described by saying that nature abhors a vacuum, so we can account for the prevalence of rumors under censorship by saying that the mental world abhors a vacuum. Mankind does not like to be kept in ignorance. A democratic people in particular cannot endure large and vital gaps in its information, even in response to exhortations from its government. Hence, lacking "all the facts, as revealed by official sources," news of lower quality rushes into circulation.

It was for this reason that the Army, the Navy, and President Roosevelt himself were plagued by successive crops of rumors that sprang up, either from nowhere or else with the help of Axis agents, each time they sought secrecy. We have seen how President Roosevelt recognized the danger from the beginning, and reminded us two days after Pearl Harbor not to spread rumors. Yet despite his plea, and patriotic efforts by the public to heed it, the rumors would not die. On the contrary, they multiplied. The prize of the crop concerned a ship filled with the bodies of 1,500 unattended, uncoffined dead from Pearl Harbor that was supposed to have docked at Brooklyn Army Base. This was no vagrant breeze of a rumor. Thousands of people heard it as unpublished gospel, and hundreds telephoned the Army Base to ask about it. Finally, even at the risk of dignifying the falsehood by denying it, both the Base Commander and the War Department said flatly that it was not true.[27]

Even so, more than a month later the tale was still alive. For when on February 23, 1942, the President again spoke to the nation he found it necessary to mention a variation of it. By this time, according to the President, there were rumors of 11,000 or 12,000 dead at Pearl Harbor. Apparently this so irritated him that he determined to put a stop to it. How? In the only way possible; namely, by disclosing officially the figures of 2,340 dead and 946 wounded [28] figures that were substantially corroborated when the full report on the damage done was published on the first anniversary of Pearl Harbor.[29]

This offers a useful object lesson. It is all very well to lecture the press to the effect that "in the absence of all the facts, as revealed by official sources," it should help suppress rumors; but the only way to kill rumors is for official sources to do enough honest and accurate revealing.

Censorship, moreover, seems to be stupid by nature. Even our unusually enlightened censorship required the *Architectural Forum* of March, 1942, to identify its pictures and text on page 150 about a new airplane engine plant only as being "in the Middle West"—and then allowed an advertisement on page 99 of the same issue, to appear with an identical illustration and the statement that it was the new Buick plant at Melrose Park, near Chicago. Even more irritating was the publication, in all kinds of technical journals—the authoritative bimonthly *Army Ordnance,* for example—of a mass of facts on plane production and the performance of weapons—all of which the War Department had asked the newspapers not to print because they were secret.

The trouble is that these decisions as to what should be censored and what should not are matters of opinion, not of fact. And naturally men's opinions differ as to the point at which a given piece of information becomes so well known, so old, or so unimportant that it is no longer worth suppressing. Yet though no one really knows when this point of diminishing returns is reached, the censor has to say Yes or No each time the question arises over some new fact. It follows that he arbitrarily decides that a piece of news may or may not be published when another censor might say just the opposite.

Here, I think, is the key to the fundamental evil of censorship; for, whether we like it or not, military censorship brings political censorship in its train. To expect to have the essential good of military censorship without the evil of political censorship is like expecting to have a garden without weeds. Political government conducts the military war, and military considerations reach into the highest realm of political decision. It is impossible to draw a dividing line between them.

Again, censorship, and in particular censorship at the source, means that the person who makes the arbitrary decision to suppress information knows more than the rest of us. Hence the censor-at-the-source feels himself in a superior position. He knows the facts, the public doesn't. From here, it is but a step to a feeling of superior wisdom as to how information should be controlled, so that news of this or that high problem of state shall make the desired impression on the people. And once that state is reached the good of censorship's protection has brought in the evil of managed news in full flavor.

Perhaps we are still too close to the war to judge our own nation's actions dispassionately. We can see how these things work in practice, however, by examining an incident in Britain's practice of censorship before we entered the war. I refer to the time when Robert St. John of the Associated Press, who covered the British retreat through Greece in 1941 and escaped with the survivors to Cairo, tried to tell the truth about what he had seen:

I wrote a rather graphic description of that day of hell in Argos. The censor did a lot of slashing when he came to that part of the story. Then we had a real knockdown argument. I tried to make my case very logical. First, all the suffering I was trying to write about was the result, principally, of the inability of the RAF to drive off the Nazi dive bombers. Second, that was due to too few British planes. Third, the only place to get more planes was from the United States. Fourth, people in the United States were still buying automobiles by the hundreds of thousands. Fifth, if the American people were aware of the death and suffering going on in Europe because of the lack of British planes and if the story of what was happening could be brought home vividly to them, they might stop buying automobiles and let airplanes be made instead. Sixth, my story of Argos gave a grim picture of that death and suffering, and therefore the British should pin medals on it as a piece of powerful propaganda, which might get them more airplanes so that it wouldn't happen again.

The censor got the idea all right, but nevertheless found reasons for suppression:

Horror stories were all right for America, but England and the rest of the Empire must not be told how bad things were. The Empire must be told that everything was in fine shape. Horror stories for America. Back-stiffening for the Empire. But the Empire listened to the radio, and it was impossible to keep the stories for America and the stories for the Empire nicely pigeonholed. Modern communications were responsible. . . . And that was the reason, he said, that the Argos story could not be told. Not completely truthfully, as I wanted to tell it. Sorry, but that's the policy.[29]

So it goes, and so it will always go as long as there are censors. The only protection the citizens of a mature democracy have is to practice eternal vigilance in confining censorship to demonstrably military considerations. Every censor should always have to defend suppression by answering these questions:

1. Which of our troops, specifically, will be endangered if the information in question is published?

2. What particular item of military strategy will be disclosed to the enemy in event of publication?

If we do this, all standard items like troop movements, ship sailings, new weapons, and forthcoming offensives obviously will come under the protection of legitimate military secrecy. So will the news of military reverses in the limited circumstances in which they might give advantage to the enemy. But censorship for reasons of morale, or to support artificially any other doctrine cherished by the official doing the censoring, would be ruled out. The importance of unending pressure for publication in the teeth of the natural tendency toward silence cannot be overemphasized. The desire to censor is not peculiar to British Colonel Blimps, nor to New Dealers, nor to West Point and Annapolis graduates who have attained flag rank. It manifests itself in lay as well as military breasts, afflicts Republicans as well as Democrats, and is indeed simply human and universal. That is why we dare not resolve the unending struggle between soldier and Fourth Estate in favor of the soldier.

Let us sum it up this way: There is no such thing as a good censorship, for that is a contradiction in terms.

THE STRATEGY OF ERROR

KARL VON CLAUSEWITZ, the Prussian scientist of war, summarizing the instructions he proposed to give His Royal Highness the Crown Prince, later Frederick William IV of Prussia, laid down these three principal objectives:

(a) To conquer and destroy the enemy's armed forces.
(b) To get possession of the . . . sources of existence of the hostile army.
(c) To gain public opinion.[1]

General von Clausewitz explained that in war public opinion is "ultimately gained" by great victories and by possession of the enemy's capital. The modern world has vastly amplified this simple and almost naïve formula. Clausewitz's successors as scientists of war, the Nazis, were especially active in elaborating it. Instead of leaving the capture of enemy public opinion until after the battles were won, they took possession before the shooting started. In this way they seemed to win battles without firing a shot, or else at a ridiculously low cost, because their victims had been reduced to jelly before the first Nazi plane roared across the border.

It would be comforting to believe that the whole evil business of war against the mind had been wiped out with Hitler and Goebbels. Unhappily, while the Nazis were the most energetic practitioners of psychological warfare, they were not the only ones. Long before the world heard of Hitler, the nations had engaged in psychological offensives of a relatively mild form; and since his disappearance they have gone right on conducting them, in accordance with another, better known maxim of Clausewitz, that war is only a continuation of international politics by other—and more openly brutal—means. As he put it: "Is not war merely another kind of writing and language for political thoughts?" And again: "War is an instrument of policy. . . . The conduct of war, in its great features, is therefore policy itself, which takes up the sword in place of the pen." The converse is also true; for, if war is a forceful means of carrying out a national policy, peacetime diplomacy, including all types of cultural, information, and propaganda programs, is only another means to that end. Whenever the war of bombs and shells ceases, the war for the mind goes right on.

Perhaps the best way to understand the present is to remember, with the added advantage of hindsight, the propaganda warfare of the Nazis before World War II. Edmond Taylor, an American correspondent in Europe, gave us the first comprehensive account of the Nazis' propaganda methods, which he named "the strategy of terror." He showed how, under skillful stimulus from Berlin, all Europe was fed on worry alternated with hope, on disillusionment followed by confusion:

I remember those inhuman diplomatic crises, more unnerving than war, that we lived through, particularly the one before Munich. I remember all those stupid, bitter political quarrels, felt like a personal grievance, between friends and within families. . . . I remember all the false hopes, all the bitter disillusionments. Above all I remember the paralyzing political despair which grew and grew until it almost overshadowed our private lives, the feeling that this world of ours would always be a madhouse and a jungle, that collective efforts to bring reason into it were fruitless, individual escape impossible.[2]

Curiously, no sooner was the Nazi ghost laid in the thundering fury of 1945's Armageddon than Hitler's prewar psychological offensive began to seem fantastic. It may be difficult for future generations to recapture the horror that lived in the Nazi strategy of terror, if, indeed, they can bring themselves to believe that the war of nerves really amounted to anything. Yet few who were abroad in those uneasy years can doubt the ghastly intensity of that seeming nightmare, that was the more terrifying because it was real. Besides, the fact remains that Adolf Hitler did divide and conquer. He so befuddled the countries round about Germany, that each nervously watched one victim after another being swallowed up, content because for the time being it was left alone. Austria, Czechoslovakia, Poland, Norway, Holland, Belgium, and France all went in this way. Hungary, Rumania, and Bulgaria voluntarily became jackals to the wolf rather than fight as the others did, when they were on the spot themselves. The most characteristic was Poland, which joined in Hitler's rape of Czechoslovakia only six months before her own turn came; and Holland and Belgium clung to the shadow of neutrality even though Hitler had long since shown that he respected no agreements, even those he made himself. No one seemed to believe that the Nazis actually meant to enslave the world.

The United States received a wholly different kind of propaganda. It was treated differently because it was situated differently. Without the weapons of today, the Nazi legions, even the vaunted Nazi Air Force, could not threaten us as they threatened their victims in Europe. Hence the Nazi propagandists did not seek to reduce us to jelly. Instead, they sought to put us to sleep. The basic Nazi theme for America was that President Roosevelt, and all who agreed with him, were warmongers, and everything would be all right if only this warmongering would stop. Hence Nazi propaganda aimed to reenforce native American sentiment against mixing in foreign trouble, to encourage every doubt that an attack on us was even thinkable.

Because its aim was not to frighten us but to lull us into unawareness of the threat inherent in the Nazi movement, the propaganda treatment applied by the Nazis to this country might be called the strategy of error rather than of terror. It sought to deceive, not to terrify. But how did it work? How was it possible for anyone in Berlin to help Americans live in a world that falsely seemed secure?

This was done by tampering subtly and skillfully with our news. It was one of the more interesting exhibits in the Nazi arsenal of skulduggery. It involved the abuse of the very standards of rapid and objective news coverage on which this country prides itself. As Elmer Davis said:

This psychological offensive seems to be a mental form of ju-jitsu —the principle of ju-jitsu being that you use your opponent's strength against him, and make him break his bones by his own instinctive reactions. . . . We are rightly proud of our news services, which have made us the best-informed people in the world; and are apt to forget that now and then routine functioning of our news system has made us the most copiously and ingeniously misinformed people in the world.[3]

Behind the Nazi use of news as an instrument of national policy lay what Adolf Hitler called "the true principle that the greatness of the lie is always a certain factor in being believed." This "principle," however, does not seem to have been remembered, as the news from Nazi and Nazi-inspired sources was gathered, edited, and read:

The great masses of a people . . . are more easily victimized by a large than by a small lie. . . . They cannot believe possible so vast an impudence in infamous distortion on the part of others; even after being enlightened they will long continue to doubt and waver, and will still believe there must be some truth behind it somewhere. For this reason some part of even the boldest lie is sure to stick.[4]

Naturally the Nazi propagandists did not let on that they were lying when they made available to American correspondents what was ostensibly news. They played our news-gathering machinery, and us, for suckers. The result was that while our editorial pages fulminated against Hitler, our news pages continued to play his game. A student of the subject, Sidney A.

Freifeld, wrote in a carefully documented analysis of the phenomenon:

If a Propaganda Ministry official were to approach a member of the American press corps in Berlin and suggest he write a nice, sympathetic article about Der Führer's love for children or nazism's peaceful intentions . . . he would in all likelihood be met with a sneer and a refusal. But let the same official state in a press conference, or write in the *Völkischer Beobachter,* that President Roosevelt is a "shameless gangster" seeking to become dictator of the world, that "Wall Street Bolshevistic bankers" are attempting to plunge unwilling Americans into war for "blood profits," or that the United States is a "Judaized plutodemocracy," and the foreign correspondent will in most cases promptly cable the story to America and thereby provide a thousand clippings for Dr. Goebbels' scrapbook.[5]

It seems farfetched, doesn't it? But what of this 1941 news item:

BERLIN, Feb. 6—(UP)—One million lice, collected to produce spotted fever vaccine, are being fed by 60 Jews, *the Nazi Party newspaper, Völkischer Beobachter, said today.*
Each Jew, the newspaper said, was appointed a share of the lice to feed on his blood and was paid three Polish zloty a day.
The newspaper said there was a rush of Jewish applicants for the job.[6]

The italics are mine. They show that Freifeld was right in his diagnosis of how Dr. Goebbels succeeded in getting space in our papers. And here is more evidence, dated 1941 and (the third) 1940:

BERLIN, May 10—(AP)—German leaders gave the deepest attention to American developments as the impression grew in Berlin that "war agitators" were gaining ground in the United States. . . .

BERLIN, Jan. 25—(AP)— . . . "Halifax lost no time to impress on the American public the urgent need for American help to England," the *Boerzen Zeitung* said. "Shortly after Roosevelt met him at the Annapolis dock he declared with the still unbroken arrogance of an English aristocrat toward the American people who once were colonists of the British that he would inform the Americans from time to time in what manner they can help. . . ."

BERLIN, July 19—(AP)—Political circles commenting today on President Roosevelt's acceptance speech, privately made no secret of their opinion [you bet they didn't] that by aiding the Axis' enemies the President is prolonging the war.

Looking back, it seems as though there had been no limit to the naïveté of seasoned American reporters in cabling home anything from subtle propaganda to outright poppycock. Like this, in 1940 and 1941:

ROME, May 28—(AP)—According to a report received here, the Germans have been experimenting with a newly bred type of omnivorous grasshopper that devours crops of all kinds, especially grain crops.

These grasshoppers, it was said, could be transported in airplanes by the millions and released over British farms in an effort to starve out the British Isles. . . .

ROME, June 2—(UP)—Among new types of war equipment that Germany is reported here to be planning to be used against Britain is a submarine trailer for transporting large numbers of troops.

According to reports current here these trailers, attached by a special cable to the stern of ocean-going submarines, are capable of carrying from 500 to 1000 fully armed soldiers.[7]

I am indebted to Sidney Freifeld for these items. They are samples of thousands upon thousands of similar items cabled from the Axis capitals and printed in our newspapers or read over our radio stations after the Nazis seized power in 1933. This kind of thing got into our papers and on our news broadcasts because the American press associations, proud of their speed in gathering the news, are usually within minutes of one another in transmitting a given item. None wants to be last. Thus, if INS used a Nazi statement, there would be pressure on AP and UP and the special correspondents to use it too. Suppose an American newspaper had received an INS dispatch from Berlin saying that So-and-so had just hinted that Hitler was soon to invade Britain. If the AP and UP papers failed to get the same news in short order the teletypes would be clacking angrily in press association headquarters; and it would not be long before the laggard correspondents in Berlin were jogged by sharp queries from home. Therefore they rarely waited to be jogged. This made for a hair-trigger sensitivity to much that Dr. Goebbels wanted to put across.

Lest we conclude that the strategy of error consists exclusively of falsehoods, we must remember that it was also the policy of the Goebbels machine, as of today's practitioners of this black art, to come out with hard, honest news, and to come out with it fast. In this way fresh audiences could be ensured and fresh evidence of reliability given to skeptical American editors.

However, the masterpiece of the Axis news managers was the construction within the Axis countries of a never-never land in which scarcely anything was what it seemed to be. The propagandists, not content with every conceivable machination to twist the news, engaged in its outright manufacture. They actually made the more important fakes real. This was news management carried to its uttermost limit. The Axis could do it because the boss propagandists were Hitler, Mussolini, and Tojo. These men had complete control of the state, they could make sure that no cabinet minister, party dignitary, general, or admiral, indeed no one in their whole domain, was above going through the motions of legitimate government activity in order to make news. And since government officials did these things, the resulting events were covered as real news even though they had been enacted only to crash American headlines. It amounted to nothing less than altering the shape of the physical world within the Axis countries, in order to falsify our mental world.

An example of the dilemma into which this kind of thing put American correspondents occurred, November 30, 1938. On that day Galeazzo Ciano, the Duce's son-in-law and Foreign Minister, addressed the Italian Chamber of Deputies. In the course of his remarks he interpolated an apparently extraneous sentence about safeguarding "with inflexible resolution the interests and natural aspirations of the Italian people." At once Fascist deputies began popping up and making their famous shouts about "Tunisia!" Blackshirts in the spectators' gallery joined in with "Nizza!" and "Savoia!" Here, then, was something that really happened. The American reporters knew that if the outbursts, apparently signifying Fascist designs on French territory, were spontaneous it would be censored. It wasn't. Well, then, it had been staged for a purpose, just as the scene itself indicated. Yet the correspondents could not say so without risking expulsion from Italy, which would be a poor service to their employers and to their readers. Besides, what proof was there? Hadn't the deputies actually made the demonstration before their eyes? It was a real event, even though the reporters were certain of its synthetic origin. So the cables were duly dispatched, and we in our innocence learned that Mussolini, having swallowed Ethiopia, was now turning his eyes upon France and her African holdings. Two American correspondents who later told the story in detail think the affair was a blind to hide Mussolini's forthcoming invasion of Albania.[8]

Again and again this kind of thing happened. Take that time when the world was shaken to its foundations as the unbelievable happened in the collapse before the Nazis of the France that had survived the Marne and Verdun. Cheerfully ready to please as ever, the Propaganda Ministry in Berlin arranged to let a select group of foreign correspondents see the stupendous show with their own eyes. One of them was Louis Lochner, Pulitzer Prize winner and veteran AP correspondent in Berlin. Going over the files of his dispatches for that last week in May, 1940, Freifeld found a remarkable pattern appearing in them. Here are some of the significant statements that were wired to our newspapers:

The object would be to drive back toward the English Channel the forces which block a direct Nazi attack on England. . . .

All are awaiting Adolf Hitler's final command to go to England. Everywhere one hears soldiers singing the "England song." . . .

. . . the Germans are trying . . . to prevent the Continental Allies from bringing effective aid to England in the event she needs it, during any German attack on the British Isles. . . .

They seem to be itching to get over to England. . . .

. . . We have also seen naval officers hastening back and forth in this area. That fact speaks volumes. These men are here for business. . . .

When correspondents entered staff headquarters no effort was made to hide highly significant maps. One commanding general had an enormous map indicating . . . how troops were to move in the offensive against England.

The Germany Army and Navy deliberately put on a show intended to convince independent and experienced reporters that the German attack was not against Paris and the rest of France so much as against England. Freifeld comments:

If this ruse could be perpetrated it would have several obvious military and psychological effects. The British might be tempted to withhold further aid to France, thereby concentrating material and men where they would be strategically less useful. The French, whom the Nazis had been making every effort to incite against their ally, would be increasingly critical of the British. Moreover, the artificial suspense and fear which might be generated in Britain would be followed by let-down and consequent effect upon national morale.[9]

So it happened. This Nazi trick contributed its share to the conquest of France and to forcing Britain to its knees at Dunkirk.

In one sense the strategy of error was beneficial, for it made us avoid the mistakes of World War I. In 1914 it was the Allies rather than Germany that propagandized us. They were able to shut us off from the German point of view by cutting the cables from Germany. Inevitably we began to assume that everything the Allies did was right. We saw the war in terms of black and white and convinced ourselves that if we joined the crusade with bands playing and flags flying the resulting military victory would both make the world safe for democracy and virtually settle international disputes for all time. What we were not able to see was the game of power politics being carried on behind the Wilsonian façade. The result was that after the victory was won we had the unpleasant shock of discovering our mistake.

The debunking process that followed not only left us greatly impressed with the power of propaganda, but swung us completely around into cynical doubt of the Allied cause. It led us to underestimate—now that the danger had safely been turned back at a cost of the lifeblood of millions of Allied soldiers—the real menace that had existed in Prussian militarism. It also left us with the comfortable feeling that we could stay out of Europe's wars by the simple process of minding our own business. All this made us substantially indifferent when in the 1930's the threat inherent in Kaiser Wilhelm's bid for conquest was revived by Japan, Italy, and Germany in far more virulent form. We did not like the aggressions against Manchuria, Ethiopia, Spain, Austria, Czechoslovakia, Poland, and all the rest, but we imagined that they did not threaten us. This made us ready and willing victims of the strategy of error.

Moreover, when the cables were cut in 1939 it made little difference, for this time there remained the shortwave radio, to which Dr. Goebbels devoted himself with such frenzied enthusiasm that we did not lack for mountains of information—and misinformation—as to the German cause. But, for all the abuses to which Dr. Goebbels subjected us, we can now take pride in the fact that we put Axis news before ourselves with no other safeguard than such editing as the newspapers and the radio cared to give it. This was in sharp contrast to the Axis authorities' careful filtering of every statement from our side before passing it on to their peoples. The Axis, furthermore, implemented this filtering process by stiff penalties, including the death sentence, for listening to foreign broadcasts. Far from doing that, we blandly permitted papers that chose to, like the *New York Times,* to print in their radio logs, right through the war, the times and dial settings at which any good American could tune in on Tokyo and Berlin! This was something radically new in the history of warfare. Imagine Caesar sending a centurion across to Britain in advance of his invasion so that the messenger might come back and explain to the legions why the British tribes wished to be left unconquered. Or imagine Napoleon after the return from Elba sending emissaries to Wellington and Blücher, or to Castlereagh, that they might return on the eve of Waterloo and explain to the survivors of the *Grande Armée* why they were wrong to fight again. What we did in leaving ourselves open to the Axis attacks on our minds was just that, translated into the modern world of mass communications. There could be no greater proof of the justice of our cause.

We also learned from our experience with the strategy of error that it would be well to revise our earlier estimate of propaganda. At first, of course, the events attending Hitler's rise seemed to confirm our World War I belief that propaganda was all-powerful. From the reoccupation of the Rhineland in 1936 to the invasion of Poland in 1939, it looked as though Hitler were winning bloodless victories through the strategy of terror. Some of us feared he was preparing the same fate for us through the strategy of error. But then came a slow and fundamental change in perspective. As the war went on we came to see that it was not the war of nerves alone that frightened Britain into Munich, that knocked over Austria, Czechoslovakia, and the Balkan satellites without a shot. It was rather the fact that the Nazi propaganda warfare was backed by the terribly real threat of the Nazi Army and the Nazi Air Force. How real that threat was soon appeared in Poland, Norway, the Low Countries, France, Yugoslavia, Greece, and in the bombing of Great Britain. It was this military power that, even before it was used, gave the propaganda of Hitler and Goebbels its strength. Not only is God on the side of the biggest battalions, but successful propaganda is on the side of the biggest air force. To Clausewitz's credit be it said, there is no propaganda so potent as that of victory.

This more temperate estimate of propaganda is, I submit, substantially accurate. It is more accurate than our blindness to propaganda during World War I. It is also more accurate than our belief after the early Axis successes that propaganda could win wars all by itself. For now, I think, we neither overrate nor underrate propaganda. We recognize it as an essential part of war—and peace—fought by mass populations in a day of modern communications; but we see that propaganda, even when waged with the skill and thoroughness of the Nazis, cannot win wars by itself. The most it can do is reenforce the military arm; and that, indeed, it must do if a modern fighting force is to function at full effectiveness.

So much for the strategy of error in war. But what of peace?

CHAPTER XV

THE STRATEGY OF TRUTH

DURING the 1920's and 1930's national press associations, like the Soviet agency Tass in Russia, Stefani in Italy, the Deutsches Nachrichten Bureau (DNB) in Germany, and Domei in Japan, were transformed from news-gathering organizations into integral parts of totalitarian governments. They became as much agents of national policy as the armies and navies.

Though this seemingly drastic change from news gathering to propaganda made the democracies aware, for the first time, that news could be used as an instrument of power politics, it was actually a change more in degree than in kind. The strategy of error described in the previous chapter and indeed the whole modern use of psychological warfare, and psychological offensives in peacetime, is an outgrowth of something that existed previously. Its roots go back to the very beginnings of mass communication. No sooner had the telegraph lines and ocean cables been laid than they were used deliberately to transmit misinformation.

Therefore, though the twentieth century dictators may have seemed to have suddenly transformed the innocent business of gathering information for newspapers into something sinister, actually the world's news agencies since their founding, except

200

in the United States, had been subservient to their national governments. Dr. Goebbels merely did a more strenuous and more efficient job than his predecessors.

The modern press association had its origin in the need of a rising industrial civilization for financial and commercial intelligence. The need led to the founding by Charles Havas, in 1836, of a financial news service in Paris. He was followed in 1849 by Dr. Bernhard Wolff, who set up an agency in Berlin, and in 1854 by Guglielmo Stefani in Turin—and later Rome. But it was Julius de Reuter, a former Prussian government messenger, who established the first press association supplying general news to newspapers rather than financial information to business clients. He succeeded in doing this in London, after various attempts on the Continent, in the years 1851–1858. By the early years of the twentieth century all technically advanced countries had similar agencies for gathering and disseminating general news.

The Associated Press, oldest of the American news agencies, traces its ancestry to the first joint news service of six New York newspapers founded under that name in 1848. In 1892 several news agencies in different parts of the country, including the New York Associated Press and the Western Associated Press, were combined into a stock corporation, and in 1900 the Associated Press was reorganized on its present cooperative basis. In the United Press Associations, E. W. Scripps revitalized in 1907 three antecedent agencies as a private, profit-making enterprise. International News Service was an outgrowth of a special wire and mail agency serving the Hearst newspapers in the early years of the twentieth century.

What differentiated the American press associations from those of the rest of the world was the fact that they did not become subservient to their national government. During the period of growth and change in the second half of the nineteenth century, peculiarly American conditions, which we shall have occasion to analyze in Chapter XVIII, gave birth to the concept of news as something that ought to be reported honestly and objectively, let the opinions fall where they may. The press associations, notably the ancestors of the present Associated Press, had an important part in this development. The fact that they served clients of all political views in all regions of the country forced them to confine their reports to the agreed facts and to present both sides of controversial events. Gradually there grew up the tradition that we now take for granted; namely, that the integrity of the news should be inviolate. Kent Cooper of the Associated Press does not exaggerate in calling this "the highest original moral concept ever developed in America and given the world." [1]

Unfortunately, all the rest of the world saw news as something that might be bent or twisted as necessary to serve diplomatic or imperial interests. Not only that, but through the dynamic enterprise of Reuter's all the world's news agencies, outside the United States, came to be gathered into an international news cartel. Reuter's operated in partnership with Havas of France and Wolff of Germany. These three linked into a world-wide network a whole regiment of lesser national news agencies, the big fellows holding the little national agencies in line through all-inclusive contractual chains. By this means Reuter's itself furnished the overwhelming proportion of news not only to Great Britain, but also to all the dominions and colonies of the empire on which the sun never set, plus Egypt, Turkey, China, and other countries in Britain's political sphere of influence. Havas had exclusive rights to France, Switzerland, Italy, Spain, Portugal, and the whole of South and Central America, right in our own back yard. Wolff took over most of what was left of Europe, including Russia, Austria-Hungary, and the Balkans.

During the time when the cartel was thus dividing the world, in the last half of the nineteenth century, a United States that was in good part insulated against the currents of world politics had only a remote interest in foreign affairs. Regrettably, when toward the end of the nineteenth century the rising importance and awareness of this country made it necessary to bring in foreign news in volume, the Associated Press, at the time the only American press association of national stature, sought to bring in foreign news economically by joining hands with the cartel. This it did in 1893, accepting its foreign news from Reuter's and feeding into the pool, through Reuter's, the news it gathered in the United States.

The cartel, AP affiliation and all, survived the First World War by the simple device of replacing the agencies that toppled with the crowned heads of Europe in 1918 by the new litter of national agencies that sprang up in their place. After that war, just as before, the world was divided into spheres of influence in which press association news was controlled by the cartel and in particular by its leading member, Reuter's.

While the cartel's coloring of the news was often, especially in Britain, a matter of subtle suggestion or even of a chauvinistic cast of thought on the part of its writers and editors, the effect was much the same as though a Dr. Goebbels had commanded it. Characteristic of the cartel's political overtones was the way in which Reuter's—which through its link with the Associated Press had a monopoly on supplying news of America to the world—somehow seemed to pass along only news that emphasized the uncouth and the bizarre in the United States, to the exclusion of the achievements that gradually came to make the United States the envy of the world. Again, a Reuter's correspondent telegraphing to London and thence through the cartel to the rest of the world about the latest developments in Greece would slant his report in the direction of Britain's imperial interests. Or consider the incident that made Kent Cooper of the Associated Press a crusader against the cartel to which his predecessors had harnessed the agency. Early in World War I, *La Nación* in Buenos Aires, as a great neutral journal, wanted to print the German as well as the Allied version of the war news. But Buenos Aires was in South America, a part of the Havas empire. And Havas refused to transmit to *La Nación* the text of the German communiqués. When a Havas representative was asked, "Why on earth don't you send from Paris the German official statement?" he answered, "We are French; we cannot do it." [2] From the point of view of shortsighted patriotism, that is no doubt a noble sentiment. From the point of view of the patriotism that seeks to save one's country from the sickening and wasteful brutality of war, it is immoral.

The breakup of the cartel began when the Associated Press left it. For four decades that included the Spanish-American and the First World War, during which the United States came to the front rank among the world's powers, the AP remained bound to the cartel by its contractual links. But after a long internal struggle, it finally, on February 12, 1934, declared its independence of the cartel and devoted itself to gathering and distributing its own news exclusively abroad as well as at home.

For a few fitful years the cartel survived. But one by one the various Italian, German and Japanese agencies were swallowed up by their totalitarian governments. And when at length World War II came, the cartel could not survive it as it had survived World War I. For the great national agencies that had ruled the cartel, and the lesser ones in smaller lands as well, themselves disappeared. Havas was crushed under the Nazi conquest of 1940, though the name was revived for a wholly new agency after the war.[3] Stefani, long since corrupted by Fascism, came to a final ignominious end when Mussolini's Italy caved in in 1943. DNB, built on the foundations of Wolff, disappeared in the smoke and rubble that swallowed Goebbels. Of all the dominating agencies in the cartel only Reuter's survived. And even before the end Reuter's had turned over a new leaf. On October 28, 1941, it became a cooperative agency owned by the entire British press, on the model of our Associated Press. In its new form it threw off at last the subtle shackles that bound it to Whitehall and Downing Street, and announced that henceforth its "integrity, independence, and freedom from bias" would at all times be fully preserved.

Curiously, little was said about the existence of the cartel during its life, and still less was said of its effect on the history of the world. It is amazing that civilized peoples did not seem to care that the vast regions of the earth had become the private preserve of the government-dominated news agencies that made up the cartel, for the effect was stupendous. The central thesis of this book as laid down in Chapter I is that mankind is condemned without hope of escape to confinement in mental worlds that correspond only in roughest outline to the real thing; and the existence of the cartel meant that the people's mental worlds were made even less accurate than they would have been if let alone, to the extent that the cartel's news reports shaded or ignored inconvenient facts. News thus doctored through the months, years, and even generations inevitably distorted, where it did not actually falsify, the concepts the peoples of the civilized world held of their fellow men in other lands.

A gradual awareness of this fact, first in the United States, in recent years in Britain, the self-governing dominions, and the small democracies, led to efforts to throw over the cartel and indeed the whole strategy of error—efforts that have yet to succeed. The objective of the crusade is to destroy not only the virulent form of the strategy of error developed by totalitarian governments, but also the subtler imperial shadings that characterized the old cartel as well. It seeks nothing less than to replace the strategy of error with the strategy of truth. It is based on the conviction that, if we are ever to lift the curse of war from mankind, all peoples everywhere must have essentially the same honest, accurate, and adequate reports on events of world import. And such a substantially unanimous view can come only through a free and equal flow of the news, as reported by independent and competing press associations, among all nations.

Perhaps, if we can once start a free flow of news across all national borders, we can develop on a world scale a tradition of objective reporting like that which has been growing in the United States for more than a century. For the separation of mankind into national groups living in disparate mental worlds that make them look at nationalistic versions of the same facts with wholly different passions, closely parallels the early nineteenth century division of the American people into violently partisan factions. Internationally, journalism today is hardly further advanced than it was in this country during that dark age of the early nineteenth century. If now it becomes possible to stimulate a tradition of objectivity in international news, if the world's newspapers and radios and moving-picture houses can learn to distribute news that is as factual and as acceptable to the newspapers of all nations, without pulling its punches, as the Associated Press's political reports of the last half of the nineteenth century were to all sorts of American newspapers at the time, then there is that much more reason to hope that this time peace may endure.

In short, what we need is an AP of the world, delivering the same news in Europe as in America, the same in Asia and Africa as in Europe. But it must be no single world-wide press association that does this; for, if man's history means anything, no monopoly of any kind can long be trusted to stay on the strait and narrow path of accuracy, objectivity, and the long-term public interest. What the world needs is not only an AP of the world but a UP and an INS of the world as well, plus still more competing agencies from Russia and Britain, France and China, and any other countries capable of developing and supporting them. Just suppose this came true. Inevitably the ensuing world-wide access to identical facts and views would make the various nations see their common crises in all their colors, as they are, rather than through the monochrome lenses of national prejudice.

Though few of us realized it at the time, the world had a chance to establish a free flow of news at the peace conference of Paris in 1919. Even before that, as long ago as 1893, the project had been entertained. In that year a World Press Conference met in Chicago to discuss, among other items, the proposition that "the press has a right and obligation to dissipate misunderstandings between nations." [4] Thereafter the subject was regularly talked about, and as regularly ignored in practice. But at the Paris Peace Conference of 1919 a handful of men earnestly preached the essentials of the strategy of truth to the men who sat at the peace table. Regrettably, the peacemakers did not understand. Woodrow Wilson himself was blind to the healing powers of objective international news, and contented himself with the vision of a League of Nations. The result was that the underlying facts of the peacemaking at Paris, like the facts about international events in later years, never reached the peoples of the world. As one reporter at Paris said a quarter of a century later, when he came upon Stephen Bonsal's record of what had really happened at the conference, "Those who served the press at Paris and Versailles in that time will realize as never before that they knew very little of the springs of the actions they chronicled." [5] No wonder that the world, lacking the facts, made a muddle of the peace.

The primary reason why the world lacked the facts was that few of the statesmen of the conference, even among the Americans and British, perceived the necessity for free access to the news at its source. To most of them such an idea seemed indecent. That was bad enough. But at the conference other decisions also were made that prevented the free and undistorted communication of news, once gathered, across all national borders. And access to the news at its source and free transmission are equally essential to the strategy of truth.

One of the few believers in the strategy of truth in Paris at the time of the conference was Kent Cooper of the Associated Press. Here is his report:

In Paris I was very much impressed by what I was able to observe of the methods by which the peace treaty was being put together. I wondered if anyone had thought about the matter of the inclusion of an article declaring for a free press and freedom of international news exchange. I had heard about the utopian approach on every other subject affecting the welfare of the peoples of the world: there were considerations of how to protect their physical health, their right to live; also about the suppression of the right to wage war and what not. But I could not find that anyone had projected for consideration the welfare of the people as to guaranteeing that they could have true, unbiased news to read in their newspapers about either world or domestic affairs.[6]

Cooper interested Colonel House in the free exchange of news, and he sought to convince President Wilson and other leaders; but nothing came of it. He merely reported to Mr. Cooper somewhat cryptically that the matter "had been taken care of privately." [7] This, it turned out, meant that Reuter's and Havas would continue their cartel and its control of the news.

Another voice crying in the wilderness of Paris was Walter S. Rogers, an expert in international communications, especially by cable and radio, who later became director of the Institute of Current World Affairs in New York. He submitted at Paris four documents designed to lay the technical groundwork for freedom of information by opening existing cable and radio systems to a full flow of information. These consisted of letters and memoranda to President Wilson, Secretary of the Navy Josephus Daniels, and George Creel, Chairman of the World War I Committee on Public Information. They were published for the first time in the 1944 annual report of Dean Carl W. Ackerman of the Graduate School of Journalism at Columbia University,[8] and they are interesting because they show, as Dean Ackerman points out, what we lost at Paris. We lost the opportunity to establish a world-wide foundation for the strategy of truth. Had it been otherwise, there might have been no World War II.

Though the statesmen of the world paid no attention, the spark of truth in world news did not die. In 1934 three members of the American Society of Newspaper Editors, Grove Patterson of the *Toledo Blade,* Casper Yost of the *St. Louis Globe-Democrat,* and William Allen White of the *Emporia Gazette,* presented the first of what has grown to be a whole barrage of resolutions calling for world freedom of news.[9] In it our two leading press associations, the United Press and the Associated Press, could hear the first tentative notes of what has since become a swelling chorus supporting their cries in the wilderness of official indifference. These press associations, and in particular their heads, Kent Cooper of the AP and Karl Bickel and Hugh Baillie of the UP, have done much to introduce to the whole world the concept of the independence and integrity of news. While Cooper has been the more vociferous campaigner, his rivals of the UP actually beat him to it in accomplishment. The UP had never in its history assumed ties with the cartel or with any other restrictive agency. Thus it escaped the chains that long irked Cooper. During World War I, in which the UP's fast and colorful services earned it a prominent position in this country, it also began to sell its news in South America in cocky disregard of the cartel. Here was a field the AP could not enter because under the cartel South America was the property of Havas. But the UP's success in doing a tidy business distributing news outside the United States was helpful to Cooper in his struggle within his own organization to break away from the cartel. Once the AP was free from the cartel it, too, aggressively sought clients in South America. Both AP and UP, and indeed INS as well, began to cultivate business in Europe and elsewhere abroad wherever they could. They became, and remain today, self-interested leaders in the crusade for a world set free for the gathering, transmission, and distribution of fast, accurate, and unbiased news on equal terms by independent, nongovernmental agencies competing with one another.

During the decade following the 1934 resolution the two larger press associations carried on the fight alone, with the help of an occasional newspaper editorial or magazine article to which statesmen, as before, paid no attention. But with the return of war in 1939, bringing a grim lesson as to the cost of the black-out in world news, interest began to pick up. In

February, 1943, the American Society of Newspaper Editors returned to the attack with another resolution calling for a "world guarantee of freedom of the press"—a call repeated at its annual meeting a year later and backed by appointment of a committee "to seek international agreement on freedom of the press." In January, 1945, the society began to move out of the field of resolutions into that of action. It sent around the world a three-man delegation consisting of Wilbur Forrest of the *New York Herald Tribune,* Ralph McGill of the *Atlanta Constitution,* and Dean Carl W. Ackerman, to propagate the idea and find out what the editors and politicians of other lands thought of it. A year later it appointed another committee to study and report on world dissemination of news.[10]

All this, however, still confined the movement to newspapermen acting in the interest of their trade. The first glimmer of light indicating that the centers of political power might also take an interest, a glimmer that had been absent even during World War I, appeared at the conference of American, British, and Soviet foreign ministers in Moscow in October, 1943. This was the conference that, by approving the concept of a general international organization, made the United Nations possible. Perhaps it is no less significant that it also issued a declaration of Allied policy toward Italy that included the purpose that "freedom of speech, of religious worship, of political belief, of the press and of public meeting shall be restored in full measure to the Italian people." That was far from a promise of world-wide freedom of news, but it hinted that freedom of the press might be worthy of inclusion among Allied war aims.

The following year, 1944, was an election year in the United States. It brought a further accolade for the newspapermen's concept in the form of planks in both Democratic and Republican platforms calling for world-wide press freedom. On September 17 Secretary of State Hull, who had been largely responsible for the success of the Moscow Conference the year before, observed, "The whole question of freedom of information has been under study in the Department of State for some time." Four days later, on September 21, the concept virtually became an American war aim when the Senate and the House, both of which had been fussing with half a dozen resolutions on the subject during the war, unanimously agreed upon Senate Concurrent Resolution 53, submitted by the chairman of the Committee on Foreign Relations, Tom Connally of Texas. Because it is a concise formulation of the sense of most resolutions on the subject, it is worth noting in full:

> *Resolved by the Senate (the House of Representatives concurring),* That the Congress of the United States expresses its belief in the world-wide right of interchange of news by news-gathering and distributing agencies, whether individual or associate, by any means, without discrimination as to sources, distribution, rates, or charges; and that this right should be protected by international compact.

Early in 1945 the Inter-American Conference at Mexico, taking action on hemispheric problems of war and peace, also adopted a resolution on the subject. It did not, unfortunately, have the force of an "international compact" as called for by the Connally resolution, for it merely recommended that individual countries take action. When a few months later the San Francisco Conference assembled to draft the United Nations Charter, the American delegation pressed for inclusion of a declaration on fundamental human freedoms, including freedom of the press. Some other delegations agreed, but the Charter as drafted and now in force makes no mention of freedom of the press or indeed any other specific freedom. It contents itself with the generalization that the purposes of the United Nations should include "promoting and encouraging respect for human rights and for fundamental freedoms for all." [11] The Economic and Social Council is authorized to make recommendations to that end.[12]

From that time to this writing not much has been done. When the United Nations Assembly held its organization meeting in London in January, 1946, Pedro López, Philippine delegate, proposed that the United Nations call an international conference on freedom of the press.[13] A subcommission of its Commission on Human Rights busied itself with an agenda for such a meeting, which was held in Geneva in March and April, 1948.[14] At the suggestion of the State Department, Richard J. Finnegan and Warren H. Pierce of the *Chicago Times* had prepared a draft treaty that in eight articles laid down the essentials that would insure free world news if only all members of the United Nations would adopt it.[15]

The convention succeeded beyond the modest hopes for it occasioned by the deep split between East and West. Three drafts of multilateral treaties, two draft articles for the projected United Nations Bill of Rights, and some 43 resolutions were adopted. In all of them there was considerable support for the Anglo-Saxon thesis of freedom. Only the so-called Indian Amendment, declaring that governments might set penalties for "systematic diffusion of deliberately false or distorted reports which undermine friendly relations between peoples and states," set a standard of official orthodoxy. The agreements have still to be accepted by the U.N., and ratified by the member nations. The principle that the gathering, transmission, and publication of news the world over shall be free still has a long way to go. But at long last a beginning has been made.

Despite the reluctance of some governments to trust the strategy of truth to which all protest their devotion, there came out of the war at least one proof of the vitality of the idea. It is not paradoxical that this development revealed its energy during the ultranationalistic years of war, for the high tide of wartime censorship made people thirst for accurate information. Hence it was only natural that American magazines and newspapers, and those of some other nations as well, should burst their national borders to find their way past all sorts of obstacles into the far corners of the world.

Formerly magazines, even where there was no language barrier, were read almost exclusively by national audiences. But during the war some of them, though little noticed among the noises of conflict, began to reach international audiences of considerable size. Where not many years before the war three millions of circulation in the United States and Canada was tops, at least one American magazine, the *Reader's Digest,* had even before the end of the war reached a circulation estimated at ten millions, of which one-fifth was reputed—the *Digest* itself is extremely chary of releasing figures—to be outside the United States and Canada. And from the end of the war the big-time American magazine publishers actively cultivated the world market.

One model for these ventures was the much abused Office of War Information's experiment in the international magazine field with *Victory* and *U.S.A.*, both issued in many editions in different languages. If the American public heard of *Victory* and *U.S.A.* at all—they were not distributed in this country or to our armed forces at congressional behest—it did so largely through the misrepresentations about them spread by Representative John Taber of Auburn, New York, and others as little able as he to comprehend what was happening in the world. These politicians and their editorial supporters called *Victory* and *U.S.A.* New Deal "propaganda," though after one false step by *Victory* the magazines did not even dare to print a picture of the President of the United States in fulfilling their task of describing America at war. The critics failed to specify, moreover, in what way these innocuous and wholly nonpolitical publications were to deliver the Arab wards of Cairo and Casablanca, the Turkish precincts of Istanbul, or the British election districts of London and Manchester to Mr. Roosevelt at election time.

Actually these magazines were far stuffier and slower than they ought to have been, thanks to the bureaucratic checks and balances under which they were put together. Nevertheless, they were snapped up by literate Arabs, Norwegians, Britishers, South Africans, Turks, Portuguese, Spaniards, Greeks, Frenchmen, Danes, Albanians, and others whenever they were placed on sale or surreptitiously distributed in their home towns. The reason was that, for all their defects, they offered glimpses through the fog of war of what was really happening in the miracle land of America. Just so since the war the State Department's Russian-language magazine *America,* circulated in the homeland of the iron curtain, has been snapped up at ten rubles a copy.

During the war, too, commercial magazines, particularly in view of the market offered by millions of homesick Americans in uniform all around the world, followed in the path of foreign publication that had been pioneered by the *Reader's Digest.* Even before the end of the war it had appeared in special British, Spanish, Portuguese, Swedish, Arabic, and Chinese editions. The others, relying more on American troops than on foreign audiences, clung largely to English editions, many in pony air-mail format. Among them were publications as diverse as *Air Force, Coronet, Detective Story, Superman, Cosmopoli-*

tan, Inside Detective, Popular Mechanics, the *New Yorker, Saturday Evening Post, Infantry Journal,* and *Science News Letter,* as well as news magazines like *Time, Life,* and *Newsweek.*[16] Newspapers too, like the *New York Times, Chicago Tribune, Chicago Sun,* and London *Daily Mail* experimented with overseas editions. In 1944 the London *Times* began to issue a full-sized air edition, printed by rotary presses in standard fashion on India paper that not only cut down weight but gave an impression remarkably clear by comparison with newsprint.

With the return of the troops, many of these wartime editions disappeared. And somehow the realities of peace dashed many a war-born dream, like that for an international *Colliers.*[17] But the news magazines put much effort into cultivating foreign readers on a permanent basis. Less than a year after the end of the war, *Time* boasted four main international editions, and soon thereafter *Life* began issuing a fortnightly edition for world-wide distribution.[18]

The habit thus being established in foreign readers of reaching for information from American or British publications, whether in English or in their own language, hints at the thirst for a more accurate understanding of the facts. This country is now the leader in international magazine publication, as in the international service of press associations. Inevitably more peoples are being exposed to the doctrine of publishing the news impartially and freely, at least to the extent common in this country. This means that, whatever the success of the crusade, in the years ahead, to get a full and free flow of competitive telegraphic news into the world's newspapers and radio, it will be backed by a growing stream of more leisured printed matter.

There is no need to analyze here the various elements that make up the strategy of truth. It must be clear from what has been said that they include at least the following: an end to censorship; independence of the media of information from government; free access to the news at its source; removal of barriers against importing printed matter, written matter, and pictures; removal of barriers against listening to foreign broadcasts; equality as among native and foreign reporters; unhindered travel everywhere by accredited correspondents; and cheap, nondiscriminating tele-communications rates.

Agreement upon these essentials is not difficult, in Anglo-Saxon countries at least. What is far more significant than this substantial unanimity of opinion, however, is the fact that even in Anglo-Saxon lands there are those who cast a fishy eye at the whole crusade for free world news, holding that it conceals a desire on the part of the American press associations, newspapers, and radio to grab more business for themselves. These agencies of information plead public service, the argument runs, but they serve the ends of private profit. Even worse, they propagate the private political and economic notions of their owners. As one cynic said to me: "Here is the old gag of the profit-motive industry demanding complete freedom from government control. These special privileges are demanded for the media of information on the naïve assumption that the media are dedicated to the public good and are, in effect, above reproach, both as corporations and as individuals. You know, of course, that this is baloney."

Is it? It would be difficult to document the thesis that our press associations preach a particular economic or political doctrine. Even so, is there not some reason for suspecting that the crusaders, who pose as knights clad in the shining armor of truth, are just so many businessmen seeking greater profits? After all, it could hardly have been pure idealism that prompted the Associated Press, at its annual meeting just before the end of the war, to place $1,000,000 a year at the disposal of Kent Cooper to spread the AP's services around the world.[19] And as the *Economist* of London wrote in sarcastic phrases:

> Mr. Cooper . . . experiences a peculiar moral glow in finding that his idea of freedom coincides with commercial advantage. In his ode to liberty there is no suggestion that when all barriers are down the huge financial resources of the American agencies might enable them to dominate the world. His desire to prevent another Goebbels from poisoning the wells will be universally applauded, but democracy does not necessarily mean making the whole world safe for the AP.[20]

In rebuttal the crusaders can point to history, with its lesson that the battle for liberty has ever been fired by the hope of private advantage. Were not Milton's own troubles over divorce the ultimate inspiration for *Areopagitica* itself? Did our American revolutionists seek to establish liberty for the Hottentots, or for themselves? In their rebellion against the British crown there was a heavy admixture of social revolution at home, prompted by the hope of economic gain. Englishmen and their descendants around the world never have been greatly interested in an abstract concept of liberty. They have always wanted specific liberties for themselves, and as often for economic as for spiritual reasons. What is there different, then, about carrying forward the battle for liberty now, until all around the world the nationalistic chains are struck off from the world's news? Suppose there is opportunity for commercial gain in striking down the barriers that block nation off from nation—is it not still a good idea? Finally, let us remember that the alternative is a continuation of, and perhaps even an accentuation of, the strategy of error.

Yet there lingers a doubt that will not down. Are we sure that Mr. Cooper's way is the only way to the strategy of truth? If we leave the crusade to the press associations, are we really going to establish the unbiased and adequate news all over the earth? Or will there still be gaps in the world's information? If by some miracle Russia should raise its iron curtain, would the capitalist American press associations report Communist activities with unqualified objectivity? If given the chance, will they pour a flood of free news into poor and backward countries as liberally as into those whose technical achievements and industrial populations provide a lush market?

Some of these doubts were formulated in the first report [21] of the Commission on Freedom of the Press, a private study group financed chiefly by *Time*, and administered by the University of Chicago. The report, written on the basis of an investigation made largely by non-newspaper personnel who had no ax to grind was devoted to the strategy of truth, and it made numerous proposals under three main heads: (1) improvement of physical facilities for international communication; (2) progressive removal of political barriers and economic restrictions on the free flow of international communications; and (3) improvement of the accuracy, representative character, and quality of news and news pictures.

Here was pointed out the fact, usually ignored by press association and newspaper crusaders for free international news, that expense or sheer lack of mechanical facilities keep news out of many less advanced corners of the world, even without political control by governments. As a partial remedy the report made the radical proposal that all American cable and radio telegraph companies, except the purely news-transmitting Press Wireless, be merged under government control and made to expand mechanical facilities. To press the removal of political barriers it urged incorporation into the framework of the United Nations a covenant "stating that the signatory nations believe in, and will do their utmost to bring about, the fullest possible flow across national borders of true information concerning all events and peoples."

To enforce this last proposal, which if put into effect would for the first time give the world free trade in news, the report suggested a mechanism that promptly called forth the ire of the newspaper professionals. The suggestion was that there be organized in all world news centers corps of correspondents including all newspaper and related workers, to handle disputes among members, or between members and host governments, subject to appeal to a unit of the United Nations Economic and Social Council—all with a view of enforcing high professional standards and scotching deliberate attempts to spread misinformation. The critics objected that history's attempts to enforce the dissemination of truth have always ended in supporting a particular orthodoxy, and so in suppressing truth rather than spreading it; the way to be free, they said, is to be free, and not to set up a disciplinary authority. This objection cannot lightly be dismissed. Yet the question remains: How are we going to prevent abuses of the strategy of truth? The newspapers are liberal with advice to labor unions that every right carries with it a corresponding responsibility. Is there no way to get the press to apply this principle to itself, to discipline its own members into exercising their freedom with a sober sense of their obligations? How are we to prevent the deliberate international window smashing that unquestionably exists? For if it is rarely to be found in the factual cables of the press associations, it is obviously marketed at a profit to large numbers of American xenophobes by columnists, commentators, and roving authors. How much does their product contribute to the strategy of truth?

Another family quarrel among believers in the strategy of truth has to do with whether the American press associations should deliver their news to the State Department, as they delivered it to the Office of War Information during the war, that the Department might cable or broadcast the American version of the truth to the dark corners of the earth where the press associations do not penetrate. Those who trust the press and distrust government point to the universal experience that government news, no matter how pure it may be, is always suspected as propaganda. As the *Manchester Guardian* said of our quarrel over the State Department plan, it was not clear whether its supporters appreciated "the rather important point that state propaganda is apt to increase, not dispel, doubts about the purity of motive." [22] Those who were troubled about the difficulty in getting information about this country spread throughout the postwar world pointed to the equally incontrovertible fact that the commercial agencies are not going to send their news into countries where it doesn't pay, and still less through the iron curtain, where they couldn't get it if they would.

During 1947 and at least early 1948 there took place an extraordinary battle over continuing the entire information program of the State Department, consisting of radio broadcasts, documentary and library services abroad, and the exchange of students and scholars. Favoring this program, known from the title of the broadcasts as the "Voice of America," was a host of witnesses. Among them were Secretary of State George C. Marshall, General Dwight D. Eisenhower, our ambassador to Russia, General Walter Bedell Smith, a great majority of the responsible newspapers, the Foreign Affairs Committee of the House, and even a committee appointed by the suspicious American Society of Newspaper Editors to investigate the program. In opposition was chiefly Kent Cooper, who now seemed to want free world news only for the press associations, and a hard-shell congressional opposition.

Why this opposition wanted to join hands with the late Dr. Goebbels, the unlamented cartel, and the Russia of today in hamstringing the effort to get news of America abroad was never made clear. Possibly somewhere underneath the surface of this intramural battle between two groups of Americans, both presumably believers in the strategy of truth, lay the present deep division between private business and government. Certainly few of the proponents of the Voice of America relished the idea of a permanent government propaganda service, even remembering that propaganda can be devoted to truth just as well as to falsehood. But that was not the issue. It was rather whether for the time being the government should fill in the cracks that private agencies ignore, whether in addition it should distribute abroad texts, documents, and similarly sober material that the press associations would find too dull for their wires and supplementary services, and, most important of all, whether it should seek to reach over the iron curtain by short-wave radio.

All one can say is that, in view of the present temper of the world, it would hardly be surprising if through the years to come Kent Cooper and his colleagues find themselves not alone in carrying information of all kinds to foreign lands. And if in the end government does settle down for a long period of years to carry a part of the burden, we shall simply have to wait and see whether, as always in the past, that leads to the distribution of nationalistically and politically colored news and views.

When all is said and done, what are the chances that the world, having invited disaster by failing to establish the strategy of truth after World War I, will force itself to establish that strategy in the uncertain years to come?

Wilbur Forrest, chairman of the American Society of Newspaper Editors' standing Committee on Freedom of Information, told the 1946 annual convention, "Nowhere in the world, not even in Russia, was the principle of a freer flow of news in the interests of postwar peace rejected." The practice, however, is something else again. On the occasion of the first anniversary of the 1945 round-the-world missionary trip of the society's three-man committee, *Editor & Publisher* solicited the help of press association correspondents abroad to survey the actual state of affairs in fifty-five nations, dominions, and dependencies.[23] This survey revealed a definite improvement over the days of the cartel, but it showed that we still have far to go before man everywhere has the right to know his world as best he can through media of information whose product is not colored officially. There are infinite gradations in this official control,

but one might take *Editor & Publisher's* report and summarize
it in a table like this:

FREE NEWS COUNTRIES		COUNTRIES CONTROLLING NEWS		
		SOME CONTROL	STRONG CONTROL	TOTAL
Europe	8	5	10	15
Middle East	0	5	1	6
Far East	5	6	1	7
Latin America	9	4	0	4
South Africa	1	0	0	0
Total	23	20	12	32

If this division is correct, then in 1946, the first year of peace,
only twenty-three countries practiced the strategy of truth, while
thirty-two still clung to one variety or another of the strategy of
error. One year later another survey [24] indicated that the trend
was away from, rather than toward, the wartime ideal of uncontrolled news. The degree of control changes almost from
day to day. But everywhere there is evidence that the ideal of a
free exchange of information, on a competitive basis, encounters
an unwillingness on the part of governments to trust the Anglo-
Saxon thesis that a complete absence of restrictions leads to the
most accurate information.

One can conclude only that universal adoption of the
strategy of truth, the great historic principle of freedom in new
form that would allow mankind to see itself far more clearly
than it does today, is still a long way off. But at least the world
is now conscious of it, and professes devotion to it. Perhaps, in
the new world that is struggling to be born, we shall yet have it.

CHAPTER XVI

NATIONS IN BLINDERS

OUR present information system consists of newspapers, magazines, radio, and moving pictures that are for the most part big-business enterprises sheltered behind a free-press principle designed to protect the individual eighteenth century pamphleteer. If we are dissatisfied with that situation, how can we better it?

The most conspicuous alternative is totalitarian journalism; and today totalitarian journalism means Russian journalism. It will not do to dismiss this Russian alternative as alien to the temperament and the traditions of the American people. In the first place, as we can see from the struggle for free world news examined in the last chapter, we now live in one world journalistically as well as physically; and the English-speaking peoples are a small minority in that world, a minority less and less insulated from the majority. We have but to look at contemporary Europe, moreover, to realize how strongly peoples there are pressing more powers upon government, because they see government as the only means of giving effect to their determination to rebuild their countries without at the same time allowing the prewar order of things to return. Nor is the tendency confined to Europe. In our own country it is obvious, from the prewar popularity of the New Deal and from our postwar struggle to find a workable balance between the old and the new that, however much we might like it otherwise, the simpler days of the past will never return.

So it is that those who in our time correspond to the great company of heroes who fought for our liberties, including freedom of the press, incline toward a view radically at variance with that of their predecessors. The liberties proclaimed in the Declaration and embedded in the Constitution—especially its Bill of Rights—were won by liberals; and a conspicuous mark of the liberal used to be his hostility to excessive government. But while our conservatives insist that this remains the identifying characteristic of the liberal today, and see nothing ridiculous in calling themselves liberals, a more fundamental quality of the liberal was and is his dissatisfaction with the *status quo,* his desire for change and improvement. He sees the golden age as lying ahead rather than in the past, and does not feel the businessman's inconsolable nostalgia for political and economic doctrines that have been outraced by events. Hence today's liberal has abandoned with hardly a qualm, as no longer suitable, his prototype's aversion to government. If he is hardly ready to reverse Jefferson's classic dictum to make it read, "That government is best which governs most," he does see in government the only force strong enough to challenge the concentration of wealth and power and the obstruction of social change that characterize most of our business enterprises.

At this point, however, our liberals stop. For when it comes to applying their favorite remedy, government, to journalism, the more discerning of them, at least, are no more enthusiastic than the rest of us. They find themselves uncomfortable at the thought of anything here resembling Soviet journalism, even in far milder form. But the awkward fact remains that government journalism is the only rival to our own that displays vitality. As we search for ways of correcting the defects of American journalism, we cannot afford to ignore it. And if we look beneath the surface of the Russian example we shall find, I think, something that interests us.

Before venturing into the mysteries of Soviet journalism, however, it will be desirable to stop briefly among the ruins of Dr. Goebbels's empire, for there we may pick up one or two pointers as to what makes government journalism effective. Let us check our prejudices at the door, and glance at a detail or two of the Nazi technics, in the professional spirit with which American staff officers examined the methods of their opposite numbers on the defeated *Wehrmacht*.

What the Nazis wanted from the press was set forth in their Twenty-five Points of 1920, the nearest thing they had to a political philosophy. Point XXIII demanded, among other things, "a German national press." To that end "all editors and contributors to newspapers employing the German language must be members of the nation," non-German newspapers must have special permission from the state to appear, and "non-Germans shall be prohibited by law from participating financially in or influencing German newspapers." [1]

The stress on a "German" press was based on the Nazis' ready acceptance of the premise that it is the function of a newspaper to be the organ of a particular point of view, to tell only a desired kind of truth. This is the direct opposite of the premise behind the Fourth Estate, which holds it to be the function of the press to serve as an independent auditor of the passing scene. It was not, therefore, the lies Goebbels published in the Nazi press that were fundamentally vicious. Rather it was his assumption that the press was a means for achieving the objectives of government.

This distinction may sound technical, almost picayune. But suppose for the sake of argument that Goebbels had happened to preach precisely our own prescription for the economic, political, and social ills of our time. Would we have objected then? Not unless we differed radically from the mass of men, who will cheerfully ignore any premise if the conclusion is agreeable. Yet a press devoted to preaching our own political gospel is no less evil, no less pernicious, than one preaching the gospel of the opposition; both identify themselves with particular causes, and in doing so betray the mission of journalism in society.

This is the first lesson we can learn from Dr. Goebbels. There are others. One is that the notorious secret daily orders he issued, which in the popular view were the means by which he made all German journals sing the official tune, were not, in fact, his primary instrument of control. When shortly before the war

I went to Germany to study the technics of control I was surprised to find that a far more powerful instrument was the Reich Chamber of Culture. This was an all-embracing, government-run combination of a trade association with a closed shop that controlled every possible approach to the German mind— from newspapers to moving pictures, from music to sculpture. The particular subdivision that dealt with the press was the Reichspressekammer, or Reich Press Chamber (and it had counterparts in radio, moving pictures, the theater, book publishing, art, and music). For comparison in the United States, imagine a merger of the American Newspaper Publishers Association, the American Society of Newspaper Editors, the American Newspaper Guild, and the mechanical unions into a single group which every last worker in the field, whether publisher, editor, advertising man, reporter, linotyper, pressman, or clerical worker, is forced to join.

This insistence on universality is what gave Dr. Goebbels his stranglehold on German news. No one could write for or edit any German newspaper or other publication without joining the writers' group of the press chamber, known as the Reich Union of the German Press. For under the journalists' law promulgated by Goebbels on October 4, 1933, it became a condition of employment for newspaper editorial workers to belong. The provisions of the law, especially Article 5,[2] were designed to make certain that only persons looked upon with favor by the Nazi hierarchy should be free to engage in newspaper work. Not only must they be orthodox politically in the first place, but they must remain constantly on their good behavior. Without a membership card in the great Nazi union of newspaper workers they could not work. And if at any time a newspaperman transgressed against the letter of the many decrees, rules, regulations, and daily propaganda orders, or even against the honor of a party dignitary in a regional office or in Berlin, he risked losing his membership card. Thereafter he was free to dig ditches or sell shoestrings for a living, but he could never again do a day's newspaper work.

The power of this closed-shop principle is incredible. Each newspaperman who works under such a system is haunted by the knowledge that by a single offense he risks his professional future and his livelihood.

The resulting fear made the non-party editor or writer toe the line as readily as the most fanatic Nazi zealot, for a frightened self-censorship set stricter standards than Goebbels himself. I discovered in talking with German newspapermen, not only those inwardly unconverted to the Nazi cause but also those who were party men, that the threat of expulsion made workers in the ranks and responsible editors alike constantly overcautious. They would refuse to print even a DNB dispatch, which was official and therefore presumably safe, if they sensed in it the slightest deviation from the previous official line.

The extreme pressure to stay on the safe side accounted for the monotone in the German press that, surprisingly enough, used to trouble Dr. Goebbels. He had avoided taking the entire German press into the party ownership precisely to preserve at least the outward signs of journalistic individuality. Yet here they were all, party organs and the rest alike, singing a single Nazi note. Repeatedly he chid the editors to be more colorful, individualistic, and aggressively varied. But always the threat of losing the right to work held them in line.

Goebbels had, of course, other means of control. His empire rested on three legs, of which the most powerful was the Chamber of Culture and the most notorious the Reichsministerium für Volksaufklärung und Propaganda. The third leg was the Nazi party propaganda organization, which kept right on functioning after party and government had for all practical purposes become one. All three—Chamber of Culture, Propaganda Ministry, and party organization—were closely intermeshed both at the top and down through the ranks, a fact signalized by Goebbels's position as head of them all—government minister, party press chief, and president of the Chamber.

We can learn from the Goebbels experiment, then, that when once one takes the plunge implicit in the liberal's cure for today's ills, and uses government as a corrective for the defects in journalism, one has started on a road whose end is frightening. This is the one respect in which the *Time* University of Chicago Commission on Freedom of the Press seems to me to err. It recommends that the government should make up for the errors and omissions of our press by going into the news business itself. It argues that there is nothing in the First Amendment or in our democratic tradition to prevent the government from participating in mass communications. The government should therefore "state its own case, . . . supplement private sources of information, and . . . propose standards for private emulation." And this, the commission blandly says, "is not dangerous to the freedom of the press." [3] In view of what happened when Dr. Goebbels embarked on this road, the rest of us may not be so sure.

Nor is the prospect of government news all that leads in this direction. The example of the powerful Nazi Chamber of Culture, little known and little understood in this country, might well give pause to the more sober heads in the American Newspaper Guild. One wonders whether the Guild membership is aware of what it headed for when it brought a labor union into the Fourth Estate. The Guild, as we shall see in the next chapter, sprang up in the great depression as the natural reaction of reporters, copy readers and other editorial men against the short-sighted mistreatment long given them by the newspaper publishers of America. Despite its continuing, aggressive pressure for more inclusive organization, the Guild obviously has a long way to go before it matches Dr. Goebbels's success in regard to universal membership; but its use of hard-boiled union tactics to gather ever more newspaper workers into the fold, and its reaching out for office and clerical employees in order to achieve more power, hardly constitutes resistance to the trend in Dr. Goebbels's direction. No doubt it is so busy fighting recalcitrant publishers that it has little time to worry about where success in its efforts must take journalism. But the Guild's leaders might well explain what, if they were left to their own devices, would keep them from gathering every last newspaper worker into the ranks. Once that goal was reached the Guild would still not include the publishers, who were forced into Dr. Goebbels's association of both workers and managers; but it would come close to Dr. Goebbels's subdivision for editorial workers, the Reichsverband der Deutschen Presse.

Without any sign of awareness, then, the Guild, by putting its energy into a drive for universality, is striving for what Dr. Goebbels achieved. Its motives obviously contrast sharply with his; but the Guild leadership might look ahead and reflect upon the political possibilities inherent in the social instrument it is creating as a by-product of its efforts to help the rank and file of newspaper employees.

For all the vaunted German efficiency and Nazi ruthlessness, Soviet journalism makes Dr. Goebbels seem an amateur in government control of the minds of the people. Whereas in Germany the Nazis took over a press that was in full being, the Soviet journalists started almost from scratch. The maximum circulation of all newspapers under the czars, just before the First World War, was 2,700,000. By 1940—that is, within a quarter-century—the Soviet government had raised this to 38,-000,000.[4] This transformation represents an achievement as stupendous as the industrialization of Russia of which it is a part. Or perhaps we should say that it seems so, for the figure of 38,000,000 circulation comes from Gosplan, the state planning agency. As with so much else concerning Soviet Russia, however, one wonders what may lie behind the official figures. And no less an authority than Joseph Stalin, in reporting on the cultural advance of Soviet Russia, cited "annual newspaper circulation" as being only 7,092,400 in 1938–1939,[5] a modest total compared with 38,000,000.

Whatever its exact dimensions, the Russian press differs sharply from ours in being almost bare of general news. It is largely functional rather than reportorial. That is, it consists for the most part of organs devoted to the interests of particular economic or social groups. One of the big dailies is *Red Star,* the Army's publication. Another is *Labor,* the trade-union paper. There are many others devoted to agriculture, the various industries, and a vast array of technical, cultural, and sporting organizations. In this devotion to a particular cause, to the interests of a particular group, we see another evidence of the basic assumption we noted in Nazi journalism, that it is the task of a publication to promote a particular interest, to propagandize something, rather than to serve as a neutral reporter of the passing scene.

Even where general news is published, as in the great Moscow dailies that are published simultaneously in other cities, there is a sharp difference from American practice. The Soviet press

follows the Continental habit of disdaining not only comic strips
and household hints but also the vast body of local, national,
and foreign news, trivial or substantial, that makes our papers
what they are. There are few items on crime—except crimes
against the state—no scandal, society, or professional sports
news, and, since there are no stock markets, no stock-market or
financial news. All this reflects the fact that to the Soviets news
is news only if it has social significance. Accordingly, speeches,
Communist Party pronouncements, reports of factories completed or production quotas exceeded, news of drives or exhibitions, resolutions of workers' committees, and technical or
industrial items that in America would be hidden in corporation
reports or trade journals, are front-page stuff in Russia. And
who is to say that the affairs of a Mary Astor, Errol Flynn, or
Charlie Chaplin are more suitable to page one than the breath-
less details of what the nonferrous metals industry is doing?

Russian newspapers now operate under the third of the Soviet
constitutions, the one adopted in 1936. In a glowing bill of
rights that begins by guaranteeing to the Soviet citizen the right
to employment, security, rest, and education, this constitution
says:

ARTICLE 125: In accordance with the interests of the working
people, and in order to strengthen the socialist system, the citizens
of the USSR are guaranteed by law:

  (a) Freedom of speech;
  (b) Freedom of the press;
  (c) Freedom of assembly and meetings;
  (d) Freedom of street processions and demonstrations.

This, together with another article recognizing freedom of
religious worship and of antireligious propaganda, is clearly
adapted from our own First Amendment. There is, however,
an additional paragraph in the Soviet free-speech article. It says:

These rights of citizens are ensured by placing at the disposal of
the working people and their organizations printing shops, supplies
of paper, public buildings, the streets, means of communication,
and other material requisites for the exercise of these rights.[6]

Behind this final paragraph lies the Soviet axiom that no freedom of any kind is possible until the slate is wiped clean of capitalism and a fresh start made with a socialist state that will eventually progress toward the classless dream-world of pure Communism. According to Soviet dogma, the fact that a socialist state exists in Russia guarantees real freedom as distinct from the illusory political freedom of democracy. To us, this thesis, which holds that freedom of the press is guaranteed by the fact that the state puts presses, paper, news services, and other facilities at the disposal of the people-journalists, is meaningless. Such a system permits only those upon whom the government looks with favor to publish news. To the Soviet mind, however, our own press freedom is meaningless, because its facilities are owned by a handful of capitalists who are themselves free, but who withhold that freedom from the mass of the people by forcing their hirelings to write only what they, the capitalists, want. To hold this view it is of course necessary to ignore the fact that in the United States the Communists can say what they please, as witness the *Daily Worker* and the *New Masses,* and that papers as different as, say, the *Washington Post* and the *Chicago Tribune* can and do say what they please. It is also necessary to ignore the fact that similar diversity in Russia would mean the death of the editors. Our liberals rightly complain that papers like the *Chicago Tribune* give far too little news that runs contrary to their editorial policy. But an equal amount of unorthodox news in a Russian paper is unthinkable. As the Soviet jurist Nikolai Krylenko—who seems since to have disappeared from circulation like so many others—himself said of the admirable but in practice largely ignored 1936 constitution:

We don't wish to be hypocrites. No worker, collective farmer or any other working person will object to the fact that any persons who might wish to bring back the capitalist system are not given either free speech or free press by our Constitution.[7]

This system, under which only those favored by the ruling group in state and Communist Party are allowed to practice journalism, is reenforced by the fact that behind both stands the criminal code, violations of which are subject to penalties ranging from imprisonment to execution by a firing squad and confiscation of all property.[8] Murder is not a capital offense in Russia. Attacks on the regime are, though it has been reported that the death penalty in peacetime has been abolished.[9]

Still another reenforcement making sure that no unpleasant notes will be sounded in the Russian press is Glavit, the supreme and ubiquitous censorship agency. According to a decree of the Soviet of People's Commissars of June 6, 1931, which as far as I can discover is still in force, Glavit was set up to maintain "all kinds of politico-ideological, military, and economic control over printed words, manuscripts, copies, pictures, etc., destined for publication or distribution, and also over radio broadcasts, lectures, and exhibitions." Glavit, which has agents in every corner of Soviet society, is furthermore empowered to forbid the editing, publishing, and distribution of works:

a) that contain agitation and propaganda against the Soviet Government and the dictatorship of the proletariat;
b) reveal state secrets;
c) arouse nationalistic and religious fanaticism;
d) have a pornographic character.

With this goes authority to control literature and all other means of public expression in early as well as finished stages; to grant or withdraw permission to open a publishing house or a newspaper or magazine; to control exports and imports of printed matter; to examine complaints, prepare lists of forbidden works, and bring transgressors to account; to maintain agents in publishing houses, newspaper and magazine offices, printing houses, radio broadcasting organizations, telegraph agencies, customhouses, post offices, and similar institutions. Always a specified number of copies of anything intended for distribution must go to Glavit before publication, and the most insignificant bit of printed matter, whether a theater program or a poster in a factory, must carry "the permissive visa of the Glavit or its local organs" in order to be published.[10]

Surely it is not possible to find here a loophole through which the slightest heresy, already made impossible by the constitutional system of allowing only safe journalists, could creep. No wonder that Soviet Russia does not find it necessary to ape Dr. Goebbels—who, incidentally, started in business long after the Russians were a going concern—by setting up a Chamber of

Culture and making all connected with journalism join it. Such a device is wholly unnecessary. Even without it the Soviet press performs magnificently as a willing and harmonious organ. Instead of the cacophony of voices that still echoes lustily in our democracy despite the theory that the boss capitalists permit only their tune to be sung, all is smoothly ordered in Russia. An American reporter, arriving in Moscow after the war with a fresh eye, had this to report:

The Soviet citizen, pushing through the crowds in the Moscow subway these hot mornings on his way to work, should be a very happy man. From reading his newspapers and listening to the radio he knows that things almost everywhere are worse than in the Soviet Union and that although his motherland is again faced with the twin bugbears of imperialism and fascism, it is protected by the mightiest army in the world.[11]

So it always was in the home of Communism. Remember the amazing way in which the war that in 1939 and 1940 had been one between grasping rival imperialisms miraculously transformed itself, on the day Hitler attacked Russia, into a glorious fight of the freedom-loving peoples against the fascist assassins of Hitlerite Germany. These surprising reversals are made far more readily than we could imagine with our own press, by virtue of the fact that there simply is no other source of information than the government press and radio. So be it:

> *Petruchio:* I say it is the moon.
> *Katharina:*   I know it is the moon.
> *Petruchio:* Nay, then you lie: it is the blessed sun.
> *Katharina:* Then, God be bless'd, it is the blessed sun;
> But sun it is not, when you say it is not;
> And the moon changes even as your mind.
> What you will have it named, even that it is.

What has been said above represents the orthodox American view of Soviet journalism, and beyond all question that view reflects the truth. What we overlook is the fact that it is not quite the whole truth. To this extent, therefore, we ourselves hold a distorted view of Russian journalism. Let us, then, without taking back one word of what has been said, look under the surface for the rest of the truth, which may reveal a factor that could be helpful in raising the standard of our own journalism.

One peculiarity of Russian newspapers that does not figure in the popular American view, though we have been told about it often enough, is the doctrine of self-criticism. This is a form of denouncing public persons and practices that is, to be sure, hardly vigorous enough to satisfy Americans, to whom the right to denounce President, Congress, and the headliners in any and all corners of American life is as necessary and as natural as it is inalienable. Russian self-criticism stops safely short of the top. Stalin receives a universal public adulation that seems to us the most nauseating kind of lickspittle, though the Russians don't seem to mind it. The top hierarchy under Stalin, too, is immune from public reproach, and policy laid down in the Kremlin is as inviolate as any primitive tribal taboo. But as far as the doctrine of self-criticism goes it is real. Walter Duranty, on the basis of his many years of observation, once summed it up in these words:

Self-criticism is the salt in the Soviet home propaganda pie. It enables any writer or speaker, high or low, to take a violent and enjoyable crack at almost anyone or anything, provided he sticks to concrete facts or remains "objective," as the Russians call it, and refrains from the unwisdom—or positive danger—of ideological criticism or covert attacks on the "party line," which would brand him with heresy and disgrace.

The Russians by nature have a streak of anarchic iconoclasm, be they never so loyal communists, and "self-criticism" gives them welcome relief from the stark rigidity of Stalinism, a relief no less delightful because it is dangerous. There have been cases when overzealous critics have been compelled to make ignominious retractions or have lost their jobs or have been expelled from the party.

But it is a splendid safety valve, none the less, and so widely used by the Moscow press in particular, which is closest, of course, to the Kremlin, that a foreign observer often wonders whether everything is "going to the bowwows," so long and grievous is the tale of mismanagement, waste, and bureaucratic error. Its chief beauty is that few save the very highest dignitaries are spared from blame.[12]

Here then is a method of achieving, within totalitarian limits, the healthy and human privilege of calling down one's betters.

It has the added advantage of providing a totalitarian press with some, at least, of the flavor and variety that Goebbels sought vainly to instill into German journalism.

There is another Russian practice that attracts the Soviet reader. This consists in reinforcing official government news with a system of amateur journalism on the part of readers. Even the great *Pravda* contains newsy items sent in by humble Bolsheviks in the factories or on collective farms or in the army. This not only makes for items as readable as the letter column in our own home-town papers, but stimulates among readers an intense loyalty toward their press. For these amateur contributions give to Soviet readers a sense of personal participation in the work of their press. Such a direct personal interest, as distinct from a spectator interest, is unknown to the readers of even our smaller and therefore more intimate American dailies. Our journals are technically far superior to the Russian ones, but somehow the Russians have won a devotion from their readers that American papers used to enjoy, but have to a considerable extent lost as they became bigger and more impersonal. Many an American publisher rests content, vastly impressed by the gratifyingly high, and ever higher, circulation figures of his paper. All too often, however, large circulations testify merely to the completeness of news coverage, the popularity of features, and the lack of rivals. The invisible and imponderable quality of devotion on the part of readers is something else again. Its existence in Russia while many American readers are cynical about their own press gives to Russian journalism, for all its totalitarian halter, a seasoning of strength that Americans might well envy.

Here we approach that positive quality in the Soviet press from which American newspapers might learn a valuable lesson. For the good will and loyalty of Russia's people to the Russian press is an outward sign of the inward substance that Soviet apologists have in mind when they insist that they, and not we, have a really free press. To us Russia's totalitarianism makes this a meaningless boast. To the Russians it derives naturally from the Soviet conception of the state, so difficult for us to understand. This conception holds that, because landlords and capitalists no longer exist in Russia, therefore everyone must be a worker; and therefore in turn there can be no occasion for what is to us the *sine qua non* of democracy, freedom for all kinds of opinion and all kinds of political groupings and parties. As one Soviet apologist put it, "In the Soviet Union there is nothing to warrant the existence of several parties, since classes with radically different interests no longer exist in our country." [13] When everyone is a worker, how can a dissident voice represent anything but treason?

That much has the familiar doctrinaire ring. But how about this further observation by the Soviet apologist? "One cannot seriously discuss the democracy of a regime and at the same time close one's eyes to the main thing: Whom does it serve? For whose benefit does it exist—for the benefit of the people or their bitterest enemies, the traitors and betrayers of the people's interests?" It is, of course, a Russian dogma that there must be class warfare as long as there is capitalism, and that capitalist countries are controlled by "traitors and betrayers of the people's interests." While that dogma no doubt goes over big behind Russia's iron curtain, it is denied by our own experience. Nevertheless the question, "Whom does the press serve?" gets to the point. Brooks Atkinson, for ten months after the war Moscow correspondent of the *New York Times,* wrote on his return a series of articles whose candor earned him a standard denunciation in *Pravda,* plus the special epithet "untalented calumniator," [14] as well as a Pulitzer Prize. But in his articles he made these not unfriendly statements: "As far as I know, the government is not imposed on the people against their will, nor is it a corrupt government that puts the personal interests of any one group ahead of what are regarded as the true interests of the state. . . . My impression is that the people of the Soviet Union generally trust and respect the wisdom and integrity of their leaders. . . . I know of no active, organized opposition to the government. . . . Apart from the normal grumbling about the hardness of living, the people seem to believe in their government." [15]

This repeats the testimony of other observers, sometimes directed more specifically toward the press. But then, press and government are for practical purposes one. Totalitarianism and all, therefore, the mass of Soviet citizens is to a large extent convinced that their press represents their interests and fights on their side.

Here is something that American publishers and editors might well mull over. For there is ample evidence that the American public, by and large, has no such conviction as to its own press. To the Soviet question, "What press have you in the United States that is wholly devoted to the interests of the people?" every American publisher would of course answer with a resounding, "Mine." But does the public agree? As noted in Chapter VI, the technological and industrial development of the last century has made the American press a largely impersonal, corporate institution from which the ordinary citizen feels himself remote. He believes in a free press, and when put to it he will fight for it. But by and large freedom of the press means to him a benefit for the press, and not for him.

This is in sharp contrast to our earlier days. Then the subscriber was willing to do battle for his paper as for himself, because he, like the Soviet citizen of today, was convinced that its sole concern was not to give him reading matter—which our press today does superbly well—but to fight his battles in the public arena. Today his paper seems instead like a journalistic General Motors, whose products are technically excellent but whose economic and political interests are not his own and are, indeed, often in sharp conflict with his own. The managers of industry and finance, the store owners and the entrepreneurs big and little, together with their women in the better residential districts, no doubt, find that the American newspaper tends to voice their sentiments. But the vast body of citizens seems to think otherwise. And it is out of this fact that there arises the conviction of today's liberals, backed by a voting majority of the people, that with some notable exceptions the American press today does not serve the people as a whole, but rather the favored few. And despite the fact that those favored few, moving in their own agreeable home and business surroundings, seem to themselves to be many, proportionately to the population as a whole they are insignificant.

If there is, then, anything we can learn from Russian journalism, it has nothing to do with state ownership or all the totalitarian trappings of which the Russians boast. All these are alien and detestable to our deepest instincts. What we have to learn, or rather relearn, is that the press ought to be devoted to the hopes and fears and desires and needs of the bulk of the

American people. Many of our publishers no doubt sincerely believe that they have the people's interests at heart. They have convinced themselves that, if the people do not go along with the doctrines preached in their editorials and columns, it is because the people have been seduced by demagogues propagandizing a false and alien political philosophy. The anomaly of this situation, in which the publishers picture themselves as devoted to the real welfare of the public while the people themselves are convinced that the publishers are often doing the opposite, seems to escape many of these who control our journalism.

The psychopathic Russian fear of an opposition, the existence of the ubiquitous censorship agency Glavit, the whole structure of the police state, indicate that the spontaneous devotion of the Russian people to the regime and its press is something less than perfect. Nevertheless, American authorities who lived in Russia before the iron curtain clanked down tell us that there is an element of popular allegiance to the Russian press. Such a faith is an indefinable and imponderable but priceless ingredient of journalism. It is one that ought to thrive far more readily in a free country than in one that is as harsh and brutal a tyranny as the world has ever seen. If our journalism is to discharge its ethical and moral as well as its technical responsibilities, it must carry the sympathy and loyalty of its readers to new heights. But how?

ALTERNATIVES

ANY attempt to improve the American press must begin with the concept of the Fourth Estate, which totalitarian journalism denies. That concept is the Anglo-Saxon contribution to the theory of journalism. It remains the one hope of a more adequate journalism in the future. As we noted long since, in Chapter IV, the Fourth Estate is by definition apart from all the rest of society. It should be free from even emotional ties to any political party, any group interest, any social or economic class. It lives in a world of its own, turning restlessly inquisitive eyes on all the other estates that make up the world of men. By virtue of being thus detached it serves the whole of society with unprejudiced testimony as to what is going on, and so helps us all to have in our minds at least a reasonable approximation of the real world we live in.

That is the ideal. But as always when man seeks to realize an ideal, the vision vanishes at his attempt to grasp it. It slips away again into the future and mocks and beckons him on from there. Because it beckons, and because our standard press seems unconscionably slow in heeding its call, many men have put forward many proposals for getting closer to the vision than we are now. Among all the possibilities, these stand out:

236

A municipal press. This envisions newspapers owned and operated by a city, just as subways or power plants may be owned by a city.

A yardstick press. This calls for government-supported newspapers comparable to the TVA, against which the performance of the private press might be measured.

A professionalized press. This envisions academic and other training for newspapermen, plus standards of admission to the profession comparable to bar examinations for lawyers.

A press without advertising. Here the idea is to make subscribers pay the whole cost of running a newspaper, and thus to free it from the need of earning its bread and butter by selling space to advertisers.

An endowed press. This somewhat similar concept envisions newspapers that are independent of their readers as well as their advertisers because, like our great private universities and research foundations, they are philanthropically underwritten.

A church press. Since the church is already devoted to our ethical as well as spiritual welfare, why not let it manage the press for the good of the community as a whole?

A labor press. This is an obvious counterbalance to the heavy concentrations of capital that control the existing press.

As far as I know this list comprises all reasonably practical suggestions for making a better press. Even so, we can dismiss most of them as obviously unsuitable. The municipal newspaper, for example, cannot meet the basic democratic requirement that the press be free from government. Its advocates falsely assume an analogy between journalism and the public utilities. Does not the newspaper operate, they ask, just like the railroad, the telegraph, or the gas company, in a primary field of public interest? It may not quite be a natural monopoly, but economically there is room for only relatively few newspapers. This takes away competition, and with it the compulsion to make the surviving papers serve all the people. Why not, then, regulate the newspapers as we regulate the power companies? Or, better, why not do what many American municipalities have done with power plants, and let the city own a newspaper? All this conveniently overlooks the unique characteristic of journalism that earned it alone, of all the business and professions, constitutional immunity from government. Perhaps that is why, even though the idea of public utility journalism is as old as that of regulating the railroads, it has for all practical purposes not been tried in the United States. In 1912 a weekly *Municipal News* was launched in Los Angeles, but Alfred M. Lee, the sociologist-historian of journalism, says of it only that it "was labeled 'that damned socialist thing' and killed by the general-circulation dailies." [1] What the murder weapon was, or what the evidence that it was murder and not death from natural causes, he does not say.

In noting that public utility or municipal journalism violates the principle of independence from government, we have already, I think, disposed of the suggestion for a yardstick press, a TVA of journalism. It is the identical suggestion, dressed in the clothes of state or Federal rather than municipal control. Like TVA itself, a single Federal newspaper, while it would no doubt raise an even more violent political tornado, might be interesting to watch. But here again, if we enlarge the suggestion into a substitute for the present daily newspapers of America, we get an even more centralized and therefore more nearly totalitarian journalism than under the more diversified municipal pattern. Finally, those who are so insensitive to democratic fundamentals as to believe that the inherent evil of government journalism would be outweighed by the good of a journalistic loud-speaker freely available to an administration they approve, should ask themselves what they would think of it were the opposition in power.

Let us therefore retreat from the uncomfortable proximity to totalitarian journalism, and pass on to the next alternative, a professionalized journalism. This has been suggested by reasoning from the fact that formerly both doctors and lawyers, like many newspapermen still, picked up their training as they went along. Today doctors and lawyers are trained in professional schools. Not only that, but before they are turned loose upon the public they must pass bar examinations or be licensed. The whole progress of medicine from witch doctoring to a science practiced on a high ethical plane is inspiring. Is there not here a pattern for journalism?

There is not. Beyond question our news staffs would benefit from further professionalization if all it meant were a wider educational background and higher technical competence, per-

haps acquired at one of the better journalism schools that have
now existed for a generation. But professionalization comparable to that of law or medicine can be dismissed offhand, like
the alternatives already reviewed, because it involves examination and licensing. This, the first shackle the authorities of
church and state put upon printing in its infancy, would mean
giving up every man's right to have his say in print regardless
of his training. We cannot license expression without killing
democracy.

In another sense, however, there is validity in the thesis that
professionalization might improve our journalism. It is largely
held within newspaper ranks that the chief fault of our press
is that the working newspapermen, who in their professional
careers have rubbed up against all sorts and conditions of men
and tend as a result to view the lot with a detachment born of
disillusionment, are not allowed to control our newspapers.
They are kept under the thumb of the businessmen who predominate among owners and publishers, who are self-interested
members of an economic aristocracy rather than detached and
objective reporters.

To find a way of giving control to the editorial professionals,
however, is not easy. One brief effort to do so was incidental
to the early history of the American Newspaper Guild, which
some of its pioneers conceived as a banding together of specialists
to promote higher ethical and technical standards. Unfortunately, this goal proved unattractive in comparison with the
economic appeal of labor unionism. In fact, the editorial employees of our newspapers, who had been indifferent toward all
the earlier sporadic attempts to organize them, entered the
Guild only under the stimulus of the great depression that began
in 1929, and at the specific invitation of the National Industrial
Recovery Act. Their reasons were well summed up in this statement, made in 1933 by reporters from three Cleveland dailies:

Squeezed between the pressures of advertisers and stockholders,
between exorbitant tolls of syndicates and press services, and the
unionized requirements of the mechanical trades, newspaper editorial employes have from the industry's infancy been the most
notoriously exploited of all producer groups in this country which
require similar standards of intelligence, skill and industry. They
have submitted to this not only uncomplainingly but in fact quite

happily, clinging to an old local room tradition which probably
never had any basis of fact whatever. It is now time that local room
staffs start living and working for something more than the byline
and pat-on-the-back. NRA holds out to them their first bona fide
opportunity to go after realities.[2]

The motive, in short, was far more to gain economic protection than to infuse spirit into the ethics and standards of
journalism. And it is difficult to view the origin of the Guild
without concluding that there was ample justification for an
economic rather than a professional motive. Heywood Broun
used to tell of a publisher who, when a city inspector insisted
that a fire escape be installed in his plant, asked angrily, "What
do you mean by interfering with the freedom of the press?"
Many of our publishers still tend to run for the shelter of the
First Amendment, shouting, "Free press! Free press!" every
time someone tries to better working conditions in any corner of
their plant. And the record shows that it took the Guild's war
against the publishers to force most of what has been achieved,
even on non-Guild newspapers, in better pay, greater job security, and a shortening of the sixty-six-hour week that was
common when I was first a reporter, during the twenties.

Still the publishers have not learned. In 1941 one young
reporter left Stanford University on the eve of his senior year,
during which he was to be editor of the undergraduate daily,
to enter the Air Corps as a private. In the Army, where he
served in China as a non-flying officer through some of the grim
days with the Fourteenth Air Force, he married and had a son;
and more than four years later he returned, a captain, to civilian
life. Finishing his work for the A.B. from Stanford, he found a
job as a reporter at twenty-six. Because of the housing shortage
he had to leave his small family temporarily in Palo Alto. Shortly
after going to work he wrote me why he felt there was still an
urgent need for collective bargaining for editorial employees:

The fellow I share a room with has just gotten a job working in
a brewery, with no previous experience and on virtually the same
shift I work here, at a wage of $71 a week. By contrast, I'm now
getting $32.50. Five-year men are getting $66. I realize that low
pay for newspapermen is an established tradition, but I certainly
don't believe that the condition should continue. After all, any

reporter shares a great deal of responsibility to the reading public, much more so, in actual practice, than an executive. Naturally, the executive is paid for experience and superior ability, but I do believe reporters and desk men should receive pay equivalent to the all-round importance of the work they do.

More than two decades of experience and observation have convinced me that the primary organizers of the American Newspaper Guild were, and are today—little as they intend it— the newspaper publishers of America. The Guild movement did not take hold because newspapermen became infected with whatever you may care to prefix to "ism." Nor did it take hold primarily because of the New Deal, or even because of the social atmosphere this generation breathes. It took hold because the men in the newsroom became convinced that they had been left behind in journalism's progress from the one-man days to the corporate big time.

If the Guild's origin is easy to understand, its present status, and still more its future possibilities, arouse less sympathy. We noted in the previous chapter the dangerous similarity between the Guild's militant struggle for an ever greater degree of organization and Dr. Goebbels's principal weapon of press control. Not only that, but the Guild has long since become an out-and-out labor union. Only one who has experienced it personally can know what it means to have a good man become more interested in the union than in his work, and to see him put the fire in his soul into the cause of the union rather than into his job. Often, indeed, the man involved is himself only partly aware of his sharply lowered usefulness, because he continues to go dutifully through the motions of doing his work. If the employer dismisses such a man he finds that the union runs to the law for help, and in all probability gets it, on the ground that the firing was animated by hostility to the union.

A final reason against anything remotely resembling greater professionalization of the press, in the sense of turning it over to an employee group like the Guild, is that to do so would hardly give the press greater independence than it has now. If newspapers are too closely identified with economic and political Tories, how shall we change matters by attaching them to a militant proletariat? Granted the temper of the times, indeed, the change would lessen rather than increase editorial independence. The concept of a pressure group like the Guild in charge of reporting and interpreting the news is grotesque. However necessary the publishers in their blindness made the Guild as an economic countermeasure, a labor union has no more business in the Fourth Estate than any other selfish interest.

Well, then, surely there ought to be some way to circumscribe the property interest in so important a public institution as the press without falling into the trap of government ownership or control, and without violating the fundamental premise of the Fourth Estate. So many have thought; and out of their thinking has come the proposal for newspapers without advertising. We noted in Chapter VI that, contrary to the popular shibboleth, the corrupting power of advertising is not the main source of the trouble. We saw that it was the newspapers' independent stake in the existing economic order rather than advertising pressure that made newspapers tend to look at the political scene with conservative eyes. Even so, what would happen if we achieved an adless press?

Let us remember that advertising is at least as old as printed journalism. It simply so happened that the newspaper-reading public has, since the beginning, refused to pay the cost of the news it demands. This is a curious reflection on man as a social and political animal. Unconsciously he realizes that he cannot live in the complex modern world without a mental reproduction of it in his head that the press helps him to build; but, overwhelming though his dependence on the press is for this service, he refuses to pay for it in full. He will buy a cocktail or an evening at the movies for more than half a dollar, but he will not pay the ten or fifteen cents daily that his newspaper would cost if it had to earn its living without the help of advertising or some other subsidy.

During the middle thirties, Clarence Leighton, editor of the *Palladium-Times* in Oswego, New York, found a way to dramatize this fact. He calculated that each of his subscribers received, during the course of a year, a volume of newsprint paper that weighed 70½ pounds. The cost of this white paper alone, without a penny for the enormous expense of gathering, editing, and printing the news, was $22. Yet the subscriber paid only $9.36, or 18 cents a week. He did not, in short, pay even half the cost of the newsprint, let alone the cost of the news printed on it. The figures have changed since the 1930's, but the principle still obtains. It is an accepted standard that a newspaper should earn roughly one-third of its revenue from what its readers pay. Another way of putting it is that a newspaper whose circulation revenue pays for both newsprint and the circulation department's own expenses can be well satisfied. So, while we damn the press for soiling its purity with advertising, it is we ourselves who force it to do so. As Walter Lippmann once remarked,[3] one might think that what the public means by a free press is one it gets for nothing.

Journalistic history does indicate that when most papers cost too much for the masses and are editorially too unsympathetic with them, then a James Gordon Bennett or a Joseph Medill Patterson will jump into the breach with a cheap paper. Still, the rising costs of the twentieth century have brought a trend toward charging the newspaper reader more for what he gets; and so far he has not rebelled. Here are some figures, published a few years ago by the American Newspaper Publishers Association, as to the wartime effect on the single-copy price of our daily newspapers: [4]

Year	1¢	2¢	3¢	4¢	5¢	7¢	10¢	25¢	Total
1942	9	185	735	32	806	4	5	1	1,777
1943	4	84	556	175	899	3	5	1	1,727
1944	3	62	398	279	974	3	5	1	1,725

The trend away from two- and three-cent papers toward four- and five-cent papers is clear. It has become stronger since the war. Another ANPA study in 1947 showed 1,252 American dailies, the overwhelming majority, selling for a nickel.[5] And while this rise was in good part caused by the postwar inflation, it at least leaves the hope that at some time in the future the press will extract from its readers full payment for what they get—always barring a repetition of the historic fact that cheap papers supported by advertising come in below when those on top are too expensive.

A few experiments in adless papers have been made. Early in

this century E. W. Scripps, a crusading editor of liberal predilections, tried it with two papers. Marlen Pew, editor of *Editor & Publisher,* later said of them:

Some twenty years ago we discussed the non-advertising paper as an ideal, to gain complete editorial freedom and high-voltage editorial power. With his cash Mr. Scripps . . . backed two non-advertising dailies, one the *Chicago Day-Book,* edited by N. D. Cochran, and the other the *Philadelphia News-Post,* of which this writer was editor. . . . These were put forth frankly as laboratory experiments. As such, both ventures were considered fairly successful. Each was discontinued for reasons which did not relate to the non-advertising principle, the outbreak of the World War being one such reason. Both definitely demonstrated that, sans advertising, a daily publication, when economically produced, can be made to pay its way and even yield a profit from circulation receipts.[6]

Pew's recollection was written before *PM* appeared. And *PM* did nothing to bear out his belief that an adless daily can earn its own way. In the early days after its founding in June, 1940, it had to be bailed out by Marshall Field, who came to its rescue with a non-journalistic fortune and soon took it over. Five years after the founding *PM* boasted that it was completing a full year in the black.[7] But only a year later, on its sixth anniversary, it appealed for 100,000 more readers. One of the announced reasons was "to meet the present deficit, occasioned by the raised cost of living." [8] The response was apparently inadequate, because less than five months later *PM* gave up the ghost that had given it life, and announced that henceforth it would take paid advertising. Because of this its founder and editor, Ralph Ingersoll, resigned.[9] It may be, of course, that if *PM* had lived up to its original purpose of being an objective newspaper instead of becoming a leftist war whoop, it might have lived in the black without advertising. We do not know. In its present form as the New York *Star* it continues to solicit advertising.

We do have, however, a hopeful if unique example of an adless publication from the magazine field. Until comparatively recently it was an axiom of the magazine business, too, that no magazine could live without advertising. The *Nation* was characteristic. For years it lived on subsidies from well-wishers.

When in 1943 these sources dried up it called on its subscribers to support it as a nonprofit service to them. The readers came through, making the *Nation* what ought to be close to the journalistic reformer's ideal; for, though it continues to take advertising, that is a minor source of income. The readers really pay its bills, if not in subscriptions, then in contributions.[10] Yet its success is hardly striking enough to inspire an aggressive newspaper publisher to try the same method of financing.

There remains, however, the extraordinary example of the *Reader's Digest*. After half a dozen years of obscurity following its modest beginning in 1921, the *Digest* began to bloom. Thereafter it grew faster, finally shooting up to more than 10,000,000, with foreign-language editions enabling it to spread beyond the boundaries of the English-speaking world, and the end is apparently nowhere in sight. Today it basks in a prosperity that makes successful commercial magazines envious. It may be, therefore, that one day some editor will hit upon a formula that will raise up a daily newspaper without advertising, a newspaper that will duplicate the so far unduplicated success of the *Reader's Digest*.

It is well, however, not to hope too much from such a newspaper, even if it appears, for there is little to indicate that its editorial content would differ greatly from that of papers with advertising. I say this because, again, newspapers are an integral part of the present economic system, and so are conservative of their own accord rather than because advertisers tell them to be. There is support for this view, furthermore, in the example of the *Reader's Digest;* for, as the *Digest* became prosperous, left-of-center Americans, seemingly by reflex action, began to suspect it. To them, apparently, no enterprise that makes money can be honest. At any rate, our liberal-minded citizens find alarming tendencies in the once worthy pages of the *Digest*. One can conclude only that the presence or absence of advertising in a publication makes little difference.

The more one considers it, the more this makes sense. Suppose a newspaper followed in the path of the *Reader's Digest*. Suppose it succeeded, and came to boast a circulation as large as that of today's metropolitan giants. Would it then necessarily speak for the submerged masses? Or would it find itself sitting pretty, and so be quite content with things as they are—except, of course, for the income taxes and possibly subversive tendencies in the White House?

Thus one more hopeful alternative to the press as we have it seems to dissolve in our hands. With it go, I fear, the related alternatives of endowed or church newspapers.

By an endowed paper I mean not a *PM* nor a *Chicago Sun* nor any other that is nourished on an outside fortune privately controlled by its publisher, but a paper supported by a corporate endowment of its own after the fashion of our large private universities or foundations. We cannot be sure what would come of such an experiment, because it has not been tried; but we do have one newspaper which meets some of the requirements, although its financial security comes from a church rather than from an autonomous fund. I refer to the *Christian Science Monitor.*

Now, the *Monitor* is an excellent newspaper. Newspapermen usually accept it, and notably its Washington and foreign service, as having standards as high as any and far better than most. Not only that, but any crusader for a better journalism would accept it as a "good" newspaper. Well, then, what do the readers think? Its circulation, which is in part national, was 159,700 on September 30, 1947. Mr. Hearst's *American* and *Record,* also published in Boston though for only a local audience, had 214,500 and 420,400 respectively. Why?

The explanation lies, I think, in the fact that an endowed press does not have to fight for its life every day. It can afford to be good rather than successful. Unfortunately, the nearer it approaches the journalistic utopia, the more it risks boring the very citizens it hopes to enlighten. Those who are sensitive to social values may not like the comics and the corruption, the blood and the cheesecake, with which the standard press baits its pages. But the common man whose century this is does like them. And the fact that he does, and prefers to patronize the less ideal but more lively press, gives that press a vitality, an influence, that an endowed press could never have. One comes, then, to this: an endowed press might approach theoretical perfection; but alas, the more perfect it was, the fewer readers it would have.

Nor is there evidence that a church press would be any lustier. For unless it became, like some of the Continental religious papers, a propaganda organ for a church-in-politics, it would have to strive toward a virtue that was as ethical and hence as dull as that of the endowed newspaper. It is impossible to say, for example, how much of the *Christian Science Monitor's* high standards come from financial security, and how much from church sponsorship. That it flourishes as it does is due to the extent that it resembles, rather than differs from, other newspapers. The same may be said for the *Deseret News,* a Salt Lake City newspaper controlled by the Mormon Church. Though smaller in circulation than the only other evening paper in town, it holds its own. But it does not differ sharply from the standard press.

We can see the whole dilemma of the religious daily in this thumbnail sketch of the early New York *World,* by the historian of journalism Frank Luther Mott:

> The New York *World* . . . was originally designed as a religious, or at least a highly moral, daily. It excluded theatre advertising, lottery reports, details of criminal trials, divorce proceedings, and everything of a sensational cast. It advertised church and Sunday School supplies, and was itself advertised in the backs of hymnals. Large sums were advanced by religious business men of New York to establish it, and its first number was issued June 14, 1860, at one cent a copy. The paper lost money rapidly and in November went to two cents to ward off disaster. . . . the original stockholders, who had already put in $200,000, became discouraged and got rid of their holdings as best they could. The ownership came into the hands of such Democratic financiers and politicians as August Belmont, the banker, and Fernando Wood, mayor of New York. . . . The religious element was no longer emphasized, and the *World* took its place as a general newspaper. Soon it was making both ends meet.[11]

There is, I think, no other conclusion than that the approach to the reform of journalism through freeing the press from dependence on commercial sustenance is not hopeful.

There remains on our list of alternatives just one, a labor press. This looks like the most hopeful of the lot, because labor's interests are close to the interests of the mass of men. Thus a labor press might represent precisely the part of the population that the standard press, because of its big-business foundation, tends to neglect.

Past attempts to found labor dailies as an antidote to the commercial press, which go back to the time of Andrew Jackson,[12] have not made much of an impression. In the first place, labor leaders had little interest in journalism for its own sake; and, in the second place, labor unions were not rich enough. They simply could not compete with the capitalists when it came to buying or organizing news services, getting up comic strips, or otherwise paying the bills of a modern newspaper. Now, however, labor has attained unprecedented political power, and collective wealth of such enormity as to make many a daily newspaper small potatoes by comparison. Therefore it ought from here on to be able to outgrow the anemia that plagued its newspapers in the past. It ought to be able, indeed, to outgrow a strictly labor press entirely, and attempt what George Seldes recommends for it: a series of daily newspapers exactly like the standard press except that they happen to be owned by labor. He puts the argument this way:

There is only one way toward a free press: first a labor press which we already have and which needs vast enlargement; second, a standard press only incidentally owned by labor, which will drive the present standard commercial (and therefore dishonest, venal and corrupt) press out of the field.[13]

But would a labor-owned standard press really drive the present press out of the field? It may not be so easy as Mr. Seldes and other enthusiasts think, for to be effective, to provide papers that the general public outside the union ranks would read, the labor press would have to make a sharp break with its past. With a few notable exceptions, like Victor Berger's *Milwaukee Leader*, labor newspapers have been monthlies and weeklies devoted to the cause of individual unions. Therefore they resemble the Nazi and Soviet press rather than the standard press, in that they are propagandizers and organizers for their unions, rather than reporters of general news. They also resemble the nineteenth century party press in this country, to which service to the cause was everything, and objective reporting something that never entered the head of a self-respecting editor.

This functional orientation of the labor press is only natural. The labor press exists to fight the battle for labor, and not to report the teeming facts of the world at large with dispassionate objectivity.

George Seldes's suggestion of labor newspapers that are in all respects like our present ones, except that they are owned by unions instead of by businessmen, is something radically different. One wonders whether it could work, because a press that represents labor and the general public at the same time is, in spite of a considerable overlapping interest, a contradiction. There will obviously be times when a public measure that is of advantage to labor, say an unrevised Wagner Act, will be to the disadvantage of the rest of us. Therefore the catch is whether a labor-owned press can switch from party organ to general newspaper. Can it cease to be a propagandizer and become what the commercial press to a great extent already is—a local newspaper serving the general public in its region? What will it do when a public issue arises over a new piece of labor-saving machinery? Will it take the short-term labor point of view and oppose it, or will it side with the long-term public interest and favor it? In short, once the labor press is dressed in the clothes of orthodox journalism, will it acquire so strong an allegiance to the general public that if necessary it will fly in the face of its labor ownership and fight it? It seems naïve to expect a newspaper that is the property of a militant pressure group to speak for individuals outside the group.

At this point the whole-souled convert to the labor cause will protest that it would be just as easy for a labor paper to fly in the face of its labor ownership as it is for a standard paper to fly in the face of its businessman ownership. Perhaps it would be, but there is, I think, a difference. The overwhelming majority of standard newspapers are not pressure-group mouthpieces. With some notable exceptions they are not owned by a copper company, a paper and power company, or any other exclusive commercial interest. Still less are they owned by the National Association of Manufacturers or the Chamber of Commerce of the United States, which would be the opposite number of a labor daily owned, say, by the UAW-CIO or the American Federation of Musicians. The difference between direct labor ownership and the loose, voluntary association with conservatism that characterizes the standard newspapers, then, places an obstacle in the way of labor dailies as an alternative. It would be hard for them to be even as independent and objective as the standard press is, because the ordinary newspaper, for all its conservative cast, is a geographical and not an ideological entity.

Perhaps in time there will be founded dailies that are under labor auspices but not directly under the thumb of the union bosses, dailies that can rise to the heights of independence. We noted earlier that in times of political peace and economic expansion the capitalist-owned press has displayed liberal tendencies, and gone to bat for its readers rather than for the forces of conservatism to which it clings in time of trouble. It may be, therefore, that when labor feels even more secure than now, some of the more daring among its editors will risk defying the union officials who control their salaries and their careers.

Thus far, however, labor journalism, again with a few exceptions, has not come within hailing distance of the standards of objectivity observed by the capitalist press it scorns, as we shall have occasion to see in the next chapter. If you read the labor press you will know what I mean. Except where they are dealing with noncontroversial records, labor editors don't pretend to be fair. They are waging war. The result is bias in the news. It ranges from bias as mild as that in the better commercial press to question begging and name calling worthy of Dr. Goebbels. If the standard press slanted its news to a fraction of the extent that the labor press does, our liberals would have the screaming heebie-jeebies.

It seems reasonable, therefore, to expect that the labor press will in the future be useful not as a substitute for the standard press but as a supplement to it. It can fill the holes left in the commercial press's presentation of the physical world. It can be more of what it already is, a watchdog. But one has to be an ardent convert indeed to see in the labor press alone the future of American journalism. To the rest of us a labor press, by definition closely allied with a militant segment of society, with one of the estates in the twentieth century body politic, cannot even take us as close to the ideal Fourth Estate as does the existing press.

But where does that leave us? We started out with dissatisfaction with our existing press, on the ground that it is no longer the tribune of the people and the palladium of their liberties that nineteenth century editors said it was; but, having exhausted all the reasonable alternatives, we seem to have nowhere else to turn. Is there, then, no way out? Are we condemned to choose between a press of growing reaction on the one hand, and the plunge into totalitarianism on the other? I think not.

AMERICA'S CONTRIBUTION:

OBJECTIVE REPORTING

PERHAPS if we look closer home instead of chasing theoretical alternatives to our present press, we shall find what we seek. In fact, if we look back down the long road journalism has traveled since the beginning, and particularly if we examine the native American contribution to it, we can find a hint as to where that road leads. We shall find, I think, that it promises to take us toward the goal we all seek.

If we look back, then, we find that during the past century American journalism has taken tremendous strides toward objective reporting. That statement may seem so obvious as to invite a "So what?" It is what the press still lacks in objectivity, and not any progress it may have made toward it in the past, that gives us concern. Nevertheless, a little reflection will show that objective reporting is the utmost that man can ask of his press and of all the rest of his information system. For the basic task of that system is simply to tell him honestly what is happening out of eyesight and out of earshot, so that the picture of the world in his head will bear at least a working resemblance to the great world in which he lives. If the fewer and bigger units that now make up our information system can make up for their smaller numbers by giving us more accurate and unbiased reports than we got from the larger number of smaller papers we had in the past, then we have gained rather than lost.

Now obviously this generation, like all others, must still ask with Pilate, "What is truth?" and no man knows the answer. We know that even disciplined reporters will look at events differently and will therefore report them differently. Nor can we hope that a single news item in a single paper or radio broadcast will represent the complex facts of the world as they are. But journalistic history may indicate that we have a right to hope to arrive in time at an approximation of objectivity, at news accounts that are honest and fair within the limits of human fallibility.

We saw long since that concentration of the press into fewer and bigger units has invalidated the factual basis on which the theory of the free press was based. But that theory revolved about a concept far different from that of objective reporting. For the principle first formulated in *Areopagitica* and gradually built up through the years presupposed no such perfection as objective reporting. It held rather that the whole truth was not to be found in any one report of an event. Truth emerges only from the sum total of reports, after all facts and all shades of opinion have been aired in the process of free reporting and free discussion.

This still holds true, and society must always hold open the door for minority publications giving expression to dissident voices. But it is equally true that what we have lost in the number of newspapers we have far more than made up in a journalistic tradition of greater objectivity. An investigation of our journalistic past, in other words, for which few of the critics of our press seem to have time, indicates that the invalidation of the theory of the free press by economic changes has been more than compensated for by changes in journalistic habits. In fact, even the present American standard of objectivity in the news, imperfect though it is, is so incomparably superior to the standards of the supposed editorial giants of the nineteenth century, and to journalism in all but a few other countries today, as to constitute a revolution in journalism.

Two and a half centuries ago there was published in the first daily newspaper to be founded in London, the *Daily Courant*, a statement of the principles of objective reporting that might still serve as a model today. The publisher, Elizabeth Mallet, promised in her initial issue of March 11, 1702, to cite the names of the foreign papers from which, after the fashion of the time, news reports were copied, so that her readers might judge their worth by their source. Then she added:

Nor will he [i.e. she, the publisher] take upon him to give any Comments or Conjectures of his own, but will relate only Matter of Fact; supposing other people to have Sense enough to make Reflections for themselves.[1]

When a month later Samuel Buckley took over as publisher he elaborated the theme:

He hopes he shall be thought to perform what he takes to be the proper and only Business of a News-Writer . . . delivering Facts as they come related, and without inclining either to one Side or the other: And this he will be found to do by representing the same Actions, according to the different Accounts which both Sides give of them. . . . And thus having fairly related, What is done, When, Where, by which Side reported and by what Hands transmitted hither; He thinks himself obliged not to launch out of his Province, to amuse People with any Comments and Reflections of his own; but leave every Reader to make such remarks for himself as he is capable of.[2]

The newspapers of eighteenth century colonial America, such as they were, followed this prescription to a considerable extent, consisting largely of items copied from the European press or from papers in other colonies—which made it natural for the printers who issued newspapers as a side line to pass on the news without comment. Local news as we know it did not exist, and only an occasional political diatribe struck off sparks of opinion.

The Revolution, however, brought a sharp change. It made objectivity highly unpopular. For example, the *Boston Evening-Post* had, down to 1775, given equal space and prominence to letters from both patriots and loyalists. But on April 24, five days after the battles of Lexington and Concord, the publishers announced that "the unhappy Transactions of the last Week are so variously related that we shall not at present undertake to give any particular Account thereof.[3] So high did feeling run, indeed, that the publishers suspended the paper entirely and retired to the safety of their job-printing business. Another colonial publisher who tried reporting both sides, James Rivington, was hanged in effigy and had his shop wrecked for his pains. Finally he turned outright loyalist and pleased his clientele by publishing only news designed to prop up the spirits of the Tories.[4]

Samuel Adams as much as anyone capitalized the violent feeling of the time, and in so doing showed the way to a new kind of journalism. Though his cause was utterly different, his method was an eighteenth century prototype of that of Dr. Goebbels. Sam Adams went in for no nonsense about reporting the news from both sides. In the spirit of our ephemeral *PM* he was far more interested in fighting for a cause than in the niceties of balanced coverage. Accordingly, a minor outbreak in the streets of Boston became, in his fiery account, the Boston Massacre, and remains that in our history books to this day.

Unhappily for journalism's devotion to objectivity, it was the Sam Adams school of reporting that thereafter came to predominate. For the lesson taught by Adams, Tom Paine, and others during the Revolution, that journalism could be a political weapon as well as a factual report, changed American journalism completely. The cause of faction and party within the country insensibly took the place of the patriot cause of the Revolution. Accordingly, there gradually emerged in post-Revolutionary America the polemical journalism of the party press. By the turn of the century printers were devoting themselves less to reporting "the same actions according to the different accounts which both sides give of them," as that first daily in London had promised, than to beating the drum for a party. Frank Luther Mott sums up the change in this fashion:

Indeed, as party feeling grew, a new reason for the existence of newspapers came to be recognized. Whereas nearly all newspapers heretofore had been set up as auxiliaries to printing establishments and had been looked upon merely as means which enterprising printers used to make a living, now they were more and more often founded as spokesmen of political parties. This gave a new dignity and a new color to American journalism.

It resulted also in the emergence of the newspaper editor.[5]

It resulted further in a brand of reporting not distinguished for its fairness, and in a tradition of biased reporting from which we still suffer to this day. For when the first national political parties took shape after 1795, American journalism, following the partisan trend, began to sink to depths of venom and bias that seem inconceivable today. President Washington himself was far from immune, and on occasion lost his temper, even as have more recent Presidents, at the violent and unjust attacks made upon him in the press.[6] And after him, throughout the first third and more of the nineteenth century, the newspapers became so vituperative and scurrilous that the journalistic attacks of later generations, including the fulminations of the *Chicago Tribune* against President Roosevelt, seem harmless pleasantries by comparison. Our authority Dr. Mott once summed up his extended research into the period in this extemporaneous statement:

Virtually no printing of news of the opposition party—indeed, one of these newspapers would be considered a traitor to its party and to its cause if it did do that. A Jackson paper wouldn't print a speech by Henry Clay; not the text of it, not even a summary of it. It might have an oblique reference to it put in merely to furnish a text for an attack upon Clay. And the same thing can be said of the Clay papers. Now, it might be thought that that very bad situation, that abuse, was corrected by the fact that we had Clay papers and we had Jackson papers, but the trouble is that most men took only their own partisan papers and the individual man would take his party paper and he would rely upon that, and he would say the opposition fellows are liars (and that's what his own editor was saying all the time).[7]

"Liar" was not the only staple name for opposition. Words like "wretch" and even "thief," together with appropriate adjectives, were common. For instance, on the death of Benjamin F. Bache, editor of the *Aurora* and grandson of Benjamin Franklin, a Boston paper paid its respects to the departed by commenting that Bache was "the equal of the most atrocious felon ever hanged at Tyburn," [8] and more along the same line. Nor was partisan journalism merely a matter of calling names. Vilification of the great men of the day included the lowest form of personal attack, such as printing the canard that Thomas

Jefferson sought his pleasure with female slaves. An example appears in the *Philadelphia Port Folio,* in which Thomas Paine is represented as addressing Jefferson in a parody of Horace that begins:

> Dear Thomas, deem it no disgrace
> With slaves to mend thy breed,
> Nor let the wench's smutty face
> Deter thee from the deed.[9]

All this neither excuses nor lessens the departures from the truth, in unjust attacks, visited by newspapers today upon the public figures and the causes they oppose. It does, however, show today's journalistic aberrations in their true proportion as diluted survivals from the dark age of American journalism, rather than as the inventions made after the inauguration of Franklin Roosevelt they are now often imagined to be. The dark age out of which our journalism has grown was well summed up by ex-President James Madison when he complained in 1828, "Could it be so arranged that every newspaper, when printed on one side, should be handed over to the press of an adversary, to be printed on the other, thus presenting to every reader both sides of every question, truth would always have a fair chance." [10] But in those days journalism gave the truth no chance at all, let alone a fair one.

Within five years of Madison's complaint there arose in American journalism something hitherto undreamed of in the free-press philosophy. Spontaneously there grew out of the social change of the time a wholly different conception of journalism. Slowly through the years since then it has grown, and has fed on other influences. If it has not yet given us the ideal Fourth Estate it has at least taken us a long way toward it. For out of the journalistic experiments of the 1830's came the beginnings of that tradition of fairness and accuracy in reporting, with opinion segregated in editorials, columns, and signed articles, that we take for granted today even though to some extent our press still practices the ways of the past.

In the early 1830's New York City supported eleven newspapers. A prominent one was Colonel James Watson Webb's *Courier and Enquirer,* with a circulation of 3,300 daily. That was exceptionally high. The papers of the time, if not purely of the violent political type described above, were addressed to mercantile audiences. In addition to political comment, they offered foreign, commercial, and important court news. This was not, however, presented remotely as it is now. Reporters were unknown. Messengers or a printer-editor gathered such scraps and items as were available, which for the most part were published as paragraphs sparing of detail.

Into this journalistic world a twenty-three-year-old job printer named Benjamin Day brought, on September 3, 1833, a four-page tabloid. Its pages, 11¼ by 8 inches, resembled our type-writing paper in size. Day named his venture the *Sun,* and sold it on the streets by the single copy for a penny instead of on the yearly $8 or $10 subscriptions charged for the existing press. Its object, he said in his first issue, was to "lay before the public, at a price within the means of every one, ALL THE NEWS OF THE DAY, and at the same time afford an advantageous medium for advertising." [11]

What was radical about the *Sun* was that it turned its back on political and mercantile news and sought seemingly trivial items of general interest to the growing lower strata of the New York population. It ignored politics as not greatly interesting to its audience. It sought news where none had ever been sought before, in the police courts and fire department, on the streets, and wherever else human stories could be found to entertain the mechanics and the masses. And whereas the existing political and mecantile papers rarely exceeded 3,000 copies a day, the *Sun* rose within four months to 5,000 and in two years to 15,000 —at that time the largest in the world.[12]

Looking back, Day's success seems surprising. Here, for example, is the flippant and colorful kind of reporting he helped to pioneer, which so pleased his numerous if humble readers:

Bridget McMunn got drunk and threw a pitcher at Mr. Ellis, of 53 Ludlow St. Bridget said she was the mother of 3 little orphans —God bless their dear souls—and if she went to prison they would choke to death for the want of something to eat. Committed.[13]

Day was moved to print this kind of thing, and all sorts of other news that hitherto had been considered beneath the dignity of the press, from a desire to succeed. He set out not to reform journalism, but to make money. Nevertheless, the result was a journalistic revolution. For soon Day, like the host of editors that took the same path in succeeding years, found it possible to boast of their freedom from political subsidy. Their only master was the reading taste of the new lower strata of newspaper buyers for more interesting news. In meeting this taste successfully it became increasingly possible for papers like the *Sun* to attract advertising. This put a foundation under their independence. Circulation bred advertising, and advertising paid for new ways of gathering the news the masses liked. Therefore, though both the established editors and the respectable upper crust of the community looked down on the new penny journalism as vulgar, it had the supreme merit of getting the press out from under the party bosses who subsidized the political press, and sent it off on a path of its own. Finally, in the decades that followed, steam presses and all sorts of other mechanical aids to journalism, now taken for granted, were brought into the service of news and ever more news.

These three—a concept of news as news rather than as a cause, the independence that came with greater advertising revenue, and vast mechanical improvements—together lifted journalism out of its dark age and started it on the path to the present.

Ben Day with his *New York Sun* was not the first to try it, but merely the first to succeed. The venture was in the heady American air of the time. Others soon took up the same challenge, and those who had the right touch established other new papers and helped carry the trend vastly further than could Day alone. Thus James Gordon Bennett founded the *Herald* in New York in 1835, and Horace Greeley the *Tribune* in 1841. In Philadelphia the *Public Ledger* appeared in 1836; and in Baltimore the *Sun,* a year later. And there were others throughout the country.

Of them all, Bennett was the most energetic and probably the most influential. He took the same journalistic path as Day, but outstripped him. He not only printed chitchat from the police courts and from all about town, but began printing the full text of reports on the more colorful court trials, and human-interests facts about criminals. From there he went on to develop a host of new sources of news, doing much, despite the scorn of his fellow editors and the raised eyebrows of the respectable, to set the broad outlines of what has since become the pattern of American news. In his first issue of May 6, 1835, Bennett expressed his creed as follows:

We . . . openly disclaim . . . all principle as it is called—all party—all politics. Our only guide shall be good, sound, practical common sense, applicable to the business and bosoms of men engaged in every-day life. We shall support no party—be the organ of no faction or *coterie,* and care nothing for any election or any candidate from President down to a Constable.

We shall endeavor to record facts on every public and proper subject, stripped of verbiage and coloring, with comments, when suitable, just, independent, fearless and good tempered. If the *Herald* wants the mere expansion which many journals possess, we shall try to make it up in industry, good taste, brevity, variety, point, piquancy, and cheapness.[14]

Such were Bennett's professions. In some ways his performance did not live up to them, for he did not always stay out of politics, and some of the things he printed, far from being in good taste, seemed scandalous to New York's early Victorian society. But in the main he carried out his intentions. He went himself to Wall Street, writing "money articles" that soon came to be widely read because they reported any financial shenanigans, names and all, with a pitiless brashness that soon earned the interest of readers in large numbers. So, too, he invaded the hitherto sacrosanct society life of the town and printed for the benefit of any curious housemaid the details of what went on at the affairs of the great. He scandalized his own trade by revealing the secrets of other editorial sanctums, earning for himself several beatings in the process—which were duly reported in the *Herald* for the delectation of New York's breakfast tables. One of his biographers thus sums up the early Bennett:

If he had a friend anywhere, none was visible to the naked eye. The *Herald's* circulation, however, kept on growing. He was turning on the light where little had shone before, and readers fast found it out.[15]

The readers not only found it out but liked it. The *Herald* soon outstripped the *Sun,* and within fifteen months had reached the incredible circulation of 30,000 a day. The new journalism paid its arch practitioner handsomely, both through circulation and through advertising, which soon began to flourish with a boom of its own.

Bennett put much of the proceeds into pioneering new methods of gathering news as well as new kinds of news. No sooner was there a Pony Express or a telegraph line than Bennett was using it to speed the transmission of news. His coverage of the Mexican and Civil wars helped set the modern pattern. He and his son helped pioneer foreign correspondence in the contemporary sense. Earlier, Bennett had led his competitors in having fast small boats meet incoming ships, which themselves now ran with steam, on regular schedules, so that European news came to New York readers far less stale than before. Since rival newspapers were forced to imitate some, at least, of Bennett's newsgathering methods, each paper's costs ran up to amounts that would have seemed incredible before.

One result of this expensive competition in news gathering was that in May of 1848 ten men representing the six most important New York papers met in the office of the *Sun* and organized the first Associated Press. It was a cooperative enterprise designed to save money for the six.[16] Here again a selfish enterprise had the incidental effect of taking American journalism further along the road toward objectivity and independence. For, as time passed, the Associated Press, living through several incarnations, came to serve far more masters than the original six. Other press associations, mostly regional, did the same. Their client newspapers belonged, however, to all schools of political thought. Hence the press associations' news reports, the same one for all papers served, had to stick to facts. Only an accurate, unbiased report was proof against complaint from editors separated by political, economic, social, and often geographical boundaries. So it was that, as early as the election of 1860, the campaign reports of the Associated Press, appearing side by side with the reports of the correspondents of individual papers, seemed strangely calm, direct, and terse;[17] for the correspondents of individual papers followed in accustomed fashion the tradition of journalism as the fighting arm of a cause rather than as an objective reporter.

At this time one Washington veteran of the Associated Press thus summed up his creed, a creed that remains a model for the American press association reporter today:

My business is to communicate facts; my instructions do not allow me to make any comment upon the facts which I communicate. My dispatches are sent to papers of all manner of politics, and the editors say they are able to make their own comments upon the facts which are sent them. I therefore confine myself to what I consider legitimate news. I do not act as a politician belonging to any school but try to be truthful and impartial. My dispatches are merely dry matters of fact and detail. Some special correspondents may write to suit the temper of their organs. Although I try to write without regard to men or politics, I do not always escape censure.[18]

Despite its recurrent crop of pioneers, American journalism is essentially slow to change. Therefore the nineteenth century's tremendous strides toward objectivity were counterbalanced by a tendency to cling to the past. Horace Greeley typified the two forces in that he made the *Tribune* one of the new penny papers, but scorned the vulgarities of Day and Bennett. In a prospectus for the *Tribune* he declared that "the immoral and degrading Police Reports, Advertisements and other matter which have been allowed to disgrace the columns of our leading Penny Papers will be carefully excluded." [19]

No doubt the pioneers of police reporting themselves could no more foresee the ultimate effect of their policy than the out-raged Greeley; but we at least, looking back, know that the trend typified by "the immoral and degrading Police Reports" helped to establish the concept of news for its own sake, and thereby made a contribution to American life that was of greater moral stature than any of the reforms Greeley preached.

Greeley was, however, also a pioneer. His political bias, far different from the calumnies of the earlier years of the century, stemmed from a zeal for social improvement. The *Tribune* under him was a political leader rather than the mouthpiece of a political group. His comment to Thurlow Weed, "I do no man's bidding but speak my own thoughts," revealed an independence we could use more of today. But Greeley was an editorial writer more than a newsman. It was his comment on the news in the daily and weekly *Tribune*, rather than the news itself, that held his readers.

The custom of segregating opinion in separate editorials had begun with the birth of the party press at the beginning of the nineteenth century. And now that the independent penny press was established, the practice of confining editorial comment to editorial columns and leaving the news objective became more firmly established, even though today we have still not reached completely opinionless news columns.

Continually during the nineteenth century the concept of the news as something apart from opinion about the news sent new roots down into the American social structure. For example, when Henry J. Raymond on September 18, 1851, launched the *New York Times* he insisted that the first business of a newspaper was to publish news rather than to print the political views of its editor as Greeley did. Even before this a fellow spirit named Samuel Bowles III was trying to do essentially the same thing with the *Springfield Republican* in Massachuetts. His father had started the paper as a political weekly—its name came from the pre-Whig party known as the National Republicans—in 1824. But the son had made it a daily twenty years later; and by February 3, 1885, he reflected in an editorial the modern concept of the news as an objective report:

> The *Republican* is a newspaper, and an independent newspaper. As its readers know, it has positive opinions and a positive way of stating them. . . .
> . . . The honest reader may take our opinion on trust, if he chooses. But if he prefers, as he ought, to compare and weigh and strike the balance for himself, we are bound to furnish him the raw material.[20]

Already many years earlier, in the fifties, Bowles had written: "There is not in New York City . . . a single party organ in existence. All are emancipated. None conceal facts lest they injure their party. None fear to speak the truth." [21] In saying this he was right in the sense that the old party organs of the dark age had disappeared. But his enthusiasm for independent journalism must have carried him away. Nearly a century later, newspapers do not yet fully live up to that ideal; but, as we shall see, during the nineteenth century they were far more partisan than they are now.

The change came slowly. In Chicago, in 1875, Melville E. Stone introduced the *Chicago Daily News* with $500 in cash and an idea that "a newspaper should be run distinctly in the interest of the public," and put the paper on its feet with the help of Victor Lawson.[22] In Kansas City five years later William Rockhill Nelson laid another stone in the foundation of honest reporting when he began publication of the *Kansas City Star* with a staff of no less than seven reporters. In an introductory editorial published twenty-nine years to the day after Raymond launched the *New York Times,* Nelson promised: "The *Star* will contain in condensed form all the news of the day, presented to its readers in an impartial and truthful manner, without exaggeration or partisan coloring."

Another pioneer who pushed the boundaries of journalism nearer to where they are today was the Hungarian-born dynamo from St. Louis, Joseph Pulitzer. According to Dr. Mott [23] he did "more toward setting the pattern of modern journalism than anyone else." Early in 1883 he took over the languishing *New York World* when its circulation had fallen to 20,000 though other papers had more than 100,000 and some had even passed 200,000. In a little more than a year he was able to celebrate the *World's* passing the 100,000 mark by having 100 guns fired in City Hall Park and giving every employee a tall silk hat.[24]

Pulitzer's contribution to objective reporting was indirect rather than direct. He carried the human interest news of Bennett still further, vied with William Randolph Hearst in appealing to the mob with yellow journalism, and in various ways multiplied the variety and size of the journalistic artillery. Yet politically he was a liberal. He took the cause of the people for his own, and gave the newspaper editorial page new power, incisiveness, and intellectual honesty.

A little nearer still to our own day yet another stone was laid in the foundation of objective reporting. In 1896 Adolph S. Ochs arrived in New York from Tennessee, where he was publisher of the *Chattanooga Times,* to take over another debt-laden New York paper, the *Times.* Following the all but universal custom of an editorial prospectus, he announced he would "conduct a high standard newspaper, clean, dignified, and trustworthy," and give the news impartially, "regardless of party, sect, or interest involved." [25] The languid *Times* was selling 9,000 copies a day while the *World,* with its far higher editorial temperature, was now up to 370,000, and Hearst's *Journal* to 385,000. Ochs introduced a sixteen-page Sunday magazine section printed on good quality paper, illustrated with halftones. Its appearance and contents were in keeping with the substantial character of his daily issue, and were in striking contrast with the colored magazines and comic supplements of the yellow-journalism Sunday editions of the *World* and the *Journal.*[26]

But most of all he returned to the ideals of the *Times's* founder, Henry J. Raymond. He based his policy on complete and objective reporting; and, against this, all the clever writing of Dana's *Sun* and the gyrations of Hearst and Pulitzer could not prevail. Within five years the sober *Times* was up to 200,000 copies daily. It began to attract advertisers. During the lifetime of its new owner it became the richest of them all. Objectivity began to pay dividends, and to a greater or less extent all other American newspapers, and even some foreign ones, began to fall into the pattern of reporting both sides more than ever before.

During the long decades of the nineteenth and twentieth centuries in which this process went on, the pressure for reader interest influenced even political reporting. The rise of the interview, another distinctively American invention, became a way of reporting all sorts of opinions as news, and hence more or less impartially. It made a hot statement from a robber baron of industry as to the wickedness of organizing labor, and a similar statement from the other side of the fence, simply accurate and truthful reports on what somebody said rather than revelations of the gospel by an editor.

World War I was another milestone, leading as it did to the introduction of foreign correspondence on the modern scale. Here again was a new kind of news, presented primarily for the interesting or useful information it contained, even though the tradition of interpretation in signed and even unsigned articles by special correspondents let opinionated matter creep in.

Science news, more business news, educational news, likewise came to their present stature, once more offering new sources of information to buttress the concept of news for its own sake. Later still came labor news, reported by specialists. And still the slow march toward objectivity goes on. As Dr. Gallup reported after the 1940 campaign, on the basis of his experience with the preelection polls of that year:

All of the newspaper members of the American Institute of Public Opinion who were supporting Willkie were promoting his candidacy in the editorial columns and yet predicting the election of Roosevelt in the news columns supplied by the Institute. Ten or twelve years ago such a situation would probably not have existed.[27]

So, gradually the American tradition of objective reporting began to take shape. Let us emphasize again that the primary reason it came into existence was the approach to news as news rather than as a weapon. With this came increasing financial independence through advertising, and a mechanical and editorial transition from the simple two- or four-page sheet to the bulky product of today. At the same time we overlook something if we ascribe progress toward objective reporting exclusively to the search for circulation and advertising. To do so reflects the materialistic philosophy of today's cynical and uneasy world. The argument that it is good business to print honest news may describe the flesh of the past century of journalistic progress, but it overlooks the spirit; for the editors and publishers of the nineteenth century had ideals as well as an interest in profits. William Rockhill Nelson was under no compulsion to give Kansas City a free Sunday newspaper, as he did when his daily prospered. But to him a newspaper was a public trust, and not merely a creature of dollars and cents.[28] Melville Stone and Victor Lawson needed no truth-in-advertising law to make them restrict the advertising columns of the *Chicago Daily News*. E. W. Scripps saw a public service as well as profits in newspapers addressed primarily to working people. In fact, the professional attitude of these men, and of the countless others who worked with them in the newspaper offices of America, was grounded in more than materialism; for these members of a still far from perfect Fourth Estate nevertheless sensed its obligations, and struggled to meet them.

That, in briefest outline, is how the concept of objective reporting grew. Without benefit of law or any other compulsion, this exceedingly powerful tradition now keeps the vast majority of American news reports free from bias, and leads editors and publishers to segregate their opinions about the news in clearly identifiable editorials, columns, cartoons, and special articles. The tradition that the news must be reported objectively is beyond question the most important development in journalism since the Anglo-Saxon press became free from authority. Moreover, there is implicit within it, I think, a wholly natural force that promises to carry us the rest of the way toward the ideal Fourth Estate.

Curiously, the critics of our press, as one man, overlook the significance, promise, and even the very existence of the tradition of objective reporting. One reason is, no doubt, the spate of frankly opinionated columns, features, and editorials that exists side by side with it in our papers. Another is the fact that the good of unbiased reporting is partly obscured by the surviving vulgarity, sensationalism, and headline thinking that still characterize the news pages of our papers. I hope I have made it clear in the brief historical sketch above that the vulgarity, growing out of an interest in the news as news, as something interesting to the mass of men, contributed notably to the rise of objective reporting. But we still cannot see the forest of objectivity for the trees of journalistic superficiality. Perhaps, if we cannot see it on today's front pages, we can appreciate it by looking back with the advantage of hindsight. To us Joseph Pulitzer, for example, is far enough in the past to be seen for what he was, both a panderer to the vulgar and a pioneer in changing the press from its nineteenth to its twentieth century form. Yet a contemporary, even in Pulitzer's later days when he was already abandoning yellow journalism to conduct one of the outstanding American liberal newspapers, could see only the bad in him. Thus, in 1903, C. C. Buel, assistant editor of the *Century Magazine,* protested earnestly to Columbia University at its soiling its hands by accepting Pulitzer money to found a school of journalism that might help raise the standards of the profession. When Pulitzer acquired the *World* in 1883, Buel declared, Bennett's *Herald*—another pioneer on the way to objective reporting—had been for many years "an easy-going prostitute in the journalistic field, with few or no imitators." But then came Pulitzer:

At first all reputable journalists were shocked, and many of them stood out against the new practices, but little by little, the tone of nearly the whole press began to change, for the *World* steadily grew in wealth and influence, and as each year new men from the colleges poured into newspaper square, journalism that could produce wealth became more and more the beacon-light of success. . . .

Pulitzer has made yellow journalism a necessity of human life, because human nature is too weak in the mass to resist the enjoyment of the sins and follies of its fellows.[29]

Buel added that Pulitzer had brought him to believe "that the fast rotary press is the greatest curse that ever fell on civilization." Perhaps that reveals the extent of his understanding of democracy.

In Europe too, even today, it is the fashion to look down upon the American press as vulgar. General assignment reporters on the American model are unknown on the Continent. Fires, police news, the courts, and all the trivia of the American press, from Hollywood scandals to kittens rescued from trees, are beneath the dignity of the Continental editor. The result is, to be sure, that Europe's newspapers are less cluttered than ours with the tinsel and baubles of the passing show. But it is equally true, and far more significant, that twentieth century Continental journalism bears a remarkable likeness in the political partisanship of its news to the American party press of the dark age in the first third of the nineteenth century. A European looks to his paper not for an unbiased report, but for a window on the world that is heavily stained with his own prejudices.

Even the relatively new Soviet press, which takes a severely holier-than-thou attitude toward our press, simply does not understand the obligation to be impartial in reporting news. For example, Tass, the Soviet news agency, in reporting the discussion during the long sessions of the Paris Peace Conference of 1946 over whether Albania should be invited to attend, told Russian readers that Anglo-Saxon speeches against the invitation "provoked *quite reasonable* objections from Vishinsky. . . . Immediately after this the Greek Prime Minister Tsaldaris made a speech in which he put forward *rude and unjust accusations* against Albania." [30]

No American reporter could have written the words I have italicized. Trained in the American tradition, he would automatically have been content simply to record what Mr. Vishinsky's objections were, letting the reader judge for himself whether they were "quite reasonable" or wholly unreasonable. In the same way he would not have made the distinctly editorial comment that Mr. Tsaldaris was "rude and unjust," but would merely have reproduced the accurate substance, if not indeed the essential words themselves, of the Greek minister's remarks.

This point is so important to a determination of what to do about the future of the American press, and is so consistently overlooked by the critics of our press, that it is well to make the contrast clearer with an American example. Two quotations do not make a case; but no one familiar with European journalism and American journalism can doubt that Tass's editorializing of the news and the following sample of American news writing are wholly representative of these two utterly different journalistic traditions. The example I choose is from my own paper, the *Hartford Courant*, although almost any spot-news story on a reasonably controversial subject from any other American paper would do as well. The item concerns a local strike, in which the two opposing sides inevitably had different opinions and different emotions as to the rights of the matter. Under the headline "Royal Union Makes Issue of Security," the story began:

Maintenance of "union security" and the method and extent of future arbitration are the two key issues in the Royal Typewriter Company contract dispute negotiations, Union President Joseph Chesery revealed Saturday when details of the dispute were aired publicly for the first time by both sides.

According to the union, negotiations have ended, and about 3500 Royal employees will vote whether or not to strike for their demands at 10 a.m. Monday in the State Theater.

After each of the six issues that follow, the management's viewpoint as stated by Charles B. Cook, company vice-president and factory manager, is found in the first paragraph; the union stand, given by Mr. Chesery, is in the second. [31]

The story went on to give the details in exactly this fashion, without any hint as to whether the reporter, or his superiors, held the management's or the union's cause to be the more just. I repeat that this is nothing unusual. It merely typifies what is done every day, in the vast majority of news stories, as a matter of course.

Prewar France made a distinction between the *journal d'information* and the *journal d'opinion;* the first was supposedly devoted to news more or less on the American pattern, while the second was frankly in the tradition of the European, and the dark-age American, method of reporting the world according to a preconceived point of view. It is true that the *journaux d'information,* like the prewar *Matin,* did publish more general news in the American pattern than other French papers. Yet the worst of today's American transgressors against objective reporting are pure by comparison. And it is precisely this that the critics of American newspapers, foreign and native alike, refuse to credit.

Instead, the critics concentrate on two things: the surviving violations of the American tradition by American newspapers, and the many editorials, columns, features, and other matter in our papers that are openly devoted to opinion. There can be little doubt that most American newspapers slant these deliberate expressions of opinion in a conservative direction. That is, as we have long since noted, what is wrong with the twentieth century press. But I submit that we cannot find ways and means of righting this balance without starting from the surprising fact that our editors and publishers go as far as they do in keeping their prejudices out of their news columns. Rather than criticize them for their remaining offenses against objectivity, we must recognize that their achievements in this direction are, when measured against the journalism of our own past and against that of most of the rest of the world even today, nothing short of extraordinary.

Yet listen to this characteristic blast from one of the press's critics, Harold L. Ickes. After the heated 1940 presidential campaign between Wendell Willkie and a Franklin Roosevelt seeking his third term, Ickes made an investigation of how fairly the battle had been reported. He "had checks made on two different days of five representative newspapers, distributed, with an eye to geographic balance, throughout the country. The object was to take a fair cross-section of the metropolitan press." The object must also have been, though Ickes does not say so, to include the *Chicago Tribune,* whose departures from purity in reporting during the New Deal campaigns were magnificently prominent. How many similar lapses he made from the dispassionate scholarship he assumes in these tests we do not know. He did, however, emerge with these results:

The checks showed that the news space assigned to the two presidential candidates varied from 60 per cent for one and 40 per cent for the other in the best of the newspapers, to 96 per cent for one and 4 per cent in the case of the worst.[32]

That last can only have been the *Tribune.* But Ickes goes on to report another sin against objective reporting; namely, that when Roosevelt and Willkie appeared at rallies in Madison Square Garden within four days of each other, coverage of the rallies by a paper as distinguished as the *Baltimore Sun* was sadly out of balance:

The *Sun,* in addition to printing the text of the speeches . . . devoted three times more news space to the meeting of one candidate than it gave to the other. It assigned five times as many staff reporters to cover the event when its favorite spoke, as it did to the opposition candidate.

Ickes cites still other examples of editorial bias in the news, and there can be no doubt that he has put his finger on a grievous journalistic fault. But note that phrase he slips in parenthetically: *in addition to printing the text of the speeches.* In other words, our papers, despite their remaining bias, have come so far toward objectivity that even during a violent campaign the bigger ones actually print every word of the opposition candidate's major speeches.

It is not accurate to say, as New Dealers sometimes did, that radio forced the practice of printing the full text of speeches and documents on the newspapers. That practice began when the *New York Times* printed official reports, documents, and speeches during World War I, winning a Pulitzer prize for it in 1918. Radio did not start in 1920, and it was 1924 before a President, Calvin Coolidge, went on the air over a network that boasted as many as three stations. As for presidential politics, they did not even begin to assume their modern place on the radio until the Hoover-Smith campaign of 1928.

It is often argued, too, that in 1936 and 1940 and 1944 most of our newspapers were defeated at the polls by Franklin Roosevelt. So they were, in so far as their editorial pages were concerned. *But they elected him by means of the objectivity of their news pages.* For, no matter what bias in reporting may remain, our anti-Roosevelt and pro-Roosevelt papers hardly differed in that for a dozen years they covered their front pages with substantially accurate accounts of everything the President said and did. This, and not the fulminations on their editorial pages, is what they really told their readers; and this is what elected him, as he used to say, again and again and again.

We can appreciate the extraordinary achievement that such honest reporting represents if we once more look back upon a standard of comparison. If the press of our day sinned in reporting, what of the account of the inauguration of Thomas Jefferson on March 4, 1801, in the *Columbian Centinel,* of which this heading is typical:

YESTERDAY EXPIRED
Deeply regretted by MILLIONS of grateful Americans
And by *all* GOOD MEN
The FEDERAL ADMINISTRATION
Of the
GOVERNMENT of the UNITED STATES:

———

Its death was occasioned by the
Secret Arts, and Open Violence;
Of Foreign and Domestic Demagogues [33]

Surely the *Baltimore Sun's* coverage of the 1940's rallies that so aroused Mr. Ickes was more objective than that.

Nor need we go back to the dark age of American journalism for a comparison. As recently as the Cleveland-Blaine campaign of 1884, when newspapers had already begun to approach their modern form, we can find political reporting of a kind that even the worst of our standard papers today would not resort to.

The *New York World,* then recently come under control of the whirlwind Joseph Pulitzer, sent a correspondent to Elmira, New York, to cover a rally for Blaine, whom it opposed. Here is what he wrote:

The City of Elmira woke up yesterday after a night of carousal to speed the parting guest, James G. Blaine, who had spent the night in the city, and the faithful Republicans were happy. Never in the history of the Rathbun House was so much whiskey sold over the bar. . . .

The work of the night before left its imprint upon his [Blaine's] feeble constitution. His face was even more blanched than ever before; not a trace of blood was visible; a dull, leaden pallor over-spread the features and the muscles hung heavy and flaccid. His most striking feature was his dull, glassy eyes, which appeared con-tracted behind the swelled lids. A more expressionless, dispirited face can hardly be imagined.[34]

The *World* was not unusual. That was just the way political news was reported at the time. Page one of Whitelaw Reid's *Tribune* ran the following bill of particulars on election day in that campaign: "Cheerful news from doubtful states: Indiana Republicans confident, New Jersey Republicans confident, Democrats alarmed. Ohio Democrats desperate. Bright prospects in Conn. Tennessee probably Republican." There were two columns in that issue on Blaine's final reception—and not a single line about Cleveland.[35]

If Harold Ickes and the rest really want to improve our press, why do they not inform themselves about its past, the better to see the way into the future, by reading items like the above? Besides, if he really wants to find bias and one-sided reporting today he will find it not in the standard press, but rather in all the labor press, the farm journals, industrial house organs, trade journals, and other mouthpieces for pressure groups. Take the *Guild Reporter,* organ of the American Newspaper Guild, which consistently maintains an attitude of superior virtue toward the daily press. One copy before me displays in the leading position on page one, in the guise of a news story and not a signed article of opinion, an item about the pub-lishers. Here the resemblance to standard journalism stops. The very headline, "Nazi Technique Used by Press," departs

from the temper common to our supposedly more biased standard press, and the article begins with these paragraphs:

The American newspaper industry last fortnight manufactured a
propaganda product which was in effect, if not in intent, an attack
against the things for which America is fighting—freedom, democracy.

It was a concerted attack built, as the totalitarians themselves build
their attacks, on demonstrated lies, and it swept across the nation
from coast to coast in page one force, an attempted blitzkrieg drive
on labor.

In the name of "patriotism," the newspapers demanded an end
to non-existent strikes in defense industry, repeal of the people's
social security, laws virtually outlawing the core of democracy—
trade unions.

In streamer stories the press made heroes and statesmen out of
the Coxes, the Smiths, the Vinsons and the Hoffmans of Congress
at a time when the CIO and AFL were doing the statesmanship and
the workers of the country were doing an heroic job in the mills,
manning them for victory, fighting for more and more production.

An hysterical editorial in the Scripps-Howard newspapers, vici-
ously libeling labor, was wildly acclaimed by the publishers as a new
declaration of independence, and thousands of reprints of it appeared as if by magic, fluttering down in propaganda missiles to
incite a misinformed public to virtual civil war.[36]

The reader will have detected, I think, the difference in flavor
between this handling of a controversial subject and the more
factual manner of a news story in the standard press, like the
Hartford Courant's report of the Royal Typewriter strike mentioned above. Again, what would our liberals say if they found
in one of the conservative papers, say the *New York Herald
Tribune,* a news story written in the spirit of this characteristic
paragraph in the *CIO News?*

The Gallup Poll (American Institute of Public Opinion) is an
institution financed by big-business publishers, to check up on the
effectiveness of their own propaganda. Its findings are usually most
encouraging to its sponsors.[37]

Or what would those who felt that *PM* gave them the real
news say if the *New York Times,* or any other standard paper,
modeled its headlines on those in *PM?* I have at hand two char-

acteristic ones. The first says, on the top of page one, "Standard Oil's Answer to Henry Wallace." [38] But under that heading is printed in huge red capitals the one word BUNK. The other example covers most of page one with the words, "Legion Fries Fish For Helping Subversives Spread Poison." But the Fish, referring to Representative Hamilton Fish, is no word at all but a drawing in red ink showing a dejected and presumably smelly fish lying on a platter.[39] We may or may not have agreed with *PM* in its opinion of Hamilton Fish. But can even those who agreed honestly say that *PM* exemplified a higher type of journalism than that of which it so consistently complained?

Our leftist press in general often presents information and views that serve as a healthy corrective for the errors of the standard press; but, far from being the journalism of the future, it is merely a throwback to the dark ages. To be sure, the bias that remains in the standard press is itself a survival from the dark ages. But, putting the two kinds of papers together, few will question that the standard press, with all its faults, is far closer than the rebels to the objectivity our information system must give us if we are to survive as a democracy.

Rather than complain about the remaining imperfections of our press, then, we ought to marvel that it is as objective as it is; and, having looked back upon more than a century's steady progress toward honest journalism, we must remind ourselves that the journey is not yet ended. The journalism of today is not America's final, best product. We are simply midway, perhaps much farther than midway, along the road. Right now our papers are still marching along that road by making still firmer the obligation to be impartial in news reports and by carrying that obligation into fresh areas hitherto reserved to opinion. They will go farther in that direction, no matter how impatiently critics who are ignorant of journalistic history damn them for their unquestioned faults, no matter how the *Chicago Tribunes* and *PMs* alike cling to the journalistic vices of the past. And our newspapers and their critics alike will find that no doctrine imported from abroad, no inspiration dreamed up in Washington, no theory invented in an academic ivory tower, points the way ahead. That way lies in following to the end the same natural, spontaneous course into the future we have followed in the past.

CHAPTER XIX

FREEDOM OF INFORMATION

ALL discussions of how to make today's journalism more adequate to today's needs end in disputes over freedom of the press. And if our press's heritage of freedom from government control is beyond price, that freedom was founded on an economic base that has vanished. Perhaps it will clear the air, therefore, to omit the term from our discussion entirely.

A convenient substitute that has gained some currency is "freedom of information." This term is used loosely to mean a number of different things, one of which is the crusade for free world news described in Chapter XV. Let us adopt it here in the sense of that more perfect journalism we all seek, whether in the world at large or within our own borders. In the pages that remain, then, freedom of information for newspapers and related media will have not only the historic sense of freedom from government, but also include *freedom from any attachment, direct or indirect, to any class, political party, economic group, or other fraction of society*. Freedom of information, then, means nothing more nor less than realizing in practice the ideal Fourth Estate.

Freedom of information requires nothing more drastic than encouraging the natural growth that has already given us the tradition of objective reporting. But extending that growth necessitates a sharp change of purpose and direction by the corporations that operate our newspapers, radio, moving pictures, and other means of mass communication; for more is involved here than continued progress toward objectivity in news reports to the point where they no longer display even occasional lapses from fairness: we shall not have freedom of information until we make a courageous leap into the future by broadening the tradition of objectivity to include not only news, but the interpretation of news.

Here is where the most significant and necessary change from present practice comes in. Editorials, columns, commentaries, features, cartoons, and special articles are by nature expressions of opinion; but to achieve freedom of information the orientation of that opinion must be more objective than it is today. Instead of arguing for a preconceived point of view, as now, they must be dedicated, in a spirit of scientific inquiry, to the search for truth.

At this point I can hear all Americans who are distressed at the preponderantly conservative animus of our information system groan as one man and say, "Good Lord, does this fellow expect us to trust those old buzzards who run the newspapers and radio to get religion of their own accord, and give us an honest slant on what is happening in their editorials, columns, and political tirades?" The only possible answer is, "Yes." I challenge anyone to find an approach more likely to carry us toward freedom of information than reliance on this indigenous American growth. Time passes. With it pass old men, and even young men whose ideas are old. We have come far in the past century. Is there any reason why the spiritual growth that has given us truth in the news should suddenly halt before it gives us objectivity in the evaluation of the news?

To begin with, we are not so badly off as our Cassandras would have us believe. When war came in 1939 President Roosevelt told us we were "the most enlightened and best informed people in all the world." We were. We still are. Despite the preponderantly conservative bias of our information media, no people, at any time in history, in any country, has had so complete, so accurate, and so fair a report on the world it lives in as the American people today. This is of enormous significance.

We still have a long way to go. But we shall have difficulty in going the rest of the way if we ignore the fact that we have already covered the greater part of the long, long road toward the ideal. Our system does function, and function far better than any other that has ever existed anywhere, despite what a Seldes or an Ickes, a Goebbels or a Molotov may say about it. No doubt you recall, for example, Henry Wallace's celebrated speech in 1942 to the effect that this is the century of the common man. At the time it was made, that speech was, to put it mildly, inadequately reported by the standard press. But *PM* and others, making much of the incident, came out with the full text, and—well, you remember the speech still, don't you? At the time, this was cited as one more proof that a capitalist press suppresses the truth. But if our press tried to suppress the Wallace speech it did not do a good job. It never does, under the American tradition. The fact is that in one way or another the American public finds out what is going on. If a too conservative press and radio ignore something that is noteworthy, it comes out anyway. Nothing is suppressed for long. Minorities, wise and foolish, public-spirited and selfish, do get their views into the open if only through minority publications. And if what they have to say is important enough, then all the resources of newspapers, radio, magazines, films, and books spread the word to the people.

The fact that our system works as well as it does ought to give us the courage to believe that it holds within itself the seeds of all we need for the future. What is conspicuously lacking is a conviction in most publishers and editors, network executives, and film producers that it is up to them to make a jump into the future like that made by the newspaper pioneers of the nineteenth century. Where is the publisher with the vision of the twenty-year-old Adolph Ochs who, when he took over the sickly *Chattanooga Times* in 1878, saw that success lay in abandoning the universally accepted habit of allegiance to a political party, political idea, religious sect, or industry? Ochs resolved instead to take the entire community for his constituency,[1] and to publish the news as it happened for the benefit of *all* the members of that constituency. The result was that the *Chattanooga Times* and the *New York Times,* with which he subsequently repeated the formula, turned into gold mines. The publishers of today who have Ochs's vision and courage stand to win similar rewards. In fact, the newspapers that take the next and final step toward independent journalism will find themselves prospering far beyond their most fantastic dreams. There is, in other words, a commercial as well as a moral reason for a change. But if the managers of today's vastly complicated information system are to win a financial reward and a world-wide esteem like that won by Adolph Ochs, they must take a forward step as positive and as radical as the one he took. They must apply to editorial policy the same standard of service to the entire community that Ochs applied to the coverage of news. Only when an entire newspaper is put together with the thought of reflecting the desires and the needs of society as a whole will the newspaper owners and managers of the twentieth century achieve the moral greatness of their predecessors of the nineteenth.

To those publishers who insist that this is precisely what they do now it must be pointed out that, like them, the editors who dipped their news in partisan colors before publishing it also fancied they were serving their fellow men. Salvation lay through the particular political doctrine they preached. Why not, therefore, present the news only as colored by that doctrine? Once we achieved objective reporting, we could see how wrong they were. So it is now. The demands our times make on the men responsible for journalism are not easy. Our publishers and editors must give up, not only outwardly but in their hearts, all liaison with economic and political groups. They must sponsor no Committee for Constitutional Government, no partisan tax doctrine or labor policy, nor any cause at all other than independent journalism. They must not hanker after political office. They must not own a paper as an incident to owning or managing some other business. They must fight until there is not a paper left in the country with the hooks of a bank in its financial nerves. They must battle for independence until no paper or power company, no department store, no great copper or chemical industry, is so much as suspected of participating in the ownership of any medium of public information.

It is difficult to see, in short, how we can realize freedom of information to the full until our publishers and editors are just that, and nothing more. Such professional independence is little enough. As we have noted long since, despite the convictions of our liberals it is not advertising or any other direct financial inducement that orients the press toward conservatism. Rather it is the fact that the men who make our newspapers live and breathe the same atmosphere as the men in the top posts elsewhere in the national economy. Therefore the severance of such economic ties with industry and finance as remain is only the beginning of independence. Our editors and publishers must also develop a healthy skepticism toward their own prejudices. They must scrupulously and suspiciously inspect the bases of their own editorial policies. If they find themselves at the club, agreeing with the manufacturers and the corporation lawyers, the brokers and the real-estate men, as to the significance of the latest political speech or as to the rights in the newest labor dispute, it is a sign that they may have wandered out of the Fourth Estate. Would the laboring men themselves agree in full with these better citizens at the club? Would the white-collar workers, the office girls, the housewives who do not live in the best residential districts? But why go on? All of us know already the difference between viewing the world from a particular point of view and viewing it with the objectivity of a Fourth Estate.

No doubt the critics of our press will want stronger medicine than a gradual, voluntary reorientation of editorial policies. Thus, when Morris Ernst comes to remedies after his cogent analysis of our information system in his book *The First Freedom,* he offers a whole drawerful of remedies—every one of which would force a change by law. His proposals range from requiring moving picture producers to sell their theater chains, and requiring newspaper chains and radio networks to split into their component parts, to loosening the copyright laws. He would also prescribe by law what advertising rates may be charged, would prohibit boiler plate in the weekly papers that still use it, limit the profits radio may make, publish the income-tax returns of radio stations, hold down transmission rates of news, and so on through a long and imposing array.[3]

Some of these legal clubs with which to beat recalcitrant publishers, radio tycoons, and movie moguls into line might prove salutary; but, if history shows anything, it is that legal compulsion alone does not bring social changes. Law had its origin in custom, and the two are still inextricably intertwined. Laws are effective only when they codify what is already the belief and the habit of the majority. This generation's passion for curing every social ill by passing a law had its great object lesson in prohibition; but we have not yet learned that law cannot travel too greatly in advance of willing observance. We cannot force journalism to serve the whole of society merely by passing laws.

Other critics of the press see hope in scientific developments. Thus it has been argued that the advent of facsimile, with its relatively cheap and simple mechanical facilities, will restore the days when there was a plenitude of newspapers because they were born as easily as they died.[3] Here again may be a healthy influence. But to hope that mechanical gadgets will reverse that whole trend toward larger, more complex, and more powerful instruments of information that is inherent in our technological developments seems hardly warranted. Why will not the same mighty newspapers, the same radio networks and advertising agencies that have absorbed or dominated existing smaller papers and independent radio programs do the same with facsimile newspapers?

At least one other critic wants to reverse the trend of the last hundred years. Kenneth Stewart, the experienced newspaperman who makes this proposal,[4] knows his subject, and no one acquainted with him can doubt his sincerity and integrity. Therefore it is distressing to find that he sees the cure for our remaining lack of objectivity in not more but less of it. Starting with the premise that no one can know the truth, that no two reporters will size up an event in quite the same terms, he has come to regard objectivity as a dream impossible of attainment. Hence he stresses the importance of what the man who gathers the news at first hand thinks about it. If 100 per cent objectivity is impossible, why not free the reporter from the burden of trying to be objective at all? Why not just let him color the news according to his own predilections? Isn't this the best way to get at the truth in an imperfect world? Mr. Stewart would of course "draw a fine distinction between conscious coloration and deliberate distortion";[5] but, as S. T. Williamson, another newspaperman, remarked, this "sets one to wondering whether it's not conscious coloration when our side does it but deliberate distortion when practiced by our ignoble opponents."

To me, it is indeed hard to see how removing the obligation to try to tell both sides of a story would do anything else than return us to the dark age of American journalism, when news stories read like the editorials of today. But we no longer have enough newspapers to make the system work. As we have seen, the steadily shrinking proportion of newspapers to population forces us to represent as many points of view as possible in a single newspaper account of an event.

Moreover, in Chapter XVIII there was quoted a sample news story, reporting what both sides said about a strike. Would that story have brought us closer to the truth if it had followed Mr. Stewart's formula of letting the reporter consciously color the story according to his own sympathies, on the side of either management or the strikers?

Try as we will, we are driven back to the conviction that the road that has brought us as far as we already are toward objectivity is the one that will carry us still closer toward it.

This native American approach to the improvement of journalism, however, puts upon our publishers and other information executives a responsibility they may well ponder. Their editorial writers, their Westbrook Peglers and Fulton Lewises, have for a decade and a half shouted to heaven that labor has betrayed the fundamental principle that for every right there is a corresponding duty, for every freedom a responsibility, without which democracy withers and dies. In this they are obviously right. But what the publishers and editors fail to see is that they themselves are just as flagrant offenders as labor against the principle that every freedom presupposes an obligation.

Freedom of the press is so deeply embedded in our social structure that we could not tear it out if we wanted to; but freedom of the press has remained an integral part of our life only because in the past the responsibility that is a part of it has been accepted. The responsibility that goes with freedom of the press is to provide a journalistic advocate for every noticeable point of view, every substantial interest, that exists in the body politic. Earlier, the relatively high proportion of newspapers to population made it easy to discharge this responsibility. With the number of outlets for opinion now limited, the responsibility of those on whom freedom of the press is conferred has changed. A new duty accompanies the historic right, the duty of fighting for the interests of the entire community.

Though this is the responsibility of today's free press, the men who control that press do not see that responsibility clearly, let alone accept it. Newspapers, commentators, moving pictures, all join with the industrialists and financiers in pleading for free enterprise, which when in harmonious balance with the facts of economic life is unquestionably the most effective system the world has ever known; but, by tending always to side with its friends at the top of the economic ladder, the press, in its strategic position, is doing more than any other element of society to endanger free enterprise. This honored term has already earned the opprobrium of large numbers of our people because it has been used as a shield to ward off all attempts to remedy economic inequalities, all attempts to restore the really free enterprise that the powerful bureaucracy of big business has stifled. Let the publishers, the editors, the columnists, and the network commentators first acknowledge the responsibility that goes with their own freedom; then the American people will heed them when they preach to labor and to other groups in modern society that there is a duty for every right.

The first requisite of editorial independence is that newspapers abandon their allegiance to political parties and fly the flag of freedom at their masthead. They have long since done so in their news columns. Now let them do it on their editorial pages.

It is of course arguable that, in a country governed by a two-party system, newspapers should attach themselves to one or the other party. But today such an alignment has a hollow ring. Many a newspaper that flies the Democratic flag preaches a political economy hardly distinguishable from that of its Republican contemporaries.

The newspaper directories now list many papers that prefix an *I* for "Independent" to the *R* or *D* denoting Republican or Democratic affiliation. This is a confession on their part that their usefulness to society requires a freedom from bias they have not yet had the courage to espouse fully; but it is contradictory to try to be at once independent and partisan. A paper that makes no bones about being Republican or Democratic is at least honest. Moreover, in theory it is just as free to criticize its party as one that pretends to partial independence. Nevertheless it is in fact hobbled by the ball and chain of bias it deliberately attaches to its own feet.

A considerable number of newspapers now list themselves simply with an *I* for "Independent." We need more of them, and a greater number that will not merely proclaim their independence but practice it. When the *Johnstown Democrat* in Pennsylvania took the plunge it began printing the words "An Independent American Newspaper" under its outmoded Democratic title, and explained editorially: "The problems America faces today, nationally and internationally, are not partisan problems. They cannot be solved by a partisan approach. No more can the problems facing this state, this county, or this city." The *Democrat's* editor, John F. James, added that he had long been convinced that newspapers cannot fulfill their duty toward their readers if they bind themselves to a party:

All of us, Republicans and Democrats alike, are quick to note the stultifying effects of the Communist line in the left-wing papers in this country as well as the government-dominated press within the Soviet Union. A strictly Democratic party line or a Republican party line can be just as hamstringing.[6]

The thesis that our newspapers should serve as advocates for one of the parties about which our political life revolves would be more tenable if the labels they chose for themselves reflected their politics more accurately than they do. It would also be more tenable if their politics matched the preferences of the voters with reasonable accuracy. But take Connecticut, the state I live in, as an example. It now supports twenty-eight daily newspapers. Of these, thirteen list themselves as Republican or Independent Republican, three as Democratic or Independent Democratic, and twelve as Independent. If readers were aware of these designations, to which neither they nor the editors pay overmuch attention, they would find a good number in flagrant contradiction to the political doctrines the papers actually preach. Two of the more glaringly conservative papers in a state of conservative newspapers cheerfully set themselves down as

Independent. Actually the twenty-eight are, with a few exceptions, overwhelmingly Republican and far to the right in the men and measures they support. Yet in the 1940 and 1944 presidential elections the people for whom these papers ostensibly spoke voted Democratic by roughly 84 and 60 per cent. Clearly, the bias of the papers did not square with the bias of the voters.

Shuffling off outworn political labels is preliminary, almost superficial, to the achievement of editorial independence and the objectivity that comes with it. Freedom from commitment to a political party is more the symbol than the substance of freedom of information for the American people. The real reason why our press should be independent editorially is implicit in the changed economic base of our journalism that cannot be emphasized too often, because it is so blandly ignored by those who defend the journalistic *status quo*. Again to choose an illustration near at hand, in 1841 the city of Hartford had a population of 9,500—13,000, including the entire township. The opinions of those 13,000 persons could be expressed in the thirteen newspapers that then existed. The proportion was one paper for every thousand inhabitants. Today Hartford has a population of about 180,000—and just two newspapers. To put it another way, there is today *one ninetieth* the chance for the divergent opinions of the city's people to find expression in the press. The only mitigating factor in this fantastically reduced opportunity for expression is more objective news coverage, plus the existence of four local radio stations—which by and large offer the same news and the same views as the newspapers.

It is difficult to escape the conclusion that either party allegiance or devotion to the interests of one economic group among the population is, today, a betrayal of the newspaper's trust. Under contemporary conditions a paper that is anything else than independent in fact as well as name is an anachronism, a relic of Horace Greeley's political journalism, of the days when type was set by hand, and readers studied the newspapers by the light of kerosene lamps.

Once the publishers get to the point where they would rather be right than Republican, our press will fulfill a function not unlike that of the independent voters. It is the independent voters who decide elections. The history of Anglo-Saxon countries under the two-party system can be told in terms of a swinging pendulum. In a given period a government that began as a fresh breath of life will grow old, tired, overfond of office, and insensitive to the needs of the people. It will keep a country too long on one side or the other of the main stream of its history. It will, that is, try to hold the pendulum too long to its side of center. Because it does so, conditions will worsen; and at length a popular upheaval will once more sweep out the old government, bring in a new, and thus start the pendulum on its swing to the other side. So it was in the United States in 1920 when, after the Wilsonian social experiments and the stimulating but exhausting excitements of World War I, the country turned, with a sigh of relief, to Republican conservatism. So it was again when, after a stretch of too much smugness and indifference, we were engulfed by the depression. Again the pendulum swung and the people chose Franklin Roosevelt. But for the war the pendulum would presumably have swung the other way once more in 1940, or surely in 1944. As this book goes to press the 1948 campaign is just beginning. But all signs point to the long overdue return to the Republicans. Whatever the decision of the electorate, it is always the loosely attached and the independent voters, not the stalwarts on either side, who send the pendulum off on a reverse swing.

This system is the genius of representative democracy. Surely it is the obligation of our press to be sensitive to the deep currents of public feeling that swing the pendulum. Surely our press ought to fight the battles of *res publicae* in substantial accord with this healthy rhythm of the people themselves. Surely this is wiser than to have the newspapers serve as appendages—obstreperous ones at times, perhaps, but nevertheless appendages —of the political parties that stand always on one side or the other of the destined national course. A press that is free in the sense that our times demand will not ask whether a man or a measure is Republican or Democratic, liberal or conservative. It will ask only what is right.

It is already clearly noticeable that in municipal affairs, to a lesser extent in state affairs, and to a varying extent in foreign affairs, newspapers do thus seek the truth, let the political labels fall where they may. Perhaps this is because party labels have by now become meaningless in municipal affairs and, in time of crisis, in foreign affairs. A paper that would not dream of supporting a Democratic candidate for President will see nothing inconsistent in supporting a Democrat for mayor, when he looks like the better man. When we look at the extraordinarily heterogeneous assortment of men and policies that make up both our national parties we wonder how newspapers can discern more virtue in one or the other of them nationally than locally. But the fact that newspapers do have greater perspicacity than this in local affairs, and do not hesitate to assert their freedom from political commitments when they editorialize on local affairs, gives hope that the growth toward objectivity is still vigorous, and that it has already begun to carry us on toward the day when editorial policies as well as news policies will be objective. It remains only for the men who own and control newspapers to become aware of the fact that the time long ago arrived when they ought to cease being advocates, and become judges.

Even a whole-souled dedication to independence on the part of our standard press will not, in this imperfect world, give us a perfect journalism. If all our papers freed themselves from commitments to preconceived outlooks or to certain factions of society, they would abandon the singing in conservative unison that is common now. Even so, a majority of them might find themselves on one side of a public debate, and that majority might be wrong. Therefore, in accordance with the basic tenet of democracy, the way must ever be kept open for minority publications raising dissident voices. If a paper like *PM* was a throwback to the dark age of American journalism because it slants its news, it nevertheless served a useful purpose by being a gadfly. A *PM* or a *CIO News* make an excellent condiment with which to swallow a daily diet of standard newspapers; but they do not begin to be substitutes for it. The man who relies on them alone lives in a hyperthyroid world full of Fascist plots; but, at least pending a more objective motivation in our standard press, such dissidents are healthy. They give meaning to the principle of a free press in its original sense. All this, however, is incidental. Our hope lies not in the lunatic fringe of journalism, but in an increasing sense of responsibility on the part of the great mass of our newspapers.

There is no need to fear that the standard papers, by making their editorial pages as objective as their news columns, will stultify themselves with an excess of ifs, buts, and on-the-other-hands. Objectivity in opinion is achieved not by emasculating editorials, but by directing every possible ounce of missionary zeal and hellfire to the service of the entire community rather than merely to a part of it. A news story is made objective by reporting both sides of a controversy. An editorial is objective by weighing both sides of a controversy with a broad perspective and a deep understanding before deciding which side to fight for. Editorially, a newspaper should be objective only as to purpose. Once it has determined what is right in a given issue, it should pull no punches. The only difference from the most vigorous present practice will be that its mind will not be largely made up in advance on political issues, political candidates, economic disputes, or anything else. Too many newspapers now get too many of their opinions first, and then look for facts to bolster them. It is the deepest obligation of newspapers in a really free world to get the facts first and let those facts determine their opinions.

Far from losing color and strength from this kind of objectivity, they would gain. They would even reverse the trend toward watering down editorials that set in as newspapers slowly changed from pamphleteering to big business. There is too much pussyfooting now. We need more, not less, of the thundering Hebrew prophets in our editorial pages. It is only the purpose of that thundering that needs to be reexamined.

None of the technics, few of the habits, of the modern newspaper need be changed to give effect to a policy of editorial independence. In fact, all that is necessary is a realization by the owners of our press that they have an obligation no less high than that of a minister, doctor, or scientist. More than two centuries ago Benjamin Franklin propounded to candidates for admission to the earliest American learned society, the Junto, this oath: "Do you love truth for truth's sake, and will you endeavor impartially to find and receive it for yourself, and communicate it to others?" Why should those who control America's information not be glad to take such an oath now, in all sincerity? Why should they not rejoice in the sense of dedication that would come from acknowledging an obligation like that of the young doctor taking the Hippocratic oath?

We have seen why it is a basic contradiction to apply to journalism a system of licensing like that in law or medicine. But a deepening sense of purpose might be imparted to neophytes of all ages in journalism and the related arts of mass communication by requiring them to take a pledge comparable to the noble oath that hands down from generation to generation the ideals of the father of medicine. That pledge might read something like this:

You do solemnly swear, each man by whatever he holds most sacred, that you will be loyal to the profession of journalism and just and generous to all men; that you will lead your lives and practice your craft in uprightness and honor; that whatsoever event, thought, or passion you may touch upon in your writing, it shall be for the good of all your fellow men to the utmost of your power, you holding yourselves far aloof from wrong, from corruption, from the tempting of others to vice; that you will exercise your skill solely for the truth as in your heart you see it and say nothing for another purpose, even if solicited, far less suggest it; that whatsoever you shall see or hear of the lives of men that promises either harm or good, you will not suppress it. These things do you swear. Let each man bow the head in sign of acquiescence. And now, if you will be true to this, your oath, may prosperity and good repute be ever yours; the opposite, if you shall prove yourselves forsworn.

Perhaps it seems pretentious thus to translate the Hippocratic oath into terms of journalism. Certainly there is one difference between administering such an oath to newly graduating doctors, and doing the same with young aspirants in journalism: doctors have the integrity of their art in their own hands; cub reporters do not. We need not fear that the young men and women who enter journalism with the hopes and ideals of youth will betray it. I have seen successive annual generations of them go out into the journalistic world, and have seen many of them turn to cynicism as they observed the men who control the great engines of communication. The young reporters hardly need an oath to truth. Rather, it is the men and women who manage, and still more those who own, the press and its allies.

The need for an oath to truth in journalism arises at the moment any man or woman enters into ownership of a newspaper, radio, or like enterprise; or becomes possessor of so much as a single share of corporate stock in one. A hint of what is needed was given in Britain when the Reuter's News Agency became independent. The new owners then pledged themselves to regard their holdings in Reuter's as a trust rather than an investment.[7] This kind of thing is needed because it is the owners, not the practitioners, of journalism that have the power to dedicate it to editorial independence. Yet, of all men associated with the calling, they are the least aware of its traditions, of its meaning to their fellow men, and of the dedication to the search for truth that alone justifies any expression of opinion in print, over the air, or on the screen.

Perhaps the most hopeful way of achieving this ideal is to put control of the press and related media into the hands of the men who do the practical work. A handful of our papers have taken steps toward this end. For example, the *Milwaukee Journal* has adopted a plan for making employee control of a majority of its stock permanent. In announcing this plan Harry J. Grant, chairman of the board, said:

My plan is in no sense a departure from the capitalistic system under a democratic form of government. It calls for perpetuity of employee stock control through the establishment of the employee trust agreement. This agreement provides that no new holdings of the Journal Company stock shall ever be issued outside the employee group, or any employee holdings be withdrawn from the trust.[8]

Of course, some of these plans still leave control in the hands of one or two top employees who are so free from a check on their decisions by the rest of the employees that they are just as conservative as if they owned the paper outright. But I repeat that this plan of financial control by a widespread group of the men who get out the paper offers the most hopeful approach to the freedom of information that is mandatory for our society because there are now so few outlets of popular expression in proportion to population.

Pending the eventual adoption of such a system I do not see how anyone connected with a newspaper or other source of information today can face his conscience, as long as it remains devoted to some cause other than that of the search for truth. Publishers can make more money by enlisting in the battle on behalf of all their fellow men, but the real, the urgent demand is spiritual. Our society cries out for it. It may not be too much to say that the solution of this century's titanic struggle to make the forms and traditions of democracy adequate to the technology and economics of our time is a reborn information system—one controlled by skilled professionals whose integrity is above reproach, and who are consciously and purposefully free from identification with any other group or interest.

Throughout man's long struggle he has achieved nothing higher than the resolve to give up all prior commitments, all prejudice, and become a seeker after truth. It was this dedication to the truth that long ago made the heroes of the free press prefer abuse, suffering, poverty, jail, and, if necessary, death, before they would write anything that betrayed what they saw as the truth. They fought for the right to be partisan. We must fight for the right not to be partisan. It is the same fight, in modern dress.

A WORD OF THANKS

THIS BOOK was begun long ago, in 1940, when I was at the Graduate School of Journalism at Columbia University. Work on it was often interrupted, not least by the war, and again when I left Columbia to return to newspaper work. As time passed, substantial changes became necessary. Indeed about all that remains of the original plan is the purpose of analyzing the position of journalism in contemporary democratic society. My object has been neither to indict the press nor to defend it, but simply to present it as honestly as I can.

Reading the final product in proof, I see how inadequate it is. Sometimes the words say things I do not mean, or leave unsaid much that I tried to say. But perhaps the whole will still contribute toward an understanding of the habits, and still more the rights and duties, of the press in the life of free men in the mid-twentieth century. I hope so. For it is still true, as Joseph Pulitzer said long ago, that our republic and its press will rise or fall together.

Despite the changes since the beginning, I wish to record here my thanks to eighteen students at Columbia who helped gather material in the early stages of the task. Some of them will find in the finished version little that reflects their labor. None of them is to be held responsible for the views expressed, which are wholly my own. Nevertheless my thanks are due, and gladly given, to the following members of Journalism 302, Section IV, at Columbia in 1942:

Elie Abel, Stanley E. Cohen, Jane Dealy Wirsig, Woodrow Wirsig, Mauri Edwards, Anthony Frances, Stuart Hale, George E. Herman, Arthur Kavaler, Richard Lang, Jack Matcha, Murray Morgan, Edmund Motyka, Arthur J. Olsen, Alan L. Otten, Adrian Spies, Milton D. Stewart, and John S. Wilson.

I also owe much to a host of others too numerous to mention here, men and women of newspapers, radio, and our universities, who gladly gave me of their time, insight, and information; to a series of secretaries who suffered through long years of retyping; and to the one who from beginning to end helped most of all, my wife.

HERBERT BRUCKER

Hartford,
September 29, 1948

FOOTNOTES

CHAPTER I

1 *New York Times,* Aug. 6, 1914, p. 6.
2 *Telegraph and Telephone Age,* Aug. 1, 1925, pp. 241–242.
3 Derrick Sington and Arthur Weidenfeld, *The Goebbels Experiment* (New Haven: Yale, 1943), p. 181.
4 Elmo Roper, "What People Are Thinking," *New York Herald Tribune,* May 9, 1946, p. 25.
5 Norman Angell, *The Public Mind* (New York: Dutton, 1927), chap. one.
6 *Editor & Publisher,* July 7, 1945, p. 5, and Dec. 8, 1945, p. 16.
7 "Bedlam Breaks Loose," *Editor & Publisher,* Sept. 10, 1932, p. 18.

CHAPTER II

1 Charles Warren, *The Making of the Constitution* (Boston: Little, Brown, 1928), p. 146.
2 Aristotle, *Politics,* Jowett transl., bk. VII, chap 4 (Oxford, 1885, Vol. I, p. 215).
3 "Annual Don R. Mellett Memorial Address in Journalism," *Editor & Publisher,* Feb. 28, 1942, p. 7.
4 Quoted in Frank L. Mott and R. D. Casey, *Interpretations of Journalism* (New York: Crofts, 1937), p. 52. Italics mine.
5 Warren, *op. cit.,* p. 186.
6 *Ibid.,* p. 217.
7 *Atlantic Monthly,* VIII, 346 (Sept., 1861).
8 *New York Times,* March 26, 1942, p. 3.

9 *Ibid.,* March 24, 1942.
10 From *Public Opinion,* copyright, 1922, by Walter Lippmann, pp. 364–365. Used by permission of The Macmillan Company, publishers.
11 Warren, *op. cit.,* pp. 605–610.
12 *The Federalist and Other Constitutional Papers,* ed. E. H. Scott (Chicago: Albert, Scott, 1894), No. LXXXIV, pp. 469–470.
13 *Freedom of the Press Today,* ed. Harold L. Ickes (New York: Vanguard, 1941), p. 3.

CHAPTER III

1 Commission on Freedom of the Press, *A Free and Responsible Press* (University of Chicago Press, 1947), p. v.
2 *Hartford Times,* April 4, 1947.

CHAPTER IV

1 *Freedom of the Press Today,* ed. Harold L. Ickes, p. 4.
2 Nov. 8, 1940, p. 1.
3 *A New English Dictionary on Historical Principles,* ed. James A. H. Murray (Oxford: Clarendon Press, 1888), Vol. III, p. 300.
4 Thomas Carlyle, *On Heroes, Hero-Worship, and the Heroic in History,* 1889 ed. (London: Chapman & Hall), p. 134.
5 *Loc. cit.*
6 Thomas Babington Macaulay, *Works* (London: Longmans, Green, 1879), V, 234.

7 William Haller, ed., *Tracts on Liberty in the Puritan Revolution, 1638–1647,* (New York: Columbia University Press, 1934), Vol. I, p. 7.

8 John Milton, *Works,* ed F. A. Patterson, Vol. IV (New York: Columbia University Press, 1931), p. 348.

9 *Ibid.,* p. 347.

10 Quoted in Mott and Casey, *op. cit.,* p. 18.

11 *Ibid.,* p. 37.

12 *Ibid.,* p. 43.

13 *On Liberty* (London: Longmans, Green, 1908), p. 10.

CHAPTER V

1 Burton Stevenson, ed., *The Home Book of Quotations,* 3rd ed. (New York: Dodd, Mead, 1937), p. 2276.

2 Quoted by Roger Howson, Librarian, in the Annual Reports of Columbia University for the Year Ending June 30, 1935, p. 387.

3 Sec. 1, p. 3.

4 *New York Times,* April 21, 1942.

5 *Ibid.,* May 4, 1942.

6 *Authority in the Modern State* (New Haven: Yale University Press, 1919), p. 54.

7 Quoted in an editorial, *St. Louis Post-Dispatch,* June 9, 1942, p. 2C.

8 Zechariah Chafee, Jr., *Free Speech in the United States* (Cambridge: Harvard University Press, 1941), p. ix.

9 Arthur Krock, *New York Times,* April 30 and May 22, 1942.

10 *New York Times,* April 28, 1942.

11 *Ibid.,* May 21, 1942, p. 6.

12 *Ibid.,* June 1, 1941, p. 1.

13 *Ibid.,* Feb. 18, 1942, p. 9.

14 *Ibid.,* May 1, 1947, Sec. 1, p. 1.

15 *Ibid.,* May 15, 1942, p. 1.

16 *New York World-Telegram,* May 15, 1942, p. 21.

17 *Manchester Guardian,* July 5, 1940, quoted in *Editor & Publisher,* July 27, 1940, p. 4.

18 *Editor & Publisher,* Sept. 28, 1940, p. xiii.

19 *Editor & Publisher,* Dec. 7, 1935, p. 29; and *New York Times,* Dec. 12, 1935, p. 2 (story beginning on p. 1).

20 Quoted in Lucy Maynard Salmon, *The Newspaper and Authority* (New York: Oxford University Press, 1923), p. 450.

21 *Ibid.,* p. 451.

22 *New York Post,* May 6, 1942, pp. 1, 3, and 33.

CHAPTER VI

1 Everett Rich, *William Allen White* (New York: Farrar & Rinehart, 1941), pp. 70–71.

2 *Emporia Gazette,* Jan. 29, 1944, p. 4.

3 *Ibid.,* Dec. 23, 1925.

4 *Editor & Publisher,* May 23, 1942, pp. 5, 34.

5 *PM,* June 18, 1940, p. 19.

6 Quoted in *Editor & Publisher,* Sept. 10, 1932, p. 36.

7 *The Brass Check* (published by the author, Pasadena, Calif., 1920), especially chaps. xliii, xliv.

8 *Freedom of the Press* (Indianapolis): Bobbs-Merrill, 1935), esp. chap. ii.

9 "Of a Defect in Our Policies"— quoted in Frank Presbrey, *The History and Development of Advertising* (Garden City, N.Y.: Doubleday, 1929), p. 35.

10 Henry Sampson, *A History of Advertising* (London: Chatto & Windus, 1875), pp. 63–64.

11 Paul Louis Hervier, "L'Évolution de la publicite," *La Nouvelle Revue,* Aug., 1906, p. 378.

12 Quoted in Sampson, *op. cit.,* p. 64.

13 *Ibid.,* p. 109.

14 Quoted in Lawrence Lewis, *The Advertisements of The Spectator* (Boston: Houghton Mifflin, 1909), p. vi.

15 Facsimile in Presbrey, *op. cit.,* p. 137.

16 Facsimile in *ibid.,* p. 157.

17 James Melvin Lee, *History of American Journalism* (Boston: Houghton Mifflin, 1923), pp. 118–119.

18 Presbrey, *op. cit.,* p. 197.

19 *The Newspaper: Its Making and Its Meaning,* by Members of the Staff of the *New York Times* (New York: Scribner, 1945), pp. 179–180.

20 Figures compiled by H. H. Hilliker, *Editor & Publisher*, Dec. 4, 1943, p. 28.

21 Address made in 1940. Copy in possession of author.

22 *Editor & Publisher*, March 7, 1942, p. 6. Its Year Books: 1943, p. 116; 1944, p. 132; 1945, p. 134; 1946, p. 16; 1947, p. 20; 1948, p. 18.

23 *Editor & Publisher*, Yearbook 1948, p. 18.

24 From Alfred M. Lee: *The Daily Newspaper in America*. Copyright, 1937, by The Macmillan Company and used with their permission, p. 711. Tabulated by him from C. S. Brigham's "Bibliography of American Newspapers, 1690–1820."

25 Figures from census and other sources, tabulated in A. M. Lee, *op. cit.*, p. 717.

26 Figures for one year earlier than corresponding population, e.g., 1899 instead of 1900.

27 *Editor & Publisher* figures, which are lower than census figures and therefore slightly out of scale.

28 Study of communities in which newspapers disappear, and role of radio in this development. Typed copy, Office of Radio Research, 1941, p. 1.

29 "Concentration and Absenteeism in Daily Newspaper Ownership," *Journalism Quarterly*, June, 1945, pp. 97–114.

30 *Editor & Publisher*, May 10, 1947, p. 69.

31 Letter to Dean Carl W. Ackerman, Graduate School of Journalism, Columbia University, Aug. 3, 1938.

32 Humbert Wolfe, *The Uncelestial City* (London: Gollancz, 1930), p. 37.

CHAPTER VII

1 *New York Herald Tribune*, Feb. 12, 1944, p. 9.

2 *New Republic*, March 6, 1944, pp. 303–304.

3 *New York Times*, Dec. 29, 1943, p. 23.

4 Testimony before the FCC, Jan. 22, 1942, of Frank Luther Mott, now Dean of the School of Journalism at the University of Missouri.

5 A. M. Lee, *op. cit.*, pp. 211–212, 215.

6 Author's tabulation from *Editor & Publisher* Year Book, 1944, p. 134.

7 *Editor & Publisher*, Nov. 21, 1942, Sec. 2, p. AP–3.

8 *Ibid.*, Oct. 9, 1943, pp. 9, 70.

9 *Ibid.*, p. 9.

10 *New York Times*, Jan. 19, 1944, p. 1; *Editor & Publisher*, March 11, 1944, p. 7.

11 *New York Times*, Aug. 29, 1942, p. 8.

12 *Ibid.*, March 10, 1944, p. 11; and March 14, p. 21.

13 *Editor & Publisher*, March 25, 1944, p. 12.

14 *Ibid.*, Dec. 1, 1945, p. 7.

15 *New York Times*, April 23, 1946, p. 16.

16 *Editor & Publisher*, May 3, 1947, p. 8.

17 Howard Wolf, "What About the Associated Press?" *Harper's Magazine*, Feb., 1943, p. 261.

18 Quoted in Thomas Porter Robinson, *The Radio Networks and the Federal Government* (New York: Columbia University Press, 1943), p. 74.

19 *Editor & Publisher*, Oct. 23, 1943, p. 9.

20 *Ibid.*, pp. 64–65.

21 *New York Times*, May 4, 1941, Sec. 1, pp. 1, 48.

22 *Broadcasting*, Jan. 25, 1943, pp. 8, 48.

23 TNEC Monograph Nov., 1943. Daniel Bertrand, W. Duane Evans, and E. L. Blanchard, *The Motion Picture Industry: A Pattern of Control* (Washington: Government Printing Office, 1941), pp. 16–17.

24 *New York Times*, July 21, 1938, p. 1.

25 *Ibid.*, Jan. 18, 1946, p. 36.

26 FCC Docket No. 6051, July, 1941.

27 Testimony in FCC Newspaper-Radio hearing, Oct. 2, 1941. Typed transcript, pp. 1402, 1407–1408. Punctuation changed slightly from stenographic record.

28 *Ibid.*, p. 1411.

29 *Ibid.*, Oct. 3, 1941, pp. 1709–1721.

30 *Freedom of the Press,* a selection of testimony from witnesses before the FCC Newspaper-Radio hearings (New York: Newspaper-Radio Committee, American Newspaper Publishers Association, 1942), p. 66.

31 Summary of Continuation of Hearings of Newspaper Ownership of Radio Before the FCC Committee, July 30 to Aug. 1 (New York: Newspaper-Radio Committee, ANPA, 1941).

32 A Comparison of News Programs, Educational Programs, and Editorial Policy of Associated and Non-Associated Media (Office of Radio Research, 1941).

33 *Editor & Publisher,* Dec. 4, 1943, p. 15.

34 *New York Times,* Dec. 31, 1943, p. 10.

35 *Broadcasting & Broadcast Advertising,* Jan. 17, 1944, p. 65.

CHAPTER VIII

1 Reprinted from *The Revolt of the Masses* by José Ortega y Gasset, by permission of W. W. Norton & Co., Inc., copyright, 1932 by the publishers, p. 54.

2 *New York Times,* June 10, 1942, p. 16.

3 *Ibid.*, Dec. 28, 1946, p. 1.

4 *Life,* Jan. 22, 1945, pp. 76, 93.

5 W. Roepke, *Die Gesellschaftskrisis der Gegenwart* (Zurich, 1942), p. 172 —quoted in Friedrich A. Hayek, *The Road to Serfdom* (University of Chicago Press, 1944), p. 126.

CHAPTER IX

1 *New Statesman and Nation,* May 23, 1942.

2 Delbert Clark, *Washington Dateline* (Philadelphia: J. B. Lippincott, 1941), p. 54.

3 *Ibid.*, p. 119.

4 *Ibid.*, p. 20.

5 Dennis Bardens, "Public Relations," *Spectator,* Feb. 13, 1944, p. 142.

6 Peter Edson, *New York World-Telegram,* Nov. 5, 1941, p. 26.

7 Press release from Senator Tydings for May 31, 1942.

8 *New York Herald Tribune,* May 3, 1942, Sec. 1, p. 1.

9 *U. S. Government Manual,* Sept., 1941.

10 *New York Herald Tribune,* Oct. 9, 1941, p. 22.

11 *Editor & Publisher,* June 20, 1942, p. 5.

12 *New York Times,* June 14, 1942, Sec. 1, p. 1.

13 *New York Times,* July 11, 1942, p. 7.

14 Address before Sales Executive Group, New York, Dec. 28, 1943. Text in author's possession.

CHAPTER X

1 Oliver Gramling, *AP: The Story of News* (New York: Farrar & Rinehart, 1940), pp. 229–230.

2 *Broadcasting,* Feb. 15, 1943, p. 45.

CHAPTER XI

1 *New York Times,* June 26, 1942, p. 19.

2 *Editor & Publisher,* June 13, 1942, p. 51.

3 Peter H. Odegard, *Pressure Politics* (New York: Columbia University Press, 1928), pp. 231–232.

4 Harold D. Lasswell, Ralph D. Casey, and Bruce L. Smith, *Propaganda and Promotional Activities* (Minneapolis: University of Minnesota Press, 1935), pp. 20–21.

5 Gorham Munson, *Twelve Decisive Battles of the Mind* (New York: Greystone, 1942), p. 11.

6 Memorandum from Milton S. Eisenhower, associate director, to OWI staff, Oct. 12, 1942. See also *N. Y. Herald Tribune,* Oct. 9, 1942, p. 19.

7 Lucy Maynard Salmon, *The Newspaper and Authority* (New York: Oxford University Press, 1923), pp. 324 ff.

8 P. T. Barnum, *The Life of P. T. Barnum* (New York, Redfield, 1855), p. 316.

9 *Ibid.*, p. 315.

10 M. R. Werner, *Barnum* (New

York: Harcourt, Brace, 1923), pp. 56–62.

11 Edmond Taylor, *The Strategy of Terror* (Boston: Houghton Mifflin, 1940), pp. 74, 87.

12 Frank Ward O'Malley, "Hot Off the Press Agent," *Saturday Evening Post*, June 25, 1921, p. 9.

13 *New York Times*, July 28 and 30, 1920.

14 Quoted in Salmon, *op. cit.*, pp. 363–364.

15 Quoted in Roscoe C. E. Brown, "The Menace to Journalism," *North American Review*, Nov., 1921; reprinted in J. W. Cunliffe and Gerhard R. Lomer, eds., *Writing of Today* (New York: Century, 1922), p. 248.

16 Edgar Sisson, *One Hundred Red Days* (New Haven: Yale University Press, 1931), p. 215; and Munson, *op. cit.*, pp. 240–241.

17 Quoted by Edgar Sisson in a letter to the author, Feb. 18, 1927.

18 Edward L. Bernays, *Propaganda* (New York: Horace Liveright, 1928), p. 28.

19 *Editor & Publisher*, Feb. 12, 1944, p. 4.

CHAPTER XII

1 Robert Sherrod, *Tarawa: The Story of a Battle* (New York: Duell, Sloan & Pearce, 1944), p. 150.

2 Quoted in Mott and Casey, *Interpretations of Journalism*, p. 458.

3 *The Idler*—quoted in *ibid.*, p. 157.

4 George Seldes, *Lords of the Press* (New York: Messner, 1938), pp. viii, 355.

5 *Fortune* Survey, Aug., 1939, pp. 64, 70.

6 George H. Gallup, "The People and the Press," in Harold L. Ickes, ed., *Freedom of the Press Today* (New York: Vanguard, 1941), p. 115.

7 Commission on Freedom of the Press, *A Free and Responsible Press* (University of Chicago Press, 1947), p. 21.

8 *Ibid.*, e.g., p. 123.

9 *Ibid.*, p. 57.

10 Supplement to *New Republic*, Aug. 4, 1920.

11 Mitchell V. Charnley, "Preliminary Notes on a Study of Newspaper Accuracy," *Journalism Quarterly*, Dec., 1936, pp. 394 ff.

13 Letter to author, March 16, 1944.

14 *Omaha Morning World Herald*, March 28, 1942, p. 1.

15 *Guild Reporter*, March 1, 1944, p. 8.

16 *N.Y. Herald Tribune*, May 4, 1942, p. 7.

17 "Newspaper Errors," *Editor & Publisher*, Aug. 23, 1941, p. 18.

18 *Muncie Evening Press*, Feb. 7, 1933. Reprinted in Mott and Casey, *op. cit.*, pp. 211 ff.

19 *Ibid.*

20 *Editor & Publisher*, Feb. 26, 1944, p. 72.

21 *New York Times*, Nov. 25, 1940, p. 1.

22 *Courier-Journal*, March 14, 1944.

23 *Louisville Times*, March 14, 1944.

24 Letter from James S. Pope to author, March 16, 1944.

25 Westbrook Pegler, "Fair Enough," *New York World-Telegram*, Sept. 3, 1943.

26 *New York Times*, June 9, 1943, p. 4.

27 *Adventures in Error* (New York: McBride, 1936), chap. viii.

28 Feb. 27, 1946, p. 26.

CHAPTER XIII

1 Arthur Krock, "In Wartime What News Shall the Nation Have?" *New York Times*, Aug. 16, 1942, Sec. 7, p. 4.

2 Letter to Harry W. Caygill, Feb. 29, 1932, quoted in H. W. Caygill, "press Censorship in the American Expeditionary Forces," (M.S. thesis, Columbia University, 1932), p. 78.

3 Macnair Wilson, *Lord Northcliffe* (Philadelphia: Lippincott, 1927), chaps. xxxv–xl.

4 Radio Censorship Policy Is Praised," *Broadcasting*, Nov. 2, 1942, p. 16.

5 *New York Times*, May 22, 1942, p. 5.

6 *Ibid.*, Nov. 29, 1943, p. 27.

7 *Ibid.*, July 28, 1945, p. 1.

8 From *The Newspaper and Authority* by Lucy Maynard Salmon. Copyright, 1923, by Oxford University Press, New York, Inc., p. 48.

9 *New Statesman and Nation*, Feb. 7, 1942.

10 Havilah Babcock, "The Press and the Civil War," *Journalism Quarterly*, March, 1929, p. 3.

11 A. M. Lee, *The Daily Newspaper in America*, p. 618.

12 Walter Millis, *The Martial Spirit* (Boston: Houghton Mifflin, 1931), p. 163.

13 James R. Mock, *Censorship 1917* (Princeton University Press, 1941), p. 42.

14 Quoted in James R. Mock and Cedric Larson, *Words That Won the War* (Princeton University Press, 1939), p. 50.

15 George Creel, *How We Advertised America* (New York: Harper, 1920), p. 4.

16 *Ibid.*, pp. 21–23.

17 "Censorship," *Fortune*, June, 1941, pp. 88, 154.

18 *Editor & Publisher*, April 12, 1941, p. 7.

19 *New York Times*, Dec. 10, 1941, p. 5.

20 *Ibid.*, Dec. 17, 1941, pp. 1, 5.

21 *Code of Wartime Practices for the American Press* (Washington: Government Printing Office, Jan. 15, 1942), p. 1.

22 *New York Times*, Dec. 10, 1943, p. 14.

23 *Ibid.*, Jan. 20, 1944, p. 6.

24 Office of Censorship release, June 12, 1942.

25 *Time*, June 22, 1942, p. 60.

26 *New York Times*, Dec. 10, 1941, p. 4.

27 *Ibid.*, Jan. 17, 1942, p. 3.

28 *Ibid.*, Feb. 24, 1942, p. 4.

29 *Ibid.*, Dec. 6, 1942, Sec. 1, p. 71.

CHAPTER XIV

1 Karl von Clausewitz, *On War*, Transl. J. J. Graham (London: Kegan Paul, 1911), Vol. III, p. 209.

2 Edmond Taylor, *The Strategy of Terror* (Boston: Houghton Mifflin, 1940), p. 3.

3 Foreword to Matthew Gordon, *News Is a Weapon* (New York: Knopf, 1942), pp. vi–vii.

4 Adolf Hitler, *Mein Kampf* (Harrisburg, Pa.: Stackpole, 1939), p. 228.

5 Sidney A. Freifeld, "The War of Nerves in the News," *Contemporary Jewish Record*, Feb., 1942, p. 19.

6 Quoted in *ibid.*, p. 38.

7 *Ibid.*, p. 35.

8 Reynolds and Eleanor Packard, *Balcony Empire* (New York: Oxford University Press, 1942), pp. 60–61, 78.

9 Freifeld, *op. cit.*, pp. 32–34.

CHAPTER XV

1 Kent Cooper, *Barriers Down* (New York: Rinehart, 1942), chap. iii.

2 *Ibid.*, p. 34.

3 *Editor & Publisher*, May 10, 1947, p. 44.

4 *Editor & Publisher*, April 12, 1947, p. 13.

5 Arthur Krock, *New York Times*, Feb. 18, 1944, p. 16.

6 Kent Cooper, *op. cit.*, p. 88.

7 *Ibid.*, p. 90.

8 Report of the Dean of the Graduate School of Journalism for the Academic Year Ending June 30, 1943 (New York: Columbia University, 1944), pp. 8 ff.

9 C. W. Ackerman, *Bulletin of the American Society of Newspaper Editors*, No. 263, June 1, 1945, p. 4.

10 *New York Times*, May 8, 1946, p. 16.

11 Art. 1, par. 3; Art. 55(c).

12 Art. 62, par. 2.

13 *New York Times*, Jan. 12, 1946, p. 5 (City ed.).

14 *Ibid.*, p. 16.

15 *Editor & Publisher*, May 15, 1948, pp. 56 ff.

16 *Editor & Publisher*, April 15, 1944, p. 11.

17 *Time*, April 1, 1946, p. 62; *New York Times*, Jan. 31 and March 31, 1947.

[18] *Time*, April 1, 1946, p. 62; *Life*, July 22, 1946, p. 19.

[19] *Editor & Publisher*, April 21, 1945, p. 15.

[20] *New York Herald Tribune*, Dec. 2, 1944, p. 3.

[21] Llewellyn White and Robert D. Leigh, *Peoples Speaking to Peoples* (University of Chicago Press, 1946).

[22] *Manchester Guardian Weekly*, Jan. 11, 1946, p. 14.

[23] *Editor & Publisher*, April 13, 1946, p. 7.

[24] *Editor & Publisher*, Feb. 7, 1948, p. 36.

CHAPTER XVI

[1] Adolf Hitler, *Speeches, April, 1922, to August, 1939*, ed. Norman H. Baynes (New York: Oxford University Press, 1942), Vol. I, p. 106.

[2] H. Schmid-Leonhardt and P. Gast, eds., *Das Schriftleitergesetz vom 4. Oktober, 1933* (Berlin: Carl Heymanns Verlag, 1934), p. 24.

[3] Commission on Freedom of the Press, *A Free and Responsible Press*, p. 81.

[4] *New York Times*, May 6, 1935, p. 12; and May 6, 1940, p. 1.

[5] *The Land of Socialism Today and Tomorrow: Reports and Speeches to the 18th Congress of the Communist Party* (Moscow: Foreign Language Publishing House, 1939), p. 31.

[6] Anna Louise Strong, *The New Soviet Constitution* (New York: Holt, 1937), pp. 154–155.

[7] *The Draft Constitution of the Soviet Union*, annotated by Pat Sloan (London: Lawrence & Wishart, 1936), p. 11; quoted in Strong, *op. cit.*, p. 111.

[8] Michael T. Florinsky, *Toward an Understanding of the U.S.S.R.* (New York: Macmillan, 1939), p. 145.

[9] *New York Times*, May 27, 1947, p. 7.

[10] From the Russian text of: *Administrative Legislation, Collection of the Most Important Decisions*, ed. S. S. Askarkhanov and S. M. Brodovich (Moscow: State Publishing House, "Soviet Legislation," 1936). Parts quoted and mentioned translated for the author by Clarence A. Manning, Assistant Professor of Slavic Languages, Columbia University.

[11] Drew Middleton, *New York Times*, June 23, 1946, p. 4.

[12] *Duranty Reports Russia*, ed. Gustavus Tuckerman, Jr. (New York: Viking, 1934), p. 204.

[13] A. Sokoloff in the *New Times*, Moscow; quoted in Brooks Atkinson, Democracy As Russia Defines It Today," *New York Times*, Sec. 6, Nov. 4, 1945, p. 14.

[14] *New York Times*, July 12, 1946, p. 1.

[15] *Ibid.*, July 7, 1946, pp. 1, 6.

CHAPTER XVII

[1] A. M. Lee, *The Daily Newspaper in America*, p. 190.

[2] Quoted in A. M. Lee, *op. cit.*, pp. 678–679.

[3] *Public Opinion*, p. 322.

[4] *New York Times*, March 4, 1944, p. 28.

[5] *Editor & Publisher*, March 8, 1947, p. 52.

[6] *Ibid.*, Sept. 10, 1932, p. 36.

[7] *Time*, June 25, 1945, p. 64.

[8] *PM*, June 18, 1946.

[9] *New York Times*, Nov. 5, 1946, p. 23.

[10] *Ibid.*, Feb. 16, 1943, p. 9.

[11] From Frank Luther Mott: *American Journalism*. Copyright, 1941, by The Macmillan Company and used with their permission, pp. 350–351.

[12] A. M. Lee, *op. cit.*, pp. 190–194.

[13] Foreword to Morris Watson, *How to Write for Your Union Paper* (San Francisco: International Longshoremen's & Warehousemen's Union, 1943), p. 7.

CHAPTER XVIII

[1] Facsimile in Willard G. Bleyer, *Main Currents in the History of American Journalism* (Boston: Houghton Mifflin, 1927), p. 17.

[2] *Ibid.*, p. 18.

[3] *Boston Evening-Post*, March 6,

1775, quoted in Bleyer, *op. cit.*, p. 86.

4 Bleyer, *op. cit.*, pp. 94–96.

5 *American Journalism,* pp. 113–114.

6 Frank L. Mott, *Jefferson and the Press* (Baton Rouge: Louisiana State University Press, 1943), p. 21.

7 Testimony at Newspaper-Radio hearings before FCC printed in a pamphlet, *Freedom of the Press* (New York: Newspaper-Radio Committee, 1942), p. 26.

8 *Ibid.,* p. 27.

9 Oct. 30, 1802. Quoted in Mott, *Jefferson and the Press,* p. 40.

10 Letter to N. P. Trist, quoted in Mott and Casey, *Interpretations of Journalism,* pp. 113–114.

11 Frank M. O'Brien, *The Story of the Sun* (New York: Doran, 1918), p. 26.

12 G. H. Payne, *History of Journalism in the United States* (New York: Appleton, 1920), p. 107.

13 Quoted in Mott, *American Journalism,* p. 223.

14 Quoted in Don C. Seitz, *The James Gordon Bennetts, Father and Son,* p. 39. Copyright, 1928. Used by special permission of the publishers, The Bobbs-Merrill Co.

15 *Ibid.,* p. 42.

16 Oliver Gramling, *AP: The Story of News,* p. 21.

17 *Ibid.,* p. 39.

18 *Ibid.,* p. 39.

19 Henry Luther Stoddard, *Horace Greeley* (New York: Putnam, 1946), p. 61.

20 Quoted in Mott and Casey, *op. cit.,* pp. 116–117.

21 Quoted in Bleyer, *op. cit.,* p. 259.

22 Merle Thorpe, *The Coming American Newspaper* (New York: Holt, 1915), p. 98.

23 *American Journalism,* p. 430.

24 *Ibid.,* p. 435.

25 *New York Times,* Aug. 19, 1896.

26 Bleyer, *op. cit.,* p. 406.

27 "The People and the Press," in Harold L. Ickes, ed. *Freedom of the Press Today,* p. 117.

28 Bleyer, *op. cit.,* p. 311.

29 Letter to John B. Pine (files of Columbia University).

30 Quoted in Drew Middleton, "A Week's News As Russia Got It," *New York Times,* Aug. 18, 1946, Sec. 6, p. 50.

31 *Hartford Courant,* June 23, 1946, p. 1.

32 Ickes, *op. cit.,* p. 9.

33 Quoted in Bleyer, *op. cit.,* p. 132.

34 *New York World,* Oct. 29, 1884, p. 1.

35 *New York Tribune,* Nov. 4, 1884, p. 1.

36 *Guild Reporter,* April 1, 1941, p. 1.

37 *CIO News,* Aug. 30, 1943, p. 4.

38 Sept. 13, 1943.

39 Sept. 23, 1943.

CHAPTER XIX

1 Gerald Johnson, *An Honorable Titan* (New York: Harper, 1946), p. 159.

2 Morris L. Ernst, *The First Freedom* (New York: Macmillan, 1946), chap. vii.

3 Eugene Katz and Alan Barth, "The Facsimile Newspaper," *American Mercury,* Oct., 1945, pp. 408 ff.

4 *News Is What We Make It* (Boston: Houghton Mifflin, 1943).

5 *Ibid.,* p. 316.

6 *Bulletin of the American Society of Newspaper Editors,* July 1, 1946, p. 4.

7 *New York Times,* Dec. 23, 1946, p. 6.

8 *Ibid.,* May 17, 1947.

INDEX

303

daniel
THRU malachi

GOD'S PROMISES ON DISPLAY

S0-BHW-179

CONTRIBUTING EDITORS:
John Hanneman
Rev. Stephen C. Magee
Doug McIntosh
Dr. Robert Rayburn

CONSULTING EDITOR:
Dr. Tremper Longman

Produced with the assistance of Christopher. D. Hudson & Associates. Contributing writers include: Gordon Lawrence, Heather Rippetoe, Laura Coggin, Stan Campbell, and Carol Smith.

Published by Barbour Publishing, Inc., P.O. Box 719, Uhrichsville, Ohio 44683 www.barbourbooks.com

Our mission is to publish and distribute inspirational products offering exceptional value and biblical encouragement to the masses.

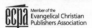

Printed in the United States of America.

DANIEL

INTRODUCTION TO DANIEL

The book of Daniel contains some of the best-known stories in the Bible, but it also provides some of the most challenging and intriguing passages to attempt to comprehend. Some of the prophets had sent warning of a judgment of God's people to come; others are present at the end of the captivity to help encourage and empower the beleaguered exiles. But Daniel goes into exile along with his countrymen and provides an insider's view of Judah's experiences in the faraway land of Babylon.

AUTHOR

Daniel came from a royal family. He is compared with Noah and Job in terms of faithfulness to God and righteousness (see Ezekiel 14:14). Daniel also demonstrates great wisdom, always giving God complete credit. Unlike Solomon, who started life strong as a young man but strayed from God as an adult, Daniel's faith and wisdom are consistent and evident throughout his long lifetime.

OCCASION

Daniel describes events that occur during one of the worst situations the people of God ever experienced. The nation of Israel had fallen to the Assyrians more than one hundred years earlier, but Judah survived. Yet Judah continues to refuse to heed God's warning and soon faces humiliating defeat themselves. The Babylonians breach the walls of Jerusalem, ransack the temple, and carry off most of the population in a series of deportations. Daniel is among the first group taken. His writing offers much assurance in that even though circumstances are bad, God is still with His people.

THEMES

From start to finish, the theme of the book of Daniel is the sovereignty of God. This theme is detected in the way the Lord interacts with individuals, controls nations, and shares with Daniel plans for the long-range future of His people.

HISTORICAL CONTEXT

Babylon was considered to be one of the most glorious and powerful kingdoms of the world at the time that Daniel was written. The palace and gardens are listed among the seven wonders of the ancient world. God uses Babylon's strong armies to conquer Judah after the people refuse to serve Him. In the process, the Babylonians kill many Judeans and take many into captivity. Yet by the end of Daniel, the Babylonian Empire has already fallen to Cyrus, leader of the Medes and Persians.

CONTRIBUTION TO THE BIBLE

In addition to some of the Bible's most beloved stories (including the fiery furnace and the lions' den), the book of Daniel is an invaluable source of information concerning various events of future history. Coupled with John's writing in Revelation, many of the symbols of the apocalyptic literature begin to cohere and make sense. Certainly, there are numerous ways to interpret the same information, and it can be difficult to do more than speculate in many places. However, Jesus quotes Daniel as a source for what to look for in the future (see Matthew 24:15-16), giving the prophet's writing the highest degree of credibility.

OUTLINE

DANIEL 1:1-21

DANIEL TAKEN TO BABYLON

Setting Up the Section

The book of Daniel describes some of the same era as 2 Kings and 2 Chronicles, yet Daniel describes this era from within the Babylonian exile. Due to persistent disregard for God's laws and other sins throughout Judah, the Lord had allowed His people to be conquered. The Babylonian armies had shown little mercy as they marched into Judah, laid siege to Jerusalem, and eventually left the city and the surrounding territory in ruins. Many people died while fighting; many others starved to death. Most of those who survived were deported to Babylon—Daniel among them. The people feel as though God has deserted them. However, Daniel repeatedly attests to the power of the one true God at work, even while His people are exiled in the idolatrous land of Babylon.

📄 **1:1–2**

A DISTRESSING BEGINNING

Daniel has one of the bleakest openings of any book of scripture. Within the first two verses, the beloved city of Jerusalem falls into the hands of one of the most terrifying empires on earth. The temple's holy items are carted away and placed among the idols of Babylon. To make things worse, it is the Lord who has given Jerusalem over to her enemies. The captivity that results is a God-designed plan to chastise His people for their ongoing rebellion. The year is 605 BC. Judah's king at the time is Jehoiakim.

This is one of the worst experiences in the history of Judah. (The northern kingdom of Israel had faced a similar end more than a century earlier at the hands of the Assyrians.) Yet despite this potentially depressing beginning, Daniel never ceases to be encouraging and optimistic. Right from the start, the theme of his book is the sovereignty of God. The Lord is in control of the nations and is working out His plan in this world. He is absolutely in control.

Critical Observation

The prophet Habakkuk confirms that God permitted the brutal Babylonian invasion as a result of the wickedness of His people (Habakkuk 1:5–11). In fact, Habakkuk tries to talk God out of impending disaster (Habakkuk 1:12–2:1). He learns, however, that the plans of God are God's alone, and that the best he can do is walk by faith, no matter what happens.

Other sources describe various horrific events associated with the fall of Jerusalem, so it is interesting to notice what Daniel focuses on in his record. Of all the dreadful and repulsive things taking place around him, he singles out the degradation of the temple (1:2). Israel's worship had become ritualistic rather than genuine, so God took worship away from them. He allowed all of the gold previously used in temple worship to be used to mock Him in the presence of false gods. It is humiliating to Judah and to the Lord.

Israel's mind-set and practice of worship as ritual had no effect on their day-to-day lives. Placing their so-called holy objects among the idols of other nations is God's way of giving them a picture of what is in their hearts. Their "worship" is no different than that of the Babylonians.

God wants to see His people redeemed. He wants Judah to repent and fall before Him in complete devotion. Therefore, He allows them to endure much heartache and lose their temple temporarily so that ultimately they might be saved.

📄 1:3–7

THE BEST IN A BAD SITUATION

After Jerusalem falls, Babylonian King Nebuchadnezzar conducts a search for some of Judah's top young people—a common practice of the time by victorious rulers. By indoctrinating the up-and-coming leaders of the defeated nation, Nebuchadnezzar hopes to ensure that new generations will settle into the Babylonian way of life rather than attempting escape or revolt.

Daniel is one of four young men from Judah mentioned by name who are taken (1:6). At the time, they are probably about fifteen or sixteen years old. Nothing is said of their parents, but the Babylonians wouldn't have thought twice about breaking up families to carry off anyone they wished.

Being handsome and without defect (1:4), Daniel and his three peers clearly have genetics working for them. But they also are noted for their quickness to learn and their aptitude for accumulating wisdom. They are expected to quickly assimilate into Babylonian culture by absorbing the language and literature of their new home. They are also given Babylonians names.

Demystifying Daniel

A change in names had spiritual as well as cultural significance. The Hebrew names all acknowledged characteristics of the awesome God of Judah:

Daniel meant, "God is my Judge."

Hananiah meant, "Yahweh is gracious."

Mishael meant, "Who is like God?"

Azariah meant, "Yahweh is my helper."

The newly assigned names, in contrast (Belteshazzar, Shadrach, Meshach, and Abednego), acknowledged various Babylonian deities: Bel, Aku, and Nego/Nebo.

Theirs was a demanding, three-year program (1:5). Nebuchadnezzar changed their names, clothes, language, home, and culture, yet he was not successful in changing their hearts.

🗋 1:8–21

PASSING THE FIRST TEST

However, there are benefits in addition to the demands for these men. The young trainees are entitled to a daily allotment of food from the king's own table—the best of the best (1:5). This is intended to be a privilege, but Daniel and his friends do not see it that way. Daniel is probably well aware of the numerous dietary restrictions in Jewish law, and the gourmet food of Babylon did not meet those standards. Also, the Babylonian food was associated with their idols.

Regardless of his motivation, Daniel determines not to defile himself with Nebuchadnezzar's choice food or fine wine (1:8). This verse is key in understanding who Daniel truly is. He is a young man, away from home and family, plunged into a new and potentially mesmerizing culture, and offered the best of everything. Many young people would quickly succumb to exotic opportunities and temptations, especially in a setting where it appears that righteous behavior does not matter. Yet Daniel never loses his resolve to live a holy life for the Lord.

He acts on his belief, and the way he does so also attests to his character. He doesn't make a big scene, attempt to manipulate anyone, or tell little white lies. He realizes this is a delicate situation—one that can get his supervisor killed if things go badly (1:10). So Daniel goes behind the scenes and makes an agreement with the delivery boy, suggesting a ten-day test period.

Daniel acts wisely, yet the text makes it clear that it is God who is at work to resolve the problem (1:9). Even as God's people are being disciplined, the Lord is at work among them, still preserving and protecting them. All the other trainees in Nebuchadnezzar's program are given the rich foods, while Daniel and his three friends stick to a vegetable and water diet (1:11–14).

After ten days, Daniel and his three friends are noticeably healthier and better nourished than their peers. Their supervisor breaths a sigh of relief and continues their vegetable diet, and they feel no more pressure to defy their religious convictions in order to fit in (1:15–16).

But the diet test is just a beginning. God gives Daniel, Hananiah (Shadrach), Mishael (Meshach), and Azariah (Abednego) great understanding and wisdom in all areas of learning and philosophy (1:17). Daniel is given a special ability to understand dreams and visions. Daniel and his friends aren't actively seeking special favor from God, yet the Lord responds to their devotion and obedience.

In the midst of destruction and misery for Judah, God is still blessing His people. And through them, others will be blessed. In this case, Daniel's supervisor comes out looking good. Before long, the young men of Judah will be influencing kings.

At the end of the three-year training period, Nebuchadnezzar interviews each of the young men who have gone through his program. Again, Daniel and his three friends are clearly exceptional. The king deems them ten times better in terms of wisdom and understanding than any of the magicians and enchanters from whom he seeks advice (1:20).

Ten times better (1:20) is not a quantitative term. Just as people today think in terms of "a perfect 10" at an Olympic event, or judge an extremely attractive person as "a 10," the number had similar meaning in ancient times. *Ten* was a number that represented fullness or completeness.

Considering their young age and circumstances, the faithfulness of Daniel and his friends is particularly amazing. And yet, both Daniel and his three friends will face far greater challenges (and successes) ahead.

Daniel demonstrates that the battle for holiness is either won or lost in the small areas of life. Instead of attempting to change circumstances that are beyond his control, he shifts his focus to simply obeying God. In fact, sometimes the desire to maintain control is the polar opposite of faith. Can you think of any areas in your life where you might need to relinquish control in order to let God act on your behalf instead?

DANIEL 2:1–49

DANIEL INTERPRETS NEBUCHADNEZZAR'S DREAM

Setting Up the Section

After going through Nebuchadnezzar's three-year training period and excelling among his fellow participants (1:3–5, 18–20), Daniel is soon put to the test. In an account that demonstrates how eccentric and brutal Babylonian leadership could be at times, the king makes a demand of his advisors that seems impossible, yet their failure will result in their deaths. As the Lord had done previously, He again provides a way out for Daniel—an act that delivers not only Daniel but also spares the entire group of Nebuchadnezzar's advisors.

📄 2:1–13

NEBUCHADNEZZAR'S CHALLENGE

Before delving into the crux of the passage, a matter of interpretation needs to be addressed. Daniel 2:1 records that this account occurs during the second year of the reign of Nebuchadnezzar, yet Daniel and his friends are put into the king's service after three years of training (1:5, 18). Because of this apparent discrepancy, some people have actually sought to dismiss the book of Daniel as unauthentic or even fictional.

However, in the Babylonian system, a king's years of service are counted the same way people today number birthdays. Even though Nebuchadnezzar might have been well into his third year chronologically, the record would have shown it as his second. This observation should be coupled with another one that explains why Daniel uses the Babylonian counting system. At this point in his narrative (from 2:4–7:28), Daniel shifts from Hebrew to Aramaic in his writing. Aramaic was a widespread language, understood by many diverse peoples. (Nebuchadnezzar's advisors, for example, were probably from different nations, and according to 2:4, they spoke in Aramaic.) Daniel reverts to Hebrew for chapters 8–12.

So in a common language, Daniel writes of a dream that had troubled Nebuchadnezzar. It is a divine dream that creates a divine disturbance, driving Nebuchadnezzar to reconcile the disturbance that he feels. He needs to make sure that the dream is interpreted correctly, so he sets forth a challenge that rattles his entire staff. Not only does Nebuchadnezzar demand an interpretation to his dream; first he wants his magicians and astrologers to tell him what he has dreamed! If they do, he will reward them handsomely with wealth and honor. But if they don't, he will have them cut into pieces and their houses destroyed (2:5–6). They attempt to negotiate a better deal, but Nebuchadnezzar will not back down from his ultimatum, and he accuses them of stalling (2:7–9).

At first, Nebuchadnezzar's demand to have someone else tell him what he (Nebuchadnezzar) had dreamed was an unusual request. He wanted a proper interpretation for his disturbing dream that he believed may have been sent by God and thought that he could completely trust the interpretation of anyone able to first relate to him his dream. It would turn out that his instinct was correct, but this was not the Babylonian way. According to Babylonian custom, the king would have related his dream and then the wise men would interpret its significance.

When Nebuchadnezzar remains adamant, his usual counselors attempt to plead and reason with him. They tell him that in the known history of the world, no one has ever expected such a thing. It is an impossible task. They say only the gods can do such a thing, and that the gods do not dwell with people (2:10–11).

The response of Nebuchadnezzar's magicians reveals their worldview. They perceive a distinct separation between gods and people. From their perspective, gods stay in their world, and it is the responsibility of humans to reach out to them. The magicians' statement sets the stage for the rest of the book of Daniel, which explains the gospel message in terms that can be understood by the Gentile world of the Babylonian culture. Daniel will go on to describe how God enters the world of humanity to rescue people. Every story told from this point forward demonstrates how God interacts with this world. The second half of Daniel's book describes more specifically how and when God will come to the world in the person of the Messiah.

The court magicians' pleas to Nebuchadnezzar are to no avail. The infuriated king immediately gives the order to have all the wise men of Babylon put to death—an order that includes Daniel, Shadrach, Meshach, and Abednego (2:12–13). This apparent crisis is divinely orchestrated to create a supposedly impossible situation through which God's plan for the world will be revealed.

📄 **2:14–23**

DANIEL'S RESPONSE

The captain of the king's guard is sent to inform Daniel of the grim news. Daniel, however, responds with discretion and discernment. He asks for a bit more time so that he might do what the king has asked (2:14–16). Even though Nebuchadnezzar had just accused his court magicians and sorcerers of attempting to stall for time (2:8), it seems that he respects Daniel's request (2:16).

Daniel gathers his three Hebrew friends, and the four of them pray (2:17–18). They realize this is a divine challenge that they face, so they turn to God for clarity. They appeal to Him for mercy and wisdom, and He provides the solution.

Daniel has a vision during the night in which God gives him the answer that Nebuchadnezzar desires (2:19). But after receiving the solution, Daniel doesn't immediately go running to the king. First he takes time to praise God, appropriately ascribing all wisdom and power to the Lord.

It appears that Daniel's prayer is also influenced by the content of the dream God reveals (a dream not yet revealed in scripture). It is God who determines times and seasons, who sets up and deposes kings as he sees fit (2:21)—all in anticipation of a Messiah to come. Daniel acknowledges God's sovereign hand in the world. Unlike the gods of the Babylonians, the Lord *does* interact with this world. Not only does He interact, but He also controls the world.

The Lord is a God of light, who exposes the things of darkness. He also reveals hidden things. God enables Daniel to be wise and discerning, and Daniel uses his wisdom to seek God's help. In return, God makes known to Daniel something that Daniel couldn't possibly discern on his own. Daniel's knowledge of Nebuchadnezzar's dream will allow many people to live who otherwise would have been put to death. So Daniel also praises God for revealing Nebuchadnezzar's dream to him (2:22–23).

📄 **2:24–43**

DANIEL'S INTERPRETATION

Daniel's praise to God is not limited to the privacy of prayer. When he is called back in to speak to Nebuchadnezzar, he gives God full credit before the king. Daniel makes it patently clear that no human—not wise men, enchanters, magicians, or diviners—could have given Nebuchadnezzar the answer he sought. Yet his God is in heaven and can reveal mysteries (2:26–28). Daniel elevates the focus from humanity to God.

Only a revelation from God could enable anyone to understand Nebuchadnezzar's dream. Through Daniel, God is letting Nebuchadnezzar know that God is at work in the world, revealing His glory. This is the Lord's world, the future is in the Lord's control, and even the ability to see and understand what the Lord is saying requires divinely inspired insight.

Demystifying Daniel

The entire book of Daniel is a revelation of the gospel. God has just demonstrated to Nebuchadnezzar the seed plot to the teaching of justification by faith. To interact with the wisdom of God and understand what He is doing, one must go to God and seek His kingdom, wisdom, and righteousness. Later portions of Daniel will reveal even more about God's plan.

Then Daniel begins to relate the specifics of what Nebuchadnezzar had dreamed. The king had seen a great statue (2:31). Even though Nebuchadnezzar is the mightiest king in the world, who had conquered every nation in his path, he is not the center of the dream; the statue is. Nor is he in control of the events in his dream; he is merely an observer. Perhaps it is the sense that someone or something is more powerful than he is that had created all the fear and anxiety behind his threats toward those who serve him.

The statue is made of different kinds of metal. The head is gold, the chest and arms are silver, the middle portions are bronze, the legs are iron, and the feet are iron mixed with baked clay (2:31–33). As Nebuchadnezzar continues to observe, he sees a rock that is cut out, but not by human hands (2:34). The rock smashes into the statue. The statue topples over and breaks into pieces, which are quickly swept away by the wind like chaff at threshing time. The rock, however, grows into a huge mountain that fills the whole earth (2:34–35).

This dream both humbled and frightened Nebuchadnezzar. This was no mere nightmare that resulted from indigestion or an active imagination. Daniel will soon make it clear that this is a divine revelation that Nebuchadnezzar had received (2:45). God is allowing Nebuchadnezzar to come face-to-face with a future not under his control, but the Lord's. As Daniel goes on to interpret the dream, Nebuchadnezzar will receive the first of several lessons concerning the sovereignty of God.

Daniel's explanation foretells four world empires. Each section of the statue represents a different nation. He starts with Nebuchadnezzar and Babylon.

For modern readers with New Testament awareness, it may sound peculiar to read that Daniel refers to Nebuchadnezzar as "king of kings" (2:36–37). Literally, the phrase refers to a king that all other kings are subject to, which is why it becomes such a meaningful messianic title for Jesus. But Daniel uses the term to affirm that Nebuchadnezzar is a dominant figure. From Babylon's inception (Genesis 10:8–12), it had always stood for defiance of God. In time, the kingdom of Nebuchadnezzar came to symbolize the kingdom of this world. So in a literal sense, Nebuchadnezzar is indeed king of kings over those who are opposed to God.

Critical Observation

During the decline of the Roman Empire, Augustine wrote a monumental work called *City of God*. His observation was that there are really only two kingdoms: the kingdom of man and the kingdom of God. Those in the kingdom of man live to serve themselves, while those in the kingdom of God live to serve the Lord.

The head of gold on the statue in Nebuchadnezzar's dream (2:32, 36–38) symbolizes Babylon. Nebuchadnezzar is the leader of the most glorious of all the kingdoms in the world. Yet it will not be a lasting kingdom.

Next on the statue are the chest and arms of silver (2:32, 39). The nations that conquer Babylon (the Medes and Persians) will be inferior to Babylon. They will be stronger, but not as glorious. Daniel is letting Nebuchadnezzar know that his days are numbered. The kingdom he has established will fall to another.

But then a third kingdom will arise after the second. The statue's belly and thighs of bronze (2:32, 39) represent Greece. Just as bronze is stronger than silver, Alexander the Great will dominate the leaders of the Medes and Persians. Yet the Greek Empire will be less glorious than the Persian Empire had been.

Stronger still will be the Roman Empire, the statue's legs of iron (2:33, 40). At a point in the future, the Romans will arise and conquer all the surrounding kingdoms. Yet again there will be a diminishing of the glory of the kingdom. In addition, this fourth kingdom will be divided. Portions will be as strong as iron, but other parts will be like clay—and iron and clay certainly don't mix well (2:43). The imagery is most appropriate. As it turns out, the mighty Roman Empire will lack unity as it is plagued by civil wars, social unrest, and moral relativism.

Demystifying Daniel

Daniel speaks only of a series of specific kingdoms to come and doesn't identify them by name. Yet history shows that the series of Babylonian, Medo-Persian, Greek, and Roman world domination provide a fitting fulfillment of Daniel's prophecy. The rock (the establishment of the kingdom of God) also seems to fit the historic scenario very well with the birth of Jesus Christ during the time of the Roman Empire.

📄 **2:44–49**

THE FINAL KINGDOM

The imagery in Nebuchadnezzar's divinely inspired dream is important. Even though four great nations are mentioned in Daniel's interpretation, they comprise a single statue. The series of nations, even though distinct from one another, represent one world system.

As Daniel continues to interpret the dream for Nebuchadnezzar, he explains that the cut rock (2:34) represents the kingdom of God (2:44). The stone smashed into the feet of the image (the Roman Empire) and the entire statue (the human world system) come crashing down. God's kingdom, ruled by Jesus, will destroy the kingdom of the world. All the combined glory and strength of humanity will not be able to stand before the kingdom of God.

Modern readers need to remember that Daniel wrote this account to remind the Jews that God is sovereign, and therefore nothing is beyond His control. Specifically, even Judah's domination by the Babylonians is part of God's plan. Nations that rise do so because God allows it. Nations that fall do so because God brings them to an end. All nations are temporary until the final kingdom of God. The rock in Nebuchadnezzar's dream produces a mountain that fills the whole earth (2:35), and it will last forever. In demonstrating to Judah that God is still in full control of their future, Daniel is also warning Babylon that they are not eternal and will see their kingdom fall one day.

Daniel's accurate recall of Nebuchadnezzar's dream, and his insightful interpretation of what it means, impresses the king. Nebuchadnezzar becomes very appreciative and accommodating. He even acknowledges the superiority of Daniel's God above all other gods and kings (2:46–47). However, Nebuchadnezzar's contrition will be short-lived. In the following section, his ego will be back in full bloom, and God will humble him again. In fact, Nebuchadnezzar will have numerous encounters with the humbling arm of God.

Meanwhile, Daniel is rewarded with many gifts and elevated to a position of power above all the other wise men of the court. At Daniel's request, Nebuchadnezzar also promotes Shadrach, Meshach, and Abednego (2:48–49). God is at work to place His people in positions of influence over the entire Babylonian world at that time.

Throughout this section, Daniel refers to God as a *revealer of mysteries* (2:19, 22, 28–29, 47). Certainly, there may be mysteries of life that people will not or cannot understand in this world. Other deep truths, however, are available to those who seek God's wisdom as Daniel did. Sometimes you might find yourself in Daniel's position, providing valid answers for someone else. Other times you may find yourself like Nebuchadnezzar—confused and seeking help. What are some of the mysteries that persistently pique your curiosity? What are some sources you might consult (people, reference materials, etc.) to help gather information as you continue to seek God's answers for your hardest questions?

DANIEL 3:1–30

THE FIERY FURNACE AND GOD'S DELIVERANCE

Nebuchadnezzar's Statue	3:1–7
The Hebrews' Dilemma	3:8–18
Nebuchadnezzar's Lesson	3:19–30

Setting Up the Section

Four men of Judah are mentioned by name as being taken from Judah to Babylon to be trained to serve King Nebuchadnezzar (1:6–7). The primary focus so far has been on Daniel. In this section, however, the attention is placed on his three friends, better known by their Babylonian names: Shadrach, Meshach, and Abednego.

📄 **3:1–7**

NEBUCHADNEZZAR'S STATUE

To get a proper perspective on this account, one must relate it to the events of Daniel 2. In chapter 2, King Nebuchadnezzar dreams of a great statue and is eventually told that he is the head. So when Nebuchadnezzar subsequently has a huge statue built of his image, there can be little doubt that the statue expresses his desire to see his dream not only fulfilled but surpassed.

Nebuchadnezzar has been told that he is the king of kings—the head of gold (2:37–38). It is commonly thought that the king's pride leads him to then make a statue of himself in complete gold. Perhaps he is so prideful that he misses the point of the dream and hears only that he is the king of kings. The statue, then, communicates that his kingdom is beautiful and will last forever.

It is not only an ambitious project but also a huge expense. The golden figure is ninety feet high and nine feet wide (3:1). It is the ultimate expression of human ego; Nebuchadnezzar is so enthralled with himself that he brings his entire staff together and has them listen to a new decree (3:2–6). A close reading reveals that the unveiling of Nebuchadnezzar's statue is shrouded in religious overtones. He is not just introducing the image as a token of remembrance; he is presenting a new religion.

The unveiling ceremony involves much religious symbolism: a dedication (3:2); music and a desire to create a worship ritual (3:5); and the act of bowing down in honor, reverence, and worship (3:5). It seems safe to presume that the image is of Nebuchadnezzar. If so, then the people are required to bow down to worship his image every time the music is played. Apparently the king believes that he is the sovereign lord of the earth and the leader of the world, and therefore he deserves worship. But in order to think in such a manner, he has to disregard the interpretation of his dream that Daniel provided—that Nebuchadnezzar's kingdom is a gift of the true God.

Demystifying Daniel

This section of Daniel introduces some obscure words. But since translations vary, it is enough to say for our purposes that the list of terms in 3:3 (*satraps*, *prefects*, and so forth) is of government leaders at various levels. And the list in 3:5 is an assortment of musical instruments of the era.

It is easy to be critical of Nebuchadnezzar's haughty attitude, but it is far more common than many might like to admit. It is a temptation for all humankind to take credit for the things with which God has blessed them. People tend to never be satisfied with what God provides and feel that they deserve more. Then, when they get more, they lose sight of the fact that every blessing is a result of the kindness and mercy of God. Nebuchadnezzar is only one example.

It seems that most people have no problem with Nebuchadnezzar's new ruling. When the music plays, they bow as they have been ordered (3:7). This naturally exposes anyone who doesn't bow, as is the case with Shadrach, Meshach, and Abednego.

Demystifying Daniel

The question that usually comes up at this point is, "Where is Daniel while all this is going on?" His three friends are left to themselves to deal with a high-pressure situation. It seems likely that Daniel would have been required to travel in his position as Nebuchadnezzar's top assistant. He might well have been in another part of the kingdom. One should also note that considerable time has probably passed between Daniel 2 and Daniel 3. Ninety-foot-tall gold statues are not quickly constructed.

📄 **3:8–18**

THE HEBREWS' DILEMMA

It takes little time for a group of Babylonians to go running to Nebuchadnezzar and tell him that certain Jews have not bowed down like everyone else. Their specific accusations bear close attention. They accuse Shadrach, Meshach, and Abednego of: (1) disregarding

Nebuchadnezzar; (2) not serving his gods; and (3) not worshiping the golden image he has set up. Nowhere in Nebuchadnezzar's decree did he stipulate that everyone had to serve his gods, but these men add it to their list of charges.

It is likely that the accusers are jealous of the prior success of Shadrach, Meshach, and Abednego, because the charges are certainly exaggerated. In reality, the three Hebrews have not disregarded the king or defied his position. They are three of Nebuchadnezzar's greatest assets and more than willing to serve on his staff. But in that culture, no king could afford to easily dismiss accusations of treason against those close to him.

Nebuchadnezzar's response to the news is immediate rage. He sends for Shadrach, Meshach, and Abednego. He personally repeats for them the mandate that had previously been announced publicly. Then he gives them an ultimatum: Either bow down and worship him now or be thrown into the fiery furnace and die (3:13–15).

Nebuchadnezzar's final comment during this brief conversation is telling. If they refuse to bow to the image, he wants to know, "What god will be able to rescue you from my hand?" (3:15 NIV).

The king has dismissed everything Daniel told him. He has established himself as a god again. He presumes his form of torture is the maximum punishment in both this world and the heavenly world. And in the greatest offense of all, he believes that the Hebrew God is impotent in comparison to him.

Critical Observation

It is always awkward for a well-meaning person to encounter a dominant superior who is angry to the point of ranting. How much more intense it must have been when the furious person was the leader of a ruthless empire who was accustomed to getting his way.

Despite the unreasonable hostility of Nebuchadnezzar, the response of Shadrach, Meshach, and Abednego remain fearless and well-reasoned. They don't feel compelled to answer him because his threats are empty in light of the power of their God. Still, they *choose* to respond and explain themselves. In doing so, they reveal four important points.

First, they fully trust God's sovereignty. Even in this difficult and threatening situation, they do not consider it foolish to trust God. Nebuchadnezzar's power pales in comparison to God's. Second, they remain true to the scriptures. This isn't just a difference of opinion between them and the king. They only disobeyed Nebuchadnezzar because they were following a higher law by refusing to bow down to any image or idol (Exodus 20:3–6). Third, they are willing to die for their faith. They know God is powerful enough to rescue them, whether or not He chooses to do so. And fourth, they remain completely submissive to God's will. Their faith is not conditional, based on a prescribed outcome. At issue is not their comfort; it is their obedience to God.

NEBUCHADNEZZAR'S LESSON

The response of Shadrach, Meshach, and Abednego is not what Nebuchadnezzar wants to hear. His very countenance changes (3:19). He had trusted these men and placed them on his elite team. Now he feels betrayed and wants to see nothing less than their total destruction. In his great fury, he orders the furnace to be heated to seven times its usual temperature—most likely, to its maximum heat (3:19–20). He has the three traitors bound (3:20), which serves no good purpose other than the psychological strategy of removing control from them, preventing them from even minimally shielding themselves from the heat. Doing his work for him are his strongest soldiers.

Critical Observation

Nebuchadnezzar is parading his strength for all to see. He wants the totality of his power to be made known so that the three young men and everyone observing will know that he is the most powerful man on earth.

The punishment for Shadrach, Meshach, and Abednego is intended to be most cruel, as is proven when a number of their captors die just from tossing the three into the flames (3:22–23). The judgment intended for the Hebrews falls instead on some of Nebuchadnezzar's most valiant warriors. As for the three who have so deeply angered the king, they are about to astonish him.

Peering into the furnace, Nebuchadnezzar sees the men walking around, but there are four figures instead of three (3:24–25). He asks his advisors for confirmation, and they assure him that only three people had gone into the furnace. But the king can clearly see four men walking around unbound and unharmed.

Not only does God preserve Shadrach, Meshach, and Abednego; He joins them in the furnace. Some people think the fourth figure may be the preincarnate Christ. Nebuchadnezzar can only speculate as to the fourth figure, calling him a son of the gods, but he definitely wants to know more.

He approaches the furnace and calls for the three to come out (3:26–27). As they do, all the Babylonian leaders gather around to inspect them. No one would even suspect the men had been near fire. Not only is their skin, clothes, and hair unaffected, but they don't even smell of smoke! Apparently all the flames had done was burn off the ropes with which they had been bound.

As a result, Nebuchadnezzar has a complete change of heart (3:28–30). At this point, he is both impressed that they have defied him and overwhelmed that their faithfulness to their God is stronger than their physical security. He correctly reaches the conclusion that no other god can deliver someone in the manner that their God has just done. Moreover, Nebuchadnezzar amends his previous mandate. From now on, he says, anyone who speaks out against the God of Shadrach, Meshach, and Abednego will receive the worst punishment conceivable.

As for the three young Hebrew men, they are again promoted (2:49; 3:30). Even though they haven't sought any tangible result from their display of faith, God allows them to prosper. Their steadfastness during great crisis is rewarded.

Take It Home

People of faith can expect occasional debates, disagreements, or conflicts with people who don't believe in God, and they can learn much from Shadrach, Meshach, and Abednego. Even at risk of their lives, the Hebrew trio refuses to compromise their beliefs. Although under great pressure, they remain remarkably calm and even understated. They don't attempt to overpower or outshout Nebuchadnezzar, or maneuver their way out of a tricky situation. They simply explain what they believe to be true and leave the outcome to God. Can you think of current examples where Christians and nonbelievers are at odds over important issues? In each instance, how well do you think the believers involved represent their God and their faith? On a personal level, what can you learn from this narrative that will help you be a better spokesperson for God?

DANIEL 4:1–37

NEBUCHADNEZZAR'S HUMBLING EXPERIENCE

Nebuchadnezzar's Second Dream	4:1–18
The Dream's Interpretation and Fulfillment	4:19–37

Setting Up the Section

The previous two chapters of Daniel have shown how God is dealing with the pride of King Nebuchadnezzar, first through Daniel and then through Shadrach, Meshach, and Abednego. This section is the final segment concerning Nebuchadnezzar, as the king recounts what he has learned. Even Nebuchadnezzar has come to realize that God is the Lord of the universe, and he opens and closes the section with a declaration about the sovereign power and glory of God.

📄 **4:1–18**

NEBUCHADNEZZAR'S SECOND DREAM

Daniel 4 is a letter to the nations that Nebuchadnezzar composes after he is finally convinced of the sovereignty of God. Coming from the pen of a Gentile king, this chapter provides some incredible transforming insights about the Lord.

The positive opening temporarily shields the fact that Nebuchadnezzar has been through a horrendous experience. However, the experience has taught him about his own sin and the nature of God, so he records the lesson for all the governors in his kingdom so they will not make the same mistake he has (4:1–2).

Nebuchadnezzar opens by acknowledging four aspects of God that he has discovered (4:3). First are the great *signs* he has observed. The Lord has communicated with the king through dreams and then provided Daniel to interpret the dreams. God even enabled Daniel to know what Nebuchadnezzar had dreamed without being told (2:5-6, 19). God had specifically communicated with Nebuchadnezzar, and the king praises Him for such an extraordinary experience.

Next Nebuchadnezzar praises God for His mighty *wonders*—God's intervention in this world. God literally changes the course of life for Nebuchadnezzar, as the king will soon explain. The story he tells will confirm the great wonders God can perform. As previously noted, the Babylonian gods were not known to step into the world of humanity, but Judah's God is undoubtedly active among His people.

Third, Nebuchadnezzar praises God's *eternal kingdom*. For the first time, the reader sees the Babylonian leader acknowledge a greater kingdom. Babylon will not be a lasting empire, but God's kingdom will have no end. Such acknowledgment reflects a significant change in Nebuchadnezzar, demonstrating the extent of his humility.

Finally, the king concedes God's *rule* over the earth. The Lord's dominion extends throughout all generations. God is the only authentic ruler of the world because no kingdom, past or present, is beyond His control.

Nebuchadnezzar begins his story by explaining that everything in his life and kingdom was going well—or so he thought (4:4). He was prosperous, contented, and happy. And then he has another dream.

The previous dream of Nebuchadnezzar's—the image made of different metal (2:31-35)—had no small effect on the king. But this one is apparently even more influential. This dream terrifies him, and he can't get it out of his mind (4:5).

Seeking some kind of clarity or insight, Nebuchadnezzar calls for his staff of wise men and describes his dream to them. But they are no more helpful in this case than they had been before (2:10-11). When they fail to understand and interpret the dream, the king calls for Daniel, who again comes through for him. Why Nebuchadnezzar always waits to ask Daniel is unknown, although his tendency to do so repeatedly proves that the Lord enlightens Daniel in ways that none of the other magicians, enchanters, astrologers, and diviners (4:6-7) can come close to matching.

Critical Observation

The Hebrew captives who had been drafted into Nebuchadnezzar's service have been given Babylonian names. Daniel's three friends—Hananiah, Mishael, and Azariah—are better known by their new names: Shadrach, Meshach, and Abednego. Daniel's name is also changed. Since Daniel 4 is from Nebuchadnezzar's perspective, Daniel's Babylonian name (Belteshazzar) is used (4:8–9, 18–19). However, in most other cases, Daniel's Hebrew name is used, and that is the name by which he is best known.

Nebuchadnezzar has made two key observations about Daniel. First, he realizes that "the spirit of the holy gods" is in him (4:9). It is not likely that Nebuchadnezzar is giving the one true God full credit here, although some translations use the upper case *G* for *gods*. This passage is within the portion of Daniel that is written in Aramaic (2:4–7:28), and translators face some difficulty putting the original language into English. Yet at the heart of the king's expression is his certainty that Daniel has been given insight by some divine source.

The second observation about Daniel is that no mystery baffles the young man. Daniel has already proven himself beyond doubt, and the king has great confidence that Daniel can interpret any dream—even one that has stumped all his peers on Nebuchadnezzar's court.

So Nebuchadnezzar lays out his dream for Daniel to hear (4:10–18). It is indeed a strange account of a great tree that flourishes for a time until a heavenly voice commands it to be chopped down. The stump and roots are left in the field, bound with iron and bronze. Then the tree appears to become a beast, sentenced to live in the field for a period of time. Finally, a declaration is made about a person being removed from power so that everyone will know that the One speaking is the Most High Lord of the universe.

It is likely that Nebuchadnezzar has a sense of what the dream means, which is probably why it troubles him so much. He may even have enjoyed the first part of the dream as he saw himself as the great tree that touched the sky and provided shelter and sustenance for so many. If so, he is surely unsettled as the dream unfolds and strange events begin to occur.

📄 **4:19–37**

THE DREAM'S INTERPRETATION AND FULFILLMENT

After Daniel hears the dream, he is unsettled himself—not because he doesn't understand the meaning, but because he *does*. He is reluctant to look the king in the eye and deliver bad news, yet Nebuchadnezzar encourages him to speak truthfully.

The last time the king had dreamed about the future, Daniel identified Nebuchadnezzar as king of kings (2:37) and the head of gold (2:38). Shortly afterward, Nebuchadnezzar built a ninety-foot statue in honor of himself (3:1). This time, however, Daniel has the responsibility of telling Nebuchadnezzar that God is going to take his kingdom away, and the king will suffer in even worse ways as well.

Daniel confirms that the tree in the dream is indeed a symbol for Nebuchadnezzar (4:20–22). He has become the most powerful man in the world, and the rest of the world is subject to him. More than being merely strong and mighty, Babylon is known for its glory. Yet as dominant as Nebuchadnezzar has become, he is still merely a human. Heavenly forces are at work over which he has no control. At a single command by a holy messenger, the great tree is cut down.

The future of the king is grim. He is going to go mad and then be driven from Babylon. God's action will be the result of the king's refusal to recognize that it is the Lord who rules. Nebuchadnezzar has acknowledged that Daniel's God is a strong God, and he notes that Daniel and his friends benefited from serving their God. But Nebuchadnezzar has always stopped short of *submitting* to Daniel's God.

Demystifying Daniel

When Daniel tells Nebuchadnezzar that the king needs to acknowledge that "heaven rules" (4:26), he is using a figure of speech that substitutes a place for a person. Similarly, someone today might say that an action made by the president is made by Washington, or the White House. Daniel isn't attempting to soften what he is saying. Indeed, he has been quite bold when speaking about God to King Nebuchadnezzar (2:27–28).

Daniel exhorts Nebuchadnezzar to cease his sin and start practicing righteousness (4:27), supposing that he might be able to avoid the judgment predicted by the dream. Daniel's approach is tactful and humble. He still respects the office of Nebuchadnezzar. He doesn't leap right to accusations and judgment; he starts with the opportunity of repentance. He lays out the option for the king to start right away to cease his wickedness and serve God by showing mercy to the weak. In that case, maybe the king's prosperity will continue.

Perhaps Nebuchadnezzar takes Daniel's words to heart for a while, but not for the long run. A year later, the king is walking on a royal rooftop and starts looking out over his kingdom. With Daniel's warning forgotten, in a moment of unrestricted pride and arrogance, Nebuchadnezzar boasts of how he is responsible for the success of Babylon (4:28–30). The words aren't completely out of his mouth before a heavenly voice decrees the removal of his royal authority. In addition, the voice says Nebuchadnezzar will spend a length of time (probably seven years) with beasts, living as an animal (4:31–32).

His sentence begins immediately. The once-arrogant king is driven away from people. He eats grass like cattle. He stays outside in the dew as his hair grows long (like the feathers of an eagle) and his nails become like bird claws (4:33).

Critical Observation

A fragmentary cuneiform tablet in the British Museum refers to Nebuchadnezzar, apparently during this part of his life. It states that "life appeared of no value to" Nebuchadnezzar, that "he does not show love to son and daughter," and that "family and clan does not exist" for him any longer.

Animals don't reason as humans do, and perhaps Nebuchadnezzar suffers in that respect as well. But eventually he raises his eyes toward heaven. In that action, he evidently submits to God, and his sanity is restored (4:34).

When he is able, he praises, honors, and glorifies God. He acknowledges God's eternal dominion and kingdom, as well as God's complete sovereignty over both the powers of heaven and the people of earth (4:34–35).

Afterward, God does indeed allow Nebuchadnezzar to prosper again. In fact, the king says he becomes even greater than before (4:36). And this time he doesn't make any attempt to take credit for his fame. Instead, he exalts and glorifies the King of heaven (4:37). Had he done so earlier, in response to Daniel's advice, he might have avoided a lot of misery.

Take It Home

Perhaps one reason that Nebuchadnezzar's strange experiences were recorded for posterity as well as for his peers at that time is to caution everyone of the importance of fully submitting to God as the Lord of the universe. It's rather easy to verbally acknowledge God, to claim to know God, or even to express love for God. However, such actions mean nothing if not accompanied by complete and humble submission to Him. On a scale of 1 (least) to 10 (most), how would you rate your submission to God in recent days? Can you tell a difference in your life when your obedience begins to lessen a bit?

DANIEL 5:1–31
DANIEL AND BELSHAZZAR

Setting Up the Section

At least six years have passed between the previous section and this one. In that time, King Nebuchadnezzar has been replaced by Belshazzar. It appears that Daniel's high-profile position in the king's court has also come to an end. Although the previous section highlights a public letter from Nebuchadnezzar warning his fellow Babylonian leaders what can happen if they defy the God of Judah, Belshazzar is either oblivious or defiant. Either way, he will suffer for it.

📄 **5:1–4**

BELSHAZZAR'S BANQUET

After the death of Nebuchadnezzar, his successor is his son Evil-Merodach. This son rules for two years until he is assassinated by Labashi-Marduk and replaced by Neriglissar. After Neriglissar, Evil-Merodach's brother-in-law, an Assyrian named Nabonidus takes control of the kingdom. As new king, Nabonidus establishes a home in the oasis that is now the location of Saudi Arabia. He appoints his son Belshazzar to reign as vice-regent and handle the business of Babylon.

The first thing the Bible records about Belshazzar is that he throws a banquet. It is no small affair, attended by a thousand of the leaders of Babylon along with their wives and concubines (5:1–3). This event may have been a kind of preparation for war, since Babylon was already under the attack of the Persians.

The banquet became the backdrop for a major misstep on the part of Belshazzar—his callous disregard for the holy Jewish objects stored in his treasury. When he sees that his wine is of a good vintage, he sends for the golden goblets that had been taken from the Jerusalem temple. They were originally set aside to be used exclusively for the worship of God. Even after Nebuchadnezzar seized Jerusalem and took the temple furnishings, he had several encounters with the God of Daniel and eventually came to have a respect for the King of heaven (4:37), decreeing that the Lord should not be mocked under penalty of death (3:29).

As Daniel will eventually make clear, Belshazzar cannot plead ignorance. He knew about Nebuchadnezzar's decrees and the holiness attached to the Jewish goblets (5:22–23). He just doesn't care. In the ultimate mockery of God, he uses the temple's sacred vessels for his party, passing out wine to impress his nobles as well as their female companions. Even worse, as they drink they praise their gods (5:4).

📄 **5:5–12**

THE WRITING ON THE WALL

Belshazzar considers Judah's God a trivial matter, but his casual and carefree attitude changes in an instant when a disembodied hand suddenly appears and begins to write on the palace wall. The king's defiance of God has been public; so, too, is God's condemnation of Belshazzar. In front of all his guests, the king turns pale, goes limp, and is gripped by fear to the point of terror. Then, after the experience of seeing the hand come and go, Belshazzar is left with a message he can't comprehend (5:5–6).

Critical Observation

Clearly, Belshazzar doesn't know what (who) he is dealing with. Yet his response of such intense fear indicates that he acknowledges something more powerful than he is. His initial fears will soon be confirmed.

He brings together all of the spiritual leaders of his cabinet to attempt to interpret the words left on the wall, promising to promote anyone who can do so to third place in the entire kingdom. (Belshazzar is responsible to Nabonidus, so the top two places are already filled.) It is a magnificent offer, yet no one is able to decipher the message (5:7–9). The sum total of the religious wisdom of the day is unable to read or understand the words, and the king has no peace.

Belshazzar thinks he is out of options. God has spoken to him, yet the leaders of Babylon can't determine what God has said. God has extended Belshazzar beyond his limits, just as he had for Nebuchadnezzar. And the answers will come from the same source: God's servant, Daniel.

The queen at the time may well have been the queen mother—possibly the widow of Nebuchadnezzar, or perhaps his daughter (5:10). In any case, she is well aware of the recent goings on within the palace. In particular, she knows of Daniel and his reputation of divine knowledge and understanding, and also his ability to interpret dreams, explain riddles, and solve difficult problems (5:12). It is the exact job description Belshazzar needs, so he takes the queen's advice and summons Daniel.

Demystifying Daniel

In addressing Belshazzar, the queen refers to "your father the king" (5:11). The usage of *father* cannot be assumed to mean a biological relationship or even a relationship in terms of one generation to the next. The word was sometimes used in referring to a person's lineage. The Jews often spoke of Abraham as their father. Similarly, Nebuchadnezzar could be considered a father by any number of offspring, not merely his biological children.

5:13–31

THE WRITING'S INTERPRETATION

Daniel had risen to the top of Nebuchadnezzar's group of advisors (2:48–49), yet he must have been sidelined when the new king came into power. Clearly, Belshazzar doesn't even know who Daniel is. Ironically, Belshazzar will get to know him the same way Nebuchadnezzar had—by bringing him in only after every other option has failed.

Belshazzar goes through the proper protocol of flattering Daniel, briefly summarizing the situation for him and offering him great rewards for his much-needed help (5:13–16). Daniel agrees to help, but not because of the proffered rewards. He is more confrontational with Belshazzar than he had been with Nebuchadnezzar, and for good reason. Nebuchadnezzar had left the world a letter outlining his sin of pride and the ultimate result. He had learned that God—not the leader of Babylon—deserved the glory for whatever good happened in the world. But Belshazzar had ignored the lesson of the past and in a matter of a few years openly defied God. Daniel will do as the king asks, but he has no desire to work for this new regime (5:17). (Of course, it will turn out that in interpreting God's message, Daniel is foretelling the fall of the existing king anyway.)

Daniel begins with a short history lesson that will put God's message into context. Nebuchadnezzar had been bestowed with the most powerful and glorious kingdom of the world—not because of anything special he had done, but because it was part of God's plan. When pride became an issue, God had removed the kingdom from Nebuchadnezzar and had driven the king out to live like an animal. Eventually, after Nebuchadnezzar lifted his eyes to heaven and acceded that God was the sovereign ruler of the world, he was reinstated into his position as king with a much clearer understanding of who God is (5:18–21).

And here is Daniel's point: He isn't telling Belshazzar anything the king doesn't already know (5:22). A mighty ruler who leaves the throne for a while to live in the fields, eat grass, and grow animal-like hair and nails is not quickly forgotten. Belshazzar knows the story, but he hasn't heeded the lesson of Nebuchadnezzar. Because Belshazzar refuses to honor God, his defiant party is the last one he will ever have.

The words the hand had written on the wall—*Mene, Mene, Tekel, Parsin* (5:25)—essentially mean, "Number," "Weigh," and "Divide." The message that no one else could determine is quite clear to Daniel: The days of Belshazzar are numbered, his life has been weighed (evaluated) by God, and because he is found deficient, his kingdom will be divided as the Medes and Persians take over. Simply put, the end is at hand for the king.

Belshazzar's response is telling. He certainly must have believed Daniel, because he restores the authority and prosperity that had been taken away from him (5:29). Yet this appears to be his *only* response. He hears a disturbing message that has been divinely delivered in an astounding manner, and he does nothing. He shows no hint of remorse, repentance, confession, or desire to change. Perhaps this is why God's punishment is much swifter than it had been with Nebuchadnezzar. It is this very night that the Medes breach the walls, take over the city, and put Belshazzar to death (5:30).

The new ruler of the kingdom is Darius the Mede. In the next section, he, too, will learn a lesson about God because of his experience with Daniel.

Take It Home

The fall of Belshazzar is particularly brutal because he failed to learn from the experience of Nebuchadnezzar who had come before him. Can you think of any spiritual lessons, either positive or negative, that you have observed in the lives of other people? To what extent do those lessons influence your personal faith? What lessons do you hope to pass on to others who might be observing the way you live?

DANIEL 6:1-28

DANIEL AND DARIUS

Setting Up the Section

The previous section ends with the demise of Babylonian King Belshazzar and his replacement by Darius the Mede. This section continues with the establishment of Darius as king and how he comes to experience the power of Daniel's God.

📄 **6:1–4**

DANIEL'S EXEMPLARY CHARACTER

Throughout the book of Daniel so far, kings have come and gone while Daniel's service to God, as well as to his human rulers, has remained consistent. It seems clear that the godly wisdom demonstrated by Daniel in his youth has carried into his senior years as well. He serves as one of three key leaders to whom another 120 officials report. This leadership structure is used by Darius so that he can protect his interests (6:2). In other words, Darius is wisely attempting to avoid losing his kingdom to a rebel group or having the wealth of his kingdom pilfered by an unscrupulous, unsupervised overseer. He is aware of the temptations inherent with power and control.

It is in this environment that Daniel's character shines. In a competitive setting with little regard for righteousness, Daniel continues to faithfully follow God. Before long, Darius has plans to reward Daniel's exceptional qualities and promote him to the top position over the entire kingdom (6:3).

Critical Observation

Daniel's integrity becomes evident in a close comparison between verses 2 and 3. At first King Darius is cautious about placing too much power in the hands of any one person (6:2). But when he sees how Daniel lives and works, he trusts him to have even more power without fear that he will misuse it (6:3).

Not surprisingly, there is a good deal of resentment when the other leaders hear that Daniel is in line to become their boss. They decide to work together, watch him closely, and get some dirt on him that they can take to Darius. But the closer they monitor his behavior, the more evident it becomes that he isn't doing anything he shouldn't do, nor is he neglecting to do anything he should be doing (6:4).

📄 6:5–12

THE CONSPIRACY AGAINST DANIEL

When Daniel's jealous peers can't find a single problem with his integrity, they change their strategy. When they closely examine his life, they see his bold faith in God and realize his spiritual consistency is all they can use against him (6:5).

Apparently *they* have no problem operating without integrity. They devise a plan to present Darius with a proposal for a law requiring his subjects to pray to no one but him for a thirty-day period. Furthermore, the law will make it clear that anyone who disobeys the injunction will be thrown into the lions' den (6:6–8). Scripture doesn't say that Darius is flattered at their proposal, but he doesn't appear to need much coaxing. It is said simply that he puts the decree into writing, which makes it an unalterable law (6:9). Not even Darius can revoke it.

Although it is a despicable attempt to get rid of Daniel, the plan is an intelligent one. Darius had structured his leadership team to protect the kingdom from disloyal people, and at face value it appears that this proposal will support the king in his desire.

Daniel is well aware of the king's signing of the decree. He understands the consequences of breaking it. He goes to pray to God in his usual place at his usual time (6:10). He has other options, such as waiting thirty days or praying in a more private location. But Daniel truly believes what he has been communicating to Nebuchadnezzar and Belshazzar: God is sovereign and in control. God's kingdom is a priority for him, and if death is a result of his commitment, so be it.

Evidently the conspirators have Daniel's home staked out. It takes little time for them to witness him in prayer and go running to Darius. First they clarify the essence of the decree that has been passed and ensure that it cannot be revoked. *Then* they inform the king that Daniel has defied the law.

Note how expertly they pervert the truth (6:11–13). They had found nothing wicked or illicit for which they could accuse Daniel. So they manipulate the legal system to pass a binding, unrighteous law. When Daniel maintains his integrity and ignores the law, his accusers present him as a wicked person, disloyal to the king.

📄 **6:13–28**

DANIEL SURVIVES THE LIONS' DEN

It appears that Darius is not fooled by their manipulation, but there is nothing he can do about it. He searches for legal loopholes but can find no way to avoid sentencing Daniel to the punishment as set forth in the decree (6:14). So when Daniel's accusers return as a group, the king has little recourse but to order Daniel thrown into the lions' den (6:15). Yet in that moment it becomes clear how much Daniel's faithfulness to his God has influenced Darius. It is admirable that Daniel displays faith that God will deliver him, whether in life or in death. But as a result of his consistent faith, even *Darius* suggests that Daniel's God might deliver him (6:16).

The lions' den is an enclosure with no visual access. Daniel is apparently lowered into it, a stone is laid over the top, and the king seals it with his signet ring. It is a fretful night for Darius. He can't sleep, won't eat, and refuses any kind of entertainment (6:17–18). He is up at dawn to return to the lions' den, and he is surprisingly optimistic. He doesn't just call out to Daniel; he asks a question that demands a response (6:19–20). And Daniel's voice assures him that, yes, God has indeed delivered him from the lions. He also sets the record straight by averring, "I have not wronged you, Your Majesty" (6:21–22 NLT).

Demystifying Daniel

Daniel has defied a Persian law and submitted to what was intended to be the Persian death penalty. So God's deliverance of Daniel is more than simply a reward for his steady faith. It is also God's divine declaration of Daniel's innocence based on the law of the Lord and an emphatic demonstration that God's law is to be feared over any human law.

Daniel is freed from the den unharmed. He has no bite marks and no scratches (6:23). God's rule of the world includes both corrupt political systems and the animal kingdom.

The people who had attempted to destroy Daniel are then rounded up and thrown to the lions, along with their wives and children (6:24). Their scheme is revealed for what it is: a malicious attempt to murder an innocent man. Historians have learned that Persian law dictated the destruction of entire families of people who were harmful to the kingdom. It may be that in a culture of violence and vengeance, it was believed that the children of an offender might attempt vengeance when they grew up.

For whatever reason the men and their families are condemned, their deaths make a certain point: The lions are hungry. Before the wicked conspirators even hit the bottom of the den, the lions overpower them and crush them (6:24). It becomes clear that Daniel had not escaped death because the animals had been overfed or drugged the night before. The king's seal is affixed to the only entrance/exit to the den. Any attempt to explain away a divine solution to Daniel's dilemma is met with a biblical counterargument.

The section concludes with a new decree, written by King Darius and sent throughout the land to people of all languages (6:26–27). The king mandates that everyone in his kingdom must show reverence to Daniel's God. Just as the Lord made Himself known to Nebuchadnezzar and Belshazzar in phenomenal ways, so, too, He persuades Darius of His unequalled power.

Critical Observation

The decree that had been designed to entrap Daniel supposedly could not be repealed (6:12, 15) and was supposed to be in effect for thirty days (6:7, 12). Perhaps King Darius waited a month before issuing his new order, although it appears to have been sent out immediately after Daniel's release. It might have been that Darius came to the conclusion that God's law effectively superseded any contradictory human law, and he repealed the first decree after all.

After his return trip from the lions' den, Daniel does quite well throughout the reign of Darius (6:28). In fact, his service continues into the rule of the next king, Cyrus.

Take It Home

In previous situations, Daniel had wisely used compromise to keep from doing something that would have gone against his beliefs (1:11–16). In this case, he wisely trusts God to see him through, and he refuses to alter his prayer habits in any way. It can be difficult to know when to yield a bit and when to stand firm. What do you think determined how Daniel decided to respond in various circumstances? Can you think of similar examples from your own life? How do you decide when it is appropriate to seek compromise and when you need to be completely unwavering in the exercise of your beliefs?

DANIEL 7:1–28

DANIEL'S FIRST VISION

Daniel's Dream of Four Strange Creatures	7:1–14
The Interpretation of the Dream	7:15–28

Setting Up the Section

The first half of the book of Daniel (chapters 1–6) is a mostly chronological narrative of Daniel's service to various kings of Babylon and Medo-Persia. The second half (chapters 7–12) contains more personal accounts of some of Daniel's dreams and visions.

📖 **7:1–14**

DANIEL'S DREAM OF FOUR STRANGE CREATURES

The book of Daniel was written during a time when the Jews had just been conquered, their temple destroyed, and most of the potential leaders taken captive and carried away. It appears that aggressive human forces are in control and that God either no longer cares or is unable to do anything to deliver His people.

But Daniel has repeatedly highlighted the ongoing sovereignty of God throughout the first half of his book. God makes it clear that even though human kingdoms are being allowed some temporary successes, they will not reign forever. The kingdom of God will arrive, it will succeed, and God will be the eternal King.

Beginning in chapter 7, Daniel shares a series of revelations to explain how God plans to bring about the end of the human kingdoms. The prophecies deal with the destruction of arrogant human rulers and the coming of the Messiah, who will sit on the throne to rule forever. Chapter 7 provides an overview of what is going to happen in the world, setting up the prophecies that follow.

The chronological progression of Daniel is interrupted at this point as the author returns to the reign of Belshazzar (7:1). In Daniel 5, the observation is made that Daniel appears to be sidelined when Belshazzar replaces Nebuchadnezzar. Perhaps Belshazzar didn't make use of Daniel during that time, but here it is evident that God did. It also appears that Daniel saw more than he recorded but only wrote down all the high points.

His vision begins with an image of the great sea (the Mediterranean) being greatly disturbed by "the four winds of heaven" (7:2). Those who sail for a living pay close attention to wind direction, partly because the direction helps determine what kind of storm to expect. In Daniel's vision, God stirs up the waters to bring about various storms of discord and confusion.

Critical Observation

For those living in the Middle East, the only great sea they knew was the Mediterranean Sea. It was the territory that all the kingdoms of the world sought to control. The Mediterranean provided a path for international shipping, sustenance for living, and protection from invading forces. It was both literally and figuratively a "great sea."

As Daniel continues to observe, four different types of "great beasts" come out of the sea (7:3). He will later be told that the beasts represent kingdoms (7:17), so his description is more to differentiate their qualities and characteristics than to detail their specific physical appearances.

The first creature is like a lion with wings like an eagle—both powerful and swift (7:4). But then its wings are plucked, and it is placed on the ground with two feet instead of four, with a human's power to reason. The implication is that the figure began as a wicked being, fell from earthly glory, and was restored to normal. Nebuchadnezzar immediately comes to mind after his account provided in Daniel 5, although some people believe this will be a king yet to come. At this point, more information is needed.

The second creature is compared to a bear—powerful and vicious, but with a tendency to be slow and lazy (7:5). It is raised up on one of its sides, perhaps indicating a walking position. And it has been feeding on another animal, having been given permission to conquer.

The third beast is described as a four-headed, four-winged leopard, meaning it is swift, fierce, and has the ability to cover a lot of territory quickly (7:6). The biblical concept of multiple heads frequently symbolizes different kingdoms or regions, so the creature is perhaps a single kingdom with four regions.

Comparisons fail Daniel while he attempts to describe the fourth creature (7:7). He can only say it is dreadful, powerful, and frightening. Its large iron teeth crush and devour its victims. It is different from any of the others in that it has ten horns. Animal horns are symbols of power, and ten is a number of completeness, so this final creature appears to have all rule and power.

This fourth beast is captivating. Daniel continues to watch it as yet another horn emerges, uprooting three of the existing ones. This new horn is different from the others. For one thing, it is smaller. Even stranger, however, is that it has eyes and a mouth, and the mouth is boasting (7:8).

Yet as fascinating as this bragging, multi-horned beast is, Daniel's eyes are drawn to an even more intriguing sight. He sees God (the "Ancient of Days") taking His seat among a number of thrones. His garments are white, symbolizing purity, as is His hair. His throne is ablaze. Fire flows from Him like a river, representing God's judgment poured out over all the earth (7:9–10). His is the throne of a judge; the other thrones are set up for those who will be watching the proceedings. (The book of Revelation speaks of great multitudes who will witness God's final judgment [Revelation 7:9–10; 19:1–3].)

Demystifying Daniel

The books that Daniel sees opened in 7:10 may be the same books mentioned in Revelation 20:11–15. God's judgment is based on the deeds recorded in these books. God notices the injustices done in this world, and they will not go unpunished.

Despite the presence of the Ancient of Days, the little horn continues its boasting. As Daniel watches, the fourth beast is killed as it speaks, and its body is thrown into a roaring fire. The other beasts are still around, but all their authority has been removed (7:11–12).

Then, in stark contrast to the boasting beast, Daniel sees another figure, whom he describes "like a son of man" (7:13–14). All the previous rulers of the world have been described as various animals (symbols of strength and power). It is clear from the text that this new figure is a special ruler, and he is somehow related to the Ancient of Days, yet he is perceived in human form. The concept of God ruling the earth in the form of a man is a profound thought, and would have been especially so to the religious leaders of Babylon and Persia.

The new ruler is given authority and power over all nations and peoples. The scope of his rule is unlimited, as is its length. His position as ruler is everlasting (7:13–14).

📄 7:15–28

THE INTERPRETATION OF THE DREAM

Even within his dream, Daniel is troubled. It must have been overwhelming to realize he was seeing what is in the future yet not fully understanding his visions. So he asks for clarification, and one of the heavenly figures (angels) helps him interpret the symbols and meaning (7:15–16).

The various beasts are kingdoms. Four of them will arise from the natural order of the earth. They will threaten and persecute the people of God, but God's kingdom will never be in doubt.

Critical Observation

The word interpreted *saints* in 7:18 can mean a couple of different things. It may be instinctive to see the word and think of people who are devoted to the lordship of God and who willingly submit to Him. However, Daniel is still writing in Aramaic throughout this section, and in that language *saints* could also mean "angels." This possibility is bolstered by later sections of Daniel that indicate an intense heavenly conflict taking place beyond what is visible on earth.

Not surprisingly, Daniel is particularly eager to learn more about the fourth beast (7:19–22). It is the most vicious and terrifying. The numerous horns, of shifting number, are mysterious. Even as he continues to watch, the boastful, outspoken horn is warring against the saints and is actually winning until the Ancient of Days puts an end to the matter by pronouncing judgment in favor of His saints.

The angel's response to Daniel reveals that the fourth creature is a cruel beast that will control ten kingdoms and conquer the world (7:23–27). Another king would arise after the others, displacing three of the existing kingdoms and supporting the beast in speaking out against God and His followers. He will even work through the legal system to change laws in his oppression of God's people. His reign of terror will last for "a time, times, and half a time" (7:25). In Aramaic, the use of the word *time* refers to the passing of one year (4:16). A common interpretation of the phrase, then, is to consider *a time* as one year, *times* as two years, and *half a time* as half a year, yielding a total of three and a half years.

Demystifying Daniel

The four beasts in Daniel's dream appear to correspond with the four sections of the great statue of Nebuchadnezzar's first dream (2:31–35). The descriptions of the four creatures lend credence to their representation of Babylon, Medo-Persia, Greece, and Rome. Much debate takes place as to the significance of the ten horns and the final, boastful horn. Many people connect this section of Daniel with John's writing in Revelation and believe that Daniel's dream describes the end-times Antichrist (called the "beast" in Revelation) and the false prophet who serves as a type of prime minister for him.

After the violent reign of this figure, God's heavenly court will assemble to strip him of power and destroy him once and for all. The people of God will then be given control of all the kingdoms of the world. God will be acknowledged as the true King, ensuring everlasting peace and contentment (7:26–27).

It is a satisfying ending, to be sure, yet the dream completely overwhelms Daniel. It is quite a burden to not only be informed of the end of the world as he knows it but to witness and experience it to a certain extent. He is deeply troubled, but he doesn't say anything about it to anyone.

Take It Home

Sometimes people feel they have witnessed the worst that humanity has to offer. In Daniel's case, he could make that claim with confidence, and he was physically shaken by the experience. Yet every time a prophet confronts his readers/listeners with bad news, it is coupled with the assurance that beyond the bad times, God will step in to restore and reward those who are faithful to Him. What are some distressing events you have recently experienced? If you could be absolutely sure that God is in control of those events, how would your perception of them change? What can you do to strengthen your awareness of God's sovereignty?

DANIEL 8:1–27

DANIEL'S SECOND VISION

Setting Up the Section

This section follows the previous one as another account from the private life of Daniel, in contrast to his interactions with various kings in chapters 1–6. This vision of Daniel's is also filled with symbols, as is his dream in chapter 7.

📄 **8:1–14**

A RAM AND A GOAT

In this chapter, Daniel returns to writing in Hebrew. The section between 2:4 and 7:28 was written in Aramaic and was a message of God's sovereignty over all nations. In chapter 8, the focus of Daniel's writing shifts to what God is planning to do *to* and *through* the nation of Israel.

Another notable observation of Daniel 8 is that it is a description of rage. The nations rage as they seek control of the world. One figure in particular rages in his attempt to take over the world. And, ultimately, the rage of God is witnessed as He punishes those who have rejected Him to embrace the world. The chapter should be approached as a description of events that are difficult to accept. However, an interpretation is provided for the vision that is specific and helpful for properly understanding its meaning.

This vision occurs during the third year of Belshazzar's reign (8:1), which is about two years after the dream Daniel previously described (7:1). The location in the vision is Susa, a city in the heart of the Medo-Persian Empire that will later become a common vacation spot for King Darius. So during the final years of the Babylonian Empire, Daniel is shown a vision of the destruction of the Persian Empire that will follow (8:1–2).

The citadel in Susa is synonymous with the success of the Persians, and the ram in the vision (8:3–4) is later identified as the Medo-Persian Empire (8:20). The ram dominates all other animals in every direction. The variance in the size of its two horns is most likely a prediction that the Medes will be the stronger of the two allied nations at first, although the Persians later gained power.

The land acquisitions of the Medo-Persians were not typically peaceful. They frequently resulted in war, death, destruction, pain, and misery. A raging ram is an appropriate symbol to represent their approach to surrounding nations.

But the ram finally meets its match in the form of a goat that shatters its two horns (8:5–7). Daniel will soon be informed that the goat represents Greece (8:21). It has a single prominent horn between its eyes (a single leader) and moves across the earth without touching the ground (indicating great speed).

The goat strikes the ram and quickly overpowers it. And when Persia comes up against Alexander the Great, it falls hard and fast. Alexander will go on to conquer most of the populated world before he is thirty. His combination of strength, speed of conquest, and youth will stand out in history. Napoleon and George Patton are two of many military leaders who studied the strategies of Alexander in designing their own battle plans.

Daniel's vision continues as he sees the goat grow in fame, but it suddenly has its large horn broken off. In place of the severed horn grows four other horns (8:8). History confirms that Alexander became quite proud and exalted himself. Yet by the age of thirty-three, he had died (the cause of which is widely disputed). After his death, the Greek nation is split into four states, each with a different leader.

God is not revealing these events to Daniel simply to give him preview of what will occur in history. These events will have a direct impact on the Jewish people. One of the four horns from the goat (Greece) starts small but quickly becomes great. Among the territories to which he turns his attention is *the Beautiful Land*—the name the Jews use for Jerusalem (8:9; Psalm 48:2).

The language that follows (Daniel 8:10–12) includes war imagery. "The host of heaven" is the army of heaven, a term sometimes applied to angels. Stars can represent large numbers of people. The horn strives to set himself up as an equal to God ("Prince of the host") by eliminating other religious ceremonies. He is associated with rebellion and a disregard for truth.

Again, history sheds light on this prophetic vision. One of the leaders who rises to power after Alexander the Great is a man named Antiochus Epiphanes. He has an intense dislike of the Jews, persecuting them, killing their high priest, and entering their temple to have pigs sacrificed to him because he believes he is the Messiah. In the ultimate insult, he corrupts and twists the entire religious system of the Jews so that it serves him.

Critical Observation

The religious corruption initiated by Antiochus Epiphanes will actually turn out to be a worse experience for the Jews than their exile. In Babylon, they mourned because they knew their temple and city were being neglected. But later, when they see their religion perverted and a false Messiah desecrating their temple, it is heart-wrenching.

Daniel overhears a heavenly conversation taking place regarding the length of time the rebellious horn will be allowed to trouble God's people (8:13–14). The answer has created a bit of confusion. It seems reasonable that 2,300 evenings and mornings should be 2,300 days, or almost six and a half years. Another possibility is that it means 2,300 *sacrifices*, with one each morning and one each evening for a total time of only half as long. But since the daily sacrifices are suspended during this time, this option doesn't seem as likely.

📄 **8:15–27**

THE INTERPRETATION OF THE VISION

Modern readers who are confused by passages such as this may be comforted to realize that Daniel also struggled to understand what he was seeing (8:15–16). First he is confused. As the angel Gabriel begins to explain the vision to him, he becomes terrified. Then when he discovers that the vision concerns a time of the end, he is so physically afflicted—almost comatose—that he needs help standing (8:17–18).

Gabriel's reference to the "time of the end" (8:19 NIV) should be interpreted from Daniel's perspective, not a modern one. The Jewish people are undergoing a time of God's discipline. They are currently exiled in Babylon, and Daniel is discovering that this won't be the worst of it. It is a couple of centuries before the horrors of Antiochus Epiphanes falls on them, but soon thereafter the consequences for the sins of Israel will come to an end.

Demystifying Daniel

When Daniel is addressed as *son of man* (8:17), it is not intended as a special title, as when it is applied to the Messiah. Rather, Daniel is among heavenly beings, so it is only logical that he would be singled out as the human in the group.

However, it is also fair to say that Antiochus Epiphanes is a picture of the end-times Antichrist (the beast in Revelation). The description in 8:23–25 is applicable to both figures: "completely wicked," "master of intrigue," and "very strong" (NIV). Both feel superior and spread deceit. Both are especially destructive because they establish their power while people feel secure. Only later do they reveal their true natures. And eventually, both will be destroyed, but not by human power (8:25). (Antiochus isn't killed; he eventually dies of tuberculosis.)

The wrath that Gabriel speaks of is God's response after God's people allow themselves to be fooled by the false religion of Antiochus (8:19). After they agree to the Greek leader's twisted religion, God will allow them to suffer the consequences. But as Daniel is about to be shown (in chapter 9), shortly afterward will come a Messiah to rescue God's people.

Daniel is assured that what he has seen is true (8:26). But then he is asked to seal the vision—not to discuss it with anyone. The reason, he will discover, is that he is about to receive another vision that will take precedence. Daniel can see some of the behind-the-scenes operations of God's kingdom, but the Lord doesn't want people motivated to come to Him out of fear. The next vision will reveal the coming of an anointed one, a Messiah, who acts out of compassion and offers salvation.

The knowledge of what is ahead for God's people overwhelms Daniel for a period of time. He is physically sick for several days. Even when he recovers and goes back to work, the vision continues to weigh on him. He will continue to struggle with what he has seen until God reveals more to him and puts his mind to rest.

Take It Home

Brazen leaders have defied God throughout history. Antiochus Epiphanes is certainly one of the worst, but there are many others. In fact, John warns God's people to watch out for anti-christs who have already come (1 John 2:18). Such people need not have widespread influence. Anyone who persistently opposes God and attempts to sway others to that belief is, by definition, an antichrist. Do you know anyone whom you would place in that category? How do you tend to respond/interact with such people?

DANIEL 9:1–27

DANIEL'S THIRD VISION

Daniel's Prayer	9:1–19
God's Response to Daniel's Prayer	9:20–27

Setting Up the Section

Continuing his record of various divine revelations he has received, Daniel describes a prayer for which he is given a most emphatic response. During his prayer, he is visited by the angel Gabriel, who tells Daniel what to expect in the future, although the symbolism used is challenging and difficult to properly interpret and understand.

📄 9:1–19

DANIEL'S PRAYER

The date that Daniel provides in 9:1 reveals that fourteen years have passed between his previous recorded vision (chapter 8) and this prayer. At the end of the previous section, Daniel is left exhausted, sick, and confused about what he has witnessed. He has been shown that God is going to bring the kingdoms of humanity to an end and that He is going to discipline the Jewish people. Seemingly, those fourteen years have been a time of searching for Daniel. He has not questioned that both discipline and judgment are deserved, yet God has promised that they will not last forever. So Daniel is seeking to discover when God will restore His glory.

Critical Observation

Jerusalem was an integral part of worship for the Jewish people. It symbolized the land God had given to His people, and the temple represented the presence of God amongst them. With the temple destroyed and the people scattered, Jerusalem was desolate at the time of Daniel's writing.

He has searched the scriptures available to him and found Jeremiah's prophecies, written prior to the invasion of Babylon, warning the people of what will come (Jeremiah 25:11–12). But along with the bad news of the coming captivity is the announcement that after seventy years the people will be allowed to return to Jerusalem.

This is encouraging news to Daniel, so he begins to pursue God in prayer. He realizes that the reason the Jews have fallen out of fellowship with God to begin with is because of their sin. So Daniel approaches God in prayer and petition, fasting, and sackcloth and ashes (9:3). His mind-set, habits, and dress are all designed to place his full focus on the Lord.

Daniel's prayer begins with confession, which is followed by a request for mercy (9:4–19). He first acknowledges the character of God (9:4). God is great and awe-inspiring because He can be counted on to keep His promises and care for His people.

God's people, however, have sinned in many ways (9:5–6). They have been wicked and rebellious, ignoring God's commandments. When God sent prophets to confront them about their sin, the people had rejected them. They had persistently lived for themselves, not for God.

Their rejection of God leads to their being scattered to various countries and their leaders driven from positions of responsibility. Daniel acknowledges that they deserve everything that has happened to them. However, in spite of the sins of the people, Daniel realizes that God remains merciful and forgiving (9:7–10).

The people have no excuse for their sinful rejection of God. The consequences of such sin are clearly spelled out in the Law of Moses (Leviticus 26:14–20). They had ignored Moses and a long series of prophets, and God had done what He said He would do (Daniel 9:11–14). The Lord's action in response to their sin is only proof of His righteousness.

Daniel then moves on to his request: He asks God to turn away His anger from Jerusalem (9:15–16). This is not a personal request. Rather, Daniel is asking God to reestablish His glory in the world. Ever since God allowed the Babylonians to conquer Jerusalem and take away the people, there has been no specific physical location where God is acknowledged and worshiped. Daniel's request is not just to get "home" but rather to see the glory of Jerusalem restored and an end to God's name being mocked by pagan nations.

Critical Observation

When Daniel (or any other Jewish person, for that matter) states that his God is more powerful than any other god, it appears to be a foolish statement to anyone outside of Judah. The Jews had been brutally defeated and were still living as captives. From all appearances, their God either doesn't care or is unable to do anything to improve the situation. Daniel's prayer is to correct such misperceptions about God.

📄 9:20–27

GOD'S RESPONSE TO DANIEL'S PRAYER

Daniel is still in prayer in the evening, when the angel Gabriel appears to him in swift flight. Daniel recognizes the angel from his previous vision (9:20–21). Ever since then, for fourteen years, Daniel must have wondered about the future. Gabriel had shared with him a description of punishment the Jews could expect in those days, but he had said nothing at the time about their salvation/deliverance (8:15–26). Finally, Gabriel has been instructed to provide Daniel with additional insight and understanding (9:22–23).

Still, what Daniel is about to hear has since been described as one of the most difficult passages in the Bible. Gabriel begins to depict a unit of time comprised of seventy sets of sevens, during which God will bring about redemption for His people (9:24). Numerous theories abound as to what this message really means. Some consider each "seven" to be a seven-year period. If so, much of what Gabriel says begins to fit a historic time line starting when a decree is passed to rebuild Jerusalem (which is described in Ezra 7:12–26) and carrying through to Jesus' ministry.

What is known for certain—what Gabriel tells Daniel—is that a ruler will appear who will again destroy the temple and the city of Jerusalem (Daniel 9:26). It will be a time of war. The destructive ruler to come will establish a covenant with the people for that final "seven" (9:27), but halfway through that period he will abolish all sacrifices and offerings, desecrating the temple with something called *an abomination that causes desolation* (NIV). But the ruler's end, already decreed, will occur shortly thereafter.

Demystifying Daniel

The *abomination that causes desolation* (NIV) means "the abomination that desolates or appalls" (9:27). It is a reference to something so detestable and repugnant that no decent, ethical, religious person will have anything to do with it. Such people will be nowhere near it, leaving that area desolate.

One understanding of this passage is that the destruction and desolation described in Daniel takes place in 70 AD, when the Romans overthrow a Jewish uprising by completely demolishing the temple. The ruler at the time is Titus. Those events fit a portion of what Daniel is told to expect, but not all.

More likely, the final "seven" is a still-future period of time. It seems logical to relate this new information that Daniel receives from Gabriel with the prophet's previous vision of the beast with the ten horns (7:19–27). If the ruler of 9:26–27 is the same as the boastful horn (7:20–22), the final "seven" will begin with the contract made by this malicious leader. He will break his covenant midway through, and great suffering will ensue for God's people. But after a period of time, God will remove him from leadership and make all things right.

Daniel's response to this new information is not recorded. However, it must have been encouraging to be assured that the predicted punishments he learned of in his previous vision will indeed come to an end and that God will make atonement for the sin of the people and provide everlasting righteousness (9:24).

Take It Home

Although the specific interpretation of future events as presented in this section may be confusing and debatable, one clear observation is that God has a plan. Events are moving toward the dates that He has specified. Even in the worst of times—especially in the worst of times— believers need to remain faithfully committed to Him. When are some recent times when your faith may not have been as strong as you wished? What are some specific truths about God that you might want to recall the next time you face similar situations?

DANIEL 10:1–12:13

DANIEL'S FOURTH VISION

Setting Up the Section

Daniel has recorded three visions so far: one of the destruction of human kingdoms and establishment of the kingdom of God (chapter 7), one of the punishment that will be inflicted on God's people because of their sin and rejection of God (chapter 8), and one of the coming Messiah who will conquer sin and provide a way of everlasting righteousness (chapter 9). In the rest of his book, Daniel records one final vision that encompasses, integrates, and further explains much of what he has already witnessed.

📄 **10:1–11:1**

THE FRAMEWORK FOR THE VISION

Daniel regularly dates his visions based on the reign of the leader at the time (7:1; 8:1; 9:1). This one is last chronologically. Darius (9:1) and Cyrus (10:1) rule Persia at the same time. Cyrus was the great king over the entire Persian Empire, which at this time included Israel. Darius may have been a subking under him as emperor. During Cyrus's first year, he passes a decree allowing the Jews to return to Judah and rebuild Jerusalem (Ezra 1:1–4). This final vision of Daniel's is two years later.

Critical Observation

Some people question why Daniel doesn't return to his homeland when he had the opportunity. No reason is given, although a couple of possibilities seem logical. First, he would have been at least in his mid-eighties, and a long journey could be difficult. Second, God had used Daniel as a consistently faithful voice in the midst of a people who had no knowledge of the Lord. Daniel had already demonstrated that he lived for the kingdom of God and not for his own well-being, advancement, or success. Perhaps his was a conscious decision to remain and serve where God had placed him.

Daniel's vision is nothing new, but it is more developed than his previous ones. As he begins to comprehend more clearly, he grows very troubled and goes into mourning, setting aside all the pleasantries of life such as wine, choice food, and lotions used to minimize the effects of the hot, arid climate (10:1–3). He is still troubled over the sin of God's people and the approaching punishment that will be the consequence. His emotions are probably heightened by the date as well, which would have coincided with the annual Passover to celebrate God's deliverance of His people in the past (10:4). Daniel is passionate about both the will of God and the people he loves on earth.

A biblical reference to the "great river" usually means the Euphrates, but Daniel clarifies that he is beside the Tigris (10:4). There he sees a heavenly figure whose description is similar to that of Jesus in Revelation 1:12–16. Some people have suggested that it is indeed a preincarnate appearance of Jesus, but the difficulty this figure faces in spiritual warfare would not have been true of the Lord (10:13). Daniel witnesses the splendor of one of God's angels, but not Jesus.

The figure is bedecked in linen (a sign of purity) and a gold belt (worn by royal leaders). His body is like beryl, a shiny and transparent gold-colored stone. His face is like lightning, his eyes like flaming torches. His arms and feet have a gleam like polished bronze. His voice is unusually powerful (10:5–6).

As impressive as this figure is, only Daniel is enabled to see him. Those with Daniel only realize something unexplainable is happening, and they run to hide (10:7). Daniel, too, is affected; he goes pale, feels entirely weak and helpless, and soon falls into a deep sleep (10:8–9). A touch of the angel helps him up, first to his hands and knees, and then to a standing position, although he is still quite wobbly (10:10–11).

The angel addresses Daniel as a man who is "highly esteemed" (10:11 NIV). God honors Daniel because his heart is not callous. The Lord values the pain that Daniel feels as a result of the people's sin.

Daniel has been fasting and praying for three weeks, and the angel had been quickly dispatched to respond to his prayers and desires. Daniel's prayers are heeded because he has set his heart on understanding and because he has humbled himself before God (10:12). Yet there has been a long delay between Daniel's petition and the angel's response, because the messenger sent to Daniel became involved in a fight with the prince of the Persian kingdom that lasted three weeks (10:12–13). Clearly this is a hostile and aggressive spiritual being, perhaps working to affect the kingdom of Persia for evil. Eventually the messenger of God, still struggling against the evil force, summons the help of Michael the archangel, the most powerful of the angels, and is able to continue on his way to Daniel.

Demystifying Daniel

This passage (10:12–14) alerts the reader to some of the truths about the unseen spiritual world. It is evident that angels are real, and both good angels and bad angels (demons) can influence the affairs of human beings.

Daniel has already heard what to expect for the Jews in the latter days, but he is about to receive another summary. Again, Daniel feels weak and unworthy to be part of such a divine moment (10:14–17). And again, he is touched by the heavenly messenger and encouraged to remain courageous and strong. As he listens, Daniel begins to regain his strength (10:18–19).

The angel is preparing to return and reengage in spiritual warfare, but first he wants to share with Daniel what is written in the Book of Truth (10:20–21). The messenger angel and the angel Michael stand opposed to the evil in the land, both in Persia and Greece. God had allowed those nations to thrive for a time, and His people had suffered. But here it is seen that God's protection is always in place. The sovereign Lord controls everything—including limiting the evil that occurs.

Demystifying Daniel

The Babylonians thought their gods had a Tablet of Destiny that supposedly foretold their history. Gabriel's reference to the Book of Truth in 10:21 may have suggested Daniel's awareness of such a Tablet, and it could have been the angel's way of assuring Daniel that God is sovereign and has the future in His hand. In any event, Gabriel is about to reveal some truth about the future to Daniel (11:2).

📖 11:2–35

THE VISION UNFOLDS

At this point, Gabriel begins to relate to Daniel a rather complex explanation of future events. It is helpful to keep in mind that as God orchestrates the events of the world, it is toward the purification of Israel and all of His followers. Some degree of purifying the nation will include punishment and persecution. God's plan includes the temporary emergence and dominance of various nations along with individual world leaders who exert a certain amount of control. Afterward, God's people will be purged and ready to serve Him.

Daniel has already been assured that no matter what takes place in world events, and as bad as things will become, God is always in control and permits evil to continue only for a limited time (9:24). With that in mind, he is then told that four more kings will arise in Persia, the fourth creating conflict against Greece (11:2). The three Persian leaders who follow Darius are Cambyses (530–522 BC), Smerdis (522 BC), and Darius I (522–486 BC). However, the Persian Empire had a total of thirteen leaders, and opinions vary as to whether the three referred to in Daniel 11:2 are the consecutive kings after Darius or the three most prominent leaders who succeed him.

Also debated is the identity of the fourth Persian king, although much evidence points to Xerxes I (486–465 BC). He is a strong king whose empire and wealth grow to large proportions. Eventually he seeks to attack Greece and incorporate the nation into his empire, but he fails miserably. His antagonism may have been the primary catalyst for the fall of Persia to Greece more than a century later.

However, almost everyone agrees that the "mighty king" who will appear and do as he pleases is Alexander the Great (11:3). The description in 11:4 fits Alexander precisely. His few family members are assassinated shortly after his death, and none of them inherit the great empire he had conquered and organized. Instead, rule goes to his four primary generals ("the four winds of heaven"), essentially segmenting the large empire into four separate kingdoms.

Two of those four kingdoms become prominent: Syria (the kingdom of the north) and Egypt (the kingdom of the south). The king of the south (Ptolemy I) and the king of the north (Seleucus I) begin as allies. Seleucus spends time with Ptolemy in Egypt while avoiding conflict with another power in the north. They fight together to defeat that opponent, and Seleucus returns to the north, settling in Babylon.

Tension forms between these two powers over the land in between them—the area of Palestine. It technically belongs to Seleucus, but Ptolemy occupies it. This tension appears to have continued to their successors, who attempt to resolve it with a marriage to unite the two kingdoms.

Ptolemy II (the successor of Ptolemy I) offers his daughter Berenice to Antiochus II Theos (the grandson of Seleucus). Antiochus agrees to the marriage, although he has to divorce his first wife, Laodice, to do so. Laodice had a son with him (Seleucus II). Antiochus and Berenice then have a son who appears to be next in line for the throne. In time, Antiochus reconciles with Laodice, which proves to be a mistake. She evidently doesn't like seeing another woman's son being groomed for leadership because she poisons Antiochus, Berenice, and their son. Laodice then occupies the throne until her son, Seleucus II, is ready to rule.

Needless to say, Laodice's actions are not well received in Egypt. Not long after the brother of Berenice (Ptolemy III Euergetes) takes the throne, he marches north to do battle against Seleucus II. He is initially successful and carries off the images of the northern gods, but subsequent battles continue between the two forces (11:5–8).

Critical Observation

This may sound like a complicated ancient history lesson. However, the details are important in demonstrating how accurate and succinct Daniel's account is, who recorded his prophecies two to four hundred years prior to the occurrence of the events.

Daniel's descriptions in 11:9–19 are pretty much self-explanatory, except for the names that are later provided for the participants. Laodice's son rules for twenty years before he dies and is replaced by his two sons, Seleucus III and Antiochus III. During the war described in 11:10, Seleucus III is murdered, leaving Antiochus III as sole leader of the northern kingdom. In the next battle that ensues, Antiochus assembles 62,000 infantry, 6,000 cavalry, and 102 elephants. He sends his army to Egypt, where they confront an opposing force of 70,000 infantry, 5,000 cavalry, and 73 elephants. The Egyptian army of Ptolemy IV Philopator is victorious, enacting a wholesale execution of the north and taking much land (including Palestine). Fifteen years later, Antiochus assembles an even larger army and begins to reacquire much of the territory he had lost (again, including Palestine). He presses on until he has gained control of Egypt. But for many years, the balance of power continues to go back and forth between the two nations.

The king of the north in Daniel 11:14–19 is still Antiochus III. The marriage of his daughter (Cleopatra I) to the king of the south (Ptolemy V) doesn't work as anticipated. Antiochus was hoping to win Ptolemy's favor. Instead, his daughter sides with her new husband rather than her father.

Stalled in his efforts against Egypt, Antiochus begins to tangle with the Roman army that is beginning to make some serious advancements in the area. The Romans first defeat Antiochus and then require him to pay heavy fines for his attacks, which place an economic strain on his country. When Antiochus returns home, he is killed by an angry mob who resents paying so much to Rome (11:18–19).

Demystifying Daniel

All the names and conflicts of this section definitely correlate with history. However, they serve the primary purpose of explaining the rise of one figure in particular: Antiochus IV Epiphanes. He is the ruler who most directly affects the people of God in their homeland.

After the death of Antiochus III, his son Seleucus IV takes over. He is the one who sends out a tax collector in an attempt to pay Rome the taxes they demanded (11:20). That tax collector, however, kills Seleucus in an attempted coup. He is unsuccessful, yet his actions leave the throne open to other contenders. The person who comes out on top is Antiochus IV Epiphanes. The rightful heir to the throne, a man named Demetrius, is being held hostage in Rome until his nation's taxes are paid. So Antiochus seizes the leadership role; he is not *given* the honor (11:21).

Still, Antiochus IV uses political savvy and false promises to gain and maintain power. When Egypt launches an unsuccessful attack attempting to regain Palestine, Antiochus takes their king captive. The brother of Egypt's king uses that opportunity to secure Egypt's throne for himself. The former king then proposes to Antiochus that they can work together to regain the Egyptian throne and rule the entire region together. Antiochus likes the idea. He signs an agreement and gives the Egyptian leader the title "prince of the covenant." But no sooner has the former Egyptian king been released than he breaks the covenant with Antiochus and forms an alliance with his brother to attempt to drive Antiochus out of Palestine. The forces of Antiochus are too strong, however, and the Egyptian attack fails (11:22–23).

In the peaceful interlude that follows, Antiochus begins to show his true colors. He begins to plunder the wealth of his own land, including the riches from the temple in Jerusalem. And when some of the Egyptians later betray their king, Antiochus is able to overpower that country as well, at the cost of many lives (11:24–26).

Yet another attempted alliance between Antiochus IV and the king of Egypt fails to work out. Antiochus returns home but then marches against Egypt again. However, this time ships from Rome are in the Mediterranean Sea with support for Egypt, and Antiochus is turned away (11:27–30).

He is not in a good mood as he returns home through Palestine, and he takes his anger out on the Jews. He not only kills Jewish people, but he seeks to destroy Judaism as well. (This is perhaps the time that Daniel had previously written about, when a figure would arrive under the pretense of peace and gain support, but would then break his promises, turn on the Jews, and sacrifice a pig to himself in their temple [9:27].)

Some Jews will be deceived and side with him. Some will be betrayed, but they will choose to remain silent rather than be confrontational. A few will resist Antiochus and fight back, many of whom will die as a result (11:31–34). This will be the beginning of the purging to purify God's people, although more is to come (11:35).

Critical Observation

One of the most notable opponents to the aggression of Antiochus IV Epiphanes is a man named Judas Maccabeus, who stands for God. He forms an army of dedicated fighters. They are unable to rid their land of Greek influence, but they do regain the temple.

📖 **11:36–12:13**

FURTHER INTO THE FUTURE

Up until this point in the vision, the events described appear to have been fulfilled by very specific events in history between Daniel's time and the modern day. In fact, the amazing accuracy has led some scholars to believe that Daniel must have lived in the second century BC and backdated his prophecy. The literary technique was not unusual at the time, but a close study of numerous additional aspects of Daniel's writing has convinced other scholars of its much earlier date, its reliability, and the reliability of his predictive prophecy. As Daniel repeatedly tells King Nebuchadnezzar, God is a revealer of mysteries (2:22, 28, 29). The precision of Daniel's visions only confirms this fact.

Beginning with 11:36, however, Daniel's prophecy makes an almost imperceptible shift. He continues to write about the king of the north and the king of the south, but the events no longer correlate to what has been recorded about Antiochus Epiphanes. In addition, his language adopts a grander scale than previously, and he begins to speak of end times.

It is difficult to state with certainty exactly what Daniel knew at the time and intended to communicate, but several scholars believe he must be writing of the last-days Antichrist, a figure who certainly can be compared with Antiochus Epiphanes in terms of deceit, hatred of God's people, and self-importance. The following comments will be based on that presumption. However, according to one school of thought, Daniel may not even have realized that his prophecy was jumping from a future Greek Empire to an even more distant future.

Many times people study the events concerning the end of the world and become scared when it seems that God cannot or will not stop the evil that is so strong and prevalent. Yet it is clear that God is always in control. In fact, He uses the events of the last days to bring about the cleansing and purging of evil that is necessary so He can establish His eternal kingdom. Just as He allowed the persecution of Israel during the reign of Antiochus IV Epiphanes, He will allow a similar purging during the final period of "seven" under the rule of the Antichrist (9:27).

The first thing revealed about this end-times figure is that he does as he pleases (11:36). He is able to carry out every notion and plan that comes to his mind. Antiochus had assumed the role of Messiah, but this figure goes one step further to position himself above *all* other gods, even the one true God (11:36–37). He will be successful, but only because God allows it.

Demystifying Daniel

Translations of 11:37 vary. Some say that the figure described has no desire for women, which would indicate that he is so consumed with himself that no other relationships matter. Other translations say that he has he has no desire for the god loved by women. In this case, the reference might be to a Babylonian fertility god named Tammuz. (The only overt biblical mention of this god is in Ezekiel 8:14.) His following was much like the one that would follow for the Greek god Adonis.

The only god that appeals to this individual is power (11:38–39). His religion is based on his ability to conquer. As he accumulates more and more power, it confirms his misassumption that he is the one and only god.

Sill, nations see the harm this figure can do, and they attempt to resist, even though they are not successful. He will go wherever he wishes. He will have strength like no king before him (11:40). Yet as he nears the land of Israel, for some reason he is unable to overtake the southeastern portions that include Edom, Moab, and Ammon. Why these areas are spared is not known. But other than the areas that God deems off-limits, the destructive leader will be allowed widespread conquest. Along with his territorial acquisitions comes economic strength as well (11:41–43). When he hears of threats, his intent is to annihilate (not merely stop) his opponents (11:44).

One observation that must have greatly disturbed Daniel's original readers is the location of this individual's headquarters. He sets up "between the glorious holy mountain and the sea" (11:45 NLT)—right in the heart of Israel. But as soon as this fact is revealed, it also confirms that his success will be limited. His time of conquest will quickly be concluded. When God finally takes action against him, his end is inevitable.

The period designated *at that time* in 12:1 is "the time of the end" (11:40). When the beast takes up residence in Israel, the great archangel Michael will depart. His presence has been to provide protection, and once that is removed, a time of unprecedented distress will occur. By this time, the Jewish people have already suffered through the rage of Antiochus IV Epiphanes and have been brutally murdered in great numbers by Hitler. But Daniel warns that what is yet to come will be even worse.

However, God is aware of which people have placed their faith in Him, and He will deliver the believers (12:1). A resurrection will take place as well, one that includes both righteous people and those who died as unbelievers. The righteous will receive rewards, including everlasting life (12:2). Those who are rewarded are identified as wise, or insightful (12:3). They are the people who understand that the world is God's and through Him are saved and find their purpose. They also share with others what they have discovered about God. Such people live forever, shining like stars in a clear night sky (12:3).

In ancient times, an official document was concealed or put in a safe place after being sealed. Gabriel instructs Daniel to close and seal what he has seen and heard (12:4). When later generations are ready to increase their knowledge, this book will be available to them.

Daniel is still on the bank of the river (10:5). At this point, he overhears two angels, one on either bank of the Tigris. One asks how long it will take to fulfill these astonishing things and is told it will be a period of three and a half years (12:5–8). Furthermore, it will be a time when the power of the holy people has finally been shattered (12:7).

Since the inception of Israel as a nation, the people had not learned to steadfastly serve God, so the Lord is going to deal with their rebellion through this persecution. The result will be a final end to the people's rebellion.

Even after seeing and hearing so much, Daniel can't help but ask what the outcome will be of all these events (12:8). What will be the result of the separating and shattering of the people?

Most people are intrigued with what will happen in the future and end-of-the-world events. Daniel is no exception. Yet even Daniel, with all his wisdom and devotion, is told to go (12:9, 13). God will see to everything in His own way and His own timing. It is not always for people to try to figure out everything He will do and when it will be done.

However, wisdom will provide understanding for the things the Lord *does* want people to know (12:10). His people can be purified and acquire greater spiritual knowledge, but intentionally wicked people will never comprehend the plan of God.

Wisdom requires patience, and Daniel's patience results in a final bit of information: The evil end-times ruler will openly persecute God's people for 1,290 days (three and a half years), beginning with his cessation of Jewish temple rites and his desecration of the temple. This is a long time for people to remain faithful to God. And even beyond the 1,290 days is another forty-five-day period during which people are to patiently persevere (12:11–12).

Demystifying Daniel

No explanation is provided for the different lengths of time mentioned in Daniel 12:11–12 (1,290 days vs. 1,335 days). Conceivably, a forty-five-day period might pass between the time God puts an end to the suffering of His people and His ultimate destruction of the person responsible for it.

The best Daniel can do in response to all he has seen is to continue on until the end (12:13). He has faithfully served his God throughout his long life. In return, he is promised rest and eventual resurrection, after which he will receive everything God has in store for him.

Take It Home

Many times people are reluctant to discuss spiritual matters with others because there is so much they don't fully understand. It should be somewhat comforting, then, to see that even Daniel doesn't completely comprehend the things of God. Still, he is expected to continue serving and speaking out faithfully. Indeed, God's people have a challenge before them to lead many to righteousness (12:3). What is your opinion of evangelism? Do you feel it is everyone's responsibility, or is it best left to the experts (pastors, teachers, scholars, etc.)? When believers don't have all the answers to life's mysteries, do you think their testimony to others is adversely affected?

THE NEAR EAST
DURING THE TIME
OF THE MACCABEES

Copyright © 2007 by Barbour Publishing, Inc.

HOSEA

INTRODUCTION TO HOSEA

In our present age, fixed truths, moral absolutes, divine imperatives, sure hope, and life-transforming power often seem to be overshadowed by uncertainty, insecurity, and subjectivism. Yet in the story of Hosea, we are confronted with the truth about God's persistent and unlikely love for an unfaithful people, the Israelites, even as we marvel at the tragic and remarkable beauty of one prophet's unconditional love for his faithless wife that exemplifies the love story between God and humanity.

AUTHOR

Hosea's prophecy may have existed first simply in spoken form, then later it may have been gathered together in written form by disciples or scribes. Still, this work is traditionally attributed to Hosea, the son of Beeri (1:1). We don't know much about the prophet's life except for the little that we learn from chapters 1 and 3.

PURPOSE

The purpose of the book of Hosea is to remind God's people of their unfaithfulness and of the judgment that will come because of that unfaithfulness. Hosea teaches that, in spite of their unfaithfulness, it is impossible to escape the love of God, who is ultimately their only hope of salvation from themselves.

OCCASION

When Hosea is called to serve as God's prophet, the nation of Israel is in a state of rebellion. Based on the kings reigning during his prophecy (1:1), we know that the nation of Israel has been split by civil war (1 Kings 12) and that Hosea is sent to the northern kingdom of Israel, which is characterized by corrupt kings, crime, and compromised morality (Hosea 4:1–2).

THEMES

Both themes of love and judgment run through Hosea's prophecy. God's saving love is faithful even in the face of unfaithfulness. Yet, the consequence of that unfaithfulness will be faced. Hosea's ministry is meant to awaken the Israelites to their own unfaithfulness to God and to call their adulterous hearts back to Him.

HISTORICAL CONTEXT

God called Hosea to the northern kingdom, or Israel, at a time when the nation was in a position of strength and wealth, probably during the later years of Jeroboam II's reign. Hosea was a contemporary of other Old Testament prophets: Amos, Isaiah, Jonah, and Micah. Already on the horizon was the Assyrian menace, and within thirty years, Israel had fallen in defeat.

HOSEA 1:1–2:1

AN UNUSUAL CALLING

Setting Up the Section

God calls Hosea to an unlikely method of ministry: Hosea becomes an example of God's message to a rebellious and unfaithful people.

📄 **1:1**

CALLED BY GOD

The book of Hosea provides its reader with some important facts that ground the story in its historical context. God calls Hosea during the reigns of Uzziah, Jotham, Ahaz, and Hezekiah, kings of Judah, and during the reign of Jeroboam II, king of Israel. Israel has split from civil war (2 Kings 13:12-13), and the people are pursuing nearly everything except God. Even their kings are often quite corrupt. Hosea is a contemporary of Amos, Isaiah, Jonah, and Micah—other Old Testament prophets charged with declaring God's love and faithfulness in the face of Israel's wayward rebellion. Yet Hosea is given a unique charge (as we will see).

📄 **1:2–2:1**

HOSEA'S FAMILY

What the Lord requires of Hosea is shocking indeed: to forsake the natural hopes he may have for a happy marriage and instead consign himself to endure the emotional anguish and dishonor of a wife who will be persistently unfaithful. Hosea fulfills God's calling in his marriage to Gomer (1:2-3).

The names that the Lord requires Hosea and Gomer to give to their children express the Lord's intention in the most decisive and unmistakable way. The name *Jezreel* declares God's intention to punish Israel for her unfaithfulness to Him. *Lo-ruhamah* means "not loved," as the Lord is prepared to not love Israel anymore because she has broken His covenant. *Lo-ammi* means "not my people." This harsh denial of their place as God's nation is ultimately what the Lord is warning this generation of Israelites about: Their fate is based on their unfaithfulness (1:4–9).

Critical Observation

The Lord's instruction to Hosea has been widely taken to mean that the Lord commands Hosea to marry a woman of ill repute, perhaps a prostitute. Some scholars maintain that the whole account of Hosea and Gomer is only a parable and not a description of what actually happened. It is a story to make a point. Another view suggests that perhaps Gomer is not a prostitute, but instead the term *adulterous wife* is used metaphorically, as *prostitution* is used metaphorically to refer to Israel's spiritual adultery. Since the most natural reading is to take the story literally, that is how it is approached here.

God uses revelation by action throughout the Bible—most obviously in the ultimate revelation of His love in the incarnate person of Jesus Christ. Jeremiah remains a bachelor his entire life, against all social expectations and his own desire, as an enacted prophecy against the people of God (Jeremiah 16:2). The death of Ezekiel's wife and the odd behavior God commands His prophet to display in connection with it are made symbolic of God's purpose and plan for His people (Ezekiel 24:15–27). Abraham was asked to sacrifice his son, Isaac (Genesis 22:1–18), as a demonstration of his faith and also to picture the future sacrifice God makes by sending His own Son to die on the cross for the salvation of all His children.

Ultimately, after God has judged and punished this generation of His people, He will return to them and restore them to Himself and renew His covenant with them. God's promise to restore His people unto relationship with Himself is fulfilled, at least in large part, in the gathering of the Gentiles into the church after Pentecost (Romans 9:22–26). It is this promise of restoration that is prophetically enacted in Hosea's relationship with Gomer (Hosea 1:10–2:1).

Take It Home

Throughout all generations, God's people are called to examine themselves and their faith—to make their calling and election sure, to strive to be certain that they belong to the people of God, not only in an outward way, but essentially and eternally.

HOSEA 2:2–23

PUNISHMENT AND RESTORATION

Setting Up the Section

Hosea describes God's coming punishment of Israel for her sin, telling of God's wrath and anger and, ultimately, His saving love that brings about the restoration of His people.

📖 2:2–13

HOSEA'S ANGRY GOD

The Old Testament prophets devote an immense amount of their preaching to what the modern church has neglected almost altogether: the judgment and the wrath of God. The centerpiece of the prophetical preaching is God's divine wrath against sin and the impending doom of those who betray His covenant and do not believe His Word. Hosea describes the punishment that God intends to put upon Israel in stark uncompromising terms: God will make Israel like a desert, blocking her path with thorn bushes; strip her naked; slay her with thirst; and ruin her vines and fig trees (2:2–13).

God wants His people to know the reality of His judgment and wrath and to attend to many false prophets in their thinking and living. The prophets of the Old Testament, like Christians today, had to contend with many whose messages were all sweet and lighthearted (Micah 2:11). Recognizing the reality of God's wrath toward sin helps make sense of a broken world, and accepting it spurs God's children to take their own lives more soberly. The suffering we experience in this world is the curse of God upon humanity because of rebellion against Him. The curses Hosea describes are the very curses God promised to visit upon His people if they betray His covenant with Israel in the days of Moses (Leviticus 26; Deuteronomy 28).

📖 2:14–23

THE PROMISE OF RESTORATION

God promises a new and tender courtship of Israel and holds forth the possibility of bringing new life in their relationship through a return to the wilderness—a place where Israel had previously experienced both judgment and cleansing. This is intended to give hope that the coming punishment is not intended to ultimately hurt the nation but instead help them and restore them to a right relationship with God (2:14–15).

Like other prophets, Hosea foretells that the eventual consequence of God's wrath will be a restoration in which a new covenant will be written on the hearts of wayward Israel (Jeremiah 31:31–34; Ezekiel 36:26–27). The Valley of Achor (or Valley of Trouble) points back to Achan's sin of taking riches God had said were off-limits when the Israelites first took the promised land (Joshua 7:26). The Israel of Hosea's day has chased after the "gifts" of her lovers. But the grace of God will reverse the curse so that what was once a marker for sin becomes a door of hope (Hosea 2:15).

Israel's hope is found in what God is going to do in their hearts. They will forever banish the name Baal from their religious life. The term *Baal* literally means "master," and it was the term used for the false gods that the Canaanites worshiped. The Israelites' acceptance of this name for God began the process of compromise and the nation's fall.

What comes out of one's mouth is a representation of what is in the heart (Proverbs 13:3; 16:23). Thus by calling God *Baal*, they are in essence showing that they have given their hearts to false worship. Yet God will cleanse them, and they will address God in terms of a deep love relationship rather then abandoning Him in false worship. Israel will call God *husband*—a term of endearment and relationship. Thus the restoration will be great (Hosea 2:16–17).

Instead of the wilderness being a place where the wild animals are a threat and a danger to mankind, it now becomes a place where the animals themselves are brought into covenant relation with the redeemed people. What Hosea describes is a restoration of the creation order in which God is going to make all things new again (2:18). It is a vision of the new heavens and the new earth (Isaiah 11:6–7; Revelations 21:1).

Despite Israel's unfaithfulness, God is going to pursue her again, and this time the marriage covenant will be stronger—one that will bring an eternal relationship. This new covenant will be one in which love will rule. It is the beginning of an unprecedented relationship of love between God and His people. It is a new covenant.

God gives righteousness, justice, love, and compassion as the means by which He obtains His bride (2:19). It is God's righteousness and justice, not Israel's, that redeems her. God is the One who pays the price to make us His own. Faithfulness becomes the summary of the other four qualities in a single word (2:20). The unfailing goodness of God is the basis for Israel's salvation.

The goal of God's wooing of the people is that they will know Him. To know God implies the deepest relationship with Him. To know God is to love Him, to be one of His people, to abandon all other gods, and to be eternally committed to Him. What God is promising here is that Israel will be bound in an unbreakable covenant, and all the people from least to greatest will know Him.

God promises to reverse the famine of 2:9 by making what has become a wilderness a land that meets the needs of His people. God is going to respond to the people's call for help by providing for them. Jezreel, the name of Hosea's firstborn, had been a warning of brokenness for Israel (1:4–5), but now it implies salvation and prosperity. The name *Jezreel* literally means "God sows" (2:21–23).

Hosea concludes this promise with a final reversal: the reversal of the names Lo-ru-hamah and Lo-ammi. God will have compassion on those who have not had compassion, and He will call those who are not His people to be His. The people's response ("You are my God") fulfills the prophecy of 2:20, that they will know the Lord, and reverses the rejection described in 1:9 ("I am not your God"). God will resolve all of the self-inflicted consequences for our sins. Rather than eternally punishing mankind, God has offered a way of salvation (2:23).

Take It Home

We are reminded by passages such as Hosea's that the stakes are high—heaven or hell (the love and favor of God or His wrath and curse; eternal life or everlasting doom). An understanding of the immensity of the issues of life or death should drive each of us to live a serious and self-examined life. In the end, our hope is in the Lord, who will renew our faith even in the midst of our own unfaithfulness.

HOSEA 3:1–5
RECONCILIATION
Love Covers a Multitude of Sins   3:1–5

Setting Up the Section

Hosea is called to reconcile with his wife despite her adultery. God draws a parallel between the story of Hosea's love for his wife and God's love for unfaithful Israel.

📖 3:1–5

LOVE COVERS A MULTITUDE OF SINS

God requires Hosea to reclaim his wife, Gomer, though she is an adulteress (3:1). This command is extraordinary considering how seriously God takes faithfulness, but He gives Hosea a model in His own love for the unfaithful Israelites. The general view of this passage is that Hosea must purchase his wife, who is on sale as a slave, perhaps for debt. God describes how the Israelites were unfaithful to Him by loving sacred raisin cakes, which were used in the worship of false deities (Jeremiah 7:18). The Lord's love cannot be extinguished even by the people's outright apostasy (Hosea 3:1).

Hosea purchases Gomer with an assortment of items—fifteen shekels of silver and five bushels of barley—which demonstrates how he had to tap all of his resources to recover his unfaithful bride. Hosea initiates a period of discipline during which his wife will live with him for many days before the resumption of full marital relations (3:3). This interim is meant to signify the exile Israel has to undergo before the restoration in the last days (3:5). The word *return* is used repeatedly throughout Hosea's prophecy—a total of twenty-two times—and is a significant theme of the message. Like Gomer's return to Hosea, Israel's return to the Lord does not come without a cost and a period of purification and exile. Israel, like Hosea's wife, is ultimately restored to her true happiness with her rightful God through a miracle of God's grace.

HOSEA 4:1-19

THE CASE AGAINST ISRAEL

Setting Up the Section

Hosea lays out God's charges against Israel, describing the people's sinfulness and God's holiness.

📄 4:1-3

THE WORD OF THE LORD

In this passage, Hosea is laying out a prophet lawsuit—a charge from the Lord that comes with evidence and judgment (4:1).

The charges are fairly straightforward and damning. "There is no faithfulness, no kindness, no knowledge of God in your land" (4:1 NLT; see Proverbs 24:2). There is instead plenty of transgression—cursing, lying, murder, stealing, adultery—that is already bringing about negative consequences for the people and even the land (Isaiah 33:9; Jeremiah 4:28). The land mourning is likely a reference to a drought (Hosea 4:3), and the death of the animals is mentioned in other Old Testament prophecies (see Jeremiah 4:25; 9:10).

📄 4:4-19

THE PRIESTS' CULPABILITY

As it had been in 2:2, God's main point in this lawsuit against Israel is that the priests have forsaken their true calling and responsibility, and they are responsible for the spiritual defection of the people and the debacle that God is about to bring upon them for their breech of the covenant (4:4).

So far as it is possible to assign particular blame for Israel's apostasy, Hosea is willing to say it is the ministers' fault that the people will perish under God's judgment. The priests have led them astray, kept them from a true knowledge of God and His covenant, and have encouraged unbelief and disobedience. But God, in His holy vengeance, now intends to bring justice.

Hosea explicitly says that the priests have perverted the law of God. In fact, under their false teaching, Israel is perishing for lack of knowledge. No doubt that teaching included a great deal of paganism (drawn from the surrounding culture), a radical undermining of the authority of God's law, and a relaxing take on the standards of holiness God requires (4:5-6).

Hosea blames the priests because they bore the greatest responsibility for the spiritual life of the people of God. Their ministry of the Word and worship, or lack thereof, had a far greater influence upon the people—for good or for ill—than the ministry of any other. Sin multiplied under and among these false teachers (4:7-8).

Demystifying Hosea

Malachi provides what may be the Old Testament's most succinct description of the calling of a priest or a minister in the Lord's reminiscence of the priestly ministry of Aaron: "True instruction was in his mouth and nothing false was found on his lips. He walked with me in peace and uprightness, and turned many from sin" (Malachi 2:6 NIV). The priests of the northern kingdom in Hosea's day are the perfect antithesis of that description and therefore are the subject of God's stern rebuke and judgment.

This greater responsibility and consequent accountability does not absolve the rest of the Israelites. God will punish both the priests and the people for their wickedness (4:9). Like Gomer, the Israelites will give themselves over to prostitution. This part of the prophecy describes how God will punish the Israelites for their persistent unfaithfulness—through depriving them of prosperity and joy and by launching a full-scale attack on the Baal cult (4:10–14).

Hosea warns Judah (Israel's southern sister) not to follow Israel in the path to destruction (4:15–19). The use of the name *Ephraim*—in reference to Israel—signifies that because of their lack of allegiance to David, the northern kingdom does not even deserve to be called Israel (4:17). Themes of drunkenness and prostitution continue as Hosea presents God's case against His people (4:18).

Take It Home

Hosea teaches us that the spiritual health of the priests and ministers of God's message is a matter of great importance and bears directly on the spiritual health and well-being of the larger community. As a body of believers, we must support, encourage, and hold our leadership accountable to the Word of God. We must pray for our leaders, knowing that our spiritual journeys are intertwined, just as Moses prayed for Levi (Deuteronomy 33:11).

HOSEA 5:1-15

THE JUDGMENT

The Point of No Return   5:1–15

Setting Up the Section

One of the solemn messages Hosea and other Old Testament prophets are called to deliver is the terrible seriousness of rebellion against God. Not only will God's people someday have to give an account for their unfaithfulness, but there will also be immediate consequences for their rebellion.

📄 **5:1–15**

THE POINT OF NO RETURN

Hosea calls again to get the people to listen—there is judgment against them, and God wants their full attention. These opening verses renew the fact that God is making a direct charge against Israel's leaders, the priests, and even the royal family (5:1-2). Tabor and Mizpah are places associated with worship of Baal. Legal imagery continues as well in the use of words like *judgment* and *testifies* (5:1, 5).

God sees everything and declares that Israel is corrupt, or unclean. This image points back to Hosea's unclean wife, whom God calls Hosea to love in spite of her unfaithfulness. The speaker in this verse can either be Hosea or Yahweh (5:3). Israel's sin is so tremendous that it prevents them from returning to God even if they want to, a concept that resurfaces in the New Testament (5:4; see Mark 3:29; 1 John 5:16).

God has even withdrawn from receiving the people's sacrifices. This is another of the curses that God long ago promised to visit upon those unfaithful to His covenant (Deuteronomy 31:18). The New Moon festivals that will devour the people and their fields (Hosea 5:7) likely refers to pagan rituals that are mentioned elsewhere (Isaiah 1:14).

Ephraim is reduced to waste, and Judah acquires a territory of Benjamin by military force (5:8-9). This action violates the sacred tribal land allotments which God's covenant had fixed and is what Hosea is probably talking about when he says Judah's leaders move boundary markers (5:10). These actions of violation provoke God's wrath (Proverbs 22:28).

God identifies Himself as the real threat to a sinful people floundering about in unfaithfulness (5:14). Not even their allegiances with Assyria will cause them as much oppression as their allegiance to idols (5:11). God is their judge and the only One who can save them from themselves (5:12-13). The consequences of the people's rebellion do not stop with destruction and despair. God withdraws Himself until they are able to repent of their sins (5:14-15).

Take It Home

The sins of Israel take hold because they are permitted to take hold. It becomes so much the habit of life as to make these people beyond the reach of even prophecies about their own destruction. These words call each of us to seriously examine our lives, to deal with sin as soon as we recognize it, and remember not to underestimate how far-reaching its affects can be. The psalmist reminds God's children: "We are the people he watches over, the flock under his care. If only you would listen to his voice today!" (Psalm 95:7 NLT).

HOSEA 6:1–11

ISRAEL REFUSES TO REPENT

Setting Up the Section

Most of Hosea's prophecy focuses on proving how Israel betrayed the Lord and His covenant and enumerating the curses which God is about to visit upon His people for their faithlessness and apostasy. Hosea also proclaims that after God is finished with His judgment, He will return to bless a future generation of His chosen people.

📄 6:1–3

THE LORD PROMISES FORGIVENESS

Finally, in the midst of the despair of God withdrawing His life-giving presence from His people, there is a glimmer of hope and forgiveness. God will return to bless His people. Hosea has been hammering away at Israel with his message of doom and the grim promise that she is about to fall under God's unrelenting judgment. And now, in the next breath, Hosea proclaims the compassion and mercy of God and His willingness to forgive His people in defiance of the wrongs they have committed against Him.

Hosea does not contemplate that his contemporaries will dodge God's wrath—they will be judged. But at some point in the future, God will return to His people with grace. The *us* (6:1–3) refers not to Hosea's contemporaries but to people in a distant time in the future. Similarly, when God said to Israel in the wilderness in Deuteronomy 4 that He will send them into exile, He isn't referring to that very group of people but to people in a distant time.

God is a God of great mercy, and He will forgive and restore human beings to fellowship with Himself, even when they are guilty of every manner of sin against Him—if they will repent (6:1). Even when they have defied His grace, spurned His commandments, and abused His gifts, His grace reaches the heights and the depths. Just as Christ was raised on the third day, so the image of Israel's revival and restoration to live in God's presence is described (6:2). If there is anything that Israel can hope in—even in the midst of God's judgment—it is God's own merciful return (6:3).

Take It Home

In the midst of judgment, God's love shines like a beacon of hope. As great as Israel's sins are— and as great as our own—the mercy of the Almighty God will sweep them away like the coming of dawn if only they repent. God is a holy God who demands justice but who also delights in mercy and freely offers grace to His people. "Who is a God like you, who pardons sin and forgives the transgression of the remnant of his inheritance? You do not stay angry forever but delight to show mercy" (Micah 7:18 NIV). "May your unfailing love rest upon us, O LORD, even as we put our hope in you" (Psalm 33:22 NIV).

📄 6:4–11

WORSHIP GONE WRONG

The tone shifts noticeably in verse 4 as Hosea returns to the main idea at hand for the Israelites—God's sorrow at their sin. God is suspicious of the people's love and desire to return to Him—their love is as ephemeral as the morning mist (6:4). God reminds them of what He has proclaimed through earlier prophets—that He requires more than empty promises and He desires acknowledgement of Himself (6:6). The word *mercy* in 6:6 is the same word rendered *love* in 6:4. In reference to God, this word translates to "grace" and "loving-kindness." But with reference to Israel, it refers to that love and loyalty that is their part of the covenant with God. Hosea's great point is that Israel has been disloyal to God and the covenant; she has failed to do her part.

Israel has come to think about her God, the living and true God who created all things and knows the hearts of His people, in the same way that the pagans around her think of their false gods and idols. The Israelites had come to believe that by offering sacrifices and performing rituals, they could ingratiate themselves with God and get Him to do good things for them, allowing them to live however they please. To worship God as Hosea's contemporaries worshiped God, with outward rituals but no inward devotion, is to be false to God. God is not interested in that kind of worship at all (6:6).

Just as God judged and banished Adam from the garden for breaking the covenant, God is banishing His people from the benefits of the covenant they have broken (6:7; see Joshua 23:16). Hosea provides a powerful image of a city "stained with footprints of blood" (6:8 NIV).

Israel has lost a sense of what worship is intended to be. Her worship had first become a true hypocrisy before it became naked paganism. Israel does not love God and does not care about what pleases Him. They leave their worship of God, do exactly as they please, commit whatever sins they desire to commit, and live between their trips to offer sacrifices a life of unrelieved disobedience and rebellion against God (6:9–10).

Take It Home

Worship is the true test of where a church, or any churchgoer, really stands before God. Worship is the test. Israel's worship had clearly gone far wrong (4:12–14). God demands more from us in our worship than just lip service. Israel's sin is the same one the Pharisees committed in Matthew 9:13. Outward rituals and religious formalities do not please God unless one's heart and life are aligned to His will.

HOSEA 7:1–16

ISRAEL'S GREAT CHALLENGE

Living by Sight	7:1–8
Blind to the Truth	7:9–16

Setting Up the Section

Hosea dwells on Israel's complete, final, and irreversible failure of faith. The people continue to be religious and call upon the Lord, but all the while they do not really put their trust completely in Him. God longs to redeem His people, but they persist in their sin. The great challenge for Israel is to admit that she has lost her faith and to return to God's truth.

7:1–8

LIVING BY SIGHT

Israel, on account of her disobedience and disloyalty to the Lord, is teetering on the brink of extinction. God's desire to "restore the fortunes" is a reference to the same healing and restoration of the covenant relationship described in 6:1 (6:11–7:2). It is the recovery anticipated in the New Year festival. Israel's real hope lies in the Sovereign God who knows how to deliver His people, as He has so often in the past. But instead of trusting in this, the people are putting faith in the sort of diplomatic maneuvering that never brings true success (7:1–2).

Israel's failure, Hosea says, is a failure of faith, and all of her terrible disobedience is evidence of the fact that she does not really believe in the Lord or trust in Him. Because their faith is weak, the Israelites continue to regularly and instinctively count more upon that which they can see and hear and touch than upon an unseen God. This faithlessness leads to a time of tumultuous political uncertainty (7:3–7).

BLIND TO THE TRUTH

Israel has for so long beckoned to the world of sight and ignored the unseen realities of the life of faith and of God's covenant, that she now has become totally blind and deaf to those realities. Her faith is so feeble that she is completely cut off from understanding what faith in God alone gives. No amount of evidence can make Israel realize what total folly she has chosen for herself (7:9-10).

Critical Observation

Israel persists in making terrible decisions that only further her destruction. Hosea pictures Ephraim in her clumsy waywardness like a dove flapping every which way (7:11). The context for what Hosea is referencing is the foreign policy decisions that Israel made to play off Egypt and Assyria (2 Kings 15:19–20; 17:3–6). Israel thinks she can find a way out of her mess, but God will see to it that all her plans are frustrated and that she gets what she deserves. He will not be mocked! Israel had hoped that Assyria or Egypt would be her savior, but lurching between the one and the other, she became hateful to both of them. Assyria will become her conqueror, and Egypt will make sport of her when she is destroyed.

The simple evidence is that Israel continues to maintain the pretence of faith in God without actually being sincere. The people do not think they are faithless—they pray and worship God. Yet Hosea says these actions are meaningless because of the intentions of their hearts to continue harboring sin. Everything we do is abundantly clear to God; He is not deceived by our calculations to look good. Just as God said to Samuel when He was anointing David king, "The LORD doesn't see things the way you see them. People judge by outward appearance, but the LORD looks at the heart" (1 Samuel 16:7 NLT).

God's revelation through Hosea concludes with another warning of final disaster and an implication that the nation will return to Egypt and God will no longer choose them to be His people (7:13-16). God is tired of the way He has been misrepresented—through lies, turning away, and evil plots (7:13-15). The wailing is a reference to the worship of Baal (see 1 Kings 18:28), and God calls them out on the duplicity of their cry for help, implying that the people are actually calling for Baal (7:14-15). Israel's arrogance and failure to call on the one true God makes them a laughingstock even among their enemies in Egypt (7:16).

Take It Home

Israel has become interested in pleasing people more than drawing near to the One who actually, and finally, holds their fortunes in His hands. They know that God is the only true deliverer, and yet they fail to practice daily on this knowledge. Their faith is so weak that they are more inclined to trust themselves and others than God. Like the Israelites of Hosea's day, our faith is weak. The greatest way for us to grow in grace is to seek God by practicing, nurturing, and exercising our faith in community, Bible study, and prayer.

HOSEA 8:1–14

REAP THE WHIRLWIND

Inevitable Judgment   8:1–14

Setting Up the Section

Hosea's prophecy continues to describe how Israel is about to reap the whirlwind of God's judgment for their unfaithfulness. His manner is serious and somber and sets the tone for the punishment to come in the chapters ahead.

📄 **8:1–14**

INEVITABLE JUDGMENT

The theme of this chapter is to prepare Israel for the punishment that she is about to receive. The trumpet signals the approaching danger. The eagle is more accurately translated as a *griffon vulture*, which signifies that death is already settling over Israel and the birds of scavenging are taking their places (8:1). Israel's cries of acknowledgment in the midst of her unfaithfulness only serve to further arouse and inflame God's anger and judgment. The people refuse to turn to God; they have "rejected what is good" (8:2–3).

God reviews Israel's rebellious ways. She has set up kings and princes He does not approve of (8:4) and uses the treasures of the land to fashion idols of gold and silver that violate the covenant and bring destruction (8:5). Jeroboam I, the first king God had not appointed or anointed, also initiated the idolatrous cult. This example is a reality that both Hosea and the people know. The reference to the monarchy also signifies Israel's attempt to do without God.

The calf-idol of Samaria refers to the two calves at Bethel and Dan (1 Kings 12:28–30), and these man-made imposters will be destroyed just as they have brought about the destruction of Israel (8:5–6). The next set of verses is a return to Israel's political misdeeds, particularly their alliances with foreigners. Hosea quotes two proverbs—"sow the wind and reap the whirlwind" and "the stalk has no head, it will produce no flour" (8:7 NIV). These proverbs seem to underscore the inevitable judgment that Hosea is prophesying—events have been set in motion by Israel's disobedience (8:7).

Hosea continues to hammer home the punishment that awaits Israel for her unfaithfulness. She will be "swallowed up" by those she believes to be potential allies, and she is now considered worthless, for she has failed in her divine purpose (8:8). The image of Israel as a wild donkey underscores her aimlessness and isolation. The reference to selling herself to her lovers returns to the themes of prostitution from Hosea's early prophecy and further illuminates how desperate she has become (8:9). The result of Israel's unfaithfulness and sin is no longer something she can deny or avoid—she is no longer a nation and certainly not a nation worthy of being claimed as God's people. She has lost herself (8:10).

In the conclusion of this chapter, Hosea returns to enumerating Israel's religious misdeeds by describing how she has turned to other gods. Altars that were intended to cleanse the people from sin became, ironically, places where their sin increased as they misused them for Baal (8:11). Even God's guidebook to the people became indecipherable to their sinful hearts—seeming like a foreign thing (8:12). God gave His law to the people, but they came to think of it as strange and far removed from the real interests and issues of their lives. Israel has lost all true regard for the law of God and all true interest in keeping God's commandments. She has made a life's work of rebelling against that law and defying it at every turn.

Hosea promises doom to Israel for her disobedience, though all along she has claimed to believe in God. No one can ever save themselves by keeping the commandments of God; but it is just as true that everyone who is truly saved by the grace of God will practice obedience to His commandments. Jesus saves us in order to sanctify us, to make us holy—being obedient to God's law. He saves us to make us zealous for good works, and by *good works* He means all that we do in obedience to His commandments.

Hosea puts it bluntly: Israel has chosen for herself the path of disobedience to God's law, and God is now preparing her doom (8:13). Throughout the Bible, it is proclaimed from the rooftops that those who are truly the people of God will love and obey His law. Those who do not, whatever they may protest to the contrary—and Israel does protest her faith in God to the bitter end—will not be numbered among God's children and will not be spared His wrath in the Day of Judgment.

Again and again, Hosea says this: Israel calls upon the Lord to save her, but she will have God only on her own terms. She has no intention of living according to the commandments of God. She wants His forgiveness and His help, but she does not want to be ruled by Him and by His law. The name *Maker* for God refers to His election of Israel from among the nations, not their physical creation (8:14; see Psalm 100:3; Malachi 2:10).

God will not listen to the prayers nor will He accept the sacrifices of people who will not do what He says. He instead promises to send fire to consume their fortresses. God's judgment will include both Judah and Israel (8:14–15).

Take It Home

One idea that sometimes gets lost in Hosea's sobering prophecy of inevitable judgment is the truth that Israel has forgotten—that obedience to God leads to blessings in this life and the life to come. Hosea is full of this simple and happy truth. Hosea is here to remind the transgressors of what their choices are really reaping and also to remind them that the way of the Lord leads to great reward. God gives us His commandments because He loves us and knows what is best for us. The only absolutely reliable plan for the achievement of happiness and self-fulfillment is the plan for living by the law of God.

HOSEA 9:1–10:15

PUNISHMENT TO ARRIVE

No Reason to Rejoice	9:1–17
The Consequences of Sin	10:1–15

Setting Up the Section

Israel tried to be like other nations by seeking to become wealthy by the same means that the nations used: the fertility cult. But Israel isn't like the other nations; Israelites are God's children, and God will not bless them to operate with this level of harlotry. When Israel embraces these pagan religious practices, they are acting in a way that is inconsistent with their own identity and calling.

9:1–17

NO REASON TO REJOICE

Israel's harvest has failed, and God commands them to stop rejoicing. Their harvest has failed because of their prostitution against God. When Hosea refers to "the wages of a prostitute at every threshing floor" (NIV), he is talking about the immoral acts that often accompany the party atmosphere at harvest in which sexual license is considered to encourage agricultural prosperity (9:1). The harvest they seek from this harlotry will not produce prosperity for the nation. In fact, their produce will not sustain them at all. God will keep the product of their harlotry from feeding the nation (9:2).

Not only is God going to prevent the harvest from sustaining the nation, but He will also drive Israel from the land. Because they have defiled themselves, they will be unfit for residence in the holy land and will instead eat defiled food in a foreign land (9:3).

They have no offerings to give that are suitable for use in worship. Because of their harlotry and the consequence that is coming, there is no sacrifice that will be acceptable to God (9:4). The "bread of mourners" refers to the fact that those who are in mourning, and who must deal with the burial of a dead body, contaminate the food they touch. Therefore, such bread is unfit for offering to God (see Deuteronomy 26:12–14).

Israel has embraced false worship and rejected God. Though they have maintained a form of ceremonial worship, they have nothing to recommend themselves to God. No matter how much they adhere to the proper forms, it is not a worship that brings glory to God (9:5). The people are suffering from the plight of famine—the food is unfit to offer to God because of its poor quality and because it comes from an environment where death and contact with the dead are common. The people, devastated, will go down to Egypt, just as Abraham did, to find relief. The famine-ravaged Israelites will seek deliverance in Egypt and will not find it (9:6).

Critical Observation

Memphis (9:6) is the Greek name for the Egyptian Mamphta, which is the capital of Egypt at this time (Isaiah 19:13; Jeremiah 2:16; 44:1; 46:14; Ezekiel 30:13). Its name means "the dwelling of Phta," the Greek Vulcan. In it is the well-known court of Apis. There, in the home of the idol to whom the rebellious Israelites look for refuge, they will be gathered to be buried. This place is a favorite burial place of the Egyptians. Hence the place of their refuge is the place of their destruction.

The false prophets had continually deceived the people, promising them that days of destruction will never come. They have escaped this day of judgment for only so long, but now it is upon them. In God's purpose, the days of judgment are inevitable. Hosea gives to the false prophets the title which they claim for themselves: "the prophet" and "the man of the spirit" (ESV). Yet, these prophets are not God's men, and they do not have the Spirit of God in them. They are mad and crazy prophets who speak destructive lies to the people. They lead the people astray (9:7–8).

The reference to Gibeah brings us back to Judges 19–21, in which a Levite's concubine is raped and murdered at Gibeah. The Levite, to obtain vengeance, cuts her body into twelve pieces and sends the pieces to the tribes of Israel to provoke their outrage. This begins a civil war and a series of grotesque atrocities. Hosea declares that the people of his day have fallen to the level of this most corrupt generation of Israel's history. They are just as judged by God (9:9).

One does not expect to find edible grapes in the desert, and such a discovery would make a real feast for a traveler. Similarly, the firstfruits of a fig tree in spring would be especially delicious to people in the ancient world. The point of both metaphors is that Israel in her youth was a special source of delight to God, yet something happened. The people went to Baal Peor and consecrated themselves to shame. Just like fruit going bad, the people, upon arrival in Israel, gave themselves over to Baal and became a stench to the One who loves them (9:10).

Demystifying Hosea

Baal Peor was the location of a shrine to Baal in the plains of Moab, some twelve miles north-east of the Dead Sea (Numbers 25:1–9). After Balaam failed to bring a curse down on Israel, the Israelites brought one down on themselves by yielding to the temptation to have sexual relations with Moabite women. A plague began in Israel, and the plague did not come to a stop until the priest Phinehas took a spear and ran it through the bodies of an Israelite man and a Moabite woman. By calling the attention of Israel to this, the people will see that their apostasy to Baal began before they entered the promised land.

Ephraim's glory will depart. As a sign of judgment, they will not be able to have children. Since children are a sign of God's blessing, God will remove the ability to be fertile. Instead of the blessing of children, Israel will bear the consequence of their sin (9:11–12).

God formed this nation to be strong and glorious, planted in a great meadow. Yet, instead of growing and becoming strong, they are leading their children out to slaughter. Rather than growing, they are acting like those who worship Baal and thus killing their children. Just as those who worship Baal sacrifice their children to him, Israel is now doing the same (9:13).

Israel had attributed their fertility to Baal, and now barrenness is the only appropriate judgment. Since they turned to Baal for life, the only logical consequence is for God to give them over to death. Thus, God will remove the fertility of the land (9:14).

Gilgal is the prototypical city of Israel—it contains every evil that the book of Hosea condemns. Gilgal is the city that prompts Yahweh to declare Israel His enemy. Gilgal is described as a cult center in 4:15 and 12:11. The rebellion that is here is so hated by God that He is going to drive the people out of the land and punish all the leaders who have led Israel into such apostasy (9:15).

Israel is so cursed that life will not be given to them. God will show them how cursed they are as a nation. They will be wanderers among the nations—exiled and forced to live as aliens and strangers in the world. They will lose their blessing, their home, and their fertility. In short, they will live cursed because they have rejected God and turned to Baal (9:16–17).

📄 10:1–15

THE CONSEQUENCES OF SIN

Israel and her reach are compared to a spreading vine (10:1), a metaphor that Jesus Himself used when describing the life of God's children. The message from Hosea is that in the midst of their prosperity, Israel grew unfaithful to her God and thus "must bear their guilt" (10:2). Hosea predicts the destruction of both the kings and the cults that have failed Israel so miserably (10:3–7). And Israel will be so distraught and desperate that, in the absence of both their false saviors, they will cry out to the mountains to cover them up and for the earth itself to consume them (10:8).

God is in control and will give Israel what she deserves—divine judgment. It is not what

God wants to do, but it is what Israel has sown with her wicked ways. The Bible is full of conditional statements like the ones here in 10:12–13. The prophet says that if Israel will trust and obey the Lord, the nation will prosper; but because she has disobeyed Him and His covenant, she is suffering and faces destruction.

Long before, when God made His covenant with Israel during the days of Moses, He had promised them that if they fully obey Him, they will be set high above all the nations and all manner of blessing will be poured out upon them. But, at the same time, the Lord promised Israel that if she betrays His covenant and proves disloyal to Him, then He will curse her and deprive her of all of those blessings (10:10–13).

The Bible is full of declarations having to do with sowing and reaping (10:12). The book of Proverbs is devoted to the theme that godly living brings blessing and prosperity and that sinful living brings ruin. In this chapter, Hosea is reminding Israel that her suffering is a result of her disobedience to God.

Critical Observation

Hosea does not say, nor does the rest of the Bible, that all of these consequences are to be visited upon the Israelites immediately. God brings the fruits of faith or unbelief to light in His own timing. Hosea's own ministry stretched over twenty or thirty years, and when he began to preach Israel's doom, she remained for some time a nation at peace and enjoyed an almost unprecedented prosperity. Only slowly, during the course of Hosea's life and work, did the judgment he prophesied begin to appear. And, of course, Israel had been in deep rebellion against the Lord for two centuries prior to Hosea's ministry.

Scripture measures blessedness and punishment in different ways than mankind is accustomed to measuring these things. To be holy and near to God, and to have one's life blessed by salvation, are the markers of true life (1 Timothy 6:19). And these joys are so strong and so great that they can lift even a much-afflicted life right out of the sorrows and pains of this world.

Hosea prophesies doom for Israel on account of her betrayal of the covenant, but the doom she suffers at the hands of Assyrian armies is but a foretaste of the judgment that awaits. The blessing that God promises to lavish on those who love and serve Him, though rich beyond words in this world, is rich beyond thought in the world to come. You will never take the measure of what faith brings or what unbelief brings until you see the full issue of each in the next world (10:14–15).

Take It Home

Does God really mean that if we are faithful we will prosper and if we are not we will suffer? If it is for the nation of Israel, is it true for all of God's children? We must trust that the ways of the Lord bring blessing (Psalm 1). Yet we also know that in this life we will encounter trials of many kinds, just as Jesus Christ did (James 1:1–3), and we should not assume that trials or suffering are consequences of our own sin (consider Job; Psalm 73; Matthew 5). Even in the midst of a suffering world and our own suffering, the joy of the Lord and His banner of love over His children preserve and protect in this world and in the world to come (Revelation 22:1–7). This is the reason for the hope that is within us (1 Peter 3:15).

HOSEA 11:1–12
GOD'S DISPLEASURE

Setting Up the Section

This chapter draws heavily on two components of Israel's history: the Exodus and the destruction of Sodom and Gomorrah.

📄 11:1–5

REVISITING THE EXODUS

Hosea warns that God will undo Israel's exodus and send His people to a new Egypt (Assyria) and into servitude to a new pharaoh (the Assyrian king). The childhood of Israel refers to the occasion when Israel was first in Egypt (11:1; see Exodus 4:22). The metaphor of Israel as God's son is distinct from the earlier terminology (Hosea 1:10) that describes the people as God's children and the corporate nation as God's adulterous wife (1:2). By calling Israel a son, God is making the point that He trained them and gave them what they needed to serve Him and do His work. This description highlights the rebellion of Israel. Another reason the reference works is because this text is used to refer to Jesus' move from Egypt back to Israel (Matthew 2:15). The uniqueness of referring to Israel as a son here is God's way of doing two things in this text: highlighting Israel's sin and foreshadowing a picture of the Messiah.

Critical Observation

Many scholars have observed that Jesus' fulfillment of Hosea 11:1 corresponds to the typology that one finds throughout Matthew, in which Jesus recapitulates the story of Israel in the way that He lived His life. Jesus spends forty days in the wilderness, just as Israel is there forty years. Jesus gives His law on a mountain, just as God gives the law at Mount Sinai. Jesus miraculously feeds His followers in the wilderness, just as Moses gives the people manna. Jesus has to walk in the path of Israel without sin so that He can be proven worthy to take the penalty for mankind.

If you look at the history of Israel, you see how through the centuries the people disregarded the prophets' messages. The more God spoke, the more they rebelled. The more God revealed Himself, the more they ran from Him. From the moment they left Egypt, they were fighting against the will and plan of God, seeking to do things their own way. The text continues to reflect upon what God did for Israel to care for the people. God cared for the needs of the nation—describing Israel as His child and His animal. Yahweh fed Israel throughout the Exodus (11:2–4). Hosea warns that the Exodus will be undone and Israel will return to its former condition of slavery. Yet this time the captivity will not be in Egypt but in Assyria (11:5).

📖 11:6–12

LESSONS FROM THE PAST

Hosea turns to another example from Israel's past—one of judgment and not redemption: the story of God's destruction of Sodom and Gomorrah. Under Assyrian domination, Israel will become like the cities that were eternally annihilated because of their rebellion against God. The image of the sword slashing through the bars probably means that when the Assyrians come, they will put an end to the boasting of the Israelites and destroy all of their vain attempts at securing their own future. All the things that they once trusted in, and all their self-focused wisdom, do nothing for them. They cannot protect themselves from what is coming (11:6).

The Israelites are deepening their rebellion against God. The reality is that the more they deepen their rebellion, the more they depend upon false religious practices to get them through. Therefore, there will not be the type of deliverance that God had provided in the past. They will feel the sting of this rebellion (11:7).

The mood of the text changes abruptly when God reveals His heart. Like a father who is facing the rebellion of a strong-willed child, God puts on the table the conflicting feelings of His love and His anger. In verse 8, He is seeking to resolve His compassion for Israel and the punishment demanded by their sin. This text is metaphorical, as God shows His love in terms that human minds can understand. God has very real feelings about the horrendous nature of sin. Zeboiim and Admah, together with Bela, are the other cities of the plain in the same region as Sodom and Gomorrah (Genesis 14:2). These cities represent the depravity that God destroyed (Genesis 19; Deuteronomy 29:23). God mentions them as a way to get the attention of the Israelites.

Hosea presents Israel as a city in danger of repeating the history of Sodom, Gomorrah, and the cities of the plain. When God says He will not unleash His anger, it does not mean that Ephraim is going to escape punishment. Rather, it means that God will not give full vent to His fury, as He did in the case of Sodom. In other words, Israel will not suffer the total, irreversible annihilation that Sodom experienced (11:9).

Hosea uses an intense image to talk of the restoration of Israel—he describes God as a lion with a mighty roar. Yet, this roar will not be to destroy Israel but to restore it. The image, like many in the prophets, is disorienting: A lion roars and the birds come to it rather than flee (11:10-11; see Numbers 24:8-9). Hosea's point here is that there is to be a new exodus in which God will again play the part of the lion and deliver His people from their enemies and into a new land. This call will bring them back. Israel will no longer be a silly dove wandering to and fro (7:11). This foretells of the day when the people will return not only from Egypt and Assyria but also from the west, the regions around the Mediterranean (11:10-11).

HOSEA 12:1-13:16

LESSONS FROM HISTORY

Setting Up the Section

Hosea continues his meditation on the history of Israel's relationship to God—tracing the nation's sin and how it has provoked God's judgment.

📄 **12:1-14**

ISRAEL'S SIN

Hosea persists in employing legal language to describe God's case against Israel—laying out God's charge against Israel (12:2). Hosea brings up examples from Israel's past, as well as Judah's, in which Jacob rebelled and wrestled to get his way (12:3-5). Hosea returns again to his crucial themes of love, justice, and patience, commanding Israel to return to the Lord in repentance as Jacob did (12:6).

The Lord unmasks Israel's pride through Hosea and warns His children never to imitate Israel in her fundamental and tragic blasphemy. God shows through Israel what pride can do and, by recording it in scripture, warns His children to stand against it. Israel's spiritual pride is plain dishonesty. It is the big lie of Israel's life. Pride is false security. Ephraim has boasted and taken credit for her economic prosperity, luxurious lifestyle, and success, when in fact it is God's favor she has enjoyed (12:8).

God shifts the focus of His complaints from the Exodus and pre-exodus to the message of the prophets. Hosea will pick up this shift in the opening of his next complaint (12:12-13). Once again, God declares that He will undo the Exodus and return Israel to the status of no longer being a nation. God speaks of a return to wilderness rather than a return to slavery. God asserts His sovereignty over them. The feast referred to in this text is the Feast of Tabernacles, or Booths (Leviticus 23:33–44). This verse looks ahead to the time when Israel's people will be scattered from their homeland (Hosea 12:9).

God's complaint has shifted to how Israel is presently ignoring His warnings—even the ones His prophet Hosea is speaking. God is warning the people, albeit sometimes in puzzling forms (visions and parables), but they are too rebellious to listen to the warnings (12:10). The obvious answer to God's rhetorical question (12:11) is that there is nothing besides sin in Gilead. *Gilead* represents all the country east of the Jordan, and *Gilgal* represents the land west of the Jordan. They both have sinned and sacrificed to Baal. And in both, God has shown forth His mercies.

Critical Observation

Hosea returns to the story of Jacob by citing incidents from Jacob's life in order to make a comparison between the patriarch and his descendants. Hosea compares Jacob's experience to the Exodus and to the ministry of the prophets. First, both Haran and Egypt are foreign lands that serve as places of refuge. Second, Jacob works like a slave for a ruthless master. In the same way, the Israelites are enslaved by Pharaoh. Just as God creates a situation in which Laban is eager to have Jacob leave (Genesis 31:1–14), God delivers Israel from the Egyptians, who are also ready to be rid of Israel after God afflicts Egypt with plagues. In both cases, the Israelites depart with the wealth of their hosts. The prophet who brings Israel out of Egypt and guards them through the wilderness is no doubt Moses (Hosea 12:12–13).

Yet, Ephraim has continually rebelled against the Lord. Hosea asserts that Ephraim has *provoked* God, a term that implies exasperating God through worshiping idols and placing one's heart away from God. These crimes are worthy of capital punishment. They will have to pay the penalty for this rebellion. Idol worship is the worst offense to God. God wants to be worshiped solely. Anything less is a provocation toward Him (12:14).

📄 13:1–16

GOD'S ANGER AGAINST ISRAEL

God continues to describe His people's unfaithfulness in terms of their idolatry. He recognizes that despite the consequences of their sin, they persist in it by making even more idols. He compares them to the morning mist, suggesting that rather than preserving them and making them a great nation as He promised to Abraham, they will surely pass away (13:1–3).

Israel is too proud to be saved, and the wrath of God is surely coming upon them. This is the culmination of Hosea's message of doom—and it describes the destruction of Israel in no uncertain and seemingly final terms. God recounts the many ways that He has been faithful in providing for and working out the Israelites' salvation—bringing them out of Egypt, caring for them in the desert, and feeding them (13:4–5).

Yet the Israelites grow proud and forget God. This is their deadly sin. Israel's chief problem is not idolatry—that is only an aftereffect. The people worship idols because they make no room for a God who deserves their loyalty and devotion. But the God of Abraham, Isaac, and Jacob demands that Israel acknowledge no one (not even Israel herself) but Him. For the nation to worship God, she would have to stop worshiping herself, and this she could not do (13:6).

God will not be mocked. The Lord had warned Israel that this would happen if she broke the covenant (Deuteronomy 6:10–12; 8:17–18). If we forget to be grateful to God for the blessings of our lives, He will take what He has given us "like a bear robbed of her cubs" (13:7–8).

The Lord solemnly makes the point and swears that Israel's boasting will be overturned, her cities in ruins, and her security gone. This is the tragedy of pride (13:9–16).

The God who gives can take away, and the God who gives and is not properly acknowledged promises to take away as part of His judgment upon dishonesty and ingratitude. This, then, is the Lord's warning through Hosea, His prophet: Pride is a hopeless illusion that will certainly be shattered (13:10–13).

Scholars disagree over the precise meaning of the ransom described by God. Some suggest that it points ahead to Christ paying the ransom for His people (13:14; see 1 Corinthians 15:55). However, in Hosea's context, those factors are in the future. Ultimately the Lord decides against paying the ransom, declaring that He will have no compassion. The images in the final verses of Hosea are truly ghastly—the people will bear their guilt, and even little ones and pregnant women will be subject to the violence (13:16).

HOSEA 14:1–9

BLESSING FROM REPENTANCE

Return to God	14:1–3
God's Response	14:4–9

Setting Up the Section

Following the total disaster and judgment described in the previous chapter, Hosea ends with the blessing and hope that his own story—of loving restoration of his unfaithful wife Gomer—parallels. Hosea's vision of Israel's restoration is partial.

📖 14:1–3

RETURN TO GOD

Hosea is still desperate to have Israel hear God's plea to return to Him. He reiterates the theme of the book—that their sins have been their downfall—and encourages them to turn to God in repentance (14:1–2). Hosea's last chapter is a reprise of a main theme of his preaching from the very beginning of the book: It is a call to repentance, an invitation to Israel to repent of her sins (14:2–3).

As Hosea has already declared, God demands sincerity of heart. Repentance is not merely the recognition of one's own sin. It will not be enough for Israel to recognize that she has disobeyed the Lord and betrayed His covenant. Even Pharaoh confessed that he had sinned in not letting Israel go from Egypt after the plague of hail. But he did not really repent. Repentance, as God requires it, is not merely sorrow and remorse for sin. Judas was so overcome by sorrow when the enormity of his betrayal of the Lord Jesus came home to him that he committed suicide, but he had no repentance.

Critical Observation

Repentance begins with a change of mind and heart about sin. Sin becomes not a thing to be loved but a thing to be abominated. In Psalm 51, David expresses the mind of every man or woman whom the Spirit of God has brought to a true repentance. Repentance wants nothing so much as to be right with God and to walk with God. Repentance is a turning away from sin to God for pardon and forgiveness. True repentance is always the fruit of a genuine faith in Christ, and it is called into being by the wonderful discovery that there is forgiveness with God. Indeed, there is no real repentance ever in the heart of a person who does not think that his sin can be removed and forgiven. Israel must believe that nothing besides God can save her (14:3). Repentance is a change of will and behavior—just as Israel denounces her sin, she also draws near to God, in whom the fatherless find compassion.

📄 14:4–9

GOD'S RESPONSE

Hosea declares that repentance is just the beginning of a great new adventure with God. God will heal Israel's waywardness and love them freely, and Israel will blossom like a flower (14:4–5). It is a beautiful picture to end a serious and solemn prophecy (14:6–8).

The final verse of Hosea is an editorial note, reminding the reader to take careful heed of the message of the book and repeating that message succinctly (14:9). The Lord Himself echoes Hosea's last word in John 15:5 when He says "Those who remain in me, and I in them, will produce much fruit" (NLT).

THE PROPHETS OF
ISRAEL AND JUDAH

| Prophet | Prophet's birthplace or primary area of ministry |

Dan

Hazor

ARAM

Mediterranean Sea

Jonah

Sea of Galilee

Aphek?

Mount Carmel

Gath-hepher

Kishon River

Megiddo

Jezreel

Lo-debar?

Beth-arbel

I S R A E L

Elijah

Abel-meholah

Tishbe?

Elisha

Samaria

GILEAD

Ahijah

*Jehu
Hosea*

Joppa

Gilgal?

Shiloh

PHILISTIA

*Isaiah
Zephaniah
Haggai
Zechariah
Malachi*

Bethel

Jordan River

Nahum

Jeremiah

Jericho

Anathoth

Elkosh

Jerusalem

Micah

J U D A H

Dead Sea

Moresheth-gath?

Tekoa

Amos

| 0 | 5 | 10 | 20 | 30 mi |
| 0 | 10 | 20 | 30 | 40 km |

Copyright © 2007 by Barbour Publishing, Inc.

N

JOEL

INTRODUCTION TO JOEL

The book of Joel is an intriguing book, beginning with the fact that we know little about the author, his historical time frame, or even whether he was writing to the northern kingdom of Israel or the southern kingdom of Judah. We are left, then, with the words themselves—the brute force of the message of the divine author.

We may be unaware of the specifics of Joel's personal information or the audience to whom he writes, yet he delivers the message of God with boldness and clarity.

AUTHOR

Joel (meaning "Jehovah is God") is a popular name in the Old Testament, with a dozen other men bearing the same name. However, little is known about the prophet Joel.

PURPOSE

Joel writes in response to a devastating attack by locusts. But the destructive insects are described as an invading army, symbolizing the potentially greater destruction awaiting those who do not heed the words of the prophet and repent. Then, beyond the immediate situation in the land, Joel writes of the Day of the Lord, when judgment will come to the enemies of God's people and Israel will eventually be restored.

THEMES

The Day of the Lord—a time, known only to God, when He will exact judgment on the nations—is a key theme throughout Joel. The concept encompasses other related themes, including the need for repentance, the certainty of coming judgment, and eventual redemption and restoration for the people of God.

HISTORICAL CONTEXT

Without any references to specific events, it is difficult to put Joel's message into a specific historical context. Some people cite the enemies of Judah that are listed (Egypt, Edom, Philistia, and Phoenicia [3:4, 19]) and suggest an early, pre-exilic date for the book. But with no mention of the northern kingdom and a specific reference to Greece (3:6), others feel the book must have been written much later—and was perhaps the last of all the Old Testament prophetic books. So, proposed dates of writing can vary by as much as six or seven centuries.

CONTRIBUTION TO THE BIBLE

Perhaps the most well-known use of Joel's prophecies is on Peter's lips on the Day of Pentecost, when the Holy Spirit comes upon the church. Joel's insight into the fresh manner in which God's Spirit will interact with human beings is a tremendous contribution to scripture (2:28–32; Acts 2:14–21).

JOEL 1:1–2:11

DESTRUCTION: PRESENT AND FUTURE

The Present Destruction — 1:1–12
The Future Destruction — 1:13–2:11

Setting Up the Section

The terrible arrival of a swarm of locusts is the catalyst for Joel's writing. In his opening section, he responds to the great destruction, calling on the people to mourn. Such a sobering event should also remind them that an even worse time of suffering is in store for those who refuse to humble themselves before God.

📄 1:1–12

THE PRESENT DESTRUCTION

It may seem slightly disconcerting that the exact nature of the problem taking place in Joel is unclear, but the terrible situation is only going to get worse. Wave after wave of locusts have overrun the nation's crops (1:4), and that is in addition to a drought (1:10–12).

For a nation characterized as drunkards (1:5), the loss of the grape harvest is particularly disheartening. Along with the failure of all the other crops (wheat, barley, fig, pomegranate, apple, and so forth), the situation is indeed dire. A disaster of this magnitude had not been witnessed by recent generations (1:2–3). The locusts are described as a lion-like nation with such numbers that they cannot be counted, invading without mercy (1:6–7).

Demystifying Joel

It is rather common in scripture (as well as in other ancient literature) to read of invading armies described as swarms of locusts. In Joel's case, it appears he has reversed the imagery. He describes a literal invasion of locusts in terms of a human army attacking (1:6–7). As far as the effects on an agrarian society, locusts could be every bit as merciless and cruel as enemy soldiers.

Joel addresses the elders of the nation (1:2) because they should have borne a special responsibility to clothe themselves with humility before God and seek His mercy on behalf of the people. Yet they are the ones who have allowed the spiritual state of the nation to decline, so they probably feel the effects of the crisis just as much as anyone. All the priests can do is mourn; the daily grain and drink offerings have been suspended during the crop failure and drought (1:8–9). All previous sources of joy have withered away (1:12).

📖 1:13–2:11

THE FUTURE DESTRUCTION

Joel exhorts the priests to demonstrate appropriate behavior, considering the situation they are in. They are to dress for mourning—in dark, rough sackcloth rather than their usual clothing. Instead of offering their usual prayers, they are to wail (1:13). Then they are to prepare the people: Declare a fast and call an assembly. The nation as a whole is to cry out to God together (1:14). Joel will soon clarify that it isn't the actions being taken that will appease the wrath of God but rather the proper attitudes by the people (2:12–13).

He describes a future destruction that he identifies as "the day of the LORD" (1:15), which he says is approaching. Joel will use this phrase several times in his short book, as do numerous other prophets. It refers to a time, known only to God, when He will exact judgment on the nations. The event will trigger much great suffering, although the end result will be the deliverance and restoration of those who remain faithful. The precise timing of that day remains a mystery. But as the people begin to attempt to cope with the devastation resulting from the locusts, their fear and confusion should put them in a somber state to ponder the severity of the Day of the Lord.

Critical Observation

The Hebrew words for *almighty* and *destruction* sound quite similar, so Joel's statement in verse 15 has added impact. Specific historic events are associated with the Day of the Lord, including Israel's fall to Assyria and Babylon's subsequent conquest of Judah.

This is a time for the people of God to come before Him with the truth. It is a time to speak to Him about their trials and to acknowledge Him as the only One who can ever provide food, shelter, safety, and joy. Such an acknowledgment should occur *before* disaster strikes, but even in the depths of their despair, God's people can call on Him for help. No such help can be found from any other source (1:16–20).

When Joel writes of *fire* (1:19–20), it is probably used as a metaphor. Perhaps the locusts are portrayed as a fire that devours all the nation's crops. Or maybe he intends to acknowledge the accompanying drought. In the heat of the Middle East, when water is short, it doesn't take long for the land to dry out and become unable to sustain plant growth—essentially the same result as fire.

Scholars are divided as to what Joel really means when he warns about the Day of the Lord and the invading army. Some believe that he continues using the army metaphor to describe actual locusts. Others think that as he begins to say more about the Day of the Lord, he speaks of a conflict involving human armies. If that is the case, the shift is subtle as his description of insect devastation in chapter 1 sets up the image of an even worse catastrophe to follow.

Either way, the coming event is in relation to the Day of the Lord. It will be a day of darkness, gloom, clouds, and blackness, and it will involve the encroachment of the largest army ever seen. At first it will be the sheer size that is noticeable: The army will appear "like dawn spreading across the mountains" (2:1–2 NIV). Only later will people realize, as Joel reveals, that this is the Lord's army with forces "beyond number" (2:11 NIV).

Demystifying Joel

Even for those who want to understand this army as a continuation of Joel's description of literal locusts, it is fair to consider it the Lord's army. Just as other prophets explain that the Assyrian and Babylonian armies had acted to fulfill the will of God, so, too, will this army of locusts.

The analogy to locusts is a fitting one. The land will lie beautiful and plush, so much so that it is compared to the Garden of Eden, but by the time the army has passed through, all that will be left is a desert wasteland. Again, a comparison to fire is appropriate to describe utter loss (2:3).

The appearance of this army will stun those who see it. The noise and destruction will dishearten all observers. Nothing can be done to stop its progress. It is described as marching straight ahead, plunging through defenses, scaling walls, and even entering private homes. The impact of the aggression will shake the earth. In response, entire nations will be in anguish and become pale with fear (2:4–11).

In this sense, the Day of the Lord will indeed be "dreadful" (2:11 NIV). And Joel's question ("Who can endure it?") must have seemed unanswerable to those hearing his description of things to come. Thankfully, Joel doesn't stop here. He provides an answer in the following section.

JOEL 2:12–32

SURVIVING THE DESTRUCTION

Setting Up the Section

After a rather distressing section pertaining to a current plague of locusts and an even worse similar scourge to come, in this section Joel at last offers some hope to the readers and listeners. Yes, the coming Day of the Lord will be dreadful, but there are things the people can do to avoid its potentially terrifying consequences.

📖 2:12–17

A CALL TO RETURN TO THE LORD

When the Day of the Lord arrives, there is nothing people can do to stop God's judgment. However, it is never too late for *God* to act. Speaking through His prophet, God provides a note of hope for those remaining in a situation that appears completely hopeless. He invites the wayward people to return to Him "even now" (2:12). However, such a return will accomplish nothing if it is based on hypocrisy or empty ceremony. God knows the hearts of people and sees through insincerity.

The people are called to return to God with all their hearts—weeping, fasting, and mourning. However, God cares little for their outward expressions of sorrow, per se. He is more intent on seeing humbled hearts than torn clothing. And God reminds His people that He is gracious, compassionate, slow to anger, and abounding in love. He doesn't *want* to send calamity on those who claim to be His people. Perhaps He will put off their impending doom (2:12–14).

In addition, the people are told to gather in a sacred assembly that should take priority over everything else. Nursing children are to attend, as are newlyweds. The priests can then intercede for the people (as should have been their role all along). The people will be reminded that their prior refusal to act as if they belonged to God has left surrounding nations with the wrong impression. When God disciplines His people for their defiant behavior, outside observers will see the consequences and perceive the Lord's corrective judgment as His absence. They will doubt the power and the concern of Israel's God, and they will scoff at His people (2:15–17).

📖 2:18–27

THE SHORT-TERM RESULT

Joel calls the people to repent—young and old, priest and populace. In return, the Lord promises to respond dramatically and bountifully. He will hear their cries and take pity on His people who have no other recourse than His mercy. He will bless their land far beyond their expectations, including ample new grain, wine, and oil. He will protect them from foreign threats. Rather than Israel being an object of scorn, it will be the other nations who falter and fall (2:18–20).

Critical Observation

The locust invasion previously described by Joel gives more impact to what he writes here about the smell arising from a retreating army (2:20). Historic accounts tell of enormous locust swarms that flew out to sea, drowned, washed up on shore, and created a terrible stench.

God will replace His people's fear with gladness and rejoicing. He will send rain and make the ground fruitful again. He will restore what the locust horde had destroyed, promising that the people will eat plentifully and be satisfied. Here, as in other places throughout scripture, rain is perceived as the blessing of God (2:21–24).

As terrible as the losses had been that resulted from the locusts, the land will recover and the people will be able to eat their fill. In return, they will praise the Lord and have a greater awareness that only He is truly God (2:25–27).

In spite of the people's previous sins, God will temper His judgment with mercy and compassion. His people will not be destroyed. It is terrific news for those who appeared to be doomed. Yet even better news is promised for the future.

📄 **2:28–32**

THE LONG-RANGE RESULT

The date of these future events is left a mystery. God's promise of the future will come "afterward" (2:28). As it turns out, some of Joel's prophecy from this section will be remembered and applied in connection with the arrival of the Holy Spirit on Jesus' followers shortly after the Lord's death and resurrection (Acts 2:14–21).

God speaks through His prophet of a great day to come, when His Spirit will pour out— not just upon Israel but also on all faithful believers (Joel 2:28). The power of God will be felt by young and old, men and women. God's plan will be known through dreams, visions, and prophecies (2:28–29). When that day arrives, the effect will be so dramatic that onlookers will presume the recipients of God's Spirit are drunk (Acts 2:13).

Demystifying Joel

When Joel 2 is quoted by Peter (Acts 2:17–21) and Paul (Romans 10:13), it becomes clear that the ultimate fulfillment of the prophecy will be a *heavenly* Jerusalem and Mount Zion. And from the New Testament perspective, another important detail is drawn out of the shadows and brought into clear light: The Lord Jesus Christ is the Son of God who died on the cross for sinners and rose again. He is the Lord of the resurrection. It is His name people must own in order to receive the fullness of salvation that comes by the grace of their merciful God.

Yet that time will also include a sense of foreboding of the coming judgment. The Day of the Lord will include the greatest of blessings for some, but it will also involve an unspeakably frightening curse for others. It will be reminiscent of the destruction of Pharaoh and his armies during the time of the exodus of God's people from Egypt. Joel provides few specifics, yet he includes hints of blood, fire, and billows of smoke (2:30). The light of the sun and moon will be affected, perhaps from the great conflict to take place. The coming of the Day of the Lord will be great for some and dreadful for others (2:31).

Yet God will ensure that those who call on His name are delivered. It will be a terrible time, but there will certainly be survivors. God is both Judge and Savior, and His justice will prevail (2:32).

Take It Home

Joel looks ahead to the Day of the Lord. How do you feel as you contemplate a day that will involve dread and judgment for some? If you remained more aware of a coming day when God will deliver those who remain faithful to Him, how might it affect your day-to-day life?

JOEL 3:1–21

THE COMING JUDGMENT

Setting Up the Section

Up to this point, Joel has primarily dealt with God's message to His own people. In this section, after God has just promised redemption and restoration of Israel, the Lord turns His attention to the judgment of other nations that have treated His people badly throughout history. Their relentless cruelty has not been overlooked. Their judgment will be harsh indeed, and although Israel had been guilty of much wrongdoing in the past, they will experience God's great forgiveness.

📖 3:1–16

GATHERING THE NATIONS

Joel continues to peer into the future as he relates God's message. The still-to-come Day of the Lord looms ahead, and God continues to describe what will happen in those days (3:1). It will include a restoration of Judah, Jerusalem, and Israel (3:1–2), and the prophet will soon go into detail about what such a recovery will entail (3:17–21). But first God will address the offenses of other nations.

The nations are to be *gathered* in a sense that sounds much like a summons to appear in court. The charges against them are quite severe. For one thing, they have ransacked the wealth of Israel (3:5). They are also guilty of scattering God's people throughout the various lands of the time. And while it is true that they were acting under the auspices of God's control, they treated their captives horribly. The remaining specific charges that are included in the narrative are some of the worst imaginable offenses, with human trafficking and child prostitution among them (3:3).

The Valley of Jehoshaphat (3:2, 12) has never been identified as a specific geographic location, in the past or present. However, the precise location is not as important as the name itself. *Jehoshaphat* means "the Lord judges." It matters little where the judging is taking place; what matters is that the time has come for justice to be exacted against those who had long persecuted God's people.

Demystifying Joel

The specific nations and offenses listed (3:4–6) present some challenges to determining the time of Joel's writing. The Philistines are among the earlier enemies of Israel, yet the reference to scattering the people points some scholars to the Babylonian captivity (3:2, 4). At that time, the temple treasury was plundered (2 Kings 25:8–17), although neither the Philistines nor Phoenicians (Tyre and Sidon) were involved. Some believe that this is a case where perhaps a number of Israel's persistent enemies are listed to represent *all* of the persecutors of God's people throughout their history.

The various nations committed numerous offenses against Israel and Judah during times when God's people had forsaken the Lord and were vulnerable. Israel's enemies presume they have gotten away with their despicable behavior, but God continues to hold them responsible for what had been done. The insulting treatment of God's people is a transgression against God. It had been God's silver and gold that was stolen. It had been God's people who were sold for wine and thrust into prostitution (3:2–6).

It will appear for a time that Israel and Judah are no more, with their populations removed and deported to faraway countries. But God will then reverse the harm that had been done. He will recall His people from the various places to which they have been sold, and He will return on them what they had done to Israel and Judah. Judah's enemies will see how it feels to witness their children sold to distant lands (3:7-8). (This prophecy comes true soon thereafter, as the Greek Empire begins to spread and various countries find themselves subjugated and/or enslaved.)

Just as God had promised to rouse His people from among the nations, Joel tells the nations to rouse their warriors. If they are going to be foolish enough to oppose the Lord of Israel, they may as well prepare for it. Their tools for everyday living ("plowshares" and "pruning hooks") should be converted into weapons of war ("swords" and "spears"). They should join forces and assemble (3:9-11).

But they will be marching toward their judgment. The gathering place will be the Valley of Jehoshaphat, where God will sit and judge their great wickedness. They will come forth in all their pride and power, but they will be approaching their own destruction.

Those who defiantly oppose God will not long stand. They will meet utter defeat. The comparisons are made to swinging a sickle and trampling grapes—two common actions the people of that time are familiar with. Just as wheat falls before a reaper's scythe, so will the enemies of Israel fall. Just as grapes are trodden on to fill the winepress with juice, so will flow the blood of those hostile peoples (3:12–13).

Critical Observation

The apostle John uses similar imagery in his apocalyptic vision recorded in Revelation. There, too, God's judgment is compared to both reaping and trampling on grapes (Revelation 14:14–20).

God's judgment of the nations is connected with the Day of the Lord, and afterward the Valley of Jehoshaphat [God's judgment] will become the "valley of decision" (3:14). Again, this event is said to be accompanied by great signs in the skies—a darkening of the sun, moon, and stars (2:10; 3:15)—and a shaking of the earth (2:10; 3:16).

As terrible as the Day of the Lord will appear to those who oppose God, people who turn to Him will find surprising security. God will be a refuge and stronghold for those who remain faithful (3:16).

📄 3:17–21

JERUSALEM RESTORED

Numerous prophets had made it clear that because of the persistent sins of the people, God will allow Jerusalem to fall to the Babylonians. Yet here, even after the city had fallen and the people had been dispersed to various lands, God will still rule from Jerusalem and Zion. The earth is still the Lord's. Nothing has been ultimately lost (3:16–17).

Joel's closing description portrays such a positive outlook for Jerusalem that it must be a reference to a yet-future time. Certainly, Jerusalem has not yet experienced a period where it could be said that foreigners will never again invade her (3:17). But someday the city will truly be holy—set apart for the glory of God. Joel's description anticipates Revelation 21–22 and the description of the New Jerusalem.

The surrounding land will also undergo a wonderful transformation. In a lush contrast to the opening description of the territory in the wake of the locust infestation, Joel foresees a time when "mountains will drip with sweet wine, and the hills will flow with milk" (3:18 NLT). While other sources refer to Canaan as a land of milk and honey, Joel provides a distinctive descriptive pairing of wine and milk. Vineyards were frequently planted on hillsides, so the description is appropriate. The addition of milk suggests abundant herds, readily sustained by the water that will never again be in short supply (3:18). In fact, the water will be associated with the presence of God—a fountain flows out of the temple to water the land.

Critical Observation

Acacias (3:18) tend to grow in arid desert areas where not much else survives. The picture of their being well watered suggests a wilderness being refreshed and capable of sustaining new life.

In contrast, those who remain hostile toward God and His people (symbolized by Israel's persistent enemies, Egypt and Edom) will lack water and life. They who had shed innocent blood will be left a desolate, desert wasteland (3:19). But Judah will be forgiven of their past sins, and God's presence will be with His people forever (3:20–21).

When the Day of the Lord arrives, one age will end and another, eternal one will begin. The Lord's coming will overwhelm the current created order and, by the plan and power of God, there will be a new heaven and a new earth fit for a renewed population of resurrected bodies. For the new Israel, the age of discipline will finally yield to the age of perfect delight.

Take It Home

In the New Testament, Paul teaches that, "in [God] we live and move and exist" (Acts 17:28 NLT). People have spent centuries attempting to understand the biology, chemistry, astronomy, and physics of creation. Yet God is bigger than everything the scientists, astronomers, and cartographers can comprehend. When people complete their lives, they still have an existence in God. God's sovereignty is not limited by what people understand to be physical realities. As you reflect on Joel's prophecies, how do you respond to the fact that no matter how grave the judgment of God will be upon the sins of some, those who place their faith in Him can count on full pardon and eternal life?

AMOS

INTRODUCTION TO AMOS

The prophet Amos was a contemporary of Old Testament prophets Hosea and Isaiah. He stood for justice in an era of Israel's history in which the nation was politically strong but spiritually weak.

AUTHOR

The first verse of this book attributes the writing to a man named Amos. Though his prophecy is directed to Israel, the northern kingdom, Amos himself is from Tekoa, a town in Judah, five miles south of Bethlehem. His work as a shepherd and gardener implies he belongs to the working class until the Lord commissions him to be one of His prophets.

PURPOSE

Amos's prophecy condemns the powerful, self-satisfied, wealthy upper class that had developed in Samaria, the capital of Israel.

OCCASION

Amos's ministry falls in the first half of the eighth century BC, during the last half of the reign of Jeroboam II (793–753 BC). Israel is enjoying a measure of domestic affluence and international power that she has not known since the reign of Solomon. Israel and Judah have expanded to the point that they nearly encompass all the land that David and Solomon controlled two centuries before. It is a time of military conquest and economic prosperity. It is also a time of moral darkness.

THEMES

Themes in the prophecy of Amos include God's sovereign power, the covenant agreement between God and Israel, and the day of the Lord's judgment.

AMOS 1:1–2:3

THE COMING LION

Setting Up the Section

The opening section of Amos is a series of oracles of judgment pronounced against Israel's neighbors: Syria (Aram), Philistia, Tyre (a city in Phoenicia), and so on. In each case, these nations are condemned not for their false religion and worship but for their various crimes against humanity. They have violated principles of morality that are universally recognized by human beings. But Amos does not preach these oracles to these nations themselves. They are rather part of Amos's sermon against Israel—Israel being, as we learn in 1:1, the focus of Amos's preaching and prophecy. The point of these oracles of judgment is that if these foreign nations cannot escape God's wrath on account of their sins, Israel most assuredly will not escape it for her similar sins.

The six nations listed in the first two chapters are the principal nations bordering on Israel, and they are the world as Israel encountered it. Syria (Aram, see 1:3–5), Philistia (1:6–8), and Tyre (1:9–10) are simply Israel's neighbors; Edom (1:11–12), Ammon (1:13–15), and Moab (2:1–3) share ancestry with Israel; and Judah (2:4–5) was once one nation with Israel.

Demystifying Amos

Uzziah was king of Judah between 791 and 740 BC. Jeroboam II (not the first Jeroboam, who was the very first king of Israel after the division of the kingdom after the death of Solomon) was king of Israel from 793–753 BC. Jeroboam II is also known as Jeroboam the Great. Apparently what we have in the book of Amos is the preaching of the prophet over a comparatively short period of time, hence the "two years before the earthquake" (1:1). That earthquake must have been very powerful, for it left its mark on Israel's history. There is mention of it again hundreds of years later in Zechariah 14:5.

Amos 1:1 reveals that even though Israel is in a time of prosperity, God's prophet knows Jeroboam's kingdom is not far from total extinction after his death. Verse 2 mentions a roar thundering from Jerusalem. This roar from Jerusalem is probably of a lion about to pounce, ready to lunge at its victim, Israel. Israel has voluntarily cut herself off from the temple in Jerusalem and its worship, but that is where the Lord's presence is represented. Part of what the Lord holds against Samaria, the capital of Israel, is the sanctuaries they have built rather than attending the temple in Jerusalem.

The recurring phrase regarding not just three sins but four is a reminder of the Lord's mercy and patience. Punishment does not happen because of the first sin, or the second, or the third. There are multiple opportunities for repentance before judgment falls (1:3).

Notice that God condemns the nations not for their false worship or religious practices but for their violations of the obligations they owe to other human beings—in Syria's case, her barbarity and inhumanity in war.

Demystifying Amos

Gaza, mentioned in verse 6, is representative of Philistia. Gaza is one of Philistia's chief cities and is accused of brutality.

In verse 9, Tyre is accused of slave trading, but the sin for which she is to be destroyed is her violation of covenant she made with another nation, apparently Israel. This is significant because it reveals a second similarity with Edom, who is also condemned for violations of brotherhood (1:11).

Edom has already been implicated in slave trading (1:6, 9), but the fourth sin for which God is angry is like Tyre's: a violation of family bonds. Edom is indeed Israel's brother, descended from Esau as Israel is from Jacob, and Isaac is the grandfather of both. But Edom has long harbored animosity toward Israel. The cities of Edom (1:12)—Teman to the south and Bozrah to the north—are mentioned to make the point that the entire country will suffer God's wrath, from top to bottom.

The last two nations, Ammon and Moab, are condemned for atrocities committed against the most vulnerable, fragile, and helpless of human beings: pregnant women and their unborn children in the first case and dead bodies in the second. And the Ammonites did this for temporal advantage, to enlarge their borders. They stepped on the weak to advantage themselves (1:13–2:3). In verse 14, Rabbah, Ammon's only significant city, receives the threat of destruction at the hand of Assyria.

The first three verses of chapter 2 complete Amos's prophecy against the surrounding nations. Moab and Edom hate each other, and evidence of this is the disrespect for dead bodies described in 2:1. The idea may have been to prevent the king's body from being resurrected.

The harsh, brutal reality of human sin that results in these kinds of cruelty—slavery, war, desecration of bodies—lies at the base of Amos's charge against these nations and the threat of divine wrath.

AMOS 2:4-16

THE PATH TO APOSTASY

Setting Up the Section

The two oracles of judgment in chapter 2—against Judah and Israel—show the progress of apostasy. Things are not as bad in Judah during Amos's ministry as they are in Israel, but eventually Judah will be guilty of all the sins that Amos accuses Israel of in verses 6–12.

At best, relations between the divided kingdoms—Israel to the north and Judah to the south—took the form of a peaceful coexistence. But more often, the two kingdoms interacted with outright hostility and sometimes war. Amos's Israelite audience would have enjoyed his message thus far. They would have been glad to hear of the Lord's judgments to befall their surrounding enemies and glad to learn that Judah is going to suffer.

While the six nations in the first section are condemned for crimes against humanity, Judah is condemned for a failure to obey God's law as revealed by Moses and the prophets. The *law*, as it is used here, means much more than simply commandments or rules—it means instruction from God about the life He has called His people to live (2:4).

The remaining verses of chapter 2 describe Israel as guilty of the same crimes against humanity that the pagan nations around her have been accused of.

Israel has blatantly disobeyed the commandments of God's Word, involving herself in incestuous and promiscuous sexual relations, especially, no doubt, in regard to fertility rites at the temples and shrines. Amos represents Israel as deliberately throwing off the claims of the Lord.

In verse 8, the garments "taken in pledge" (or as collateral for a debt), according to God's law, are to be returned at night to the debtor (Exodus 22:26–27). According to this description, however, the Israelites do not return these garments but instead use them at altars, making their religious life the context for their disobedience. Moreover, fines are to be according to the Law of Moses, a vehicle for making restitution, not for enriching the wealthy, who are drinking them up in orgies at their sanctuaries.

The Amorites, mentioned in verse 9, are inhabitants of the region before it became known as Canaan.

In verses 10–12, Israel's sins are against God's goodness. He has done so much for them, and they are repaying Him with selfish indifference to His will. God has spoken to His people through His prophets and used the plight of Nazirites, who consecrated themselves only to God.

Verse 12 twists the oracle from what God has done for His people to the way in which they have repaid His goodness. That which God has provided, Israel has ignored or disobeyed. Nazirites vow not to drink wine, yet the Israelites force them to do it in an act of cruel blasphemy. Or perhaps, more likely, this statement is to be taken metaphorically to describe Israel's utter indifference to the spiritual challenge and example of such godly people.

Critical Observation

In both Judah and Israel, the mistreatment of God's revelation is the first cause of the disaster that is about to befall them both. Judah receives the truth from God but chooses instead the traditions of culture. And what is true to a degree in Judah is entirely true in Israel.

Verses 13–16 describe God's wrath as inescapable, regardless of anyone's earthly wealth, power, or talent. As before, with the other nations, God's judgment will come in the form of an attack by a stronger nation. This will prove to be Assyria, of course, just a few decades later. The Assyrian's theory of conquest is the complete devastation of a nation, the depopulation of its territory, and the terrorization of its remnants.

Take It Home

Amos's prophecy raises the issue of how much the people of God incorporate the practices of the culture around them. This issue is still relevant for the church today, with people of faith landing on both sides of the balance. How much is our faith affected by the cultural customs we incorporate?

AMOS 3:1–15

WITHIN BUT WITHOUT

Setting Up the Section

In this section, the indictment that Amos has drawn up against Israel in 2:6–16 is expanded, clarified, and proved. Israel believes she, as Yahweh's people, was delivered from bondage in Egypt on eagles' wings, but her rebellion, disobedience, and unbelief render her the object of God's wrath, not His care and protection.

The opening words of chapter 3 are repeated in 4:1, 5:1, and 8:4. Amos speaks to Israel as one nation, though the nation has long ago been divided and its people have been addressed separately already in this prophecy. The verses following will make it clear, however, that Israel, the northern kingdom, is chiefly in Amos's view.

In some translations of verse 2, God claims that Israel is the only nation He has *known*. In others, the word *chosen* is used. Either word points out the covenant relationship God has with these people.

The questions in verses 3–6 make a point. In verses 4–5, the coming of God's judgment is certain. Just as nature moves when it has purpose and need, so will God's justice move on His people. Verse 6 refers to the blowing of a trumpet, a ram's horn, which would have been familiar to the people of Amos's day. While the preceding questions rhetorically point to a "no" answer, the questions in verse 6 point to a "yes" answer. Perhaps the last question makes the main point—these people are not expecting disaster and do not see themselves in Amos's question.

With verse 7, Amos switches from rhetorical questions to direct statements. Yahweh not only does bring disaster upon the unrighteous, but He communicates His intention to do so through His prophets. Just as one pays attention when a lion roars, so the Lord's prophet cannot ignore or fail to deliver His Word (3:8).

The pagan nations around Israel, mentioned in chapter 1, are invited to observe Israel's life to see whether the sins of Samaria deserve God's judgment (3:9–10). The point here is that Israel's sins are so egregious that even the wicked nations around her will stand in judgment of her.

The picture painted in verse 11 is that Israel's strongholds and fortresses—the things she has trusted for protection—will prove little obstacle to the Assyrians. Neither will Israel's wealth be her protection. According to verse 12, the wealthy in Samaria, who indulge themselves on fine and comfortable furniture, will be swept away. Only a few will survive.

Demystifying Amos

Verse 13 introduces a new oracle. It is directed to Israel, referring to the nation as the *house of Jacob*. Jacob was the son of Isaac, grandson of Abraham. He had twelve sons, and the tribes of Israel were tracked according to each son. In referring to Israel this way, the heritage of the nation is brought to mind, including their covenant of obedience to God.

Verses 14–15 combine the image of Bethel, a name which means "house of God," with a variety of other houses. When the house of God falls, no house remains. Israel's great houses are monuments to her corruption and her ill-gotten wealth.

AMOS 4:1–13

THE POINT OF NO RETURN

Setting Up the Section

Chapter 4 begins a new indictment against Israel that opens with a call to the upper-class women.

Bashan was known for the size and quality of its livestock (Deuteronomy 32:14; Psalm 22:12). In Amos 4:1, the women are likened to animals fattening themselves on rich pasture. They live their lives for pleasure, yet the poor remain oppressed. They make demands of their husbands for the household service they should be providing.

There are a variety of opinions about the meaning of the hooks in verse 2. What is certain is that the reference is to the women of Israel being humiliated by their enemies.

We do not know the location of Harmon, mentioned in verse 3. Some have supposed it to be a dump where the women's bodies will be thrown after their deaths. Other translations simply refer to it as a fortress or palace. In either case, the breaks in the walls are an important element of the description. What should have protected these women becomes simply a portal through which they are undone.

In verse 4, Amos taunts the Israelites by saying that all they are accomplishing with their worship is the multiplying of their sins and the deepening of their judgment. He exaggerates their practices as if they are doing almost nothing but making pilgrimages to Bethel and Gilgal. The implicit question becomes: What good is all of this doing?

The description in verse 5 reveals the unbelief and self-absorption of these people. Their inappropriate worship—freewill offerings are to be private, yet they brag about them—makes matters worse, not better. This theme of inauthentic ritual is strong with Old Testament prophets.

Verse 6 begins a new section that continues through verse 11, marked by the first-person pronoun *I* and the refrain that the people have not returned to God even with all He has done to draw them back. There is a deliberate contrast between what Yahweh has done and what Israel is doing. Israel has been busy rebelling against the Lord; the Lord has been busy seeking to bring her to repentance.

All of the catastrophes listed in this section have been signs of God's wrath, and Israel has ignored them all. According to verses 12–13, the God whose justice and judgment Israel must now face is the sovereign Lord who controls nature. She cannot withstand the Lord when He comes against her in judgment.

Take It Home

Amos is particularly difficult for the modern reader. Like Israel in the eighth century BC, we are a prosperous people. Also, in our scientific age, we are much less likely to connect events in the world with the action of the Almighty. But every Bible reader, sooner or later, has to decide how to understand that God is both merciful and wrathful.

AMOS 5:1–27

REPENTANCE AND THE DAY OF THE LORD

Setting Up the Section

This book begins by condemning the nations that surround Israel for their sins and with a promise of God's judgment. If these other nations will not escape God's wrath, how much more judgment must Israel face, a nation who has sinned against God's grace? Chapter 5 is an eloquent plea addressed to the nation of Israel, in hopes that at least some of her people will hear it and respond.

The poetry of verses 1–3 follows the form of a Hebrew funeral dirge. At this time, Israel is at the height of her prosperity under Jeroboam II. Like the virgin mentioned in verse 2, it seems that Israel's best days are ahead. But verse 3 reveals that her military strength will be wrecked and her soldiers slaughtered in battle.

Instead of empty rituals, God wants His people to seek Him (5:4–5). Bethel, Gilgal, and Beersheba are important sites in Israel's history. Apparently all three cities held shrines to which Israelites made faithful pilgrimages—even Beersheba, which lay at the southernmost end of Judah. But the people had been commanded to go to Jerusalem to worship. Amos is once again pointing out the futility of Israel's religious practices. Her people worship, but instead of following God's guidelines, they make their own rules. They offer worship that offends the Lord rather than pleases Him.

The "house of Joseph," mentioned in verse 6, is a reference to the northern kingdom of Israel. Regions were often identified by their principal tribe. In this case, that tribe is Ephraim, made up of the descendants of one of Joseph's sons.

Verses 7–11 have a unique structure. Verse 7 characterizes Israelite life as unjust and unrighteous, something that Amos has already established. Verses 8–9 function as a kind of doxology. The verses describe God in terms of His power and majesty. He alone can save Israel from the disaster that looms. Then, the characterization that began in verse 7 continues in verses 10–11. By the middle of verse 11, the announcement of judgment begins.

Verses 12–13 reveal that, in essence, the religion of the Israelites does not touch their lifestyles; they are heedless of the claims of justice and God's law. Verses 14–15 state what the people need to do if they indeed want to be the people of God they claim to be. The last half of verse 14 reveals the state of mind of the Israelite people—they mistakenly believe God to be on their side, even while they are disconnected from their true spiritual state.

Take It Home

Amos 5:14–15 has great application for us in that it offers a clear account of what God requires of His people.

If the people do not turn back to their God, the destruction will be so great that farmers will have to be summoned to wail because there will not be enough professional mourners to go around (5:16). Yahweh will pass through Israel as her destroyer, reminiscent of the angel of death passing through Egypt long before (5:17).

Verses 18–20 include the earliest recorded use of the expression *Day of the Lord*. It will occur many more times in the prophets of the Old Testament and again in the New Testament. But clearly, it is already a familiar phrase by this time as a religious figure of speech. Because of their disconnection from God's view of their spiritual state, the Israelites think that the Day of the Lord will bring happiness and triumph to them when, in fact, it will bring disaster.

Amos has already said that the Lord won't accept Israel's sacrifices. However, in verses 21–24, he says the Lord won't accept Israel's praise, either. This continues the theme in Amos that God is looking for meaningful relationships with His people, not empty worship. Because the people have refused to hear this message, God indicates that it is time for His justice to flow as naturally, strongly, and completely as water flows down a mountain.

Verse 25 can be seen as a rhetorical question, in which case the assumed answer is no. We don't know if the people neglect to offer sacrifices on their journey because they are disobedient or because the rituals of sacrifice are not implemented yet.

The prophet continues making the point that Israel's sacrifices are disconnected from her faith relationship with God (5:25–26). The people of Israel seem to think that as long as they offer Yahweh sacrifices, all will be well, no matter their obedience in other areas of life. Amos is reminding them that their own history is the disproof of that idea.

Verse 27 refers to a place beyond Damascus, which is Assyria. Assyria does eventually defeat the northern kingdom of Israel.

AMOS 6:1–14

A HARD TRUTH

Setting Up the Section

Amos continues to focus on the northern kingdom in this section. The influential and the rich who live and work in the capital cities are the target of Amos's condemnation. Both their complacency and their coming judgment are described.

As he has done before, Amos, at the opening of chapter 6, presents Israel as serenely confident of God's approval without good reason to be so confident. Zion, a synonym for the capital city of Judah, seems to be a reference to the whole southern kingdom. Samaria, capital city of the northern kingdom, is used in the same way to represent the whole kingdom of Israel.

The cities mentioned in verse 2 may have fallen during Amos's lifetime or before. Either way, he lifts these cities up as a reality check to Israel, that trusting in her own supremacy may be a futile effort. Amos accuses his nation of bringing a "reign of terror" by its disobedience (6:3 NIV).

Verses 4–8 describe the affluence of the wealthy in Israel. The average Israelite may have eaten meat only three times a year, the poor even less. Only the rich can afford to spend time playing and listening to music. The reference to David suggests that the people think of themselves and live as if they are kings. And they drink so much wine that they don't bother to pour it first into cups; they take it straight from the bottle. The anointing of the body was common in the ancient Near East, especially after bathing. It soothed the skin and served as a protection against both heat and lice. The rich added expensive spices and perfumes to the oil. The wealthy who have prospered the most in their rebellion against the Lord will be the first to suffer the Assyrian wrath. That is always the conqueror's way, of course: Cut off the head, and the body will fall easily enough. What God wants His people to also notice, though, is how the body—the innocent and the poor—suffers the consequences of the head's actions and choices.

Israel's military self-confidence will be turned into a cruel joke. The picture in verses 9–10 is that of ten men who have survived the terrors of the siege so far and are found taking refuge together in a single home—probably a large home. This is a picture of the wealthy of Samaria, but even these will die, probably of disease, a feature of siege warfare, as suggested in verse 10. The few remaining survivors hope that Yahweh will consider the judgment sufficient and, if they keep a low profile, perhaps He will not bring upon them any further punishment. But according to verse 11, their defeat is certain.

Two supremely unnatural and absurd activities—running horses up cliffs or plowing the rocks (or the sea; either reading is possible) with oxen—serve as analogies to point out how preposterous and unreasonable Israel's behavior has been (6:12–13). Defying the Lord successfully is just that impossible. To deal with it, God sends brutal conquest by another power (6:14). At this moment, during Jeroboam's reign, the other nations of the region are relatively impotent, including Egypt and Assyria. In that vacuum, Israel's power seems impressive. All of that will change quickly. Lebo Hamath, mentioned in verse 14, is Israel's northernmost boundary and Arabah her southernmost. So the description is one of total defeat.

Take It Home

What honest Christian cannot find himself or herself in Amos's words? How many times have we found ceremony replacing godliness in our own lives? How many times have we caught ourselves going through motions in respect to our faith and the things of God?

AMOS 7:1-17

THE CONTEST FOR THE TRUTH IN THE CHURCH

Setting Up the Section

While the prophecy thus far has included accusations and condemnations, this chapter marks a change. Here, Amos begins to describe a series of visions. Much of the rest of his prophecy will follow this same form.

Each of Amos's visions opens in the same way—attributing his vision to the Lord. Locusts represent an unstoppable agricultural disaster in the ancient world. In this first vision, this swarm of locusts is to fall at a difficult time in harvest, destroying the fruit of the second planting (7:1). This is the part of the harvest that is reserved for the farmers themselves. Without it, neither they nor their livestock will have food to carry them over to the next harvest.

In verses 2–3, God is described as relenting. This is not the first time in scripture the picture is painted of God desisting from a planned course of events in response to human appeal. Moses interceded for Israel when Yahweh threatened to destroy His people (Exodus 32:9–14). Here Amos is the intercessor, and as a result of his intercession, there will be no swarm of locusts (Amos 7:2–3).

Critical Observation

Repeatedly throughout this section, Amos refers to the nation of Israel as *Jacob*. This is a common custom in the writings of the Old Testament. Nations are sometimes identified by the name of their ancestors. Jacob is the forebear of the twelve tribes of Israel.

The vision described in verses 4–6 is of fire sweeping over the land. Amos again appeals to the Lord, and the Lord, even in His wrath, again relents.

In the third vision, a plumb line illustrates the deviation of Israel from the true path (7:7–8). A plumb line is a string with a weight tied to one end. A person holds it upright vertically, and the weight drops the string straight down toward the ground. Anything that isn't straight will look crooked next to the plumb line. God will set a straight line beside Israel, and her crookedness will be evident to all. This time Amos is given no opportunity to intercede. The Lord has determined to punish Israel as Amos has described throughout this prophecy.

The objects of God's divine wrath are mentioned in verse 9—the false places of worship and the royal families who have abandoned God's covenant and forsaken their responsibilities to lead God's people in the ways of righteousness.

Amos's message in verse 9 is the last straw for the priest Amaziah. Amaziah not only wants to punish Amos, but he wants to discredit him and get rid of him (7:10). The quickest path to this goal is creating trouble for Amos with the current government. For Amaziah to say that the land cannot bear Amos's words is simply to say that these words should not be tolerated.

Demystifying Amos

Amaziah is the chief priest at the sanctuary at Bethel, one of the major sanctuaries set up in the northern kingdom in opposition to Jerusalem. Amaziah is not a descendant of Aaron, and therefore, under Mosaic Law, he should not have held that position. No doubt he takes personally Amos's condemnation of Israelite life and worship. The accusation that Amaziah brings against Amos is suited to provoke the maximum response from the king. Jeroboam had reigned for a long time, and almost certainly there was opposition to him abroad in the land. Upon Jeroboam's death a few years later, his son is assassinated, further suggesting that there had been political intrigue already during the later years of Jeroboam's reign, so he would have been alert to any threat to his throne. Amos is certainly no political conspirator. He has not spoken treasonously against the king, he has taken no action against the king himself, and he has not conspired with anyone else to do so. But the Lord's public condemnations of the king and of the nation through His prophet could easily be taken in that way, and so they provide Amaziah with a pretext for his charge.

In verse 11, Amaziah exaggerates, as do most people who wish to cast someone else in a bad light. Amos never predicts that Jeroboam will die by the sword (in fact, he died of natural causes), but Amos had said enough about the nation's sins and God's impending judgment by military conquest that it was only a small step to saying that Amos predicted Jeroboam's death.

The treatment that Amos receives reveals animosity and superiority on the part of Amaziah (7:12–13). The insinuation is that Amos is preaching in Israel because the money is better in the wealthy north. Amaziah is judging Amos by his own standards. He thinks of his own work as simply a job, and he imagines it to be the same for Amos. In verses 14–15, however, Amos clarifies the issue. He is not a prophet for hire; he is called by God. This sets him apart from Amaziah, a bureaucrat doing the king's bidding.

Demystifying Amos

The temple in Jerusalem is the only authorized center of Israel's worship. But to keep Israelites loyal to the northern kingdom and to prevent them from advertising Israel's illegitimacy by traveling to Jerusalem three times a year for worship, sanctuaries were set up at Bethel and elsewhere (1 Kings 12:25–33). Most of the old Mosaic ritual is still visible in Bethel, but the *yahweh* who is worshiped at Bethel is a god of Amaziah's devising, not the living God who revealed Himself to Israel at the Red Sea and gave His law to her at Mount Sinai.

While Amaziah wants Amos to stop prophesying against Israel, he receives not only a prophecy against Israel but also against his own family (7:16–17). Verse 17 is a ferocious judgment pronounced against Amaziah for his false ministry. His wife will become a prostitute to survive, his children will be killed, his property will be despoiled, and the nation to which he purported to provide spiritual leadership to will be destroyed. The last line of the curse is the explanation of the previous four: Israel will be conquered and its people sent into exile. The other punishments can all be explained as typical effects of military conquest and exile. In any case, events will prove which of the two men has been speaking the truth and is a servant of the true living God.

AMOS 8:1–14

TOO LATE

Setting Up the Section

Chapter 8 opens with a basket of ripe fruit. While Amos may be seeing a physical bowl of fruit, he is likely seeing a vision. Significant to this scene is that the fruit is ripe. In this way, the fruit is an image of Israel.

In describing the basket he sees, Amos says it includes ripe fruit. Typical fruit for Amos's region and era included figs, olives, and grapes.

Amos has already referred to music in Israel's temple worship (5:23), but when the Lord's judgment falls, the only music to be heard at Israel's sanctuaries will be wailing. Dead bodies will be scattered everywhere (8:3).

Verse 4 begins with a call to listen. This is the formula that Amos uses repeatedly to begin new sections of his prophecy (see 3:1; 4:1; 5:1).

We are again given a description of Israel as religiously scrupulous, at least outwardly—the people observe the Sabbath and the other festival days punctiliously—but they are morally bankrupt (8:5-6). They don't do business on the Sabbath, but they can't wait for it to be over so they can resume their acts of greed. They were able to buy off the poor, because the poor people were reduced to pennilessness after paying high prices for food and, in turn, became desperate for money.

Critical Observation

From the beginning of His covenant with Israel, Yahweh reminds His people that He will be a protector of the poor and will hold anyone accountable who misuses them. Twice before in Amos, we have heard the Lord use the word *swear.* In 4:2 He swears by His holiness, and in 6:8 He swears by Himself. Here, in 8:7, He swears by the "Pride of Jacob." Earlier in verse 6:8, God states that He abhors the pride of Jacob. In this earlier instance (noted in some translations by a lowercase *p* in pride), the reference is to the haughtiness of Israel trusting in her own strength. Here (noted by some translations by an uppercase *P* in Pride), it is a reference to God Himself.

The Nile River, mentioned in verse 8, rose and fell every year and often caused great damage by its flooding. It is a useful illustration of the convulsion to come in the land of Israel. An enemy will sweep over Israel like floodwaters and leave nothing but devastation behind. The same expression is used again in 9:5.

In verse 10 we read of the Israelites mourning, wearing sackcloth, and shaving their heads. Amos compares their mourning to that found at the funeral of an only son, which would have been understood by Amos's listeners to be an ultimate and bitter loss.

According to verse 12, the Israelites will stagger from one sea to another. This reference implies the Dead Sea to the Mediterranean, which is a way of saying that this will affect all of Israel. The famine will be so severe that it will consume not only the old and weak but also the young and strong (8:13).

In verse 14, Samaria's shame is a contrast to the mention of Jacob's pride in verse 7. It refers to the false gods who have been added to Yahweh's worship at Israel's shrines. To swear by a god is to commit themselves to the reality of those gods and their power to help them. Yahweh is saying, "You chose those gods over me, let them save you now." They can't! Israel's lack of true repentance shows that in that same day, they will still be found calling on other gods and looking to their idols as well as to Yahweh.

AMOS 9:1–15

FUTURE BLESSING

Setting Up the Section

The theme of this conclusion is that no one can escape God's wrath. God punishes unfaithfulness, and no person can get in His way.

Verses 1–4 contain the fifth and last of the visions that God gives Amos—this one of the destruction of the temple. (The first four visions are recorded in chapters 7–8.) The pillars of the temple support the roof, and the cut stone thresholds are at the bottom of the great doors. The picture here is of the complete collapse of the temple from top to bottom. One of Israel's sanctuaries is in view, probably the principal one at Bethel. The picture of the building collapsing on the worshipers indicates that Israelite worship is conducted in some significant measure inside the sanctuary, in the Canaanite fashion, not outside in the court in the orthodox fashion prescribed in the Law of Moses.

The structure of verse 2 is a common biblical figure of speech that uses two extreme parts together. In this case, heaven and hell are extremes that communicate that all of God's creation is included. There is nowhere to hide. The mountain mentioned in verse 3, Mount Carmel, was known for its thickly wooded mountainside honeycombed with caves. For Amos's contemporaries, this image would serve to reinforce the pervasiveness of God's judgment, as would the reference to *exile* (or *captivity*) in verse 4. Even an enemy nation will not be powerful enough to keep God's judgment at bay.

The Nile's rising and falling is used as an image of destruction in 8:8. Here, in 9:5, the Nile serves as another image of the totality of the Lord's judgment—like a flood that covers the land before it recedes, it leaves nothing but destruction behind.

Verses 5–6 have a hymnlike quality in their mention of God's power and their images of water and the heavens.

With verse 7, the Lord begins to speak in the first person, asking two rhetorical questions that place Israel, spiritually speaking, on equal ground with all others. First, Israel is no more exempt from God's judgment than the people of Cush, a reference to Ethiopia. Israel, by her lack of faith and her betrayal of God's covenant, has become just like these other people instead of the people of God she was called to be. Since the Philistines and the Arameans (NIV) (or Syrians, KJV) were hated enemies of Israel, the comparison would have been particularly galling to Amos's audience.

There is a hopeful element to verses 8–10. The kernels of grain that fall through the sieve to the ground represent the believing remnant of Israel. The pebbles—those who don't believe—will be caught in the sieve and thrown out. They will die by the sword— Amos's last reminder that the Lord's wrath will come upon Israel in the form of military conquest.

In verse 11, Amos first sees David's kingdom (his "tent" NIV) as destroyed but then as renewed and rebuilt. The restoration of David's dynasty is another way of speaking about the Messiah and His kingdom, as the Messiah is, in all biblical prophecy, the future of David's dynasty and the hope of his kingdom.

Edom was a particularly bitter enemy of Israel. Here it represents the nations of the world that, in the last days, will be subject to the kingdom of God (9:12). David was the only king of Israel who not only conquered Edom but held it. So Edom makes a particularly good representative for the nations of the world that will become subject to David's descendant, the Messiah.

Verses 13–14 describe a time of unprecedented bounty. The picture is of fields so fertile and harvests so large that the reapers will still be gathering the grain as the soil is being turned over for the next planting. And the image of wine flowing downward from the hills where the grapes are grown is, again, a picture of unimaginable plenty.

Critical Observation

We have this picture very often in the prophets and as early as Jacob's blessing of Judah in Genesis 49:10–12: The Messiah will restore the world to its pure state, as it was in Eden before the fall. Additionally, there will be peace, enabling the people of God to pursue their life's work without fear.

Amos closes with a promise that when the people of God are restored and resettled in the promised land to enjoy the blessings and benefits of God's favor, they will never be judged again. The judgment of the nation is upon them. This has been Amos's primary theme from the beginning of the book, but when the Day of Judgment is passed and Israel is restored, it will be for good.

Take It Home

Amos's prophecy concerns all the people of God, Jews and Gentiles alike. The living, faithful church—whether Jewish or Gentile—is the true Israel of God, as we are often told in the New Testament. Also, the promise here is primarily a promise of eternal salvation, of the life of heaven, and of the complete fulfillment of human life as it will be experienced at the consummation of all things. Amos's description of the future here is simply another version of that description of heaven that John gives us at the end of the book of Revelation. Amos ends with a promise of a wonderful day, a day of fulfillment, joy, and perfect satisfaction for every human being who is numbered among the true people of God when history comes to its close.

OBADIAH

INTRODUCTION TO OBADIAH

The book of Obadiah is the shortest of the Old Testament, yet its brief message has numerous applications far beyond its relevance to Edom. Obadiah provides a warning to anyone who mistakenly believes that sin will go unnoticed (and unpunished), but he also offers confidence that for those who continue to seek God, the Lord is able to both forgive and deliver.

AUTHOR

Personal facts are scarce concerning the prophet Obadiah. He provides no family references or pertinent locations that enlighten the reader as to his biography. Even his name (meaning "worshiper of the Lord") was a common one in his day. At least a dozen Old Testament men are named Obadiah.

PURPOSE

Obadiah has a single purpose in writing: to bring God's message of judgment to the people of Edom. The nation's deeply rooted sense of pride will result in its certain downfall.

THEMES

Obadiah highlights the problems that arise from unbridled arrogance and self-centeredness. Edom (the descendants of Esau) has family ties to Israel (the descendants of Jacob), so Edom's sadistic glee in response to the previous troubles of the Israelites does not go unnoticed; they will be judged for their actions.

HISTORICAL CONTEXT

With so few clues provided, it is difficult to determine a precise date for the writing of Obadiah. But the conflict between Edom and Israel was ongoing and had existed throughout their entire histories. If the event referred to in verses 11–14 is the Babylonian destruction of Jerusalem (586 BC), then Obadiah was most likely written during the exile.

CONTRIBUTION TO THE BIBLE

Obadiah is a seldom-quoted book. Even the New Testament writers, who cited many of the Old Testament prophetic writings, are silent in regard to Obadiah. Yet the message of this short writing has practical applications that make it a significant contribution to scripture.

BOOK OF OBADIAH

THE PROBLEM WITH TAKING JOY IN THE SUFFERING OF ONE'S ENEMIES

Setting Up the Section

The concise writing of Obadiah is a pointed accusation against the nation of Edom, whose people had survived while they saw Judah fall to powerful enemies. More than that, Edom had taken perverse pleasure in seeing their enemies suffer and had even acted aggressively against Judah during a vulnerable time. What Edom didn't realize, however, was that Judah's fall was a result of God's judgment on His people. Obadiah now reveals that God will certainly judge Edom as well and that judgment will be severe.

📄 1–14

JUDGMENT IN STORE FOR EDOM

Israel and Edom had a long and interwoven history. Sometimes they had joined as allies against a common enemy. More often, however, the original rivalry between Jacob (Israel's forefather) and Esau (Edom's forefather) created ongoing conflicts between the two nations.

The timing of Obadiah's writing is debated, but it is clear that Judah has experienced a bitter defeat at the hands of enemies (verse 11). The Edomites foolishly believe they are exempt from a similar outcome. Edom was located along a span of wilderness that stretched from the southern tip of the Dead Sea to the northern portion of the Red Sea. It was mountainous territory where the inhabitants lived among rocky cliffs, confident of their security and the impenetrability of their cities. It is as if they feel untouchable, high among the stars (verses 3–4).

But from their heights of arrogance, they are about to fall and become small among the nations (verse 2). They may dwell above much of the world, but God is higher still and will bring them down (verse 4).

Demystifying Obadiah

Israel had requested permission to travel through Edom during their exodus from Egypt, but the Edomites had marched out with a large and powerful army to deny them passage (Numbers 20:14–21). Later, when Israel was an established nation of its own, the Edomites waited until other people attacked Israel and then invaded and took prisoners (2 Chronicles 28:16–21). And when Jerusalem eventually fell to the Babylonians, the Edomites cheered and celebrated (Psalm 137:7–8).

During a typical theft, the robber(s) will leave behind some of the person's belongings, but Edom's loss will be total. Even worse, those whom Edom considers their close friends and allies will prove deceitful. The very people whom they trust enough to sit around the table and share a meal with will destroy them with alarming treachery. The wisdom and power of the most accomplished descendants of Esau will not be adequate to anticipate this trouble nor deliver their countrymen from a horrifying slaughter (verses 5–9).

God disciplines those He loves, which is a difficult concept for outsiders to understand. When nonbelievers observe God's people undergoing a period of corrective discipline, they tend to presume that God has no abiding love for those who worship Him. Some even take a perverse pleasure in celebrating the suffering of God's people, but it is never wise to gloat over those whom the Lord has called His special possession. He will stand up for them in the day when He comes to judge and will bring upon the heads of their enemies the very vengeance those people had sought for them. Edom will learn this lesson too late, as they find themselves covered with shame and destroyed (verses 10–14).

📄 15–21

DELIVERANCE IN STORE FOR JACOB

Jesus will later teach that, "So in everything, do to others what you would have them do to you," saying that this so-called Golden Rule "sums up the Law and the Prophets" (Matthew 7:12 NIV). The prophet Obadiah records how the Edomites have treated God's people despicably, and God's pronouncement of their judgment is, "As you have done to Israel, so it will be done to you" (Obadiah 15 NLT).

After contributing to the (temporary) defeat of Jerusalem, the Edomites had apparently celebrated with strong drink. But the cup of God's wrath (see Isaiah 51:17) is in store for them to drink. Edom represents all the nations who have opposed God—they all will one day completely disappear from existence, while Jerusalem is restored. The house of Esau will have no survivors (Obadiah 16–18).

Critical Observation

While Obadiah's prophecy focuses on Edom, other Old Testament prophetic books include prophecies against these people (Jeremiah 49:7–39; Ezekiel 35:1–15; Malachi 1:1–4).

Mount Zion (Jerusalem) will be delivered, once again holy and home to the house of Jacob (Israel). Surrounding land that had been ceded to other nations will be reclaimed and restored. People will be called out of exile to resettle in their homelands. Deliverers will be assigned to help govern, but the kingdom will be the Lord's (verses 19–21).

The short book of Obadiah confirms what many other prophets teach in greater detail. The Day of the Lord will one day bring judgment on all who persistently defy God and live in disobedience, while bringing deliverance and restoration to those who repent and seek God's mercy. What appears to be injustice is only temporary. God is aware of every deed and attitude of every person, and He will punish or reward accordingly.

Take It Home

Obadiah's message to Edom is a relevant lesson for many people today. Even though Edom and Israel were ongoing enemies, it becomes clear that God was displeased for one side to take delight in the suffering and downfall of the other. Can you think of times when you have taken pleasure in seeing someone "get what was coming to him or her"? The command to "love your enemies" (Matthew 5:44) begins by being more sensitive to others' pains and problems. What can you do in the weeks to come to develop a stronger empathy with those you don't normally get along with?

JONAH

INTRODUCTION TO JONAH

Jonah is the only prophet who is recorded as having run away from God. In this way, Jonah is not known for his piety but for his prodigality. Jonah, in his rebellion, disobedience, and hardness of heart, is a man who typifies the rebellion of Israel as described by other prophets. Ironically, the name *Jonah* means "dove," a bird often associated with peace.

AUTHOR

Very little is said of the prophet Jonah outside of the book of Jonah itself. It does seem safe to conclude that the Jonah in 2 Kings 14:25 is the same person who is the subject of the book of Jonah, especially since both are identified as the son of Amittai.

The book of Jonah does not name its author. While it is about Jonah, there is no specific claim as to whether Jonah actually wrote it.

PURPOSE

The book stood to reveal to Israel the possibility of repentance, even for those whom Israel would have considered the most wicked. The point was, if repentance is a possibility for the most wicked, then repentance is a real possibility for Israel herself as well.

OCCASION

Jonah is a prophet in the northern kingdom of Israel during the first half of the eighth century BC. His predecessors are Elijah and Elisha. The ministries of Hosea and Amos immediately follow that of Jonah.

THEMES

Throughout the book of Jonah runs the theme of second chances, worked out through opportunities for repentance, some taken and some wasted. Hand in hand runs the theme of those who choose to obey God and those who don't.

HISTORICAL CONTEXT

Jonah is associated in 2 Kings 14:25 with the reign of King Jeroboam, a time of prosperity for Israel. Assyria, whose capital city is Jonah's target of Nineveh, has already begun to exercise her dominance in the Near East, but for a time her control will wane, allowing Israel to expand her borders. Israel's empowerment at this time may have been a factor in her lack of repentance. This makes the story of Jonah all the more pointed, in that a nation Israel considered to be wicked repents before God when His own people won't.

CONTRIBUTION TO THE BIBLE

In the New Testament, Jesus mentions Jonah (Matthew 12:39-41; 16:4; Luke 11:29-32). When asked for a sign, Jesus refers the religious leaders to the sign of Jonah that already exists. He points out the parallel of Jonah's three days in the fish and the Son of man's three days in the heart of the earth.

OUTLINE OF JONAH

JONAH 1:1–17

JONAH AND THE SAILORS

Setting Up the Section

At the opening of Jonah's story, he is given a divine commission to go to the great city of Nineveh, capital city of Assyria and a potential threat to Israel (see Genesis 10:8–11).

📖 1:1–3

RUNNING FROM GOD

The description of Nineveh as *great* in verse 2 probably refers to its size and its influence, but its sins were great as well. Its wickedness has come to God's attention, and Jonah is to be God's messenger. But instead of doing what God instructs him to do, Jonah catches a ship heading in the opposite direction (1:1-3).

The city of Nineveh is located on the Tigris River, more than five hundred miles to the northeast of Israel. But Jonah goes west toward Tarshish, which seems to have been located on the western coast of Spain. Jonah flees from God's presence, a truth repeated twice in verse 3. Jonah is not trying to flee the literal presence of God, but he is attempting to avoid his role as a prophet.

1:4–11

A POWERFUL STORM

But God does not let Jonah flee. He hurls a storm in Jonah's path—a storm so great that it terrifies veteran sailors and threatens the ship (1:4–5). The sailors begin casting the cargo overboard in an effort to save the ship and their own lives. At the same time, each sailor is praying to his gods for deliverance. These pagan sailors would have worshiped gods they thought influenced the seas on which they traveled.

As the sailors gather the cargo to throw overboard, they find Jonah deep in sleep (1:5). The ship's captain is irritated to find Jonah sleeping while the rest of the crew members work to stay alive during the storm. He doesn't ask Jonah to help cast the cargo overboard, but he does command Jonah to pray to his God (1:6). The text does not reveal if Jonah obeys the captain's orders.

The captain and the sailors understand the storm to be a religious matter. When praying doesn't stop the storm, they try another religious technique: casting lots to find the person whose sin has caused the problem (1:7). The lots land on Jonah and identify him as the culprit.

The sailors are in fear for their lives, but in spite of the imminent danger, and the likely urge to throw him overboard, they interrogate Jonah, asking about his origin, purpose, and heritage (1:8). In his answer, Jonah separates himself religiously from the sailors but apparently reveals insight into his mission. From his responses, the sailors immediately know that Jonah has indeed caused the storm and that his sin has endangered the entire ship's crew (1:9–10).

The response of the sailors—appalled at Jonah's disobedience—shows that even the pagans are shocked at how this man has chosen to defy God. They, too, are experiencing the consequences of Jonah's actions, so they ask Jonah what to do to appease the wrath of his God (1:11).

1:12–17

GOD'S PROVISION

Jonah tells the sailors to throw him overboard and the sea will calm (1:12). Given the intensity of the storm, this request would have made his death seem a certainty. Some believe this shows repentance on Jonah's part, but others feel that Jonah wants to die to avoid God's command to confront Nineveh. The sailors could have responded quickly to Jonah's instructions, yet because they are reluctant to cause his death, they make one more risky attempt to save him by rowing for the rocky shore (1:13). When they conclude that Jonah's solution is their only alternative, they pray once more before casting him into the sea (1:14). Many scholars agree that at this point the sailors are praying to Jonah's God. Having prayed, they pick up the prophet and cast him into the sea (1:15).

As Jonah sinks beneath the waves, the winds cease and the sea calms down. This confirms for the sailors that Jonah's God is the only true God. Thus, at the end of the chapter, we see the sailors worshiping by sacrificing and declaring their faith in God (1:16). In trying to avoid preaching to the Ninevites, Jonah has unwillingly preached to the sailors, and they have come to faith in his God.

The fish that God provides for Jonah has become the focus of this story, yet it is simply a provision of the Lord (1:17). The miracle is not the fish itself or in the details of how the fish swallows Jonah; the miracle is God's grace toward Jonah, saving him from almost certain death in order that Jonah may receive all that God's call on his life has to offer.

Critical Observation

Jesus refers back to Jonah's plight in the belly of the fish in Matthew 12:39–41, comparing Jonah's three days and nights to the three days and nights the Son of man spends in the earth. This is called the sign of the prophet Jonah.

JONAH 2:1–10

JONAH AND HIS PSALM

Jonah's Petition   2:1–9
Jonah's Deliverance   2:10

Setting Up the Section

Jonah 2:1 picks up the story from under the sea. Verses 2–9 present Jonah's prayer in psalm format.

📄 2:1–9

JONAH'S PETITION

Jonah's descriptions of what is happening to him in the water affirm that he knows God is in control and responsible (2:2–3). The word *Sheol* typically means "grave" but sometimes has connotations of the underworld. Nevertheless, Jonah's words reveal that he acknowledges death as an imminent threat.

Jonah mentions seeing the temple, most likely the temple in Jerusalem (2:4).

In verses 5–7, Jonah describes his situation with graphic detail. He acknowledges God's rescue. In verses 8–9, he appears to contrast Gentile pagans with his own belief in God. This sense of separateness, and even at times superiority, speaks to the core of Jonah's dilemma. God called him to preach to a wicked place, to those who were enemies to his own people. His unwillingness reveals his inability to see how much God values even those who have not yet come to know Him.

2:10

JONAH'S DELIVERANCE

There is little emphasis on the actual fish itself here, perhaps because the fish is obedient to his commission. Jonah's prayer is answered, and he is not only expelled from the fish but also returns to dry land (2:10).

Take It Home

In chapters 1 and 2, the pagan sailors are the ones who seem to act with pure hearts, acknowledging the true God and worshiping with sacrifices and declarations of faith. Jonah, on the other hand, acts rebelliously by disobeying God, and in doing so he endangers many people. It is easy for those of us who consider ourselves to be on God's side to assume that our attitudes will be right. We must always be vigilant, however, that we are acting as servants of the Lord.

JONAH 3:1–10

JONAH AND THE CITY

A Second Chance   3:1–3
Nineveh's Repentance   3:4–10

Setting Up the Section

In chapters 1 and 2, Jonah's sin is apparent yet still somewhat subtle and passive. But this changes in chapters 3 and 4, for Jonah's preaching and the repentance of Nineveh reveal his sinfulness in its ugliest dimensions. In the following chapters, all appearances of piety vanish in the account of the prodigal prophet.

3:1–3

A SECOND CHANCE

God commands Jonah for the second time to deliver His message to the Ninevites (3:1–2). It is almost a repetition of the command given to him in 1:2. This time Jonah obeys the Lord. Verse 3 describes Nineveh, perhaps including its suburbs, as large; the mention of a three-day journey refers to how long it will take to walk around it.

3:4–10

NINEVEH'S REPENTANCE

Jonah's message is simple, to the point, and frightening: In forty days, Nineveh will fall (3:4). Just like the sailors in chapter one, the people of Nineveh take Jonah's words of imminent divine judgment seriously—they believe. The faith of the Ninevites is not simply a fear of judgment. They call a fast and put on sackcloth—a sign of helplessness and despair (3:5). The text specifies that the belief and repentance starts with the common people and rises upward to Nineveh's leadership (3:6).

Because the king also believes Jonah's warning, he makes every effort to assure total compliance to the citywide repentance. He begins by personally repenting. The king then makes a proclamation which requires all of Nineveh to fast and to abstain from drinking water (3:6–7). Both men and animals are to be covered with sackcloth, and all the people are to call upon God and stop their wicked ways and violence (3:8).

The wicked ways of the Ninevites are not detailed, except for use of the word *violence* (3:8). Nineveh's motivation is that God may change His mind (3:9). God had instructed Jonah to deliver not a promise of things to come but a warning. The Ninevites understand God's message correctly. God takes note of Nineveh's repentance because it involves more than mere words or token gestures. The Ninevites have changed more than outward appearances; they have changed their evil ways (3:10).

Critical Observation

Jesus' reference to the repentance of the Ninevites is particularly informative (Matthew 12:38–41). If the Ninevites can repent with so little evidence, then surely the problem with the Jewish leaders, scribes, and Pharisees was not a lack of evidence. Like Jonah, the Jewish leaders, scribes, and Pharisees did have evidence but refused to believe that God would act in a way unexpected by them—and thus no evidence was enough to change their willful rejection.

JONAH 4:1–11

JONAH AND THE SHADE

Jonah's Anger Against God   4:1–3
The Plant and the Prodigal   4:4–11

Setting Up the Section

Had Jonah been any other prophet in the history of Israel, he would have been overjoyed with the results of his ministry—the repentance of the great city of Nineveh. In chapter 4, Jonah blurts out his reasons for rebelling against the command of the Lord. The events in this chapter reveal Jonah's sin.

📖 **4:1–3**

JONAH'S ANGER AGAINST GOD

In spite of the repentance of Nineveh, Jonah is angry with God (4:1). Jonah is not hesitant to explain, and he protests to the Lord in prayer (4:2). Jonah is angry with God because He shows grace toward the Ninevites, who are enemies of Israel. Instead of learning this lesson about God's loving and merciful character, he complains that he would rather die than live (4:3).

THE PLANT AND THE PRODIGAL

God acknowledges Jonah's anger toward Him (4:4) and presses on with another experience: the giving and the taking away of a plant.

Jonah goes outside the city, where he makes a shady booth from which he can watch the spectacle of the destruction of Nineveh (4:5). God causes a plant to grow, and for the first time in the narrative, Jonah is described as being happy (4:6). With the advent of the worm that eats the plant, and with the arrival of the scorching wind, Jonah loses his comfort and his happiness (4:7–8). Jonah could have chosen to walk away from his suffering and join the Ninevites in their worship of God, but he allows his anger to keep him in discomfort and isolation. He once again begs God to let him die.

For the second time in this chapter, God offers the opportunity for Jonah to examine his anger; and again, Jonah chooses anger over any other emotion (4:9). He is so adamant about his anger that he insists upon keeping it and wishes to die.

God has the final word in the book of Jonah, and His last words press to the heart of the matter. He wants Jonah to see that just as Jonah had compassion on the plant, God had compassion on the people (4:10). God wants Jonah to examine his feelings for the plant—they were strong, even though Jonah had nothing to do with the plant's growth or existence.

The book of Jonah does not end nicely and neatly. We are left somewhat suspended by God's final words of rebuke. We are never told if Jonah repents.

Take It Home

Jonah had rejected the principle of grace. Resisting and rejecting the grace of God is just as great and just as common a sin today as it was in Jonah's time. God's grace takes unexpected forms. He was gracious to Jonah, saving him by means of the great fish. God is gracious to His children by using even pain and adversity in their lives. May we today embrace God's grace however it is bestowed upon us.

MICAH

INTRODUCTION TO MICAH

Sometimes called the prophet of the poor, Micah is a contemporary of Isaiah and speaks a similar message, though, as recorded in the Bible, shorter. King Hezekiah initiates sweeping spiritual and moral reforms in Judah in response to the preaching of Micah and Isaiah, but unfortunately these reforms are short-lived.

AUTHOR

The first verse of this book ascribes the authorship to Micah, a prophet about whom we know very little outside of what is revealed through this prophecy. The prophet is mentioned in only one other place in the Bible, in Jeremiah 26:17–19. In this account, Micah is described as a prophet during the reign of King Hezekiah. When Micah prophesied a bad end for Jerusalem, the king repented, saving Jerusalem from the destruction Micah had prophesied.

PURPOSE

Micah prophesies to stir his readers to action. His writing takes the form of three oracles of judgment. This judgment falls on his countrymen, who act as oppressors, as well as on his society in general, which is filled with corruption. Micah also reminds his people of God's restoration (as do other Old Testament prophets), which awaits them in the future.

OCCASION

The first verse of this prophecy identifies the monarchies under which Micah prophesies—Jotham, Ahaz, and Hezekiah. This places Micah in the eighth century BC. The prophecy references the destruction of Samaria and the invasion of Sennacherib in 701 BC, which would agree with that chronology.

THEMES

While Micah's prophecy is not a theological treatise, running through it are the themes of God's sovereignty, His consistency of nature, and the destiny of the remnant of the faithful.

MICAH 1:1–16

THE JUDGMENT TO COME

Setting Up the Section

Micah begins with the announcement of judgment because of sins against God and unfaithfulness to God's covenant. This is a major theme of the prophets, leading up to the destruction of the northern kingdom in 722 BC and the devastation and exile of the southern kingdom some 150 years later. This lesson also reveals the nature of God's divine justice, the ferocity of divine wrath, and the final and conclusive judgment of all people at the end of the world.

The kings listed in 1:1 reign from 742 BC to 686 BC. It is widely thought that Micah mentions only the southern kings—though he mentions the northern kingdom (Samaria) as well as the southern (Jerusalem)—because he did not regard the northern kings as legitimate and did not want to dignify them by mentioning them by name.

The call goes out to the entire earth, even though the message concerns Samaria primarily and Jerusalem to a lesser degree. They are all being summoned to a trial to face the Judge of all the earth (1:2). In verse 3, the Lord appears from heaven as an avenging judge.

The specific sins will be enumerated in chapters 2 and 3 and again in chapter 6. But here the case is put generally as rebellion (1:5). The capital cities are mentioned both to represent the entire nation and because it is where the living embodiment of the corruption that has destroyed the nation originated. The punishment on Samaria and Jerusalem foreshadows punishment for all people who worship idols (1:6–7). The meaning of the second half of verse 7 could be that, because idols are bought with the revenues of the cult prostitutes, the conquerors whom God will use to punish Israel will break them up not only for their precious metals but also for spending the money earned from them on the same prostitutes.

The description in verse 8 of the prophet stripped of clothes is not a picture of penitence but of exile. Exiles, barefoot and naked, tramp miserably away from home in long lines under the supervision of enemy soldiers. The same idea is expressed with the howling of the jackal. Jackals howl in the waste places, in the wilderness, and that is what Judah will be reduced to. The gate is the place in the community where announcements are publicly made (1:9).

The following verses (1:10–16) mention several Judean towns, all of them within fourteen kilometers of Micah's hometown of Moresheth. All of the names are omens—they are given some special significance by means of a play on the name, either on the meaning or the associations of the name, or on its sound.

The first name, Gath, is significant because the city does not exist at this time, having been destroyed by Sargon (1:10). The idea, as any Israelite would immediately realize, is that the house of David is now falling, just as the house of Saul had done before. Dust is a symbol of abject humiliation and defeat (1:10; see Genesis 3:14). Verse 11 continues the name-play. The idea in verses 11–12 is that the towns of Judah are hoping for help from the capital, but it is under siege. Lachish is apparently the place where idolatry got its foothold in Judah, spreading outward from there (1:13). With the loss of Lachish, which is a key defensive point and, in fact, holds out longer in 701 BC than the other towns and villages of Judah, the nation must expect to pay tribute. The idea of verse 14 is that towns that belong to Judah and contribute to her must now be paid for instead, as they are in enemy hands. Again in the name-play of the verses above, the allusion in verse 15 is literary, not literal. As David had to flee from Saul to the cave of Adullam (see 1 Samuel 22:1), so the sons of David—the kings and the nobles (the glory of Israel)—will be driven out.

Micah sees the future destruction of Judah on account of her sins, and he considers that the appropriate response is to mourn with true sincerity (1:16). But in this culture, there were professional mourners, so it wasn't always done with as great a depth of feeling. An official mourner does not grieve the loss of a husband as a loving wife does, or of a child as her parents do.

MICAH 2:1–13

FROM OPPRESSION TO HOPE

Setting Up the Section

This next oracle is a pronouncement of judgment against the leadership of Judah. But it goes beyond simply promising judgment against the northern kingdom (1:6–7) and the southern kingdom (1:8–16). This oracle specifically identifies one of the sins for which Israel will be judged.

The reference to the light of morning alludes to the time of day when the courts meet (2:1). The indication here is that the people in power are controlling the courts, which should be a place of justice for all, not just the powerful. But the first part of verse 2 explains how the powerful are taking others' physical property and taking advantage of the people. In this culture, if you take away a person's land, you take away that person's livelihood. Consequences include becoming a day laborer at best and potentially a slave.

Those in power are gaining possession of people's fields by lending money to the landowners and then foreclosing. The result of this is the evacuation of the middle class—most people in prosperous Israel are in the middle class in these days—and the creation of a large poor class serving a smaller, but much wealthier, ruling class. The violation here is in coveting others' property instead of recognizing their ownership and ignoring the fact that, regardless of what one might own and what others might own, all things belong to God and are to be used in His service and for the accomplishment of His will.

The people mentioned in verse 3 indicate a group acting with corporate solidarity. The people who are being ruined by these wealthy land barons are not completely innocent themselves, though. The entire social and religious fabric is rotten, not just the leaders and people in power. Because of this, the Assyrians will come and take the land itself, the very possession the Lord had promised to Israel (2:4). The sacred land of Israel will be distributed to infidels, people who had curried the favor of the Assyrians. This section clearly indicates that this takeover will be done with the help of God.

Critical Observation

God's judgment, as described in chapter 1, is an example of "an eye for an eye and a tooth for a tooth." While this kind of judgment can sound brutal, at the heart of it is the principle that a punishment should fit the specific crime. An eye for an eye is harsh. But it is more equitable than a life for an eye. Here are other examples of punishments that specifically fit the transgressions: Esther 7:9–10; Psalm 7:15–16; Ezekiel 36:6–7; Matthew 26:52.

Micah 2:6 launches an oracle against the false prophets and against the leadership of the people who favor these prophets and approve of their teaching. In its original writing, the imperative not to prophesy is directed to more than one person. This suggests that Micah is not the only one preaching against the sins of the day. We know that Isaiah and Hosea were contemporaries of Micah. There is also a remnant of faithful people who would have repeated the teaching of these faithful men.

The first half of verse 7 shows what the false prophets are teaching, and the second half reveals Micah's response to that teaching. The message of the false prophets amounts to an assurance that because God is love, Israel has nothing to fear. But Micah explains that while God is gracious, He is also a God of judgment to those who do not believe in or obey Him. And because Micah's generation is such an unbelieving and disobedient people, He is going to be a God of judgment to them, not a God of grace and mercy. He will reach out to them if they cry out to Him for mercy and forsake their evil ways, but they will not.

Micah includes some specifics. When men return from battle, as in verse 8, they are confident, assured, at peace, and not expecting trouble. But the leadership pillages them.

In other words, the leadership treats the people just like the enemy does. Women are being evicted from their homes, and the descriptions of those homes indicate the people of Judah are, at this time, prosperous and comfortable (2:9). The listeners are instructed to leave, to flee what is coming as a result of sin (2:10). Unfortunately, that means they must go away into exile.

Micah mocks the message preached by the false teachers as simply another version of what people want to hear (2:11). He is being properly cynical of the base motives of the false teachers.

Historically there have been two different interpretations of verses 12–13. Some see the verses as a further prophecy of woe and judgment. Most, though, take the verses to be a message of hope and consolation, a promise of at least a temporary deliverance—a direct prophecy of the deliverance of Jerusalem from Sennacherib's invading army in 701 BC. The sheep pen, or fold, is Jerusalem (2:12). The Shepherd of Israel is gathering His flock to protect it from marauders.

Demystifying Micah

The force of verse 13 lies in the description of the Lord as breaking open the way. Micah's contemporary listeners would have noticed a similarity to David's reference to the Lord breaking out against His enemies (the Philistines) in 2 Samuel 5:20, 24. In other areas of scripture, God is the One who breaks open a way to save His people. The second half of verse 13 is a spiritual picture of this procession out of the city; the Lord at the head of His people (eventually not the human king, but the King Shepherd of Israel, the Christ).

MICAH 3:1–12

JUDGMENT ON THE LEADERSHIP

Setting Up the Section

Chapter 3 contains three oracles of judgment of equal length and identical in form, with the same theme in every case—corrupt leadership.

Micah is the person speaking in verse 1. He uses imagery to show that the leaders are, in effect, consuming people for their own gain (3:2–3). (We've seen already in chapter 2 how they steal people's houses and render them destitute.) There is a startling new development in this oracle—the fact that the Lord will punish these false teachers in keeping with their crimes (3:4). The oppressed cry out to these leaders, and they do not answer or help them. So, when the leaders cry out to God for help, He will not answer them. This indicates a point of no return.

In verse 5, the prophet speaks for the Lord rather than on his own behalf, with the following verses addressing the false prophets. Verse 6 specifically mentions divination, or fortune-telling, something that is forbidden to people of God (Deuteronomy 18:10). It is considered a betrayal of the sufficiency of God's revelation and a serious mistaking of the way to live a life pleasing to God.

In Micah's day, these false prophets held equal status with God's prophets, if not higher because of the popularity of their message. Yet, one hundred years later, these same false prophets will be walking through the ruins of Jerusalem like unclean lepers (3:7). But Micah is filled with God's Spirit and with the power to speak on His behalf to the people (3:8).

Verses 9–12 make up the third oracle against the corrupt leadership of the people. This last oracle speaks to the leadership in general, adding the priests, by name, to the leaders and false prophets.

Micah continues railing against the leaders for their unjust ways (3:9–10). Both the civic leaders and the religious leaders are accused of taking bribes instead of following God for justice (3:11). Verse 12 is the only verse in the Old Testament that is cited word for word somewhere else in the Old Testament (Jeremiah 26:18), some one hundred years later. The Lord relents because of Hezekiah's faithfulness, and this prophecy does not come to pass.

MICAH 4:1–13

ZION'S FUTURE

Setting Up the Section

While Jerusalem is still being addressed in chapter 4, the mood of the message changes. Micah 4–5 contains the first of the oracles of salvation. These are oracles of an eventual deliverance, unlike the apparent near-terms deliverance described in 2:12–13. These oracles describe a new epoch that lies beyond the judgment that Micah is prophesying for Israel and Judah in the near future.

The prediction that opens chapter 4 is similar to other instances in the Old Testament prophets such as Isaiah 2:2–4 and Hosea 3:5. The opening mention of the last days is used in the New Testament also to refer to the future when God will bring all prophecies to fruition (1 Timothy 4:1; 2 Timothy 3:1; 1 Peter 1:5; Jude 18). There is debate about whether these days refer to a time before Christ comes again or the time after Christ actually has returned.

In the opening verses of this fourth chapter, Micah overhears the nations and reflects on what he has seen and heard and what will come of it: The law of God will be embraced by the nations and the result will be peace, to the point that weapons will be retooled for growing food. This is a refreshing contrast to the forms of justice Micah has just condemned. The final verse of this segment has been described as a liturgical response on the part of the righteous: Until this vision is a reality, God's people will participate by faith.

Demystifying Micah

Almost every ancient Near Eastern religion and deity had a mountain dedicated to it, and most often a temple stood on that mountain (or hill, as the case may be). In this era, the mountain symbolizes God's bringing of order over chaos, access to heaven, and His presence on earth. All of this is the context for Micah's prophecy in verses 1–5: The Lord's mountain rising above the others means that Yahweh will reign supreme as the nations come to recognize and honor Him as the true God.

The opening phrase of verse 6—*in that day*—refers to the events of 4:1–5. The prophet is anticipating the reality of the exile that has already been prophesied. God's remnant will be made up of the weakest ones of society, and He will use those people to rebuild His strong nation (4:6–7). This can be seen as a foreshadowing image of what God will do through Christ—born in a stable yet God in human flesh. In fact, in the next verse, God directly addresses Jerusalem as He will later address Bethlehem (5:2). Eventually, the depleted people of God will become the nucleus of something far greater, stronger, and more permanent in the future. Judgment will come first; deliverance, salvation, and triumph later. Indeed, much later—far beyond the horizon of the people to whom Micah is preaching this message.

Take It Home

The response of the faithful in verse 5 reminds Christians of all eras that we are to bear witness to Micah's vision of the peace that comes from God's sovereignty. We can participate in it in advance, by living according to this same law in our lives today. We can whet our appetite—and that of the culture around us—for what is to come by living by faith in the reality we believe for the future.

Verses 9–13 contain two parallel sections: Each refers to *now* (4:9, 11), moving from the present distress of God's people to a future deliverance; each has a command (4:10, 13); each has a promise that is the rationale for obedience (4:10, 13); and each takes a similar view of present circumstances as being the outworking of a plan that people do not understand.

The suffering of the people in the coming captivity is foreshadowed in verses 9–10. Some Bible translations interpret *king* and *counselor* as a reference to human figures and thus interpret the question in verse 9 as sarcasm. But if verse 9 parallels verse 11, it suggests that these words are a reference to God. In this understanding, the question is rhetorical. Has God perished? Of course not.

There is a twist in verses 11–13. While these nations think they are destroying Israel on their own, in reality God is using them to punish and purify His people. While their actions are being used by Him at this time, eventually He will punish these nations for both their actions and their intentions.

God's plan and purpose is to bring eventual salvation out of the present distress and judgment. He will eventually order Israel to take action instead of simply writhing in agony (4:9, 13). But for now, Israel must pass through judgment until these nations—which, in their hubris, seek to destroy God's people and God Himself—will be destroyed. The commands of verses 10 and 13 are a summons that, in the meantime, those who belong to the faithful remnant are to step out in faith and endure the judgments of the Lord, knowing that vindication is in His hands.

MICAH 5:1–15

THE COMING CHAMPION

Setting Up the Section

The first verse of chapter 5 actually completes the closing thought from chapter 4. With verse 2, then, Micah begins a hopeful oracle regarding a champion who will come from Bethlehem. Verses 2–4 discuss the rule and triumph of the Messiah Himself, and verses 5–6 describe those who rule in His name. The ideal king of the ancient Near East is a shepherd king, one who provides for and cares for his people. The Messiah will be such a king.

The idea in verse 1 of Israel's leader being stricken on the cheek is an image of Hezekiah's total humiliation. He is so defenseless that he cannot even protect his face. He cannot defend his people—it's as if they have no king at all. It is in this context of Israel's humiliation and the demonstration of her powerlessness against a mighty foreign army that the great messianic prophecy is given. Once again, Micah is moving from the present distress of Israel—in this case, the Assyrian invasion of 701 BC—to a future deliverance.

Demystifying Micah

The Assyrian invasion in 701 BC is the context of this oracle. This is demonstrated by several things: 1) In verses 5–6, Nimrod, that is Babylon, is an inferior power, so this must be when Babylon is subject to Assyria, not later when it rules over the former Assyrian Empire; 2) in the verses following verse 5, Assyria is used as the representative of the forces of hostility to the kingdom of God, which makes sense if it is the great enemy of the people of God in the day of this prophecy; and 3) the term *leaders*, or *principle men,* at the end of verse 5 is rarely used, but it is one the Assyrian king Sargon used for his leaders.

Beginning with verse 2, Micah addresses the city of Bethlehem. With the advantage of hindsight, we know that Micah is about to share words related to the coming of Christ. The mention of old or ancient times seems to be a reference to the Messiah's bloodline—the ancestry of Jesse and David. It will be a new start from the original root.

The idea of verse 3 is that Israel's distress will continue until the Messiah comes. The *remnant*, or the *rest*, is the same idea as in Isaiah 11:11–12 and Zechariah 10:10, the gathering of those who have been dispersed because of exile or defeat.

In verse 4, the Messiah is called a shepherd, and this shepherd will protect His people from the *Assyrian*, as if describing an individual (5:5–6), but the name represents the enemies of the kingdom of God. The use of the number seven is a depiction of the idea of perfection (5:5). Then, the number eight offers the idea of even more than perfect. The Messiah's kingdom will have all the necessary leaders and the very best of them; the enemy will be no match for them. The golden age will be a messianic age. The consummation of the kingdom of God in the world will be brought to pass by the rule of this coming king.

The previous oracle links the earlier prophecies with the coming of the Messiah. In the oracle beginning in verse 7, the Messiah will expand His kingdom through the nations of the world by means of the remnant.

Dew is life-giving water that comes from God—humans are powerless to create or control it (5:7). This water comes from the Lord to and for people, and when it comes, it covers everything. This sets up the promise that comes next. As before in Micah, a parallel structure appears in verses 7–8. Each verse has as its subject the remnant among the nations, and each has a description in simile form of what the remnant will be—like dew and like showers in the first case; like a lion and like a young lion in the second. Each concludes with an explanation of the descriptions—in the first case, an image of salvation; and in the second, judgment and destruction.

The promise for the remnant includes a new strength for the group (5:9). But this eventual blessing can come only when God punishes His own people in order to purify them (5:10–14). The destruction in Micah's own day comes by means of the Assyrian invasion, and it will continue with the exile to Babylon (which has already been foretold by Micah). The specific details of the destruction highlight God's anger at Israel's worship of false gods. The word translated *destroy* or *demolish* in verse 14 is the same word used in Leviticus concerning the punishment of sin in the camp in order to maintain a holy people (Leviticus 17:10; 20:3).

MICAH 6:1–16

MORE ACCUSATIONS

Setting Up the Section

The first oracle in chapter 6 is a kind of lawsuit God brings against the people. Then the chapter closes with a pronouncement of Israel's sentence.

The opening phrase of the chapter highlights that these are the Lord's words spoken through Micah. The following case or lawsuit against the people is a common theme in the Prophets. The Lord is the plaintiff, witnesses are called, the evidence is presented, and a judgment is rendered.

The mountains in verse 2 are personalized and called upon as witnesses for several reasons: First, they are the original witnesses of the covenant God made with His people when they entered the promised land (Deuteronomy 27:12–13). Also, Micah indicates that they are enduring and unchanging, outlasting a thousand generations of God's people, and can therefore bear witness to the everlasting validity of God's covenant with His people.

God defends Himself against the complaint of His people, as they essentially blame Him instead of themselves for the present calamity (6:3). This extends the metaphor of God trying His people before a court, and here He is making His case. In the next two verses (6:6–7), Israel replies, saying it will perform rituals and sacrifices. But as seen often in the Prophets, God responds strongly, saying He doesn't want such things. Instead, we read one of the most well-known verses in Christian history, because it succinctly states God's desires for His people (6:8). It is a magnificent account of what true covenantal life involves and requires, and what God's gracious salvation must and will bring to pass in the lives of those who trust in Him. This idea expressed in verse 8 represents one of Micah's chief emphases. The failure of Israel's faith is demonstrated in the people's indifference to justice and mercy toward others, especially toward those who are poorer or weaker than themselves.

Critical Observation

In the Old Testament, a call to remember carries the idea of participation (6:5). In remembering, the people are reliving and reclaiming events of the past. This is very much the same thing that is involved, or is to be involved, in the Lord's Supper when we are told to "do this in memory of the Lord." We are to bring what He did into our present experience.

Verse 9 is a summons to the city to listen to what the Lord has decided. In the legal analogy, this is the sentencing phase of the oracle. The rod mentioned in this verse is a picture of the Assyrians, who will attack and who will function as God's chastisement of His people.

Demystifying Micah

An *ephah* (6:10) equals twenty-two liters or about a half-bushel. Lack of technological expertise made the manufacture of precise weights and measures impossible. All you needed to make an unfair profit was an ephah that actually held less than it should, so then you would get the price for a full ephah while giving less than an ephah to your customer. There was little a customer could do in the day before weights and measures inspectors. Besides, as Micah says in chapter 2, the authorities were in the pocket of the cheating merchants.

Verses 10-13 catalog Israel's sins, beginning with cheating in business practices. The wealthy who are called out in verse 12 are the royal family, the land barons, and the military elite. We have already heard of their unjust treatment of the middle class in 2:2, 8-9 and 3:11. What comes next is the righteous sentence of the Judge they have ignored (6:13). The actions to avoid God's punishment will be futile; verses 14-15 show how normal activities for sustenance and comfort will no longer suffice.

In the final verse of this chapter, we see the only mention of kings by name in a prophetic message. It suggests that the sins of Omri and Ahab, more than a century before Micah's time, had by this time served as a paradigm for falling away from faith and engaging in injustice (6:16; see 1 Kings 16:23-30).

The judgments pronounced in verses 13-16 are the very curses that God long before (all the way back to Deuteronomy and Leviticus) promised to visit upon His people if they proved unfaithful to His covenant with them.

MICAH 7:1-20
EVENTUAL HOPE

Setting Up the Section

While Micah's prophecy is full of solemn accusations and bleak acknowledgments, it ends with a sense of triumph. It is Micah's statement of faith.

Chapter 7 opens with an image that anyone in Micah's agricultural society would understand—a vinedresser and orchard manager who, after long and patient labor, finds his vineyard stripped by vandals. God feels the same way when He comes to delight in His people and finds, instead, so much sin. The last part of verse 2 can sound like a manhunt, but it is actually a reference to the way in which fellow countrymen are mistreating each other (7:1-2).

Micah again specifically calls out the leaders and judges for their sins (7:3). In verse 4, he calls the best of them a briar, and a group of them like a hedge of briars, again an agricultural reality for the original audience. Briars only keep people or animals from harvesting ripe fruit—they leave painful digs and scratches on those who try. In this case, the briars are obstructing justice.

The watchmen in verse 4 won't help protect anyone, and this repeats the idea that one should not trust in his own protection, because God is the only source of protection, safety, and peace. Further, even the most intimate human relations snap under the strain of the terror of enemies, and each one looks out for oneself, as is happening to these people (7:6). This is a fitting sentence for a nation that preys upon its brothers (7:5-6).

Micah watches in hope for the Lord and waits for God his Savior (7:7). The appropriate response to such a moral and spiritual catastrophe is just so: to wait upon the Lord.

Take It Home

The instruction to wait on the Lord is found in a great many other such passages: Psalms 37:7; 38:15; Lamentations 3:26; and many more. People must humbly submit and wait upon the Lord's outcome. It is not ours to worry or fret, or to take matters in our own hands by doing what the Lord forbids. We must simply wait upon the moving of God. In the meantime, a proper spiritual posture for the believer is to always look to God to redress wickedness and, in the meantime, serve Him faithfully. Micah watches in hope for the Lord, and he waits for God his Savior. This is the most appropriate response in the midst of a moral and spiritual catastrophe.

The next section of verses (7:8–13) opens almost like a psalm, with Jerusalem telling her enemy not to gloat. She is being punished justly for her sins; but precisely because the Lord always does what is right, the remnant within Israel who acknowledges their sin and repents will once again enjoy the Lord's favor. Though she sits in darkness now, she will again sit in the light. And, then, those who were the instrument of her downfall will reap their just punishment.

In verse 11, the prophet speaks to Jerusalem, but the idea of walls here is not to imply defensive fortifications. These walls are more like the wall that surrounds a vineyard. Their mention speaks to Jerusalem's prosperity, not her self-defense.

Verse 12 indicates the universal reach of Yahweh's salvation—not just to one people, but all people. This is the fulfillment of God's ancient promise to Abram (Genesis 15:18) in a new and still more glorious form—the promise extends not just to the area but to the people in that area. God's justice will see to it that nations that leave Israel desolate will suffer a compensatory desolation (Micah 7:13). This last judgment is described in highly figurative language, just as it is everywhere else in the Bible.

With verse 14, the prophet turns from representing the Lord to Jerusalem and begins to represent the people in prayer to God. Addressing God as Shepherd is appropriate in several ways. In the ancient Near East, a king's role was to resemble that of a shepherd, caring for and protecting his people.

Bashan and Gilead are both known for their rich pastures, and thus they build upon the image of a shepherd (7:14). They are places fit for a king's sheep to graze. Israel doesn't possess these places anymore; they have been lost to her because of her infidelity to God. But Micah is asking that Israel be restored. It is not a presumptuous request, because God has already promised that Israel's former dominion will be restored to her (4:8). Micah's prayer is that God's Word, His promise, will come true.

The Lord interrupts and speaks in verse 15, promising to show His people in the future wonders of His grace and power such as He showed Israel when He brought them out of Egypt and through the wilderness. The stories of the Exodus are faith affirming for the people of Israel. They remember God's mighty acts as He freed His people and miraculously led them toward the land He had promised them.

After the brief interlude in which God speaks, Micah takes over again in verses 16–17. In these verses, the images of nations with deaf ears and hands on mouths represent a sense of awe and even a sense of being put in one's place. In fact, all the images in these verses are of people who recognize the greatness of Israel's God.

The final three verses of Micah's prophecy include three terms for sin (*sin, transgression,* and *iniquities*) and six descriptions of God's character: His pardons, His forgiveness, His ability to let go of anger, His delight in showing mercy, His compassion, and His faithfulness. These terms are reminiscent of the Exodus account in which God identifies Himself to Moses (Exodus 34:6). Micah sings the praises of the true God while educating his listeners and readers about the character of God.

Take It Home

An unworthy, undeserving, but repentant people can hope in a glorious future precisely because of God's unchanging mercy and because of His fidelity to His promise. Micah's prophecy reminds us all that while we will experience God's chastisement, there is hope for every heart that has the ability and the willingness to repent.

NAHUM

INTRODUCTION TO NAHUM

Nahum is a book that calls into reckoning Judah's enemy, Nineveh. A careful reading of this book reveals that the author has a high view of God and His Word; he preaches against idolatry, immorality, injustice, and all manner of sin.

AUTHOR

We don't know many facts about Nahum, but there is no reason to doubt he is the primary author of the material that bears his name. From his writing style we can assume he was born into a family with enough means to provide him literary training.

OCCASION

Nahum witnessed the reduction of his nation to vassalage during the early campaigns of Assyria. These events, a prelude and a means to the judgment of both Judah and Nineveh, are part of the process that accomplishes the restoration of God's people.

PURPOSE

Nahum writes his short prophecy (1) to announce the doom of Nineveh and the demise of the mighty Assyrian Empire and (2) to bring a message of consolation to an oppressed Judah.

THEMES

The most basic theological perspective of Nahum is that of God's sovereignty. God is seen as supreme over nature and nations. He moves in just judgment against His foes but with saving concern for those who put their trust in Him. God is shown to be jealous and to abhor sin, but He is also long-suffering and has distinct purposes for His redeemed people.

HISTORICAL CONTEXT

The origin and setting of Nahum's prophecy can be deduced from the earliest and latest events mentioned: the fall of Thebes (663 BC) in Nahum 3:8 and the fall of Nineveh (612 BC), an event that is predicted throughout the book. The book of Nahum is intimately bound up with this period of dramatic change.

NAHUM 1:1–15

THE DOOM OF NINEVEH DECLARED

Setting Up the Section

Nahum begins his prophecy with a notice of its central focus—Nineveh (1:1)—and then turns his attention to a description of Nineveh's certain doom (1:2–15). Throughout the book, Nahum's prophecies deal with Nineveh's doom, its eventual defeat, and its destruction. In the opening section, doom is declared to be certain, because it has been decreed by the sovereign and just Judge of the world, who deals equitably with all.

📄 **1:1–10**

A HYMN TO THE SOVEREIGN GOD

Nahum begins his prophecy with a two-part hymn that sets forth the theme of the section and depicts selected key elements of God's nature. The hymn emphasizes that God is a God of justice, who will punish the wicked and avenge His own (1:2). Further, He is a sovereign and mighty God who, although He is long-suffering, will defeat His guilty foes (1:3–6) and, though He is beneficent, will destroy those who plot against Him (1:7–10). The rehearsal of these general truths concerning the character and work of God provides a foundation for their application to the world situation of Nahum's day.

143

Nineveh, having plotted against God's people and afflicted God's people, will experience His judgment, while a previously punished Judah will know relief from affliction and be restored to peace and joy (1:12–15).

In the majestic hymn to Yahweh in verses 2–10, critical scholars have recognized the skeleton of an acrostic based on the Hebrew alphabet. The acrostic is difficult to trace in that the prescribed letter of the alphabet may occur within the line rather than as the first letter. However, the hymnic nature of verses 2–10 is undeniable.

By calling his prophecy a vision, Nahum underscores the fact that what he says is not of his own invention but is that which God has specially revealed to him. At the outset, then, Nahum makes clear that his words are not his own insights based upon his observations of the events of his time. Rather, they are nothing less than the message given to him by the sovereign God, whose word he must deliver however difficult it might be.

Nahum's prophecy is directed at Nineveh, as is made clear at the start. It begins with an indication of its theme: God is a God of justice who will punish the wicked and avenge His own (1:2).

Critical Observation

Nahum's employment of the idea of jealousy is in harmony with the familiar scriptural motif of the husband and the wife. This motif is often applied in the Bible to God's relationship to Israel. Israel had been the object of God's eternal love. She had been brought into the family of God in the exodus from Egypt. He had cared for her and nourished her in the testing of the wilderness and had brought her safely into the land of inheritance.

Thus vengeance becomes a key to understanding Nahum's prophecy. Because God is holy, He cannot let sin go unpunished. Because only God is perfectly holy, just, and wise, only He can exact the proper punishment (see Psalm 94). The last line of Nahum 1:2 is important for understanding the process of God's vengeance: It is not always immediate. At times He holds in reserve His wrath against His foes until the proper occasion.

Having drawn the reader's attention to a sovereign and just God who deals in judgment with the ungodly (1:2), Nahum further develops this theme as his hymn to Yahweh continues. The first part of the hymn (1:2–6) is drawn largely from traditional Exodus themes underscoring God's wrath against an unbelieving enemy. The second part (1:7–10) comes from a wider spectrum of praises to God for His defense of His own while defeating the enemy.

In all this, Nahum gives a graphic picture of the limitless and invincible power of God. Having painted such a poignant portrait, Nahum returns to the subject of the destruction of God's foes (1:8–10). God, in His judicial wrath, will come against them like a victorious commander pursuing his foes to the farthest recesses of the earth. Indeed, God's enemies will come to understand that He will overturn their insolent plotting against Him so thoroughly that, like men entangled in thorns or overcome with their own drunkenness, they will be easily overthrown. God's fiery wrath will consume them like fire. They will not devise their devious plot a second time.

The ruins of Nineveh show abundant evidence of the intensity of the conflagration that consumed the fallen city. Whatever application these verses have to God's enemies in general, it is obvious that Nahum's prophetic pronouncements have a particular relevance for Nineveh.

GOD'S JUSTICE FOR NINEVEH AND JUDAH

With the completion of the hymn, Nahum turns to the two nations and their capitals that are the subject of his prophecies. The latter half of his hymn has been directed against those who plot against God. Keying in on that term, Nahum turns to the supreme example of such activity: Assyria and its capital city of Nineveh. In four short verses, Nahum brings God's charges against Nineveh—it will be judged regardless of its seemingly limitless strength (1:11–12, 14). This judgment will result in a respite for Judah in its affliction (1:12–13). The section closes with a stirring message of good news: Because wicked Nineveh has been judged, a repentant Judah may once again worship God in peace (1:15).

This short section is distinct from the previous hymn in 1:2–10. In a dramatic structural shift from hymnic to narrative style, Nahum turns to Nineveh in application of the teaching of his hymn. Nineveh/Assyria is identified as a plotter, an identification that seems obvious in the light of the military exploits of its most prominent kings. The word translated in verse 11 as *wickedness* (NIV) is often translated *worthlessness*. It speaks of a character of life so totally reprobate that the term came ultimately to apply to Satan himself (2 Corinthians 6:14–15).

The initial phase of Nahum's messages against Nineveh follows in Nahum 1:12–14. For Nineveh, there is the solemn affirmation that her long night of cruel domination is soon to end. Nahum's use of the word *name* is particularly appropriate, as it here connotes *existence* (1:14). Nineveh/Assyria is to be destroyed and left without descendant.

So hopeless is Nineveh's case and so devastating will be her demise that she will not even have a memorial left to her greatness, nor will anyone erect a monument to her memory. Because of her debased activity, she has gained such contempt for herself that her demise will bring to the lips of the observers of her fall a sigh of relief and a song of rejoicing (1:15).

With the pronouncement of the irreversible decision of divine judgment, there is a good word for Judah (1:13). Nahum's prophecy is a near-historical realization of Isaiah's. Isaiah foresees the day when an oppressed Israel will be freed at last from oppressors and invaders, and its people will not only hear the message of the Lord's salvation but also experience the everlasting serenity that comes with His presence in royal power in their midst (Isaiah 52:1–10).

The emphasis of Isaiah and Nahum on God's good news becomes an important motif for the New Testament revelation. Jesus' birth is announced as an occasion of glad tidings (Luke 2:10), and Christ announces that His ministry is in initial fulfillment of the message of salvation and joy that Isaiah prophesied (compare Luke 4:16–21 with Isaiah 61:1–2). Peter makes clear to Jew and Gentile alike that Christ has effected their full salvation, with the result that God's full peace can be enjoyed by all (Acts 10:34–43), a message of good news that Paul likewise affirms (Ephesians 2:14–18). It is no wonder, then, that Paul later builds on the theme of the message of good news and peace that Christ has provided both as scriptural evidence for the Jew and as a challenge to all believers to bear the gospel to a needy mankind (Romans 10:9–15; see Isaiah 52:7; Nahum 1:15).

NAHUM 2:1–13

THE DOOM OF NINEVEH DESCRIBED

Setting Up the Section

Having declared Nineveh's certain doom and Judah's sure relief, Nahum turns to the chief consideration of his prophecy: the fall of Nineveh. The whole section is filled with the book's basic thesis: God will punish wicked Nineveh and restore His own people. This theme is developed with regard to Nineveh by means of a long narrative section (2:3–10) and a woe oracle (3:1–7).

📖 2:1–2

GOD WILL PUNISH WICKED NINEVEH AND RESTORE HIS OWN

The fate of Nineveh is carried forward in the announcement of the arrival of its attacker. In the light of the critical announcement, Nahum issues a fourfold command. Each of the imperatives in verse 1 produces a staccato effect and lends urgency and dramatic appeal to the scene. Nahum's admonitions are probably to be understood as irony, perhaps with a touch of sarcasm. Because Nineveh's doom has already been announced (chapter 1), all such efforts are obviously destined for failure as God restores His own (2:2).

FIRST DESCRIPTION OF NINEVEH'S DEMISE

Nahum now turns from his introductory theme to the first of two descriptions of Nineveh's certain destruction. The section contains two parts: (1) a description of the attackers (2:3–6) and (2) the consequences of the attack (2:7–10). It is marked by several distinctive literary features by which the poet makes skillful plays on words.

Nahum's description of the attack against Nineveh begins with a consideration of its attackers (2:3–6). In these verses, there is a clear pattern describing the siege: the enemy's assembling of his forces (2:3), the initial advance (2:4), the all-out attack (2:5–6), and its aftermath (2:7–10). The scene progresses from one of preparation and advance to one of conflict.

As the account unfolds, the attackers have gained entrance to the city, for the Assyrians are seen as being captured and led away into exile, while the women, pleading for mercy and bewailing their fate, are led away moaning.

The inevitable consequences that follow the city's capture are then detailed in verses 8–10. The fate of the fallen city is in view. Conquered Nineveh is said to be like a pool of water. The simile is effective and appropriate. Mighty Nineveh lay in a favorable location that has blessed her with an adequate water supply. But now the blessing has turned into a curse at the hands of the enemy, whose siege has left Nineveh a "leaking water reservoir" (2:8 NLT). The panicked masses flee from the waters and the crumbling city.

Demystifying Nahum

In remarkable agreement with Nahum's prophecy that there is no end to Nineveh's treasures is the factual account in the Babylonian Chronicle that the spoil taken at Nineveh's capture is "a quantity beyond counting." The city is completely sacked.

THE DISCREDITED CITY

Contemplating the demise of arrogant Nineveh, Nahum utilizes a taunt song, a literary form common in the ancient Near East. Using an extended metaphor (or allegory), Nineveh is ironically compared to a lion's den, now no longer the lair of an invincible predator or a den of refuge for its cubs but reduced to ashes. Nineveh will be judged for its selfishness, rapacity, and cruelty.

Nahum can now ask, "Where?" The mighty lion of the nations (Assyria) used to proceed at will from its impenetrable lair (Nineveh) to return its prey to its pride (the citizens of Nineveh). Where is all of that now?

Like Nahum's first oracle (chapter 1), this section ends with a pronouncement of judgment for Nineveh/Assyria, but it includes a message of hope for Judah (2:12–13). Nahum's second oracle is not yet through, however, and before he adds a further note of good news (3:19), he will again consider the defeat and demise of Nineveh, detailing the reasons for the divine sentence (3:1–7).

NAHUM 3:1–19

THE DOOM OF NINEVEH DETAILED

Setting Up the Section

With the completion of the first description of Nineveh's doom, capped by a taunt song castigating the discredited city (2:3–13), the demise of Nineveh is rehearsed again, this time underlining the reasons for the devastation (3:1–7). Nahum will build upon that description with another taunt song, which will occupy the greater portion of the third chapter (3:8–19).

📄 3:1–7

SECOND DESCRIPTION OF NINEVEH'S DEMISE

Nahum writes his second description of Nineveh's certain doom in the form of a woe oracle. The initial *woe* is a word drawn from a lamentation liturgy for the dead. As utilized by the prophet, while containing a prophetic declaration and description of the coming judgment, it also constitutes a formal denunciation of the doomed city. Woe oracles normally contain three elements: invective (3:1, 7), threat (3:2–3, 5–6), criticism (3:4).

In verses 2–3, Nahum moves to a vivid description of the coming battle. Whether reporting what he has seen in a vision or merely envisioning the future scene, his portrayal is done with picturesque brevity using vivid images.

This nation who had brought havoc and ruin to so much of the ancient Near East will now face death and destruction. Here again a notable crux occurs. Does the statement relative to Nineveh's harlotry (3:4) explain the death and destruction described in the previous verses, or does it initiate the following declaration of God's judgment against the city?

Further, Nineveh will be pelted with filth (3:6). The word translated *filth* denotes that which is detested. A strong word, it is usually reserved for contexts dealing with aberrations connected with pagan worship. The word carries with it the idea of the loathing that all such detestable practices produce; the thought is that despoiled Nineveh will be treated as a detested and abominable thing.

The woe reaches its climax with a sarcastic appraisal of Nineveh's hopeless plight: Nineveh is destroyed, destitute, and devoid of mourners (3:7).

A COMPARISON OF NINEVEH AND THEBES

Before Ashurbanipal's victory, Thebes seemed unconquerable. As described in verse 8, Thebes was surrounded by a strong defensive wall and a water system that included lakes, moats, canals, and the Nile. Thebes had been able to boast of the help of not only all Egypt but also its seventh-century allies: Sudanese Cush, Put (perhaps the fabled land of Punt in coastal Somaliland), and Libya. None of these, however, supplied strength and protection for Thebes at all.

Verses 12–13 depict the hopelessness of Nineveh's defensive measures. Nahum says the city's massive fortifications will crumble as readily before the eager attackers as first-ripe figs fall into the mouths of those who shake the trees. Further, its famed defenders will prove to be no more successful in protecting the city than untrained and weak women.

A CONCLUDING CONDEMNATION OF NINEVEH

With verse 14, Nahum approaches the end of his prophecy. The verses that follow form the second portion of an extended taunt song that functions as satire. This short section contains two short commands given in irony—verse 14 through the first part of verse 15, then the last part of verse 15 through verse 17. Verses 18–19 are a final gibe that forms both a concluding denunciation and a doleful dirge.

Nahum's sarcasm is evident throughout. He prophesies that Nineveh will know the besieger's fiery torch and sword as the enemy sweeps through the city like a horde of devouring locusts. Nineveh's merchants and officials flee and leave her alone, leaderless, and ill-equipped to meet the advance of the army that is about to surround her.

As Nahum approaches the end of his prophecy, Nineveh's leaders are compared to shepherds who have nodded off to sleep and allowed the sheep (the Ninevites) to be scattered (in flight or in exile) and subjected to harm. Even worse, no one comes to gather them. The choice of this motif as the final one for the book may suggest, as many commentators have observed, that the "sleep" of the shepherds/officials is death (3:18).

Critical Observation

Nahum's words have been dramatically precise in their fulfillment. They find corroboration in the findings of archaeologists who note the hasty strengthening of the walls at strategic defensive positions.

The fall of the city due to water (1:8; 2:8) has been attested both by archaeologists and ancient historians. Unusually heavy rains were known to have given difficulty to Nineveh, which was served by three rivers: the Tigris, the Khosr, and the Tebiltu. A high-water season and a sudden storm, accompanied by the swelling of any or all three rivers, would account for the fulfillment of Nahum's prophecy.

Nahum also predicts the burning of the city (1:10; 2:13; 3:15), a fact confirmed by archaeological excavation. Nahum's emphasis on the destruction of Nineveh's temples (1:14) is also confirmed by the excavations at Nineveh. Minute details concerning the events of the final days before Nineveh's fall—such as the drunkenness (1:10; 3:11), cowardice, degeneracy (3:4), and the desertion (2:8; 3:17) of the city by its leadership—are also abundantly recorded in the ancient traditions. Nahum's prophecies concerning the final slaughter of Nineveh's citizens (3:3) and the looting of the city (2:9–10), its utter destruction (2:10; 3:7), and the virtual disappearance of its people (3:17–19) are facts confirmed in the ancient records.

Nahum once more utilizes a rhetorical question to conclude the section, here with sobering effect. Had anyone escaped Nineveh's cruelty? The implied negative answer guarantees the universal rejoicing over Nineveh's demise. This last use of a rhetorical question (a double one, in the light of verse 18) is one of five such instances that have been woven into the book's fabric. Twice, rhetorical questions introduce the poet's satirical taunt song (2:11; 3:8). Three times a rhetorical question closes a unit with striking effect: underscoring God's irresistible judgment of sin (1:6) and emphasizing Nineveh's much-deserved destruction (3:7, 19).

Take It Home

Israel no doubt joined in the exultation and took comfort in the good news (3:19). Her dreaded enemy has faced God's judgment, a reminder of God's promise concerning His judgment of all Israel's foes. May Nahum's words, as well as those of God's prophets, teach all God's people to trust fully in Him, the Shepherd and overseer of souls.

HABAKKUK

INTRODUCTION TO HABAKKUK

Like Nahum, Habakkuk begins by referring to his message as an *oracle*, or a message placed upon his heart by God. Like Nahum, Habakkuk assures his readers that what he is about to relate is not from his own ingenuity but is from God. Unlike Nahum, however, Habakkuk does not state that his message is specifically directed at any one individual or group of people, though he will devote a great deal of space to a denunciation of the Chaldeans, which is a representation of the Babylonians.

AUTHOR

We don't know anything more about Habakkuk than what can be gleaned from this book. We do know, however, that his authorship of this message was accepted from very early on.

PURPOSE

The book of Habakkuk is less of a prophet preaching to his people and more of a prophet speaking to his God. Habakkuk asks probing questions which lead from the current state of Judah to the eventual future of the kingdom.

OCCASION

While Habakkuk may differ from the other prophets in terms of whom he addresses in his message, he is similar in that he is troubled by the disobedience of his people. In Habakkuk's case, however, rather than pleading with God for more time or with the people for more attention, he questions why God's judgment hasn't already fallen on his nation.

THEMES

While judgment and the eventual vindication of Israel is a part of Habakkuk's message, as with other Old Testament prophets, he also addresses themes such as faith in God's sovereignty.

OUTLINE

HABAKKUK 1:1–17

THE PROPHET'S PERPLEXITIES

Setting Up the Section

Habakkuk plunges into a rehearsal of his spiritual wrestling with God. In so doing, he tells his readers of his perplexities as to the divine working and of God's answers to his questions (1:2–2:20). This chapter will consider Habakkuk's superscription, his two questions, and God's answer to the first.

📖 1:1–4

HOW CAN GOD DISREGARD JUDAH'S SIN?

Immediately after the notice of the source of his prophecy (1:1), Habakkuk at once plunges into a dramatic rehearsal of a time when the impact of Judah's unchecked sin overwhelmed him. His questioning of God forms the backdrop for the examination of the relation of God's holy standards to the operation of the divine providence that follows later.

The nature of Habakkuk's complaint to God, begun in the invocation (1:2) and elaborated in the statement of the problem (1:3–4), can be better appreciated when one examines the words he uses to describe his perception of Judahite society. They depict a society characterized by the general spiritual and ethical havoc that exists where such sin abounds.

Habakkuk is disturbed by God's silence with regard to his country's injustice and his own cries for help and intervention. His questions and doubts have an extra emotional and spiritual dimension. He is an unhappy, perplexed, and frustrated prophet.

📄 1:5–11

GOD WILL JUDGE JUDAH

To the emotional and dramatic cry of the prophet, God gives a dramatic, amazing answer—God is already at work on the problem. He will send the Chaldeans (Babylonians) to chastise Judah (1:5–6). God then supplies some additional details as to the martial abilities of the violent Chaldeans (1:7–11).

Critical Observation

The term *Chaldea* is used in reference to the tribes that lived in southernmost Mesopotamia. They made up the biggest part of Babylonia. By at least 705 BC, Chaldean king Merodach-Baladan took the title "King of Babylon," with the result that the terms *Chaldean* and *Babylonian* became used interchangeably in the Old Testament.

God's reply mirrors the words Habakkuk had used. God tells Habakkuk to look at the nations (1:5). God is already at work in and behind the scenes of earth's history to set in motion events that will change the whole situation. And when Habakkuk learns what is to happen, he will be utterly amazed. In fact, he probably will not be able to believe it.

The reason for Habakkuk's astonishment becomes apparent in verse 6: God will raise up the Chaldeans. Verses 5–6, revealing Habakkuk's astonishment at God's sending the Chaldeans to judge His people, are crucial to understanding the setting of the book.

By telling Habakkuk of the Chaldeans' future prominence, the Lord reassures him of His sovereign control of the details of history. Since God's prophet will be surprised at the announcement about the Chaldeans, God goes on to supply a brief résumé of their character and potentially devastating power (1:6–11).

Contrary to Habakkuk's complaint, God assures His prophet that He sees all that comes to pass and hears the prayers and complaints of His people. Habakkuk's own word is sent back to him. Has Judah done violence? It shall in turn suffer violence at the hands of a violent nation whose well-trained and battle-seasoned army will move forward with such precision that the whole striking force will march as one to achieve its objectives, at the same time taking many captives (1:9).

Although the language is hyperbolic throughout verses 6–11, in light of the ancient records it is not inappropriate. Many texts could be cited concerning the Chaldeans' successful campaigning. The picture of Chaldean armed might is of one who holds all his foes in contempt and mocks them. Such a nation knows no god but strength (1:10).

Habakkuk is informed, however, that God's avenging host is not without responsibility. The Chaldeans will be held guilty for their actions. Had Habakkuk listened as carefully to the last line of God's answer as he did to the extended description of Judah's chastiser, he might have avoided the second perplexity that gripped his soul, the report of which is contained in the verses that follow (1:12–17).

1:12–17

HOW CAN GOD EMPLOY THE WICKED?

God's answer and extended description of his agent of judgment against Judah puzzles His prophet. Habakkuk simply cannot reconcile God's use of the Chaldeans, a people more corrupt than those they are to judge, to punish His people. He begins his second perplexity with an invocation in which he expresses his consternation (1:12). Faced with the prospect of destructive judgment, perhaps even the death of the nation itself, Habakkuk cries out to Israel's God, the Holy One of her salvation, who alone is her refuge in such times.

The precise understanding of Habakkuk's impassioned words, "we will not die" (1:12), is difficult to grasp, but most see it as a statement of confidence in God.

Despite that confidence in God, Habakkuk has reservations concerning the situation. His reservations are detailed in verses 13–17. While he understands the necessity of Judah's judgment and the Chaldeans' role, he cannot comprehend why a holy God plans to use a nation more wicked than the nation He desires to punish. Not only does God's announcement seem out of character for a holy God, but also the use of the Chaldeans provokes another thought. Once this plan is put into operation, will not a helpless mankind always be at the mercy of these God-commissioned agents of chastisement (1:13–17)?

Adopting fishing imagery, Habakkuk portrays the scenario that God has set in motion as one of fishermen (Chaldeans) who use their powerful hooks and nets (military might and methods) to catch helpless fish and creatures of the sea (the various conquered peoples). The success of these fishermen will only cause them to rejoice and have their appetites whetted for still greater pleasures.

Habakkuk's fears are not unfounded, for the Chaldean war machine was effective enough to gain for them political dominance across the northern part of the Fertile Crescent and through the Levant to the borders of Egypt.

Critical Observation

Habakkuk takes his place beside many others—such as Job, the psalmist Asaph (Psalm 73), Jeremiah, and Malachi—who question God as to His fairness in handling the problems of evil and injustice. Like these other questioners, Habakkuk will be shown the necessity of fully trusting in God.

HABAKKUK 2:1-20
GOD'S SOVEREIGNTY

Instructions	2:1–4
The Chaldeans	2:5–20

Setting Up the Section

Habakkuk offers God's reply to his complaint, communicates an essential and time-less message about faith for all people, provides insight into the operations of divine government, and reveals the ultimate fate that will befall the wicked Chaldeans.

📄 2:1–4

INSTRUCTIONS

Habakkuk ends his complaint with a renewed statement of his confidence in God (2:1). He also reports his intention to assume the role of a watchman. As the city watchman mans his post atop the walls to look for the approach of danger or a messenger, or to keep watch over current events, Habakkuk will assume the role of a prophetic watchman, taking his post to watch for the Lord's reply.

Before God's specific points of reply are given to Habakkuk, He has preliminary instructions for His prophet. The Lord's commands are intended to prepare Habakkuk for the revelation of crucial issues relative to the operations of divine government that will introduce the discussion of the whole matter of Habakkuk's concern: the disposition of the voracious Chaldeans (2:5–20).

Critical Observation

The place of Habakkuk 2:4 in the history of biblical interpretation can hardly be overestimated. Its threefold citation in the New Testament (Romans 1:17; Galatians 3:11; Hebrews 10:38) attests to its basic importance to the Christian revelation.

Accordingly, verse 4 is best taken with what follows. Though it forms the essence of the divine revelation that is to be heralded to all, it is woven into the structure of verse 5, both verses thus serving as the basis for the woes that follow.

Habakkuk is told in verse 2 to write the issue of the divine reply upon tablets. He is to communicate a message of lasting importance. Everyone who reads or hears these words is to consider themselves a herald of a significant communication intended for all people everywhere. Probably the precise words are to be found in verse 4, the latter part of which is of crucial significance. The message is to be written plainly so those who pass by might be able to understand it and bear the news to others.

Habakkuk now is told the basic guiding principles upon which the operation of divine government unalterably proceeds until the coming of that final appointed time (2:3). The revelation of these truths will make clear the culpability of the Chaldeans (2:5), whose woe is pronounced in the rest of the chapter (2:6–20).

📖 2:5–20

THE CHALDEANS

Beginning with verse 5, God's answer takes the form of a logical argument: If it is true that the arrogant have ungodly desires and never come to enjoy the blessings of God, how much more certain is it that the qualities accompanying such an attitude will ultimately betray them? The underlying implication is clear: The Chaldeans' selfishness and success will be their undoing.

The first woe: The plundering Chaldean will be despoiled (2:6–8).

Each of the five woes, beginning in verse 6, pertains to one or more of the Chaldeans' sins. The first woe centers on the Chaldeans' rapacity. The language recalls their multiplying of wealth at the expense of others. The depth of the Chaldeans' insensitivity toward others may be seen in that they add to their riches by extorting pledges from their debtors, something condemned in the Torah and a violation against all mankind. The charge, only an example of the Chaldeans' unjust activities, provides entrée into the following metaphor taken from the world of finance.

Verse 7 reveals that those who had been so oppressed will arise suddenly and send collectors who will press their claims for back payment with a force equal to that of the Chaldeans' former violence. The chief point is that the plundering Chaldean will eventually know the effects of plunder himself. He who has so misused others—conquering, looting, and enslaving many—will himself experience the conqueror's heel and learn the sorrow of those whose people and possessions have been carried off as booty.

The second woe: The plotting Chaldean will be denounced (2:9–11).

The second woe underscores the Chaldeans' capacity for cunning schemes against mankind. Building upon the imagery in the first woe, the Chaldean is portrayed as one who achieves wealth through violence and evil means. Verse 11, with its stone walls and beams, is a reference to the Chaldeans' building projects. In the end, the Chaldeans will have no lasting empire.

The third woe: The pillaging Chaldean will be destroyed (2:12–14).

The image of construction found in the second woe is continued in the third. The chief materials used in constructing the city are seen for what they are: bloodshed and injustice. Such conduct is an affront to a holy and righteous God. It marks the Chaldeans as those who, unlike the righteous who reflect God's standards, are arrogant and presumptuous.

Babylon (and all such wicked people) will be judged, not only for her unbridled arrogance, but also because God's purposes include a universal experiencing of His own glory. The words of verse 14 are adapted from Isaiah 11:9. Isaiah's prophecy looks ahead to the great messianic era in all its fullness and perfection; Habakkuk uses it to validate the pronouncement of the destruction of the Neo-Babylonian Empire.

The fourth woe: The perverting Chaldean will be disgraced (2:15–17).

The tie between the third and fourth woes is not as pronounced as between the first and second or the second and third. However, they do have in common a reference to a city or town (2:12, 17).

The fourth woe begins with an invective formed with a strong allegory. The Chaldean is a man who gives his neighbor a drink in seeming hospitality. The apparently innocent cup contains a draught of wrath, for it is designed to get its partaker drunk. The allegory depicts the giver of the drink as one who is forced to imbibe of his own drink and suffer the disgrace of exposure. Several familiar biblical motifs and expressions are contained in verses 15–16. The cup as a motif of judgment is well attested elsewhere. Particularly enlightening for the understanding of Habakkuk's fourth woe is Jeremiah's use of the cup to portray God's relation with Babylon (Jeremiah 51:6–8).

Habakkuk makes the same point, although the image is slightly different. The Chaldean now knows the shame he has brought on others. Therefore, he is given a sarcastic command: "Go on! Drink and expose yourself!" (2:16). The last imperative is graphic. It means to show oneself as uncircumcised. Not even in the marks of his body can the Chaldean claim covenant relationship with Yahweh.

The reason the Chaldean must drink the cup follows in verse 17. His will be a wanton disregard of the value of the natural world, the animal kingdom, and civilized humanity.

The scene shifts to the animal kingdom. It, too, will suffer violence at the hands of the Chaldeans. The natural and animal worlds are often made unwilling participants in mankind's sin and greed. It is a crime that has increasingly plagued human society. Such thoughtless conduct by the Chaldeans indicates again their godless arrogance and selfish presumption for which punishment must come.

The fourth woe is closed with a reiteration of the charge made against the Chaldean in the first. He will have a callous disregard even for the sanctity of human life. In his quest for power, he will destroy everything that stands in his way, be it lands, cities, or those who dwell in them.

The fifth woe: The polytheistic Chaldean will be deserted by his idols (2:18–20).

In drawing the woe oracles to a close, Habakkuk deliberately changes the order he has previously employed by beginning with the reason for the threatened judgment (2:18).

The religious orientation of the Chaldean is now examined and shown to be without foundation. His idolatrous polytheism is seen to be worthless. Since idols are only mankind's creation, to put one's trust in them is to trust one's own creation rather than the Creator.

Before going on to give the most crucial reason for the doom of the polytheistic Chaldean, Habakkuk delivers an invective and a threat (2:19).

The fifth woe ends with a pronouncement that displays the vast difference between Israel's God and the gods of Babylon. Unlike those gods, who have neither life nor word of guidance for their followers, Yahweh is a living God. The gods of Babylon (and their devotees) can only remain silent before Him.

The invective and threat against Babylon (2:19) thus have more than sufficient cause. Since the Chaldeans worship gods of their own creation (2:18) rather than the Creator, controller, and consummator of history, their condemnation is certain. This is their most besetting sin. The verdict is final. Habakkuk can be assured that the Chaldeans will be judged, for they will violate the standards of God.

Verse 20 has another application. Because the idolatry that leads to the neglect and rejection of God is a universal problem, all the earth is to be silent before the living God.

HABAKKUK 3:1–19

THE PROPHET'S PRAYER AND GOD'S EXALTATION

Setting Up the Section

A perplexed prophet had awaited and received God's instructions in chapter 2. In humble response, Habakkuk turns in prayer and praise to God.

3:1–2

THE PROPHET'S PRAYER

Having heard and understood God's principles of judgment and their application, Habakkuk returns to the matter of Judah's judgment. What follows is his prayer psalm, a composition to be set to music for use in worship.

In verse 2, Habakkuk begins his prayer with a cry and a statement of praise that reflect his fear of God. The choice of the word *Lord* (Yahweh) rather than a more general term probably emphasizes the fact that Habakkuk addresses his words to Israel's covenant God. He has heard of Yahweh's past mighty deeds. Habakkuk has in mind the Exodus, the subject of verses 3–15.

In accordance with God's message of the near chastisement of Judah, Habakkuk prays for God's miraculous intervention. He asks that (as in the past) God will renew His deeds and thus again make known His work of redemption. With an aching heart, he urges God to be compassionate in the coming turmoil.

3:3–15

THE REDEEMER

Habakkuk has prayed for God's mercy in the midst of judgment. He does so on the basis of his consideration of God's past redemptive acts for His people, some of which he now rehearses for all to contemplate. The prayer-psalm-poem consists of two distinct works (3:3–7 and 3:8–15). The first poem deals with Israel's movement up from the Sinai Peninsula, on the way to the Jordan River crossing.

In a graphic simile, the brilliance of God's glory is detailed. The association of the glory of the Lord with Sinai is unmistakable; the point here, however, may be that the same glory that was seen at Mount Sinai and traveled with the people on their journeys

(Exodus 40:34–38) now moves in surpassing brilliance ahead of them. This first poem closes with a consideration of God's initial strikes against the enemy (Habakkuk 3:6–7). The land of the Midianites is identified primarily with the southern part of Transjordan, and evidence now exists that Cushan was also located there.

The second poem is a victory ode that sings of the mighty strength of Israel's Redeemer. His power is displayed at the waters of testing (3:8–9), unleashed in the natural world (3:9–11), and viewed by the enemy (3:12–15). Whereas the first two sections deal in a general way with the entire Exodus event, the final section fixes its attention on the initial stage of the Exodus.

Addressing God personally, Habakkuk asks whether His actions against the waters are out of anger. All three words for wrath here characterize God's judicial activity against anything that opposes His will. Yahweh is portrayed metaphorically as Israel's mighty warrior who appears in His battle chariot, armed with bow, club, arrows, and spear (3:8–11). This is no cosmic battle between deities; Yahweh comes as Israel's champion against human opponents.

The reference to waters here probably refers to God's activities in the entire Exodus event. The theme of water is prominent not only in the triumph at the Red Sea (Exodus 14) but also in passing through the Jordan (Joshua 3–4).

The scene changes from preparation to engagement in battle. The predominant image in this description of nature's response is the agitation of cosmic waters. The description in verses 9–10 fits well with the details of the crossing of the Jordan. The drama of warfare continues in verse 11 with a hyperbolic description.

Habakkuk had begun his prophecy with a perplexity as to why God tolerates injustice (1:2–3). When he is informed of God's intention to use the godless Chaldeans to bring judgment to His people (1:5–11), the prophet is all the more perplexed (1:12–2:1). The words of the ancient epic poem that he now considers remind him of the just nature of God.

The poem closes with details that provide a follow-up to the previous scene (3:14–15). The enemy's warriors storm out against the people of God like brigands coming upon the helpless. If, as suggested above, verse 8 deals primarily with the events toward the end of the Exodus experience, verse 15 produces the basis for the whole chain of events: the great deliverance from Egypt. The double psalm thus ends on a note of redemption. Israel's God, who brought them through the waters of testing with a mighty power that left all nature in convulsion, and who led His people in triumph, is the One who has been with them since the deliverance out of Egypt.

THE PROPHET'S PLEDGE TO THE REDEEMER'S PURPOSES

Habakkuk ends his prophecy with affirmations of personal commitment and praise. Having been dramatically reminded of the past exploits of God against the wicked and His saving intervention on behalf of His people, the prophet is overwhelmed. Now that he understands who God is and the principles and methods of His activities, it is enough for Habakkuk. He will trust Him through the coming hour of judgment and rejoice no matter what may happen (3:16–18). The words for *rejoicing* here represent strong emotions; Habakkuk used them previously to express his anxiety over the unbridled avarice of the Chaldeans (1:14–15). Here he underscores his repentant heart and triumphant faith. Together these words express his resolve not merely to rest in the Lord's will through everything that will come to pass but to rejoice fully in his saving God.

Borrowing phraseology from the repertoire of ancient Hebrew poetry, he closes the account of his spiritual odyssey on a high note of praise (3:19). The order is significant. Whatever strength he has he owes to the One who is his strength; but basic to everything is the fact that Yahweh is his Lord and his Master, the center of his life.

Habakkuk 3:8–15 constitutes a victory song commemorating the conquest itself and points to the basis of that success in the Exodus event, particularly in the victory at the Red Sea. After Habakkuk pleads for mercy in the midst of wrath (3:2) and reviews God's past record (3:3–15), his reverential trust in God is renewed. Israel's great Redeemer is his also. He will trust in the Lord no matter what happens (3:16–19). He who had acted both in judgment and deliverance for Israel in the past can be counted on to do so once again, both for Israel and His prophet. Thus Habakkuk's final prayer of praise to Israel's Redeemer stands not only as a unified composition but also as the climax to the whole prophecy.

ZEPHANIAH

INTRODUCTION TO ZEPHANIAH

Zephaniah denounced the materialism and greed that exploited the poor. He was aware of world conditions and announced God's judgment on the nations for their sins. Above all, God's prophet had a deep concern for God's reputation and for the well-being of all who humbly trust in Him.

AUTHOR

Although some concern has been raised with regard to many passages in the book that bears his name, Zephaniah has generally been accepted as the author of most of this book. Zephaniah traces his patrilineage four generations to a certain Hezekiah. Jewish and Christian commentators alike have commonly identified this Hezekiah with the king by that name, though this is not conclusive.

PURPOSE

Zephaniah speaks out for God and against wickedness. He writes to inform and warn his people of God's coming judgment, not only against all the world, but also against Judah and Jerusalem. Zephaniah also writes to give the people details of the fearsome events of the Day of the Lord that must come because of sin and because of the Lord's undying concern for His people who have humble and contrite hearts.

OCCASION

The occasion for Zephaniah's prophecy lies in the deplorable spiritual and moral condition of Judah in the early days of Josiah's reign. Taking the throne as an eight-year-old, Josiah finds himself the head of an immoral society. As Zephaniah writes, he is cognizant of the conditions that will surely spell the end of Judah itself (2 Kings 23:26–27).

THEMES

Zephaniah is best remembered for his presentation of God as the sovereign and just judge of all. It is He who punishes the wickedness of people and nations, particularly those who have opposed His people.

HISTORICAL CONTEXT

Few scholars have failed to accept that this book's author, as the first verse states, prophesied during the reign of Josiah (640–609 BC). Most discussions about the setting of the book of Zephaniah concern which period of Josiah's reign provides the backdrop, though many favor Josiah's early reign, because many of the problems that Zephaniah describes in his nation would have been corrected in Josiah's reforms.

ZEPHANIAH 1:1–18

THE ANNOUNCEMENT OF THE DAY OF THE LORD

Pronouncements of Judgment — 1:1–6
Exhortations Based on Judgment — 1:7–13
Teachings Concerning the Day of the Lord — 1:14–18

Setting Up the Section

Zephaniah begins his prophecy with notices of his reception of the word of the Lord, his ancestry, and the time of his ministry (1:1). He then announces the coming of God's worldwide judgment and supplies important details concerning the devastation of that coming Day of the Lord (1:14–18).

📄 1:1–6

PRONOUNCEMENTS OF JUDGMENT

God's prophet warns of a universal judgment that will one day descend upon the earth and all that is on it. The pronouncement is solemn; its phraseology is at first reminiscent of the flood (Genesis 6:17; 7:21–23). The disaster envisioned here, however, is more cataclysmic, for every living thing that dwells on the land, air, and sea dies. Man's sin is weighty, involving not only himself but his total environment (1:2-3).

Zephaniah alludes also to the Creation. His catalog of death is arranged in inverse order to God's creative work: mankind, beast, the creatures of the air, and those of the sea (see Genesis 1:20-27). The coming destruction will begin with humanity, who has denied the Creator and involved in his sin all that is under his domain (1:6). Because of their idolatry and apostasy, Judah and Jerusalem will find God's hand of chastisement stretched out against them (1:4-6).

Demystifying Zephaniah

Baal is a god associated with the storm and fertility; his veneration, together with licentious worship rites, is a constant source of temptation to Israel. Fascination with Baal had been a prime reason for the fall of the northern kingdom and will prove to be so for Judah as well. Although Zephaniah's denunciation of those who worship the hosts of heaven on the rooftops is a further indication of the turn that the worship of Baal often took, the adoration of Baal and the stars was a besetting sin in Judah when Josiah came to the throne.

1:7-13

EXHORTATIONS BASED ON JUDGMENT

In the light of the pronouncements of judgment, Zephaniah issues exhortations to Judah. Since the coming of judgment is certain, it is time for them to examine their spiritual condition. The unit is made up of two sections, each introduced by an imperative (1:7, 11) followed by additional details (1:8-9, 12-13). Accordingly, verse 10 is a hinge verse that proceeds on the basis of the time framework of verses 8-9 and predicts the lamentation of the merchants upon which the call for wailing is issued (1:11).

In view of the certainty and severity of coming judgment, Zephaniah advises silence and submission, fear and consecration. The motive for his call for silence follows in verse 7—the Day of the Lord. Although Zephaniah delays his description of the terrors of the Day of the Lord until the next section (1:14-18), the seriousness of that time is underscored in a dramatic metaphor of a sacrificial banquet. The sacrifice itself is Judah and Jerusalem.

Critical Observation

The metaphor of the sacrificial banquet provides a ray of hope in the clouds of doom. Although judgment is coming, there is still time. By acknowledging God as their Master and by responding in fear to the prospect of judgment in repentance from sin and repudiation of idolatry, God's people can join a believing remnant in coming to the feast as guests acceptable to Him. There is hope after all.

But there is also caution. Guests who remain unrepentant, and hence unclean, will be disqualified and will discover that they are not only invited guests but also victims. God has summoned others (the Chaldeans or Babylonians) who will destroy Judah, Jerusalem, and the unrepentant people who inhabit them (1:8–13).

In verse 8, Zephaniah gives a further message with regard to that coming day. Israel's leadership has adopted a foreign lifestyle, including its dress. There could be a veiled threat here. Do they prefer foreign attire? They will soon see the specter of foreign uniforms throughout the land. The threat is literally carried out (for examples, see 2 Kings 23:31–35; 24:10–16; 25:1–21).

Additional charges follow in verse 9, this time leveled against all the citizens of Judah and Jerusalem who have adopted pagan customs in their worship. In this case, the custom involves avoiding contact with the threshold of the temple by leaping over it. The practice had originated among the priests of the god Dagon, during the incident of the collapse of his statue before the ark of the Lord (1 Samuel 5:1–4). The verse goes on to report that the citizenry had perpetrated deeds of violence and deceit against the less fortunate in order to achieve their ambitions.

Further information concerning the sacrifice on the Day of the Lord is in Zephaniah 1:10. Although lamentation will come from all parts of the city, Jerusalem's greedy merchants will particularly be affected. From the Fish Gate through areas of commercial activity will come a great cry. Zephaniah tells the merchants to wail over their lost wealth (1:11).

Zephaniah concludes by reporting that God's judgment will be thorough. God's instruments of invasion will seek out every corner of Jerusalem in carrying away its treasures. If not in theory, at least in practice, the people of Judah behave like full-fledged pagans.

Take It Home

Whereas today's believers may applaud Zephaniah's warning to his fellow countrymen as well given due to the apostasy, immorality, and injustice of that time, we must apply Zephaniah's words to ourselves. A far more insidious danger lurks today: Apathy and inactivity will ultimately take their toll. Those who sit back and do nothing are just as culpable as those who engage in evil.

TEACHINGS CONCERNING THE DAY OF THE LORD

Zephaniah's exhortations based on the surety of the coming judgment are amplified with further information concerning the Day of the Lord (1:14–18). In language bordering on the later apocalyptic genre, he tells of frightful conditions in the natural world and terrible destruction throughout the earth.

Zephaniah declares that the Day of the Lord is near. He previously used that fact to provide grounds for submission to the Lord (1:7). Now he supplies added details to provide a further reason for the citizens of Judah and Jerusalem to repent and submit to God. He describes conditions that will exist primarily in the final stages of the Day of the Lord. But the prophecy must be viewed as one vast event. Some matters that he mentions will soon take place during Jerusalem's fall in 586 BC; others will be repeated in various historical epochs (AD 70), until the whole prophecy finds its ultimate fulfillment in the end times. Keeping such distinctions in mind enables one to keep a clear perspective as to both the meaning of the text and the effect the prophecy must have had upon Zephaniah's hearers. However much the events detailed here may have full reference only to the final phase of the Day of the Lord, they are an integral part of the prophecy and can occur anywhere along the series.

For this section of describing the Day of the Lord, Zephaniah has drawn upon the works of Isaiah, Jeremiah, Ezekiel, and Joel, but he is particularly indebted to Joel (see Joel 2:1–11).

Because of wrath against sin, the earth will experience great distress and anguish. Other prophets report that so severe will be the testing of the eschatological day that it will be called "the time of Jacob's trouble" (Jeremiah 30:7). Zephaniah makes a similar prediction and adds that the day will bring great anguish to all who experience it (Zephaniah 1:15).

Zephaniah goes on to describe conditions in the land and in nature (1:15). Destruction will dot the landscape; everything will be a desolate waste. Once again, Zephaniah draws upon phraseology employed by Job in describing a wasteland (Job 38:27). From the physical world, Zephaniah turns to the socio-political realm in verse 16. That day will be a time of great warfare. Zephaniah concludes by observing the tragic cost in human life and experience that all this will effect (1:17–18).

There is a play on words and ideas in verse 17. Because it is a day of distress and anguish, God will cause distress to mankind. So intense will be the conditions, that people will grope like blind men. How appropriate the punishment, since the charge against them is that they are spiritually blind (Exodus 23:8; Matthew 15:14; Romans 2:19; 11:25; Ephesians 4:18; 1 John 2:11). The effect of these tragic conditions is that human life (flesh and blood) is reduced to a thing of no value, with even corpses being treated as despicable refuse (Jeremiah 9:20–22; 16:1–4; 25:32–33).

The chapter closes with a reiteration of two prominent themes: (1) the self-indulgent greed of the godless wealthy and (2) the certain judgment of all men and nations (1:18).

ZEPHANIAH 2:1–15

DETAILS CONCERNING THE DAY OF THE LORD

Instructions in Light of That Day	2:1–3
Pronouncements of Judgment	2:4–15

Setting Up the Section

In light of the horrifying spectacle of the judgment of the Day of the Lord, Zephaniah presses his fellow countrymen to gather in repentance and humility before God. Utilizing images drawn from the process of separating straw from chaff, Zephaniah gives them a spiritual message designed to achieve the safety and deliverance of those who repent and put their trust in the Lord.

📄 **2:1–3**

INSTRUCTIONS IN LIGHT OF THAT DAY

In the opening of this section, Zephaniah uses straw and its collection to symbolize the assembling of people (2:1–2). He employs the concept of threshing to point to the necessity of being broken before God. He uses the idea of chaff in connection with the speed and ease with which it is blown away: Like chaff, the Day of Judgment is rapidly approaching; like chaff, wayward sinners will be destroyed in the Day of the Lord.

To *gather together* (2:1) means to come together in genuine repentance and submission to the will of God. Zephaniah's plea is urgent, for God's decree is settled and will soon be put into effect.

The second portion of Zephaniah's prophecies (2:4–3:20) is made up of pronouncements (2:4–3:7), an exhortation (3:8), and teachings (3:9–20). After his preoccupation primarily with the fate of his people in the first part of the book, Zephaniah turns his attention to the foreign nations (2:4–15). He began the first major portion of his prophecy by similarly considering all nations (1:2–3). Here he deals with specific nations that are tied to Judah's situation geographically and politically—Philistia (west), Moab and Ammon (east), Cush (south), and Assyria (north). Some translations refer to Cush as Ethiopia. The Cushites do eventually settle in that area, but for Zephaniah, Cush would have more likely referred to Ethiopia.

📄 **2:4–15**

PRONOUNCEMENTS OF JUDGMENT

Philistia

Philistine presence in Canaan had been reported since the days of the early patriarchs. The region was made up of city-states—Gaza, Ashkelon, Ashdod, Ekron, and Gath—four of which are mentioned in verse 4.

Zephaniah calls these Philistine settlers *Kerethites*, a name associated with the Philistines (perhaps an early tribe or a branch of the Philistines). According to Zephaniah, the prosperous seacoast district will become pastureland dotted with caves for Israelite shepherds and folds for their flocks. It will belong to the remnant of Judah (2:5-7).

Moab and Ammon

Zephaniah's pronouncements of judgment turn to Judah's eastern neighbors across the Jordan River, the nations of Moab and Ammon. Like the Philistines, these nations are numbered among Israel's traditional foes. Zephaniah's is not the first curse against this people.

Demystifying Zephaniah

According to Genesis 19:30–38, both Moab and Ammon are descendants of Lot, Abraham's nephew. They are conceived incestuously with Lot's daughters through a scheme set by the young women. Later in Israel's history, the Ammonites join the Moabites in hiring Baalam to curse the Israelites. Both nations harass the Israelites in the days of the judges, and Saul and David fight against them.

Zephaniah condemns both nations for their pride and their blasphemous insults against God and His people. He predicts that both nations, who have often worked together, will be treated like Sodom and Gomorrah—the whole area will be turned into a perpetual wasteland, overrun with weeds and pocked by salt pits (2:9).

Cush

Building on the concept of universal judgment in the preceding verse, Zephaniah tacks on the notice that the judgment of Cush, too, is part of the punishment that will overtake all peoples (2:12). Zephaniah's use of the term *Cushites* refers to Ethiopia, a part of Egypt. As the Cushite dynasty had passed, so also will Egypt and, one day, all earthly powers that stand in opposition to the Lord.

Assyria

In verses 13–15, Zephaniah's fourth message against the foreign powers swings around to the north—Assyria's capital city, Nineveh, will be rendered desolate, fit only for animals. Assyria's rapacity, pride, and cruelty demand her destruction. The reason for the demise of Assyria in general and of Nineveh in particular is given in verse 15—haughtiness. Centuries later, the city's ruins are unrecognizable.

ZEPHANIAH 3:1-20

FINAL WORDS

Setting Up the Section

Although the judgments in Zephaniah's prophecy and the pronouncement of woe upon Jerusalem at the opening of this chapter are not encouraging, the prophet's message is not yet complete. Before the final word has been said, his readers will come to understand that the day of the Lord's judgment, however dark, is but the path to a brighter day.

📄 **3:1–7**

JUDGMENT FOR JERUSALEM

Zephaniah concludes his messages on judgment by turning to his own nation and to the holy city in particular. In delivering his pronouncement against Jerusalem, Zephaniah utilizes the form of the woe oracle, including invective (3:1), reason (criticism) for Judah's punishment (3:2–4), and implied threat (3:5–7).

The judgment begins with a woe in which Zephaniah calls Judah's capital a rebellious and defiled city where oppression is the order of the day. These words describe a lifestyle and social structure at variance with God's character and laws. Zephaniah charges God's people with refusing to obey God's commandments and with unwillingness to learn from chastisement (3:2). They have neither concern nor time for God and His standards.

Even the priests of Jerusalem are defiled. They who were charged with the purity of God's house and the sanctity of His law have violated both. With bold metaphors, Zephaniah exposes Jerusalem's leaders for what they are (3:3).

Zephaniah reminds his hearers of Judah's ultimate leader (3:5–7). In contrast to Jerusalem's corrupt leadership, the Lord is righteous. Unlike the wicked who know no shame, He does no iniquity. With the light of each new day, He brings evidence of His unfailing justice.

Take It Home

God's righteousness may also be seen in His merciful dealings with His people in attempting to woo them back to Himself (3:6–7). Yet rather than demonstrating a desire for repentance, Judah and Jerusalem display only an increased bent for shameless corruption. How do we respond today when God calls us back to Himself? In particular, how do we respond if returning to the Lord requires us to leave a life that is comfortable and profitable for us?

3:8-13

ADDITIONAL TEACHINGS CONCERNING THE DAY OF THE LORD

Beginning with verse 9, Zephaniah turns from judgment to its outcome—God's blessing of the people of the world. In a vivid and varied metaphor, the prophet portrays a courtroom scene in which God rises first as witness on His own behalf and before the assemblage, and then presides as judge to deliver His righteous sentence. The double emphasis on judgment and hope is prominent in 3:9-20. Rather than being irreconcilable themes, judgment and hope are two aspects of one divine perspective.

Structurally, verses 9-13 provide a further reason for the exhortation to wait for the Lord (3:8). The first reason has to do with God's determination to gather the nations for the long-awaited judgment. The second deals with God's promises to a humble and purified future remnant. This section thus carries the author's thoughts to information concerning a future day that will provide the grounds for the closing admonitions of the book (3:14-20).

3:14-20

HOPE IN LIGHT OF THAT DAY

Verses 14-20 form a closing unit of instructions concerning the Day of the Lord. For Jerusalem, faced with the divine sentence against her, Zephaniah has words of instruction that will doubtless be carried out: Sing for joy, shout out loud, be glad, and rejoice. The commands are happy ones, heaped up to underscore the great expectation of the joyous times that lay beyond the immediate punishment. Although the command is aimed at the future Jerusalem, the message will not be lost on the godly worshipers of Zephaniah's own day.

The promise of release from fear is accompanied by words of encouragement not to let either fright or anxiety grip their hearts (3:16-17). Such assurances form a striking contrast with Zephaniah's earlier prophecy that the Day of the Lord will be filled with such horror that even the bravest of warriors will cry out bitterly (1:14).

In a climactic finish to all that he has prophesied, Zephaniah reveals the personal promises of Israel's Redeemer. Though from a literary standpoint verses 18-20 provide a further reason for the commands concerning rejoicing in verse 14, their force must not be missed: God Himself is speaking. The Lord's opening assurance here stands in stark contrast to His pronouncements at the beginning of the book (3:18). Unlike the earlier announcement of God's gathering of the nations together so as to sweep them from the face of the earth (1:2-4), the Lord will gather up those who have been driven away from Jerusalem and, therefore, from the opportunity to partake of Israel's periods of festivity. In God's providence, His sinning people had been punished by being carried away into exile as booty to their conquerors. Now judgment has given way to hope. God will regather His chastised and cleansed people in order to lead them home.

A threefold promise follows in verse 19, part of which is repeated in verse 20, emphasizing Israel's own festive future. The certainty of Israel's newly acquired felicity is assured.

Zephaniah closes his prophecy on the highest of notes. Not only is that which he has just recorded (3:18-20) the word of the Lord, but the whole prophecy is as well. God Himself has spoken.

HAGGAI

INTRODUCTION TO HAGGAI

Haggai's message, so effective in shaking the Jews of 520 BC from their lethargy, has an abiding relevance for all who fail to seek first the kingdom of God and His righteousness. The book of Haggai consists of four addresses.

AUTHOR

We know very little about Haggai outside of the four months of ministry described in this writing. He is mentioned in the book of Ezra.

PURPOSE

Haggai's purpose is clear. The exiles who returned to Jerusalem after their captivity in Babylonia have failed to complete the temple. Haggai calls these citizens to repentance and to action.

OCCASION

Haggai dates his first recorded revelation to the first day of the sixth month of the second year of the Persian king Darius Hystaspes (522–486 BC). Haggai's ministry falls between the sixth and eleventh months of Darius's second year. After years of exile in what was first Babylonia and then Persia, some of the Jewish exiles are allowed to return home. Their city is in ruins as is the temple, their center for worship. Throughout their history, the spiritual well-being of these people has been typified by the state of their place of worship. There is much in need of repair.

THEMES

Themes in Haggai include those familiar to other prophets—repentance, obedience, and worship. In Haggai's writings, however, these themes are built around the temple and all it means to the community of Jews.

HISTORICAL CONTEXT

In a day of profound discouragement and misplaced priorities after the Jews' return from Babylonian exile, the prophet Haggai sounds a call of rebuke, exhortation, and encouragement to his contemporaries. They have begun to rebuild their homes and businesses and to establish their statehood as a Jewish community but have been derelict in tending to the construction of the temple and making the Lord the central focus of all their hopes and dreams.

The prophets Haggai and Zechariah were contemporaries in Jerusalem at the end of the sixth century BC. This setting can be precisely identified; no other biblical author, with the exception of Ezekiel, ties his ministries and messages more closely to a chronological framework.

HAGGAI 1:1–15

REBUILDING THE TEMPLE

The Exhortation to Rebuild — 1:1–11
The Response of God's People — 1:12–15

Setting Up the section

The opening superscription provides the setting for the first oracle of the prophet (1:2–11) and identifies him and the immediate recipients of his message.

Haggai, whose name means something like "festive" or "festival," appears (apart from self-references in this treatise) only in Ezra 5:1 and 6:14. Since the oracle is transmitted on the first day of the month, a festival day (Numbers 10:10; 28:11), the prophet's name itself is revelatory of the occasion.

📄 1:1–11

THE EXHORTATION TO REBUILD

Zerubbabel son of Shealtiel, named in verse 1, is the second in a line of Jewish governors. According to Jeremiah, Gedaliah was the first governor (Jeremiah 40:7). The last mentioned in the Bible was Nehemiah (Nehemiah 8:9). The term *governor* suggests an overseer. Joshua the son of Jehozadak is here designated the high priest.

Verses 2–6 highlight the indifference of the people. The prophet chides the returned exiles and their fellow countrymen for putting their own interests ahead of the Lord and the temple. The result has been calamitous, for the more they seek self-satisfaction, the less they achieve it.

In verse 2, God's reference to the Jews as *these* (or *this*) people (rather than *my* people) implies alienation from God. The real issue is clear: The Jews who have returned from exile in Persia are more concerned for their own well-being than for honoring God by building His dwelling place among them (2:4–9). Throughout their history, establishing

God's dwelling had been an essential religious touchstone.

In verses 3–5, God, speaking through the prophet, shifts His attention from Zerubbabel and Joshua to the people at large, asking if it is appropriate for them to build their own houses even though they have protested building Yahweh's house. He challenges them so they might understand the connection between their negligence of God's house and their lack of success in everyday life (1:6).

Haggai gives four examples of the futility of selfish effort. There may be metaphorical overtones to this statement, but it also has literal meaning. Evidently the crops have failed, and now, when the fall harvest should be underway, prospects are grim.

Critical Observation

In verse 2—and elsewhere in 1:5, 7, 9, 14; 2:4, 6–9, 11, 23—Haggai refers to God in a way that describes His almighty power. This description is particularly important to the prophets, such as Zechariah and Malachi, who minister after the exiles' return and must encourage tiny, defenseless Judah in the face of imperial Persia's enormous might.

The exhortation in verse 5 is repeated in verse 7. In light of the preceding indictment (1:2–6), the people need to reflect on their ways. Their indifference leads to instruction so that the impasse might be resolved and the temple construction begun. The prophet points out that the people have sown much but harvested little and looked for much but received little (1:6, 9). Furthermore, they suffer from a lack of food, drink, clothing, and resources—a condition attributed to the drought the Lord brought upon the land, the effects of which are again listed in the same order: food, drink, protection, and productivity (1:10–11).

The cause of this disastrous condition, hinted at in verse 4, is articulated in verse 9: God's house is in ruins. The command to rebuild (1:8) is in strong antithesis to those who, in verse 2, insist that the time for rebuilding Yahweh's house has not yet come.

In verse 7, after the normal introductory formula, Haggai once more urges Zerubbabel, Joshua, and presumably the people to remember with seriousness their past failures and the remedy about to be announced.

Demystifying Haggai

Lack of any reference to stone or other materials does not mean the temple is a wooden structure, for clearly there is abundant stone from the demolished temple of Solomon lying all about. Ezra records a letter from Tattenai, governor of Trans-Euphrates (western Asia), containing a complaint to King Darius that the Jews, thanks to Haggai and Zechariah, are already rebuilding the temple with stones and timber (Ezra 5:8).

As though to reinforce His point that the promised glory has been frustrated by Judah's indolence and self-centeredness, Yahweh reiterates that the people have sought much for themselves but with meager results (1:9). As long as the temple remains unfinished, the people can continue to expect poverty and lack of fulfillment (1:10–11).

THE RESPONSE OF GOD'S PEOPLE

The first oracle, which ends with this section, consists of an address (1:2–11) and a response (1:12–14), bracketed by an introductory and concluding date formula (1:1, 15).

Haggai's stern rebuke and urgent appeal to the leaders and citizens has the desired effect, for they immediately resume construction on the temple, which had been set aside for sixteen years. Though fear is a factor, more important is Yahweh's pledge to be with them, and the supernatural stirring of their spirits to carry out His mandate (1:12–14). Within a month, they organize themselves, make their plans, marshal their labor force, and begin the work (1:15).

The people here are referred to as a remnant. The notion of a remaining few who will survive both apostasy and judgment to become the nucleus of a restored nation is pervasive in the Old Testament.

Verse 13 is an assurance of God's presence among the people. This assurance finds expression in His supernatural movement among them. Governor, priest, and people alike respond to the kindling of their dormant spirits by setting to work.

The date here reveals a twenty-three day interval between the time the message to rebuild is first proclaimed (1:1) and the time of its execution (1:14). We can't know with certainty the reason for the delay, but it may have been as simple as tending to harvest (1:11).

HAGGAI 2:1–23

LOOKING AHEAD

Setting Up the Section

In this chapter comes the message that the unpromising beginning of a second temple will someday give way to one whose magnificence and glory far transcends that of Solomon's. Yahweh is with His people and will, in line with His ancient covenant promises, reenact the Exodus and restoration to such a degree that the temple will become a place of pilgrimage from all nations. Yahweh will bring in the day of peace.

📄 2:1–9

THE GLORY TO COME

Virtually all students of Haggai agree that 2:1–9 (or 1:15–2:9) constitutes a single and undivided oracle, though opinions differ on its placement in the book. The oracle as a whole contains language that is markedly concerned with end times, especially in verses 6–9.

Critical Observation

Significantly, this word of Yahweh comes on the twenty-first of Tishri (October 17), which is precisely the seventh day of the Feast of Tabernacles. Exactly 440 years earlier (Tishri, 960 BC), Solomon had finished and dedicated his temple (1 Kings 6:38; 8:2), to which the prophet is about to compare the one under present construction. Twenty-six days have passed since construction began, and already the differences are becoming painfully evident.

No one will be more aware of the contrast between Solomon's temple and the structure under construction than those old enough to have experienced the Solomonic temple so ruthlessly destroyed by the Babylonians sixty-six years earlier. To these people, Haggai addresses his question. He concludes that they view the new building as inconsequential compared with the old.

In verses 4–5, Haggai speaks one more word of encouragement to the leaders and the people, urging them to be strong in boldness and confidence. The somewhat veiled allusion to Moses and Joshua in verse 4 (most appropriate in view of the name of the present high priest) becomes more transparent in verse 5, with its reference to the Exodus. Just as Yahweh had been with His people in the ancient days, so He will be with them now.

Haggai thus harks back to the past but also anticipates future redemption and glory. This provides an entry into the end-times message of verses 6–9.

In this first extended apocalyptic vision of the book, Haggai describes the tremendous upheavals that will attend the epiphany of Yahweh in the last days.

In verse 6, the objects of the shaking—heavens, earth, sea, and land—draw attention to Yahweh's violent intervention in the past and suggest that He will do so once more, and in just a little while.

These phenomena will accompany the new exodus and new covenant as well, as both Haggai (2:6–7) and other prophets attest. There will be a shaking of the natural structures and of men and nations. These cataclysmic events will cause the peoples to bring their precious belongings to the holy city and temple. Once this has come to pass, Yahweh will fill the temple with His glory. The house's glory will be greater than before (2:9).

The real glory of the final temple will not consist of material things. This may, in fact, be the primary thrust of verse 8. Haggai affirms that its glory will consist not of silver and gold but of God's presence (2:4–5) in the temple and among His people (2:7).

📄 **2:10–19**

THE PROMISED BLESSING

Many scholars divide the third oracle (2:10–19) into two sections—2:10–14 and 2:15–19. They do this because of the assumption that "this people" of verse 14 refers not to Judah but to Judah's enemies in the land. However, "this people" is a perfectly appropriate description of the Jews, especially since Haggai has already used this description (1:2).

The third oracle is dated on the twenty-fourth of Kislev (or December 18, 520 BC), about three months after the work on the temple had begun again in earnest (1:15) and two months after its pitifully modest prospect begins to become apparent (2:1, 3). The people have deluded themselves into thinking that holiness is gained merely by association with holy things (2:11–12) and have failed to consider that unholy associations render one unclean (2:13–14).

The specific occasion for the oracle is unclear, but it could well have been delivered as a warning against cooperation with the Samaritans and others in the work of the temple, and the religious influence the non-Jews wielded.

If so, it is clear why the hypothetical set of questions posed by Yahweh are targeted to the priests, the religious leaders. Verse 12 asks if a person can make unholy things into holy things simply by touching them with holy hands. The meats mentioned here, if profane because they are gifts from pagan kings, will remain profane no matter who touches them. The gifts of pagan kings, no matter the spirit in which they are given, cannot become clean and acceptable to Yahweh just because they come in contact with the sacred sites and rituals of the covenant people. Such gifts should, therefore, be politely refused. To fail to do so is to render oneself unclean (2:14).

Verses 13-14 represent a converse case. Granted, unclean things don't become clean by virtue of their association with the clean. However, will things that are clean become contaminated by the unclean? The answer is an unqualified *yes*. The example is the corruption caused by contact with a corpse. The dead body mentioned here isn't linked with something in the immediate context of this passage. The point is that God's people can pollute, and have polluted, themselves because of their ungodly associations (2:14).

Take It Home

While it is impossible to know precisely what calls forth these words of denunciation, the context of the book suggests that it is the people's self-centeredness and inverted priorities (1:2–4, 9), and their tolerance and acceptance of assistance of their pagan neighbors—assistance that involves even the presentation of sacrificial animals. Haggai's prophecy speaks to us today, not so much in terms of the food we eat, but in terms of the priority we place on our faith and the spiritual practices that sustain that faith.

The community's moral and spiritual defilement described in the previous passage calls for divine discipline (2:10-14). From the very beginning of their postexilic life, before the foundations of the temple were laid some sixteen years earlier, the people had suffered Yahweh's wrath because of their self-service (2:16-17). This chastening marks their whole life until Haggai, called by God, urges them to forsake their shortsighted materialism and resume the work of building a house for Yahweh.

The language of failed expectation here is like that of Haggai 1. Yahweh visited the people with drought, a generic term fleshed out in the blight, mildew, and hail of the present passage (1:11; 2:17).

In verses 18-19, Haggai refers back not to the initial groundbreaking for the temple in 536 BC (2:15) but to the renewal of construction exactly three months earlier. This reference provides a backward glance focused on the refounding of the temple and subsequent events. In spite of this backward glance, however, verses 18-19 relate to the present and future. The date of the laying of the foundation is the date of the oracle, the twenty-fourth day of the ninth month (2:18). The seed has already been sown, and the fruit trees promise rich production in the season to come, but the growing season is a future event. In the midst of December, there is little on which to subsist. Verse 19 contains a promise of better days ahead. Even though the vestiges of the people's previous disobedience remain to make their existence most uncomfortable, all this will change. God will begin a new age of prosperity.

ZERUBBABEL THE CHOSEN ONE

This fourth and final message of Haggai is received and delivered on the very same day as the third, but to Zerubbabel alone. The apocalyptic language focuses on the destruction of all things hostile to the rule of Yahweh, a destruction that cannot be separated from the last clause of 2:19. In verse 19, the promise to bless from that very day finds its expression in the end-times hope outlined in verses 20–23. In terms reminiscent of his second oracle, the prophet speaks of a shaking of heaven and earth and the overthrow and shattering of human kingdoms (2:6–7).

The difference in the two addresses is the results of the shaking. In 2:7 it results in tribute to Yahweh in His temple. Here, it is a defeat of the nations so severe in its results that no one and nothing remains but Yahweh and His own sovereign ruler.

Continuing with His focus on the future, the prophet introduces the climax of his message by relating it to "that day" (2:23). Since the context indisputably is apocalyptic in nature, the Zerubbabel to whom the oracle is directed cannot be the governor whom Haggai has so frequently addressed. Rather, one must see Zerubbabel as a prototype of one to come who will be Yahweh's servant and chosen vessel.

Demystifying Haggai

Zerubbabel the governor is a descendant of Jehoiachin, most likely his grandson (1 Chronicles 3:17–19; Matthew 1:12). Because of this, using his name in this oracle has prophetic significance. Zerubbabel is a link in the Davidic monarchy. It is to this monarchy that God promises eternal reign. When someone of that bloodline became governor of Judah, it must have seemed to the restored community that God's ancient covenant promise—that there would never fail to be a son of David on the throne (2 Samuel 7:16; Psalm 89:24–37)—had come to pass.

ZECHARIAH

INTRODUCTION TO ZECHARIAH

The books of Haggai, Zechariah, and Malachi were composed in the postexilic period of Israel's history to offer hope to a people whose national and personal lives had been shattered by the Babylonian destruction of Jerusalem and captivity of the people. Zechariah goes beyond Haggai's burden for the immediate, earthly situation of the postexilic community and sees, through a vision and dream, the unfolding of divine purpose for all of God's people and for all the ages to come.

AUTHOR

At least thirty people mentioned in the Bible bear the name *Zechariah*, which means "the Lord remembers." The prophet and author of this book, however, is further identified as being the son of Berekiah and grandson of Iddo (1:1). He was born during Judah's captivity in Babylon and returned to Jerusalem with a group led by Zerubbabel. Iddo was a priest during that time (Nehemiah 12:1-7), and Zechariah eventually succeeds his grandfather in that role.

Some people propose that the latter portion of Zechariah (chapters 9-14) likely has a different author. They cite a variation in writing style and the author's inclusion of historical events that span beyond a single lifetime. Yet those variations are not evidence enough to sway the beliefs of other scholars, who continue to maintain that the book has a single author.

PURPOSE

After about seventy years of exile in a foreign land, God's people are released to return to their homeland, only to discover that the walls and temple of Jerusalem have been demolished. Projects are planned for reconstruction, but the people need much encouragement and faith during this period. As both prophet and priest, Zechariah brings assurance of God's faithfulness and hope for the future of His people.

THEMES

Zechariah adopts an already existent apocalyptic tradition of writing from which he draws heavily and to which he makes a significant contribution. The apocalyptic format receives immeasurable momentum from the trauma of the exile, a calamity that not only shook the social and political structures of Judah but also threatened to undermine the covenant faith itself. So Zechariah shifts the focus from the present to the future, from the local to the universal, and from the earthly to the cosmic and heavenly.

HISTORICAL CONTEXT

The release of the people of Judah was in conjunction with the overthrow of the Babylonians by the Medes and Persians. Zechariah begins his ministry in the eighth month of the second year of the Persian king Darius (1:1)—520 BC. Zechariah's final chronological reference (7:1) is to the ninth month of the fourth year of Darius (518 BC). If one accepts that Zechariah is the sole author of the book, the latter date presumably marks the occasion for all the oracles and other messages of chapters 7–14.

The opposition to the rebuilding projects in Judah occurs prior to Darius, and serious antagonism of the Jewish people does not arise again until Xerxes (486 BC). It is safe to assume, therefore, that work on restoring the temple goes unimpeded during the two years of Zechariah's ministry.

CONTRIBUTION TO THE BIBLE

Rich in apocalyptic imagery and packed with messianic prediction and allusion, Zechariah's writings become a favorite of the New Testament evangelists and apostles. No minor prophet excels Zechariah in the clarity and triumph by which he looks to the fulfillment of God's program of redemption.

OUTLINE

ZECHARIAH 1:1–3:10
ZECHARIAH'S NIGHT VISIONS, PART I

Setting Up the Section

The overall message of Zechariah, though occasionally obscure, is largely clear and plain. The prophet seeks to comfort his discouraged and pessimistic compatriots, who are in the process of rebuilding their temple and restructuring their community, yet who view their efforts as making little difference in the present and offering no hope for the future. Zechariah challenges members of the restored remnant to work confidently and to fully expect that what they do will be crowned with success when God, true to His Word, will bring to pass the fulfillment of His ancient promises to their forefathers. This section introduces the book and covers the first four of eight visions the prophet sees in a single night.

📄 **1:1–6**

INTRODUCTION

The rather lengthy introduction to the book of Zechariah is clearly intended as a preface to all the night visions that follow (chapters 1–6), if not the entire book. This is evident from the fact that 1:7 is also an introduction, perhaps for the first vision only, but more likely for all eight visions that follow.

Zechariah, here identified as the son of Berekiah and grandson of Iddo (1:1), is also mentioned in Ezra (5:1; 6:14) and Nehemiah (12:16). However, both of those citations imply that the prophet is the son of Iddo, and neither mentions Berekiah. It is likely that Zechariah's father died young and Zechariah was raised by his grandfather. This would also explain why Zechariah succeeds Iddo as priest (Nehemiah 12:10–16).

"The second year of Darius" refers to 520 BC, and the "eighth month" is October/November, so Zechariah's visions are only a month prior to Haggai's final vision, which would have been December 18, 520 BC (Haggai 2:10, 20). Zechariah is likely quite young, and his ministry may have extended well beyond his people's return from exile.

Zechariah begins his book with a solemn exhortation to learn from history. God had been extremely displeased with the generations past (1:2) because they had stubbornly refused to heed the appeal of their prophets to turn to the Lord (1:3–4). *Ways* and *practices* (deeds) refer not to incidental sins but to a whole pattern of rebellion and disloyalty.

Zechariah next turns his attention to the calamity that overcame their ancestors because of their failure to heed the prophets' warnings. Both they and the prophets who had warned them had long since passed away (1:5), but God's Word had come to pass. The wicked nation had been overthrown according to the terms of the covenant, and those who lived to see it had been forced to admit that God brought to pass everything He had threatened (1:6).

The message of Zechariah will be precisely the same as that of his prophetic predecessors. His people must turn to the Lord in covenant affirmation if they expect God to reciprocate (1:3).

Critical Observation

Zechariah's use of *the LORD Almighty* (NIV) as a title for God (three times in 1:3) is most striking. In this book, the prophet uses the title fifty-three times. Yet such usage coincides with other prophets at work at the same time. Malachi uses the title twenty-four times, and Haggai uses it fourteen times in only thirty-eight verses. In light of the emergence of universal empires at the time, Judah needs to be reminded that the Lord is indeed almighty. He is the Lord of hosts— Lord even of those mighty worldly powers.

📄 **1:7–17**

VISION ONE: THE FOUR HORSEMEN

The second introduction to the book of Zechariah (1:7) embraces all the visions to follow (1:8–6:16). The next introductory passage does not appear until chapter 7. The date equates to February 15, 519 BC, in the modern calendar—approximately three months after the initial call of Zechariah (1:1) and two months after Haggai's last revelation (Haggai 2:10, 20). Significant events around this time that may have bearing on elements of Zechariah's first vision are (1) the return of Darius to Persia from Egypt (through Palestine) and (2) the approaching of New Year's day, a time when Zerubbabel will be crowned as Judah's king, restoring a Davidic successor to the throne (Haggai 2:20–23).

It appears that Zechariah is recounting a series of dream-visions from a single night. These dreams are not random or from his own imagination because they are presented in a historical and chronological sequence on one hand, and in an interlocking literary pattern on the other. Similarities are found between visions #1 and #8, #2 and #7, #3 and #6, and #4 and #5.

Both Zechariah's first and eighth (1:8; 6:1–8) visions feature four kinds of horses. Much effort has been made to connect the two visions, but the colors of the horses are not the same, and there is no reason to assume that the horses in both visions must match. In the first vision, either the man on the red horse dismounts and stands in the ravine, or the horse itself stands there with the rider still on him. Hebrew grammar favors the former, as does the description in 1:10. As for the three horses in the background, it is not certain whether or not they have riders. Presumably they do, because verse 11 indicates more than one speaker.

Critical Observation

The myrtle is a particularly appropriate element of this vision. A fragrant, decorative shrub that sometimes reaches the size of a tree, it is used in connection with the Feast of Tabernacles and in postbiblical times in betrothal celebrations. Its perpetual greenness and aromatic qualities provide a suitable setting for the inauguration of the Lord's domain, which is everlasting and pleasant in every way.

It seems that Zechariah stands with an interpreting messenger-angel and that both of them hear the answer to Zechariah's question as given by the man among the myrtles (the angel of the Lord). His response is confirmed by the riders of the horses. Overwhelmed by his own response, the angel of the Lord addresses the Lord Himself to ask about the conclusion of the seventy years of discipline. The Lord's answer is directed to the messenger/interpreter beside Zechariah, for it is the prophet who had raised the inquiries about the vision he had seen. That messenger in turn speaks to Zechariah, commanding him to deliver the Word of God to his people (1:14).

The mission of the rider of the red horse (and presumably all four horsemen) is to walk across the whole earth (1:10). To walk about on the earth is to assert sovereignty over it (see Genesis 13:17; Job 1:7; Ezekiel 28:14). Here the Lord, through the symbolism of four cavalry charges, announces that He is Lord of all.

The result of the horsemen's roaming the earth is that the land is at rest and quiet (1:11). It is therefore a suitable time for the Lord to end the judgment of the seventy-year exile by displaying His compassion for His elect people (1:12). His jealousy for Judah (1:14) is, after all, an expression of His singular interest in her and His determination to restore His people. The mention of Zion reflects the Davidic reign as part of the messianic program of redemption.

The nations, on the other hand, have become the object of the Lord's judgment. God had indeed been a little angry at His people (1:15), but the enemies of God's people brought about a measure of retribution beyond what God would have imposed.

This vision has clear implications for the end times, but it also relates to the historical circumstances of the late sixth century BC. The peace established by Cyrus strengthened and expanded under Darius, who put down rebellions associated with his ascension to the throne. Cyrus and Darius did not realize, however, that their universal peace was brought about by the Lord, God of Israel. The horses of Darius are, in fact, the horses of the Lord.

Still, the conditions are suitable for the seventy-year exile to be over. Jeremiah first refers to a seventy-year period, dating its end with the demise of the Babylonian (Chaldean) kingdom (Jeremiah 25:11–12). It is clearly understood, however, that the seventy years have a flexible starting and concluding date because their termination is also connected to the completion of the second temple (Zechariah 1:16). It may also be noted that the completion of Jerusalem's second temple takes place in 516 BC, exactly seventy years after the destruction of Solomon's temple in 586 BC.

Zechariah records in 1:13 that the Lord had spoken "kind and comforting" words to the interpreting angel. Those words are revealed in the oracle that follows the vision (1:16-17). God promises to either *turn* or *return* to Jerusalem (the intended translation is uncertain, as is whether the tense is present or future. But either interpretation would have been good news for the people of God).

We know from Haggai that God promises to bless His people, beginning with the ceremony of laying the temple foundation (Haggai 2:18-19). The work of reconstructing the temple began about five months prior to Zechariah's night visions (Haggai 1:15), but it is far from finished. The good news given to Zechariah is that what had been started will now be brought to fruition. Indeed, not only will the temple be rebuilt, but also the reconstruction will include outlying cities in addition to Jerusalem. They will become abundantly prosperous (1:16-17).

1:18–21

VISION TWO: THE FOUR HORNS

Just as Zechariah's first and eighth visions complement each other with similar themes and perspective, so, too, his second and seventh visions are a matched pair. They each have two parts, and both are concerned with the nations. This second vision has no accompanying oracle.

The connections between this vision and the first one are also striking. The fact that the first vision is of four horses and this one describes four horns and four craftsmen is significant. The horses of the first vision are God's instruments of dominion over all the earth (1:10-11); the four craftsmen will reduce the nations to defeat.

Zechariah's second vision contains two elements (four horns and four craftsmen), so the interpretation is divided into two parts. In response to the query about the horns (1:19), the angelic interpreter first asserts that they are scatterers of Judah, Israel, and Jerusalem. Under further interrogation, he adds that the horns are associated with the nations. The nations had used their horns (military might) to effect the dispersion of God's people (1:21).

As for the craftsmen, the messenger reports that their task is to bring down those nations, to nullify the effect of their great power (1:21). The ultimate result will presumably reverse the scattering so that the dispersed can return again to their land.

The listed order of those attacked is somewhat puzzling: Judah, Israel, and Jerusalem (1:19). Later, only Judah is mentioned (1:21). If Judah is seen as central, then Israel may denote the nation in its broadest sense and Jerusalem in its narrowest. The order indicates, then, that the scattering is total.

Some people attempt to identify four specific nations or events to associate with the horns. But what is suggested here (and elsewhere) by the number four is the universal character of the persecution of God's people by the nations. Israel's struggle against the nations had persisted from their settlement in Canaan until the fall of Jerusalem to the Babylonians. But the final destruction had been so climactic and irreversible that it stands out in Zechariah's text.

There is no reason to attempt to identify any particular forces to associate with the craftsmen. The word *craftsmen* used can apply to any skilled artisan regardless of his medium. But in this case, the way the word is used in the original language suggests that these four particular craftsmen are also destroyers, or devastators. They have come forth to throw down the arrogant nations that had scattered God's elect. After the Babylonian horn is cut off by the instruments of Darius, the rebuilding promised in Zechariah's first vision can take place.

📖 **2:1–13**

VISION THREE: THE SURVEYOR

Zechariah's third and sixth visions both have to do with measuring and/or dimensions, with a focus narrowed down from international interests to Jerusalem itself. In this vision, only Zechariah and one other unidentified man are participants.

It was necessary to reestablish the ancient boundary lines of Jerusalem preparatory to the city's full reoccupation. Zechariah witnesses a form of surveying, as the properties are measured out for redistribution.

Critical Observation

Before the fall of Jerusalem, Jeremiah had been told to anticipate the day when houses, fields, and vineyards would once more be bought there (Jeremiah 32:6–15). It had always been God's intent for His people to reclaim the land. Ezekiel, too, had been shown a similar scene, but the surveyor in his vision measured out the land with a reed (rod) rather than a cord (Ezekiel 40:3).

The task of the man in this third vision is to measure Jerusalem by breadth and length (2:2). The reason breadth comes first in this instance may be due to the orientation of the city. In fact, only here and in Ezekiel 40–48 are "breadth and length" designated rather than "length and breadth."

The interpreting messenger-angel appears again, this time to provide further information to Zechariah ("young man") than he had already obtained from the surveyor (2:4). This secondary messenger appears only in the first and third visions. In a sense, he is an interpreter for the interpreter. In this case, he urgently commands the first angel to go to Zechariah and provide the meaning of the vision. What is about to happen is imminent, and those who hear the message cannot be slow to act upon the news.

Zechariah is informed that the surveyor is in the process of laying out allotments in and around Jerusalem in preparation for the burgeoning population that will live there. In the absence of the walls that formerly stood, the old boundary lines will need to be redrawn. Jerusalem will be reoccupied by such a vast population that the walls that once enclosed it will be inadequate (2:4).

This prophecy has definite end-times significance, but it is also relevant for Zechariah's own circumstances. It is impossible to know a great deal about the construction and configuration of the walls about Jerusalem in the postexilic period. For the greater period of time, there were no walls—none sufficient, at least, to provide protection.

Demystifying Zechariah

It should not be assumed that Jerusalem had been continually without walls between the Babylonian conquest (586 BC) and the restoration work overseen by Nehemiah (completed in 445 BC). Ezra refers to walls existing during the time of King Artaxerxes (464–424 BC) that were most likely constructed during the earlier reign of Xerxes (Ezra 4:12). And Nehemiah's appeal to Artaxerxes was that the walls of Jerusalem had been destroyed and needed to be rebuilt (Nehemiah 1:3; 2:4–5). Everyone knew that the Babylonians had leveled the walls of Jerusalem, so Nehemiah's surprise at hearing that the walls were missing suggests that the walls had been replaced for a time and destroyed yet again.

Early Jerusalem housed only six thousand to eight thousand inhabitants. One estimate of the city's population in 700 BC is twenty-four thousand. And it is unlikely that preexilic Jerusalem ever contained as many as forty thousand people. Yet the people who returned from exile in 538 BC numbered 42,360 Jewish citizens, 7,337 slaves, and 200 singers (Ezra 2:64–65). Add to that crowd of people a group of animals exceeding eight thousand (Ezra 2:66–67). Admittedly, not all of them would have settled within the city limits of Jerusalem, but it seems that many did (Ezra 2:70; 4:4).

Eighty years later, Ezra himself leads about five thousand more individuals back to Judah (Ezra 8:1–14), most of whom apparently settle in or about Jerusalem (Ezra 8:31–32). Yet when Nehemiah arrives thirteen years after that, he finds that any former walls have been reduced to rubble. With the ruin of the walls, the population of the city had evidently evacuated (Nehemiah 7:4). After Nehemiah sees to the repairs, he conducts a lottery to repopulate Jerusalem (Nehemiah 11:1–2).

But regardless of the shifting population and varying conditions of the walls of Jerusalem during ancient times, Zechariah learns of a future when there will be no need of walls to protect the great population of the city. The Lord Himself will be a wall of fire and a source of glory for all the inhabitants (2:5).

The oracle following Zechariah's third vision (2:6–13) is a summation of the first three visions as a whole. It serves as both a warning to Babylon (2:6–9) and a promise of blessing to Judah (2:10–13).

The land of the north (2:6) is soon clearly identified as Babylon (2:7). Yet by Zechariah's time, the Babylonian exiles have already returned, so it appears that Zechariah is describing a future, more widespread regathering of God's people. In the language of the prophets, *Zion* (2:7, 10) is a key term used to refer to the end-times kingdom. And *the four winds* (2:6) suggest that exiles will be returning from all directions, not only from the north.

The *apple of God's eye* (2:8) is a reference to either the opening of the eye or the pupil. Either way, the eye is one of the most important and vulnerable parts of the body. This bold metaphor warns that to strike a blow at Zion is equivalent to striking at the Lord, attempting to wound Him in a most sensitive area. God will surely respond to such aggression. Long ago God had told Abraham, "I will bless those who bless you and curse those who treat you with contempt" (Genesis 12:3 NLT). That pledge is never abrogated and proves to be in force even with respect to the postexilic community of Judah.

The warning directed toward Babylon is closely associated with the blessing of Judah. The blessing of God's people can ultimately occur only after all hostile powers have been put down. The two parts of the oracle are also connected by the literary themes of "daughter of Babylon" versus "daughter of Zion" (2:7, 10). The personification of Zion suggests not only the corporate nature of Judah's existence as one people of the Lord but also the tenderness that God feels toward them as their Father. The names *Zion* and *Jerusalem* are frequently used synonymously.

Zion's response to the promised redemption in 2:6–9 is a ringing cry of joy. The reason for such unmitigated joy is that the Lord is coming and will live in Zion's midst (2:10). Both Haggai and Zechariah share this theology of divine presence, a note that was especially meaningful in the days of the regathered community struggling to build a temple worthy of God's dwelling place. But Zechariah is particularly concerned with orienting this theological truth to the age to come, when all nations (not just Israel and Judah) will join themselves to the Lord and be His people (2:11). In addition, God will take the land of Judah as His special allotment in all the created universe. Zechariah's reference to "the holy land" (2:12) is unique to this verse in scripture.

Demystifying Zechariah

One of the major tenets of ancient Israel's faith that distinguishes the nation from the paganism of the ancient world is her concept of the nearness of her God as opposed to the aloofness of the gods of the nations. The Lord is utterly transcendent, but the revolutionary contribution of Israel's theology is the awareness that God also lives among His people, even if invisible. Adam and Eve in the garden, Moses leading the Israelites, the psalmists, and the prophets all recognized the Lord as One who dwelled in their midst. The same message continues in the New Testament. Early in his Gospel, John identifies God's Word as One who becomes flesh and makes His dwelling among us (John 1:14).

Of interest here is the increasingly narrow parameter of the Lord's inheritance, from the whole earth to the Jerusalem temple. This narrowing of compass runs parallel, however, to an increasing broadness of His saving activity. He becomes not just the God of Abraham, Isaac, and Jacob, but the God of the nations.

📄 3:1–10

VISION FOUR: THE PRIEST

Zechariah's fourth vision is quite different from most of the others in a number of ways. Only it and the following one (4:1–4) deal with actual identifiable human beings. The usual introduction formula that precedes a vision is lacking. There is no interpreting messenger in this case. And there appears to be an absence of standard formulaic language in the vision.

The person identified in the vision is Jeshua (3:1), a high priest with whom Zechariah is personally acquainted. The same figure appears later in Zechariah (6:11), in Haggai (Haggai 1:1), and frequently in Ezra (2:2; 3:2, 8; 4:3; 5:2; 10:18) and Nehemiah (7:7; 12:1, 7, 10, 26). He is a direct descendant of Aaron through Zadok, founder of the line of priests established by David and Solomon (1 Chronicles 6:3, 8–15). His father, Jehozadak, had gone into Babylonian exile in 586 BC, so by Zechariah's night visions in 519 BC, Jeshua must certainly have been an old man.

In the vision, Jeshua appears in a state of ritual impurity, so much so that he is being condemned for it by Satan in the presence of the Lord (3:1). The accusation is not stated, but it may be inferred from 3:3: He is unfit for the priestly ministry. The accuser and the accused are both standing, the former at the right side of the latter, not unlike in a modern courtroom. The judge is the messenger/angel of the Lord.

Critical Observation

A comprehensive biblical theology deduces that the devil was incarnated in the serpent of the temptation account in Genesis 3. How and why he became the adversary remains a mystery, but it is plain throughout scripture that he is subservient to the sovereignty of God and that his pernicious conduct as the accuser is something permitted to him by an all-wise God. The commonly held position, that primitive Israelite theology regarded Satan as a previously upright being employed by God for high and holy ends and then he departed from that role in historical times to become the adversary of God, finds no support in the Bible. In fact, the New Testament teaching is the opposite: "The devil has been sinning from the beginning" (1 John 3:8 NIV). The doctrine of a personal devil or accuser, known by name as Satan, only gradually emerged in Old Testament revelation. When it originated is not known.

When Satan challenges Jeshua's right to function under these circumstances, the judge speaks up, perhaps even before Satan can open his mouth, and rebukes the accuser to his face (3:2). The rationale for the rebuke is that Satan has overlooked the fact that the Lord, who had chosen Jerusalem, had also declared Jeshua to be a brand snatched from the fire (3:2). When it looked as though all was lost where the covenant community and its worship were concerned, the Lord graciously stepped in and rescued a remnant by which He will reconstitute a believing people.

According to the law, the accusation of Satan is valid; the uncleanness of a priest attempting to minister can lead to his excommunication (Leviticus 22:3). Jeshua (and the entire remnant nation for that matter) may appear impure, but the elective grace of God is still in effect. It is precisely at this point of the priest's need that the Lord speaks, commanding those attending him to remove Jeshua's filthy clothing and replace it with fine garments (Zechariah 3:4). Simultaneously, the Lord verbally absolves Jeshua's iniquity in an act of grace.

Zechariah is also a priest, and he speaks out as he recognizes the need for a proper headdress for Jeshua (3:5; see Exodus 28:36–38). Such interruption of a vision by the one receiving it is not common among other prophets, but it occurs rather frequently in the book of Zechariah.

By investing Jeshua with pure, clean clothes and a spotless turban, the Lord has prepared the priest for a larger role in the covenant community, provided Jeshua responds to God's act of grace by assuming the task to which his reinstatement has called him.

Jeshua must meet two conditions, one having to do with his way of life and the other with his specific vocation as priest. First, he must walk in the ways of the Lord. Second, he must keep the requirements of the particular office to which he has been called (3:7).

Then, with a sharp command, the Lord addresses both Jeshua and his companions who sit before him. It is likely that the seated figures are a sign concerning the coming of the branch and the restoration of Israel as a priestly nation (3:8). Zechariah will later aver that this messianic branch/servant will build the temple of the Lord (6:12–13). It seems likely, then, that the stone placed before Jeshua (3:9) must be taken to be the foundation of the second temple.

It isn't uncommon for a stone to be used as a messianic symbol throughout the Bible (see Isaiah 28:16). But the stone in Zechariah's oracle is unique; it has seven eyes (3:9). In biblical numerology, the number seven signifies fullness or completeness, so the seven eyes suggest omniscience or undimmed vision. In the following vision, Zechariah will identify the seven eyes as the eyes of the Lord that take in everything that is happening on the earth (4:10). And, in addition to the eyes, the stone is about to be inscribed by the Lord.

Demystifying Zechariah

It seems evident that the stone in 3:9 is the cornerstone of a building, most likely the temple of the Lord. In the ancient Near Eastern world, cornerstones frequently bore inscriptions to identify the builder and the purpose of the building. The eyes on the stone are to be the divine signature of the Lord as the architect and builder of the structure. The statement of purpose is a reference to the temple as a place of expiation of sin.

In summary, Zechariah's fourth vision describes a day of redemption in which Jeshua (typical or representative of Israel as a priestly people) will be cleansed of his impurities and reinstalled in his capacity as high priest. This presupposes a temple in which this can take place, so Jeshua will build such a structure. This temple will only be a model for one yet to come, one whose cornerstone is the Lord Himself. That cornerstone contains the glorious promise of the regeneration of the nation, a mighty event of salvation that will be consummated in a single day.

Take It Home

The book of Zechariah is not the simplest portion of scripture to understand and apply. How do you feel about having to work a bit harder to comprehend what is going on? Do you enjoy the challenge of deeper thought and extra study, or do you prefer more clear-cut portions of the Bible? Based on what you've seen in Zechariah so far, how would you describe it to a friend?

ZECHARIAH 4:1–6:15
ZECHARIAH'S NIGHT VISIONS, PART II

Setting Up the Section

This section continues to present the visions of Zechariah. This opening series of visions helps provide a basis for understanding the prophet's writings that follow them.

📖 4:1–14

VISION FIVE: A GOLD LAMPSTAND AND TWO OLIVE TREES

Zechariah's fifth vision forms a matching pair with his fourth, both in juxtaposition and subject matter. Both deal with cultic persons or objects (the high priest and the menorah, respectively), both mention historical persons who were Zechariah's contemporaries (Jeshua and Zerubbabel), both refer to temple building, and both reach their climax on a strong messianic note.

The prophet sees in this vision a golden lampstand (menorah) flanked by two olive trees, the whole of which symbolizes the Spirit of the Lord. The messenger who speaks to Zechariah (4:1), a principal figure in the previous visions (except for the fourth), returns now and awakens the prophet. Since Zechariah continues in a visionary state, he is not waking from sleep, but his sensibilities have been so heightened as to be comparable to a man waking from a slumber.

Zechariah immediately recognizes the golden lampstand, as any priest would. The menorah was traditionally located on the south side of the Holy Place in the temple. Its purpose was to illuminate the interior of the Holy Place (Exodus 25:37), and it also represented the illumination of the presence of the Lord Himself.

However, the lampstand of Zechariah's vision is different from the menorah described in Exodus (4:2–3). First, it appears to have a general vessel for storing the oil located somewhere above its center. The oil for this lampstand is not poured into the lamps by the Levites but comes from the reservoir, a second difference. And finally, its connection to the olive trees is a third difference. The trees directly yield their oil without the need for plucking and crushing olives, and the oil appears to flow from the olive trees to the reservoir and then into the cups with no human hand or effort whatsoever.

Critical Observation

The major source of lamp oil in ancient Palestine was the olive, so it is not surprising that two olive trees appear in Zechariah's vision to provide that fuel. It is important to note that the trees are not to the left and the right of the menorah, but they flank the reservoir. The oil could not go straight to the cups but had to be mediated through the upper container that received it directly from the trees.

Baffled by what he has seen, the prophet proceeds to ask several questions of the interpreting messenger (4:4-6, 11-14). This time the interpretation of the vision is divided by the oracular response section (4:7-10). Zechariah first inquires as to the menorah and then, following the oracle, asks about the two olive trees (4:11). The question from the interpreting messenger (4:5) is not to infer that Zechariah is ignorant, but instead it confirms that the prophet cannot possibly understand what he is seeing without supernatural insight.

Everything Zechariah has seen so far, the messenger explains, is the Word of the Lord to Zerubbabel (4:6). This is the first time that Zerubbabel is mentioned in Zechariah's book, and he is named only three more times, all in the oracle section that immediately follows. In fact, it seems that the reason this vision has its interpretation divided by the oracle is to maintain the emphasis on Zerubbabel.

Critical Observation

Old Testament theology is not clear concerning the person of the Holy Spirit, the third person of the Godhead who is so central to New Testament revelation. Yet we read of the Spirit of God moving over the primordial waters during creation (Genesis 1:2), the tabernacle workers being filled with God's Spirit to do their creative work (Exodus 28:3; 31:3), and the Spirit's power and insight providing for the work of Israel's judges (Judges 3:10; 6:34; 11:29; 13:25; 14:6, 19; 15:14, 19) and prophets (2 Kings 2:15–16; Ezekiel 2:2; 3:12, 14; 8:3; 11:1, 5). Particularly relevant is the reference to the Spirit of the Lord in the commissioning oracle of Isaiah 11:1–5, one recognized by all scholars as messianic and eschatological, or pertaining to end times. The language in that passage is reflected in Zechariah 3–6. The branch in Zechariah 3:8 provides the same messianic allusion as the sprout from the root of Jesse in Isaiah 11:1.

The Spirit of the Lord will empower Zerubbabel, the branch (6:12), to accomplish mighty works, including the completion of the temple (4:7-8), the assumption of rulership (Haggai 2:23; Zechariah 6:13), and the reduction of iniquity and sinful forces (Haggai 2:21-22; Zechariah 3:9).

Zechariah has faithfully described what he has seen, yet he cannot understand its significance (4:11-12). For a second time, the interpreting messenger underlines the prophet's inability to comprehend by asking him if indeed he fails to discern these aspects of the vision (4:13). At this point, the messenger reaches the climax of the dialogue by declaring that the olive trees are the two anointed ones who stand by the Lord of the earth (4:14). It is important to connect these two anointed ones with the trees that symbolize them. They are not just anointed, but they are anointed with the oil of these trees.

Officials who were anointed in Old Testament Israel were the high priest, the king, and, on occasion, prophets. In Zechariah's own time and perspective, the two anointed ones would likely refer to Jeshua and Zerubbabel. Both are direct descendants of the heads of their lines, Aaron and David. Both have already been singled out for their involvement in the restoration of the postexilic community (Haggai 1:1, 12, 14; Zechariah 3; 4:6). And both have been given evidence of having been chosen by God (Haggai 2:23; Zechariah 3:2).

The significance of Zerubbabel is confirmed in the oracle portion of this vision (4:7–10). Zechariah is confident that the mountainous project of rebuilding can be completed with God's help—so much so that he addresses the mountain of obstacles (4:7). He is convinced that Zerubbabel will be able to face the mountain, level it to a plain, and completely achieve the rebuilding committed to his charge (4:9).

As if his message to Zerubbabel is not clear enough so far, Zechariah is most explicit as to what overcoming mountains and raising capstones are all about. He calls to mind that Zerubbabel has already, nearly twenty years earlier, made preparation for the temple foundation. Now the hands that had begun the work will complete it, a promise repeated in 6:12–13 and fulfilled four years later, in 515 BC (Ezra 6:15).

This fifth vision of Zechariah's is seemingly tied to earlier visions. The seven eyes of the Lord that "range throughout the earth" (4:10 NIV) seem connected to the seven eyes on the engraved stone in vision four (3:9). And the reference to running "to and fro" through all the earth conveys a similar image as Zechariah's first vision, where the four horses walk throughout the earth (1:8–11).

📄 5:1–4

VISION SIX: THE FLYING SCROLL

Zechariah's sixth vision has several things in common with his third one. Both have a national focus and highlight the centrality of Judah in the restoration program. In contrast to other visions, a solitary individual is the recipient of these two. Both have an emphasis on length and breadth measurements, be it the city of Jerusalem (2:2) or an unusual scroll (5:1–2). And they both feature movement: The man of vision three is on the move to accomplish his task, and the scroll in this vision is flying.

Scrolls from this era were typically made of leather or parchment, consisting of single sheets sewn together and rolled around wooden rollers at either end. Writing would ordinarily be on the inside, with only the description of its contents or other brief notations written outside the roll. Usually the length of a scroll would be many times its width, the width being the measurement of a single sheet from top to bottom (seldom exceeding eight to twelve inches). The length of a scroll would rarely be more than twenty-five to thirty feet.

The measurements of the scroll are so different from the norm that one must realize immediately that the dimensions are really not of the scroll itself but of something described within the scroll. Thus the thirty feet by fifteen feet (5:2) either defines an actual area or refers to something or some place whose length is twice its width. Among biblical objects or places that fit such criteria are the Holy Place in the tabernacle (Exodus 26:31–35), the porch of Solomon's temple (1 Kings 6:3), and the great bronze altar of the temple (2 Chronicles 4:2). All three of these options have to do with the sanctuary, the place where the Lord meets with His people.

The connection of the scroll with the dwelling place of the Lord leads to the conclusion that the scroll contains the covenant document that binds God and the nation together. The interpretation of the vision (5:3–4) is filled with covenant terminology and motifs that make it certain that the scroll either is the Jewish Torah or contains covenant texts of the Torah. The unidentified speaker immediately equates the scroll with the *curse*—a technical term referring to the sanctions of covenant documents.

The flying scroll of Zechariah mentions only two of the covenant stipulations (5:3), although those two represent the entire law. One has to do with interpersonal, human relations, and the other deals with the individual's responsibility before God. Someone who steals violates the eighth commandment (Exodus 20:15), a breach, therefore, of the entire second half of the law. He who swears falsely in the name of the Lord violates the third commandment (Exodus 20:7), a statute that is representative of the first part of the law. Whoever breaks either or both parts has sinned grievously, having violated the covenant that the Lord has made.

The purging (banishing) mentioned in 5:3 is explained in 5:4. The scroll, the Lord says, is something He has authored and sent out. It is a message but also a weapon by which He will judge His recalcitrant people. It is His powerful Word that accomplishes the objective for which it is sent, whether that be salvation or condemnation (Isaiah 55:11). Using a verb normally found in situations of hospitality, Zechariah states that the scroll will spend the night in the homes of the thief and of him who swears falsely in the Lord's name. It will remain there until its intended mission is accomplished. The covenant breaker will discover that his sins against God and against others will lead inexorably to utter devastation (Zechariah 5:4).

One more instructive parallel should be drawn between this vision and Zechariah's third one. In the third vision, the surveyor is about the business of building, the result of which is a city with no wall of protection other than the Lord Himself, the "wall of fire" (2:5). Here the scroll does not build but, to the contrary, destroys—leaving no wall, roof, or foundation. In the first case, the remnant people who trust confidently in the Lord will find adequate shelter in His presence among them. In the present case, the thief and blasphemer will know nothing of this protective grace but only the wrath of a holy God whose covenant mercies have been spurned (see Habakkuk 2:9–11).

📖 5:5–11

VISION SEVEN: THE EPHAH

This is one of the most perplexing of the night visions of Zechariah, not only because of the bizarre nature of what is being presented, but also due to conundrums of grammar and syntax. An *ephah* (5:6) was a familiar unit of solid or liquid measure approximately equal to five gallons. But due to the description in the vision, several translations refer instead to the *container* for the measurement ("basket," "vessel," "measuring basket," etc.).

In this vision, as in the fifth one (4:1), the interpreting angel takes the initiative to introduce the scene (5:5). Zechariah sees "the lead cover of the basket" (5:7 CEV). In the context, this can only mean a cover for the ephah (5:8). He then sees one woman within the ephah (to be differentiated from two others mentioned later) (5:9). It is when the cover is raised that the woman therein becomes visible to the prophet.

Because these are visions, Zechariah is not seeing objects necessarily to scale. For a woman to be contained in a five-gallon vessel is, in actual life, impossible. Similarly, the dimensions of the scroll in the previous vision are disproportionate and exaggerated, but they clearly communicate a message.

At last the woman is identified—she is called *Wickedness* (5:8). The woman's danger is most apparent, for no sooner has the interpreting messenger pronounced her name than he slams the heavy cover down upon the ephah to be certain that she cannot escape (5:8). In the original Hebrew, the urgency is magnified: The messenger *threw* the woman into the ephah and *threw* the lead weight upon its top. The ephah has become not only a means of conveyance but also a cage.

Once the woman is secure, the ephah takes flight, supported by two women with stork-like wings (5:9). The fact that the bearers are also women is consistent with the feminine flavor of the entire vision. The reference to the wind in their wings is no doubt intended as a double entendre. The same word translated *wind* also means "spirit." So the same spirit that empowers Zerubbabel in temple building (4:6) is now at work transporting Wickedness to her destination.

The stork was among the list of unclean birds for the Israelites, one that could not be eaten because it was an abomination (Leviticus 11:13, 19). Yet even people in ancient times recognized its affectionate care for its young and its appropriate name (in the original language, "loving, faithful, constant"). So Zechariah's paradoxical picture of an unclean bird is appropriate considering the cargo and mission of the women with stork-like wings—providing tender care of their charge as they fulfilled the mandate of the Lord.

Wanting to understand the destination of the flying ephah, Zechariah learns that the location is Shinar (Babylonia), where the stork-like women will build Wickedness a house and settle her there (5:10–11). Reference to Shinar is tantamount to Babylon. It was at Babylon, in the land of Shinar, that the rebel human race erected a great ziggurat, or tower, the purpose of which was to frustrate God's mandate to fill the earth (Genesis 11:4; see 1:28; 9:1). From that time, Babylon became synonymous with arrogant human independence.

According to various biblical writers, Babylon—whether past, present, or future—is the paradigm of wickedness and of hostility to the gracious purposes of God. From Zechariah's perspective, Babylon's role must have been exclusively future. By 520 BC, Babylon had been swallowed up by the irrepressible Persian Empire.

Transporting Wickedness to Shinar/Babylon is returning her to where she belongs. She had come from Babylon and had dogged the steps of God's people for centuries, leading at last to their destruction and captivity. But in the day of restoration, she will submit meekly to the Lord of all the earth and settle into the house built especially for her until the day of her final disposition, something Zechariah does not explicitly address.

📄 6:1–8

VISION EIGHT: THE CHARIOTS

Of all Zechariah's visions that appear to complement one another, the first and the last are most similar, effectively serving as bookends that envelop the whole series. Each concerns four principle objects (horses/horsemen in the first, chariots in this one). The objects in both are sent to do the bidding of the Lord. The interpreting messenger is key in both to disclose the vision and explain its meaning. A valley/ravine is present in both (presumed in the final vision, which is set between two mountains). And both visions share a cosmic, universalistic interest.

Various forms of the verb meaning "come forth," or "go forth" (6:1), appear fifteen times in seventy-seven verses, and with increasing frequency. Its first usage is in the third vision, again in the fifth, twice in the sixth, four times in the seventh, and seven times in this final vision. The pattern suggests an intensely heightened sense of activity. This flurry of action throughout the visions, occasioned by the Lord's work of renewal and redemption, comes to a peaceful end at last when His sovereignty is established.

This time what Zechariah sees going forth are four chariots that emerge from between two mountains (6:1–3). In the Old Testament, a chariot was not just a mode of transportation; its primary use was as a war machine. The four chariots in the vision reflect the worldwide extent of their travels. They are sent forth to reclaim all the earth for the Lord, a result that follows the splitting of the mountain in the Day of the Lord (6:1; 14:10). Zechariah witnesses the arrival of the four chariots between the two mountains, having come there from heaven. Once they are sent forth, there will be peace in Jerusalem (14:11) and throughout the whole earth (6:7–8).

Demystifying Zechariah

The chariots are to go throughout the earth, though it doesn't appear that they are dispatched north, south, east, and west. Due to the geography of Palestine, one must go north even to go to the northwest or northeast. Assyria, Babylon, and even Persia were all considered "north" of Palestine, even though they don't appear quite that way on a map.

There can be little doubt that Zechariah's vision pertains to the nations and circumstances of his own times, but it cannot be limited to that era because of the presence of its eschatological and apocalyptic characters. The picture here is one of final and universal dominion of the Lord over His creation. How that will take place is a major part of the message of the oracles of Zechariah in the chapters that follow (7–14).

📖 6:9–15

A CONCLUDING ORACLE

Zechariah records an oracle that appears to serve as a comment on, and climax to, the night visions as a whole. It does not belong with the series that commences with chapter 7, because that collection is dated more than a year later (7:1). The central portion of Zechariah's writing so far, the content of the fourth and fifth visions, focuses on the elevation of Jeshua and Zerubbabel to positions of honor and influence. Not surprisingly, then, those same two persons are the central concern of this final, summarizing oracle.

The identities of the men listed in 6:10 are not clear. There is at least some chance that, in terms of their names, they are priests who were given their assignment here. They are to take silver and gold to fashion a crown for Jeshua the high priest. The word used for *crown* denotes a regal crown rather than the expected headdress for a priest (turban, mitre, diadem, etc.), so this particular crowning of the priest must have had regal implications.

The Word of the Lord through Zechariah is directed specifically to Jeshua (6:12), thus distinguishing him from another man called the branch (6:12). There is no doubt as to the identity of the branch. Converging lines of identification within Zechariah (4:7–10) and elsewhere (Isaiah 11:1; 53:2; Jeremiah 33:15; Haggai 2:23) make it certain that Zerubbabel is in view. As a direct offspring of the line of David, he is well-qualified to sit on the royal throne of Judah, a responsibility clearly stated in 6:13.

Demystifying Zechariah

Translations of Zechariah vary as to whether the presumed priests are instructed to fashion a *crown* (singular) or *crowns* (plural). The plural form seems to be appropriate. Jeshua wears one as priest, and Zerubbabel (the branch) wears another as king.

Priest and king come together in 6:13. The harmony between the two figures clarifies that two separate persons are in view. Jeshua and the branch (Zerubbabel) are both the center of attention. Both are crowned and enthroned, charged with administering, under the Lord, the affairs of their respective civil and religious realms. The two complement each other. The quality of office is anticipated in the fifth vision, where Zerubbabel and Jeshua appear as olive trees and anointed ones of the Lord (4:11–14).

In addition to being important leaders in their own time, Jeshua and Zerubbabel are also symbolic, anointed ones whose messianic significance is unmistakable (Haggai 2:23; Zechariah 3:2–5, 8; 4:14; 6:11–13). They point toward something far more remarkable and transcendent than anyone could have anticipated. Beginning with David is the undeniable presumption that royal and priestly rule will someday merge in one individual. This anointed one of the Lord will reign from Zion and be heir of all the nations (Psalm 2:2, 6–8). As universal ruler, he will also be a priest after the line of Melchizedek (Psalm 110:4).

Apart from Psalm 110, no Old Testament passage comes as close as this one to uniting the royal and priestly offices. With this in mind, the harmony between the two takes on a greatly enhanced meaning. Jeshua and Zerubbabel are messianic forerunners whose persons and functions prototypically portray the One to come who dies as servant, intercedes as priest, and will return as king.

Take It Home

It can be a struggle to make sense of Zechariah's visions. Part of the difficulty lies in the fact that the visions contain a number of objects that may have had a great significance for his original audience but are quite foreign to modern readers. How might this awareness influence you the next time you are discussing your faith with someone else? For example, could it be that you find yourself using words or phrases that are meaningful to you but unfamiliar to your listener, causing him or her to struggle more than necessary in attempting to comprehend?

ZECHARIAH 7:1–14:21

ZECHARIAH'S ORACLES

Setting Up the Section

A clear break exists between the content of Zechariah 7 and the material that precedes it. Based on the dates Zechariah provides (1:7; 7:1), the oracles of this section begin about twenty-two months later. Unfortunately, the biblical record is silent about the impact of Zechariah's previous visions. Apart from the tantalizingly brief historical references here, there is very little that can be known at all about that period of time. Still, Zechariah has much more relevant information to record.

7:1–8:23

ORACLES CONCERNING HYPOCRITICAL FASTING

This portion of Zechariah lies between the night visions of chapters 1–6 and the self-designated oracles of chapters 9–14. The prophet's topic is fasting, a theme elaborated in both negative and positive manners. Zechariah does not specifically designate this section as an oracle, as he does in following passages, but its formal character defines it as such.

It is evident that progress is well under way on the temple by the date of this oracle (7:3). The priesthood is active there with some degree of formality and legitimacy, although it is also clear that the temple is not completely finished (8:9).

A group of travelers arrives to inquire about a religious matter (7:2–3). For a number of years, the travelers' community had fasted and wept in the fifth month (in observance of the destruction of Solomon's temple, a disaster that had occurred almost exactly seventy years earlier). The next anniversary is just a few months away, and they are asking if it is appropriate to create holy days to observe occasions that had arisen in the post-Mosaic period.

Yet what may have appeared to be an innocent query about the propriety of fasting is instead a question fraught with hypocrisy. In fact, God's response is a sharp rebuke. Their fasting and mourning, not only on the fifth but also during the seventh month, had for seventy long years been an empty exercise designed to enhance not the Lord but rather those who engaged in it in a hypocritical manner. Their religion had become one of outward show with no inner content. God points out that just as they eat and drink for their own satisfaction, so, too, do they fast (7:6). Their religious activity is centered on themselves, not their holy and loving God.

Demystifying Zechariah

The unspecified observance of the seventh month (7:5) evidently dates back to the murder of Gedaliah, the Jewish governor appointed by Nebuchadnezzar after the fall of Jerusalem (Jeremiah 40:5). He had come from an honored family, one that enjoyed the confidence of good King Josiah. However, some anti-Babylonian survivors of Jerusalem's destruction and exile formed a conspiracy to assassinate him (Jeremiah 41:1–2). Gedaliah's death was an extremely traumatic event for the community already crushed nearly to annihilation by the loss of the temple, the ruin of the holy city, and the deportation of most of its leadership.

In 7:7, Zechariah is not asking about the authenticity and accuracy of the earlier prophetic writings but rather if his own contemporaries are willing to obey those words. The Negev was in the south of Judah and consisted largely of desert. For the Negev to be populated, times of unusually suitable climatic conditions and freedom from hostility were necessary. This is even truer of the Shephelah (lowlands, or foothills) between Judah and the western plains. Zechariah's point is very apparent: If mighty and prosperous Jerusalem and Judah had been overthrown for failing to heed the warnings of earlier prophets, it is essential for his own audience to pay strict attention to those words, as their community is struggling for its survival. This is no time for hypocritical self-indulgence.

The Lord then reviews the basis for true worship, including fasting, by appealing to earlier canonical principles that provide its moral and spiritual framework (7:8–10). Such appeals to justice, mercy, compassion, and proper treatment of one another were abundant throughout the texts available to the people of that time, especially in the writings of Moses.

Past generations had responded to the word of witness from the prophets by "giving a shoulder of stubbornness" and "making their ears heavy"—the literal translations of the phrases in 7:11. The result was predictable: The Lord sent great wrath against them (7:12–14). The land had become desolate as a result, so much so that it appeared to be virtually uninhabited (Ezekiel 36:32–36). What had once been a place flowing with milk and honey had become a desert devoid of life and pleasure. Unless Zechariah's audience understands the abhorrence with which the Lord views superficial and self-serving religious observance, they can expect the same calamitous results as those experienced by their forefathers.

Critical Observation

Note the number of times Zechariah uses the name *Lord Almighty* (or *Lord of hosts*) as the name for God in his writing, and particularly throughout this section. As he describes things that appear humanly impossible, each usage of this name is an affirmation that such things can indeed come to pass by the resources of the Almighty One.

But the future appears more positive for Judah. When the Lord makes His abode in Jerusalem, the city will be radically transformed (8:1-3), including a repopulation to fill the city (8:4-5). In anticipation of the skepticism that Zechariah's message will surely elicit, the Lord makes it clear that He is speaking and that nothing is too difficult for Him (8:6).

References to the east and west (8:7) indicate the rising and setting of the sun, suggesting that future immigrants to Jerusalem will come from places throughout the world, not just the nearby surrounding areas. After the Lord has verified that He will dwell in the midst of Jerusalem (8:3), He promises to bring His people back to do the same (8:8).

Therefore it is important for the people to shoulder the responsibilities requisite to the fulfillment of God's promise. Their deliverance and return will depend wholly on God's grace (8:7-8), but present and future prosperity in the land will be directly related to their obedience and hard work. So the section in 8:9-13 is bracketed with the Lord's repeated challenge to "let your hands be strong" (NIV).

The reference here is to the rebuilding that commenced during the second year of Darius and not to the initial attempts at construction in 536 BC (8:10-12). Zechariah alludes to the days of social and economic distress in Judah (unemployment, no payment of wages, social unrest, etc.) before the people rearranged their priorities and began to put the Lord and His temple at the center of their community life. But apparently the preaching of the prophets had been effective (8:11), so the latest generations do not suffer the same consequences that their ancestors faced. The remaining remnant of the nation will possess the land during a peaceful, productive time (8:12).

Israel had been a curse (8:13) to other nations in the sense that the people had failed to engagingly attract those nations to the one true God. But now, the Lord says, they will be a blessing. There is no need to look any further than to the Jewish Messiah, Jesus Christ, to see what untold blessing Israel has been to the world.

The painful experience the Lord had previously brought on Judah had been a disciplinary action to produce consciousness of sin and a desire for repentance, and it had accomplished its intent. The Lord was then able to do good again to Judah, and the people could live where truth and justice were restored and valued (8:14-17).

In yet another example of the careful craftsmanship with which Zechariah arranges his material, the final portion of this oracle (chapters 7-8) comes full circle to the theme with which it began: the concern for fasting. At the beginning, only one city sent its representatives (7:2); but at the end, all the languages of the nations will be represented (8:23). And fasting in sorrow will be turned into feasting for joy (7:3; 8:19).

To begin with, there will be a mass pilgrimage of the people of the earth to seek the Lord at Jerusalem (8:20-22), to beseech His leniency and mercy when He might be inclined otherwise. It is impossible to know what prompts the desire, but the wording indicates a great urgency. Zechariah pictures movement on a universal scale—many peoples and strong nations (8:22).

At a ten-to-one ratio, other people will outnumber the Jews who return to seek the face of the Lord (8:23). The number *ten* is not to be taken literally but rather is symbolic in the Bible of totality or comprehensiveness. So urgent will be their desire, that they will hold onto the people of God (literally, "clutch at the sleeve" NLT) with no intention of letting go.

It is particularly interesting that the reason the nations will want to join themselves to the Jews is that they will have heard that God is with Israel. As the field of interest becomes much broader than Israel, a different name for God is used. *Yahweh* (the Lord Almighty), which has been used so frequently by Zechariah, is here changed to the generic *Elohim*. It suddenly becomes obvious to all the nations that their god is Israel's God. What they have been seeking through the millennia of human history has at last been found (Philippians 2:11; see Isaiah 45:23).

📖 9:1–11:17

AN ORACLE CONCERNING THE LORD'S SOVEREIGNTY

After Zechariah's night visions (1–6) and his oracles on fasting (7–8), the final chapters (9–14) comprise a final main division. This last section consists of two parts: an oracle concerning the nations (9–11) and an oracle concerning Israel (12–14). Chapter 9 begins with his anticipation of the coming of the true King.

For the first time in the book (with the possible exception of 5:5–11), the prophet directs a message about or against pagan nations. But he does so to provide a backdrop to the coming of the messianic King who will take His royal throne as a result of conquest.

The Word of the Lord against Israel's enemies is described as a march through those nations that will terminate at the temple in Jerusalem (9:8). No sooner has this march of the Lord commenced than it commands the attention of all the surrounding peoples, including Israel (9:1-2). It is uncertain how Hadrach (the point of origin) is related to Damascus, but Damascus is clearly to the south. Third in line is Hamath, a territory to the west and north of Damascus, roughly the territory of modern-day Lebanon. Tyre and Sidon lay west and northwest of Damascus on the Mediterranean coast, and they may be more familiar than some of the other locations because their names are often symbolic of human pride. Zechariah notes that Tyre has amassed and hoarded great revenues of silver and gold but will soon see its power and possessions taken away (9:3-4).

Next on the list are a series of Philistine city-states: Ashkelon, Gaza, Ekron, and Ashdod (9:5-6). The once-proud Philistia will be shamed and embarrassed. The blood and abominable things (9:7) are references to their religious perversions, which no doubt include slaughtering animals considered by Israelites as unclean and eating meat that has not been properly drained of its blood. However, too little is known of the Philistines to determine precisely what practices are in mind here.

Yet Zechariah declares that Philistia will be thoroughly chastened and purified, becoming a remnant for God, like a clan in Judah (9:7-8). By Zechariah's time, the Jebusites have been totally assimilated into Judah. One day Ekron (perhaps representing all of Philistia) will have the same privilege. The Philistines (and by extension the preceding nations as well) will feel the awesome wrath of the Lord, but those who are left—a small remnant—will then be included within the covenant of God.

The march ends at Jerusalem with the Lord, triumphant in His procession, standing guard over His house (the temple). Then He surrounds it with His presence so that no hostile force can ever again oppress His people (9:8). It is a sure thing. What God sees in advance must surely come to pass.

Demystifying Zechariah

This portion of scripture is eschatological literature. Although it is grounded in the present time of the prophet (and uses well-known place names), Zechariah views the future in very stylized and conventional patterns. His point is that the Lord will manifest Himself in the last days as a vanquishing hero. One should not, therefore, look to precise historical events of which this is an account, nor should one anticipate a future scenario in which God will literally march from Hadrach to Jerusalem, establishing His dominion over all opposition.

The following passage of scripture (9:9-13) is one of the most messianically significant passages in the Bible, in both the Jewish and Christian traditions. Judaism sees in it a basis for a royal messianic expectation, while Christianity sees a prophecy of the triumphal entry of Jesus Christ into Jerusalem on the Sunday before His crucifixion (Matthew 21:5; John 12:15). Both agree that a descendant of David is depicted here, one who, though humble, rides as a victor into his capital city of Jerusalem.

On first reading, it appears that the Christian interpretation does not square exactly with Zechariah's prophecy. Although Jesus is described as entering Jerusalem in precisely the manner envisioned by Zechariah in 9:9, He dies within days of the event, never having made any active claim to the throne of David. The New Testament account shows that the servant who will someday be exalted as King must first suffer and die on behalf of those who will make up His kingdom in the ages to come.

After seeing that Jesus' triumphal entry is a historical prototype of an eschatological event that must yet take place, that distinction can be detected in the Zechariah passage. Zechariah provides a clear difference in tone and emphasis between 9:9 and 9:10. The coming One is first described as humble or lowly (9:9), a most inappropriate way to speak of One whose triumph is complete in every respect. Only in 9:10 is that triumph translated into universal dominion. This is precisely why any devotee of Bible study must consider the backdrop of the entire revelation of God, Old Testament and New Testament alike.

Using the metaphor of imprisonment, the Lord says He will release Zion's prisoners from the waterless pit (9:11). This is a backward reference to the release and restoration of the Babylonian exiles. God had released them because of the covenant He had made with His people long ago, sealed with blood, the sign of the covenant. He had promised to do so in the great blessings sections of the covenant texts of Leviticus 26:40–45 and Deuteronomy 30:1–10.

To return "twice as much" (9:12 NIV) suggests a double portion of blessing. A specific manifestation of that blessing, one much in line with the militaristic theme of the whole oracle, is the use the Lord will make of Judah, Ephraim (Israel), and Zion (9:13). He will bend Judah as one draws a bow, using Ephraim as an arrow. Zion will be stirred up against Yawan (Greece), used as a sword in the Lord's hand. Defended by the Lord of hosts, His chosen ones will both devour and subdue their enemies. Such bold imagery suggests that the death of the Lord's foes is in some sense an offering to Him (9:14–15).

The eschatological character of the oracle is underlined again in 9:16 by the use of the classic phrase *in that day*. Thus, the references to Hadrach, Damascus, and even Greece must be viewed as having end-times significance. At the end of this section of his oracle, the prophet bursts out in an expostulation of praise (9:17).

The focus then shifts to the elect people of the King. In a second exodus, they will come from all the nations to the promised land, where they will share His dominion with Him. Things had been bleak, indeed, as the whole history of Israel and Judah can attest, but there is now hope in light of the restoration from exile and particularly in light of God's gracious promises concerning the age to come.

All the Lord's people need to do is ask for rain, the showers of His blessing (10:1), and it is certain to come. God previously withheld the autumn and spring ("latter") rains, but Judah had adamantly remained in rebellion against Him. The result was the exile, a time of drought and despair, "a waterless dungeon" (9:11 NLT). But it is the Lord who makes thunderstorms, so Zechariah offers hope that the latter rain of prosperity will indeed arrive.

Zechariah is still looking to the future, because in his own day, Judah had suffered a devastating crisis of leadership in both her spiritual and political life. Throughout their history, Israel and Judah had turned to illicit religious channels such as teraphim, augurers, and dreamers (10:2), all of whom delivered nothing but falsehood and emptiness.

Demystifying Zechariah

Teraphim were small household images thought to represent supernatural powers and to be a means of eliciting information from the spirit world (Genesis 31:19, 34–35; 1 Samuel 19:13, 16; Hosea 3:4). Many times, *teraphim* is translated simply as "idols." *Augurers* may also be called "diviners"—people who sought supernatural disclosure by examining animal livers, shaking (casting lots with) arrows, or other methods (Ezekiel 21:21).

Zechariah condemns all forms of divination. The result of such an abysmal search for guidance had been the aimless wandering of the people like sheep (10:2–3). The allusion to sheep afforded the prophet a shift from consideration of *spiritual* leadership to that of the kings in the *political* realm. Kings of the time were commonly described as shepherds, and the Old Testament record is replete with references to the kings of Israel, beginning with Saul (1 Samuel 28:3–7), who seek after illicit channels of revelation and end up leading the people to ruin and dispersion. Because of this history of wicked leadership, the Lord is angry (Zechariah 10:3).

Yet in the middle of 10:3, the focus shifts from past and present to future, and from a negative assessment of Judah's leadership to a positive one. Judah is the Lord's flock, and He will care for it. Then, far from being the meek and easily bullied sheep of the past, they will become a charger on which the Lord can ride to battle.

God foresees Judah as the source of four elements: the cornerstone, the peg, the bow, and the ruler (10:4). These should be interpreted in the context of the warfare that prevails here rather than in terms of construction, architecture, or anything else.

Cornerstone (or *corner tower*) occurs as a metaphor for a leader such as a king or governor. It seems that Zechariah is alluding to a future human figure who will provide the very foundation for a revived kingdom structure. Paul understands this One to be Christ, the chief cornerstone (Ephesians 2:20).

Peg can refer to a tent peg. More likely in this instance, it can also indicate a peg in the wall from which items are hung. A person who bears the weight of responsibility might be said to be a peg (Isaiah 22:20–24). Zechariah is writing of someone to serve as a stout hook on which all of Judah's hopes for the future can be suspended.

Battle bow as a personal epithet is otherwise unknown in the Bible. But a helpful reference is that of 9:13, where the Lord says He will bend Judah as a warrior bends a bow. Since Judah is the *source* (10:3–5), the actual bow must be someone who comes out of Judah—an idea that is consistent with Old Testament messianic theology.

As for the *ruler* to come from Judah, it is somewhat surprising that Zechariah doesn't use the expected word that means king or prince. Instead he uses a term usually reserved for oppressive, tyrannical rule. From the perspective of God's foes, His total and violent domination will cast Him as someone to whom they must submit against their will. This impression gains support in 10:5, where the aforementioned rulers (and perhaps the cornerstone, peg, and battle bow as well) will be like warriors treading down in the mud of the streets. They will prevail over their foes because the Lord will be with them (10:5).

Ephraim (Israel) had previously appeared in a metaphor as an arrow projected by the Lord from the bow of Judah (9:13), and the result had been a lavish celebration of victory. Here again, Ephraim's heart will rejoice as with wine, as will that of Israel's offspring, celebrating God's glorious triumph over all opposition (10:6-7).

Zechariah shares a well-established tradition when he looks at the eschatological deliverance of Israel in terms of exodus (see Isaiah 43:1-7; Haggai 2:4-5). In this case, the process of regathering will begin when the Lord signals (sometimes translated *whistles*) for His people to return (Zechariah 10:8). Once they gather, they will multiply as they did in the days of Moses, and the pitiful postexilic remnant will once more become the mighty and innumerable host of God (2:4; 8:4-5).

The people are compared to a bag of seed sowed among the nations. Alive once more, they will return to the Lord and to the land (10:9). The reference to Egypt and Assyria (10:10) represents the universal distribution of the exiles of all ages. Gilead and Lebanon were both nearby, but they are never designated as falling within the land of promise. They merely accommodate the overflow of refugees that will fill the land of Palestine.

Like the original Exodus, this returning influx of people passes safely through the "sea of distress" (10:11). *Nile* is a name for Egypt. Both Egypt and Assyria will cease to be threats to the people of God.

Demystifying Zechariah

Zechariah 11 is one of the most difficult passages in the entire book. The protagonists are not always identified, the speakers and roles are confusing, and the whole temporal orientation is uncertain. The section opens with a poem filled with symbolism.

As Zechariah continues, it soon becomes apparent that the objects he mentions under the guise of trees and animals are the same as the ones he calls shepherds. The poem in 11:1-3, then, turns out to be a lament for the destruction of the evil shepherds who, as already noted, represent kings (11:8, 17). So the cedar tree of Lebanon, the oak of Bashan, and the fir (pine) tree are symbols of powerful rulers. The fact that three trees are mentioned leads one to suspect that the three shepherds of 11:8 are relevant to the total interpretation.

In a most unusual development, God commands Zechariah to undertake a series of actions, doing so in the place of the Lord Himself (11:4-16). First he is to shepherd the flock of slaughter (11:4). The flock had been bought and sold by strangers (probably foreign kings), and the sheep were unprotected by their own shepherds. In what appears to be an incredibly harsh statement, it seems that even the Lord has withdrawn His compassion (11:6). This, of course, is precisely what had taken place in the last decades of Israel's and Judah's history leading up to their respective captivities by the Assyrians and Babylonians.

Critical Observation

The fact that the Lord completes the chastisement begun by foreign oppressors does not exonerate His people from responsibility for their evil ways. God acts out of a spirit of correction, but they act out of spiteful selfishness and depravity. The Lord, then, can condemn foreign nations for their hostility toward His people even though He may have allowed their aggression as part of a greater purpose.

Shepherding the flock may have meant that Zechariah was reliving the Lord's dealings with His people in allegory (if only in his own mind) so he could report in a fresh way what Israel's history was really all about. An indispensable instrument for the job is the shepherd's staff, so Zechariah takes two of them, one named *Pleasantness* (or *Favor*) and the other *Binders* (or *Union*) (11:7). The former name speaks of the relationship between the Lord and His people (11:10) and the latter of that between Israel and Judah (11:14).

Zechariah also eradicates the three shepherds—another clue that he is reliving the Lord's own experience in Israel's history and that his removal of the leaders is symbolic. *One month* (11:8) is best viewed as meaning a short time rather than a specific point in history when three key leaders all fell within a literal period of thirty days.

The dying, perishing, and cannibalism mentioned in 11:8–9 had been a somber part of history. When God withdrew His compassion, surrounding aggressive nations had shown little mercy to Israel and Judah. Jeremiah had predicted Judah's gruesome resorting to cannibalism (Jeremiah 19:9) and later reflected on its fulfillment (Lamentations 2:20).

To dramatize that the fall of Jerusalem and exile of Judah were tantamount to the breaking of the Lord's covenant, Zechariah takes the staff named Pleasantness and breaks it in two (11:10–11). Yet for God to break His covenant with His people is not to suggest an irreparable breach, for the Old Testament witness pervasively attests to the inviolability of that fundamental relationship. What is meant is that the benefits of the covenant—in this case, the benefit of protection from conquest and deportation—have been withheld.

Zechariah, standing in for the Lord, had been a good shepherd to the flock of Israel and Judah when no one else had. Yet when the time comes for him to be compensated for his services, he is offered thirty pieces of silver (11:12)—the pittance paid for a slave who had been gored to death (Exodus 21:32). This is actually the Lord being appraised, and only His service is considered, not His intrinsic value. Therefore, the silver is like refuse because of the insulting attitude it represents (11:13).

Critical Observation

Potters' shops were usually located near refuse pits, where the shards and other unusable or broken materials were cast (Jeremiah 18:2; 19:1–2). The place of the potter, then, was not only a place of creation and beauty but also one of rejection and ruin. It became a metaphor for a scrap heap.

Thirty pieces of silver being cast down in the house of the Lord brings to mind the incident with Judas recorded in Matthew 27:3–5. Just as the Lord is priced at only thirty silver shekels as far as His service to Israel is concerned, so Jesus is later viewed by Judas and his generation as having no more value than a slave. In this sense, the rejection of the Lord in Zechariah 11:13 is a prophecy fulfilled in Matthew 27:9.

Having accomplished this part of his commission, Zechariah takes the second staff (Binders) and cuts it in two (11:14), signifying the unbinding of the brotherhood of Israel and Judah. Indeed, Israel had ceased to exist as a separate entity at the Babylonian deportation and was not reestablished as a nation until the twentieth century.

Once again the Lord commands Zechariah to dramatize his message by taking up the implements of an unwise shepherd (11:15). Although Zechariah was previously reliving the *history* of his people, at this point his orientation is exclusively *future* in both historical and eschatological terms. It is fruitless to try to identify the foolish shepherd. It is best, perhaps, to see the figure as the whole collective leadership of Israel from Zechariah's time forward, culminating at last in the epitome of godless despotism, the individual identified in the New Testament as the Antichrist (Matthew 24:5, 24; 2 Thessalonians 2:3–4; 1 John 2:18, 22).

Fundamental to the work of a shepherd should be his concern for any sheep that might have separated from the flock and gone their own way (Isaiah 53:6; Matthew 18:12–14). Yet the foolish shepherd will not seek the scattered ones nor heal the broken ones. He will even stop nourishing the healthy sheep. So thorough and cruel will be his disposition of these defenseless ones that he will rip their very hoofs from them (Zechariah 11:15–16).

The Lord is not oblivious to the shepherd who so abuses and exploits his people, however. The woe-judgment that comes upon him will be a sword that wounds his arm and his right eye (11:17). Without the arm to carry the sheep and the eye with which to search and find, the shepherd truly is worthless—not only in a moral sense but in a practical, functional sense as well. Why the shepherd is not killed is unclear, but he is so severely incapacitated that he can no longer function.

Although this particular oracle ends on a pessimistic note, Zechariah's message as a whole has not ended. In the following, final oracle, he offers glorious hope of a triumphant shepherd yet to come.

📄 12:1–14:21

AN ORACLE CONCERNING ISRAEL

The final great oracle of Zechariah, embracing all of chapters 12–14, stands in sharp contrast with what has immediately preceded in chapter 11 as it picks up the eschatological themes of chapters 9–10. This section introduces a cosmic, universalistic motif and focuses on the messianic aspect of the end-times redemption, going so far as to identify the Lord Himself as the messianic figure (12:10–14; 13:7–9). One of the clues that the oracle's thrust is eschatological is the focus on *Israel* rather than *Judah*. Israel, from Zechariah's standpoint, is a thing of the past.

The opening description of the Lord is one of Creator (12:1). His grand actions underline His creative and redemptive role. Here at the brink of a new age, it is important to realize that the same God who brought everything into existence is well able to usher in the new creation of a restored people in a renewed and universal kingdom.

The mighty Lord will use His chosen people Judah as an instrument by which He does battle with the nations and brings them under His dominion. This is what is meant in describing Jerusalem as an "intoxicating drink" (12:2 NLT). The nations will drink of Jerusalem—partake of her in hostility and conquest—but they will end up inebriated.

Jerusalem is also a stone of burden (12:3). God's people are likened to pillage being carried off by victors, but they will be heavier than the looters bargained for, so heavy and jagged that they will lacerate the shoulders of those who try to spirit them away. Drunken and scarred, the nations come in for further judgment. The Lord will confuse their horses and cavalrymen. Their horses will be blinded, but God will open His own eyes on behalf of the house of Judah (12:4).

When all this comes to pass, Judah's rulers will realize that the people of Jerusalem have been their greatest strength. The Lord of hosts used them as a discomfit to their enemies and has guaranteed that the nation will survive. The rulers will themselves become a "firepot among pieces of wood" and a "flaming torch among sheaves" (12:5-6 NASB), incinerating all the surrounding woods that threaten Israel.

In addition to Jerusalem, even tents and humble habitations throughout Judah will enjoy pride of place among God's people (12:7). In that day, the Lord will defend the residents of Jerusalem in such a powerful way that even the weakest among them is comparable to the great warrior King David. And in an even more startling hyperbole, the dynasty of David is compared to God (12:8).

Demystifying Zechariah

One must not allow any literary device such as hyperbole (great exaggeration) to determine one's understanding of the theological content in a passage such as 12:8. All that is intended is an argument to magnify the Lord's glorious redemption of His people. The weak become strong and the strong become stronger—as powerful as God Himself if the syllogism requires it to be so.

Once the Lord has accomplished His work of judgment on the nations and secured Judah and Jerusalem from them (12:9), He will begin a work of grace among the redeemed. The spirit of grace will pour out on God's people, though they little deserve it. In fact, the Lord must extend His grace to enable His people to seek it in the first place.

Grace, however, is an abstraction. It must take shape from some occasion or action that produces an awareness of the need for divine favor. Zechariah cites one such action: "They will look on [the Lord], the one they have pierced" (12:10 NIV). But the prophet's references to the Lord shift immediately from *me* to *Him*. This is an extremely difficult text within the confines of its Old Testament setting. The most satisfying resolution is to accept a change in pronoun as a grammatical, stylistic feature without a change of the subject. From the Lord's viewpoint, it is *me* that is the focus; from the standpoint of the people, it is *Him*.

Yet that raises another question, this one a theological concern. The people of the Old Testament know nothing of a mortal God, One who can be fatally wounded as in this passage. Zechariah's audience likely presumes that the Lord has been pierced in a figurative way, in the sense that they have wounded His holiness and violated His righteousness.

By New Testament times, however, Zechariah 12:10 was considered clearly messianic in both Jewish tradition and Christian theology. The verse anticipates the day when the royal house of David and all Jerusalem will receive from the Lord a spirit of grace, enabling people to seek His forgiveness for millennia of waywardness. They will look to the Lord, the One they have mortally wounded by their heartbreaking behavior, a look that produces in them a sense of great sorrow. The only sorrow comparable is that of the loss of a firstborn son in death (Genesis 22:2), and such sorrow is a sign of genuine repentance.

Critical Observation

The great weeping of Hadad-rimmon (12:11) is believed to be the expression of sorrow that took place after the violent and premature death of King Josiah, when he foolishly interposed his tiny army between the Egyptians and the Assyrians (2 Kings 23:29–30). The tragic event was commemorated from that time on (2 Chronicles 35:25).

Nathan (12:12) was the third son of David. Though the kings of Judah after Solomon until the exile were all descendants of Solomon (1 Chronicles 3:10–16), a change occurred at that point, and royal descent began to be traced through Nathan.

Usually community or corporate repentance is standard, but in this case it appears that each member and entity of the community feels individually culpable and must individually give account before God (12:11–14). Judah's lamentation of repentance will result in their forgiveness, followed by purification and cleansing (13:1) described with the metaphor of an artesian well that gushes forth. The cleansing is widespread and removes sin and iniquity, idols in the land, false prophets, and the underlying spirit of impurity that has been so pervasive (13:1–2).

The charlatan prophets will attempt to downplay any involvement in false prophesying. They will deny having had visions, change their apparel, and lie about their participation. But even after removing the traditional hairy cloak of a prophet (13:4), the false prophets will be exposed by the marks on their chests—incisions made by many Canaanite religious practitioners to impress various deities by their acts of wholesale devotion (13:5–6). Their feeble lies will not be convincing.

Problems in the priesthood (13:1–2) and among the so-called prophets (13:2–6) are followed by Zechariah's attention to the monarchy (13:7–9). Again he refers to Israel's kings as *shepherds*. After a bold assertion by the Lord that the shepherd-king is an associate comes a poignant command to strike the leader so that the flock will become scattered. This action will cause not only the leaders of the community to suffer the blow of the Lord's righteous indignation but also the flock (described as insignificant or "little").

The scattering of the sheep, far from being an accidental consequence of the striking of the shepherd, is for the purpose of ridding the flock of the elements that must be purged (13:7). Afterward, only one-third remain. That remnant will pass through a refining process designed to equip them to have minds and hearts that are open and responsive to the sovereign claims of the Lord (13:8–9).

Demystifying Zechariah

Zechariah's original hearers perhaps considered these statements an eschatological repetition of their exile: The shepherd-kings of Israel will suffer the wrath of God, the flock-people will endure pestilence and sword, and the surviving community will be scattered. Then, from the dispersed population will emerge a purified remnant that knows the Lord. But clearly the New Testament evangelists, and Jesus Himself, regarded the Zechariah text as a messianic testimonial (Matthew 26:31; Mark 14:27). It may be that New Testament usage is intended as a maxim to indicate simply that when shepherds are struck down, sheep invariably scatter. After all, Jesus never says directly that He is fulfilling this prophecy; He simply affirms the aphorism of the cause and effect established by the removal of a shepherd from His flock. More likely, however, this is an instance where messianic truth, communicated by a text, may never have been so intended by the original prophet-author.

This oracle, as well as the entire prophecy of Zechariah, ends on the grand and glorious note of the sovereignty of the Lord and the establishment of His universal and eternal kingdom. Triumph comes through tribulation, so the prophet speaks of the Day of the Lord in the context of struggle and conflict (14:1–2). Restoration and dominion cannot come until all the forces of evil that seek to subvert it are put down once and for all. So the nations of the whole earth come against Jerusalem, defeat her, and divide their spoils of war in her very midst.

It is important to note that it is the Lord who gathers the nations (14:2), not only to purify His people in tribulation, but also to provide an occasion for the destruction of their enemies. Zechariah has already described a scene in which Jerusalem is attacked but suffers no loss (12:1–9). But in chapter 14, the deliverance of Jerusalem will be coincident with the triumphant coming of the Lord. The effect of His coming is not only victory for His people (14:3) but also the establishment of His earthly kingdom (14:9–11). Zechariah thus distinguishes between the kingdom of the Lord's universal, unchallenged dominion and a preliminary one in which His lordship prevails and His people are secure only as He exercises direct and forcible predominance.

Shortly after the defeat and pillaging of Jerusalem, the Lord will go forth to do battle, which will bring about cataclysmic changes in the terrain itself, as well as in the patterns of light and darkness and in the seasons (14:3–7). When all seems lost, the Lord leads His people forth and parts the Mount of Olives by the very act of treading on it (14:4), not unlike the way Moses parted the Red Sea to deliver the Israelites. The splitting of the mountain creates a new valley through which the people will flee (14:5). This is no mere earthquake, however, but a shaking of the whole universe as the Lord comes in judgment. This will occur on a day known only to God (14:7).

One result will be life-giving waters that flow from Jerusalem, half to the Dead Sea and half to the Mediterranean Sea (14:8). The meaning of the Hebrew indicates that these are not waters that give life but waters that are alive—moving, fast-flowing, and sparkling.

The Jewish Shema (Deuteronomy 6:4–5) is the very heart of Israel's covenant faith— a confession of the Lord's self-consistency as well as His uniqueness and exclusivity. Zechariah makes unmistakable reference to the Shema in 14:9. The original statement of monotheism, however, breaks out of an exclusively Jewish viewpoint and speaks of the oneness of God on a universal scale. There is no reference to *our* God because the Lord will be the one and only God of *all* the nations.

However, Jerusalem will continue to be the center from which the grace of God will radiate to all the earth. To express the continued centrality of Israel, Zechariah visualizes the leveling of the remainder of the Holy Land and the elevation of Jerusalem so that the city stands high above in a position of eminence and security (14:10).

Demystifying Zechariah

Geba was in the northernmost extent of Judah, and Rimmon was in the far south (14:10). So the whole land, from northern hill to southern height, would become as level as the Arabah— the southern extension of the Great Rift depression south of the Dead Sea, an area unexcelled for flatness.

The prophet isn't trying to provide precise delineations of the eschatological city, but he does want his generation to understand that the idealism of the future is rooted and grounded in the present, in actual history and geography. People will once more occupy Jerusalem, and the city will never again be destroyed (14:11).

All those who have persecuted and tormented God's people, however, will be inflicted with a horrible plague or pestilence of some kind that attacks both humans and animals (14:12–15). In addition to the plague's grotesque physical consequences, it will trigger a panic among the people, causing them to lash out and destroy one another. It appears that the plague and its related events best fit chronologically with the conflict described in 14:3–8, prior to the elevation of Jerusalem (14:9–11).

After the great fire that marks the beginning of the Lord's reign, the survivors among the nations acknowledge Him as King (14:9) and come regularly to offer Him homage (14:16). This is not to suggest, however, that they have undergone conversion in the religious sense (14:17–19). The word used for *worship* in verse 16 can mean only to bow down or do obeisance.

The particular occasion of pilgrimage is the Feast of Tabernacles, one of the three annual events in Israel's calendar when the Lord's able-bodied people are to appear before Him at the central sanctuary. Immediately after the celebration, the Levites will lead the assembly in a great ceremony of covenant renewal (Nehemiah 9:1–38) that culminates in a solemn commitment by the people to reaffirm their covenant allegiance to the Lord (Nehemiah 9:38; 10:29). It is evident that the Zechariah passage should also be viewed against a covenant background (Zechariah 14:17).

In the Bible, Egypt is frequently a symbol of the world at large (Isaiah 27:13; Revelation 11:8). Therefore, it is not distinguished here from the nations just mentioned but appears as a synonym for them (Zechariah 14:18–19).

In closing, Zechariah describes a number of transformations to take place "in that day" (14:20–21). The horse is considered an unclean animal, yet in the Day of the Lord, horses will wear bells bearing the inscription "HOLY TO THE LORD." Lowly pots used formerly as receptacles for ashes (Exodus 27:3) will be elevated to function as the holy bowls before the altar used for sacrifice. These examples point to the fact that "there will no longer be a Canaanite in the house of the LORD Almighty" (14:21 NIV).

The Canaanite, of course, symbolizes what is most reprehensible to God. The Canaanites are a cursed people (Genesis 9:25) and are to be annihilated by the conquest of Israel (Joshua 3:10). To think of their participation in the worship of God at all is scandalous, and to envision their doing so within the holy precincts of the temple is incomprehensible. Yet in the Day of the Lord, all are welcome because they all will be the people of God.

It is impossible to improve on Paul's assessment of the transformation that will characterize that glorious day: "There is neither Jew nor Greek, there is neither slave nor free man, there is neither male nor female; for you are all one in Christ Jesus" (Galatians 3:28 NASB).

Take It Home

Zechariah makes any number of noteworthy points in his final oracles, but perhaps one of the most relevant to today is the ease with which hypocrisy can infiltrate worship habits. Until such hypocrisy was removed, God would not respond. According to Zechariah, earlier generations had ignored the problem and suffered for it; later generations would repent and receive God's blessings. Do you think hypocrisy is a problem in today's church? Do you detect any instances where people in church settings seem more focused on themselves than on God's presence? What do you think is the best way for individuals and congregations to prevent hypocrisy from becoming a problem?

MALACHI

INTRODUCTION TO MALACHI

The book of Malachi is a summons to repentance and revival. In six disputations, the prophet summons the people to forsake their spiritual doldrums and halfhearted commitment to the Lord and return to an active faith and the practice of devotion to God.

AUTHOR

Some have wondered if Malachi's name, which means "my messenger," could be a title rather than a name. But there is no reason to believe that Malachi is written by anyone other than Malachi himself.

PURPOSE

Malachi addresses his people—the small group of exiled Jews who return from Babylonia. He confronts his people for keeping the best for themselves and leaving their leftovers for God. He calls his people back to their commitment and faith, particularly in light of the future judgment awaiting those who do not repent.

OCCASION

The concerns raised by Ezra and Nehemiah in their work of reformation are some of the same that Malachi mentions: spiritually mixed marriages, the neglect of tithing, disregard for keeping the Sabbath, the corruption of the priesthood, and social injustice. Some scholars suggest that it is likely Malachi preached before the reforms of Ezra and Nehemiah, preparing the way for them.

THEMES

Malachi uses the disputation form: Certain people raise a point, which is then contradicted by the prophet or, better, by the Lord speaking through the prophet. Malachi is not the only prophet to use this device. We find it in one form or another in Amos, Micah, and Ezekiel, as well as in Isaiah and Jeremiah. But only Malachi raises it to the organizing principle of his prophecy.

The covenant that God made with His people in the Pentateuch is fundamental to the message of Malachi. Malachi presumes this covenant is to establish a living relationship between the Lord and His people. Beginning in 1:1, Malachi uses the name *Israel* for the people of God. The covenant name has been applied to what remains of the people of God. The northern tribes, who were specifically referred to as Israel during the days of the divided kingdom, are no more, but Israel lives on in the remnant of the entire nation that returns from exile, primarily the descendants of the tribes of Judah and Benjamin.

HISTORICAL CONTEXT

A small company of Jews returns to Jerusalem from Babylon after the exile. The city is still largely in ruins from its destruction fifty years before. By Malachi's time, any enthusiasm and hopefulness has faded. The people are past believing that God is going to do anything grand on their behalf. It is now a time of spiritual discouragement, complaining, and a growing indifference to God's law of perfunctory worship.

So the situation Malachi faces is the same situation faced by Ezra when he came to Jerusalem in 458 BC, eighty years after the first return of exiles from Babylon, and by Nehemiah when he came to Jerusalem in 445 BC.

OUTLINE

MALACHI 1:1–2:9

ISRAEL AND THE PRIESTS

God's Call on Israel   1:1–5
The Contemptuous Priests   1:6–2:9

Setting Up the Section

Malachi opens with a statement about nations rather than individuals. The Israelites, descendants of Jacob, are God's people, as opposed to the Edomites, descendants of Jacob's brother, Esau.

📖 **1:1–5**

GOD'S CALL ON ISRAEL

Verse 1 identifies this writing as an oracle, one given through Malachi, a name that is Hebrew for "my messenger." The oracle is addressed to the nation of Israel. In this writing, the people who make up that nation are also referred to as *Judah* (2:11; 3:4) and *Jacob* (1:2; 2:12; 3:6).

In the first few verses, the term *hate* probably refers to a rejection. God selected Israel and rejected Edom as His chosen people.

Demystifying Malachi

Edom, though a little country, was often used as an emblem for all the enemies of Israel. At no point in Israel's history is Edom an ally, as are (at one time or another) most of the other nearby nations. Prophets such as Ezekiel and Obadiah speak against Edom (Ezekiel 25:12–14; Obadiah 1:1–7). The region is gradually overrun and by the middle/late fifth century has become a non-nation, but verse 5 indicates that in Malachi's time, the Edomites have not yet been thoroughly destroyed.

📖 **1:6–2:9**

THE CONTEMPTUOUS PRIESTS

This section, containing Malachi's second disputation, concerns Israel's priests' neglect of their duties. The people are complicit in this neglect, as Malachi will say, but the priests are more responsible. This disputation, the longest in the book, takes up twenty-three of a total fifty-five verses.

Critical Observation

As a demonstration that Malachi is not calling Israel to a new set of standards but calling her back to the ancient covenant, three texts from Numbers and Deuteronomy are woven through this disputation: Numbers 6:23–27 (the Aaronic benediction); Numbers 25:12–13 (the Levitical covenant of peace); and Deuteronomy 33:8–11 (Moses' blessing of the tribe of Levi and his enumeration of the priests' responsibilities). Malachi's people would have immediately recognized the ironic comparison that is being made.

Malachi 1:6 credits God with the message. The phrase "says the LORD Almighty" (or "says the LORD of hosts") is used often in this disputation. Malachi is attacking the priests, after all. They would be almost certain to react badly to Malachi's criticism, so it is important for him to emphasize that his message is from the Lord.

According to verse 8, the priests are violating the law that requires the best and the first of all the people's property be given to God. The firstborn, the firstfruits, and the most excellent of one's property belongs to God. This is a test of faith because the best animals are, of course, the best breeding stock, and in order to give that stock away to God, one has to believe it is better to honor the Lord than to seek material prosperity.

Malachi doesn't give a detailed reason the priests consent to let the people bring less than their best. It is to the priests' benefit that the people bring in the appropriate offerings. After all, part of these offerings provides sustenance for the priests, who are forbidden to own land. Ignorance is not the problem. The law is specific and emphatic on this point. The priests and the people would have never considered making these kinds of offerings to a dignitary, yet they are skimping on worship.

The doors mentioned in verse 10 are those to the temple courtyard. The sacrifices are offered outside.

Take It Home

We tend to think that lukewarm is better than cold, and something is better than nothing. But when it comes to worship, this is not God's perspective. He holds His people to a high standard. This is a common theme in the Old Testament Prophets. God doesn't want our worship if we are giving it begrudgingly, halfheartedly, and only out of a sense of duty. He doesn't want our worship if it is not an act of true faith.

Verse 11 describes a time when the whole world will worship the Lord. Malachi is interested in the future fulfillment of the plan of salvation. In contrast, according to verses 13–14, the priests are guilty of doing their jobs in a spirit of boredom, and the people seem to prefer it that way.

The moniker "great king" is a common title in some ancient texts and refers to the king over all the other lesser kings—the emperor (1:14). The Lord is the great King who will enforce the penalties of His covenant upon those who betray its requirements.

Demystifying Malachi

The requirement of giving a male animal—while it certainly foreshadows the greater sacrifice of Christ, who is a male, and is made necessary by the representative role of the male in society—is a kindness on the Lord's part. The females are needed to give milk and bear young, but only a few males are needed for breeding. So in this sense, less is lost to the flock when males are sacrificed.

Verse 1 of chapter 2 begins the curses threatened upon the priests for their unbelief and disobedience. According to verse 2, a primary role of the priests—pronouncing blessing—will become futile. The priests will pronounce blessing, as with the Aaronic benediction (Numbers 6:23–27), but the people will get curses instead.

The first curse is particularly heavy for the priest because a man became a priest by family line only (2:2). If descendants are cut off, the family will lose the right to the sacred office. The second curse is one of degradation and dishonor. Priests had to be cleaner than anyone else, and here God Himself is throwing dung in their faces (2:3).

The text of the covenant in verse 4 is found in Numbers 25:11–13, and its language is spread throughout Malachi 2:1–8, as is the blessing of Levi found in Deuteronomy 33:8–11 (Malachi 2:7). No Israelite would have missed the connection.

We read what kind of preacher and teacher a minister ought to be in 2:6–7—Malachi says that a faithful minister turns many from sin and communicates the knowledge and the instruction of the Lord. He does this, Malachi says, because he himself walks with the Lord. Contrarily, verses 8–9 reveal the hearts of the priests in this day. They teach without power, even tailor their messages to certain people's advantage and to others' disadvantage. These verses make it clear that the people have stumbled and the law is up for sale. Israel is sinking into spiritual doldrums and, from there, might eventually sink into spiritual death.

MALACHI 2:10–3:5

THE SINS OF THE PEOPLE

Setting Up the Section

Malachi's third disputation returns to the sins of the people, specifically the marital unfaithfulness among the people of God. The same format is followed as in the previous disputations: The Lord asserts through His prophet that His people have violated the covenant (2:10–13). This is followed by the people's questioning reply, the Lord's response (2:14), and the implication (2:15–16).

📄 **2:10–16**

REBELLION

In verse 10, Malachi reminds the people of their special relationship to God, their Father. Israel must live in obedience to God and in union with one another as brothers and sisters, at least in God's family. In this, the Israelites are breaking faith.

Verse 11 reveals the sin of Malachi's people to be spiritual intermarriage. Jews are marrying outside the faith. The fact that Judah is blamed for the sin suggests that it is a national sin, widespread and generally countenanced. The problem with these marriages is religious, not racial or ethnic. Members of other peoples are welcomed into Israelite life and society and into marriage with Israelites so long as they accept the faith of Israel.

Malachi looks to the Lord to enforce the curses of the covenant upon the violator (2:12). The people may have thought that as long as they continue to offer their sacrifices it didn't matter if they also took part in pagan rituals. But God doesn't need their offerings, and He doesn't want them unless they are symbols of faith and trust.

The tears mentioned in verse 13 probably refer to loud displays of emotion during sacrifices. Many religions of the day believed that these protestations of earnestness would influence God to act. What is scorned here is emotion intended to manipulate God.

In verse 14, the same word is used of two kinds of marital sins—improper intermarriage and improper divorce. Marriage is regarded as a covenant. It takes on features like that of God's covenant with His people; it requires fidelity on the part of the covenant partners.

The wife of one's youth probably reflects the fact that many, if not most, marriages in these days are arranged before the children grow to be adults (2:14). Notice the egalitarian language at the end of verse 14: The wife is referred to as a *partner*, not an underling.

2:17–3:5

SELF-DECEIT

The failure of the people identified in this sixth disputation is doubt of the Lord's justice. The Lord's reply is a promise of a divine messenger to cleanse His people, to restore true worship, and to enact justice. Malachi again addresses the need for the reform of the priesthood and the purification of Israel's worship.

In verse 17, the statement that those who do evil are good in the eyes of God is a statement of irony. It is not likely that anyone is actually saying or even thinking this. The point is that it doesn't seem that God is doing anything about this evil. Does it matter to Him?

The opening verse of chapter 3 answers the concern of 2:17. God will respond, and His response will be in the form of a messenger. The word translated *messenger* here is the same used in 1:1.

The ministry of the messenger described in 3:2–5 is clearly the ministry of a divine figure. He does the things that only the Lord has the power and the authority to do.

The day of the Lord's coming, mentioned in 3:2, is a concept found frequently in the Old Testament Prophets. It refers broadly to a time when the Lord will appear as a conquering judge to punish the wicked and vindicate the righteous, ushering in a new era of blessing. But here, as elsewhere in the Prophets, there is a surprising reversal. The assumption of the people is that the Day of the Lord will be a great day for them. They will be delivered from their enemies and granted prosperity. But here Malachi asks who will be able to endure this day. For those who have kept the covenant, the Day of the Lord will be welcome deliverance. For those who have broken it, it will be a time of judgment and curses.

Demystifying Malachi

A refiner's fire functions to purify metal. Malachi draws this image from the everyday life of Israel. The prophets often use this image to describe either the Lord's elimination of the impurities from His people or His purifying of them. The launderer's soap was a form of lye used to soak the dirt out of clothes. Both fire and lye are agents by which what deserves to remain is separated from what does not.

Verses 4–5 conclude this disputation with a description of renewed worship and re-formed justice—right worship *and* right living. Verse 5 catalogs some of the sins that are commonplace in Malachi's time. Seven violations of the covenant law are mentioned, a sampling of the way in which the people show contempt for God.

MALACHI 3:6–4:6

THE FUTILITY OF THE PEOPLE

Selfishness	3:6–12
Self-Sufficiency	3:13–4:3
Restoration Ahead	4:4–6

Setting Up the Section

This section contains Malachi's final two disputations. The first one addresses the people's failure to give ample offerings to God. The second one involves the promise of vindication for those who have put their faith in God.

📄 **3:6–12**

SELFISHNESS

Verses 6–12 contain the fifth of Malachi's six disputations. As in the second dis-putation, we find two questions put by the people instead of just one. The subject in both disputations is broadly the same—Israel's begrudging offerings—though in the second disputation the emphasis falls on the priests' failure, and here it falls on the people's failure.

Verses 6–7 focus on God's immutability. It is God's immutability that explains why Israel, though she has violated God's covenant with her generation after generation, has not been destroyed. The Lord is a merciful God, faithful to His covenant and to the promises He made to be Israel's God.

Verse 8 addresses tithes and offerings. The tithe is the requirement to give a tenth of one's income to the Lord. The offerings are gifts above the tithe. Giving of these things is a symbol of recognition that all one has belongs to God.

Verses 9–11 reveal other failures of the people. Either they are holding back part of what they owe by law or not everyone is giving a tithe. Since the tithes are the allotment of the priests and Levites, the people's disobedience causes them hardship.

The floodgates mentioned in verse 10 are a reference to rain, the lack of which has blighted Israel's crops. But verse 11 reveals another layer of meaning. Rain is a symbol of all manner of blessing. Agricultural abundance is an image frequently employed by the prophets to describe the blessing of the new age.

Take It Home

To some, verses 10–12 sound like promises that if we live righteous lives, we will be rich. The fact is, it is plainly understood by faithful people in the Old Testament that God is not promising riches to the pious, at least not in this world. They struggle, as we do today, with the obvious fact that often we find wicked people richer than godly people.

As Christians, we worship a God who is faithful to His promises. It is our responsibility to trust and obey, no matter how we might calculate the costs and likely benefits. God often makes us trust Him before He will show us His blessing.

📄 3:13–4:3

SELF-SUFFICIENCY

In the sixth and final disputation, the people complain that God is not vindicating them by rewarding the righteous or punishing the wicked. The Lord's reply, through Malachi, is that He will most definitely vindicate His people. That day will come, and any doubts about the importance of trusting the Lord and obeying Him will be forever put to rest.

Given that Malachi has confronted his people about their disobedience, verse 14 seems ironic. The people complain about carrying out requirements, but in light of Malachi's charges against the people, what are all the requirements they have carried out?

The mourning they mention was probably the same kind of ritual mourning mentioned in 2:13. Malachi condemns the people for a show of mourning and penitence before the Lord that is nothing but an attempt to manipulate Him.

In verse 15, the idea of challenging or testing God refers to those who openly do what God forbids. Their actions test to see if God will respond. The people here called *evildoers*, or *wicked*, are simply those who are doing other kinds of evil than the insolent and complaining Israelites are doing.

Verse 16 contains the only narrative in the book of Malachi. The people described here (obviously a distinct minority among Israel as a whole) are pious, faithful, and devout. They stir one another up to love and good deeds, and the Lord takes special notice of their spiritual conversation.

The *scroll* (or *book*) *of remembrance* mentioned in verse 16 is probably a document that contains the names of all those who ascribe to some written commitment to the Lord. Another possibility is that it is a scroll akin to "the books," in which are written the record of the lives of men and women, or even to "the book of life," in which are found the names of those whom God has saved.

Fire, mentioned in the first verse of chapter 4, is an image often used to describe the effects of the Lord's judgment. Malachi has already referred to a refiner's fire in 3:2. This is a metaphor.

The fire renders the wicked stubble (4:1). *Stubble*, used here as a term of agriculture, is what is left when everything valuable has been taken away—the leftovers after the field has been cut down with a scythe.

Verse 2 contains a complex figure of speech in the "sun of righteousness" that "will rise with healing in its wings."

There is the image of reversal of fortune in 4:3. The wicked, who generally ride in triumph over the righteous in this world, will be trampled under the feet of the righteous in the Day of the Lord. This, too, is a frequently employed image of divine judgment. The prosperity of the wicked is overtaken in a moment.

📄 **4:4–6**

RESTORATION AHEAD

Verse 4 mentions the Law of Moses, which summarizes the focal point of the first three disputations. Verses 5–6 mention the Day of the Lord, which is a focus of the last three.

Demystifying Malachi

Verse 5 contains a promise of the coming of Elijah, the quintessential prophet. Does this mean he will return in person? In Matthew 11:7–10 and 17:10–13, we read Jesus' interpretation of this text. In both cases, Jesus mentions John the Baptist as the "Elijah" of whom Malachi speaks.

The sense of verse 6 is not merely that when the Messiah and the Day of the Lord come they will usher in a new harmony in family relationships. The mention of parents and children is a way of saying that when the Day of the Lord comes, He will turn everyone back to faithfulness to the covenant. This is a promise of great revival.

Take It Home

If God is for us, who can be against us? This is Malachi's point from the beginning. Our enemies cannot prevail, and our Edoms can do us no harm with the Lord on our side. Let us then live for Him and walk with Him in the covenant He has so graciously made with us; let us rest in His love. If we have blessings, they have come from His hand.

CONTRIBUTING EDITORS:

Stan Campbell has a MA from Wheaton College and has been a full-time writer in Christian publishing for over 10 years and active in a church ministry for twenty years. Among his almost three dozen books are *The World's Easiest Guide to Understanding the Bible* and *Bible to Go: Genesis to Revelation in One hour.*

Robert L. Deffinbaugh, Th.M. graduated from Dallas Theological Seminary with his Th.M. in 1971. Bob is a teacher and elder at Community Bible Chapel in Richardson, Texas, and a regular contributor to the online studies found at Bible.org.

Stephen Leston, is pastor of Kishwaukee Bible Church in DeKalb , IL. He is passionate about training people for ministry and has served as a pastor at Grace Church of DuPage (Warrenville, IL) and Petersburg Bible Church (Petersburg, AK).

Eugene H. Merrill is Distinguished Professor of Old Testament Studies at Dallas Theological Seminary where he has served on the faculty since 1975. The author of scores of books and articles, mainly of a historical and exegetical nature, Dr. Merrill holds the PhD in Old Testament studies from Bob Jones University, the MA in Jewish Studies from New York University, and the MPhil and Ph.D. in Middle Eastern Studies from Columbia University. He is an active churchman and preaches and teaches abroad on a regular basis.

Richard D. Patterson was chairman of the Department of Biblical Studies and professor of Semitic Languages and literatures at Liberty University, Lynchburg, Virginia. He contributed to The Expositor's Bible Commentary. He also has written numerous articles for *Grace Theological Journal, the Journal of the Evangelical Theological Society,* and other scholarly journals. (A.B., Wheaton College; M.Div., Northwest Baptist Theological Seminary; Th.M. Talbot Theological Seminary; M.A., Ph.D., University of California Los Angeles)

Robert Rayburn holds a Master of Divinity degree from Covenant Theological Seminary and a doctorate in New Testament from the University of Aberdeen, Scotland. His commentary on Hebrews was published in the *Evangelical Commentary of the Bible.*

CONSULTING EDITOR:

Tremper Longman is the Robert H. Gundry Professor of Biblical Studies at Westmont University. He has taught at Westmont since 1998 and taught before that for 18 years at the Westminster Theological Seminary in Philadelphia. Dr. Longman has degrees from Ohio Wesleyan University (B.A.), Westminster Theological Seminary (M.Div.), and Yale University (M.Phil.; Ph.D.). He has also been active in the area of Bible translation, in particular he serves on the central committee that produced and now monitors the New Living Translation.

WITH SPECIAL THANKS TO BIBLE.ORG

Bible.org is a non-profit (501c3) Christian ministry headquartered in Dallas, Texas. In the last decade, bible.org has grown to serve millions of individuals around the world and provides thousands of trustworthy resources for Bible study including the new NET BIBLE® translation.

Bible.org offers thousands of free resources for:
• Spiritual Formation and Discipleship
• Men's Ministry
• Women's Ministry
• Pastoral Helps
• Small Group Curriculum and much more...

Bible.org can be accessed through www.bible.org

Look for All 12 Volumes in the

QUICKNOTES SIMPLIFIED BIBLE COMMENTARY SERIES

ALSO AVAILABLE: